The Baseball Hall of Fame

A Fan's Perspective

David W. Gue

Dedication

This book is dedicated to my faith in God, wife Kathy, son Ryan and granddaughter Arya, who provide everything good in life.

Great friends George, Pat and Jimmy for listening and providing valuable feedback.

To the fans who love the game, and the individuals that have given their lives to Baseball.

May the great players, coaches and managers receive their worthy place in the Baseball Hall of Fame while able to enjoy the honor.

Special thanks to Tommy & Cheryl John and Jeff Santo.

Table of Contents

Preface

One of the goals of every Baseball fan is to visit the Baseball Hall of Fame in Cooperstown, NY. I was able to achieve that goal by visiting it with my wife Kathy and son Ryan in December of 1996. I enjoyed every minute, looking over the exhibits, video footage, and many of the statistics available but fell far short of what I had really wanted to see.

Every year since my visit in 1996, I waited anxiously to see who was elected by the Baseball Writers Association of America (BBWAA). I had a goal to attend the ceremonies when one of my three all-time favorite individuals were elected, Ron Santo, Buck O'Neil, and Tommy John. Growing up in the suburbs of Chicago, I gravitated towards each of these individuals. Every year from 1997 through 2006, my disappointment grew as I saw all three being bypassed. I shared Ron's and Bucks heartaches when the new inductees were announced, and they were not one of them. I assumed Tommy John been elected due to his great career and the surgery that bears his name since most of his greatest success being achieved in Los Angeles and New York. It wasn't just being great players, but they were high-quality individuals. Ron Santo was the first ballplayer I ever met at seven years old with my Grandpa Louie. The memory of how nice Ron was and took time to talk to a seven-year-old fan and signed the program my grandpa bought is as fresh in my mind as if it happened yesterday

Tommy John was my favorite White Sox player in the 1960's. I would watch the White Sox in the evening on WGN, and it seemed every time I saw him pitch, he would throw a shutout, or lose to a shutout. If the White Sox had any offense when Tommy pitched for the White Sox, he would have had over 300 wins for his career. Instead, he barely had enough run support to achieve the modest record of 82 wins and 80 losses in his seven years with Chicago. My admiration of Tommy was the way he pitched, his interaction with young fans, and how he always made time to sign everyone's request for an autograph. He let youngsters know he really cared.

The third member of my heroes was Buck O'Neil. I met Buck in 1968 when he was buying a car from my grandfather, Louis Spataro, at the car dealership in Chicago, IL. They knew each other from their ball playing days barnstorming in the mid 1930's. Grandpa was a pretty good pitcher who played against O'Neil, and some of the other great Negro League players in the 1930's. Grandpa and I went to many Cubs games and would always look for Buck. The two of them talked about the good old days and laughed a lot. Grandpa passed in 1972, and I didn't see Buck until he was interviewed throughout the 1994 documentary Baseball by Ken Burns. I had never forgotten Buck, but my admiration was rekindled due to the documentary. Then I realized Buck had not been enshrined in the Baseball Hall of Fame. I saw him wait every year for the BBWAA to finally elect him to his rightful status of being a Hall of Famer, but it never happened.

My parents, Glen and Eve Gue, raised myself and three brothers, Ken, Mike and Rob in the Christian faith and supported us in the best ways they could. Dad often worked multiple jobs to support the family while Mom stayed home making sure there was a steady presence at home when we came home from school. That was normal in the town where we grew up. In addition, if we disrespected a neighbor, we would get called on it immediately and scolded, but when we got home...oh boy did we get it. The town had a moral compass that promoted equality, faith, honoring your parents, education, hard work, and the best of values. One feeling expressed by those that grew up there is "How Blessed to have our parents and others to raise us right."

Though I continued to play baseball and softball into my late 20's, I stopped when I met my future wife, Kathleen Soukup in 1985. Meeting her is another story of faith and I thank the Lord every day for her. After a 15-month courtship, we were married in 1986. Together, we made decisions, planned our future, and had a son Ryan in 1988. Kathy supported my ideas, education, career decisions, and was a dream come true. Yes, it was love at first sight for me and the love of my life and best friend.

When the baseball strike wiped out the 1994 World Series for the first time in 90 years, the game went into a downward spiral. The catalyst was the strike, but included escalating ticket prices, lack of fan appreciation by the players, rising costs of concessions & merchandise, along with many other factors. For the first time in my life, I was losing my passion for baseball.
After watching Ken Burns Documentary Baseball in 1994, I began thinking of all those not in the Hall of Fame but should be. Watching it over and over during the down time, I began seeing the game in a different light. I still loved the game but often regressed to the pre-1990 years when you could get an autograph from the players without being charged. Though my friends and I continued to follow baseball, we rarely talked about the trip to Cooperstown to see the induction ceremonies. When baseball resumed in 1995, again I began listening to Ron Santo and Pat Hughes calling Cubs

games on the radio. Ron was called a "Homer" as he bled Cubbie Blue and wore his emotions for all to see. Everyone could tell Ron loved the Cubs and the fans loved him for it. Ron and all his fans couldn't wait to hear his name called as a newly elected member of the baseball Hall of Fame. Ron tried but couldn't hide his disappointment when it didn't happen. My growing admiration for Buck O'Neil, after watching the documentary Baseball over and over, began igniting the embers of my passion to try and do something about the biases being done to Ron and this former player, coach, scout, and great ambassador of the game for eight decades. I couldn't believe both were being overlooked for the Hall of Fame and kept thinking of ways I could help. Soon I progressed from watching my favorite television and sports shows to going to the library, watching alternative Media, and looking at history through the eyes of others. The deeper I researched and found what I believed the truth really was, the more I began formulating new opinions. I started to understand why the best people are often overlooked and why there are so many injustices in the world. I realized there was the victors' side, the losers' side, and the truth somewhere in the middle. I began to question everything to find the truth, to see if it agreed with what I was taught.

In the meantime, the continual omission of O'Neil, John, and Santo fueled my desire to bring out the hypocrisy of the current Hall of Fame election system. Seeing the hurt in Santo's eyes and hearing Buck hide his disappointment with dignity and praise for his Negro League contemporaries, continued stoking the fire inside me to do something to correct these injustices. Both Santo and O'Neil were eventually elected but only after each had passed. They never had the opportunity to enjoy their celebrity in the place they should have called home for years.

I no longer trusted the BBWAA as I believed the current system of election for the Hall of Fame is too biased in favor of the Sportswriters, or their sub-committees and could be manipulated to keep certain individuals out of the Hall while allowing those with lesser career statistics in. I statistically analyzed careers and put together charts that would provide induction criteria versus voting percentages equitable for pitchers, hitters, fielders, managers, and a combination category for players who became managers and great coaches as well. These charts were developed after Santo passed away and I continued to remain silent with my thoughts and the system I created until a conversation I had with an older sports enthusiast. We were talking about baseball when the topic of the Hall of Fame came up. We both threw out names of who should have been elected along with a few we felt should not have been. One name that came to both of us was Tommy John. Neither one of us could believe he wasn't already enshrined until we looked it up. Sure, enough he wasn't. Here was my third hero who deserved to be enshrined but wasn't and felt the need to help correct this injustice.

Tommy had Hall of Fame statistics and helped revolutionize the game by enduring an injury, surgery, and perfecting a recovery to allow him to pitch again. I do not know if it was Divine Intervention or not, but George encouraged me to see if I could get in touch with Tommy John, to get permission to write about him before proceeding with this book. By some phenomenon, I found his phone number and called leaving a message on his voice mail. He later returned my call and agreed to endorse the book I wanted to write. Corresponding with Tommy, and his lovely wife Cheryl, made my respect, appreciation, and admiration grow tremendously. At 80 years of age, this wonderful individual deserves to be inducted with the greats in the Baseball Hall of Fame.

During the research of the book, I reached out to the Santo family to get their permission to include Ron as part of a chapter in the book because of my personal thoughts and feelings about him. Jeff said they were all happy that their father was recognized being elected and had only thanks and praise for the Hall of Fame. Though I respect the class and kindness of the Santo family, it didn't change my belief that he should have been elected years earlier so Ron could have enjoyed the status and celebrity of being one of the best of all-time and been able to deliver his own speech.

Introduction

By David Gue

Baseball's significance in American History Baseball has a long history of shaping American values. For decades, it was often referred to as the national pastime as the wave of baseball's popularity in the late 19th century to the current day, was mostly because the game had a way of connecting men with their youth. And generations. As large metropolitan cities and factories began to boom across America, people looked for ways to reduce the tensions of their gradually busier lives. Even though baseball was popular among many socio-economic classes, it could be remarkably appealing to the poor as it seemingly offered hope of achieving an American dream of money and fame if one could become a professional player. These historical references show that from the late 19th century until the present day, baseball had become a common sport to which many people of different backgrounds could relate.

By the 20th century, early sports journalism played a big role in elevating the status of baseball in America. Dedicated baseball writers in local newspapers and national journals kept Americans informed about their favorite teams and players. It has been pointed out that many sports writers of this time worked in unity with athletes and baseball promoters to produce articles that were favorable to the game. Eventually, names like Ty Cobb, Walter Johnson and several other players rose to a heroic level of prominence among the public. A fundamental element in this early baseball reporting was the communication concerning players' statistics that further established them as heroes among the public. The progress of box scores allowed for the comparison of personal statistics and helped establish an "valid marker of greatness" among players.

The substantial importance of an individual player statistics and records in baseball established a desire for "clean," heroes. This directs the ideals of integrity and innocence within the game of baseball. Like American history, baseball history has struggled to live up to the ethical ideals as it once excluded all non-white players from entering the league under a "gentlemen's agreement". There has been widespread testimony of the use of amphetamines or drugs that helped boost player energy to make it through a season. Players have been on record as saying they used amphetamines to be able to play after a night out and was the result of peer pressure. Flaws aside, the Baseball Hall of Fame expresses the ideal of purity. Given the statistical and moral standards needed for individuals to gain entry, there has always been an implied preference for all inductees to reflect the ideal of pureness. The ideals of baseball purity are threatened when there are concerns of players using steroids, or performance enhancing drugs (PEDs), which can give them an unsanctioned advantage over other players. Steroids did not officially become banned in Major League Baseball until 1991 but it was not until 2003 that the players' union agreed to allow survey testing of players to gauge the occurrence of steroid use in the game. There were no punishments for results of the survey testing, but the league mandated testing of all players for the 2004 season with penalties after about 5-7% of the survey tests came back positive for steroids in 2003.

There are a variety of views on this issue among fans and players as Major League Baseball did not take a definite position. When asked what advice he'd give writers on how to handle Hall of Fame voting, current league commissioner Rob Manfred recently said the only advice he was comfortable giving was "everyone should keep in mind the difference between players who tested positive and were disciplined on the one hand, and players where somebody has surmised that they did something on the other". Ultimately, having been left for the Baseball Writers Association of America (BBWAA) to decide the legacy of these players. The BBWAA is the main voting body that elects individuals to the Hall of Fame. Each of the members covers baseball for a newspaper, magazine, or major website for the entire year. Members are required to be with the organization for 10 years before being eligible to participate in the Hall of Fame voting. They can also continue to vote for at least 10 years after ending their active membership. In addition, the BBWAA also votes on yearly league honors like Most Valuable Player and Rookie of the Year. A player must receive at least 75% of the BBWAA vote to be elected to the Hall of Fame. Players failing to receive 75% of the vote must receive a minimum of 5% of the vote to remain on the ballot for next year. If a player(s) receives less than the minimum 5%, they will be removed from the ballot starting the next year and become dependent on other committees for election. The BBWAA allows writers to vote for up to 10 players each year. The Baseball Hall of Fame also has a voting guideline, referred to as the "character clause,"

which states: "voting shall be based upon the player's record, playing ability, integrity, sportsmanship, character, and contributions to the team(s) on which the player played. There is no such voting guideline for any other hall of fame honoring athletes of a major American sport. Interpretation of how this character clause should apply varies among BBWAA voters. However, there has not been much literature focusing on the BBWAA. Some current and former members have offered internal criticism of the organization over issues like membership selection. As caretakers to the public institution of the Baseball Hall of Fame, the voting habits of BBWAA writers need to be evaluated for the sake of accountability. Not only should the public understand the reasoning behind voting decisions, but the oratory supporting those decisions should also be reviewed to ensure it is done in a fair and ethical manner. Furthermore, if the voting rhetoric of the BBWAA is not legitimate and ethical, the Hall of Fame's election process should be suspected and changed to ensure its integrity. Truthfulness is a universal standard requiring statements to be based on fact and reality. Thus, whether combined in analysis, or applied separately, the values of truth, rightness and sincerity set a strong standard for acceptable discussion. These three concepts form a solid framework for investigating the legitimacy of an argument.

Having universally agreed-upon standards like the proposed Hall of Fame Criteria Charts, truth, rightness and sincerity helps establish accountability among collective parties. Strong debate works best when there is an expectation for everyone to play by the same rules, regardless of power or influence. When considering the historical relationship between sports journalists and the public, writers had a large share of influence simply because their newspaper allowed them to regularly mass produce messages in a way not yet available to the public. The BBWAA writers claim Hall of Fame voting is more vulnerable to public challenges based on principles like truth, rightness, and sincerity. The analysis of accuracy asked the question of whether the writer had the proper authority or insight to definitively make a certain claim. Beliefs on Ethical Persuasion While analysis through the lenses of truth, rightness and sincerity helps address the merit of a claim, additional criteria are required to evaluate the potential societal impact. Words exchanged in public forums can have a strong impact on public perception and emotion surrounding an issue. Such effects can be magnified depending on the number of people who hear the message and the frequency of its communication. Special attention should also be given to communication aimed at persuading the public to form a consensus on an opinion or take a specific course of action. This type of communication can be especially powerful, warranting some accountability to make sure such statements are presented in an ethical manner. Beyond simple communication, it is the position of this study that BBWAA writer voting explanations are also meant convince others that their ballot decisions are justified.

Writers who listed those verifying sources helped boost the credibility of their claims. Lack of available specifics about which players did or didn't use PEDs led some writers to speculate. When based on verifiable facts, speculation could be acceptable and provide useful information to the public about the issue. However, writers were expected to clarify speculative claims as opinion, not fact, to ensure the public knew the change.

The Hall of Fame has for years presented exhibits addressing the exclusion of non-white ball players while celebrating the history 16 of the segregated Negro Leagues). In a similar way, reflection on the history of baseball's Steroids Era might provide a teachable moment for the public. However, beyond being an honorable museum, others like Hall of Famer Joe Morgan have argued that the Baseball Hall of Fame is a place for the league's best players to be honored for the way they played the game. By allowing entry to players who may have cheated, it could give the idea that illegal behavior can be rewarded. Voting for them should be the result of evaluating their careers within the context of the time they played in Baseball. With that being said, history is still history and should never be censored from the game. Those that fall short due to Character Clause Violations should still have their records included but not be glorified by having a plaque, or bust with those individuals that played the game clean and without reproach.

A Fan's View of the Baseball Hall of Fame

Since Major League Baseball set up the first Sports Hall of Fame Museum in 1936, it was meant to be for the top guys, the stars, the ones with an immense career of achievements. The Cooperstown Baseball Hall of Fame Museum, located in Cooperstown, New York is the mecca for baseball fans who enjoy the complete history of the game. Since 2007, the Museum attendance has fallen from annual attendance topping 400,000 in the peak years of the late 1980's and early 1990's to 236,406 in 2022. In addition, following the 2007 Induction Ceremonies, when an estimated crowd of 82,000 fans came to attend the Cal Ripken and Tony Gwynn Hall of Fame Induction Ceremonies, attendance has fallen to an estimated total of 35,000 in 2022. This 57.4% drop in attendance represents an enormous decline of the history of America's so-called "National Pastime" that needs to be addressed.

This book is not about which players are in the Hall of Fame but who deserve to be there for their impact on the game. In the 148-year history of the game, only 278 players (less than two per year) have been elected to the Hall of Fame. This low total suggests to the fans that visiting the Hall of Fame is a "one and done" day trip. There is so much history that isn't in the Museum due to having such a low number of inductees. The belief is that fans would stretch their visits over a few days, maybe even a week, if there was enough of their favorite players in the Hall. Their extended stays would be a benefit for the museum, the communities, and incentive for the creation of other businesses. If The Baseball Hall of Fame made visiting a "destination for the fans", attendance would increase in the off seasons so they could continue getting their baseball fix throughout the year. This can be achieved by restructuring the current election system to incorporate the immense database of almost 150-years of the history of the game. The Hall of Fame Total Points Charts created for this book present an automatic Induction Score that will allow players to forgo the BBWAA Election process. For the superstars, being inducted when their five-year waiting period is over would eliminate wasted time for those greats. It would speed up the time for the many great players that have waited for the mandatory five-year waiting period before the BBWAA could even vote them in. If not elected in their allotted time, they are then referred to other committees, only to have to wait many additional years before being elected and allowed to enjoy their status as part of this very elusive club. Many of the individuals that were always well deserving, were of failing health or deceased and able to become longtime representatives of the Jall of Fame. These charts quantify the various statistics for pitching, hitting, fielding, managing and peripheral parts of the game that separate in a non-bias method that is equal for all. This information is needed for the electors to make sound decisions in a time frame allowing the fans to enjoy their favorites while still fairly fresh in their minds. Baseball, the longest recorded history of a professional sport in the United States, should be the example other sports follow.

"The Baseball Hall of Fame - A Fan's Perspective" is more than a subjective understanding about who should be in the Baseball Hall of Fame and who shouldn't be. This one-of-a-kind publication, thoroughly and concisely, examines the current and former paths players have taken to ultimately receive the "Hall of Famer" moniker, as well as other deserving players who have been snubbed by the writers and various committees. The author proposes solutions to reform the voting process instead of simply complaining about the current election methods. This leads to debates on individuals who aren't in the Hall of Fame due to various reasons which have rules on non-baseball related issues and at times, that affects which players get in. There's always the debate of whether on-field production should supersede any potential wrongdoings off the field. There should be a clear and precise definition for "The Character Clause" that eliminates this being a debate. Any offenses while employed in the game of Baseball should be documented just as much as the awards and accolades each individual has received during their careers. American History sometimes is fraught with inaccuracies and deception that portrays individuals to a certain narrative of the writer(s). This should never happen in sport, but it often does. Any player that fails the Character Clause should have their statistical information and biography included in a section of the Museum for all to review but omit having a plaque in the Hall of Fame. In today's day and age, the average fan can look up all they want to know about almost any individual on the internet. This is their right to be a fan and do not want others censoring their knowledge.

This visual, oral, and written history of each player recording their achievements needs to be pristine in accuracy and without omission. It appears to the average fan that selected players get in on their first try while others have to wait a while, or fail to get in at all, until the fraternity of the BBWAAs, and to some extent the Veterans Committee, allow them entrance into their hallowed halls. Over the years, The Baseball Hall of Fame has made questionable decisions about who they induct and who stays a spectator. There are deserving stars who've been ignored while lesser individuals have been elected for various biased reasons. However, the Baseball Writers

The Baseball Hall of Fame

Association of America (BBWAA) has voted in several individuals to the Hall of Fame whose numbers don't merit inclusion-based on the Statistical Charts created in this book. This can be corrected with the development of the Induction Charts as guidelines and eliminate many players getting into the Hall of fame by working the voters and media to consequently get in via familiarity. The fact that writers are voting for these players leads to a bit of bias based on how some may personally feel about a player. Once a player is taken off the BBWAA balloting, they wait to be included on the ballot for the Veterans Committee which tends to put in guys just because of their age and favoritism.

Baseball fans wish to see the past, present and future of the game's players that are loved by millions over several generations. The statistical analysis and thorough research will test the baseball confidence of even the most knowledgeable patrons of the game. Each individual will have a biography that lists their achievements, family background, and history while in service of the game of Baseball. Whether the individual was exclusively a player, a coach, a manager, or a combination of the three, their accomplishments and time in the game are quantified in the Hall of Fame Points category. Each of these trademarked categories are responsible for generating statistical data that separates the superstar players that should be Inducted without having the BBWAA "elect them", the great players that fall within range of being great and can be elected by the BBWAA, and very good players that just didn't measure statistically to be reviewed for being elected. However, statistics for good and very good players are listed so fans can see how their favorite players compared against all the others. The book outlines individuals that had shortened careers, but close statistically and should be elected by the BBWAA.

Individuals like Don Mattingly, Will Clark, Thurman Munson, and others whose careers were shortened due to injury, family issues, death, or other instances should never be penalized if they have the minimum time of ten years played and have accumulated many achievements. They were revered by their fans during their careers and could be tremendous ambassadors for many years. Let them enjoy their celebrity and do not punish them for not meeting the expectations of the ruling elite. All three listed above had shortened careers which prevented them from accumulating the sexy statistics the BBWAA seem to enjoy. Mattingly lost production and retired early due to a congenital back issue, Clark cut his career short in order to spend time with his autistic son, and

A Fan's Perspective

Munson's career was cut short due to his tragic death. All three have long deserved to be in the Baseball Hall of Fame.

Two other great careers that should be recognized are Elston Howard and Don Newcombe. These two great players didn't acquire the statistics needed to be Inducted per the Statistic Charts in this book but were very close and should have been elected many years ago. Both individuals started out playing in the Negro Leagues and spent two years in the United States Military before making their marks in Major League baseball. Both were class acts and helped ease integration as an accepted standard in Baseball. Howard did it as being the first African American to integrate the New York Yankees, playing behind legend Yogi Berra. If Howard had his career starting in the 1970's, his statistics would have been much greater as he could have rotated the designated hitter position with legends Mickey Mantle and Roger Maris. On any other team, Howard would have been a superstar and a no-brainer Hall of Fame electee.

The passage of time should never alter the assessment of an individual's career to mean they are less than Hall-worthy, whether they are in the Hall of Fame, or still waiting to get in. What was exceptional in the different eras should not be diminished but elevated and remembered as the game matures. A few well-deserving 19th century players have been excluded from the Hall for the simple reason they have been forgotten. Jim McCormick, Bobby Mathews, and Tony Mullane are three pitchers who excelled in the early years of the game but have since been forgotten when the Baseball Hall of Fame opened 60 years after Baseball became a professional sport. Since then, pitching statistics changed, batting statistics changed, equipment became better, players bigger, etc.… as the Dead-Ball ERA (the period of inside-game dominance") of play emphasizing pitching, speed, and batsmanship that was established in the first 40 years of the game slowly disappeared. Skills such as bunting were very common, doubles, and triples were more publicized than home runs. This style lasted until the home run became dominant with the emergence of Babe Ruth where a home run could generate multiple runs with one swing of the bat.

Colonel Jacob Rupert, part owner of the Yankees, saw a great opportunity and purchased Ruth from the Red Sox after the 1919 season after noticing how the fans enjoyed the crack of the bat more than the three hits usually needed to produce a run. With Ruth belting home runs, attendance went from 619,164 fans for the Yankees in 1919 and more than doubled to 1,289,422

The Baseball Hall of Fame

fans in 1920. This led to what is usually called the "the lively ball" era period in Major League Baseball beginning in 1920 and continues to the present day. The name "live-ball era" comes from the dramatic rise in offensive statistics, as a direct result of a series of rule changes (introduced in 1920) that were informally said to have made the ball "livelier". The live-ball era was the era in which baseball regained relevance and exploded in popularity. Since 1920, the rabbit ball was kept in place. Offense exploded in those two seasons to 5.37 runs and 0.59 home runs per game. The 1930 season was particularly outrageous, as Hack Wilson, Babe Ruth, Lou Gehrig and Chuck Klein all topped 40 home runs and the league's batting line was an absurd .296/.356/.434. In 1931 was the year when the cork center was replaced by a "cushion cork" pill that was a mixture of cork and ground rubber. Scoring and home runs promptly went down to 4.81 runs and 0.43 home runs per game. There continued to be slight differences between the balls being used in the American and National League for the next couple years, but the two leagues agreed to a standardized ball in 1934.

This era draws almost parallel to the emergence of the Steroid ERA of the late 1990's which saw home run totals explode and the game see a resurgence at turnstiles after the disastrous elimination of the World Series in 1994. Should the statistics of the players from 1930 & 1931 seasons be subtracted from the players that benefited back then? It was the owners and officials that promoted this, and it is believed by many the owners knew about the steroids in the late 1990's as they were enjoying the resurgence of profits the home runs seemed to draw from the fans. Did the owners and officials turn a blind eye to the increase of home runs and physical change in some players? Once a reporter found an over-the-counter performance enhancing supplemental drug, Androstenedione, on the locker of Mark McGwire in 1998, the same individuals, McGwire, and Sammy Sosa, who thrilled the fans with their season-long race to beat the home run record of 61 by Roger Maris had become a stigma against the game.

When Barry Bonds finished his record-breaking season with his 73rd homer and shattered the slugging percentage record that Babe Ruth had owned for 81 years Bonds finished the 2001 season with a .328 batting average, a career-high 137 RBIs and a slugging percentage of. 863 when the cries of "Steroid ERA" began to take form. After Bonds hit a new record of 73 home runs, the media made Bonds, McGwire, Sosa, and others listed in the Mitchell report, the focal point of the investigation in the use of performance enhancing drugs (PED's). The owners continued to enjoy the profits while the Media now had their new story line. Maybe it was because the media hated Bonds, maybe they needed a good story, or whatever the reason, the media made Bonds the poster child for steroid use. Over a few years Bonds physical transformation was noticeable, but it did not make him a better hitter. Steroids do not improve hand-eye-coordination? That's not how steroids work. Steroids make it possible for players to train longer to get the repetitions in to become netter players. Steroids help the body recover from not just injuries, but the everyday wear-and-tear on the body faster. In turn, this allows an athlete to train longer, building more strength and muscle mass by giving them extra stamina to tear down more muscles and rebuild them over the same period of time as an athlete not using PEDs. That's what makes it possible for a baseball player to hit the ball further; by allowing them to train to be stronger.

Statistical Analysis and Baseball Cards

Baseball Statistics play an important role in evaluating the progress of a player or team. Henry Chadwick, a sportswriter in New York, developed the box score in 1858. This was the first way statisticians were able to describe the sport of baseball by numerically tracking various aspects of game play. The creation of the box score has given baseball statisticians a summary of the individual and team performances for a given game. These have been accumulated over the course of a Baseball Season and quantified for the Fan's viewing and collecting pleasure.

Since the flow of a baseball game has natural breaks to it, and normally players act individually rather than performing in groups, the sport lends itself to easy record-keeping and statistics. Statistics have been recorded since the game's earliest beginnings as a distinct sport in the middle of the nineteenth century, and as such are extensively available from leagues such as the National Association of Professional Base Ball Players and the Negro leagues, although the consistency to which these records have been kept and the standards with respect to which they were calculated (and their accuracy) has varied.

Since the National League (which along with the American League constitutes contemporary Major League Baseball) was founded in 1876, statistics in the most elite levels of professional baseball have been kept to a reasonably consistent standard which has continually evolved in tandem with advancement in available technology. The practice of keeping records of player achievements was started in the 19th century by Henry Chadwick. Based on his experience with the sport of cricket, Chadwick devised the predecessors to modern-day statistics including batting average, runs scored, and runs allowed.

Throughout modern baseball, a few core statistics have been traditionally referenced – batting average, RBI, and home runs. To this day, a player who leads the league in all of these three statistics earns the "Triple Crown". For pitchers, wins, ERA, and strikeouts are the most often-cited statistics, and a pitcher leading his league in these statistics may also be referred to as a "triple crown" winner. General managers and baseball scouts have long used the major statistics, among other factors and opinions, to understand player value. Managers, catchers and pitchers use the statistics of batters of opposing teams to develop pitching strategies and set defensive positioning on the field. Managers and batters study opposing pitcher performance and motions in attempting to improve hitting. Scouts use stats when they are looking at a player who they may end up drafting or signing to a contract.

Commonly Used Statistical Data

Commonly used statistics with their abbreviations are explained here. The explanations below are for quick reference and do not fully or completely define the statistic; for the strict definition.

Offensive Statistics

- **AB – At bat:** A plate appearance, does not include bases on balls, being hit by pitch, sacrifices, interference, or obstruction.
- **BA** – Batting average is the hits divided by at bats (H/AB).
- **BB** – Base on balls (also called a "walk"): hitter not swinging at four pitches called out of the strike zone and awarded first base.
- **H – Hit:** reaching base because of a batted, fair ball without error by the defense
- **HBP** – Hit by pitch: times touched by a pitch and awarded first base as a result.
- **HR** – Home runs: hits on which the batter successfully touched all four bases, without the contribution of a fielding error.
- **K** – Strike out (also abbreviated *SO*): number of times that a third strike is taken or swung at and missed, or bunted foul. Catcher must catch the third strike or batter may attempt to run to first base.
- **OBP** – On-base percentage: times reached base (H + BB + HBP) divided by at bats plus walks plus hit by pitch plus sacrifice flies (AB + BB + HBP + SF)
- **OPS** – On-base plus slugging: on-base percentage plus slugging average
- **PA** – Plate appearance: number of completed batting appearances.
- **R** – Runs scored: number of times a player crosses home plate
- **RBI** – Run batted in: number of runners who score due to a batter's action, except when the batter grounded into a double play or reached on an error
- **SLG** – Slugging percentage: total bases achieved on hits divided by at-bats.
- **TB** – Total bases: one for each single, two for each double, three for each triple, and four for each home run [H + 2B + (2 × 3B) + (3 × HR)] or [1B + (2 × 2B) + (3 × 3B) + (4 × HR)]
- **SB** – Stolen base: number of bases advanced by the runner while the ball is in the possession of the defense.
- **CS** – Caught stealing: times tagged out while attempting to steal a base.

The Baseball Hall of Fame

Pitching statistics

BB – Base on balls times pitching four balls, allowing the batter to take first base.

BF – Total batters faced: opponent team's total plate appearances.

CG – Complete game: number of games where player was the only pitcher for their team.

ERA – Earned run average: total number of earned runs multiplied by 9, divided by innings pitched.

G – Games (AKA "appearances"): number of times a pitcher pitches in a season

GF – Games finished: number of games pitched where player was the final pitcher for their team as a relief pitcher

GS – Starts: Games pitched where player was the first pitcher for their team.

H (or HA) – Hits allowed: total hits allowed

HB – Hit batsman: times a batter is hit with a pitch, allowing runner to advance to first base

IP – Innings pitched: the number of outs a team gets while a pitcher is pitching divided by 3.

K (or SO) – Strikeout: number of batters who received strike three

L – Loss: number of games where pitcher was pitching while the opposing team took the lead, never lost the lead, and went on to win

SHO – Shutout: number of complete games pitched with no runs allowed.

SV – Save: number of games where the pitcher enters a game led by the pitcher's team, finishes the game without surrendering the lead, is not the winning pitcher, and either (a) the lead was three runs or fewer when the pitcher entered the game; (b) the potential tying run was on base, at bat, or on deck; or (c) the pitcher pitched three or more innings

W – Win: number of games where pitcher was pitching while their team took the lead and went on to win, also the starter needs to pitch at least 5 innings of work (also related: winning percentage)

WHIP – Walks and hits per inning pitched: average number of walks and hits allowed by the pitcher per inning

Typical Baseball Card Statistics:

Position Players

AB	= At Bats	**R**	= Runs
H	= Hits	**2B**	= Doubles
3B	= Triples	**HR**	= Home Runs
RBI's	= Runs Batted In	**BB**	= Base on Balls
BA	= Batting Average	**OBP**	= On Base Percentage
SLG%	= Slugging Percentage	**OBPS**	= On Base + Slugging%
NBP	= Hit by Pitch	**Sac**	= Sacrifices

Pitching Statistics

G	= Games Pitched	**IP**	= Innings Pitched
W	= Games Won	**L**	= Games Lost
PCT.	= Winning Percentage	**SV**	= Games Saved
GS	= Games Started	**CG**	= Complete Games
GF	= Games Finished	**SHO**	= Shutouts
BB	= Bases on Balls	**H**	= Hits
WHIP	= (BB + Hits)/Innings Pitched	**HB**	= Hit Batters

These are the typical statistics the typical fan views and expects. Each chart for the Hall of Fame Statistical Point Totals is based off of 12 of the above statistics. No current Sabermetrics were used in the calculations for the three categories: Career– Post Season Pts.– World Series Pts.

Hall of Fame Elections Delayed

By The

Baseball Writers of America (BBWAA)

John Jordan "Buck" O'Neil Jr.

John Jordan "Buck" O'Neil Jr. was born Nov. 13, 1911, in Carrabelle, Florida. He was the second of three of three children born to John Jordan O'Neil (1873–1954) a sawmill worker, and Louella Campbell (1884–1945) a restaurant manager. The family later moved to the Newton Community, in Sarasota, Florida in 1923. O'Neil spent much of his childhood and worked the celery fields in Sarasota while his father ran a pool hall in Newtown. It was there that O'Neil received his first taste of professional baseball. As a 12-year-old, O'Neil began his semi-professional career as a member of the Sarasota Tigers and traveled throughout Florida. He took his nickname "Buck" from the Miami Giants semi-pro team co-owner Buck O'Neal.

O'Neil, the grandson of a slave, wanted to continue his education following completion of the eighth grade but was not allowed to enroll because Florida had only four high schools specifically for African Americans. Sarasota High School was not one of the four schools so O'Neil moved to Jacksonville with relatives and attended Edward Waters College. Here O'Neil completed high school and spent two years of college courses earning a baseball and football scholarship O'Neil completed two years of college before leaving school to play baseball.

To support himself, O'Neil shined shoes and worked as a box boy. Buck related a pivotal moment in his life to Steve Wulf of Sports Illustrated, "I was considered a good box boy because, while most of the box boys could only carry two crates at a time, I was big and strong enough to carry four. I did that for about three years, at $1.25 a day. One day I was having lunch by myself next to a big stack of boxes, and it was so hot, I said out loud, 'Damn, there has got to be something better than this.'" That "something," Buck decided, was baseball.

Negro League Baseball Career

Leaving Florida in 1934 until1938, O'Neil played on various teams, including the Miami Giants, New York Tigers, and the Shreveport Acme Giants. In addition, he played in many semi-professional "barnstorming" experiences (playing interracial exhibition games). The effort paid off, and in 1937, O'Neil signed with the Memphis Red Sox for their first year of play in the newly formed Negro American League. That same year, he played for one month with the Zulu Cannibal Giants, a barnstorming team. The Giants, owned by Harlem Globetrotters founder Abe Saperstein, wore straw skirts instead of

The Baseball Hall of Fame

uniforms, but the team paid well, and the players didn't have to wear war paint as some "African-themed" teams did.

In 1938, his contract was sold to the Monarchs the following with O'Neil earning a spot as the first baseman for the Kansas City Monarchs, one of the elite teams of the Negro Leagues. From 1939 to 1942, Kansas City won four consecutive Negro American League pennants. O'Neil told *Sports Illustrated* about the glory years of the Monarchs: "We were like the New York Yankees. We had that winning tradition, and we were proud. We had a strict dress code—coat and tie, no baseball jackets. We stayed in the best hotels in the world. They just happened to be owned by black people. We ate in the best restaurants in the world. They just happened to be run by blacks. And when we were in Kansas City, well, 18th and Vine was the center of the universe. We'd come to breakfast at Street's Hotel, and there might be Count Basie or Joe Louis or Billie Holiday or Lionel Hampton.

O'Neil's baseball career was interrupted for two years (1944 and 1945) during World War II when he joined the U.S. Navy after the close of the 1943 season. He served his enlistment in a naval construction battalion in New Jersey. In 1944, with the United States deeply involved in World War II, he was stationed at Subic Bay in the Philippines and worked as a bosun loading and unloading ships. Although he was proud to serve his country, O'Neil regretted the fact that he was not a member of the Monarchs in 1945 when Jackie Robinson played in Kansas City before signing with the Brooklyn Dodgers.

Following the end of World War II, O'Neil returned to the Monarchs in 1946 and became a member of Satchel Paige's All Stars. Paige's team, made up of Negro League stars, played a team of white major league players known as Bob Feller's All Stars in a 14-game barnstorming series. He also won the batting title that year and married Memphis schoolteacher Ora Lee Owens on January 17,1946. O'Neil remained devoted to her until her death on, November 2, 1997. Buck and Ora Lee shared a love for children, but one thing always surprised longtime friend Jim Wilson. They never had any children of their own.

In 1946, the first baseman led the NAL with a .353 batting average and followed that in 1947 with a .350 mark in 16 games. O'Neil played in three East-West All-Star Games in three different seasons and two Negro World Series. In 1948, O'Neil was named player-manager of the Monarchs. He led Kansas City to league pennants in 1948, 1950, 1951, and 1953 and two Negro World Series titles. Alfred "Slick" Surratt, who played outfield for O'Neil, told Mark Goodman of *People Weekly* about O'Neil's managerial style: "He knew what it took to win a ball game, and he gave you confidence in yourself. After every game, he'd go over the game with us, whether we'd won or lost."

A Fan's Perspective

O'Neil had a career batting average of .288 between 1937 and 1950, including four .300-plus seasons at the plate, as well as five seasons in which he did not top .260. O'Neil remembered that the players who performed in those exhibitions had a mutual respect for the abilities of their opponents with the Negro League All Stars winning most of the games played.

Major League Baseball

When Tom Baird sold the Monarchs at the end of the 1955 season, O'Neil resigned as manager. In 1956, O'Neil became a scout for the Chicago Cubs and traveled throughout the South searching for talented African American baseball players. He is credited with bringing formidable talents such as Ernie Banks, Lou Brock, Oscar Gamble, Lee Smith, and Joe Carter to the Cubs. In 1962, O'Neil made history by becoming the first African American coach in the major leagues. Although he had broken through an important barrier, Buck realized the Cubs were never going to make him manager of the team, so he chose to return to scouting. O'Neil remained with the Cubs until 1988, capping a 33-year career with the organization. Later, O'Neil returned to Kansas City in 1989 and joined the Kansas City Royals as a scout until his death.

Championed Negro League History

In 1990, O'Neil began raising money for a museum to preserve and celebrate the history of the Negro Leagues. O'Neil was adamant about the need to preserve memories of the Negro Leagues: "It's very important that we know our history. We have to do that ... this is not a sad story. It's a celebration!" he said, according to the *Pittsburgh Post-Gazette*. His efforts led to the opening of the Negro League Baseball Museum in Kansas City, Missouri. As a co-founder of the museum and one of the most articulate and engaging spokesman for the Negro Leagues, O'Neil began to appear regularly on radio and television programs. In 1994, he was featured prominently on Ken Burns's PBS documentary "Baseball." O'Neil was a key contributor to the segment titled "Shadow Ball," which chronicled the greatness of the Negro Leagues, but also the pain of discrimination and exclusion from the major leagues. Burns told People Weekly's Goodman that "He's the conscience of the program. Because of his dignity, lack of bitterness and sense of humor, Buck made a wonderful envoy for the game." O'Neil's presence in the documentary made him a media celebrity.

In the late 1990s O'Neil served as the chairman of the Negro Leagues Baseball Museum Board of the Directors, and was a member of the Veterans' Committee of the National Baseball Hall of Fame in Cooperstown, New York. He worked as a spokesman to secure pensions for surviving Negro League players and to preserve the history of the Negro Leagues. O'Neil often stated that "Negro League baseball was like the white major leagues, serious baseball, well organized. There were 16 Negro League ball clubs, each with at least 15 players—the Monarchs had 18 players. There were all those people putting on the games, booking agents, traveling secretaries, trainers. Baseball was black entertainment and was important to black communities. For his efforts, O'Neil came to be considered an "architect" of the game, as Brock described him in the Columbia Daily Tribune. "He helped shape the game. But even greater, he shaped the character of young black men. He touched the heart of everyone who loved the game." He was, perhaps the greatest ambassador baseball has ever known," in the words of Jane Forbes Clark, chairperson of the Baseball Hall of Fame, as quoted in *Sporting News.*

Baseball Hall of Fame

O'Neil was a member of the 18-member Baseball Hall of Fame Veterans Committee from 1981 to 2000 and played an important role in the induction of six Negro league players from 1995 to 2001 during the time the Hall had a policy of inducting one Negro leaguer per year. O'Neil was nominated to a special Hall ballot for Negro league players, managers, and executives in February 2006, but he fell one vote short to gain admission; however, 17 other Negro league figures were selected. Yet O'Neil took the news in stride. "Shed no tears for Buck," O'Neil announced to his fans after hearing the news, according to the *Pittsburgh Post-Gazette.* He pointed to past sorrows caused by racial discrimination that kept him from gaining the education he wanted, admitting "That hurt." From his perspective, he explained "not going into the Hall of Fame, that ain't going to hurt me that much, no." O'Neil bore no grudge.

He hosted the induction ceremony in Cooperstown with characteristic charm and grace. "Sometimes, I think God may have kept me on this Earth for a long time so I could bear witness to the Negro Leagues," O'Neil once told the *Kansas City Star.* When 17 Negro Leagues legends were inducted into the Hall of Fame in 2006, O'Neil came to Cooperstown for the Induction Ceremony and spoke on their behalf. "I've done a lot of things I really liked doing," O'Neil said in his speech. "But I'd rather be right here, right now, representing the people who helped build a bridge across the chasm of prejudice." God's been good to me. They didn't think Buck was good enough to be in the Hall of Fame. That's the way they thought about it and that's the way it is, so we're going to live with that. Now, if I'm a Hall of Famer for you, that's all right with me. Just keep loving old Buck. Don't weep for Buck. No, man, be happy, be thankful.

His fans rallied and promised to make amends for what they perceived to be an error in judgment. Buck O'Neil will be remembered as one of the finest players in the Negro Leagues and a legend in the game of baseball. Through his willingness to share his memories of the Negro Leagues, fans everywhere have a greater understanding and deeper appreciation for a significant period in baseball history. To honor his legacy, the Negro Leagues Baseball Museum began raising money to open the John "Buck" O'Neil Education and Research Center in Kansas City.

Death & Legacy

On August 5, 2006, O'Neil was admitted to a Kansas City hospital after complaining that he did not feel well. He was admitted for fatigue and was released three days later only to be re-admitted on September 17. On September 28, Kansas City media reported O'Neil's condition had worsened. On October 6, O'Neil died at the age of 94 due to heart failure and bone marrow cancer. During the ESPN opening day broadcast of the 2007 Kansas City Royals, on April 2, 2007, Joe Morgan announced the Royals would honor O'Neil by placing a fan in the Buck O'Neil Legacy Seat in Kauffman Stadium each game who best exemplifies O'Neil's spirit. The seat itself has been replaced by a red seat amidst the all-blue seats behind home plate in Section 101, Row C, Seat 1. Due to the renovations and section renumbering in 2009 the seat number is now Section 127, Row C, Seat 9, and the seat bottom is now padded. The first person to sit in "Buck's seat" was Buck O'Neil's brother, Warren G. O'Neil (1917–2013), who also played in the Negro American League.

- On March 31, 2007, O'Neil was posthumously awarded MLB's first annual Beacon of Life Award at the inaugural MLB Beacon Awards luncheon
- The Lifetime Achievement Award was created in 2008 with a statue dedicated in the Hall of Fame and named after Buck O'Neil. The award honors "an individual whose extraordinary efforts enhanced baseball's positive impact on society, broadened the game's appeal, and whose character, integrity and dignity are comparable to the qualities exhibited by O'Neil."
- O'Neil was posthumously awarded the Presidential Medal of Freedom by President George W. Bush.

The Baseball Hall of Fame

On November 5, 2021, O'Neil was selected to the final ballot of 10 candidates for consideration by the Early Days Committee during voting for induction to the Hall of Fame. Candidates needed to receive at least 12 of 16 votes (75%) for election, with the results to be announced in December. On December 5, the Hall of Fame announced that O'Neil had been elected with 13 votes. Buck O'Neil was formally enshrined on July 24,2022, as an executive, with his niece Angela Terry accepting the nomination and delivering a speech on his behalf.

Summary Analysis

O'Neil was the first African American coach and scout in Major League Baseball with the Cubs with a great eye for talent. He helped tremendously with the development of Cub Great, Ernie Banks, and scouted and assisted in the signing of future Hall of Famers Like Lou Brock, Billy Williams, and Lee Smith along with many other talents.

Though his playing statistics were good, not often great, Buck O'Neil's contributions to baseball spanned eight decades. He was masterful in identifying talent and was a skilled coach. O'Neil was a player who assisted in breaking down barriers for others and made it his life's mission to honor the legacy of the Negro Leagues. It's no wonder that baseball is considered America's pastime, Buck was one of the main architects of the game of Baseball and helped shape it. He was extremely important in influencing the character of young Black men and showed dignity and grace to White America. O'Neil touched the heart of all who loved the game and provided everyone a voice that could be heard on and off the field. Those that were close to him will forever seek to walk in the shade of his shadow, and the future generations have a role model to emulate.

Buck O'Neil was a hero of this writer since the mid-1960's due to his sparkling personality, grace, and love for others that was present every day. He was the only individual that could not be put in a Numerical Point Total due to the inaccuracies of Negro League record keeping, never playing in the MLB, and this writer's inability to quantify his contributions over eight-decades. The BBWAA and Baseball Hall of Fame, by not electing this great man while he was alive, is the biggest injustice ever done. His election into the Hall of Fame should have happened prior to Buck O'Neil appearing in the Baseball Documentary from 1994, which finally made everyone know his true value.

Ron Santo

Ronald Edward Santo was born on February 25, 1940, as the second born to Louie and Vivian Santo, who also had a daughter named Abilene. Ron's parents divorced when he was a young boy, as Ron lived with his mother and sister. His mother married John Constantino a few years later, giving Santo a male role model whom he became very close to, often referring to Constantino as Dad. Ron grew up to be a talented multi-sport star athlete in southeastern Seattle, Washington and attended Franklin High School. He excelled at football, basketball, and baseball and played organized youth baseball in the Babe Ruth League and grew up near Sick's Stadium, home of the Pacific Coast League's Seattle Rainiers. Ron had summer jobs there as a batboy, groundskeeper and clubhouse attendant while playing three sports in high school. At age 14, he made the Seattle all-star team that advanced to the 1954 Babe Ruth World Series.

Santo made the varsity baseball team as a freshman playing third base through his junior year. During his sophomore year at Franklin, Santo and Dave Kosher, who was a bird-dog scout for the Chicago Cubs, became close friends. In Santo's senior year, the team's starting catcher was lost to an injury and Ron had such a strong throwing arm, he took over the position. In 1958, Santo started to attract the attention of big-league scouts as a catcher. He received the Hearst All Star Award and, in competition with other Hearst Award winners, was selected as a catcher for a national all-star team that played the New York All Stars in New York. His talent impressed the many scouts who were in attendance with the Cubs lead scout, Roy "Hardrock" Johnson being one of them. He offered Santo a signing bonus of $20,000 and told Santo he would sign him as a catcher, because "I don't think you can play third base in the big leagues." Although other teams offered more money, Santo chose Chicago as he believed the Cubs would provide the shortest path to the majors, Also, he felt a sense of loyalty to Kosher, who believed in him and encouraged him from the start.

After signing with the Cubs in 1959, Santos' amateur career ended, and his professional career began. Santo concealed a secret even though he didn't realize he had one. This secret was found during a routine physical just before his minor league career began. It was then that doctors diagnosed Santo with Type 1 juvenile diabetes. At the time of the diagnosis, the life expectancy of a juvenile diabetic was thought to be about 25 years. Santo was 18 and educated himself about the disease and taught himself how to administer insulin injections. Santo enjoyed his success despite battling the disease since he was a teenager, Santo came out in public with the secret of his diabetes in August 1971. He explained why he hadn't gone public about it before, by telling reporters, "I didn't want anyone to know about diabetes because I felt that people would think that I was using it as an alibi if I was going bad. But I want to make it clear that being a diabetic hasn't affected my career in the slightest. If I take care of myself properly, I'm as good physically as any other player." Although most players and media knew of his condition, they respected his wishes to not make it public. The disease eventually necessitated the amputation of the lower half of both Santo's legs.

In 1960, Santo married his high school sweetheart Judy Scott. Together, the couple had three children, sons Ron Jr. and Jeff, and a daughter Linda but divorced in 1982. Santo married his second wife Vicki in 1983 and remained married until his death December 3, 2010, after a battle with bladder cancer. After spending most of his adult life associated with the Chicago Cubs, the team and all its fans mourned the death of this beloved figure and self-avowed "greatest Cubs fan." The Bleacher Report released a ranking of the 50 most beloved announcers in baseball history, in which Santo was placed 16th. He personified the Chicago Cubs for more than 50 years as a player, a broadcaster, and an icon. His legend is a testimony to his love of the game.

Baseball Career

Ron Santo was an American Major League Baseball third baseman who played for the Chicago Cubs from 1960 through 1973 and the Chicago White Sox in 1974. Santo was an All-Star for nine seasons during his 15-year career led the National League (NL) n triples one time, walks four times, and on-base percentage two times. On the field, Santo developed into a star at the plate and with the glove. He was named to his first All-Star Game in 1963 and won the first of five straight Gold Glove Awards in 1964. From 1963-70, Santo averaged almost 29 homers and 106 RBI per season. He also led the NL in walks four times between 1964 and 1968 and paced the league in on-base percentage twice in that same span.

Chicago Cubs Career (1959 to 1974)

Santo was signed as a free agent by the Chicago Cubs in 1959, and made his debut on June 26, 1960. Santo was moved to third base and immediately made an impact in the minors, hitting .327 with 87 RBI for Double-A San Antonio in 1959. With Hall of Famer, Rogers Hornsby, the Cubs' hitting instructor, and future Hall of Famer Billy Williams, a fellow rookie. Williams and Santo formed a solid friendship. After a week of inactivity, Santo was installed as the catcher and began hitting the ball all over the park. At the conclusion of the three-week camp, Hornsby assembled the prospects in the bleachers. He went down the line, critiquing each player: "You might as well go home"; "You won't get by A ball"; "Forget A ball, you won't get past C ball." He got to Santo and said, "You can hit in the big leagues right now." He made similar comments to Williams, the only other player Hornsby said would make the major leagues. These were all of the top prospects for the Cubs, but Rajah was right. Of the whole group, only Santo and Williams made it to the major leagues. Santo's rise through the system took just a year and three months, as he excelled at San Antonio of the Texas League (Double-A) and Houston of the American Association (Triple-A). In anticipation that he would replace Alvin Dark, the Cubs third baseman, who was winding down his career, Santo had been moved from catcher back to third. In San Antonio he learned how to field the position. At first, he was having a hard time with his throwing. But manager Grady Hatton, a former third baseman, worked with him. "He helped me tremendously at third, especially in correcting my throwing," said Santo. "I had been taking my time, daring the runner to beat my throw. It was strictly high-school stuff. Grady taught me to come up throwing and get rid of the ball immediately." The next season, Santo had 32 RBI in 71 games with Triple-A Houston before getting the call to the majors. In his June 26,1960 debut against the Pirates, Santo had three hits and five RBI in the doubleheader and never appeared in another minor league game.

In 1961 he set a Cubs record with 41 double plays at third base, breaking the previous mark of 33 set by Bernie Friberg in 1923. Santo finished fourth in the National League Rookie of the Year vote that season despite appearing in only 95 games. The next season, Santo firmly entrenched himself at third base by hitting 23 home runs and driving in 83 runs. In 1962 he led the National League in assists for the first time with 332, setting the team record for assists at third base, breaking the mark of 323 set by Randy Jackson in 1951. Santo continued to lead the NL in assists every year through 1968, breaking Ned Williamson's major league record of leading the league six times Brooks Robinson went on to lead the American League eight times. Mike Schmidt eventually tied Santo's NL mark of seven. In 1963 Santo broke the modern NL record with 374 assists at third base, passing Tommy Leach's 1904 mark of 371. In 1966, he set the all-time league record with 391, the previous record being Billy Shindle's 382 in 1892; his total was 99 higher than that of league runner-up Ken Boyer. Santo broke his own record in 1967 with 393 assists, which remained the NL record until Schmidt posted 404 in 1974. He also finished fourth in the 1967 NL Most Valuable Player Award voting results. Santo's assist totals from 1963 through 1968 were the six highest by an NL third baseman between 1905 and 1973. He also led the NL in putouts every year from 1962 through 1967 and again in 1969, tying the league record shared by Pie Traynor and Willie Jones in leading the league seven times.

He batted .300 or more and hit 30 or more home runs four times each, and is the only third baseman in MLB history to post eight consecutive seasons with over 90 runs batted in (RBI) (1963–70). Also was a Gold Glove Award winner for five consecutive seasons. He led the NL in total chances eight times, in games, putouts and assists seven times each, and in double plays six times. From 1966 to 1974, he held the NL record for assists in a single season. He also set NL records for career assists (4,532), total chances (6,777) and double plays (389) at third base, all of which were eventually broken between 1986 and 1988 by Mike Schmidt. His NL total of 2,102 games at third base is 52 short of Eddie Mathews' league record, and he ranks sixth in putouts (1,930) and ninth in fielding percentage (.954).

Chicago White Sox

The 1973 season was the last on the North Side for Santo. The Cubs at one time celebrated their core of youthful talent. But now they started trading players away, among them Jenkins, Hundley, and Beckert. Santo was believed to be on his way to the California Angels, but vetoed a trade as allowed under the Players Association contract because he had ten years in the league and five with the same team. Santo did approve of a trade to the White Sox on December 11.

Although the trade caused much celebration on the South Side, it proved to be premature euphoria. Santo spent most of the 1974 season as a utility infielder, spelling Bill Melton at third base or Jorge Orta at second. His primary position was that of designated hitter. Santo retired as a player on December 13, 1974, and said his new job as vice president of sales at Torco Oil would occupy much of his time. He added that his confidence on the baseball diamond had been shaken by his diminished role the past year. His role with the White Sox may have been even harder for him to adapt to after starring for the Cubs for 14 seasons. For his career, he smacked 342 home runs and drove in 1,331 runs. His career fielding percentage was .954, with 4,581 assists. In 1999 he was named to the Cubs All-Century Team. His number 10 was retired on September 28, 2003. For his career, he smacked 342 home runs and drove in 1,331 runs. His career fielding percentage was .954, with 4,581 assists. In 1999 he was named to the Cubs All-Century Team and number 10 retired on September 28, 2003.

Achievements

- 5-Times National League Golden Glove Winner: (1964 – 1968).
- 9-Times National League All-Star: (1964 – 1969, 1971- 1973).
- 7-Times Received Most Valuable Player Votes National League: (1963-1969).
- 2-Times led National League in Games Played: (1963 & 1965).
- 1-Time led National League in Triples: (1964).
- 4-Times led the National League in Bases on Balls: (1964, 1965-1968).
- 2-Times led the National League in On-Base Percentage: (1964 & 1966).
- 3-Times led the National League in Sacrifice Hits: (1963, 1967 & 1969).

Hall of Fame BBWAA

Santo first became eligible for election to the Baseball Hall of Fame in 1980 but was named on less than four percent of all ballots cast by the Baseball Writers' Association of America (BBWAA), and was removed from the ballot in subsequent years; he was re-added to the ballot in 1985 following widespread complaints about overlooked candidates. After receiving 13 percent of the vote in the 1985 election, his vote totals increased in until he received 43 percent of the vote in his final year on the 1998 ballot.

Subsequent Committees

Following revamped voting procedures for the Veterans Committee, Santo finished third in 2003, tied for first in 2005, and again finished first in voting for 2007 and 2009 inductions, but fell short of the required number of votes each year.

Golden Era Committee

Santo's next opportunity for admission came during the voting in 2011 by the new 16-member Golden Era Committee which considers every three years, ten candidates identified by the Historical Overview Committee from the 1947 to 1972 era. Although Santo became a widely supported candidate for selection, his initial poor showing in balloting has been attributed to various factors, including a longtime tendency of BBWAA voters to overlook third basemen as only three of the over 120 players elected were third basemen, and only Pie Traynor had been elected by the BBWAA.

Also, the fact that Santo's best years occurred in the pitching-dominated 1960s has been cited as a factor that led the voters to perhaps overlook him. Another possible reason that was suggested was that voters had not focused sufficiently on Santo's high walk totals and defense. These aspects of play are perhaps more valued by sabermetrics — newer methods of evaluating a baseball player's productivity — than they have been by BBWAA voters in the past.

Others have also commented that two Cubs players who were in their prime during Santo's prime years have already been honored by the Hall of Fame (Ferguson Jenkins and Billy Williams), and the Cubs also featured a third Hall of Famer, Ernie Banks, who was arguably past his prime, yet the team never won a pennant. However, the late 1960s Cubs were far from the only team in baseball history with multiple Hall of Famers that did not win a pennant or a World Series. Santo also fell short of such traditional standards of Hall election as 3,000 hits and 500 home runs; however, by the time his career ended, only two third basemen (Brooks Robinson and Lave Cross) had even collected 2,500 hits, and only one (Eddie Mathews) had reached the 500-home run plateau. Bill James ranked Santo among the 100 greatest players of all time (sixth among third basemen), believed his election to the Hall of Fame was long overdue.

Even though Santo was disappointed at being bypassed by the Hall of Fame, on the day his jersey number 10 was retired by the Cubs, the optimistic and emotional "old Cub" told the cheering Wrigley Field crowd, "This is *my* Hall of Fame!" During Ryne Sandberg's Hall of Fame acceptance speech in 2005, Sandberg reiterated his support for Santo's selection, saying, "...for what it's worth, Ron Santo just gained one more vote from the Veterans Committee.

Hall of Fame Election

On December 5, 2011, the 16-member Golden Era Committee began voting on ten candidates selected by the BBWAA screening committee whether Santo would be elected to the National Baseball Hall of Fame's Class of 2012. Williams, Santo's long-time teammate and friend, had made a fresh case for Santo, emphasizing his personal struggle with diabetes during his career, and his post-retirement charitable work to try to find a cure. Santo received 15 of the 16 possible votes and was the only one of the ten Golden Era Ballot candidates to be elected to the Hall of Fame by the committee's first vote. Santo's widow Vicki accepted the plaque on Induction Day and spoke about his love of the Cubs and his devotion to people with diabetes.

Retired number at Wrigley Field

Santo broke Eddie Mathews' NL record of 369 career double plays at third base in 1972, and in 1973 he broke Mathews' league records of 4,284 assists and 6,606 total chances. Schmidt passed Santo's record for double plays in 1986, his record for assists in 1987, and his mark for total chances in 1988. During his 14-season run with the Cubs, Santo hit 337 home runs, then the eighth most by a NL right-handed hitter; his 1,071 career walks with the Cubs remain the team record for a right-handed hitter. He was the first third baseman to hit 300 home runs and win five Gold Gloves.

Santo became the first player in major league history to wear a batting helmet with protective ear flaps, when in 1966, in the midst of trying to break the Cubs' modern consecutive-game hitting streak record of 27 games, Santo was sidelined for nearly two weeks following a pitch thrown by the Mets' Jack Fisher. The beaning fractured his cheekbone and ended his consecutive playing streak. When he returned, he wore an improvised ear flap on his batting helmet in order to protect the injury; ear flaps have since become standard equipment on batting helmets. In 1999, he was named to the Cubs All-Century Team and on September 28, 2003, Santo's jersey No. 10 was retired by the Cubs organization, making him the third player so honored. In April 2004, Santo was inducted into the inaugural class of the Washington Interscholastic Activities Association Hall of Fame as a graduate of Seattle's Franklin High School. After Santo's death, Cubs Chairman Tom Ricketts announced that Santo would be honored by the Cubs in the 2011 season as the Cubs wore a patch on the sleeve of their jersey with the number 10 on it from spring training to the end of the year.

The Baseball Hall of Fame

Summary Analysis

Ron Santo's 107.500 Hall of Fame Point Total listed in the statistical analysis section of this book is less than 2.500 off the required 110.00 for induction proposed in this book. However, since the BBWAA likes to use the "Character Clause" as a crutch to keep individuals they do not like from being elected to the Hall of Fame, Ron Santo was one player who has always demonstrated extreme character in dealing with fans. Over the years Santo played for the Cubs and White Sox, and this writer attended many games observing Santo signing autographs, balls, etc... for the young and old fans every game.

As a youngster growing up in the 1960's and 1970's, Ron Santo was the perfect role model I followed. As proven by the statistical analysis provided in this book, Ron Santo should not have had to wait until his death to be elected but should have been elected within the first ten years after of his retirement. If he had been, he could have enjoyed almost 30 years of being recognized as one of the best players the sport of Baseball ever produced. Ron deserved to give his own Hall of Fame speech.

This writer lived and died every year when Santo failed to be elected to the Baseball Hall of Fame and is in the opinion that Ron Santo's failure to be elected by the various committees and BBWAA while he was still living was one of the most grievous injustices the Hall of Fame ever experienced. His career statistics alone were Hall of Fame worthy, but it was his heartfelt passion for the game he loved his interaction with the fans, 20 years as a die-hard Cub announcer, and his charitable work endorsing the Juvenile Diabetes Research Foundation's annual Ron Santo Walk to Cure Diabetes in Chicago made him an icon to the fans. His endorsement has helped raise over $65 million for the foundation. In 2002, he was named the Juvenile Diabetes Research Foundation's "Person of the Year". Individuals like Ron Santo being enshrined in the Baseball Hall of Fame is one of the main reasons fans would go there.

John, Tommy (The Bionic Man)

John realized that prior to 1974, injured pitchers just faded away with this type of injury and felt he really had nothing to lose but everything to gain so he told Dr. Jobe to "Let's do it,". The type of surgery had entered Jobe's mind a few years before he first tried it as he knew several hand surgeons who were doing work transplanting ligaments and giving people back the use of their fingers after a severe injury. Jobe had wondered whether the same could work in the elbow, but no one had done it as of now. Repairs to some major ligaments, like those of the knee, had been done but the surgery was extensive, and the repair never returned the player back to the normal level. Even with surgery, the injury itself was often career-ending. It took an opportunity like Tommy John for Dr. Jobe to try something that was never successfully done.

The surgery was relatively simple and after a few months of recovery, John was throwing again and looking positive. However, there was a setback when Tommy began having severe pain in the elbow, requiring Dr. Jobe to go back inside the elbow. The ulnar nerve had become trapped inside scar tissue and was causing pain. To relieve the pain, Dr. Jobe moved the nerve in a common surgery called transposition, though the setback made John miss the entire 1975 season. This surgery was the most dramatic change in the history of baseball with Dr. Jobe and Tommy John not getting the credit they deserve for the surgery and recovery procedures they developed. The impact on baseball as a result of the surgery pioneered by Dr. Jobe, and Tommy John is truly too large to understand. Over several decades, this operation has withstood the test of time, over and over again successfully returning high-level throwers back to baseball. There are very few procedures with such longevity that have withstood the test of time. The impact on baseball has been so large that it is now taken for granted that a professional thrower can successfully return back to his career as a result of this surgery.

Johns' legacy is safe, with or without the honors of the Baseball Hall of Fame.
John returned to the Dodgers in 1976, the fourth starter in their rotation after spending all of the previous year on the disabled list. On April 16, he made his comeback against the Braves at Fulton County Stadium. Though he allowed three runs in five innings and took the loss, it was the first time any pitcher had started a game following UCL reconstruction surgery. Five days after the Atlanta game, in a 1–0 loss to the Houston Astros, John threw seven scoreless innings. On June 13, he

threw his first complete game since the injury, also against the Expos, whom he held to three runs in a 6–3 victory. He threw a four-hit shutout against the Padres on July 23 and a 10-hit shutout against the Cincinnati Reds on September 14. John would make 31 starts for the Dodgers in 1976, posting a 10–10 record, a 3.09 ERA, 91 strikeouts, 61 walks, and 207 hits allowed in 207 innings pitched. In recognition of John's accomplishments, the Sporting News awarded him its NL Comeback Player of the Year Award, and John also won the Fred Hutchinson Award, presented annually to a player who shows outstanding character and courage.

Career Turning Point

John was never a sexy pitcher. Even though John had three twenty plus seasons of wins, aside from a few years leading the league in shutouts, and back-to-back seasons with the Los Angeles Dodgers leading the NL in winning percentage, John never stood out as a statistical super star. Tommy John's Hall of Fame Point Total of 139.300 is considerably higher than the 110.000 Induction Criteria proposed in this book. There is no one with more wins than John that has not been elected to the Hall of Fame. Beyond his pitching stats, John is obviously notable for being the first recipient and namesake of Tommy John surgery. The procedure revolutionized baseball and saved countless careers, with John proof of the concept. In addition, he won 164 games after surgery.

Tommy John NOT BEING elected to the Baseball Hall of Fame is a Travesty done by the BBWAA and Baseball that needs to be corrected immediately while he is still living. Tommy John should have been inducted 6 years after retirement so he could have enjoyed the fruits of his outstanding career and revolutionary namesake surgery. I can think of no one more deserving than this fine gentleman to be a role model for generations to follow. However, a Cooperstown's tribute would certainly be something long overdue and celebrated. Tommy, now at age 81, deserves the Aristocrats of Baseball to put him in the Hall of Fame where he could be side by side with some of the careers, the team of John and Dr. Jobe, pioneered and saved.

Tommy's Faith and Family

On August 13, 1981, John was out in the dusk of the bullpen, throwing between starts to loosen his arm. Abruptly a bat boy approached and told him he had a call. "Take a number," he said, "and I'll call back." After a few finishing pitches, Tommy was walking toward the Yankee dugout when he noticed Jeff Torborg waving for him to hurry. "Sallys on the phone,' he was told and says it's an emergency. His son, Travis, was unconscious in a Point Pleasant, N.J., hospital and had a fractured skull that required 90 minutes of surgery to relieve pressure on his brain. Sally John had taken their three children, while the Yankees were on the road, to a family friend's beach house. They were on the third floor where Travis had pushed through a window screen and fallen and bounced off of a station wagon in the driveway. At the time Tommy had received the call, Travis's life was hanging by a thread and was unconscious. There was an air controllers' strike at the time, so Tommy could not get a flight to Newark that night. He phoned a friend, Bob Zankl, who owned a small plane that was not available but helped Tommy charter a plane. After having arrived at a small airport near Point Pleasant shortly after midnight, Tommy John learned that doctors had arranged for Travis to be taken by helicopter that morning to Manhattan and the N.Y.U. Medical Center. 'Tommy and Sally had to go to another helicopter but were informed by the doctors they were not sure Travis would still be alive when they got there.

Travis had survived the flight and tests soon showed no brain damage, but he remained unconscious. To be close to the hospital, Tommy and Sally moved into the Grand Hyatt Hotel a few blocks away. Their two other children, 6-year-old Tami and 4-year-old Tommy, were taken by Sally's sister, Judy Reed, to her Covington, Ind., home. At this point, John said that "baseball didn't mean anything to us.' Hour after hour, Tommy and Sally talked to Travis, even though he was in a coma. "We told Travis that we loved him, that his sister and brother loved him. "The doctors told us that someone in a coma can understand what they hear but they can't respond. And whenever we mentioned his sister and brother, the machines connected to him would show that his heartbeat was faster. He must have received more than 2,000 letters and cards, most of them from strangers, and we read them to him when he was in a coma. The world was aware of Travis John's battle as President Reagan sent a note, along with notes from former Presidents Jimmy Carter and Richard Nixon. The day after the accident, the Johns started to hear from many fans of the Yankees and numerous baseball people. He also got presents, letters, and wires from a lot of entertainers that knew Tommy when he was with the Dodgers.

One day Travis woke up from the coma with his eyes open, but hardly moved. A few days later Reggie Jackson visited Travis John's bedside. Some people of the Muppets learned how much Travis loved the Muppets and sent over some puppets and when Reggie stopped by that day, he took one of the puppets and started acting silly and put on a show. Travis couldn't even laugh then but seemed to understand. Soon he was a little boy again and soon he was down on the floor, learning to walk again, taking a few steps each day. One day Travis got his legs to move, the next day he was able to take a few steps then soon seven or eight and continued to progress from there. On September 13, 1981, Travis was released to go home and sat in the back seat with his mother, while Tommy drove. As Tommy drove into the driveway, 'Travis,' Sally said, 'we're home.' "Bicycle," Travis said. "Bicycle." His mother smiled. Travis had remembered that his bicycle was in the garage. Once inside their home, Travis reached into his toy box and tossed a few balls around in his playroom. Then he leapt onto some overstuffed pillows on the floor and stared at the TV set. Tommy put on a video cassette of "The Muppet Movie" which was Travis's favorite before his accident. "Until he went to bed that night,' Tommy John remembered, 'I think he watched that movie three times".

Travis had remembered his little world and Tommy was so welcome and relieved that his little boy was back. With Travis' recovery, Tommy's psychological state started to return to normal as well. In his first start after Travis's accident, Tommy's mind drifted and made It difficult to think about how to pitch. After Travis started to get better, so did Tommy, who had the ability to force himself to concentrate when he had to. He is a very strong and spiritual individual that prays regularly and not only when prayers are needed. In addition, he also prays in thanks when prayers are answered. As Travis continued recovering, John thanked everyone who had offered up prayers and any assistance for this miraculous recovery of his beloved son.

Unfortunately, Tommy John was no stranger to tragedy as he has endured the passing of his father in 1987, his died in mother in 2009 due to an auto accident, but his faith was strongly tested because of the untimely passing of his youngest son, Taylor Simmons John on March 9, 2010, as a result of a seizure and heart failure caused by an overdose of prescription drugs. Prior to his stint on Broadway, Taylor played Gavroche for one year in the national touring company of Les Misérables. At the time of his passing, Taylor worked as a teacher's assistant at Deerpath Middle School in Lake Forest, Illinois. as well as an accomplished Broadway singer. Taylor was a regular singing the national anthem in ballparks around the country. The death of a child is devastating and often described to as the worst experience a parent can endure. A child's death causes a profound family crisis. It shatters core beliefs and assumptions about the world and the expectations about how life should unfold. The overwhelming suffering and intense emotions that flood the days, weeks, months, and years following the loss is called grief.

The pain of grief is extremely intense as parents digest the finality of never seeing their child again and the loss of future hopes and plans. While memories of the child flood their mind, they also experience a deep emptiness and unimaginable void in their lives. Grief impacts a parent's whole identity as well as the identity and security of other members of the family. Some emotions of grief can be shared with others, while other intense feelings of loneliness or guilt, may never be put into words. The ways in which feelings and emotions of grief are experienced and expressed differ from person to person. One parent may need to talk a great deal about the loss and the pain, while another may become quiet and withdrawn. Some try to avoid facing their pain by holding feelings inside and acting as though they are fine. Tommy always handled his grief with dignity and faith.

The Miracle for Tommy John

On December 12, 2020, COVID struck Tommy and his wife Cheryl, and he could barely walk when they returned to their home in La Quinta, California. Cheryl didn't know how she got him in the house but did. On the morning of the 13th, Tommy tried to stand up but fell and sliced his forehead open. Cheryl tried to get him up as he was wedged between their bed and a dresser. Cheryl went out to the garage to get a baseball bat so she could try and help him up but couldn't. Then she dialed 911 and told not to move him. When the ambulance came, they asked Cheryl if they were in a domestic relationship because they saw the bat. They took him to Eisenhower Health Center in La Quinta and sent him home the next day. Cheryl said, "He couldn't stand up or go to the bathroom, had the worst bed sores ever as the hospital never checked him, but they sent him home five times. Cheryl was looking at Tommy and he looked like he was dying, and she felt helpless. Tommy was approximately 280 pounds and Cheryl couldn't lift him. The hospital even dropped him on the ground the last time he went into the hospital. At the same time, Cheryl was trying to fight off pneumonia but would not allow herself to be sick enough because she knew that Tommy needed to be taken care of. Cheryl couldn't taste, or smell for four months but Tommy was her love and he needed her. Tommy John would be in and out of Eisenhower Health Center for five weeks but was thankful it wasn't five weeks and one day. Tommy had two huge blood clots in the upper and lower lobes of his lung. Cheryl texted a friend, Dr. Dan Oakes, who sent all the necessary information to

The Baseball Hall of Fame

Dr. Antreas Hindoyan, a Cardiologist, at Keck Medical Center of the University of Southern California Health Sciences.

Cheryl received a telephone call at 3:30 in the morning from Dr. Hindoyan. He told her to "Get him out of that hospital immediately" as the doctor ordered an ambulance to pick Tommy up as he believed he was in grave condition. The ambulance was waiting, and they transported him to Keck Medical and by 6:00 am Tommy in surgery where two massive blood clots were broken up in his lung. The quick-thinking Dr. Hindoyan had saved Tommy's life. However, another COVID curveball came up when Tommy came down with Guillain-Barré syndrome. This affects the nerves which left John paralyzed in his lower extremities for almost eight months. Tommy is still dealing with the disease and has to use a walker to get around. John feels he is getting better daily as he feels his strength coming back. He was in a wheelchair for almost eight months, but it didn't stop Cheryl and Tommy's wedding day. He could not walk but he lay in the back of their SUV, and Cheryl stood outside the car, in the lot at the County Clerk's office and they asked the Justice to come out and marry Tommy and Cheryl, which they gleefully did. Cheryl gushed, "We're happy!" "And we're happy!" John said. Friends introduced Cheryl and Tommy 12 years ago with this being the second marriage for the both of them. He turned 79 on May 22, 2022, and was treated to a surprise party at his apartment clubhouse with approximately 60 guests, including his son Tommy John III, son- In-Law, and retired Chicago Bears

Tommy & Cheryl John

long snapper, Patrick Mannelly, granddaughter Tyler Mannelly. His daughter Tamara Mannelly was away on business but was not able to attend. John has teamed with his son, Tommy John III, who advocates through speaking engagements and his Performance and Healing Center in San Diego, that the year-round nature of sports can be detrimental to the body's long-term sustainability in competitive athletics. Tommy Sr. is extremely proud of what he did, which was supposed to open doors for a professional. However, the younger John feels the surgery named after his father is being overdone on young ball players. So, if it can be Tommy John and son trying to prevent the namesake surgery, because he cannot stand that his name is attached to something that is happening more to kids than adults.

In baseball's enduring struggle to understand the root cause of the Tommy John epidemic, there have been losses and victories. All that is missing is an actual answer, leaving teams to digest correlations and presumptions. The Major League level dictates that pitchers go out there and get outs and do the best you can for yourself and for the team. Coaches could start teaching in high school, or the minors, pitching to contact could be done to mitigate the possible damage done to elbows in the future. That not one new piece of information leads to transformational change is not surprising. There is no concise precision so far in the attempt to save pitching elbows. Every team has its own approach and even a study like this one has its own questions. While it adds to the conversation, it does not prove a causation.

Tommy John has been a great Ambassador of the game from the time he threw his first professional pitch until now. He was above average during his long career; very dependable, consumed innings, and regardless of any surgery named after him, is a guy whose baseball career alone simply says he's a Hall of Famer. He coached in the minor leagues and would pull a pitcher aside after a game to go through each hit he gave up, asking what pitch he threw. Most couldn't do it, and John couldn't understand why. He didn't want them to merely throw, but to think their way through the game, like he did. It was the biggest reason he was successful, he says, and allowed him to play long after his physical skills had declined, when he was throwing no faster than 85 mph. That's not the way the game is played now, he says. Though he rarely watches any part of a game, he has strong opinions of today's MLB. He doesn't care much for automation of umpires in the minor leagues and feels that an umpire is a part of baseball and should remain so. John scoffs at instant replay and do not get him started on bat flips and says whoever did that to show him up would have been hit the next time up with the ball in their side. Tommy also thinks it's troubling how often benches clear these days. He suggests allowing batters to charge the mound while punishing teams when they empty the dugout during any sort of confrontation. That, he says, would cause batters to think twice before charging. He still loves the game at its core, though. He'll talk for hours to those who ask him about baseball's yesteryear, about playing in the World Series and how, deep into his 40s, he had just two pitches in his arsenal at the very end. He'll also talk passionately about how children should be playing far less baseball, with 57 percent of the Tommy John elbow ligament replacement surgeries done today on kids ages 13 to 18. That's far too young to have to endure that, he says.

There are many more changes the game of baseball has undergone since he broke in the majors in 1964. A few of the changes John is not entirely a fan of are the designated hitter, lowering of the mound, the recently introduced pitch clock. The latter, he feels, is not needed if the if more pitchers and hitters played to contact. There are far too many strikeouts and walks which eat up time. Teach the players early on to choke up for better bat control with two strikes, learn to bunt more efficiently, hit and run, steal bases. Instead of always looking for a three-run home run, learn to play small ball. And last but not least, pitch counts can be misleading. Don't try and throw as hard as you can for as long as you can, pitchers need to pace themselves better and only try for the strikeout when it is needed. If anyone knows about the art of pitching, Tommy John knows.

Statistical Review of Potential First Basemen for the Hall of Fame

Player	Years Played	Career Pts.	Post Season Pts.	World Series Pts.	Add-On Pts.	Mil/LT Pts.	Total HOF Pts.	Votes. Needed	Comments
Players Needing to be Inducted									
Allen, Dick	15	60.000	2.650	0.000	59.000	0	121.65	0	Inducted
Garvey, Steve	19	56.000	10.900	7.800	51.000	0	125.700	0	Inducted.
Helton, Todd	17	96.000	1.650	4.635	30.000	0	132.285	Elected	2024
Hernandez, Keith	17	50.750	5.400	4.500	61.000	0	121.650	0	Inducted
Mattingly, Don	14	47.000	11.050	0.000	62.000	0	120.050	0	Inducted.
Pujols, Albert	22	145.00	15.050	5.250	92.000	0	257.300	0	Inducted.
Players Needing to be Voted into the Hall of Fame by the BBWAA									
Berkman, Lance	15	70.725	10.250	10.500	15.000	0	106.000	4	Election
Clark, Will	15	60.000	9.850	1.650	26.000	0	97.500	13	Election
Delgado, Carolos	17	68.250	9.900	0.000	15.000	0	103.150	17	Election
Galarraga, Andre	19	64.250	2.200	0.000	25.000	0	91.450	19	Election
Konerko, Paul	18	66.500	7.350	4.450	12.000	0	90.300	20	Election
Olerud, John	17	64.250	10.050	3.450	22.000	0	99.750	11	Election
Oliver, Al	18	60.500	3.700	1.500	26.000	0	91.700	19	Election
Texiera, Mark	14	54.000	5.150	1.900	37.000	0	98.050	12	Election
Players Not Meeting the Statistical Requirements									
Cash, Norm	17	53.000	4.150	5.300	18.000	0	77.450	N/A	DMR
Clark, Jack	18	54.500	6.950	7.650	20.000	0	89.100	N/A	DMR
Cooper, Cecil	17	44.000	1.800	2.100	24.000	0	71.900	N/A	DMF
Daubert, Jake	15	40.000	0.000	2.350	25.000	0	67.350	N/A	DMR
Dykes, Jimmy	12	43.750	0.000	6.650	10.000	0	60.400	N/A	DMR
Fielder, Prince	12	46.250	4.200	0.750	28.000	0	79.200	N/A	DMF
Gonzalez, Adrian	15	49.750	7.250	0.000	31.000	0	88.000	N/A	DMR
Grace, Mark	16	58.250	7.150	4.100	18.000	0	87.500	N/A	DMR
Judge, Joe	20	42.500	0.000	5.500	10.000	0	68.000	N/A	DMR
Kluzewski, Ted	15	45.500	0.000	10.500	14.000	0	70.000	N/A	DMR
Lee, Derrek	15	51.250	3.300	1.500	26.000	0	82.050	N/A	DMF
Martinez, Tino	15	44.750	8.050	6.800	4.000	0	63.600	N/A	DMR
Powell, Boog	17	45.500	6.500	4.450	17.000	0	73.450	N/A	DMF
Sievers, Roy	17	41.700	0.000	0.000	23.000	0	64.700	N/A	DMR
Vaughn, Maurice	12	50.000	3.050	0.000	16.000	0	69.050	N/A	DMF

Hall of Fame Statistical Requirements:

All Players achieving the total of 110.000, or greater, Total Hall of Fame Points, shall be Inducted after five (5) years of retirement. This provision can be waived due to the death by a 75% vote of the 25 Panel BBWAA's. Individuals receiving less than the required 110.000 Hall of Fame Points are eligible for Election after five (5) years of retirement. A 25 person BBWAA will determine the Players that will be Inducted and vote on the Players needing to be elected. An example of those needing to be elected are as follows: Player "A" has a total of 95 Hall of Fame Points and will need 15 of the (25) BBWAA votes to be Elected in the following year.

The Baseball Hall of Fame

First Basemen Needing to be Inducted

1. Dick Allen
2. Steve Garvey
3. Keith Hernandez
4. Don Mattingly
5. Albert Pujols

110.000 Hall of Fame Statistical Induction Criteria

Allen, Dick "Richie"

Personal Life

Richard Anthony Allen was born to Coy Allen & Era Rhodes Craine Allen on March 8, 1942, in Crescentdale, PA. After his parents divorced, Allen was educated in the Baptist tradition at the First Baptist Missionary Church in Chewton, Pennsylvania. Allen was the second youngest of nine children and raised by his mother.

Dick Allen was a highly gifted, multi-sport athlete at Wampum High School. He was a starting guard on the basketball team with his older brothers, Hank and Ronnie. All three earned All-State honors in basketball in 1958 and 1960, and the team won the Division B state championship with Dick earning All-American honors. Allen's talent, exceptional instincts, and strong desire to win captured the attention of scouts. Era Allen served as her son's negotiator and let Dick to sign with the Phillies in 1960 for an estimated $70,000. The first thing Dick did was buy his mother a new house.

Allen married Barbara Moore in 1962 with the couple having two sons, Richard and Eron and divorced in 1981. Allen married Willa King in 1987, spending his final years living in Wampum, Pennsylvania with her.

Baseball Career

Allen began his career in the New York-Pennsylvania League in 1960. In 1963, Allen was expected to play in the major leagues, but the Phillies relocated their Triple-A farm club and decided to integrate the team. Allen experienced racial segregation and pressure daily with racial taunts from the crowd and threatening notes on his car. However, he overcame his fear to be voted Most Valuable Player, hitting .289 and leading the International League with 33 home runs and 97 RBIs. Allen was called up to the Phillies on September 3, 1963, and played in ten games. In 1964, Allen played third base, a position he had never played regularly, Allen was adept with the bat, but his fielding was a sore spot with fans. He made 41 errors at third base in 1964 with the Phillies fans booing him unmercifully.

By September 20 the Phillies had built a 6½-game lead with 12 to play but lost ten games in a row. On the final day, the Phillies needed a win. Allen went 3-for-5 with two home runs in a 10-0 win over the Reds but the Cardinals beat the New York Mets and clinched the pennant. During the final two weeks, Allen hit .429 and had an 11-game hitting streak. Allen had done his part finishing the 1964 season with a .318 average, 29 homers, and 91 RBIs. He led the league with 125 runs scored and the only Philie to start all 162 games earning the National League Rookie of the Year Award.

Allen, always delivered with the bat, played wherever his teams needed him but was often misunderstood. The 1966 season solidified Allen's status as a baseball superstar as he hit .317, with 40 home runs, 110 RBIs, and played in 141 games. He led the league in slugging and finished fourth in the National League MVP voting. On August 24, 1967, Allen was at home working on his 1950 Ford and his right hand slipped and went through the headlight. Two tendons were cut, and a nerve was severed limiting him to 122 games. The Doctors gave Allen a 50-50 chance of ever playing again but Allen came back and had a good year in 1968 hitting 33 HR's and 90 RBIO's.

On October 7, 1969, the Phillies traded him to the St. Louis Cardinals in March 1970. Allen played in 122 games, hit .279 with 34 HRs, and 101 RBI's but the Cardinals management were convinced Allen was prone to injury and didn't devote himself to healing quickly enough. So, they moved him while his value was at a premium to the Los Angelos Dodgers where he played a year and then traded to the Chicago White Sox as the team was looking for more pitching. In 1972, Allen carried the White Sox into pennant contention and was credited for revitalizing Baseball on Chicago's South Side. The White Sox drew only 833,891 fans to Comiskey Park in 1971, but in 1972 attendance spiked to almost 1.8 million fans. Allen was the most dominant player in the American League and led the league with 37 home runs, 113 RBIs, batted.

The Baseball Hall of Fame

Allen finished his career with a .292 average, 351 home runs, and 1,119 RBIs and 1,848 hits. He was one of baseball's top sluggers of the 1960s and early 1970s. Allen played in the Phillies system from 1960 to 1969 and again in 1975 and 1976. In his career he played with the Cardinals, Dodgers, White Sox, and the Athletics.

Achievements

In 1964, Allen was elected the National League Rookie of the Year.

1-Time led the National League in Runs & 1-Time 200 hits in a season in 1964.

2-Times led the American League in Home Runs: (1972 & 1974).

1-Time led the American League in Runs Batted in & Bases-On-Balls:(1972).

2-Times led the League in On-Base %: (1967 NL & 1974 AL).

4-Times led the League in OPS %: (1966 NL & 1972 &1974 AL).

4-Times led the League in Slugging % %: (1966-1967 NL & 1972 &1974 AL).

7-Times League All-Star: (NL – 1965-1967 & 1970 & AL 1972-1974).

7-Times Received NVP Votes: (NL 1964-1967 & AL 1972 (Won) -1974).

Hall of Fame

Dick Allen was on the 1983 balloting by the Baseball Writers' Association of America but only received 3.7% and was dropped. He returned in 1985 and remained on the ballot until 1997 never received more than 18.9% of the vote. Allen was considered in 2014 but fell one vote short of being elected. The Golden Days Committee (1950–1969) voted in December 2021, with Allen once again falling short of election.

Summary Analysis:

Allen had 121.650 career statistical points. His being overlooked for election has been an injustice by the BBWAA and deserves to be inducted into the Baseball Hall of Fame.

First Baseman Potential Hall of Fame Inductee

Allen, Dock

Positions	Born:	March 8, 1942
First Baseman	Died:	December 20, 2020
Third Baseman	From:	Wampum, PA
Left Fielder	Bats:	Right
	Throws:	Right

Height:	5'11" USC 180 cm
Weight:	187 lbs. 84 Kg.
Debut:	September 3, 1963
Last Game:	June 19, 1977

Year	Age	Tm	Lg	G	PA	AB	R	H	2B	3B	HR	RBI	SB	CS	BB	SO	BA	OBP	SLG	OPS	TB	HBP	Awards
1963	21	PHI	NL	10	25	24	6	7	2	1	0	2	0	0	0	5	0.292	0.280	0.458	0.738	11	0	
1964	22	PHI	NL	162	709	632	125	201	38	13	29	91	3	4	67	138	0.318	0.382	0.557	0.939	352	0	MVP-7,RoY-1
1965	23	PHI	NL	161	707	619	93	187	31	14	20	85	15	2	74	150	0.302	0.375	0.494	0.870	306	2	AS,MVP-28
1966	24	PHI	NL	141	599	524	112	166	25	10	40	110	10	6	68	136	0.317	0.396	0.632	1.027	331	3	AS,MVP-4
1967	25	PHI	NL	122	540	463	89	142	31	10	23	77	20	5	75	117	0.307	0.404	0.566	0.970	262	1	AS,MVP-19
1968	26	PHI	NL	152	605	521	87	137	17	9	33	90	7	7	74	161	0.263	0.352	0.520	0.872	271	1	
1969	27	PHI	NL	118	506	438	75	126	23	3	32	89	9	3	64	144	0.288	0.375	0.579	0.949	251	0	
1970	28	STL	NL	122	533	459	88	128	17	5	34	101	5	4	71	138	0.279	0.377	0.560	0.937	257	2	AS
1971	29	LAD	NL	155	649	549	82	162	24	1	23	90	8	1	93	113	0.295	0.395	0.468	0.863	257	1	
1972	30	CHW	AL	148	605	506	90	156	28	5	37	113	19	8	99	126	0.308	0.420	0.603	1.023	305	1	AS,MVP-1
1973	31	CHW	AL	72	288	250	39	79	20	1	16	41	7	2	30	51	0.316	0.394	0.612	1.006	153	1	AS,MVP-35
1974	32	CHW	AL	128	525	462	84	139	23	1	32	88	7	1	57	89	0.301	0.375	0.563	0.938	260	1	AS,MVP-23
1975	33	PHI	NL	119	481	416	54	97	21	3	12	52	11	2	58	109	0.233	0.327	0.385	0.712	160	2	
1976	34	PHI	NL	85	339	298	52	80	16	1	15	45	11	4	37	63	0.268	0.346	0.480	0.826	143	0	
1977	35	OAK	AL	54	200	171	19	41	4	0	5	31	1	3	24	36	0.240	0.330	0.351	0.681	60	1	
162 Game Avg.				162	678	586	102	171	30	7	33	104	12	5	83	144	0.292	0.378	0.534	0.912	313	1	
PHI (9 yrs)				1070	4511	3985	687	1143	204	64	204	685	86	33	517	1023	0.290	0.371	0.530	0.902	2087	9	
CHW (3 yrs)				348	1422	1218	213	374	71	9	85	242	33	11	189	266	0.307	0.398	0.589	0.988	718	3	
LAD (1 yr)				155	649	549	82	162	24	1	23	90	8	1	93	113	0.295	0.395	0.468	0.863	257	1	
STL (1 yr)				122	533	459	88	128	17	5	34	101	5	4	71	138	0.279	0.377	0.560	0.937	257	2	
OAK (1 yr)				54	200	171	19	41	4	0	5	31	1	3	24	36	0.240	0.330	0.351	0.681	60	1	
NL (11 yrs)				1347	5693	4943	867	1433	245	70	251	846	99	38	681	1254	0.29	0.375	0.526	0.901	2601	12	
AL (4 yrs)				402	1622	1389	232	415	75	9	90	273	34	14	213	302	0.299	0.39	0.56	0.95	778	4	
15 Yrs				1749	7315	6332	1099	1848	320	79	351	1119	133	52	894	1556	0.292	0.379	0.534	0.912	3379	16	**Career Pts.**
				4.500	0.000	0.000	4.500	2.500	0.000	0.000	6.750	4.500	1.500	0.000	3.000	0.000	5.500	5.500	8.000	9.250	4.500	0	**60.000**

Post Seasonal Play

Year	Age	Tm	Lg	G	PA	AB	R	H	2B	3B	HR	RBI	SB	CS	BB	SO	BA	OBP	SLG	OPS	TB	HBP	
1976	34	PHI	NLCS	3	12	9	1	2	0	0	0	0	0	0	2	2	0.222	0.417	0.222	0.639	2	0	
				3	12	9	1	2	0	0	0	0	0	0	2	2	0.222	0.417	0.222	0.639	2	0	**Post Season Pts.**
				0.250	0.000	0.000	0.250	0.250	0.000	0.000	0.000	0.000	0.000	0.000	0.250	0.000	0.000	1.400	0.000	0.250	0.000	0.000	**2.650**

World Series Play

Year	Age	Tm	Lg	G	PA	AB	R	H	2B	3B	HR	RBI	SB	CS	BB	SO	BA	OBP	SLG	OPS	TB	HBP	
None		None		0	0	0	0	0	0	0	0	0	0	0	0	0	0	0	0	0	0	0	
				0.000	0.000	0.000	0.000	0.000	0.000	0.000	0.000	0.000	0.000	0.000	0.000	0.000	0.000	0.000	0.000	0.000	0.000	0.000	**World Series Pts.**
																							0.000

Yearly Points Leading the League

Category	Times	Points	Total
MVP	1	7	7
Rookie of Year	1	5	5
Triple Crown	0	5	0
Golden Gloves	0	3	0
All-Star	7	2	14
Games	0	2	0
Totals			28

Category	Times	Points	Total
B.A.	0	3	0
Runs	1	2	2
H.R.'s	2	3	6
R.B.I's	1	3	3
Hits	0	2	0
T.B.	0	2	0
Totals			11

Category	Times	Points	Total
T.B.	1	2	2
B.O.B.	1	2	2
OBP%	2	2	4
SLG%	3	2	6
OBPS%	4	2	8
Totals			22
Grand Total Add-On Points			36

Hall of Fame Points	
Career Points	60.000
Post Season Points	2.650
World Series Points	0.000
Career Add-On Points	59.00
Writers Association Pts.	0.000
Military/Lifetime Achievement	0.000
Grand Total HOF Points	122.65

Steve "Mr. Clean" Garvey

Personal Life

Steven Patrick Garvey was born December 22, 1948 in Tampa, Florida, to Joe Garvey and Mildred Winkler. He graduated from George B. Chamberlain High School in 1966 excelling in baseball and football. He batted .472 in his junior year and .465 as a senior which attracted the attention of Baseball scouts as well as College Football coaches'.

Steve Garvey's married Cindy Truhan in 1971 with the couple having two daughters, Krisha and Whitney. They divorced in 1985. Garvey married Candace Thoms in 1989 and they have three children. Together, the Garvey's have a total of nine children.

Baseball Career

Garvey was selected by the Minnesota Twins in the June 1966 amateur draft in the 3rd round but decided to attend Michigan State University. Upon completion of his MSU career, the Dodgers selected Garvey in the first round of the 1968 draft and assigned him to Ogden. In 1969 at Albuquerque, he was batting .373, 14 home runs, and 85 RBIs when the Dodgers called him up, making his debut on September 1, 1969.

Garvey began the 1970 season with the Dodgers but was optioned to Spokane at the end of April and recalled in September. Garvey improved his average to .269, but his fielding at third base remained a problem. In 1972, Garvey had made a league-leading 28 errors. It was teammate, Bill Buckner, that led to Garvey's break at stardom. Garvey began the 1973 season on the bench but as the team suited up for a June 23 contest, manager Walter Alston was faced with lineup issues. He had players injured and needed someone to play left field. Buckner suggested that he could play left field and use Garvey at first base. The experiment worked as Garvey batted .304 while improving his fielding percentage to .993 after the transition to first base.

In 1974, Garvey was batting .338 with 11 home runs and 46 RBIs when the Fans began to notice and started to write Garvey in for the All-Star game. He won by nearly 20,000 votes and became one of only two players to have started an All-Star Game as a write-in vote. By years end, he had a 200-hit season, 21 home runs, 111 RBIs, and a .312 batting average, only eight errors at first base, and won the N L MVP award.

A Fan's Perspective

From 1969 through 1982, Garvey batted .301, 1968 hits, 211 home runs, 992 runs-batted-in, .340 OBP%, .446 Slugging %, and an OPS of .759. 8-Time All-Star, 8-Time received MVP votes, and won the award in 1974.

In 1983, the San Diego outbid the Dodgers in hope that Garvey's would provide a role model for the younger players. His "box office appeal" helped San Diego increase its season ticket sales by 6,000 seats in his first year. On April 15, 1983, Garvey returned to Dodger Stadium as a member of the Padres playing his 1,117th consecutive game, tying the National League record. On July 29, 1983, he was batting .294 with 14 home runs and 59 RBIs when the streak ended at 1207 consecutive games played when he broke his thumb. Garvey recovered to play the entire 1984 season without committing an error. His offensive numbers continued to decline as he batted.284 with only eight home runs. It was Garvey's second season in San Diego, however, that would be his highlight in a Padres uniform. In 1984, Garvey became the only first baseman in MLB history to commit no errors while playing 150 or more games!

Led by Garvey, the Padres won their first National League pennant over the Chicago Cubs in 1984. Garvey made his final appearance in a game on May 23, 1987, with his final numbers being 2,599 base hits, 272 home runs, 1,308 RBIs, and a .996 fielding %.

The Baseball Hall of Fame

Achievements

- 2-Times Led the National League in hits: (1978 & 1980).
- 9-Times received MVP votes:(1974- Won, 1975 – 1981 & 1984).
- 5-Times member of National League Pennant Winners: (LA Dodgers 1974, 1977, 1978 & 1981 and 1984 San Diego Padres).
- 2 -Times Member of World Champion LA Dodgers: 1977 & 1981).
- 2-Times Led National League in Hits: (1978 & 1980).
- 5-Times 100+ RBIs in a season: (1974, 1977 - 1980).
- 10-Times National League All Star: (1974-81 & 1984-85).
- 6-Times led the National League in Games played: (1977, 1978, 1980, 1981 - 1985).
- 6-Times hit .300 seven times 20, or more home runs: (1974, 1977 – 1980, 1986).
- 4-Times National League Golden Glove Winner: (1974-1977).

Hall of Fame

Steve Garvey was on the (BBWAA) ballot for 15 years (1993–2007). His highest was 42.6% in 1995 and received 21.1% in his final year. He was considered by the Expansion Era Committee for 2011 and 2014, In 2017, the Modern Baseball Era Committee voting, the for 2018 voting, the 2019 voting by the Modern Baseball Era's committee, and the 2023 voting but didn't receive the required votes.

Summary Analysis

Steve Garvey 125.7 Hall of Fame points should have been enough to elect him five years after retirement. Not being elected in his first four years of eligibility is an injustice done by the BBWAA. Garvey was one of the most dependable baseball players in the 70s & 80s and believed to be a first ballot Hall of Fame electee. That was until his image was tarnished by a self-described mid-life crisis in the late 1980s. The press turned on him and he has yet to be elected. A player should never be penalized for his private non-baseball-related life. Steve Garvey is a Hall-of-Famer and needs to be inducted, or elected, so he can enjoy the status of being one of the best.

A Fan's Perspective

Garvey, Steve

First Baseman Potential Hall of Fame Inductee

Positions	Born:	December 22, 1948	Height:	5' 10"	USC	178	cm
First Baseman	From:	Tampa, Fla.	Weight:	192	lbs.	87	Kg.
Third Baseman	Bats:	Right	Debut:	September 1, 1969			
	Throws:	Right	Last Game:	May 23, 1987			

Year	Age	Tm	Lg	G	PA	AB	R	H	2B	3B	HR	RBI	SB	CS	BB	SO	BA	OBP	SLG	OPS	TB	HBP	Awards
1969	20	LAD	NL	3	3	3	0	1	0	0	0	0	0	0	0	1	0.333	0.333	0.333	0.667	1	0	
1970	21	LAD	NL	34	100	93	8	25	5	0	1	6	1	1	6	17	0.269	0.310	0.355	0.665	33	0	
1971	22	LAD	NL	81	249	225	27	51	12	1	7	26	1	2	21	33	0.227	0.290	0.381	0.673	86	0	
1972	23	LAD	NL	96	317	294	36	79	14	2	9	30	4	2	19	36	0.269	0.312	0.422	0.734	124	1	
1973	24	LAD	NL	114	366	349	37	106	17	3	8	50	0	2	11	42	0.304	0.328	0.438	0.766	153	3	
1974	25	LAD	NL	156	685	642	95	200	32	3	21	111	5	4	33	66	0.312	0.342	0.469	0.811	301	3	AS,MVP-1,GG
1975	26	LAD	NL	160	704	659	85	210	38	6	18	95	11	2	33	66	0.319	0.351	0.476	0.827	314	3	AS,MVP-11,GG
1976	27	LAD	NL	162	696	631	85	200	37	4	13	80	19	8	50	69	0.317	0.363	0.450	0.813	284	1	AS,MVP-6,GG
1977	28	LAD	NL	162	696	646	91	192	25	3	33	115	9	6	38	90	0.297	0.335	0.498	0.834	322	1	AS,MVP-6,GG
1978	29	LAD	NL	162	689	639	89	202	36	9	21	113	10	5	40	70	0.316	0.353	0.499	0.852	319	1	AS,MVP-2
1979	30	LAD	NL	162	697	648	92	204	32	1	28	110	3	6	37	59	0.315	0.351	0.497	0.848	322	2	AS,MVP-14
1980	31	LAD	NL	163	704	658	78	200	27	1	26	106	6	11	36	67	0.304	0.341	0.467	0.808	307	3	AS,MVP-6
1981	32	LAD	NL	110	461	431	63	122	23	1	10	64	3	5	25	49	0.283	0.322	0.411	0.732	177	1	AS,MVP-25
1982	33	LAD	NL	162	660	625	66	176	35	1	16	86	5	3	20	86	0.282	0.301	0.418	0.718	261	1	
1983	34	SDP	NL	100	425	388	76	114	22	0	14	59	4	1	29	39	0.294	0.344	0.459	0.802	178	3	
1984	35	SDP	NL	161	653	617	72	175	27	2	8	86	1	2	24	64	0.284	0.307	0.373	0.680	230	1	AS,MVP-20
1985	36	SDP	NL	162	699	654	80	184	34	6	17	81	0	0	35	67	0.281	0.318	0.430	0.748	281	3	AS
1986	37	SDP	NL	155	584	557	58	142	22	0	21	81	1	2	23	72	0.255	0.284	0.408	0.692	227	1	
1987	38	SDP	NL	27	78	76	5	16	2	0	1	9	0	0	1	10	0.211	0.231	0.276	0.507	21	1	
162 Game Avg.				162	658	614	79	181	31	3	19	91	6	4	33	70	0.294	0.329	0.446	0.775	274	2	
LAD (14 yrs)				1727	7027	6543	852	1968	333	35	211	992	77	57	367	751	0.301	0.337	0.459	0.796	3004	20	
SDP (5 yrs)				605	2439	2292	291	631	107	8	61	316	6	5	112	252	0.275	0.309	0.409	0.717	937	9	
19 Yrs				2332	9466	8835	1143	2599	440	43	272	1308	83	62	479	1003	0.294	0.329	0.446	0.775	3941	29	**Career Pts.**
				9.250	0.000	0.000	5.500	6.750	0.000	0.000	4.500	8.000	1.000	0.000	0.500	0.000	5.500	2.000	2.500	3.750	6.750	0.000	**56.000**

Post Season Play

Year	Age	Tm	Lg	G	PA	AB	R	H	2B	3B	HR	RBI	SB	CS	BB	SO	BA	OBP	SLG	OPS	TB	HBP	
1974	25	NLCS	NL	4	19	18	4	7	1	0	2	5	0	0	1	1	0.389	0.421	0.778	1.199	14	0	
1977	28	NLCS	NL	4	16	13	2	4	0	0	0	0	1	0	2	1	0.308	0.400	0.308	0.708	4	0	
1978	29	NLCS	NL	4	18	18	6	7	1	1	4	7	0	1	0	1	0.389	0.389	1.222	1.611	22	0	
1981	32	NLDS	NL	5	19	19	4	7	0	1	2	4	0	0	0	2	0.368	0.368	0.789	1.158	15	0	
1981	32	NLCS	NL	5	21	21	2	6	0	0	1	2	0	0	0	4	0.286	0.286	0.429	0.714	9	0	
1984	35	NLCS	NL	5	21	20	1	8	1	0	1	7	0	0	1	2	0.400	0.429	0.600	1.029	12	0	
				27	114	109	19	39	3	2	10	25	1	1	4	11	0.358	0.381	0.697	1.078	76	0	**Post Season Pts.**
				0.600	0.000	0.000	0.600	0.800	0.000	0.000	1.000	1.000	0.250	0.000	0.250	0.000	1.200	1.000	2.000	1.400	0.800	0.000	**10.900**

World Series Play

Year	Age	Tm	Lg	G	PA	AB	R	H	2B	3B	HR	RBI	SB	CS	BB	SO	BA	OBP	SLG	OPS	TB	HBP	
1974	25	LA	NL	5	21	21	2	8	0	0	0	1	0	0	0	3	0.381	0.381	0.381	0.762	8	0	
1977	28	LA	NL	6	25	24	5	9	1	1	1	3	0	1	1	4	0.375	0.400	0.625	1.025	15	0	
1978	29	LA	NL	6	25	24	1	5	1	0	0	0	1	0	1	7	0.208	0.24	0.25	0.49	6	0	
1981	32	LA	NL	6	26	24	3	10	1	0	0	0	0	0	2	5	0.417	0.462	0.458	0.92	11	0	
1984	35	SD	NL	5	21	20	2	4	2	0	0	2	0	0	0	2	0.200	0.200	0.300	0.500	6	0	
				28	118	113	13	36	5	1	1	6	1	1	4	21	0.319	0.342	0.407	0.749	46	0	**World Series Pts.**
				1.000	0.000	0.000	0.800	1.200	0.000	0.000	0.250	0.400	0.250	0.000	0.250	0.000	1.200	0.250	0.000	0.400	1.800	0.000	**7.800**

Yearly Points Leading the League

Category	Times	Points	Total
MVP	1	7	7
Rookie of Year	0	5	0
Triple Crown	0	5	0
Golden Glove	4	3	12
All-Star	10	2	20
Games	6	2	12
Totals			51

Category	Times	Points	Total
B.A.	0	3	0
Runs	0	2	0
H.R.'s	0	3	0
R.B.I's	0	3	0
Hits	0	2	0
S.B.	0	2	0
Totals			0

Categor	Times	Points	Total
T.B.	0	2	0
B.O.B.	0	2	0
OBP%	0	2	0
SLG %	0	2	0
OBPS%	0	2	0
Totals			0
Grand Total Add-On Points			51

Hall of Fame Points	
Career Points	56.000
Post Season Points	10.900
World Series Points	7.800
Career Add-On Points	51.00
Writers Association Pts.	0.00
Military/Lifetime Achievement	0.00
Grand Total HOF Points	125.7

Keith Hernandez

Personal Life

Keith Hernandez was born on October 20, 1953, in San Francisco to his father John Hernandez (1922–1992), and Mother Jacqueline Hernandez. He and brother, Gary grew up in San Bruno. He attended the College of San Mateo and played baseball in 1971 before being drafted in the 42nd round of the draft by the St. Louis Cardinals.

He was married to Susan Broecker from 1979 – 1983 with the couple having daughters, Jesse, Melissa, and Mary. Hernandez was married to Kai Thompson from 2005 to 2011.

Baseball Career

Hernandez began his professional career in 1972 and moved up with the Cardinals until he made his big-league debut on August 30, 1974. In 14 late-season games with St. Louis, he batted .294 with a .441 slugging percentage. Hernandez ended up splitting 1975 between Tulsa and the Cardinals. Though he had a .996 fielding percentage with only two errors in 507 chances, Hernandez struggled with major league pitching.

As Hernandez made his presence known as a batter, he quickly gained a reputation as one of the slickest fielders in the game, as evidenced by his 11 consecutive Gold Glove Awards (1978-1988). In 1979, his fourth full season with the Cardinals, Hernandez had a breakout campaign, capturing the National League batting title with a .344 batting average, leading the league in doubles (48), and runs scored (116) and shared the National League MVP Award with Pittsburgh's Willie Stargell.

A Fan's Perspective

In the Cardinals' 1982 world championship season, Hernandez batted .299 and drove in 94 runs. He helped the Cardinals past the Atlanta Braves in a three-game sweep of the National League Championship Series, and during the seven-game World Series triumph over Milwaukee, he drove in eight runs. The Cardinals decided that Hernandez was causing more problems than what he was worth to them, and on June 15, 1983, traded him to the Mets. Amid the controversy, Hernandez's play stayed sharp; he batted .306 in 95 games for a dismal Mets team and won his sixth consecutive NL Gold Glove.

Upon Hernandez's arrival in New York, he was determined to get along with manager Davey Johnson, to make the Mets legitimate contender for a championship. In 1984, Hernandez's first full season with the Mets, he batted .311 with 15 home runs and earned a spot on the National League All-Star team for the first time since 1980. He won another Gold Glove, a Silver Slugger Award and finished second in the National League MVP voting. That season the Mets won 90 games, 22 more than they had won the previous season. Hernandez's efforts, combined with the maturing youngsters proved to be the spark that the Mets were looking for.

In 1985, the Mets won 98 games and finished second in their division. In 158 games Hernandez batted .309 with 91 RBIs and had a .997 fielding percentage with some uncertainty at the beginning of the 1986 season. Hernandez was a target in a massive investigation of drug and on March 1, Commissioner Peter Ueberroth suspended Hernandez and seven other players for a year but offered to lift the suspensions if the players agreed take a number of steps, including contributing 10 percent of their salaries to antidrug programs, and undergoing drug tests for the rest of their careers.

Hernandez agreed to the alternative and played the 1986 season. He proceeded to bat .310, with 83 RBIs, won his ninth consecutive Gold Glove voted a starter in the All-Star Game for the first time. The Mets were 108-54 and won first-place in the East Division finish. The 1986 post season was Hernandez's second career playoff appearance, and the Mets defeated the Astros in six games, and he had seven hits and three RBIs in the six NLCS games. The World Series against the Boston Red Sox was a classic with the Mets falling behind in games 6 & 7. Hernandez drove in key runs in both games and the Mets won the world championship.

The Baseball Hall of Fame

Achievements

- 5-times National League All-Star: (1979, 1980, 1984, 1986 & 1987).
- 8-Times received National League MVP Votes: (1979 (Won) -1986).
- 11-time National League Gold Glove Winner: (1978-1988).
- 2-time National League Silver Slugger Award Winner: (1980 & 1984).
- 1-Time National League Batting Average Leader (1979).
- 1-Time National League On-Base Percentage Leader (1980)
- 2-Times National League Runs Scored Leader (1979 & 1980).
- 1-Time National League Base-On-Balls Leader: (1986).
- 2-Time World Series Winner (Stl. Cardinals (1982) & N. Y. Mets (1986).

The 1989 season saw Hernandez's skills began to fade dramatically as he hit just .233 with four home runs, due partly to a broken kneecap. After the season the Mets let Hernandez go and he signed with the Cleveland Indians for two years. He played a final season with the Cleveland Indians but played in only 43 games in an injury-plagued 1990 season and announced his retirement and had back surgery in 1991.

Hall of Fame

Hernandez was on the Hall of Fame Ballot starting in 1995 until 2004 when he received 4.3% of the votes and expiration of the ballot. He peaked at 10.4% in 2000 but never seemed to get much support from the BBWAA. He was up for election by the Contemporary ERA in 2023 and failed to secure enough votes.

Summary Analysis

Hernandez's has a 121.650 Hall of Fame Point Total. He should have been inducted within six years of the end of his playing career. Though he was suspended for cocaine use, his career totals and fielding excellence were Hall of Fame Worthy. He paid the penalties for his transgression and Hernadez deserves to take his place among the greats in the Baseball Hall of Fame.

A Fan's Perspective

Hernandez, Keith **First Baseman Potential Hall of Fame Inductee**

Positions: First Baseman

Born:	October 20, 1953	Height:	6'0" USC 183
From:	San Francisco, CA	Weight:	180 lbs. 81
Bats:	Left	Debut:	April 30, 1974
Throws:	Left	Last Game:	July 24, 1990

Year	Age	Tm	Lg	G	PA	AB	R	H	2B	3B	HR	RBI	SB	CS	BB	SO	BA	OBP	SLG	OPS	TB	HBP	Awards
1974	20	STL	NL	14	41	34	3	10	1	2	0	2	0	0	7	8	0.294	0.415	0.441	0.856	15	0	
1975	21	STL	NL	64	207	188	20	47	8	2	3	20	0	1	17	26	0.25	0.309	0.362	0.671	68	0	
1976	22	STL	NL	129	428	374	54	108	21	5	7	46	4	2	49	53	0.289	0.376	0.428	0.803	160	3	
1977	23	STL	NL	161	645	560	90	163	41	4	15	91	7	7	79	88	0.291	0.379	0.459	0.837	257	1	
1978	24	STL	NL	159	633	542	90	138	32	4	11	64	13	5	82	68	0.255	0.351	0.389	0.741	211	2	GG
1979	25	STL	NL	161	698	610	116	210	48	11	11	105	11	6	80	78	0.344	0.417	0.513	0.93	313	1	AS,MVP-1,GG
1980	26	STL	NL	159	690	595	111	191	39	8	16	99	14	8	86	73	0.321	0.408	0.494	0.902	294	4	AS,MVP-11,GG,SS
1981	27	STL	NL	103	444	376	65	115	27	4	8	48	12	5	61	45	0.306	0.401	0.463	0.864	174	2	MVP-20,GG
1982	28	STL	NL	160	694	579	79	173	33	6	7	94	19	11	100	67	0.299	0.397	0.413	0.81	239	2	MVP-17,GG
1983	29	TOT	NL	150	633	538	77	160	23	7	12	63	9	5	88	72	0.297	0.396	0.433	0.829	233	2	MVP-21,GG
1983	29	STL	NL	55	244	218	34	62	15	4	3	26	1	1	24	30	0.284	0.352	0.431	0.784	94	0	
1983	29	NYM	NL	95	389	320	43	98	8	3	9	37	8	4	64	42	0.306	0.424	0.434	0.858	139	2	
1984	30	NYM	NL	154	657	550	83	171	31	0	15	94	2	3	97	89	0.311	0.409	0.449	0.859	247	1	AS,MVP-2,GG,SS
1985	31	NYM	NL	158	682	593	87	183	34	4	10	91	3	3	77	59	0.309	0.384	0.43	0.814	255	2	MVP-8,GG
1986	32	NYM	NL	149	652	551	94	171	34	1	13	83	2	1	94	69	0.31	0.413	0.446	0.859	246	4	AS,MVP-4,GG
1987	33	NYM	NL	154	676	587	87	170	28	2	18	89	0	2	81	104	0.29	0.377	0.436	0.813	258	4	AS,GG
1988	34	NYM	NL	95	384	348	43	96	16	0	11	55	2	1	31	57	0.276	0.333	0.417	0.75	145	1	GG
1989	35	NYM	NL	75	244	215	18	50	8	0	4	19	0	3	27	39	0.233	0.324	0.326	0.649	70	2	
1990	36	CLE	AL	43	145	130	7	26	2	0	1	8	0	0	14	17	0.2	0.283	0.238	0.521	31	1	
162 Game Avg.				162	664	572	87	169	33	5	13	83	8	5	83	79	0.296	0.384	0.436	0.821	249	2	
STL (10 yrs)				1165	4724	4076	662	1217	265	50	81	595	81	46	585	536	0.299	0.385	0.448	0.833	1825	15	
NYM (7 yrs)				880	3684	3164	455	939	159	10	80	468	17	17	471	459	0.297	0.387	0.429	0.816	1358	16	
CLE (1 yr)				43	145	130	7	26	2	0	1	8	0	0	14	17	0.2	0.283	0.238	0.521	31	1	
NL (16 yrs)				2045	8408	7240	1117	2156	424	60	161	1063	98	63	1056	995	0.298	0.386	0.44	0.826	3183	31	
AL (1 yr)				43	145	130	7	26	2	0	1	8	0	0	14	17	0.2	0.283	0.238	0.521	31	1	
17 Yrs				2088	8553	7370	1124	2182	426	60	162	1071	98	63	1070	1012	0.296	0.384	0.436	0.821	3214	32	Career Pts.
				6.750	0.000	0.000	5.500	3.750	0.000	0.000	2.000	4.500	1.000	0.000	4.500	0.000	5.500	5.500	2.500	5.500	3.750	0.000	50.750

Post Season Play

Year	Age	Tm	Lg	G	PA	AB	R	H	2B	3B	HR	RBI	SB	CS	BB	SO	BA	OBP	SLG	OPS	TB	HBP	
1982	28	STL	NLCS	3	14	12	3	4	0	0	0	1	0	0	2	3	0.333	0.429	0.333	0.762	4	0	
1986	32	NYM	NLCS	6	29	26	3	7	1	1	0	3	0	0	3	6	0.269	0.345	0.385	0.729	10	0	
1988	34	NYM	NLCS	7	32	26	2	7	0	0	1	5	1	0	6	7	0.269	0.406	0.385	0.791	10	0	
				16	75	64	8	18	1	1	1	9	1	0	11	16	0.281	0.387	0.375	0.762	24	0	Post Season Pts.
				0.400	0.000	0.000	0.250	0.400	0.000	0.000	0.250	0.400	0.250	0.000	0.600	0.000	0.600	1.200	0.250	0.400	0.400	0.000	5.400

World Series Play

Year	Age	Tm	Lg	G	PA	AB	R	H	2B	3B	HR	RBI	SB	CS	BB	SO	BA	OBP	SLG	OPS	TB	HBP	
1982	28	STL	NL	7	31	27	4	7	2	0	1	8	0	0	4	2	0.259	0.355	0.444	0.799	12	0	
1986	32	NYM	NL	7	32	26	1	6	0	0	0	4	0	0	5	1	0.231	0.344	0.231	0.575	6	0	
				14	63	53	5	13	2	0	1	12	0	0	9	3	0.245	0.349	0.340	0.689	18	0	World Series Pts.
				0.600	0.000	0.000	0.400	0.400	0.000	0.000	0.250	0.600	0.000	0.000	0.600	0.000	0.400	0.400	0.000	0.250	0.600	0.000	4.500

Yearly Points Leading the League

Category	Times	Points	Total
MVP	1	7	7
Rookie of Year	0	5	0
Triple Crown	0	5	0
Golden Glove	11	3	33
All-Star	5	2	10
Games	0	2	0
Totals			50

Category	Times	Points	Total
B.A.	1	3	3
Runs	2	2	4
H.R.'s	0	3	0
R.B.I's	0	3	0
Hits	0	2	0
S.B.	0	2	0
Totals			7

Category	Times	Points	Total
T.B.	0	2	0
B.O.B.	1	2	2
OBP%	1	2	2
SLG%	0	2	0
OBPS%	0	2	0
Totals	0		4
Grand Total Add-On Points			61

Hall of Fame Points	
Career Points	50.750
Post Season Points	5.400
World Series Points	4.500
Career Add-On Points	61.000
Writers Association Pts.	0.000
Military/Lifetime Achievement	0.000
Grand Total HOF Points	121.65

Don "Donnie Baseball" Mattingly

Personal Life

Donald Arthur Mattingly was born April 20, 1961 in Evansville, Vanderburgh County, Indiana to Bill Mattingly and Mary Louise Mattingly. Don has three brothers Randy, Jerry, Michael Mattingly, and one sister, Judy Mattingly. The Mattingly's excelled in sports from an early age thanks to their father. Jerry earned all-state honors as he helped Rex Mundi High School to the 1964 IHSAA state basketball semifinals. Don's older brother, Randy, played quarterback at the University of Evansville and drafted by Cleveland in the fourth round of the NFL Draft. Jerry earned all-state honors at Rex Mundi High School in 1964 and was recruited to play for the University of Evansville.

Don Mattingly graduated from Reitz Memorial High School in Evansville, Indiana, and was selected by the Yankees in the 1979 amateur draft. Mattingly is ambidextrous and pitched both right-handed and left-handed in Little League Baseball and played first base. He was a member of the 1973 Great Scot Little League championship team in Evansville, Indiana. When her played American Legion baseball for Funkhouser Post #8, Mattingly played at second base, throwing right-handed. Playing for Reitz Memorial High School's baseball team, Mattingly led the school to a state record 59 straight victories through the 1978–79 season. The Tigers won the state championship in 1978 and finished as the runner-up in 1979. Mattingly was All-State in 1978 and 1979. During the four years he played in high school, Mattingly batted .463, leading the Tigers to a 94–9–1 win–loss record. He still holds Reitz Memorial records for hits (52), doubles (29), triples (25), runs batted in (RBIs) (140), and runs scored (99). His 25 triples are also an Indiana state record. A multisport athlete, Mattingly was selected to the SIAC all-conference basketball team in 1978. Following his high school career, Mattingly accepted a scholarship to play baseball for the Indiana State Sycamores. His father had informed Major League Baseball (MLB) teams that his son intended to honor that commitment and would not sign a professional contract. In the 1979 draft, Mattingly lasted until the 19th round when he was selected by the New York Yankees.

Mattingly married Kim Sexton on September 8, 1979, and they divorced after his playing career ended in 2007. Mattingly and Kim share three sons: Taylor, Preston, and Jordon. Taylor was drafted in the 42nd round (1,262nd overall) of the 2003 Major League Baseball draft by the New York

Yankees, and Preston was chosen in the supplemental round (31st overall) of the 2006 MLB draft by the Los Angeles Dodgers.

Mattingly remarried on December 10, 2010, to Lori McClarney, in his hometown of Evansville, Indiana. The wedding, and managing the Phoenix Desert Dogs of the Arizona Fall League, prevented him from attending the 2010 winter meetings. In 2014, Don and Lori welcomed a son, Louis, into their family.

Professional Career

Mattingly began his professional career in Minor League Baseball with the Oneonta Yankees of the Class A-Short Season New York–Penn League in 1979. He batted a league-leading .358 in 1980. Despite Mattingly's hitting ability, concerns existed about his lack of speed and power. Mattingly was batting .325 in the Triple-A International League when he made it to the majors late in the 1982 season. Debuting with the Yankees in 1982 after four seasons in Minor League Baseball, he emerged as the Yankees' starting first baseman after a successful rookie season in 1983.

Between 1984 and 1989 he posted a batting line of .327/.372/.530 batting line and averaged 27 homers and 114 RBIs. That slugging percentage was the best in baseball over that span, as was his extra base hit total (428) and RBI total. He was the American League batting champ in 1984 and was the MVP in 1985 and knocked in 145 runs. Mattingly's career was separated into two distinct halves, the 1983 to 1989 pre-back injury career who was one of the best in all of baseball with an average year of 185 hits, 23 home runs, 102 runs-batted-in, .320 batting average, and an OPS of .878 with five golden gloves. The post-back injury from 1990 to 1995 with an average year of 142 hits, 9.7 home runs, 63.7 runs-batted-in, .286 batting average, and an OPS of .809 with four golden gloves. He was on the trajectory to be a no doubt selection to the National Baseball Hall of Fame until the congenital disk deformity sapped his power and brought his career to a premature end at the tender age of 34.

Achievements

- 6-Times American League All-Star:(1984-1989)
- 7-Times Received MVP Votes: (1984,1985 Won-1987,1989,1993 & 1994).
- 9-Times American League Gold Glove Winner: (1985-1989, 1991-1994)
- 3-Times American League Silver Slugger Award Winner: (1985-1987).

The Baseball Hall of Fame

- 7-Time American League Batting Average Leader: (1984).
- 1-Time American League Slugging Percentage Leader & OPS % Leader: (1986).
- 2-Times American League Hits Leader: (1984 & 1986).
- 2-Times American League Total Bases Leader: (1985 & 1986).
- 2-Times 20-Home Run Seasons: (1984, & 1989) & 3-Times 30-HR: (1985 - 1987)
- 5-Times 100 RBI Seasons: (1984-1985 Led AL, 1986, 1987 & 1989).
- 2-Times 100 Runs Scored Seasons: (1985 & 1986).
- 3-Times 200 Hits Seasons: (1984, 1985 & 1986).

Hall of Fame

After retiring following the 1995 season at the age of 34, Mattingly went on to receive just 28.2% of the vote in his first year on the ballot in 2001. Though he received enough votes to remain on the ballot for the maximum 15 years, Mattingly never received another total as high as that first year. Mattingly was on the Hall of Fame ballot from 2001 to 2015. Mattingly's was later named a finalist on the Modern Era Ballot in 2017 and later became eligible to be inducted into the Hall of Fame via the Contemporary Baseball Era Players Committee. He was shortlisted for the 2018, 2020, and 2022 Modern Baseball Era ballot ballots, but did not receive enough votes for election.

Summary Analysis

Mattingly's Statistical Hall of Fame Points is 120.050, over the Induction Score of 110.000 and he should have been at least elected within six years of the end of his playing career. A career shouldn't be measured by perceived milestones of the BBWAA but through the actual statistics achieved during a career. In addition, career ending injuries, such as Mattingly's congenital back, should be considered with the overall career numbers. He deserves to take his place among the greats in the Baseball Hall of Fame.

Mattingly, Don **First Baseman Potential Hall of Fame Inductee**

Positions	Born :	April 20, 1961	Height:	6' 0"	USC	183	cm
First Baseman	From:	Evansville, IN	Weight:	175	lbs.	79	Kg.
Outfielder	Bats:	Left	Debut:	September 8, 1982			
	Throws:	Left	Last Game:	October 1, 1995			

Year	Age	Tm	Lg	G	PA	AB	R	H	2B	3B	HR	RBI	SB	CS	BB	SO	BA	OBP	SLG	OPS	TB	HBP	Awards
1982	21	NYY	AL	7	13	12	0	2	0	0	0	1	0	0	0	1	0.167	0.154	0.167	0.321	2	0	
1983	22	NYY	AL	91	305	279	34	79	15	4	4	32	0	0	21	31	0.283	0.333	0.409	0.742	114	1	
1984	23	NYY	AL	153	662	603	91	207	44	2	23	110	1	1	41	33	0.343	0.381	0.537	0.918	324	1	AS,MVP-5
1985	24	NYY	AL	159	727	652	107	211	48	3	35	145	2	2	56	41	0.324	0.371	0.567	0.939	370	2	AS,MVP-1,GG,SS
1986	25	NYY	AL	162	742	677	117	238	53	2	31	113	0	0	53	35	0.352	0.394	0.573	0.967	388	1	AS,MVP-2,GG,SS
1987	26	NYY	AL	141	630	569	93	186	38	2	30	115	1	4	51	38	0.327	0.378	0.559	0.937	318	1	AS,MVP-7,GG,SS
1988	27	NYY	AL	144	651	599	94	186	37	0	18	88	1	0	41	29	0.311	0.353	0.462	0.816	277	3	AS,GG
1989	28	NYY	AL	158	693	631	79	191	37	2	23	113	3	0	51	30	0.303	0.351	0.477	0.828	301	1	AS,MVP-15,GG
1990	29	NYY	AL	102	428	394	40	101	16	0	5	42	1	0	28	20	0.256	0.308	0.335	0.643	132	3	
1991	30	NYY	AL	152	646	587	64	169	35	0	9	68	2	0	46	42	0.288	0.339	0.394	0.733	231	4	GG
1992	31	NYY	AL	157	686	640	89	184	40	0	14	86	3	0	39	43	0.288	0.327	0.416	0.742	266	1	GG
1993	32	NYY	AL	134	596	530	78	154	27	2	17	86	0	0	61	42	0.291	0.364	0.445	0.809	236	2	MVP-19,GG
1994	33	NYY	AL	97	436	372	62	113	20	1	6	51	0	0	60	24	0.304	0.397	0.411	0.808	153	0	MVP-18,GG
1995	34	NYY	AL	128	507	458	59	132	32	2	7	49	0	2	40	35	0.288	0.341	0.413	0.754	189	1	
162 Game Avg.				162	701	636	91	195	40	2	20	100	1	1	53	40	0.307	0.358	0.471	0.830	300	2	
14 Yrs				1785	7722	7003	1007	2153	442	20	222	1099	14	9	588	444	0.307	0.358	0.471	0.830	3301	21	**Career Points**
				4.500	0.000	0.000	3.750	3.750	0.000	0.000	3.000	4.500	0.500	0.000	1.500	0.000	8.000	3.750	3.750	5.500	4.500	0	47.000

Post Season Play

Year	Age	Tm	Lg	G	PA	AB	R	H	2B	3B	HR	RBI	SB	CS	BB	SO	BA	OBP	SLG	OPS	TB	HBP	
1995	34	NYY	ALDS	5	25	24	3	10	4	0	1	6	0	0	1	5	0.417	0.440	0.708	1.148	19	0	
				5	25	24	3	10	4	0	1	6	0	0	1	5	0.417	0.440	0.708	1.148	19	0	**Post Season Pts.**
				0.200	0.000	0.000	0.200	0.200	0.000	0.000	0.200	0.200	0.000	0.000	0.200	0.000	2.500	2.150	2.500	2.500	0.200	0.000	11.050

World Series Play

Year	Age	Tm	Lg	G	PA	AB	R	H	2B	3B	HR	RBI	SB	CS	BB	SO	BA	OBP	SLG	OPS	TB	HBP	
				0	0	0	0	0	0	0	0	0	0	0	0	0	0	0	0	0	0	0	**World Series Pts.**
				0.000	0.000	0.000	0.000	0.000	0.000	0.000	0.000	0.000	0.000	0.000	0.000	0.000	0.000	0.000	0.000	0.000	0.000	0.000	0.000

Yearly Points Leading the League

Category	Times	Points	Total	Category	Times	Points	Total	Categc	Times	Points	Total	Hall of Fame Points	Points
MVP	1	7	7	B.A.	1	3	3	T.B.	1	2	2	Career Points	47.000
Rookie of Year	0	5	0	Runs	0	2	0	B.O.B.	0	2	0	Post Season Points	11.050
Triple Crown	0	5	0	H.R.'s	0	3	0	OBP%	1	2	2	World Series Points	0.000
Golden Glove	9	3	27	R.B.I's	1	3	3	SLG %	1	2	2	Career Add-On Points	62.00
All-Star	6	2	12	Hits	2	2	4	OBPS%	0	2	0	Writers Association Pts.	0.000
Games	0	2	0	S.B.	0	2	0	Totals			6	Military/Lifetime Achievement	0.000
Totals			46	Totals			10	Grand Total Add-On Points			62	Grand Total HOF Points	120.05

The Baseball Hall of Fame

Albert "The Machine" Pujols

Personal Life

José Alberto Pujols Alcántara was born January 16, 1980 to Bienvenido Pujols (mother unknown) as an only child and raised in Santo Domingo, Dominican Republic, mostly by his grandmother, America Pujols. Pujols, his father, and his grandmother immigrated in 1996 to Washington Heights in New York City. Pujols played baseball at Fort Osage High School in Independence and was named an All-State athlete twice.

Albert Pujols married Diedre on January 1, 2000. and have five children, daughter Isabella, son Albert Jr, daughter Sophia, son Ezra, daughter Esther. They divorced on August 18, 2022, after being separated since April 4, 2022. The first daughter Isabella was adopted by Albert and born with down syndrome condition, which inspired Albert to create the Pujols family nonprofit foundation to assist those living with down syndrome in the Dominican Republic, the United States and World-Wide.

Albert Pujols married Nicole Fernandez on February 5, 2023, the daughter of Lionel Fernandez, former President of the Dominican Republic.

Professional Career

Pujols began his minor league career in 2000 playing third base with the Peoria Chiefs of the single-A Midwest League. He batted .324 with 128 hits, 32 doubles, six triples, 17 home runs and 84 RBI, in 109 games. He finished the 2000 season with the Memphis Redbirds in the AAA Pacific Coast League (PCL), and after appearing in three regular season games with them, he batted .367 in the playoffs and was named the postseason Most Valuable Player (MVP) as the Redbirds won their first PCL title.

During spring training in 2001, the Cardinals activated him to the Opening Day roster, and he started all season at third base, right field, left field, or first base.

At midseason, Pujols became the first Cardinals rookie since 1955 to make the All-Star Game. He finished the season batting .329, 194 hits, 37 home runs, 112 runs, and set an NL rookie record with 130 RBI's. He was unanimously named the NL Rookie of the Year after and becoming the fourth

MLB rookie to hit .300 with 30 home runs, 100 runs, and 100 RBI's. The Cardinals advanced to the playoffs as the National League wild card team. Pujols spent most of 2002 in left field and began the season batting cleanup but was moved in May to the third spot in the lineup, where he remained for the rest of his Cardinals career. Pujols finished the year batting .314 (seventh in the NL) with 185 hits, 40 doubles, 34 home runs, 118 runs scored, and 127 RBI's. He became the first player in major league history to hit over .300 with at least 30 home runs, 100 runs scored, and 100 RBIs in his first two seasons. Pujols finished second in the MVP voting. In 2002, the Cardinals won the NL Central title to reach the playoffs and completed a three-game sweep of the Diamondbacks in the 2002 NLDS but lost in five games in the NL Championship Series.

In 2003, from July 12 to August 16, Pujols had a 30-game hitting streak, tied for the second-longest in Cardinals' history. On July 20, Pujols hit his 100th career home run, a game-winner in a 10–7 victory over the Dodgers. He became the fourth major leaguer to hit his 100th home run in his third season. Pujols hit his 114th home run on September 20 tied him for the most home runs by a player in his first three seasons. In 157 games, Pujols hit 43 home runs. 124 RBI's, batting .359, and he led the league in runs (137), hits (212), and doubles (51). Pujols again finished second in MVP voting.

After 2011 Pujols left via free-agency and signed with the California Anges. It is here that Pujols career can be separated into two stages:

Stage 1 – Cardinal ERA – Ages 21-31	**Stage 2 – ERA (11 Years) – Ages 32-42)**
• Games – 1705	Games – 1484
• Runs - 1291	Runs - 652
• Hits – 2073	Hits – 1376
• HR's - 445	HR's - 275
• RBI's - 1329	RBI's - 939
• B. A. - .328	B.A.'S - .256
• OBP - .420	OBP - .345
• SLG – .617	SLG. - .453
• OBPS – 1.037	OBPS - .798

The Baseball Hall of Fame

Achievements

- 2001 National League Rookie of the Year Award.
- 11-Times All-Star (2001, 2003-2010, 2015 & 2022).
- 13-Times Received MVP Votes (2001-2012, & 2014 Winning in 2005, 2008 & 2009).
- 2-Times National League Gold Glove Winner (2006/1B & 2010/1B).
- 6-Times Silver Slugger Award Winner (2001, 2003, 2004 & 2008-2011).
- 1-Time National League Batting Average Leader (2003).
- 1-Time National League On-Base Percentage Leader (2009).
- 3-Times National League Slugging Percentage Leader (2006, 2008 & 2009).
- 3-Times National League OPS Leader (2006, 2008 & 2009).
- 5-Times National League Runs Scored Leader (2003-2005, 2009 & 2010).
- 1-Time National League Hits Leader (2003).
- 4-Times National League Total Bases Leader (2003, 2004, 2008 & 2009).
- 2-Times National League Home Runs Leader (2009 & 2010).
- 20-Home Run Seasons: 18 (2001-2012, 2014-2017, 2019 & 2022).
- 30-Home Run Seasons: 14 (2001-2012 & 2015, 2016).
- 40-Home Run Seasons: 7 (2003-2006, 2009, 2010 & 2015).
- 100 RBI Seasons: 14 (2001-2010, 2012, 2014, 2016 & 2017).
- 100 Runs Scored Seasons: 10 (2001-2006 & 2008-2011).
- Won two World Series with the St. Louis Cardinals in 2006 and 2011.

Hall of Fame

Albert Pujols is eligible to be elected by the BBWAA in 2026 for Induction in 2027.

Summary Analysis

Albert Pujols Hall of Fame Point Total is 260.300. This makes him the perfect example of a superstar that currently still needs to be elected to the BBWAAs for the Baseball Hall of Fame. He should be Inducted within six years of the end of his playing career.

A Fan's Perspective

Pujols, Albert — First Baseman Potential Hall of Fame Inductee

Positions: First Baseman, Third Baseman, Left Fielder	**Born:** January 16, 1980
From: Santo Domingo, Dominican Republic	**Bats:** Right **Throws:** Right
Height: 6'3" / 190 cm	**Weight:** 235 lbs / 106 Kg
Debut: April 2, 2001	**Last Game:** October 4, 2022

Year	Age	Tm	Lg	G	PA	AB	R	H	2B	3B	HR	RBI	SB	CS	BB	SO	BA	OBP	SLG	OPS	TB	HBP	Awards
2001	21	STL	NL	161	678	590	112	194	47	4	37	130	1	3	69	93	0.329	0.403	0.61	1.013	360	9	1,SS
2002	22	STL	NL	157	675	590	118	185	40	2	34	127	1	4	72	69	0.314	0.394	0.561	0.955	331	9	MVP-3
2003	23	STL	NL	157	685	591	137	212	51	1	43	124	5	1	79	65	0.359	0.439	0.667	1.106	394	10	AS,MVP-2,SS
2004	24	STL	NL	154	692	592	133	196	51	2	46	123	5	5	84	52	0.331	0.415	0.657	1.072	389	7	AS,MVP-3,SS
2005	25	STL	NL	161	700	591	129	195	38	2	41	117	16	2	97	65	0.33	0.43	0.609	1.039	360	9	AS,MVP-1
2006	26	STL	NL	143	634	535	119	177	33	1	49	137	7	2	92	50	0.331	0.431	0.671	1.102	359	4	AS,MVP-2,GG
2007	27	STL	NL	158	679	565	99	185	38	1	32	103	2	6	99	58	0.327	0.429	0.568	0.997	321	7	AS,MVP-9
2008	28	STL	NL	148	641	524	100	187	44	0	37	116	7	3	104	54	0.357	0.462	0.653	1.114	342	5	AS,MVP-1,SS
2009	29	STL	NL	160	700	568	124	186	45	1	47	135	16	4	115	64	0.327	0.443	0.658	1.101	374	9	AS,MVP-1,SS
2010	30	STL	NL	159	700	587	115	183	39	1	42	118	14	4	103	76	0.312	0.414	0.596	1.011	350	4	AS,MVP-2,GG,SS
2011	31	STL	NL	147	651	579	105	173	29	0	37	99	9	1	61	58	0.299	0.366	0.541	0.906	313	4	MVP-5
2012	32	LAA	AL	154	670	607	85	173	50	0	30	105	8	1	52	76	0.285	0.343	0.516	0.859	313	5	MVP-17
2013	33	LAA	AL	99	443	391	49	101	19	0	17	64	1	1	40	55	0.258	0.33	0.437	0.767	171	5	
2014	34	LAA	AL	159	695	633	89	172	37	1	28	105	5	1	48	71	0.272	0.324	0.466	0.79	295	5	MVP-17
2015	35	LAA	AL	157	661	602	85	147	22	0	40	95	5	3	50	72	0.244	0.307	0.480	0.787	289	6	AS
2016	36	LAA	AL	152	650	593	71	159	19	0	31	119	4	0	49	75	0.268	0.323	0.457	0.78	271	3	
2017	37	LAA	AL	149	636	593	53	143	17	0	23	101	3	0	37	93	0.241	0.286	0.386	0.672	229	2	
2018	38	LAA	AL	117	498	465	50	114	20	0	19	64	1	0	28	65	0.245	0.289	0.411	0.7	191	2	
2019	39	LAA	AL	131	545	491	55	120	22	0	23	93	3	0	43	68	0.244	0.305	0.430	0.734	211	8	
2020	40	LAA	AL	39	163	152	15	34	8	0	6	25	0	0	9	25	0.234	0.27	0.395	0.665	60	1	
2021	41	TOT	MLB	109	296	275	29	65	3	0	17	50	2	0	14	45	0.236	0.284	0.433	0.717	119	5	
2021	41	LAA	AL	24	92	86	9	17	0	0	5	12	1	0	3	13	0.198	0.25	0.372	0.622	32	3	
2021	41	LAD	NL	85	204	189	20	48	3	0	12	38	1	0	11	32	0.254	0.299	0.460	0.759	87	2	
2022	42	STL	NL	109	351	307	42	83	14	0	24	68	1	2	28	55	0.27	0.345	0.550	0.895	169	10	AS
162 Game Avg.				162	686	601	101	178	36	1	37	117	6	2	72	74	0.296	0.374	0.544	0.918	327	6	
STL (12 yrs)				1814	7784	6619	1333	2150	469	15	469	1397	85	37	1003	759	0.326	0.417	0.614	1.031	4062	87	
LAA (10 yrs)				1181	5053	4613	561	1180	214	1	222	783	31	6	359	613	0.256	0.311	0.447	0.758	2062	34	
LAD (1 yr)				85	204	189	20	48	3	0	12	38	1	0	11	32	0.254	0.299	0.460	0.759	87	2	
NL (13 yrs)				1899	7988	6808	1353	2204	472	15	481	1435	86	37	1014	791	0.324	0.414	0.609	1.023	4149	89	
AL (10 yrs)				1181	5053	4613	561	1180	214	1	222	783	31	6	359	613	0.256	0.311	0.447	0.758	2062	34	
22 Yrs				3080	13041	11421	1914	3384	686	16	703	2218	117	43	1973	1404	0.296	0.374	0.544	0.918	6211	123	**Career Pts.**
				15.500	0.000	0.000	36.750	18.500	0.000	0.000	21.000	20.000	1.000	0.000	8.300	0.000	5.500	4.500	8.250	8.250	18.730	0.000	**145.000**

Post Seasonal Play

Year	Age	Tm	Lg	G	PA	AB	R	H	2B	3B	HR	RBI	SB	CS	BB	SO	BA	OBP	SLG	OPS	TB	HBP
2001	21	STL	NLDS	5	20	18	1	2	0	0	1	2	0	0	2	3	0.111	0.200	0.278	0.478	5	0
2002	22	STL	NLDS	3	13	10	3	3	0	1	0	3	0	0	3	1	0.300	0.462	0.500	0.962	5	0
2002	22	STL	NLCS	5	22	19	2	5	1	0	1	2	0	0	2	5	0.263	0.364	0.474	0.837	9	1
2004	24	STL	NLDS	4	18	15	4	5	0	0	2	5	0	0	3	0	0.333	0.444	0.733	1.178	11	0
2004	24	STL	NLCS	7	32	28	10	14	2	0	4	9	0	0	4	3	0.500	0.563	1.000	1.563	28	0
2005	25	STL	NLDS	3	13	9	4	5	2	0	0	3	0	0	4	0	0.556	0.692	0.778	1.470	7	0
2005	25	STL	NLCS	6	25	23	3	7	0	0	2	6	0	0	1	3	0.304	0.320	0.565	0.885	13	0
2006	26	STL	NLDS	4	16	15	3	5	1	0	1	3	0	0	1	4	0.333	0.375	0.600	0.975	9	0
2006	26	STL	NLCS	7	29	22	5	7	1	0	1	3	0	0	7	3	0.318	0.483	0.500	0.983	11	0
2009	29	STL	NLDS	3	13	10	0	3	0	0	0	1	0	0	3	1	0.300	0.462	0.300	0.762	3	0
2011	31	STL	NLDS	5	23	20	2	7	3	0	0	1	1	1	2	4	0.350	0.409	0.500	0.909	10	0
2011	31	STL	NLCS	6	27	23	5	11	4	0	2	9	0	0	4	4	0.478	0.556	0.913	1.469	21	0
2014	34	LAA	ALDS	3	13	12	1	2	0	0	1	2	0	0	1	1	0.167	0.231	0.417	0.647	5	0
2021	41	LAD	NLWC	1	1	1	0	0	0	0	0	0	0	0	0	0	0.000	0.000	0.000	0.000	0	0
2021	41	LAD	NLDS	2	3	3	0	2	0	0	0	0	0	0	0	0	0.667	0.667	0.667	1.333	2	0
2021	41	LAD	NLCS	6	14	13	2	3	0	0	0	0	0	0	1	5	0.231	0.286	0.231	0.516	3	0
2022	42	STL	NLWC	2	8	8	0	2	0	0	0	0	0	0	0	1	0.250	0.250	0.250	0.500	2	0
				72	289	249	45	88	14	1	19	46	1	1	38	37	0.333	0.421	0.578	0.999	144	1	**Post Season Pts.**
				1.600	0.000	0.000	0.200	1.400	0.000	0.000	1.800	2.000	0.250	0.000	1.600	0.000	1.000	1.800	1.400	1.000	1.400	0.000	**15.050**

World Series Play

Year	Age	Tm	Lg	G	PA	AB	R	H	2B	3B	HR	RBI	SB	CS	BB	SO	BA	OBP	SLG	OPS	TB	HBP
2004	24	STL	WS	4	17	15	1	5	2	0	0	0	0	0	1	3	0.333	0.412	0.467	0.878	7	1
2006	26	STL	WS	5	21	15	3	3	1	0	1	2	0	0	5	3	0.200	0.429	0.467	0.895	7	1
2011	31	STL	WS	7	33	25	8	6	1	0	3	6	0	1	6	8	0.340	0.424	0.640	1.064	16	2
				16	71	55	12	14	4	0	4	8	0	1	12	9	0.255	0.388	0.545	0.933	30	4	**World Series Pts.**
				0.600	0.000	0.000	0.800	0.600	0.000	0.000	0.800	0.600	0.000	0.250	0.600	0.000	0.400	1.000	0.800	1.000	1.000	0.000	**8.250**

Yearly Points Leading the League

Category	Times	Points	Total		Category	Times	Points	Total		Categ	Times	Points	Total
MVP	3	7	21		B.A.	1	3	3		T.B.	0	2	0
Rookie of Year	1	5	5		Runs	5	2	10		O.O.B.	0	2	0
Triple Crown	0	5	0		H.R.'s	2	3	6		OBP%	1	2	2
Golden Glove	2	3	6		R.B.I's	1	3	3		SLG %	3	2	6
All-Star	11	2	22		Hits	2	2	2		OBP%S	3	2	6
Games	0	2	0		S.B.	0	2	0		Totals			14
Totals			54		Totals	0		24		Grand Total Add-On Points			92

Hall of Fame Points

Career Points	145.000
Post Season Points	15.050
World Series Points	8.250
Career Add-On Points	92.000
Writers Association Pts.	0.000
Military/Lifetime Achievement	0.000
Grand Total HOF Points	**260.300**

The Baseball Hall of Fame

Berkman, Lance "Big Puma"

Personal Life

William Lance Berkman (born February 10, 1976), was born in Waco, Texas, to Cynthia Ann Thomas and Larry Gene Berkman with two sisters, Jennifer, and Brook. Berkman graduated from Canyon High School and received a scholarship to Rice University from 1994-1997 batting a collective .385 with 67 home runs and 272 RBI.

Berkman married Cara Baker on October 3,1998 with the couple having four children. Hanna Leigh, Carly Ann, Katie Mae, and Abigail Primm.

Baseball Career

The Houston Astros selected Berkman 16th in the first round of the 1997 MLB draft. He went to Class A and in 1999, was called up to the Astros.   As a switch-hitter, Berkman ranks second all-time in OPS, slugging (.537), third in OBP (.406) and sixth in homers. In 1,879 games, Berkman batted .293, 1,146 runs, 422 doubles, 30 triples, 366 home runs, 1,234 RBI, and a .406 on-base percentage, a .537 slugging percentage, OPS of .943, and a .991 fielding percentage. In 52 postseason games, he hit .317, 9 HR's, 41 RBIs, .949 OPS, .410 average and 1.084 OPS in 11 World Series games.

Achievements:

- 2-Times 40 plus home run seasons: (2002 & 2006).
- 5-Times 100 plus runs scored: (2001-2004, & 2008).
- 6-Times All-Star: (2001, 2002, 2004, 2008 & 2011).
- 6-Times 30, or more home runs: (2001, 2002, 2004, 2006, & 2007).
- 6-Times Top Ten of MVP Award Voting: (2001, 2002, 2004, 2006, 2008 & 2011).

Hall of Fame

Lance Berkman received just five votes, in 2018, and fell off the ballot.

Summary:

Based on the 106.000 Career Statistical Points presented in this book, Berkman needs to be elected to the Hall of Fame by the BBWAA.

A Fan's Perspective

Berkman, Lance | **First Baseman Potential Hall of Fame Inductee**

Positions	Born:	February 10, 1976	Height: 6' 1" USC 185 cm
First Baseman	From:	Waco, TX	Weight: 220 lbs 99 Kg.
Outfielder	Bats:	Both	Debut: July 16, 1999
	Throws:	Right	Last Game: September 17, 2013

Year	Age	Tm	Lg	G	PA	AB	R	H	2B	3B	HR	RBI	SB	CS	BB	SO	BA	OBP	SLG	OPS	TB	HBP	Awards
1999	23	HOU	NL	34	106	93	10	22	2	0	4	15	5	1	12	21	0.237	0.321	0.387	0.708	36	0	
2000	24	HOU	NL	114	417	353	76	105	28	1	21	67	6	2	56	73	0.297	0.388	0.561	0.949	198	1	RoY-6
2001	25	HOU	NL	156	688	577	110	191	55	5	34	126	7	9	92	121	0.331	0.43	0.62	1.051	358	13	AS,MVP-5
2002	26	HOU	NL	158	692	578	106	169	35	2	42	128	8	4	107	118	0.292	0.405	0.578	0.982	334	4	AS,MVP-3
2003	27	HOU	NL	153	658	538	110	155	35	6	25	93	5	3	107	108	0.288	0.412	0.515	0.927	277	9	
2004	28	HOU	NL	160	687	544	104	172	40	3	30	106	9	7	127	101	0.316	0.45	0.566	1.016	308	10	AS,MVP-7
2005	29	HOU	NL	132	565	468	76	137	34	1	24	82	4	1	91	72	0.293	0.411	0.524	0.934	245	4	MVP-14
2006	30	HOU	NL	152	646	536	95	169	29	0	45	136	3	2	98	106	0.315	0.42	0.621	1.041	333	4	AS,MVP-3
2007	31	HOU	NL	153	668	561	95	156	24	2	34	102	7	3	94	125	0.278	0.386	0.51	0.896	286	8	
2008	32	HOU	NL	159	665	554	114	173	46	4	29	106	18	4	99	108	0.312	0.42	0.567	0.986	314	7	AS,MVP-5
2009	33	HOU	NL	136	563	460	73	126	31	1	25	80	7	4	97	98	0.274	0.399	0.509	0.907	234	1	
2010	34	TOT	MLB	122	481	404	48	100	23	1	14	58	3	2	77	85	0.248	0.368	0.413	0.781	167	0	
2010	34	HOU	NL	85	358	298	39	73	16	1	13	49	3	2	60	70	0.245	0.372	0.436	0.808	130	0	
2010	34	NYY	AL	37	123	106	9	27	7	0	1	9	0	0	17	15	0.255	0.358	0.349	0.707	37	0	
2011	35	STL	NL	145	587	488	90	147	23	2	31	94	2	6	92	93	0.301	0.412	0.547	0.959	267	3	AS,MVP-7
2012	36	STL	NL	32	97	81	12	21	7	1	2	7	2	0	14	19	0.259	0.381	0.444	0.826	36	2	
2013	37	TEX	AL	73	294	256	27	62	10	1	6	34	0	0	38	52	0.242	0.34	0.359	0.7	92	0	
162 Game Avg.				162	674	560	99	164	36	3	32	106	7	4	104	112	0.293	0.406	0.537	0.943	300	14	
HOU (12 yrs)				1592	6713	5560	1008	1648	375	26	326	1090	82	42	1040	1121	0.296	0.41	0.549	0.959	3053	134	
STL (2 yrs)				177	684	569	102	168	30	3	33	101	4	6	106	112	0.295	0.408	0.533	0.94	303	20	
TEX (1 yr)				73	294	256	27	62	10	1	6	34	0	0	38	52	0.242	0.34	0.359	0.7	92	3	
NYY (1 yr)				37	123	106	9	27	7	0	1	9	0	0	17	15	0.255	0.358	0.349	0.707	37	3	
NL (14 yrs)				1769	7397	6129	1110	1816	405	29	359	1191	86	48	1146	1233	0.296	0.409	0.548	0.957	3356	154	
AL (2 yrs)				110	417	362	36	89	17	1	7	43	0	0	55	67	0.246	0.345	0.356	0.702	129	6	
15 Yrs				1879	7814	6491	1146	1905	422	30	366	1234	86	48	1201	1300	0.293	0.406	0.537	0.943	3485	160	Career Pts.
				4.500	0.000	0.000	5.500	2.500	0.000	0.000	6.750	6.750	1.000	0.000	5.500	0.000	5.500	9.250	8.000	10.500	4.500	0.000	70.250

Post Seasonal Play

Year	Age	Tm	Lg	G	PA	AB	R	H	2B	3B	HR	RBI	SB	CS	BB	SO	BA	OBP	SLG	OPS	TB	HBP	
2001	25	HOU	NLDS	3	12	12	0	2	0	0	0	0	0	0	0	4	0.167	0.167	0.167	0.333	2	0	
2004	28	HOU	NLDS	5	25	22	5	9	1	0	1	3	0	1	3	6	0.409	0.480	0.591	1.071	13	0	
2004	28	HOU	NLCS	7	30	24	7	7	2	0	3	9	1	0	5	4	0.292	0.400	0.750	1.15	18	0	
2005	29	HOU	NLDS	4	18	14	4	5	1	0	1	5	0	0	3	4	0.357	0.500	0.643	1.143	9	1	
2005	29	HOU	NLCS	6	25	21	2	6	2	0	1	3	0	0	4	3	0.286	0.400	0.524	0.924	11	0	
2010	34	NYY	ALDS	3	4	4	2	2	1	0	1	2	0	0	0	1	0.500	0.500	1.500	2.000	6	0	
2010	34	NYY	ALCS	4	15	12	1	3	0	1	0	2	0	0	3	2	0.250	0.333	0.417	0.750	5	0	
2011	35	STL	NLDS	5	22	18	4	3	1	0	1	4	1	0	2	3	0.167	0.286	0.389	0.675	7	1	
2011	35	STL	NLCS	6	23	20	4	6	0	0	0	2	1	0	2	2	0.300	0.391	0.300	0.691	6	1	
				35	151	127	25	37	8	1	8	28	2	1	19	27	0.291	0.383	0.606	0.989	77	3	Post Season Pts.
				0.800	0.000	0.000	0.800	0.600	0.000	0.000	0.800	1.200	0.250	0.000	0.800	0.000	0.600	1.000	1.600	1.000	0.800	0.000	10.250

World Series Play

Year	Age	Tm	Lg	G	PA	AB	R	H	2B	3B	HR	RBI	SB	CS	BB	SO	BA	OBP	SLG	OPS	TB	HBP	
2005	29	HOU	NL	4	19	13	0	5	2	0	0	6	1	0	5	5	0.385	0.526	0.538	1.065	7	0	
2011	35	STL	NL	7	31	26	9	11	1	0	1	5	0	0	5	7	0.423	0.516	0.577	1.093	15	0	
				11	50	39	9	16	3	0	1	11	1	0	10	12	0.410	0.520	0.558	1.078	22	0	World Series Pts.
				0.400	0.000	0.000	0.600	0.600	0.000	0.000	0.250	0.600	0.250	0.000	0.600	0.000	2.000	2.000	1.000	1.400	0.8	0.000	10.500

Yearly Points Leading the League

Category	Times	Points	Total	Category	Times	Points	Total	Categ	Times	Points	Total
MVP	0	7	0	B.A.	0	3	0	T.B.	0	2	0
Rookie of Year	0	5	0	Runs	0	2	0	B.O.B.	0	2	0
Triple Crown	0	5	0	H.R.'s	0	3	0	OBP%	0	2	0
Golden Glove	0	3	0	R.B.I's	1	3	3	SLG %	0	2	0
All-Star	6	2	12	Hits	0	2	0	OBPS%	0	2	0
Games	0	2	0	S.B.	0	2	0	Totals			0
Totals			12	Totals			3	Grand Total Add-On Points			15

Hall of Fame Points	
Career Points	70.250
Post Season Points	10.250
World Series Points	10.500
Career Add-On Points	15.00
Writers Association Pts.	0.00
Military/Lifetime Achievement	0.00
Grand Total HOF Points	106.000

The Baseball Hall of Fame

Clark, Will "The Thrill"

Personal Life

William Nuschler Clark Jr. was born March 13, 1964, to William Nuschler Sr. and Letty Jane (Hubert). Will has a brother Scott and a sister Robin. Clark attended Mississippi State University and played for the USA at the 1984 Summer Olympics

Clark married Lisa White in 1994 and have a son Trey and a daughter, Ella. The Clarks son, Trey, was diagnosed with Pervasive Developmental Disorder.

Baseball Career

In 1985, Clark was drafted by the San Francisco Giants in the 1st round with the second overall pick and made his pro debut with the Fresno Giants on June 21st. In1986, Clark was the Giants first baseman and hit .287 with 11 homers. Clark was a consistent star until he retired in 2000 to spend time with family. He left with 284 HR's, 1205 RBIs, 1,186 runs, and 2,176 hits. He was a career .303/.384/.497 with a career OPS+ of 137.

Achievements:

- 1-Year Led the League in games played, RBI's and Base-On-Balls (1988).
- 1-Year Led the League in Slugging % & Total Bases: (1991).
- 6-Times All-Star: (1988-1992, & 1994). & 2-Time won Silver Slugger (1989 & 1991).
- 5-Times received MVP Votes: (1987-1989, 1991 & 1994).
- 1-Time received a Golden Glove Award: (1991)
- 1-Time Led the League in Runs Scored: (1989),

Hall of Fame Candidacy

In 2006, Clark received 23 votes for 4.4% and was removed from the ballot. In 2018 Game ERA voting he once again failed to achieve the votes needed.

Summary Analysis

Will Clark 97.500 Hall of Fame Point Total listed in the statistical analysis section of this book and should be voted in by the BBWAA due to his Amateur, Olympic, MLB records.

A Fan's Perspective

Clark, Will — First Baseman Potential Hall of Fame Inductee

Positions: First Baseman

Born:	March 13, 1964	Height: 6' 2" USC 188 cm
From:	New Orleans, LA	Weight: 175 lbs. 79 Kg.
Bats:	Left	Debut: April 8, 1986
Throws:	Left	Last Game: October 1, 2000

Year	Age	Tm	Lg	G	PA	AB	R	H	2B	3B	HR	RBI	SB	CS	BB	SO	BA	OBP	SLG	OPS	TB	HBP	Awards
1986	22	SFG	NL	111	458	408	66	117	27	2	11	41	4	7	34	76	0.287	0.343	0.444	0.787	181	3	RoY-5
1987	23	SFG	NL	150	588	529	89	163	29	5	35	91	5	17	49	98	0.308	0.371	0.580	0.951	307	5	MVP-5
1988	24	SFG	NL	162	689	575	102	162	31	6	29	109	9	1	100	129	0.282	0.386	0.508	0.894	292	4	AS,MVP-5
1989	25	SFG	NL	159	675	588	104	196	38	9	23	111	8	3	74	103	0.333	0.407	0.546	0.953	321	5	AS,MVP-2,SS
1990	26	SFG	NL	154	678	600	91	177	25	5	19	95	8	2	62	97	0.295	0.357	0.448	0.805	269	3	AS
1991	27	SFG	NL	148	622	565	84	170	32	7	29	116	4	2	51	91	0.301	0.359	0.536	0.895	303	2	AS,MVP-4,GG,SS
1992	28	SFG	NL	144	601	513	69	154	40	1	16	73	12	7	73	82	0.300	0.384	0.476	0.860	244	4	AS
1993	29	SFG	NL	132	567	491	82	139	27	2	14	73	2	2	63	68	0.283	0.367	0.432	0.799	212	6	
1994	30	TEX	AL	110	469	385	73	128	24	2	13	80	5	1	71	59	0.329	0.431	0.501	0.932	195	3	AS,MVP-15
1995	31	TEX	AL	123	537	454	85	137	27	3	16	92	0	1	68	50	0.302	0.389	0.480	0.869	218	4	
1996	32	TEX	AL	117	512	436	69	124	25	1	13	72	2	1	64	67	0.284	0.377	0.436	0.813	190	5	
1997	33	TEX	AL	110	450	393	56	128	29	1	12	51	0	0	49	62	0.326	0.400	0.496	0.896	195	3	
1998	34	TEX	AL	149	636	554	98	169	41	1	23	102	1	0	72	97	0.305	0.384	0.507	0.891	281	3	
1999	35	BAL	AL	77	294	251	40	76	15	0	10	29	2	2	38	42	0.303	0.395	0.482	0.877	121	2	
2000	36	TOT	MLB	130	507	427	78	136	30	2	21	70	5	2	69	69	0.319	0.418	0.546	0.964	233	7	
2000	36	BAL	AL	79	310	256	49	77	15	1	9	28	4	2	47	45	0.301	0.413	0.473	0.886	121	4	
2000	36	STL	NL	51	197	171	29	59	15	1	12	42	1	0	22	24	0.345	0.426	0.655	1.081	112	3	
162 Game Avg.				162	679	588	97	178	36	4	23	99	5	4	77	98	0.303	0.384	0.497	0.880	292	5	
SFG (8 yrs)				1160	4878	4269	687	1278	249	37	176	709	52	41	506	744	0.299	0.373	0.499	0.872	2129	32	
TEX (5 yrs)				609	2604	2226	381	686	146	8	77	397	8	3	324	335	0.308	0.395	0.485	0.880	1079	18	
BAL (2 yrs)				156	604	507	89	153	30	1	19	57	6	4	85	87	0.302	0.404	0.477	0.881	242	6	
STL (1 yr)				51	197	171	29	59	15	1	12	42	1	0	22	24	0.345	0.426	0.655	1.081	112	3	
NL (9 yrs)				1211	5075	4440	716	1337	264	38	188	751	53	41	528	768	0.301	0.375	0.505	0.880	2241	35	
AL (7 yrs)				765	3208	2733	470	839	176	9	96	454	14	7	409	422	0.307	0.397	0.483	0.880	1321	24	
15 Yrs				1976	8283	7173	1186	2176	440	47	284	1205	67	48	937	1190	0.303	0.384	0.497	0.880	3562	59	**Career Pts.**
				5.500	0.000	0.000	5.500	3.750	0.000	0.000	4.500	5.500	1.000	0.000	3.000	0.000	6.750	5.500	5.500	8.000	5.500	0.000	**60.000**

Post Season Play

Year	Age	Tm	Lg	G	PA	AB	R	H	2B	3B	HR	RBI	SB	CS	BB	SO	BA	OBP	SLG	OPS	TB	HBP	
1987	23	SFG	NL-CS	7	28	25	3	9	2	0	1	3	1	1	3	6	0.360	0.429	0.560	0.989	14	0	
1989	25	SFG	NL-CS	5	22	20	8	13	3	1	2	8	0	0	2	2	0.650	0.682	1.200	1.882	24	0	
1996	32	TEX	AL-DS	4	19	16	1	2	0	0	0	0	0	0	3	2	0.125	0.263	0.125	0.388	2	0	
1998	34	TEX	AL-DS	3	12	11	0	1	0	0	0	0	0	0	1	2	0.091	0.167	0.091	0.258	1	0	
2000	36	STL	NL-DS	3	14	12	3	3	0	0	1	4	0	0	1	3	0.250	0.357	0.500	0.857	6	1	
2000	36	STL	NL-CS	5	20	17	3	7	2	0	1	1	0	0	2	1	0.412	0.500	0.706	1.206	12	1	
				27	115	101	18	35	7	1	5	16	1	1	12	16	0.347	0.416	0.584	1.000	59	2	**Post Season**
				0.600	0.000	0.000	0.600	0.600	0.000	0.000	0.600	0.800	0.250	0.000	0.600	0.000	1.200	1.400	1.400	1.200	0.600	0.000	**9.850**

World Series Play

Year	Age	Tm	Lg	G	PA	AB	R	H	2B	3B	HR	RBI	SB	CS	BB	SO	BA	OBP	SLG	OPS	TB	HBP	
1989	25	SFG	NL	4	17	16	2	4	1	0	0	0	0	0	1	3	0.250	0.294	0.313	0.607	5	0	
				4	17	16	2	4	1	0	0	0	0	0	1	3	0.250	0.294	0.313	0.607	5	0	**WS Points**
				0.250	0.000	0.000	0.250	0.250	0.000	0.000	0.000	0.000	0.000	0.000	0.250	0.000	0.400	0.000	0.000	0.000	0.250	0.000	**1.650**

Yearly Points Leading the League

	Times	Points	Total	Category	Times	Points	Total	Categr	Times	Points	Total
MVP	0	7	0	B.A.	0	3	0	T. B.	1	2	2
Rookie of Year	0	5	0	Runs	1	2	2	B.O.B.	1	2	2
Triple Crown	0	5	0	H.R.'s	0	3	0	OBP%	0	2	0
Golden Glove	1	3	3	R.B.I's	1	3	3	SLG %	1	2	2
All-Star	5	2	10	Hits	0	2	0	OBP5%	0	2	0
Games	1	2	2	S.B.	0	2	0	Totals			6
Totals			15	Totals			5	Grand Total Add-On Points			26

Hall of Fame Points	
Career Points	60.000
Post Season Points	9.850
World Series Points	1.650
Career Add-On Points	26.00
Writers Association Pts.	0.000
Military/Lifetime Achievement	0.000
Grand Total HOF Points	97.500

Carlos Delgado

Personal Life

Carlos Juan Delgado Hernández (born June 25, 1972) in Aguadilla, Puerto Rico to Carlos "Cao" Delgado and Carmen Digna Hernandez. He attended Agustín Stahl Middle School and José de Diego High School, from which he graduated in 1989.

He married Betzaida García in 2005. They have a son, Carlos Antonio, and in 2010 adopted a daughter, Mariana Isabel.

Baseball Career

Delgado signed with the Blue Jays in 1988 and sent to St. Catharine's, Ontario, the New York-Pennsylvania League affiliate. He played in their minor leagues until a major league debut on October 1, 1993. From 1997 on, he became one of the most productive sluggers in the major leagues and hit at least 30 home runs in ten consecutive seasons. On September 25, 2003, Delgado became the 15th major league player to hit four home runs in one game and is the only player to hit four home runs with only 4 at-bats in a game. In 2,035 games over 17 seasons, Delgado posted a .280 batting average, with 1241 runs, 483 doubles, 18 triples, 473 home runs, 1,512 runs batted in, 1,109 bases on balls, .383 and .546 slugging% He finished with a .9and, a 992 fielding %. In ten postseason games, he hit .351 with eight runs, three doubles, four home runs, 11 RBIs and six walks. He is one of only six players in Major League history to hit 30 home runs in ten consecutive seasons.

Hall of Fame

Delgado's Hall of Fame candidacy ended in his only appearance on the Baseball Hall of Fame ballot in 2015 when Delgado received just 3.8% of the vote and was removed.

Summary Analysis

Based on the 103.150 Hall of Fame career statistical points presented in this book, Delgado needs to be eventually elected by the BBWAA for Baseball Hall of Fame as he has met the requirements.

A Fan's Perspective

Delgado, Carlos
Positions
First Baseman

First Baseman Potential Hall of Fame Inductee

Born:	June 25, 1972
From:	Aquidilla, Puerto Rico
Bats:	Left
Throws:	Right

Height:	6' 3"	USC	190
Weight:	215	lbs.	97
Debut:	October 1, 1993		
Last Game:	May 10, 2009		

Year	Age	Tm	Lg	G	PA	AB	R	H	2B	3B	HR	RBI	SB	CS	BB	SO	BA	OBP	SLG	OPS	TB	Awards
1993	21	TOR	AL	2	2	1	0	0	0	0	0	0	0	0	1	0	0.000	0.500	0.000	0.500	0	
1994	22	TOR	AL	43	159	130	17	28	2	0	9	24	1	1	25	46	0.215	0.352	0.438	0.791	57	
1995	23	TOR	AL	37	99	91	7	15	3	0	3	11	0	0	6	26	0.165	0.212	0.297	0.509	27	
1996	24	TOR	AL	138	563	488	68	132	28	2	25	92	0	0	58	139	0.270	0.353	0.490	0.843	239	
1997	25	TOR	AL	153	595	519	79	136	42	3	30	91	0	3	64	133	0.262	0.350	0.528	0.878	274	
1998	26	TOR	AL	142	620	530	94	155	43	1	38	115	3	0	73	139	0.292	0.385	0.592	0.978	314	MVP-21
1999	27	TOR	AL	152	681	573	113	156	39	0	44	134	1	1	86	141	0.272	0.377	0.571	0.948	327	MVP-12,SS
2000	28	TOR	AL	162	711	569	115	196	57	1	41	137	0	1	123	104	0.344	0.470	0.664	1.134	378	AS,MVP-4,SS
2001	29	TOR	AL	162	704	574	102	160	31	1	39	102	3	0	111	136	0.279	0.408	0.540	0.948	310	
2002	30	TOR	AL	143	628	505	103	140	34	2	33	108	1	0	102	126	0.277	0.406	0.549	0.955	277	
2003	31	TOR	AL	161	705	570	117	172	38	1	42	145	0	0	109	137	0.302	0.426	0.593	1.019	338	AS,MVP-2,SS
2004	32	TOR	AL	128	551	458	74	123	26	0	32	99	0	1	69	115	0.269	0.372	0.535	0.907	245	
2005	33	FLA	NL	144	616	521	81	157	41	3	33	115	0	0	72	121	0.301	0.399	0.582	0.981	303	MVP-6
2006	34	NYM	NL	144	618	524	89	139	30	2	38	114	0	0	74	120	0.265	0.361	0.548	0.909	287	MVP-12
2007	35	NYM	NL	139	607	538	71	139	30	0	24	87	4	0	52	118	0.258	0.333	0.448	0.781	241	
2008	36	NYM	NL	159	686	598	96	162	32	1	38	115	1	1	72	124	0.271	0.353	0.518	0.871	310	MVP-9
2009	37	NYM	NL	26	112	94	15	28	7	1	4	23	0	0	12	20	0.298	0.393	0.521	0.914	49	
162 Game Avg.				162	689	580	99	162	38	1	38	120	1	1	88	139	0.280	0.383	0.546	0.929	317	
TOR (12 yrs)				1423	6018	5008	889	1413	343	11	336	1058	9	7	827	1242	0.282	0.392	0.556	0.949	2786	
NYM (4 yrs)				468	2023	1754	271	468	99	4	104	339	5	1	210	382	0.267	0.351	0.506	0.857	887	
FLA (1 yr)				144	616	521	81	157	41	3	33	115	0	0	72	121	0.301	0.399	0.582	0.981	303	
AL (12 yrs)				1423	6018	5008	889	1413	343	11	336	1058	9	7	827	1242	0.282	0.392	0.556	0.949	2786	
NL (5 yrs)				612	2639	2275	352	625	140	7	137	454	5	1	282	503	0.275	0.363	0.523	0.886	1190	
17 Yrs				2035	8657	7283	1241	2038	483	18	473	1512	14	8	1109	1745	0.280	0.383	0.546	0.929	3976	Career Pts.
				6.750	0.000	0.000	6.750	3.000	0.000	0.000	10.500	10.500	0.500	0.000	4.500	0.000	3.750	5.500	9.250	10.500	6.750	78.250

Post Season Play

Year	Age	Tm	Lg	G	PA	AB	R	H	2B	3B	HR	RBI	SB	CS	BB	SO	BA	OBP	SLG	OPS	TB	
2006	34	NYM	NL	3	14	14	3	6	0	0	1	2	0	0	0	3	0.429	0.429	0.643	1.071	9	
2006	34	NYM	NL	7	29	23	5	7	3	0	3	9	0	0	6	3	0.304	0.448	0.826	1.274	19	
				10	43	37	8	13	3	0	4	11	0	0	6	6	0.351	0.442	0.757	1.199	28	Post Season Pts.
				0.250	0.000	0.000	0.250	0.400	0.000	0.000	0.400	0.600	0.000	0.000	0.400	0.000	1.200	1.800	2.000	1.600	1.000	9.900

World Series Play

Year	Age	Tm	Lg	G	PA	AB	R	H	2B	3B	HR	RBI	SB	CS	BB	SO	BA	OBP	SLG	OPS	TB	
None				0	0	0	0	0	0	0	0	0	0	0	0	0	0	0	0	0	0	World Series Pts.
				0.000	0.000	0.000	0.000	0.000	0.000	0.000	0.000	0.000	0.000	0.000	0.000	0.000	0.000	0.000	0.000	0.000	0.000	0.000

Yearly Points Leading the League

Category	Times	Points	Total	Category	Times	Points	Total	Category	Times	Points	Total
MVP	0	7	0	B.A.	0	3	0	T.B.	1	2	2
Rookie of Year	0	5	0	Runs	0	2	0	B.O.B.	0	2	0
Triple Crown	0	5	0	H.R.'s	0	3	0	OBP%	1	2	2
Golden Glove	0	3	0	R.B.I's	1	3	3	SLG %	0	2	0
All-Star	2	2	4	Hits	0	2	0	OBPS%	0	2	0
Games	2	2	4	S.B.	0	2	0	Totals			4
Totals			8	Totals			3	Grand Total Add-On Points		15	

Hall of Fame Points	
Career Points	78.250
Post Season Points	9.900
World Series Points	0.000
Career Add-On Points	15.00
Writers Association Pts.	0.000
Military/Lifetime Achievement	0.000
Grand Total HOF Points	103.15

Galarraga, Andres "The Big Cat"

Personal Life

Andrés José Padovani Galarraga was born June 18, 1961, in Caracas to Francisco & Juana Padovani. He has three brothers Orlando, Alfonso, Francisco, and a sister Haide.

Galarraga married Eneyda on Valentine's Day 1984. The couple have three children Katherine, Andria, and Andrianna.

Baseball Career

Galarraga played in the Minor Leagues from 1979 until he made his major-league debut on August 23, 1985. He started to establish himself in 1986 and in 1988, he blossomed hitting .302 with 29 home runs, 92 RBIs, and 99 runs scored, leading the league in hits 184. and doubles 42. After the 1991 season, he was traded to the St. Louis Cardinals and Galarraga broke his wrist in the second game of 1992 and hit .243. 10 home runs and 39 RBIs. Don Baylor persuaded him to sign Galarraga with Colorado following his release by the Cardinals and his career took off as he became a fan favorite.

Achievements

- Five-time National League All-Star: (1988, 1993, 1997, 1998 & 2000).
- Two-time National League Golden Glove winner: (1989 & 1990).
- Led National League in Hits (184 in 1988)
- Led National League in Total Bases (329 in 1988) and Doubles (42 in 1988)
- Led National League in Batting average (.370 in 1993), Home Runs (47 in 1996)
- Twice led National League in RBIs (150 in 1996 and 140 in 1997)

Hall of Fame

In 2010, Galarraga appeared on the BBWAA Ballot and received 1.5% and removed from the ballot. In 2023 Game ERA he failed to achieve the votes to be elected.

Summary Analysis

Galarraga's Hall of Fame Point Total listed in the statistical analysis is 91.45. His election should be dependent on the Baseball Writers Association of America (BBWAA).

A Fan's Perspective

Galarraga, Andres — First Baseman Potential Hall of Fame Inductee

Positions First Baseman	**Born:** June 18, 1961	**Height:** 6' 3" USC 190 cm
	From: Enrique Faimi (Caracus, Venezuela)	**Weight:** 235 lbs. 106 Kg.
	Bats: Right	**Debut:** August 23, 1985
	Throws: Right	**Last Game:** October 3, 2004

Year	Age	Tm	Lg	G	PA	AB	R	H	2B	3B	HR	RBI	SB	CS	BB	SO	BA	OBP	SLG	OPS	TB	HBP	Awards
1985	24	MON	NL	24	79	75	9	14	1	0	2	4	1	2	3	18	0.187	0.228	0.280	0.508	21	1	
1986	25	MON	NL	105	356	321	39	87	13	0	10	42	6	5	30	79	0.271	0.338	0.405	0.743	130	3	
1987	26	MON	NL	147	606	551	72	168	40	3	13	90	7	10	41	127	0.305	0.361	0.459	0.821	253	10	
1988	27	MON	NL	157	661	609	99	184	42	8	29	92	13	4	39	153	0.302	0.352	0.540	0.893	329	10	AS,MVP-7,SS
1989	28	MON	NL	152	636	572	76	147	30	1	23	85	12	5	48	158	0.257	0.327	0.434	0.761	248	13	GG
1990	29	MON	NL	155	628	579	65	148	29	0	20	87	10	1	40	169	0.256	0.306	0.409	0.715	237	4	GG
1991	30	MON	NL	107	400	375	34	82	13	2	9	33	5	6	23	86	0.219	0.268	0.336	0.604	126	2	
1992	31	STL	NL	95	347	325	38	79	14	2	10	39	5	4	11	69	0.243	0.282	0.391	0.673	127	8	
1993	32	COL	NL	120	506	470	71	174	35	4	22	98	2	4	24	73	0.370	0.403	0.602	1.005	283	6	AS,MVP-10
1994	33	COL	NL	103	449	417	77	133	21	0	31	85	8	3	19	93	0.319	0.356	0.592	0.949	247	8	MVP-10
1995	34	COL	NL	143	604	554	89	155	29	3	31	106	12	2	32	146	0.280	0.331	0.511	0.842	283	13	MVP-16
1996	35	COL	NL	159	691	626	119	190	39	3	47	150	18	8	40	157	0.304	0.357	0.601	0.958	376	17	MVP-6,SS
1997	36	COL	NL	154	674	600	120	191	31	3	41	140	15	8	54	141	0.318	0.389	0.585	0.974	351	17	AS,MVP-7
1998	37	ATL	NL	153	648	555	103	169	27	1	44	121	7	6	63	146	0.305	0.397	0.595	0.991	330	25	AS,MVP-6
1999		Did not play in major or minor leagues (Injured)																					
2000	39	ATL	NL	141	548	494	67	149	25	1	28	100	3	5	36	126	0.302	0.369	0.526	0.895	260	17	AS
2001	40	TOT	MLB	121	445	399	50	102	28	1	17	69	1	3	31	117	0.256	0.326	0.459	0.784	183	12	
2001	40	TEX	AL	72	271	243	33	57	16	0	10	34	1	0	18	68	0.235	0.310	0.424	0.734	103	9	
2001	40	SFG	NL	49	174	156	17	45	12	1	7	35	0	3	13	49	0.288	0.351	0.513	0.863	90	3	
2002	41	MON	NL	104	334	292	30	76	12	0	9	40	2	2	30	81	0.260	0.344	0.394	0.738	115	9	
2003	42	SFG	NL	110	293	272	36	82	15	0	12	42	1	3	19	61	0.301	0.352	0.489	0.841	133	2	
2004	43	ANA	AL	7	11	10	1	3	0	0	1	2	0	0	0	3	0.300	0.364	0.600	0.964	6	1	
162 Game Avg.				162	640	581	86	167	32	2	29	102	9	6	42	144	0.288	0.347	0.499	0.846	119	290	

19 Yrs	G	PA	AB	R	H	2B	3B	HR	RBI	SB	CS	BB	SO	BA	OBP	SLG	OPS	TB	HBP	Career Pts.
	2257	8916	8096	1195	2333	444	32	399	1425	128	81	583	2003	0.288	0.347	0.499	0.846	4038	178	
	8.00	0.00	0.00	5.50	4.50	0.00	0.00	8.00	9.25	1.50	0.00	1.50	0.00	4.50	2.50	5.50	6.75	6.75	0.00	**64.25**

Post Seasonal Play

Year	Age	Tm	Lg	G	PA	AB	R	H	2B	3B	HR	RBI	SB	CS	BB	SO	BA	OBP	SLG	OPS	TB	HBP
1995	34	COL	NL-DS	4	18	18	1	5	1	0	0	2	0	0	0	6	0.278	0.278	0.333	0.611	6	0
1998	37	ATL	NL-DS	3	13	12	1	3	0	0	0	0	0	0	1	3	0.250	0.308	0.250	0.558	3	0
1998	37	ATL	NL-CS	6	27	21	1	2	0	0	1	4	0	0	6	6	0.095	0.296	0.238	0.534	5	0
2000	39	ATL	NL-DS	3	13	10	1	2	1	0	0	1	0	0	2	4	0.200	0.385	0.300	0.685	3	1
2003	42	SFG	NL-DS	2	5	5	0	0	0	0	0	0	0	0	0	1	0.000	0.000	0.000	0.000	0	0

4 Yrs (5 Series)	G	PA	AB	R	H	2B	3B	HR	RBI	SB	CS	BB	SO	BA	OBP	SLG	OPS	TB	HBP	Post Season Pts.
	18	76	66	4	12	2	0	1	7	0	0	9	20	0.181	0.289	0.258	0.547	17	1	
	0.400	0.000	0.000	0.250	0.250	0.000	0.000	0.250	0.400	0.000	0.000	0.400	0.000	0.00	0.000	0.000	0.000	0.250	0.000	**2.200**

World Series Play

Year	Age	Tm	Lg	G	PA	AB	R	H	2B	3B	HR	RBI	SB	CS	BB	SO	BA	OBP	SLG	OPS	TB	HBP	World Series Pts.
None Played In	0	0	0	0	0	0	0	0	0	0	0	0	0	0	0	0	0	0	0	0	0	
	0.000	0.000	0.000	0.000	0.000	0.000	0.000	0.000	0.000	0.000	0.000	0.000	0.000	0.000	0.000	0.000	0.000	0.000	0.000	0.000	**0.000**

Yearly Points Leading the League

Category	Times	Points	Total	Category	Times	Points	Total	Categ.	Times	Points	Total
MVP	0	7	0	B.A.	0	3	0	T. B.	0	2	0
Rookie of Year	0	5	0	Runs	0	2	0	B.O.B.	0	2	0
Triple Crown	0	5	0	H.R.'s	1	3	3	OBP%	0	2	0
Golden Glove	2	3	6	R.B.I's	2	3	6	SLG %	0	2	0
All-Star	4	2	8	Hits	1	2	2	OBPS%	0	2	0
Games	0	2	0	S.B.	0	2	0	Totals			0
Totals			14	Totals			11	Grand Total Add-On Points		25	

Hall of Fame Points	
Career Points	64.250
Post Season Points	2.200
World Series Points	0.000
Career Add-On Points	25.000
Writers Association Pts.	0.000
Military/Lifetime Achievement	0.000
Grand Total HOF Points	91.450

Konerko, Paul

Personal Life

Paul Konerko was born March 5, 1976 in Providence, Rhode Island, to Henry[1] ("Hank") and Elena Konerko. He has three brothers Peter, Trace, and Haus. In 1994, Konerko was named the High School Player of the Year

Konerko married Jennifer Wells in 2004 with the couple having three children: sons Nicholas & Owen and a daughter Amelia.

Baseball Career

He was selected by the Los Angeles Dodgers with the 13th pick in the first round of the 1994. From 1995 until 1998, Konerko was with the Dodgers before being traded July 4,1998 to the Cincinnati Reds. Konerko again was traded on November 11, 1998, to the Chicago White Sox. Starting in 1999, Konerko was their everyday first baseman and became one of the better hitters in the majors. In 2,349 games, 18 seasons, Konerko had a .283 batting average 2,340 hits, 1,162 runs, 439 home runs, 1412 RBI, 921 bases on balls, .354 on-base percentage, .486 slugging percentage, and won a World Series with the Chicago White Sox in 2005

Achievements

- 6-time AL All-Star (2002, 2005, 2006 & 2010-2012) & 5-times received MVP votes.
- 20-HR Seasons: 13 (1999-2002 & 2006-2012)
- 30-HR Seasons: 7 (2001, 2004,2005, 2007, 2010 & 2011) & 2-40-HR Seasons.
- 100 RBI Seasons: 6 (2002, 2004-2006, 2010 & 2011)

Hall of Fame Candidacy

In 2020, his first year of Hall of Fame eligibility, Konerko received 2.5% of the votes and removed from future ballots. He becomes eligible in 2032 via the ERA Committee.

Summary Analysis

Konerko has a 90.300 Hall of Fame Point Total but has demonstrated extreme character in dealing with fans and needs to be elected by the BBWAA.

A Fan's Perspective

Konerko, Paul **First Baseman Potential Hall of Fame Inductee**

Positions	Born:	March 5, 1976	Height:	6'2" USC 188 cm
First Baseman	From:	Providence, R.I.	Weight:	220 lbs. 99 Kg.
	Bats:	Right	Debut:	September 8, 1997
	Throws:	Right	Last Game:	September 28, 2014

Year	Age	Tm	Lg	G	PA	AB	R	H	2B	3B	HR	RBI	SB	CS	BB	SO	BA	OBP	SLG	OPS	TB	HBP	Awards
1997	21	LAD	NL	6	8	7	0	1	0	0	0	0	0	0	1	2	0.143	0.250	0.143	0.393	1	0	
1998	22	TOT	NL	75	239	217	21	47	4	0	7	29	0	1	16	40	0.217	0.276	0.332	0.608	72	3	
1998	22	LAD	NL	49	158	144	14	31	1	0	4	16	0	1	10	30	0.215	0.272	0.306	0.578	44	2	
1998	22	CIN	NL	26	81	73	7	16	3	0	3	13	0	0	6	10	0.219	0.284	0.384	0.668	28	1	
1999	23	CHW	AL	142	564	513	71	151	31	4	24	81	1	0	45	68	0.294	0.352	0.511	0.862	262	3	
2000	24	CHW	AL	143	586	524	84	156	31	1	21	97	1	0	47	72	0.298	0.363	0.481	0.844	252	10	
2001	25	CHW	AL	156	650	582	92	164	35	0	32	99	1	0	54	89	0.282	0.349	0.507	0.856	295	9	
2002	26	CHW	AL	151	630	570	81	173	30	0	27	104	0	0	44	72	0.304	0.359	0.498	0.857	284	9	AS
2003	27	CHW	AL	137	495	444	49	104	19	0	18	65	0	0	43	50	0.234	0.305	0.399	0.704	177	4	
2004	28	CHW	AL	155	643	563	84	156	22	0	41	117	1	0	69	107	0.277	0.359	0.535	0.894	301	6	MVP-16
2005	29	CHW	AL	158	664	575	98	163	24	0	40	100	0	0	81	109	0.283	0.375	0.534	0.909	307	5	AS,MVP-6
2006	30	CHW	AL	152	643	566	97	177	30	0	35	113	1	0	60	104	0.313	0.381	0.551	0.932	312	8	AS,MVP-22
2007	31	CHW	AL	151	636	549	71	142	34	0	31	90	0	1	78	102	0.259	0.351	0.490	0.841	269	3	
2008	32	CHW	AL	122	514	438	59	105	19	1	22	62	2	0	65	80	0.240	0.344	0.438	0.783	192	7	
2009	33	CHW	AL	152	621	546	75	151	30	1	28	88	1	0	58	89	0.277	0.353	0.489	0.842	267	10	
2010	34	CHW	AL	148	631	548	89	171	30	1	39	111	0	1	72	110	0.312	0.393	0.584	0.977	320	5	AS,MVP-5
2011	35	CHW	AL	149	639	543	69	163	25	0	31	105	1	1	77	89	0.300	0.388	0.517	0.906	281	8	AS,MVP-13
2012	36	CHW	AL	144	598	533	66	159	22	0	26	75	0	0	56	83	0.298	0.371	0.486	0.857	259	7	AS
2013	37	CHW	AL	126	520	467	41	114	16	0	12	54	0	0	45	74	0.244	0.313	0.355	0.669	166	4	
2014	38	CHW	AL	81	224	208	15	43	8	0	5	22	0	0	10	51	0.207	0.254	0.317	0.572	66	4	
162 Game Avg.				163	656	579	80	161	28	1	30	97	1	0	64	96	0.279	0.354	0.486	0.841	282	7	
CHW (16 yrs)				2268	9258	8169	1141	2292	406	8	432	1383	9	3	904	1349	0.281	0.356	0.491	0.847	4010		
LAD (2 yrs)				55	166	151	14	32	1	0	4	16	0	1	11	32	0.212	0.271	0.298	0.569	45	2	
CIN (1 yr)				26	81	73	7	16	3	0	3	13	0	0	6	10	0.219	0.284	0.384	0.668	28	1	
AL (16 yrs)				2268	9258	8169	1141	2292	406	8	432	1383	9	3	904	1349	0.281	0.356	0.491	0.847	4010	101	
NL (3 yrs)				81	247	224	21	48	4	0	7	29	0	1	17	42	0.214	0.275	0.326	0.601	73	3	
18 Yrs				2349	9505	8393	1162	2340	410	8	439	1412	9	4	921	1391	0.279	0.354	0.486	0.841	4083	104	**Career Pts.**
				9.250	0.000	0.000	5.500	5.500	0.000	0.000	9.250	9.250	0.000	0.000	3.000	0.000	3.750	3.000	4.500	6.750	6.750	0.000	**66.500**

Post Season Play

Year	Age	Tm	Lg	G	PA	AB	R	H	2B	3B	HR	RBI	SB	CS	BB	SO	BA	OBP	SLG	OPS	TB	HBP	
2000	24	CHW	ALDS	3	10	9	1	0	0	0	0	0	0	0	1	1	0.000	0.100	0.068	0.168	0	0	
2005	29	CHW	ALDS	3	12	12	3	3	0	0	2	4	0	0	0	1	0.000	0.100	0.000	0.100	9	0	
2005	29	CHW	ALCS	5	22	21	2	6	1	0	2	7	0	0	1	4	0.250	0.250	0.750	1.000	13	0	
2008	32	CHW	ALDS	4	17	16	3	5	0	0	2	2	0	0	1	1	0.286	0.318	0.619	0.937	11	0	
				15	61	58	9	14	1	0	6	13	0	0	3	7	0.241	0.279	0.569	0.840	33	0	**Post Season Pts.**
				0.400	0.000	0.000	0.400	0.400	0.000	0.000	0.600	0.600	0.000	0.000	0.250	0.000	2.500	0.000	1.200	0.600	0.400	0.000	**7.350**

World Series Play

Year	Age	Tm	Lg	G	PA	AB	R	H	2B	3B	HR	RBI	SB	CS	BB	SO	BA	OBP	SLG	OPS	TB	HBP	
2005	29	CHW	N.L.	4	19	16	1	4	1	0	1	4	0	0	2	3	0.250	0.368	0.500	0.868	8	1	**World Series Pts.**
				0.250	0.000	0.000	0.250	0.250	0.000	0.000	0.250	0.250	0.000	0.000	0.250	0.000	0.400	0.600	0.325	1.300	0.325	0.000	**4.450**

Yearly Points Leading the League

Category	Times	Points	Total	Category	Times	Points	Total	Categ	Times	Points	Total
MVP	0	7	0	B.A.	0	3	0	T.B.	0	2	0
Rookie of Year	0	5	0	Runs	0	2	0	B.O.B.	0	2	0
Triple Crown	0	5	0	H.R.'s	0	3	0	OBP%	0	2	0
Golden Glove	0	3	0	R.B.I's	0	3	0	SLG%	0	2	0
All-Star	6	2	12	Hits	0	2	0	OBPS%	0	2	0
Games	0	2	0	S.B.	0	2	0	Totals			0
Totals			12	Totals			0	Grand Total Add-On Points			12

Hall of Fame Points	
Career Points	66.500
Post Season Points	7.350
World Series Points	4.450
Career Add-On Points	12.00
Writers Association Pts.	0.000
Military/Lifetime Achievement	0.000
Grand Total HOF Points	90.300

The Baseball Hall of Fame

Olerud, John "Johnny O"

Personal Life

John Garrett Olerud, Jr. born August 5, 1968, to Lynda and John E. Olerud, a physician from Lisbon, North Dakota. Olerud went to Interlake High School in Bellevue, Washington. He went to Washington State University and was a consensus All-American first baseman, pitcher and named the College Player of the Year.

In 1990, he married Kelly Plaisted, November 22, 1998. The couple had three children, daughters Jordan and Jessica and a son Garrett. Jordan tragically passed away at the age of 19 on March 1, 2020, due to a rare chromosomal disease.

Baseball Career

Olerud broke into MLB with the Toronto Blue Jays in 1989, and became the team's full-time first baseman. In 1993, Olerud had a breakout season, when he led the American League in batting average (.363). He had 1,275 base-on-balls, 500 doubles, 255 home runs, 1,408 runs scored, 1,230 RBIs, and recorded a career .995 fielding percentage.

Achievements

- 2-time All-Star (1993 & 2001) & a 3-time Gold Glove Winner (2000, 2002 & 2003)
- AL Batting Average Leader (1993) & On-Base Percentage Leader (1993)
- AL OPS Leader (1993) & 200 Hits Seasons: 1 (1993)
- 20-Home Run Seasons: 5 (1993, 1997, 1998, 2001 & 2002)
- 100 RBI Seasons:4 (1993,1997,2000&2002), 2-100 Runs Seasons:(1993& 1999).
- Won two World Series with the Toronto Blue Jays (1992 & 1993)

Hall of Fame Candidacy

In 2011, Olerud received 4 votes for 0.7% and was removed from the ballot. He becomes eligible by the Contemporary Baseball Era Committee in 2023.

Summary Analysis

His 99.750 Hall of Fame Point Total statistical analysis. John Olerud was a great hitter, fielder, and pitcher and should be elected to the Baseball Hall of Fame by the BBWAA.

Olerud, John — First Baseman Potential Hall of Fame Inductee

Positions	Born:	August 5, 1968	Height:	6' 5"	USC 196 cm
First Baseman	From:	Seattle, WA	Weight:	205 lbs.	92 Kg.
	Bats:	Left	Debut:	September 3, 1989	
	Throws:	Left	Last Game:	October 2, 2005	

Year	Age	Tm	Lg	G	PA	AB	R	H	2B	3B	HR	RBI	SB	CS	BB	SO	BA	OBP	SLG	OPS	TB	HBP	Awards
1989	20	TOR	AL	6	8	8	2	3	0	0	0	0	0	0	0	1	0.375	0.375	0.375	0.750	3	0	
1990	21	TOR	AL	111	421	358	43	95	15	1	14	48	0	2	57	75	0.265	0.364	0.430	0.794	154	1	RoY-4
1991	22	TOR	AL	139	541	454	64	116	30	1	17	68	0	2	68	84	0.256	0.353	0.438	0.791	199	6	
1992	23	TOR	AL	138	537	458	68	130	28	0	16	66	1	0	70	61	0.284	0.375	0.450	0.825	206	1	
1993	24	TOR	AL	158	679	551	109	200	54	2	24	107	0	2	114	65	0.363	0.473	0.599	1.072	330	7	AS,MVP-3
1994	25	TOR	AL	108	453	384	47	114	29	2	12	67	1	2	61	53	0.297	0.393	0.477	0.869	183	3	
1995	26	TOR	AL	135	581	492	72	143	32	0	8	54	0	0	84	54	0.291	0.398	0.404	0.802	199	4	
1996	27	TOR	AL	125	469	398	59	109	25	0	18	61	1	0	60	37	0.274	0.382	0.472	0.854	188	10	
1997	28	NYM	NL	154	630	524	90	154	34	1	22	102	0	0	85	67	0.294	0.400	0.489	0.889	256	13	
1998	29	NYM	NL	160	665	557	91	197	36	4	22	93	2	2	96	73	0.354	0.447	0.551	0.998	307	4	MVP-12
1999	30	NYM	NL	162	723	581	107	173	39	0	19	96	3	0	125	66	0.298	0.427	0.463	0.890	269	11	
2000	31	SEA	AL	159	683	565	84	161	45	0	14	103	0	2	102	96	0.285	0.392	0.439	0.831	248	4	GG
2001	32	SEA	AL	159	679	572	91	173	32	1	21	95	3	1	94	70	0.302	0.401	0.472	0.873	270	5	AS
2002	33	SEA	AL	154	668	553	85	166	39	0	22	102	0	0	98	66	0.300	0.403	0.490	0.893	271	5	GG
2003	34	SEA	AL	152	634	539	64	145	35	0	10	83	0	1	84	67	0.269	0.372	0.390	0.761	210	6	GG
2004	35	TOT	AL	127	500	425	45	110	20	1	9	48	0	0	61	61	0.259	0.359	0.374	0.733	159	8	
2004	35	SEA	AL	78	312	261	29	64	13	1	5	22	0	0	40	41	0.245	0.354	0.360	0.714	94	6	
2004	35	NYY	AL	49	188	164	16	46	7	0	4	26	0	0	21	20	0.280	0.367	0.396	0.763	65	2	
2005	36	BOS	AL	87	192	173	18	50	7	0	7	37	0	0	16	20	0.289	0.344	0.451	0.795	78	0	
	162 Game Avg.			162	657	551	83	162	36	1	18	89	1	1	92	74	0.295	0.398	0.465	0.863	256	6	
	TOR (8 yrs)			920	3689	3103	464	910	213	8	109	471	3	8	514	430	0.293	0.395	0.471	0.866	1462	32	
	SEA (5 yrs)			702	2976	2490	353	709	164	2	72	405	3	4	418	340	0.285	0.388	0.439	0.827	1093	26	
	NYM (3 yrs)			476	2018	1662	288	524	109	5	63	291	5	2	306	206	0.315	0.425	0.501	0.926	832	28	
	NYY (1 yr)			49	188	164	16	46	7	0	4	26	0	0	21	20	0.280	0.367	0.396	0.763	65	2	
	BOS (1 yr)			87	192	173	18	50	7	0	7	37	0	0	16	20	0.289	0.344	0.451	0.795	78	0	
	AL (14 yrs)			1758	7045	5930	851	1715	391	8	192	939	6	12	969	810	0.289	0.39	0.455	0.845	2698	60	
	NL (3 yrs)			476	2018	1662	288	524	108	5	63	291	5	2	306	206	0.315	0.425	0.501	0.926	832	28	
	17 Yrs			2234	9063	7592	1139	2239	500	13	255	1230	11	14	1275	1016	0.295	0.398	0.465	0.863	3530	88	Career Pts.
				8.000	0.000	0.000	5.500	4.500	0.000	0.000	3.750	6.750	0.500	0.000	6.750	0.000	5.500	8.000	3.750	6.750	4.500	0.000	64.250

Post Season Play

Year	Age	Tm	Lg	G	PA	AB	R	H	2B	3B	HR	RBI	SB	CS	BB	SO	BA	16.75	SLG	OPS	TB	HBP	
1991	22	TOR	ALCS	5	22	19	1	3	0	0	0	3	0	0	3	1	0.158	0.273	0.158	0.431	3	0	
1992	23	TOR	ALCS	6	25	23	4	8	2	0	1	4	0	0	2	5	0.348	0.400	0.565	0.965	13	0	
1993	24	TOR	ALCS	6	28	23	5	8	1	0	0	3	0	0	4	1	0.348	0.464	0.391	0.856	9	1	
1999	30	NYM	NLDS	4	19	16	3	7	0	0	1	6	0	0	3	2	0.438	0.526	0.625	1.151	10	0	
1999	30	NYM	NLCS	6	29	27	4	8	0	0	2	6	0	0	2	3	0.296	0.345	0.519	0.863	14	0	
2000	31	SEA	ALDS	3	13	10	2	3	0	0	1	2	0	0	2	1	0.300	0.462	0.600	1.062	6	1	
2000	31	SEA	ALCS	6	23	20	3	7	3	0	1	2	1	0	2	2	0.350	0.391	0.650	1.041	13	0	
2001	32	SEA	ALDS	5	20	17	1	3	0	0	0	1	0	0	3	5	0.176	0.300	0.176	0.476	3	0	
2001	32	SEA	ALCS	5	21	19	2	4	0	0	1	3	0	0	2	4	0.211	0.286	0.368	0.654	7	0	
2004	35	NYY	ALDS	4	16	14	2	3	2	0	0	0	0	0	1	2	0.214	0.313	0.357	0.670	5	1	
2004	35	NYY	ALCS	4	13	12	1	2	0	0	1	2	0	0	1	1	0.167	0.231	0.417	0.647	5	0	
2005	36	BOS	ALDS	3	9	7	0	2	1	0	0	0	0	0	2	0	0.286	0.444	0.429	0.873	3	0	
				57	238	207	28	58	9	0	8	32	1	0	27	27	0.280	0.363	0.440	0.803	91	3	Post Season Pts.
				1.200	0.000	0.000	0.800	1.000	0.000	0.000	0.800	1.400	0.250	0.000	1.200	0.000	0.600	0.800	0.400	0.600	1.000	0.000	10.050

World Series Play

Year	Age	Tm	Lg	G	PA	AB	R	H	2B	3B	HR	RBI	SB	CS	BB	SO	BA	OBP	SLG	OPS	TB	HBP	
1992	23	Tor	A.L.	4	13	13	2	4	0	0	0	0	0	0	0	4	0.308	0.308	0.308	0.615	4	0	
1993	24	Tor	A.L.	5	22	17	5	4	1	0	1	2	0	0	4	1	0.235	0.364	0.471	0.835	8	0	
				9	35	30.0	7	8	1	0	1	2	0	4	4	5	0.267	0.343	0.400	0.743	12	0	World Series Pts.
				0.400	0.000	0.000	0.250	0.400	0.000	0.000	0.250	0.250	0.000	0.000	0.250	0.000	0.600	0.250	0.000	0.400	0.400	0.000	3.450

Yearly Points Leading the League

Category	Times	Points	Total	Category	Times	Points	Total	Categor	Times	Points	Total
MVP	0	7	0	B.A.	1	3	3	T. B.	0	2	0
Rookie of Year	0	5	0	Runs	0	2	0	B.O.B.	0	2	0
Triple Crown	0	5	0	H.R.'s	0	3	0	OBP%	1	2	2
Golden Glove	3	3	9	R.B.I's	0	3	0	SLG %	0	2	0
All-Star	2	2	4	Hits	0	2	0	OBPS%	1	2	2
Games	1	2	2	S.B.	0	2	0	Totals			4
Totals			15	Totals			3	Grand Total Add-On Points		22	

Hall of Fame Points	
Career Points	64.250
Post Season Points	10.050
World Series Points	3.450
Career Add-On Points	22.000
Writers Association Pts.	0.000
Military/Lifetime Achievement	0.000
Grand Total HOF Points	99.750

Oliver Jr., Al

Personal Life

Albert Oliver Jr. (born October 14, 1946) Albert Oliver Jr. was born on October 14, 1946, in Portsmouth, Ohio to Albert Oliver Sr., and Sallie Jane (née Chambers). Oliver had a sister Paula, and a brother James who went to Portsmouth High School.

On April 8, 1970, Oliver married Donna Allen with the couple having a son Aaron. They divorced on December 17, 1986. Oliver married Patricia Harris on August 16, 1996.

Baseball Career

Oliver was signed by the Pirates as a free agent in 1964 and progressed through the Pirates farm system. Oliver made his MLB debut on September 23, 1968. and batted .300 or more eleven times with 2,743 hits, 2368 games, 1326 RBI, and finished with a .303 BA. Pittsburgh won five National League East division titles from 1970 through 1975 and won the World Series Championship in 1971. Oliver was one of the best hitters of the 1970s and '80s, amassing 2,743 hits and a .303 lifetime batting average.

Achievements:

- Led N.L in games played 1980 & Led N.L in hits, RBIs, B.A. & T.B. 1982.
- 7-Time All-Star in 1972, 1975, 1976, 1980, 1981 1982 & 1983.
- 10-Times received MVP votes in 1972 - 1974, 1976, 1978 - 1983.
- 3-Time3 Silver Slugger 1980-1983 & World Series Champion 1971 with the Pirates,

Hall of Fame Candidacy

Oliver became eligible for the Baseball Hall of Fame in 1991 but fell off the ballot. He was on the ballot in 2007, 2008, and 2010 but didn't get enough votes. Oliver is eligible for the Hall of Fame via the Classic Baseball Era Committee in 2025.

Summary Analysis

Al Oliver's 91.700 Hall of Fame Point Total. Due to his numbers and consistency, the BBWAA should vote Oliver into the Baseball Hall of Fame

A Fan's Perspective

Oliver Jr., AL — **First Baseman Potential Hall of Fame Inductee**

Positions		**Born:** October 14, 1946	**Height:** 6' 0" **USC** 183 cm
First Baseman		**From:** Portsmouth, OH	**Weight:** 195 lbs. 88 Kg.
Outfielder		**Bats:** Left	**Debut:** September 23, 1968
		Throws: Left	**Last Game:** October 5, 1985

Year	Age	Tm	Lg	G	PA	AB	R	H	2B	3B	HR	RBI	SB	CS	BB	SO	BA	OBP	SLG	OPS	TB	HBP	Awards
1968	21	PIT	NL	4	8	8	1	1	0	0	0	0	0	0	0	4	0.125	0.125	0.125	0.250	1	0	
1969	22	PIT	NL	129	502	463	55	132	19	2	17	70	8	5	21	38	0.285	0.333	0.445	0.778	206	13	RoY-2
1970	23	PIT	NL	151	609	551	83	149	33	5	12	83	1	1	35	35	0.270	0.326	0.414	0.740	228	14	
1971	24	PIT	NL	143	573	529	69	149	31	7	14	64	4	3	27	72	0.282	0.317	0.446	0.763	236	5	
1972	25	PIT	NL	140	612	565	88	176	27	4	12	89	2	4	34	44	0.312	0.352	0.437	0.789	247	5	AS,MVP-7
1973	26	PIT	NL	158	690	654	90	191	38	7	20	99	6	0	22	52	0.292	0.316	0.465	0.779	303	5	MVP-23
1974	27	PIT	NL	147	661	617	96	198	38	12	11	85	10	1	33	58	0.321	0.358	0.475	0.832	293	5	MVP-7
1975	28	PIT	NL	155	666	628	90	175	39	6	18	84	4	2	25	73	0.280	0.309	0.454	0.763	285	5	AS
1976	29	PIT	NL	121	481	443	62	143	22	5	12	61	6	2	26	29	0.323	0.363	0.476	0.839	211	5	AS,MVP-12
1977	30	PIT	NL	154	622	568	75	175	29	6	19	82	13	16	40	38	0.308	0.353	0.481	0.834	273	4	MVP-16
1978	31	TEX	AL	133	568	525	65	170	35	5	14	89	8	9	31	41	0.324	0.358	0.490	0.848	257	2	MVP-14
1979	32	TEX	AL	136	538	492	69	159	28	4	12	76	4	5	34	34	0.323	0.367	0.470	0.836	231	4	
1980	33	TEX	AL	163	709	656	96	209	43	3	19	117	5	7	39	47	0.319	0.357	0.480	0.838	315	5	AS,MVP-11,SS
1981	34	TEX	AL	102	448	421	53	130	29	1	4	55	3	0	24	28	0.309	0.348	0.411	0.759	173	2	AS,MVP-16,SS
1982	35	MON	NL	160	687	617	90	204	43	2	22	109	5	2	61	59	0.331	0.392	0.514	0.906	317	4	AS,MVP-3,SS
1983	36	MON	NL	157	664	614	70	184	38	3	8	84	1	3	44	46	0.300	0.347	0.410	0.757	252	2	AS,MVP-19
1984	37	TOT	NL	119	460	432	36	130	26	2	0	48	3	4	27	36	0.301	0.343	0.370	0.714	160	1	
1984	37	SFG	NL	91	360	339	27	101	19	2	0	34	2	2	20	27	0.298	0.339	0.366	0.705	124	3	
1984	37	PHI	NL	28	100	93	9	29	7	0	0	14	1	2	7	9	0.312	0.360	0.387	0.747	36	0	
1985	38	TOT	MLB	96	280	266	21	67	11	1	5	31	1	0	12	24	0.252	0.286	0.357	0.643	95	1	
1985	38	LAD	NL	35	85	79	1	20	5	0	0	8	1	0	5	11	0.253	0.294	0.316	0.611	25	0	
1985	38	TOR	AL	61	195	187	20	47	6	1	5	23	0	0	7	13	0.251	0.282	0.374	0.656	70	1	
162 Game Avg.				162	669	619	83	188	36	5	15	91	6	4	37	52	0.303	0.344	0.451	0.795	279	6	
PIT (10 yrs)				1302	5424	5026	689	1490	276	56	135	717	54	34	263	443	0.296	0.335	0.454	0.789	2283	61	
TEX (4 yrs)				534	2263	2094	283	668	135	13	49	337	20	21	128	150	0.319	0.358	0.466	0.824	976	13	
MON (2 yrs)				317	1351	1231	160	388	81	5	30	193	6	5	105	103	0.315	0.370	0.462	0.832	569	6	
LAD (1 yr)				35	85	79	1	20	5	0	0	8	1	0	5	11	0.253	0.294	0.316	0.611	25	0	
SFG (1 yr)				91	360	339	27	101	19	2	0	34	2	2	20	27	0.298	0.339	0.366	0.705	124	1	
PHI (1 yr)				28	100	93	9	29	7	0	0	14	1	2	7	9	0.312	0.360	0.387	0.747	36	0	
TOR (1 yr)				61	195	187	20	47	6	1	5	23	0	0	7	13	0.251	0.282	0.374	0.656	70	1	
NL (14 yrs)				1773	7320	6768	886	2028	388	63	165	966	64	43	400	593	0.3	0.342	0.449	0.79	3037	68	
AL (5 yrs)				595	2458	2281	303	715	141	14	54	360	20	21	135	163	0.313	0.352	0.459	0.811	1046	14	
18 Yrs				2368	9778	9049	1189	2743	529	77	219	1326	84	64	535	756	0.309	0.344	0.451	0.795	4083	92	**Career Pts.**
				9.250	0.000	0.000	5.500	9.250	0.000	0.000	3.000	8.000	1.000	0.000	1.000	0.000	6.750	2.500	3.000	4.500	6.750	0.000	**60.500**

Post Seasonal Play

Year	Age	Tm	Lg	G	PA	AB	R	H	2B	3B	HR	RBI	SB	CS	BB	SO	BA	OB%	SLG	OPS	TB	HBP	
1970	23	PIT	NLCS	2	9	8	0	2	0	0	0	1	0	0	1	0	0.250	0.333	0.250	0.583	2	0	
1971	24	PIT	NLCS	4	13	12	2	3	0	0	1	5	0	0	1	3	0.250	0.308	0.500	0.808	6	0	
1972	25	PIT	NLCS	5	21	20	3	5	2	1	1	3	0	0	0	4	0.250	0.250	0.600	0.850	12	1	
1974	27	PIT	NLCS	4	16	14	1	2	0	0	0	1	0	0	2	2	0.143	0.250	0.143	0.393	2	0	
1975	28	PIT	NLCS	3	13	11	1	2	0	0	1	2	0	0	2	0	0.182	0.308	0.455	0.762	5	0	
1985	38	TOR	ALCS	5	9	8	0	3	1	0	0	3	0	0	0	0	0.375	0.444	0.500	0.944	4	0	
				23	81	73	7	17	3	1	3	15	0	0	6	9	0.233	0.291	0.425	0.636	31	1	**Post Season Pts.**
				0.600	0.000	0.000	0.250	0.400	0.000	0.000	0.400	0.600	0.000	0.000	0.400	0.000	0.000	0.000	0.400	0.250	0.400	0.000	**3.700**

World Series Play

Year	Age	Tm	Lg	G	PA	AB	R	H	2B	3B	HR	RBI	SB	CS	BB	SO	BA	OBP	SLG	OPS	TB	HBP	
1971	24	PIT	NL	5	21	19	1	4	2	0	0	2	0	0	2	5	0.211	0.286	0.316	0.602	6	0	
				5	21	19	1	4	2	0	0	2	0	0	2	5	0.211	0.286	0.316	0.602	6	0	**World Series Pts.**
				0.250	0.000	0.000	0.250	0.250	0.000	0.000	0.000	0.250	0.000	0.000	0.250	0.000	0.000	0.000	0.000	0.000	0.250	0.000	**1.500**

Yearly Points Leading the League

Category	Times	Points	Total
MVP	0	7	0
Rookie of Year	0	5	0
Triple Crown	0	5	0
Golden Glove	0	3	0
All-Star	7	2	14
Games	1	2	2
Totals			16

Category	Times	Points	Total
B.A.	1	3	3
Runs	0	2	0
H.R.'s	0	3	0
R.B.I's	1	3	3
Hits	1	2	2
S.B.	0	2	0
Totals			8

Categ	Times	Points	Total
T. B.	1	2	2
B.O.B.	0	2	0
OBP%	0	2	0
SLG %	0	2	0
OBPS%	0	2	0
Totals			2

Grand Total Add-On Points   26

Hall of Fame Points	
Career Points	60.500
Post Season Points	3.700
World Series Points	1.500
Career Add-On Points	26.000
Writers Association Pts.	0.000
Military/Lifetime Achievement	0.000
Grand Total HOF Points	**91.700**

The Baseball Hall of Fame

Teixeira, Mark "Tex"

Personal Life

Mark Charles Teixeira was born April 11, 1980, to Margaret "Margy" Canterna and John Teixeira in Severna Park, Maryland. He played baseball for Mount Saint Joseph High School in Baltimore chose to play college baseball for Georgia Tech where in 2000 he won the Dick Howser Trophy as the national collegiate baseball player of the year.

He married Leigh Williams on December 7, 2002, and the couple have a daughter Addison Leigh, and two sons, Jack Gordan and William Charles.

Baseball Career

In 2001, Teixeira was selected by the Texas Rangers with the fifth overall pick and began the 2002 season in the Florida State League. He then moved up to Double-A and batted .316 with a .994 OPS and hit 10 home runs in 48 games. As a rookie in 2003, Teixeira hit .259 with 26 home runs, 84 RBI, and a .811 OPS. From 2004 through 2011, Teixeira hit 30, or more home runs per year, driving in over 100 as well. Teixeira played 14 seasons in Major League Baseball and was one of the most prolific switch hitters in MLB history. Teixeira was a great player since high school and a major contributor to his team's success winning a World Championship with the Yankees in 2009.

Achievements:

- 3 -Times Major League Baseball All-Star (2005, 2009, 2015)
- 5 - Times Gold Glove Award (2005, 2006, 2009, 2010, 2012)
- 3 - Times Silver Slugger Award (2004, 2005, 2009).

Hall of Fame Candidacy

In 2022. Teixeira received 23 votes for 4.4% and was removed from the ballot. In 2018 Game ERA voting he once again failed to achieve the votes need to be elected.

Summary Analysis

Teixeira has a 98.050 Hall of Fame Point Total. Throughout high school, college, and professional careers, he was a great hitter and fielder. He should be by the BBWAA.

Texiera, Mark — First Baseman Potential Hall of Fame Inductee

Positions	First Baseman	Born:	April 11, 1980
		From:	Annapolis, MD
		Bats:	Both
		Throws:	Right
Height:	6' 3"	USC	190 cm
Weight:	225 lbs.		102 Kg.
Debut:	April 1, 2003		
Last Game:	October 2, 2016		

Year	Age	Tm	Lg	G	PA	AB	R	H	2B	3B	HR	RBI	SB	CS	BB	SO	BA	OBP	SLG	OPS	TB	HBP	Awards
2003	23	TEX	AL	146	589	529	66	137	29	5	26	84	1	2	44	120	0.259	0.331	0.48	0.811	254	14	RoY-5
2004	24	TEX	AL	145	625	545	101	153	34	2	38	112	4	1	68	117	0.281	0.37	0.56	0.929	305	10	MVP-18,SS
2005	25	TEX	AL	162	730	644	112	194	41	3	43	144	4	0	72	124	0.301	0.379	0.575	0.954	370	11	AS,MVP-7,GG,SS
2006	26	TEX	AL	162	727	628	99	177	45	1	33	110	2	0	89	128	0.282	0.371	0.514	0.886	323	4	GG
2007	27	TOT	MLB	132	575	494	86	151	33	2	30	105	0	0	72	112	0.306	0.4	0.563	0.963	278	7	
2007	27	TEX	AL	78	335	286	48	85	24	1	13	49	0	0	45	66	0.297	0.397	0.524	0.921	150	3	
2007	27	ATL	NL	54	240	208	38	66	9	1	17	56	0	0	27	46	0.317	0.404	0.615	1.02	128	4	
2008	28	TOT	MLB	157	685	574	102	177	41	0	33	121	2	0	97	93	0.308	0.41	0.552	0.962	317	7	MVP-20
2008	28	ATL	NL	103	451	381	63	108	27	0	20	78	0	0	65	70	0.283	0.39	0.512	0.902	195	3	
2008	28	LAA	AL	54	234	193	39	69	14	0	13	43	2	0	32	23	0.358	0.449	0.632	1.081	122	4	
2009	29	NYY	AL	156	707	609	103	178	43	3	39	122	2	0	81	114	0.292	0.383	0.565	0.948	344	12	AS,MVP-2,GG,SS
2010	30	NYY	AL	158	712	601	113	154	36	0	33	108	0	1	93	122	0.256	0.365	0.481	0.846	289	13	MVP-19,GG
2011	31	NYY	AL	156	684	589	90	146	26	1	39	111	4	1	76	110	0.248	0.341	0.494	0.835	291	11	MVP-19
2012	32	NYY	AL	123	524	451	66	113	27	1	24	84	2	1	54	83	0.251	0.332	0.475	0.807	214	7	GG
2013	33	NYY	AL	15	63	53	5	8	1	0	3	12	0	0	8	19	0.151	0.27	0.34	0.609	18	1	
2014	34	NYY	AL	123	508	440	56	95	14	0	22	62	1	1	58	109	0.216	0.313	0.398	0.711	175	6	
2015	35	NYY	AL	111	462	392	57	100	22	0	31	79	2	0	59	85	0.255	0.357	0.548	0.906	215	6	AS,MVP-28
2016	36	NYY	AL	116	438	387	43	79	16	0	15	44	2	0	47	105	0.204	0.292	0.362	0.654	140	2	
162 Game Avg.				162	699	603	96	162	35	2	36	113	2	1	80	125	0.268	0.36	0.509	0.869	307	10	
NYY (8 yrs)				958	4098	3522	533	873	185	5	206	622	13	4	476	747	0.248	0.343	0.479	0.822	1686	58	
TEX (5 yrs)				693	3006	2632	426	746	173	12	153	499	11	3	318	555	0.283	0.368	0.533	0.901	1402	42	
ATL (2 yrs)				157	691	589	101	174	36	1	37	134	0	0	92	116	0.295	0.395	0.548	0.943	323	7	
LAA (1 yr)				54	234	193	39	69	14	0	13	43	2	0	32	23	0.358	0.449	0.632	1.081	122	4	
AL (14 yrs)				1705	7338	6347	998	1688	372	17	372	1164	26	7	826	1325	0.266	0.357	0.506	0.863	3210	104	
NL (2 yrs)				157	691	589	101	174	36	1	37	134	0	0	92	116	0.295	0.395	0.548	0.943	323	7	
14 Yrs				1862	8029	6936	1099	1862	408	18	409	1298	26	7	918	1441	0.268	0.360	0.509	0.869	3533	111	Career Pts.
				4.500	0.000	0.000	4.500	2.500	0.000	0.000	8.000	6.750	0.500	0.000	3.000	0.000	2.500	3.750	5.500	8.000	4.500	0.000	54.000

Post Seasonal Play

Year	Age	Tm	Lg	G	PA	AB	R	H	2B	3B	HR	RBI	SB	CS	BB	SO	BA	OBP	SLG	OPS	TB	HBP	
2008	28	LAA	ALDS	4	20	15	4	7	0	0	0	1	0	0	4	3	0.467	0.550	0.467	1.017	7	0	
2009	29	NYY	ALDS	3	13	12	3	2	0	0	1	1	0	0	1	1	0.167	0.231	0.417	0.647	5	0	
2009	29	NYY	ALCS	6	31	27	2	6	1	0	0	4	0	0	3	8	0.222	0.290	0.259	0.550	7	0	
2010	30	NYY	ALDS	3	14	13	2	4	1	0	1	3	0	0	1	2	0.308	0.357	0.615	0.973	8	0	
2010	30	NYY	ALCS	4	17	14	1	0	0	0	0	0	0	0	3	4	0.000	0.176	0.000	0.176	0	0	
2011	31	NYY	ALDS	5	21	18	2	3	2	0	0	1	0	0	2	5	0.167	0.286	0.278	0.563	5	1	
2012	32	NYY	ALDS	5	22	17	1	6	0	0	0	1	1	0	5	2	0.353	0.500	0.353	0.853	6	0	
2012	32	NYY	ALCS	4	18	15	1	3	1	0	0	0	0	0	3	1	0.200	0.333	0.267	0.600	4	0	
				34	156	131	16	31	5	0	2	11	1	0	22	26	0.237	0.346	0.321	0.666	42	1	Post Season Pts.
				0.800	0.000	0.000	0.400	0.600	0.000	0.000	0.250	0.600	0.250	0.000	1.000	0.000	0.000	0.600	0.000	0.250	0.400	0.000	5.150

World Series Play

Year	Age	Tm	Lg	G	PA	AB	R	H	2B	3B	HR	RBI	SB	CS	BB	SO	BA	OBP	SLG	OPS	TB	HBP	
2009	29	NYY	AL	6	27	22	5	3	1	0	1	3	0	0	2	8	0.136	0.296	0.318	0.614	7	3	
				6	27	22	5	3	1	0	1	3	0	0	2	8	0.136	0.296	0.318	0.614	7	3	World Series Pts.
				0.250	0.000	0.000	0.400	0.250	0.000	0.000	0.250	0.250	0.000	0.000	0.250	0.000	0.000	0.000	0.000	0.000	0.250	0.000	1.900

Yearly Points Leading the League

Category	Times	Points	Total	Category	Times	Points	Total	Categ	Times	Points	Total
MVP	0	7	0	B.A.	0	3	0	T.B.	2	2	4
Rookie of Year	0	5	0	Runs	1	2	2	B.O.B.	0	2	0
Triple Crown	0	5	0	H.R.'s	1	3	3	OBP%	0	2	0
Golden Glove	5	3	15	R.B.I's	1	3	3	SLG %	0	2	0
All-Star	3	2	6	Hits	0	2	0	OBPS%	0	2	0
Games	2	2	4	S.B.	0	2	0	Totals			4
Totals			25	Totals			8	Grand Total Add-On Points			37

Hall of Fame Points	
Career Points	54.000
Post Season Points	5.150
World Series Points	1.900
Yearly Add-On Points	37.00
Writers Association Pts.	0.000
Military/Lifetime Achievement	0.000
Grand Total HOF Points	98.05

The Baseball Hall of Fame

Statistical Review of Potential Second Basemen for the Hall of Fame

Player	Years Played	Career Pts.	Post Season Pts.	World Series Pts.	Add-On Pts.	Mil/LT Pts.	Total HOF Pts.	Needed HOF Votes	Comments
Players Needing to be Inducted									
None									Inducted
Players Needing to be Voted into the Hall of Fame by the BBWAA									
Cano, Robinson	17	74.000	7.000	0.750	22.000	0	103.750	7	Need Voting
Kent, Jeff	17	72.500	6.900	6.500	17.000	0	101.900	9	Need Voting
Players Not Meeting the Statistical Requirements									
Allen, Newt	20	15.500	3.650	5.500	8.000	40.000	72.650	N/A	DMR
Doyle, Larry	14	35.250	0.000	5.150	20.000	0	60.400	N/A	DMF
Franco, Julio	23	57.500	3.300	0.000	4.000	0	64.800	N/A	DMR
Grich, Bobby	17	40.500	2.150	0.000	26.000	0	68.650	N/A	DMR
Kinsler, Ian	14	41.750	8.000	7.950	14.000	0	61.700	N/A	DMF
Knoblauch, Chuck	12	42.000	4.600	5.685	16.000	0	68.650	N/A	DMR
Lopes, Davey	16	33.500	7.650	7.650	16.000	0	60.950	N/A	DMR
Pedroia, Dustin	14	35.000	7.100	3.200	38.000	0	83.300	N/A	DMR
Randolph, Willie	18	43.250	3.700	5.100	14.000	0	66.050	N/A	DMF
Scales, George	20	41.250	0.000	0.000	2.000	0	83.250	N/A	DMR
Utley, Chase	16	43.250	7.450	9.035	14.000	0	73.735	N/A	DMR
Whitaker, Lou	19	56.750	2.400	2.400	26.000	0	89.150	21	DMR
White, Frank	18	35.000	2.950	2.500	34.000	0	74.550	N/A	DMR

Hall of Fame Statistical Requirements:

All Players achieving the total of 110.000, or greater, Total Hall of Fame Points, shall be Inducted after five (5) years of retirement. This provision can be waived due to the death by a 75% vote of the 25 Panel BBWAA's. Individuals receiving less than the required 110.000 Hall of Fame Points are eligible for Election after five (5) years of retirement. A 25 person BBWAA will determine the Players that will be Inducted and vote on the Players needing to be elected. An example of those needing to be elected are as follows: Player "A" has a total of 95 Hall of Fame Points and will need 15 of the (25) BBWAA votes to be Elected in the following year

Second Basemen Needing to be Inducted

None Reached the 110.000 Hall of Fame

Statistical Induction Criteria

Cano, Robinson

Personal Life

Robinson José Canó Mercedes was born October 22, 1982 in San Pedro de Macoris, Dominican Republic to José Cano and Claribel Mercedes - Robinson. He has a younger brother Gregory, and grew up in the Dominican Republic. He attended San Pedro Apostol High School and played for the school's baseball and basketball teams.

Cano is not married but had a relationship with Jacqueline Castro, a daughter, Garia Sofia, and a son, Robinson Miguel Cano Castro, who lives with his mother.

Baseball Career

After graduating from high school, Canó signed with the Yankees on January 5, 2001 and moved up their system until called up to on May 3, 2005. He finished the year with 14 HRs, 62 RBIs, and a .297 Batting Average. From 2005 through 2017, Cano became one of four players to have won a World Series and a WBC. Cano signed with the Mariners and played for them from 2014 to 2018. In 2018, he tested positive for PED's and was suspended from MLB for 80 games for PED's. On December 3, 2018, the Mariners traded Canó to the New York Mets. On November 18, 2020, Canó was suspended 162 games after testing positive for PED's after the 2020 season. After serving the one-year suspension in 2021, Cano played for three teams in 2022.

Achievements:

- 5 time Silver Slugger Award winner & Two-time Gold Glove Award winner
- 8 time MLB All-Star (2006, 2010–14, 2016, 2017)

Hall of Fame Candidacy

Cano will be eligible for Hall of Fame voting in 2028.

Summary Analysis

Cano's Hall of Fame Point Total is 103.75. However, with two suspensions for PED's, the character clause should be enacted with his statistics being listed among greats of the game, but denied a plaque. Failing a second time shows no integrity or remorse.

A Fan's Perspective

Cano, Robinson Second Second Baseman Potential Hall of Fame Inductee

Positions		Born:	October 22, 1982	Height:	6' 0"	USC	183	cm
Second Baseman		From:	San Pedro de Macorsis, Dominican Republic	Weight:	228	lbs.	103	Kg.
		Bats:	Left	Debut:	May 3, 2005			
		Throws:	Right	Last Game:	July 27, 2022			

Year	Age	Tm	Lg	G	PA	AB	R	H	2B	3B	HR	RBI	SB	CS	BB	SO	BA	OBP	SLG	OPS	TB	HBP	
2005	22	NYY	AL	132	551	522	78	155	34	4	14	62	1	3	16	68	0.297	0.320	0.458	0.778	239	3	RoY-2
2006	23	NYY	AL	122	508	482	62	165	41	1	15	78	5	2	18	54	0.342	0.365	0.525	0.890	253	2	AS,MVP-22,SS
2007	24	NYY	AL	160	669	617	93	189	41	7	19	97	4	5	39	85	0.306	0.353	0.488	0.841	301	8	
2008	25	NYY	AL	159	634	597	70	162	35	3	14	72	2	4	26	65	0.271	0.305	0.410	0.715	245	5	
2009	26	NYY	AL	161	674	637	103	204	48	2	25	85	5	7	30	63	0.320	0.352	0.520	0.871	331	3	MVP-17
2010	27	NYY	AL	160	696	626	103	200	41	3	29	109	3	2	57	77	0.319	0.381	0.534	0.914	334	8	AS,MVP-3,GG,SS
2011	28	NYY	AL	159	681	623	104	188	46	7	28	118	8	2	38	96	0.302	0.349	0.533	0.882	332	12	AS,MVP-6,SS
2012	29	NYY	AL	161	697	627	105	196	48	1	33	94	3	2	61	96	0.313	0.379	0.550	0.929	345	7	AS,MVP-4,GG,SS
2013	30	NYY	AL	160	681	605	81	190	41	0	27	107	7	1	65	85	0.314	0.383	0.516	0.899	312	6	AS,MVP-5,SS
2014	31	SEA	AL	157	665	595	77	187	37	2	14	82	10	3	61	68	0.314	0.382	0.454	0.836	270	6	AS,MVP-5
2015	32	SEA	AL	156	674	624	82	179	34	1	21	79	2	6	43	107	0.287	0.334	0.446	0.779	278	3	
2016	33	SEA	AL	161	715	655	107	195	33	2	39	103	0	1	47	100	0.298	0.350	0.533	0.882	349	8	AS,MVP-8
2017	34	SEA	AL	150	648	592	79	166	33	0	23	97	1	0	49	85	0.280	0.338	0.453	0.791	288	4	AS
2018	35	SEA	AL	80	348	310	44	94	22	0	10	50	0	0	32	47	0.303	0.374	0.471	0.845	146	4	
2019	36	NYM	NL	107	423	390	46	100	28	0	13	39	0	0	25	69	0.256	0.307	0.428	0.736	167	5	
2020	37	NYM	NL	49	182	171	23	54	9	0	10	30	0	0	0	24	0.316	0.352	0.544	0.896	93	1	
2021									Did not play in major or minor leagues (Suspended)														
2022	39	TOT	NL	33	104	100	5	15	1	0	1	4	0	0	4	25	0.150	0.183	0.190	0.373	19	0	
2022	39	NYM	NL	12	43	41	3	8	0	0	1	3	0	0	2	11	0.195	0.233	0.268	0.501	11	0	
2022	39	SDP	NL	12	34	33	1	3	0	0	0	1	0	0	1	10	0.091	0.118	0.091	0.209	3	0	
2022	39	ATL	NL	9	27	26	1	4	1	0	0	0	0	0	1	4	0.154	0.185	0.192	0.377	5	0	
162 Game Avg.				162	682	627	90	189	41	2	24	93	4	3	44	87	0.301	0.351	0.488	0.839	306	6	
NYY (9 yrs)				1374	5791	5336	799	1649	375	28	204	822	38	28	350	689	0.309	0.355	0.504	0.860	2692	54	
SEA (5 yrs)				704	3050	2776	389	821	159	5	107	411	13	10	232	407	0.296	0.353	0.472	0.826	1311	25	
NYM (3 yrs)				168	648	602	72	162	37	0	24	72	0	0	36	104	0.269	0.315	0.450	0.765	271	6	
SDP (1 yr)				12	34	33	1	3	0	0	0	1	0	0	1	10	0.091	0.118	0.091	0.209	3	0	
ATL (1 yr)				9	27	26	1	4	1	0	0	0	0	0	1	4	0.154	0.185	0.192	0.377	5	0	
AL (14 yrs)				2078	8841	8112	1188	2470	534	33	311	1233	51	38	582	1096	0.304	0.355	0.493	0.848	4003	79	
NL (3 yrs)				189	709	661	74	169	38	0	24	73	0	0	38	118	0.256	0.3	0.422	0.723	279	6	
17 Yrs				2267	9550	8773	1262	2639	572	33	335	1306	51	38	620	1214	0.301	0.351	0.488	0.839	4282	85	Career Pts.
				8.000	0.000	0.000	6.750	8.000	0.000	0.000	5.500	8.000	0.500	0.000	1.500	6.750	6.750	3.000	4.500	6.750	8.000	0.000	74.000

Post Season Play

Year	Age	Tm	Lg	G	PA	AB	R	H	2B	3B	HR	RBI	SB	CS	BB	SO	BA	OBP	SLG	OPS	TB	HBP	
2005	22	NYY	ALDS	5	21	19	3	5	3	0	0	5	0	1	2	4	0.263	0.333	0.421	0.754	8	0	
2006	23	NYY	ALDS	4	15	15	0	2	0	0	0	0	0	0	0	1	0.133	0.133	0.133	0.267	2	0	
2007	24	NYY	ALDS	4	16	15	3	5	1	0	2	3	0	1	1	1	0.333	0.375	0.800	1.175	12	0	
2009	26	NYY	ALDS	3	12	12	1	2	0	0	0	1	0	0	0	1	0.167	0.167	0.167	0.333	2	0	
2009	26	NYY	ALCS	6	29	23	4	6	1	2	0	4	0	0	4	3	0.261	0.414	0.478	0.892	11	2	
2010	27	NYY	ALDS	3	12	12	3	4	0	1	0	1	0	0	0	0	0.333	0.333	0.500	0.833	6	0	
2010	27	NYY	ALCS	6	24	23	5	8	1	0	4	5	0	0	1	3	0.348	0.375	0.913	1.288	21	0	
2011	28	NYY	ALDS	5	24	22	2	7	2	0	2	9	0	0	2	4	0.318	0.375	0.682	1.057	15	0	
2012	29	NYY	ALDS	5	23	22	1	2	2	0	0	4	0	0	1	3	0.091	0.130	0.182	0.312	4	0	
2012	29	NYY	ALCS	4	18	18	0	1	0	0	0	0	0	0	0	3	0.056	0.056	0.056	0.111	1	0	
				45	194	181	22	42	10	3	8	32	0	2	11	23	0.232	0.299	0.453	0.752	82	2	Post Season Pts.
				1.000	0.000	0.000	0.600	0.800	0.000	0.000	0.800	1.400	0.000	0.000	0.600	0.000	0.000	0.000	0.600	0.400	0.800	0.000	7.000

World Deries Play

Year	Age	Tm	Lg	G	PA	AB	R	H	2B	3B	HR	RBI	SB	CS	BB	SO	BA	OBP	SLG	OPS	TB	HBP	
2009	26	NYY	WS	6	23	22	0	3	0	0	0	1	0	0	0	5	0.136	0.130	0.136	0.267	3	0	0.6
				6	23	22	0	3	0	0	0	1	0	0	0	5	0.136	0.130	0.136	0.267	3	0	World Series Pts.
				0.250	0.000	0.000	0.000	0.250	0.000	0.000	0.000	0.250	0.000	0.000	0.000	0.000	0.000	0.000	0.000	0.000	0.000	0.000	0.750

Yearly Points Leading the League

Category	Times	Points	Total	Category	Times	Points	Total	Category	Times	Points	Total
MVP	0	7	0	B.A.	0	3	0	T.B.	0	2	0
Rookie of Year	0	5	0	Runs	0	2	0	B.O.B.	0	2	0
Triple Crown	0	5	0	H.R.'s	0	3	0	OBP%	0	2	0
Golden Glove	2	3	6	R.B.I's	0	3	0	SLG %	0	2	0
All-Star	8	2	16	Hits	0	2	0	OBPS%	0	2	0
Games	0	2	0	S.B.	0	2	0	Totals			0
Totals			22	Totals			0	Grand Total Add-On Points			22

Hall of Fame Points	
Career Points	74.000
Post Season Points	7.000
World Series Points	0.750
Career Add-On Points	22.000
Writers Association Pts.	0.000
Military/Lifetime Achievement	0.000
Grand Total HOF Points	103.750

Kent, Jeff

Personal Life

Jeffrey Franklin Kent was born March 7, 1968, in Bellflower, California to Alan, a police officer, and Sherry Kent. He has two younger brothers, Eric and Adam. Kent graduated from Huntington Beach's Edison High School in 1986. He accepted on an academic scholarship at the University of California at Berkeley.

Kent met his wife Dana in high school and married before 1995. The couple have four children, a daughter. Lauren, and three sons, Hunter, Colton, and Kaeden.

Baseball Career

Kent played college baseball at the University of California, Berkeley and was selected in the 20th round of the 1989 MLB draft by the Toronto Blue Jays and began his in Class-A. Kent continued to move until 1992, when he made the Blue Jays. He became a regular role in the line-up but on August 27 he was traded to the Mets but earned a World Series ring despite the trade. Starting in 1997 in San Francisco, Kent's career took off and was rewarded with the National League MVP Award in 2000 Kent

Achievements:

- 5-Time All-Star (1999–2001, 2004–05) & 4-Time Silver Slugger (2000–2002, 2005)
- 7-Times in MVP: (1997 - 2000 (won), 2002, & 2005).
- 8 times with 100, or more RBI's. (1997–2002, 2004 & 2005). All-time leader in home runs as a second baseman (377).

Hall of Fame Candidacy

Kent became eligible for the National Baseball Hall of Fame in 2014 and the BBWAA voters gave Kent less than the needed votes until 2023 and removed from the ballot. Kent will be eligible in December 2025 via the Contemporary Baseball Era.

Summary Analysis

Kents Hall of Fame Point Total was 101.900, just short of the Induction Criteria of 110.000. Kent' should be elected to the Baseball Hall of Fame.

Second Baseman Potential Hall of Fame Inductee

Kent, Jeff

Positions		Born :	March 7, 1968	Height:	6' 1"	USC	185	cm
Second Baseman		From:	Bellflower, CA	Weight:	185	lbs.	83	Kg.
First Baseman		Bats:	Right	Debut:	April 12, 1992			
Third Baseman		Throws:	Right	Last Game:	September 27, 2008			

Year	Age	Tm	Lg	G	PA	AB	R	H	2B	3B	HR	RBI	SB	CS	BB	SO	BA	OBP	SLG	OPS	TB	HBP
1992	24	TOT	MLB	102	343	305	52	73	21	2	11	50	2	3	27	76	0.239	0.312	0.430	0.741	131	7
1992	24	TOR	AL	65	222	192	36	46	13	1	8	35	2	1	20	47	0.240	0.324	0.443	0.767	85	6
1992	24	NYM	NL	37	121	113	16	27	8	1	3	15	0	2	7	29	0.239	0.289	0.407	0.696	46	1
1993	25	NYM	NL	140	544	496	65	134	24	0	21	80	4	4	30	88	0.270	0.320	0.446	0.765	221	8
1994	26	NYM	NL	107	452	415	53	121	24	5	14	68	1	4	23	84	0.292	0.341	0.475	0.816	197	10
1995	27	NYM	NL	125	514	472	65	131	22	3	20	65	3	3	29	89	0.278	0.327	0.464	0.791	219	8
1996	28	TOT	MLB	128	477	437	61	124	27	1	12	55	6	4	31	78	0.284	0.330	0.432	0.762	189	2
1996	28	NYM	NL	89	361	335	45	97	20	1	9	39	4	3	21	56	0.290	0.331	0.436	0.766	146	1
1996	28	CLE	AL	39	116	102	16	27	7	0	3	16	2	1	10	22	0.265	0.328	0.422	0.749	43	1
1997	29	SFG	NL	155	651	580	90	145	38	2	29	121	11	3	48	133	0.250	0.316	0.472	0.789	274	13
1998	30	SFG	NL	137	594	526	94	156	37	3	31	128	9	4	48	110	0.297	0.359	0.555	0.914	292	9
1999	31	SFG	NL	138	585	511	86	148	40	2	23	101	13	6	61	112	0.290	0.366	0.511	0.877	261	5
2000	32	SFG	NL	159	695	587	114	196	41	7	33	125	12	9	90	107	0.334	0.424	0.596	1.021	350	9
2001	33	SFG	NL	159	696	607	84	181	49	6	22	106	7	6	65	96	0.298	0.369	0.507	0.877	308	11
2002	34	SFG	NL	152	682	623	102	195	42	2	37	108	5	1	52	101	0.313	0.368	0.565	0.933	352	4
2003	35	HOU	NL	130	552	505	77	150	39	1	22	93	6	2	39	85	0.297	0.351	0.509	0.860	257	5
2004	36	HOU	NL	145	606	540	96	156	34	8	27	107	7	3	49	96	0.289	0.348	0.531	0.880	287	6
2005	37	LAD	NL	149	637	553	100	160	36	0	29	105	6	2	72	85	0.289	0.377	0.512	0.889	283	8
2006	38	LAD	NL	115	473	407	61	119	27	3	14	68	1	2	55	69	0.292	0.385	0.477	0.861	194	8
2007	39	LAD	NL	136	562	494	78	149	36	1	20	79	1	3	57	61	0.302	0.375	0.500	0.875	247	5
2008	40	LAD	NL	121	474	440	42	123	23	1	12	59	0	1	25	52	0.280	0.327	0.418	0.745	184	7
162 Game Avg.				162	672	599	93	173	39	3	27	107	7	4	56	107	0.290	0.356	0.500	0.855	299	9
SFG (6 yrs)				900	3903	3434	570	1021	247	22	175	689	57	29	364	659	0.297	0.368	0.535	0.903	1837	51
NYM (5 yrs)				498	1992	1831	244	510	98	10	67	267	12	16	110	346	0.279	0.327	0.453	0.780	829	28
LAD (4 yrs)				521	2146	1894	281	551	122	5	75	311	8	8	209	267	0.291	0.367	0.479	0.847	908	28
HOU (2 yrs)				275	1158	1045	173	306	73	9	49	200	13	5	88	181	0.293	0.350	0.521	0.870	544	11
CLE (1 yr)				39	116	102	16	27	7	0	3	16	2	1	10	22	0.265	0.328	0.422	0.749	43	1
TOR (1 yr)				65	222	192	36	46	13	1	8	35	2	1	20	47	0.240	0.324	0.443	0.767	85	6
NL (17 yrs)				2194	9199	8204	1268	2388	540	46	366	1467	90	58	771	1453	0.291	0.357	0.502	0.859	4118	118
AL (2 yrs)				104	338	294	52	73	20	1	11	51	4	2	30	69	0.248	0.325	0.435	0.761	128	7
17 Yrs				2298	9537	8498	1320	2461	560	47	377	1518	94	60	801	1522	0.290	0.356	0.500	0.855	4246	125	**Career Pts.**
				9.250	0.000	0.000	8.000	5.500	0.000	0.000	8.000	10.500	1.000	0.000	2.500	0.000	4.500	3.000	5.500	6.750	8.000	0.000	**72.500**

Post Season Play

Year	Age	Tm		G	PA	AB	R	H	2B	3B	HR	RBI	SB	CS	BB	SO	BA	OBP	SLG	OPS	TB	HBP
1996	28	CLE	ALDS	4	9	8	2	1	1	0	0	0	0	0	0	0	0.125	0.125	0.250	0.375	2	0
1997	29	SFG	NLDS	3	12	10	2	3	0	0	2	2	0	0	2	1	0.300	0.417	0.900	1.317	9	0
2000	32	SFG	NLDS	4	17	16	3	6	1	0	0	1	1	0	1	3	0.375	0.412	0.438	0.849	7	0
2002	34	SFG	NLDS	5	22	19	1	5	2	0	0	1	0	0	2	7	0.263	0.364	0.368	0.732	7	1
2002	34	SFG	NLCS	5	22	19	3	5	0	0	0	0	0	0	2	4	0.263	0.364	0.263	0.627	5	1
2004	36	HOU	NLDS	5	24	22	3	5	3	0	0	3	0	0	2	5	0.227	0.292	0.364	0.655	8	0
2004	36	HOU	NLCS	7	30	25	3	6	2	0	3	7	0	0	3	5	0.240	0.367	0.680	1.047	17	2
2006	38	LAD	NLDS	3	13	13	2	8	1	0	1	2	0	0	0	1	0.615	0.615	0.923	1.538	12	0
2008	40	LAD	NLDS	1	1	1	0	0	0	0	0	0	0	0	0	0	0.000	0.000	0.000	0.000	0	0
2008	40	LAD	NLCS	5	8	8	0	0	0	0	0	0	0	0	0	4	0.000	0.000	0.000	0.000	0	0
				42	158	141	19	39	10	0	6	16	1	0	12	30	0.277	0.333	0.404	0.737	67	4	**Post Season Pts.**
				1.000	0.000	0.000	0.600	0.800	0.000	0.000	0.600	0.800	0.250	0.000	0.600	0.000	0.400	0.400	0.250	0.400	0.800	0.000	**6.900**

World Series Play

Year	Age	Tm	Lg	G	PA	AB	R	H	2B	3B	HR	RBI	SB	CS	BB	SO	BA	OBP	SLG	OPS	TB	HBP
2002	34	SFG	N.L	7	31	29	6	8	1	0	3	7	0	0	1	7	0.276	0.290	0.621	0.911	18	0
				7	31	29	6	8	1	0	3	7	0	0	1	7	0.276	0.290	0.621	0.913	18	0	**World Series Pts.**
				0.250	0.000	0.000	0.400	0.400	0.000	0.000	0.600	0.400	0.000	0.000	0.250	0.000	0.800	0.000	1.000	0.800	0.600	0.000	**5.500**

Yearly Points Leading the League

Category	Times	Points	Total
MVP	1	7	7
Rookie of Yea	0	5	0
Triple Crown	0	5	0
Golden Glove	0	3	0
All-Star	5	2	10
Games	0	2	0
Totals			17

Category	Times	Points	Total
B.A.	0	3	0
Runs	0	2	0
H.R.'s	0	3	0
R.B.I's	0	3	0
Hits	0	2	0
S.B.	0	2	0
Totals			0

Catego	Times	Points	Total
T.B.	0	2	0
B.O.B.	0	2	0
OBP%	0	2	0
SLG %	0	2	0
OBPS%	0	2	0
Totals			0
Grand Total Add-On Points			17

Hall of Fame Points	
Career Points	72.500
Post Season Points	6.900
World Series Points	5.500
Career Add-On Points	17.00
Writers Association Pts.	0.000
Military/Lifetime Achievement	0.000
Grand Total HOF Points	101.9

The Baseball Hall of Fame

Statistical Review of Potential Shortstops for the Hall of Fame

Player	Years Played	Career Pts.	Post Season Pts.	World Series Pts.	Add-On Pts.	Mil/LT Pts.	Total HOF Pts.	Needed HOF Votes	Comments
Players Needing to be Inducted									
None						0		0	Inducted
Players Needing to be Voted into the Hall of Fame by the BBWAA									
Vizquel, Omar	24	60.250	6.850	3.650	39.000	0	109.750	1	Need Voting
Players Not Meeting the Statistical Requirements									
Campaneris, Bert	19	39.500	2.950	5.500	26.000	0	73.900	N/A	DMF
Concepcion, Dave	19	38.750	6.300	5.900	33.000	0	83.950	N/A	DMR
Fernandez, Tony	17	39.750	6.100	0.000	24.000	0	69.850	N/A	DMR
Garciaparra, Omar	14	38.550	10.050	0.000	25.000	0	73.600	N/A	DMF
Lundy, Dick	12	34.500	0.000	2.100	10.000	24.000	70.600	N/A	DMR
Ramirez, Hanley	15	45.500	9.300	0.000	21.000	0	75.800	N/A	DMR
Renteria, Edgar	16	44.250	5.850	8.200	16.000	0	74.300	N/A	DMR
Rollins, Jimmy	17	51.500	5.510	5.820	25.000	0	87.830	N/A	DMR
Stephens, Vern	15	41.000	0.000	1.500	29.000	0	71.500	N/A	DMF

Hall of Fame Statistical Requirements:

All Players achieving the total of 110.000, or greater, Total Hall of Fame Points, shall be Inducted after five (5) years of retirement. This provision can be waived due to the death by a 75% vote of the 25 Panel BBWAA's. Individuals receiving less than the required 110.000 Hall of Fame Points are eligible for Election after five (5) years of retirement. A 25 person BBWAA will determine the Players that will be Inducted and vote on the Players needing to be elected. An example of those needing to be elected are as follows: Player "A" has a total of 95 Hall of Fame Points and will need 15 of the (25) BBWAA votes to be Elected in the following year.

Shortstops Needing to be Inducted

No Players Have Reached the

110.000 Hall of Fame Statistical Induction Criteria

Vizquel, Omar

Personal Life

Omar Enrique Vizquel González : was born April 24, 1967 to Omar Vizquel Sr. and Eucharis. He has a younger brother Carlos and a younger sister, Gabriel. Vizquel.

In 1992 Vizquel married Nicole and the couple has two children, a son Nicholas and a daughter Caylee. They later divorced and Vizquel married Blanca Garcia in 2014.

Baseball Career

Vizquel started his career with the Leones del Caracas of the Venezuelan Winter League. He was signed by the Mariners in 1984 and made his Major League debut on April 3, 1989. From 1989 through 2012, Vizquel played for the Mariners, Indians Giants, Rangers, White Sox, and Blue Jays for a total of 24 years in the MLB. He had a career BA of 272 BA, with 404 SB, 2,877 hits, the most double plays made while playing shortstop, he had the highest career fielding percentage by a shortstop (0.9846) with at least 1,000 games played, lowest number of errors in a season by a shortstop (tie) (3 in the 2000 season). his .985 fielding percentage is tied for highest all-time, the all-time leader in games played, and the all-time leader in double plays turned.

Achievements

- 11-time Gold Glove recipient Three-time All-Star (1998, 1999 & 2002)
- Won two American League Championships (with Cleveland, 1995, 1997)

Hall of Fame Candidacy

Vizquel appeared on the ballot for the National Baseball Hall of Fame since 2018. He, received 52.6% in 2020 before going down to 19.5% to in 2023, his 6th year of eligibility.

Summary:

Vizquel has a Hall of Fame Point Total of 109.750 and almost enough for automatic Induction. However, two allegations against the Character Clause have delayed his voting into the Baseball Hall of Fame. Until they are settled, his candidacy should be delayed until the allegations are resolved.

A Fan's Perspective

Vizquel, Omar — Shortstop Potential Hall of Fame Inductee

Positions	Born:	April 24, 1967
First Baseman	From:	Caracas, Venezuela
	Bats:	Both
	Throws:	Right

Height:	5' 9"	USC	175
Weight:	180	lbs.	81
Debut:	April 3, 1989		
Last Game:	October 3, 2012		

Year	Age	Tm	Lg	G	PA	AB	R	H	2B	3B	HR	RBI	SB	CS	BB	SO	BA	OBP	SLG	OPS	TB	HBP	Awards
1989	22	SEA	AL	143	431	387	45	85	7	3	1	20	1	4	28	40	0.22	0.273	0.261	0.534	101	1	
1990	23	SEA	AL	81	285	255	19	63	3	2	2	18	4	1	18	22	0.247	0.295	0.298	0.593	76	0	
1991	24	SEA	AL	142	482	426	42	98	16	4	1	41	7	2	45	37	0.23	0.302	0.293	0.595	125	0	
1992	25	SEA	AL	136	527	483	49	142	20	4	0	21	15	13	32	38	0.294	0.34	0.352	0.692	170	2	
1993	26	SEA	AL	158	630	560	68	143	14	2	2	31	12	14	50	71	0.255	0.319	0.298	0.618	167	4	GG
1994	27	CLE	AL	69	322	286	39	78	10	1	1	33	13	4	23	23	0.273	0.325	0.325	0.65	93	0	GG
1995	28	CLE	AL	136	622	542	87	144	28	0	6	56	29	11	59	59	0.266	0.333	0.351	0.684	190	1	GG
1996	29	CLE	AL	151	623	542	98	161	36	1	9	64	35	8	56	42	0.297	0.362	0.417	0.779	226	4	GG
1997	30	CLE	AL	153	642	565	89	158	23	6	5	49	43	12	57	58	0.28	0.347	0.368	0.715	208	2	GG
1998	31	CLE	AL	151	660	576	86	166	30	6	2	50	37	12	62	64	0.288	0.358	0.372	0.73	214	4	AS,GG
1999	32	CLE	AL	144	664	574	112	191	36	4	5	66	42	9	65	50	0.333	0.397	0.436	0.833	250	1	16,GG
2000	33	CLE	AL	156	717	613	101	176	27	3	7	66	22	10	87	72	0.287	0.377	0.375	0.753	230	5	GG
2001	34	CLE	AL	155	693	611	84	156	26	8	2	50	13	9	61	72	0.255	0.323	0.334	0.657	204	2	GG
2002	35	CLE	AL	151	663	582	85	160	31	5	14	72	18	10	56	64	0.275	0.341	0.418	0.759	243	8	AS
2003	36	CLE	AL	64	285	250	43	61	13	2	2	19	8	3	29	20	0.244	0.321	0.336	0.657	84	0	
2004	37	CLE	AL	148	651	567	82	165	28	3	7	59	19	6	57	62	0.291	0.353	0.388	0.741	220	1	
2005	38	SFG	NL	152	651	568	66	154	28	4	3	45	24	10	56	58	0.271	0.341	0.35	0.691	199	5	GG
2006	39	SFG	NL	153	659	579	88	171	22	10	4	58	24	7	56	51	0.295	0.361	0.389	0.749	225	6	GG
2007	40	SFG	NL	145	575	513	54	126	18	3	4	51	14	6	44	48	0.246	0.305	0.316	0.621	162	1	
2008	41	SFG	NL	92	300	266	24	59	10	1	0	23	5	4	24	29	0.222	0.283	0.267	0.55	71	0	
2009	42	TEX	AL	62	195	177	17	47	7	2	1	14	4	0	13	27	0.266	0.316	0.345	0.66	61	0	
2010	43	CHW	AL	108	391	344	36	95	11	1	2	30	11	7	34	45	0.276	0.341	0.331	0.673	114	2	
2011	44	CHW	AL	58	182	167	18	42	7	1	0	8	1	2	9	18	0.251	0.287	0.305	0.592	53	0	
2012	45	TOR	AL	60	163	153	13	36	5	1	0	7	3	2	7	17	0.235	0.265	0.281	0.546	43	0	
162 Game Avg.				162	656	578	79	157	25	4	4	52	22	9	56	59	0.272	0.336	0.352	0.688	82	3	
CLE (11 yrs)				1478	6542	5708	906	1616	288	39	60	584	279	95	612	586	0.283	0.352	0.379	0.731	2162	28	
SEA (5 yrs)				660	2355	2111	223	531	60	15	6	131	39	34	173	208	0.252	0.309	0.303	0.612	639	7	
SFG (4 yrs)				542	2185	1926	232	510	78	18	11	177	67	27	180	186	0.265	0.329	0.341	0.671	657	12	
CHW (2 yrs)				166	573	511	54	137	18	2	2	38	12	9	43	63	0.268	0.324	0.323	0.647	165	2	
TEX (1 yr)				62	195	177	17	47	7	2	1	14	4	0	13	27	0.266	0.316	0.345	0.66	61	0	
TOR (1 yr)				60	163	153	13	36	5	1	0	7	3	2	7	17	0.235	0.265	0.281	0.546	43	0	
AL (20 yrs)				2426	9828	8660	1213	2367	378	59	69	774	337	140	848	901	0.273	0.338	0.355	0.692	3070	37	
NL (4 yrs)				542	2185	1926	232	510	78	18	11	177	67	27	180	186	0.265	0.329	0.341	0.671	657	12	
24 Yrs				2968	12013	10586	1445	2877	456	77	80	951	404	167	1028	1087	0.272	0.336	0.352	0.688	3727	49	Career Pts.
				15.500	0.000	0.000	9.250	10.500	0.000	0.000	1.000	3.750	4.500	0.000	3.750	0.000	2.500	2.000	0.000	2.000	5.500	0.000	60.25

Post Season Play

Year	Age	Tm	Lg	G	PA	AB	R	H	2B	3B	HR	RBI	SB	CS	BB	SO	BA	OBP	SLG	OPS	TB	HBP	
1995	28	CLE	ALDS	3	15	12	2	2	1	0	0	4	1	0	2	2	0.167	0.286	0.250	0.536	3	0	
1995	28	CLE	ALCS	8	29	23	2	2	1	0	0	2	3	0	5	2	0.087	0.241	0.130	0.372	3	0	
1996	29	CLE	ALDS	4	18	14	4	6	1	0	0	2	4	2	3	4	0.429	0.500	0.500	1.000	7	0	
1997	30	CLE	ALDS	5	22	18	3	9	0	0	0	1	4	0	2	1	0.500	0.550	0.500	1.050	9	0	
1997	30	CLE	ALCS	8	29	25	1	1	0	0	0	0	0	0	2	10	0.040	0.143	0.040	0.183	1	1	
1998	31	CLE	ALDS	4	16	15	1	1	0	0	0	0	0	0	1	0	0.067	0.125	0.067	0.192	1	0	
1998	31	CLE	ALCS	6	27	25	2	11	0	1	0	0	4	1	1	3	0.440	0.481	0.520	1.001	13	1	
1999	32	CLE	ALDS	5	24	21	3	5	1	1	0	3	0	0	2	3	0.238	0.304	0.381	0.685	8	0	
2001	34	CLE	ALDS	5	23	22	2	9	1	1	0	6	1	0	1	1	0.409	0.435	0.545	0.980	12	0	
				44	203	175	20	46	5	3	0	18	17	3	19	26	0.263	0.342	0.326	0.668	57	2	Post Season
				1.000	0.000	0.000	0.600	0.800	0.000	0.000	0.000	0.800	1.000	0.000	0.800	0.000	0.400	0.600	0.000	0.750	0.600	0.000	6.850

World Series Play

Year	Age	Tm	Lg	G	PA	AB	R	H	2B	3B	HR	RBI	SB	CS	BB	SO	BA	OBP	SLG	OPS	TB	HBP	
1995	28	CLE	WS	6	26	23	3	4	0	1	0	1	1	0	3	5	0.174	0.269	0.261	0.53	6	0	
1997	30	CLE	WS	7	35	30	5	7	2	0	0	1	5	0	3	5	0.233	0.303	0.300	0.603	9	0	
				13	61	53	8	11	2	1	0	2	6	0	6	10	0.208	0.289	0.283	0.571	15	0	Pts.
				0.400	0.000	0.000	0.600	0.400	0.000	0.000	0.000	0.250	1.200	0.000	0.400	0.000	0.000	0.000	0.000	0.000	0.400	0.000	3.650

Yearly Points Leading the League

Category	Times	Points	Total
MVP	0	7	0
Rookie of Year	0	5	0
Triple Crown	0	5	0
Golden Glove	11	3	33
All-Star	3	2	6
Games	0	2	0
Totals			39

Category	Times	Points	Total
B.A.	3		0
Runs	2		0
H.R.'s	3		0
R.B.I's	3		0
Hits	2		0
S.B.	2		0
Totals			0

Catego	Times	Points	Total
T.B.	0	2	0
B.O.B.	0	2	0
OBP%	0	2	0
SLG%	0	2	0
OBPS%	0	2	0
Totals			0
Grand Total Add-On Points			39

Hall of Fame Points	
Career Points	60.250
Post Season Points	6.850
World Series Points	3.650
Career Add-On Points	39.000
Writers Association Pts.	0.000
Military/Lifetime Achievement	0.000
Grand Total HOF Points	109.750

The Baseball Hall of Fame

Statistical Review of Potential Third Baseman for the Hall of Fame

Player	Years Played	Career Pts.	Post Season Pts.	World Series Pts.	Add-On Pts.	Mil/LT Pts.	Total HOF Pts.	Needed HOF Votes	Comments
Players Needing to be Inducted									
Beltre, Adrian	23	95.250	3.750	5.700	26.000	0	130.700	Elected	2024
Players Needing to be Voted into the Hall of Fame by the BBWAA									
Boyer, Ken	15	47.500	0.000	3.000	44.000	0	106.500	4	Need Voting
Players Not Meeting the Statistical Requirements									
Bando, Sal	16	39.000	7.500	1.050	20.000	0	67.650	N/A	DMR
Bell, Buddy	18	45.900	0.000	0.000	26.000	0	71.900	N/A	DMF
Cey, Ron	17	46.000	6.250	6.400	12.000	0	70.650	N/A	DMR
Eliot, Bob	15	46.060	0.000	7.3850	16.000	0	69.445	N/A	DMR
Evans, Darrell	21	72.250	4.350	1.250	11.000	0	88.850	22	DMR
Gaetti, Gary	20	51.000	3.350	4.550	15.000	0	73.900	N/A	DMF
Glaus, Troy	13	38.25	7.450	11.100	11.000	0	67.800	N/A	DMR
Hack, Stan	16	40.500	0.000	6.350	20.000	0	66.850	N/A	DMR
Madlock, Bill	15	40.250	5.650	6.400	18.000	0	70.300	N/A	DMR
Nettles, Craig	22	57.000	4.600	3.650	21.000	0	86.250	24	DMR
Ventura, Robin	16	42.000	3.350	1.725	22.000	0	69.075	N/A	DMF
Williams, Matt	17	43.500	5.950	6.450	28.000	0	83.900	N/A	DMR
Wright, David	14	46.750	7.200	2.325	20.000	0	76.250	N/A	DMR

<u>Hall of Fame Statistical Requirements:</u>

All Players achieving the total of 110.000, or greater, Total Hall of Fame Points, shall be Inducted after five (5) years of retirement. This provision can be waived due to the death by a 75% vote of the 25 Panel BBWAA's. Individuals receiving less than the required 110.000 Hall of Fame Points are eligible for Election after five (5) years of retirement. A 25 person BBWAA will determine the Players that will be Inducted and vote on the Players needing to be elected. An example of those needing to be elected are as follows: Player "A" has a total of 95 Hall of Fame Points and will need 15 of the (25) BBWAA votes to be Elocted in the following year.

Third Basemen Needing to be Inducted

1. Adrian Belte – Elected for 2024

110.000 Hall of Fame Statistical Induction Criteria

The Baseball Hall of Fame

Kenton "Ken" Boyer

Personal Life

Kenton Lloyd "Ken" Boyer was born on May 20, 1931, in Liberty, Missouri. He was the fifth of 14 children of Vern and Mabel Boyer. He attended Alba High School with two of his brothers, Clete, and Cloyd, who also reached the major leagues.

Boyer married Kathleen Oliver in April 1952 with the couple having four children – Susie, David, Danny and Janie.

Baseball Career

After graduating high school in 1949, the Cardinals signed and sent him to the Class D League. The Cardinals shifted him to third base in 1951 after serving in the U.S. Army from 1951 to 1953. In 1954, he played in the Texas League and Boyer made his major league debut on April 12, 1955. In his 15-year MLB career, he was a .287 hitter with 2,143 hits, 282 home runs and 1,141 RBI, 1,104 runs scored, and played in 2,034 games with the Cardinals, Mets, White Sox, and Dodgers from 1955 – 1969.

Achievements:

- 11-Time All-Star: (1956, 1959-1964) & 1-Time Led the N.L. in fielding PCT: (1965)
- 5-Time Golden Glove Winner: (1958-1961 & 1963).
- 8-Times received MVP Votes: (1955, 1958-1964).
- 1 Time World Series Champion with the Cardinals in 1964.
- 5-Time .300 Batting Average (1956, 1958, 1959,1960 & 1961.

Hall of Fame Candidacy

Boyer became eligible for election in 1975 but never received more than 5% of the vote and was dropped. Boyer was restored in 1985 and peaked at 25.5% in 1988.

Summary Analysis

Based on the 102.5 career statistical points, Boyer should have been elected while he was still alive.

Boyer, Ken   **Third Baseman - Potential Hall of Fame Inductee**

Positions	Born :	May 20, 1931	Height:	6'1" USC 185 cm
Third Baseman	Died:	April 4, 2004	Weight:	190 lbs. 86 Kg.
Centerfield	From:	Liberty, MO	Debut	April 12, 1955
	Bats:	Right	Final Game:	August 9, 1969
	Throws:	Right		

Year	Age	Tm	Lg	G	PA	AB	R	H	2B	3B	HR	RBI	SB	CS	BB	SO	BA	OBP	SLG	OPS	TB	HBP	Awards
1951	20	min	A	151	623	565	87	173	28	7	14	90	11		41	59	0.306	0.354	0.455	0.809	257	1	
1952	21										Military Service												
1953	22										Military Service												
1954	23	min	AA	159	714	634	116	202	42	7	21	116	29	10	63	82	0.319	0.378	0.506	0.885	321	1	
1955	24	STL	NL	147	574	530	78	140	27	2	18	62	22	17	37	67	0.264	0.311	0.425	0.735	225	1	
1956	25	STL	NL	150	639	595	91	182	30	2	26	98	8	3	38	65	0.306	0.347	0.494	0.841	294	1	AS,MVP-28
1957	26	STL	NL	142	598	544	79	144	18	3	19	62	12	8	44	77	0.265	0.318	0.414	0.732	225	1	
1958	27	STL	NL	150	632	570	101	175	21	9	23	90	11	6	49	53	0.307	0.360	0.496	0.857	283	3	MVP-13,GG
1959	28	STL	NL	143	633	563	86	174	18	5	28	94	12	6	67	77	0.309	0.384	0.508	0.892	286	2	10,GG
1960	29	STL	NL	151	616	552	95	168	26	10	32	97	8	7	56	77	0.304	0.370	0.562	0.932	310	4	AS,AS,MVP-6,GG
1961	30	STL	NL	153	664	589	109	194	26	11	24	95	6	3	68	91	0.329	0.397	0.533	0.930	314	1	AS,AS,MVP-7,GG
1962	31	STL	NL	160	691	611	92	178	27	5	24	98	12	7	75	104	0.291	0.369	0.470	0.838	287	1	AS,AS,MVP-1R
1963	32	STL	NL	159	693	617	86	176	28	2	24	111	1	0	70	90	0.285	0.358	0.454	0.812	280	2	AS,MVP-13,GG
1964	33	STL	NL	162	707	628	100	185	30	10	24	119	3	5	70	85	0.295	0.365	0.489	0.854	307	2	AS,MVP-3
1965	34	STL	NL	144	605	535	71	139	18	2	13	75	2	7	57	73	0.260	0.328	0.374	0.702	200	1	
1966	35	NYM	NL	136	534	496	62	132	28	2	14	61	4	3	30	64	0.266	0.304	0.415	0.719	206	0	
1967	36	TOT	MLB	113	384	346	34	86	12	3	7	34	2	3	33	47	0.249	0.312	0.361	0.673	125	0	
1967	36	NYM	NL	56	194	166	17	39	7	2	3	13	2	1	26	22	0.235	0.335	0.355	0.690	59	0	
1967	36	CHW	AL	57	190	180	17	47	5	1	4	21	0	2	7	25	0.261	0.287	0.367	0.654	66	0	
1968	37	TOT	MLB	93	268	245	20	63	7	2	6	41	2	2	17	40	0.257	0.302	0.376	0.678	92	1	
1968	37	CHW	AL	10	25	24	0	3	0	0	0	0	0	0	1	6	0.125	0.160	0.125	0.285	3	0	
1968	37	LAD	NL	83	243	221	20	60	7	2	6	41	2	2	16	34	0.271	0.317	0.403	0.720	69	1	
1969	38	LAD	NL	25	36	34	0	7	2	0	0	4	0	0	2	7	0.206	0.250	0.265	0.515	9	0	
162 Game Avg.				162	659	594	88	171	25	5	22	91	8	6	57	81	0.287	0.349	0.462	0.810	274	2	
STL (11 yrs)				1667	7052	6334	988	1855	269	61	255	1001	97	69	631	859	0.293	0.356	0.475	0.832	3011	19	
LAD (2 yrs)				108	279	255	20	67	9	2	6	45	2	2	18	41	0.263	0.308	0.384	0.693	98	1	
NYM (2 yrs)				192	728	662	79	171	35	4	17	74	6	4	56	86	0.258	0.312	0.400	0.713	265	0	
CHW (2 yrs)				67	215	204	17	50	5	1	4	21	0	2	8	31	0.245	0.272	0.338	0.611	69	0	
NL (15 yrs)				1967	8059	7251	1087	2093	313	67	278	1120	105	75	705	986	0.289	0.351	0.468	0.816	3374	20	
AL (2 yrs)				67	215	204	17	50	5	1	4	21	0	2	8	31	0.245	0.272	0.338	0.611	69	0	

15 Yrs	G	PA	AB	R	H	2B	3B	HR	RBI	SB	CS	BB	SO	BA	OBP	SLG	OPS	TB	HBP	Career Points
	3034	8274	7455	1104	2143	318	68	282	1141	105	77	713	1017	0.287	0.349	0.462	0.810	3443	20	47.500
	6.750	0.000	0.000	4.500	3.750	0.000	0.000	4.500	5.500	1.000	0.000	2.000	0.000	4.500	3.000	3.000	4.500	4.500	0.000	47.500

Post Season Play

																			Post Season Pts
0	0	0	0	0	0	0	0	0	0	0	0	0	0	0	0	0	0	0	0
0.000	0.000	0.000	0.000	0.000	0.000	0.000	0.000	0.000	0.000	0.000	0.000	0.000	0.000	0.000	0.000	0.000	0.000	0.000	0.000

World Series Play

Year	Age	Tm	Lg	G	PA	AB	R	H	2B	3B	HR	RBI	SB	CS	BB	SO	BA	OBP	SLG	OPS	TB	HBP	WS Points
				7	30	27	5	6	1	0	2	6	0	0	1	5	0.222	0.241	0.481	0.723	13	0	WS Points
				0.250	0.000	0.000	0.400	0.250	0.000	0.000	0.400	0.400	0.000	0.000	0.250	0.000	0.000	0.000	0.250	0.400	0.400	0.000	3.000

Yearly Points Leading the League

Category	Times	Points	Total		Category	Times	Points	Total		Categor	Times	Points	Total
MVP	1	7	7		B.A.	0	3	0		T.B.	0	2	0
Rookie of Year	0	5	0		Runs	0	2	0		B.O.B.	0	2	0
Triple Crown	0	5	0		H.R.'s	0	3	0		OBP%	0	2	0
Golden Glove	5	3	15		R.B.I.'s	0	3	0		SLG %	0	2	0
All-Star	11	2	22		Hits	0	2	0		OBPS%	0	2	0
Games	0	2	0		S.B.	0	2	0		Totals			0
Totals			44		Totals			0		Grand Total Add-On Points			44

Hall of Fame Points	
Career Points	47.500
Post Season Points	0.000
World Series Points	3.000
Career Add-On Points	44.000
Writers Association Pts.	0.000
Military/Lifetime Achievement	8.000
Grand Total HOF Points	102.500

The Baseball Hall of Fame

Statistical Review of Potential Catchers for the Hall of Fame

Player	Years Played	Career Pts.	Post Season Pts.	World Series Pts.	Add-On Pts.	Mil/LT Pts.	Total HOF Pts.	Needed HOF Votes	Comments
Players Needing to be Inducted									
None						0		0	Inducted
Players Needing to be Voted into the Hall of Fame by the BBWAA									
Howard, Elston	15	23.250	4.250	10.100	37.000	0	94.600		Need Voting
Mauer, Joe	15	46.995	2.750	0.000	45.000	0	94.750	Elected	2024
Molina, Yadier	19	34.250	8.550	7.230	47.000	0	97.030		Need Voting
Munson, Thurman	11	24.500	5.050	8.950	35.000	0	93.500		Need Voting
Players Not Meeting the Statistical Requirements									
Freehan, Bill	15	26.000	2.800	1.000	37.000	0	66.800	N/A	DMR
McCann, Brian	15	47.255	2.750	0.000	14.000	0	64.050	N/A	DMF
Parrish, Lance	19	33.750	3.750	4.600	25.000	0	67.100	N/A	DMR
Piersynski, A.J.	19	31.750	7.250	3.150	25.000	0	67.150	N/A	DMR
Posey, Buster	12	35.250	6.150	3.500	34.000	0	78.900	N/A	DMR
Posada, Jorge	17	42.500	15.700	6.150	10.000	0	74.350	N/A	DMR
Torre, Joe	18	49.250	0.000	0.000	40.000	0	89.250	N/A	DMR

Hall of Fame Statistical Requirements:

All Players achieving the total of 110.000, or greater, Total Hall of Fame Points, shall be Inducted after five (5) years of retirement. This provision can be waived due to the death by a 75% vote of the 25 Panel BBWAA's. Individuals receiving less than the required 110.000 Hall of Fame Points are eligible for Election after five (5) years of retirement. A 25 person BBWAA will determine the Players that will be Inducted and vote on the Players needing to be elected. An example of those needing to be elected are as follows: Player "A" has a total of 95 Hall of Fame Points and will need 15 of the (25) BBWAA votes to be Elected in the following year.

Catchers Needing to be Inducted.

Joe Maurer – Elected for 2024

No Players Have Reached the

110.000 Hall of Fame Statistical Induction Criteria

Howard, Elston

Summary Analysis

Based on his 94.600 Hall of Fame Point Total listed in this book, Howard be elected as he was one of the best players and helped transition baseball in the integration process.

Personal Life.

Elston Gene Howard was born February 23, 1929, in St. Louis, Missouri to Emmaline Webb and Travis Howard. Howard was a standout athlete at Vashon High School.

Howard married Arlene Henley in 1954 with the couple having three children, son Elston Jr. and daughters Cheryl and Karen.

Baseball Career

In 1948, Howard signed with the Kansas City Monarchs in the Negro League and played there until the Yankees signed him on July 19, 1950. They assigned him to the Central League where he missed the 1951 and 1952 seasons due to military service but played in the Triple AAA leagues in 1953 & 1954. Howard made the Yankees in 1955 but due to the Yankees having Yogi Berra, he played various positions until 1960 when he became mostly a catcher, as Berra moved to the outfield. Howard was the first African-American Yankee and if not for the two years of time lost to military service, the color barrier, and being stuck behind Berra, he would have fashioned a Hall of Fame career. At his peak, he put up Hall of Fame numbers for a catcher. In 1963, Howard became the first African American to with the AL MVP award.

Achievements:

- 12-time All-Star (1957 to 1965, From 1961 thru 1963 he was selected twice)
- 2-Time (2)-time Golden Glove Winner (1963 & 1964)
- 5-times received MVP points (1958, 1960, 1961,1963(winning), 1964 & 1967).
- 4-time World Series Champion with the New York Yankees (1956, 1958, 1961 & 1962)

Starting in 1974, Howard was on the Hall of Fame Ballot for 15 years with his highest percentage of 20.7 % in 1981. He will once again become eligible in 2025.

Howard, Elston — Catcher - Potential Hall of Fame Inductee

Positions		Bio		Physical		Debut / Career	
Positions		Born:	February 23, 1929	Height:	6' 2"	USC	188 cm
Catcher		Died:	December 14, 1980	Weight:	196 lbs.	88 Kg.	
Left Fielder		From:	St. Louis, Missouri	Debut: N. L.		May 1, 1905	
First Baseman		Bats:	Right	Debut: MLB.		April 14, 1955	
		Throws Right		Last Game:		September 29, 1968	

Year	Age	Tm	Lg	G	PA	AB	R	H	2B	3B	HR	RBI	SB	CS	BB	SO	BA	OBP	SLG	OPS	TB	HBP	
1948	19	KCM	NAL	20	84	80	16	20	5	3	1	13	1	1	3	N/A	0.250	0.286	0.425	0.711	34	1	
1949	20	KCM	N/A	N/A	N/A	N/A	N/A	N/A	N/A	N/A	N/A	N/A	N/A	N/A	N/A	N/A	N/A	N/A	N/A	N/A	N/A	N/A	
1950	21	KCM	N/A	N/A	N/A	N/A	N/A	N/A	N/A	N/A	N/A	N/A	N/A	N/A	N/A	N/A	N/A	N/A	N/A	N/A	N/A	N/A	
1951	22							Did not play in major or minor leagues (Military Service)															
1952	23							Did not play in major or minor leagues (Military Service)															
1955	26	NYY	AL	97	305	279	33	81	8	7	10	43	0	0	20	36	0.290	0.336	0.477	0.812	133	1	
1956	27	NYY	AL	98	316	290	35	76	8	3	5	34	0	1	21	30	0.262	0.312	0.362	0.674	105	1	
1957	28	NYY	AL	110	381	356	33	90	13	4	8	44	2	5	16	43	0.253	0.283	0.379	0.663	135	0	AS
1958	29	NYY	AL	103	406	376	45	118	19	5	11	66	1	1	22	60	0.314	0.348	0.479	0.827	180	0	AS,MVP-17
1959	30	NYY	AL	125	475	443	59	121	24	6	18	73	0	1	20	57	0.273	0.306	0.476	0.783	211	3	AS
1960	31	NYY	AL	107	361	323	29	79	11	3	6	39	3	0	28	43	0.245	0.298	0.353	0.651	114	0	AS,AS
1961	32	NYY	AL	129	482	446	64	155	17	5	21	77	0	3	28	65	0.348	0.387	0.549	0.936	245	3	AS,AS,MVP-10
1962	33	NYY	AL	136	538	494	63	138	23	5	21	91	1	1	31	76	0.279	0.318	0.474	0.791	234	1	AS,AS
1963	34	NYY	AL	135	531	487	75	140	21	6	28	85	0	0	35	68	0.287	0.342	0.528	0.869	257	6	AS,MVP-1,GG
1964	35	NYY	AL	150	607	550	63	172	27	3	15	84	1	1	48	73	0.313	0.371	0.455	0.825	250	5	AS,MVP-3,GG
1965	36	NYY	AL	110	418	391	38	91	15	1	9	45	0	0	24	65	0.233	0.278	0.345	0.623	135	1	AS
1966	37	NYY	AL	126	451	410	38	105	19	2	6	35	0	0	37	65	0.256	0.317	0.356	0.673	146	1	
1967	38	TOT	AL	108	345	315	22	56	9	0	4	28	0	0	21	60	0.178	0.233	0.244	0.478	77	3	MVP-17
1967	38	NYY	AL	66	216	199	13	39	6	0	3	17	0	0	12	36	0.196	0.247	0.271	0.518	54	2	
1967	38	BOS	AL	42	129	116	9	17	3	0	1	11	0	0	9	24	0.147	0.211	0.198	0.409	23	1	
1968	39	BOS	AL	71	229	203	22	49	4	0	5	18	1	1	22	45	0.241	0.317	0.335	0.652	68	1	
162 Game Avg.				162	591	543	63	149	22	5	17	77	1	14	37	846	0.274	0.321	0.427	0.748	232	3	
NYY (13 yrs)				1492	5487	5044	588	1405	211	50	161	733	8	13	342	717	0.279	0.324	0.436	0.760	2199	24	
BOS (2 yrs)				113	358	319	31	66	7	0	6	29	1	1	31	69	0.207	0.279	0.285	0.564	91	2	
KCM (1 yr)				20	84	80	16	20	5	3	1	13	1	0	3	0	0.250	0.286	0.425	0.711	34	1	
AL (14 yrs)				1605	5845	5363	619	1471	218	50	167	762	9	14	373	786	0.274	0.322	0.427	0.749	2290	26	
NAL (1 yr)				20	84	80	16	20	5	3	1	13	1	0	3	0	0.250	0.286	0.425	0.711	34	1	
15 Yrs				1625	5929	5443	635	1491	223	53	168	775	10	14	376	786	0.274	0.321	0.427	0.748	2324	27	Career Pts.
				3.750	0.000	0.000	1.500	1.000	0.000	0.000	2.500	2.500	0.500	0.000	0.000	0.000	3.000	1.500	2.000	3.000	2.000	0.000	23.250

Post Season Play

Year	Age	Tm	Lg	G	PA	AB	R	H	2B	3B	HR	RBI	SB	CS	BB	SO	BA	OBP	SLG	OPS	TB	HBP	
1948	19	KCM	ALC	7	28	26	4	6	1	0	1	2	0	0	1	0	0.231	0.286	0.385	0.670	10	1	
				7	28	26	4	6	1	0	1	2	0	0	1	0	0.231	0.286	0.385	0.670	10	1	Post Season Pts.
				0.250	0.000	0.000	0.250	0.250	0.000	0.000	0.250	0.250	0.000	0.000	2.500	0.000	0.000	0.000	0.250	0.000	0.250	0.000	4.250

World Series Play

Year	Age	Tm	Lg	G	PA	AB	R	H	2B	3B	HR	RBI	SB	CS	BB	SO	BA	OBP	SLG	OPS	TB	HBP	
1955	26	NYY	WS	7	28	26	3	5	0	0	1	3	0	0	1	8	0.192	0.222	0.308	0.530	8	0	
1956	27	NYY	WS	1	5	5	1	2	1	0	1	1	0	0	0	0	0.400	0.400	1.200	1.600	6	0	
1957	28	NYY	WS	6	12	11	2	3	0	0	1	3	0	0	1	3	0.273	0.333	0.545	0.879	6	0	
1958	29	NYY	WS	6	20	18	4	4	0	0	0	2	1	0	1	4	0.222	0.263	0.222	0.485	4	0	
1960	31	NYY	WS	5	15	13	4	6	1	1	1	4	0	0	1	4	0.462	0.533	0.923	1.456	12	1	
1961	32	NYY	WS	5	22	20	5	5	3	0	1	1	0	0	2	3	0.250	0.318	0.550	0.868	11	0	
1962	33	NYY	WS	6	23	21	1	3	1	0	0	1	0	0	1	4	0.143	0.217	0.190	0.408	4	1	
1963	34	NYY	WS	4	15	15	0	5	0	0	0	1	0	0	0	3	0.333	0.333	0.333	0.667	5	0	
1964	35	NYY	WS	7	29	24	5	7	1	0	0	2	0	0	4	6	0.292	0.414	0.333	0.747	8	1	
1967	38	BOS	WS	7	20	18	0	2	0	0	0	1	0	0	1	2	0.111	0.158	0.111	0.269	2	0	
				54	189	171	25	42	7	1	5	19	1	0	12	37	0.246	0.308	0.386	0.692	66	3	World Series Pts.
				1.800	0.000	0.000	1.400	1.400	0.000	0.000	1.000	1.000	0.250	0.000	0.600	0.000	0.400	0.000	0.000	0.250	2.000	0.000	10.100

Yearly Points Leading the League

Category	Times	Points	Total	Category	Times	Points	Total	Categor	Times	Points	Total
MVP	1	7	7	B.A.	0	3	0	T.B.	0	2	0
Rookie of Year	0	5	0	Runs	0	2	0	B.O.B.	0	2	0
Triple Crown	0	5	0	H.R.'s	0	3	0	OBP%	0	2	0
Golden Glove	2	3	6	R.B.I's	0	3	0	SLG %	0	2	0
All-Star	12	2	24	Hits	0	2	0	OBPS%	0	2	0
Games	0	2	0	S.B.	0	2	0	Totals			0
Totals			37	Totals			0	Grand Total Add-On Points			37

Hall of Fame Points	
Career Points	23.250
Post Season Points	4.250
World Series Points	10.100
Career Add-On Points	37.000
Writers Association Pts.	0.000
Military/Lifetime Achievement	20.000
Grand Total HOF Points	94.600

Molina, Yadier "Yadi"

Personal Life.

Yadier Benjamín Molina was born on July 13, 1982, in Bayamón, Puerto Rico to Gladys Matta and Benjamín Molina, Sr. He is attended Maestro Ladislao Martínez High School in Vega Alta. His two older brothers, Bengie and José, also had lengthy MLB careers.

Molina married his wife Wanda Torres in 2007 and the couple have three children. On September 4, 2008, they have two sons and a daughter.

Baseball Career

The St. Louis Cardinals took Molina in the fourth round of the 2000 MLB draft. Molina began his career in 2001 and moved up in the system making his debut in the Major Leagues in 2004 on June 3. For the year he appeared in 51 games, batted .267, had two home runs and 15 RBIs in 151 plate appearances. From 2007 through 2019, Molina had one of the best stretches of offensive and defensive catching in baseball. Molina collected 1740 hits, 140 home runs, 803 runs batted in, .288 batting average, .342 OB%, and .415 SLG%. The Cardinals reached the playoffs seven times.

Achievements:

- Nine (9)-time Golden Glove Winner (2008, 2009 - 2015, & 2018).
- Ten (10)-time All-Star: (2009-2015, 2017, 2018, & 2021).
- Five-times received MVP points (2009, 2011, 2012, 2013, & 2016)
- Silver slugger award 2013.
- Two-time World Series Champion with the St. Louis Cardinals: (2006 & 2011).

Hall of Fame Candacy

Yadier Molina will become eligible to be elected to the Baseball Hall of Fame in 2027.

Summary Analysis

Based on Molina's Hall of Fame Score of 97.030 listed in this book, he should be elected to the Baseball Hall of Fame.

Catcher - Potential Hall of Fame Inductee

Molina, Yadier

Position: Catcher
Born: July 13, 1982
From: Bayamon, Puerto Rico
Bats: Right
Throws: Right

Height: 5'11" USC 180 cm
Weight: 225 lbs. 102 Kg.
Debut: June 3, 2004
Last Game: October 5, 2022

Year	Age	Tm	Lg	G	PA	AB	R	H	2B	3B	HR	RBI	SB	CS	BB	SO	BA	OBP	SLG	OPS	TB	HBP	Awards
2004	21	STL	NL	51	151	135	12	36	6	0	3	15	9	1	13	20	0.267	0.329	0.356	0.684	46	0	
2005	22	STL	NL	114	421	385	36	97	15	1	8	49	2	3	23	30	0.252	0.295	0.358	0.654	138	2	
2006	23	STL	NL	129	461	417	29	90	26	0	6	49	1	2	28	41	0.216	0.274	0.321	0.595	134	8	
2007	24	STL	NL	111	396	353	30	97	15	0	6	40	1	1	34	43	0.275	0.34	0.368	0.708	130	3	
2008	25	STL	NL	124	435	444	37	135	18	0	7	56	0	2	32	29	0.304	0.349	0.392	0.74	174	1	GG
2009	26	STL	NL	140	544	481	45	141	23	1	6	54	9	3	50	39	0.293	0.366	0.383	0.749	184	6	AS,MVP-23,GG
2010	27	STL	NL	136	521	465	34	122	19	0	6	62	8	4	42	51	0.262	0.328	0.342	0.671	159	7	AS,GG
2011	28	STL	NL	139	518	475	55	145	32	1	14	65	4	5	33	44	0.305	0.349	0.465	0.814	221	1	AS,MVP-21,GG
2012	29	STL	NL	138	563	505	65	159	28	0	22	76	12	3	45	55	0.315	0.373	0.501	0.874	253	5	AS,MVP-4,GG
2013	30	STL	NL	136	541	505	68	161	44	0	12	80	3	2	30	55	0.319	0.359	0.477	0.836	241	3	AS,MVP-1,GG,SS
2014	31	STL	NL	110	445	404	40	114	21	0	7	38	1	1	28	28	0.282	0.333	0.386	0.739	156	6	AS,GG
2015	32	STL	NL	136	530	488	34	132	23	1	4	61	3	1	32	59	0.27	0.31	0.35	0.66	171	0	AS,GG
2016	33	STL	NL	147	581	534	56	164	38	1	8	58	3	2	39	63	0.307	0.36	0.427	0.787	228	6	MVP-23
2017	34	STL	NL	136	543	501	60	137	27	1	18	82	9	4	28	74	0.273	0.312	0.439	0.751	220	4	AS
2018	35	STL	NL	123	503	459	55	130	20	0	20	74	4	3	29	66	0.261	0.314	0.436	0.75	200	9	AS,GG
2019	36	STL	NL	113	452	419	45	113	24	0	10	57	6	0	33	56	0.27	0.312	0.399	0.711	167	5	
2020	37	STL	NL	42	156	145	12	38	2	0	4	16	0	0	6	21	0.262	0.303	0.359	0.662	52	5	
2021	38	STL	NL	121	473	440	45	111	19	0	11	66	1	0	24	79	0.252	0.297	0.37	0.667	163	5	AS
2022	39	STL	NL	78	270	262	10	56	8	0	5	24	2	0	5	40	0.214	0.233	0.302	0.535	79	3	
162 Game Avg.				163	623	568	57	158	30	1	13	74	5	3	39	67	0.277	0.327	0.399	0.726	227	6	

19 Yrs				G	PA	AB	R	H	2B	3B	HR	RBI	SB	CS	BB	SO	BA	OBP	SLG	OPS	TB	HBP	
				2224	8554	7817	777	2168	408	7	176	1022	71	37	562	922	0.277	0.327	0.399	0.726	3118	76	Career Pts.
				8.000	0.000	0.000	2.500	3.750	0.000	0.000	2.500	3.750	1.000	0.000	1.000	0.000	3.000	1.500	1.000	2.500	3.750	0.000	34.250

Post Season Play

Year	Age	Tm	Lg	G	PA	AB	R	H	2B	3B	HR	RBI	SB	CS	BB	SO	BA	OBP	SLG	OPS	TB	HBP	
2004	21	STL	NLDS									Did not play in series											
2004	21	STL	NLCS	1	4	4	0	1	0	0	0	0	0	0	0	0	0.250	0.250	0.250	0.500	1	0	
2005	22	STL	NLDS	3	13	13	1	3	0	0	0	3	0	0	0	1	0.231	0.231	0.231	0.462	3	0	
2006	22	STL	NLCS	6	22	22	1	7	3	0	0	0	0	0	0	2	0.318	0.318	0.455	0.773	10	0	
2006	23	STL	NLDS	4	13	13	0	4	1	0	0	1	0	1	0	2	0.308	0.308	0.385	0.692	5	0	
2006	23	STL	NLCS	7	26	23	2	8	1	0	2	4	0	0	3	2	0.348	0.429	0.652	1.075	15	0	
2008	26	STL	NLDS	3	13	13	0	4	1	0	0	0	0	0	0	1	0.308	0.308	0.385	0.692	5	0	
2011	28	STL	NLDS	5	20	19	1	4	0	0	0	1	1	0	1	5	0.211	0.250	0.211	0.461	4	0	
2011	28	STL	NLCS	6	26	24	5	8	3	0	0	2	0	0	2	3	0.333	0.385	0.458	0.843	11	0	
2012	29	STL	NLCS	1	4	4	0	0	0	0	0	0	0	0	0	0	0.000	0.000	0.000	0.000	0	0	
2012	29	STL	NLDS	5	23	17	3	2	0	0	0	1	0	0	5	1	0.118	0.348	0.118	0.465	2	1	
2012	29	STL	NLCS	7	28	28	2	11	1	0	0	2	0	0	0	1	0.393	0.393	0.429	0.821	12	0	
2013	30	STL	NLDS	5	20	17	2	5	1	0	1	1	0	0	3	0	0.294	0.400	0.529	0.929	9	0	
2013	30	STL	NLCS	8	25	22	2	5	0	0	0	1	0	0	3	4	0.227	0.320	0.227	0.547	5	0	
2014	31	STL	NLDS	4	15	15	2	3	1	0	0	0	0	0	0	3	0.200	0.200	0.267	0.467	4	0	
2014	31	STL	NLCS	2	7	6	0	2	0	0	0	0	0	0	0	0	0.333	0.333	0.333	0.667	2	0	
2015	32	STL	NLDS	3	8	8	0	1	0	0	0	0	0	0	0	2	0.125	0.125	0.125	0.250	1	0	
2019	36	STL	NLDS	5	23	21	1	3	0	0	0	2	0	0	1	2	0.143	0.174	0.143	0.317	3	0	
2019	36	STL	NLCS	4	14	12	1	2	0	0	1	1	0	0	0	1	0.167	0.286	0.417	0.702	5	2	
2020	37	STL	NLWC	3	14	13	2	6	1	0	0	2	0	0	1	1	0.462	0.500	0.615	1.115	8	0	
2021	38	STL	NLWC	1	4	4	0	0	0	0	0	0	0	0	0	0	0.000	0.000	0.000	0.000	0	0	
2022	39	STL	NLWC	2	8	8	0	1	0	0	0	0	0	0	0	2	0.125	0.125	0.125	0.250	1	0	
				83	330	306	25	80	14	0	4	24	1	1	19	36	0.261	0.311	0.346	0.657	106	3	Post Season Pts.
				1.800	0.000	0.000	0.800	1.400	0.000	0.000	0.400	1.000	0.250	0.000	0.800	0.000	0.400	0.250	0.000	0.250	1.200	0.000	8.550

World Series Play

Year	Age	Tm	Lg	G	PA	AB	R	H	2B	3B	HR	RBI	SB	CS	BB	SO	BA	OBP	SLG	OPS	TB	HBP	
2004	21	STL	WS	3	3	3	0	0	0	0	0	0	0	0	0	1	0.000	0.000	0.000	0.000	0	0	
2006	23	STL	WS	5	20	17	3	7	1	0	0	1	0	0	3	1	0.412	0.5	0.529	1.029	9	0	
2011	28	STL	WS	7	29	24	1	8	2	0	0	9	0	0	4	5	0.333	0.414	0.417	0.83	10	0	
2013	30	STL	WS	6	24	23	0	7	1	0	0	2	0	0	1	8	0.304	0.333	0.348	0.681	8	0	
				21	76	67	4	22	5	0	0	12	0	0	8	8	0.328	0.395	0.403	0.798	27	0	World Series Pts.
				0.800	0.000	0.000	0.250	0.800	0.000	0.000	0.000	0.600	0.000	0.000	0.400	0.000	1.400	1.000	0.000	0.980	1.000	0.000	7.230

Yearly Points Leading the League

Category	Times	Points	Total		Category	Times	Points	Total		Category	Times	Points	Total
MVP	0	7	0		B.A.	0	1	0		T.B.	0	2	0
Rookie of Year	0	5	0		Runs	0	2	0		B.O.B.	0	2	0
Triple Crown	0	5	0		H.R.'s	0	3	0		OBP%	0	2	0
Golden Glove	9	3	27		R.B.I's	0	2	0		SLG%	0	2	0
All-Star	10	2	20		Hits	0	2	0		OBPS%	0	2	0
Games	0	2	0		S.B.	0	2	0		Totals			0
Totals			47		Totals			0		Grand Total Add-On Points			47

Hall of Fame Points	
Career Points	34.250
Post Season Points	8.550
World Series Points	7.230
Career Add-On Points	47.000
Writers Association Pts.	0.000
Military/Lifetime Achievement	0.000
Grand Total HOF Points	97.030

Munson, Thurman "Tugboat"

Personal Life

Thurman Lee Munson (June 7, 1947 – August 2, 1979) was born in Akron, Ohio to Darrell Vernon Munson and Ruth Myrna Smylie as the youngest of four children. Munson attended Lehman High School.

On September 2, 1968, Thurman married Diana in Canton, Ohio. They have three children, daughters Kelly and Tracy and a son Michael.

Baseball Career

Munson was selected by the Yankees with the fourth overall pick in the 1968 Baseball draft. In 1969, he earned a promotion to the New York Yankees and In 1970 was the American League Rookie of the Year. At the start of the 1976 season, Munson was named the Yankees team captain. He was a clutch hitter who had a career .357 batting average in the postseason with three HR's, 22 RBI, 19 runs and a .373 batting average in the World Series. On August 2, 1979, Munson died after crashing his plane and receiving spinal damage and a broken neck from the impact.

Achievements:

- AL Rookie of the Year (1970)
- 7-Times received MVP votes: (1970, 1973-1978 – Winning in 1976).
- 3 times Gold Glove Award: (1973-1975) & 7 time All Star: (1971 & 1973-1978).
- 3 American League Pennants & 2 World Series titles: (2006 & 2011)

Hall of Fame Candidacy

Munson was eligible for the Baseball Hall of Fame in 1985 and didn't receive more than 9.5% of the vote and was taken off the ballot. He will become eligible in 2025.

Summary

Munson had a 93.500 Hall of Fame total point score. At the time of his death, he was still one of the best at his position and should be elected by the BBWAA.

Munson, Thurman

Catcher - Potential Hall of Fame Inductee

Positions		Born : June 7, 1947		Height:	5' 11" USC	180 cm
Catcher		Died: August 2, 1979		Weight:	190 lbs.	86 Kg.
		From: Akron, Ohio		Debut:	August 8, 1969	
		Bats: Right		Last Game:	August 11, 1979	
		Throw Right				

Year	Age	Tm	Lg	G	PA	AB	R	H	2B	3B	HR	RBI	SB	CS	BB	SO	BA	OBP	SLG	OPS	TB	HBP	Awards
1969	22	NYY	AL	26	97	86	6	22	1	2	1	9	0	1	10	10	0.256	0.330	0.349	0.679	30	0	
1970	23	NYY	AL	132	526	453	59	137	25	4	6	53	5	7	57	56	0.302	0.386	0.415	0.801	188	7	MVP-19,RoY-1
1971	24	NYY	AL	125	517	451	71	113	15	4	10	42	6	5	52	65	0.251	0.335	0.368	0.703	166	7	AS
1972	25	NYY	AL	140	568	511	54	143	16	3	7	46	6	7	47	58	0.280	0.343	0.364	0.707	186	3	
1973	26	NYY	AL	147	576	519	80	156	29	4	20	74	4	6	48	64	0.301	0.362	0.487	0.849	253	4	AS,MVP-12,GG
1974	27	NYY	AL	144	571	517	64	135	19	2	13	60	2	0	44	66	0.261	0.316	0.381	0.697	197	1	AS,MVP-26,GG
1975	28	NYY	AL	157	661	597	83	190	24	3	12	102	3	2	45	52	0.318	0.366	0.429	0.795	256	6	AS,MVP-7,GG
1976	29	NYY	AL	152	665	616	79	186	27	1	17	105	14	11	29	38	0.302	0.337	0.432	0.769	266	9	AS,MVP-1
1977	30	NYY	AL	149	638	595	85	183	28	5	18	100	5	6	39	55	0.308	0.351	0.462	0.813	275	2	AS,MVP-7
1978	31	NYY	AL	154	667	617	73	183	27	1	6	71	2	3	35	70	0.297	0.332	0.373	0.705	230	3	AS,MVP-22
1979	32	NYY	AL	97	419	382	42	110	18	3	3	39	1	2	32	37	0.288	0.340	0.374	0.714	143	0	
162 Game Avg.				162	672	608	79	177	26	4	13	80	5	6	50	65	0.292	0.346	0.410	0.756	249	5	

11 Yrs	G	PA	AB	R	H	2B	3B	HR	RBI	SB	CS	BB	SO	BA	OBP	SLG	OPS	TB	HBP	
	1423	5905	5344	696	1558	229	32	113	701	48	50	438	571	0.292	0.346	0.410	0.756	2190	42	Career Pts.
	2.500	0.000	0.000	2.000	1.000	0.000	0.000	1.500	2.000	0.500	0.000	0.500	0.000	5.500	2.500	1.500	3.000	2.000	0.000	24.500

Post Season Play

Year	Age	Tm	Lg	G	PA	AB	R	H	2B	3B	HR	RBI	SB	CS	BB	SO	BA	OBP	SLG	OPS	TB	HBP	
1976	29	NYY	ALCS	5	23	23	3	10	2	0	0	3	0	1	0	1	0.435	0.435	0.522	0.957	12	0	
1977	30	NYY	ALCS	5	22	21	3	6	1	0	1	5	0	0	0	2	0.286	0.273	0.476	0.749	10	0	
1978	31	NYY	ALCS	4	18	18	2	5	1	0	1	2	0	0	0	0	0.278	0.278	0.500	0.778	9	0	
	14	63	62	8	21	4	0	2	10	0	1	0	3	0.339	0.333	0.500	0.833	31	0	Post Season
	0.400	0.000	0.000	0.250	0.400	0.000	0.000	0.400	0.400	0.000	0.000	0.000	0.000	1.000	0.400	0.800	0.600	0.400	0.000	5.050

World Series Play

Year	Age	Tm	Lg	G	PA	AB	R	H	2B	3B	HR	RBI	SB	CS	BB	SO	BA	OBP	SLG	OPS	TB	HBP	
1976	29	NYY	WS	4	17	17	2	9	0	0	0	2	0	0	0	1	0.529	0.529	0.529	1.059	9	0	
1977	30	NYY	WS	6	27	25	4	8	2	0	1	3	0	0	2	8	0.320	0.370	0.520	0.890	13	0	
1978	31	NYY	WS	6	28	25	5	8	3	0	0	7	1	0	3	7	0.320	0.393	0.440	0.833	11	0	
	16	72	67	11	25	5	0	1	12	1	0	5	16	0.373	0.417	0.493	0.909	33	0	Word Series
	0.600	0.000	0.000	0.600	0.800	0.000	0.000	0.250	0.600	0.250	0.000	0.400	0.000	1.800	1.400	0.250	0.800	1.200	0.000	8.950

Yearly Points Leading the League

Category	Times	Points	Total	Category	Times	Points	Total	Categ.	Times	Points	Total
MVP	1	7	7	B.A.	0	3	0	T. B.	0	2	0
Rookie of Year	1	5	5	Runs	0	2	0	B.O.B.	0	2	0
Triple Crown	0	5	0	H.R.'s	0	3	0	OBP%	0	2	0
Golden Glove	3	3	9	R.B.I's	0	3	0	SLG %	0	2	0
All-Star	7	2	14	Hits	0	2	0	OBPS%	0	2	0
Games	0	2	0	S.B.	0	2	0	Totals			0
Totals			35	Totals			0	Grand Total Add-On			35

Hall of Fame Points	
Career Points	24.500
Post Season Points	5.050
World Series Points	8.950
Career Add-On Points	35.000
Writers Association Pts.	0.000
Military/Lifetime Achievement	20.000
Grand Total HOF Points	93.500

The Baseball Hall of Fame

Statistical Review of Potential Left Fielders for the Hall of Fame

Player	Years Played	Career Pts.	Post Season Pts.	World Series Pts.	Add-On Pts.	Mil/LT Pts.	Total HOF Pts.	Needed HOF Votes	Comments
Players Needing to be Inducted									
None						0		0	Inducted
Players Needing to be Voted into the Hall of Fame by the BBWAA									
Belle, Albert	12	63.250	5.950	6.850	28.000	0	104.050	16	Need Voting
Foster, George	18	47.250	4.550	5.150	42.000	0	98.950	12	Need Voting
Holliday, Matt	15	63.000	8.500	4.650	24.000	0	100.150	10	Need Voting
Players Not Meeting the Statistical Requirements									
Alou, Moises	17	60.500	4.100	8.950	12.000	0	85.550	N/A	DMR
Anderson, Garrett	17	50.250	4.500	2.350	16.000	0	75.100	N/A	DMR
Carter, Joe	16	53.500	4.150	4.000	19.600	0	79.700	N/A	DMR
Howard, Frank	16	42.000	0.000	3.700	26.000	0	71.700	N/A	DMR
Johnson, Bob	13	62.250	0.000	0.000	20.000	0	82.250	N/A	DMR
Kellar, Charlie	13	45.000	0.0000	10.930	16.000	0	77.930	N/A	DMF
Magee, Sherry	16	56.250	0.000	1.4850	31.000	0	88.735	N/A	DMR
Williams, Ken	14	52.750	0.000	0.000	10.000	0	62.750	N/A	DMR

<u>Hall of Fame Statistical Requirements:</u>

All Players achieving the total of 110.000, or greater, Total Hall of Fame Points, shall be Inducted after five (5) years of retirement. This provision can be waived due to the death by a **75% vote of the 25 Panel BBWAA's**. Individuals receiving less than the required 110.000 Hall of Fame Points are eligible for Election after five (5) years of retirement. A 25 person BBWAA will determine the Players that will be Inducted and vote on the Players needing to be elected. An example of those needing to be elected are as follows: Player "A" has a total of 95 Hall of Fame Points and will need 15 of the (25) BBWAA votes to be Elected in the following year.

Left Fielders Needing to be Inducted

No Players Have Reached the

110.000 Hall of Fame Statistical Induction Criteria

Belle, Albert "Joey"

Personal Life

Albert Jojuan Belle born August 25, 1966, and his fraternal twin, Terry, were born on August 25, 1966, in Shreveport, Louisiana, to Albert Belle Sr., and Carrie Belle. He played college baseball at Louisiana State and made 1st team All-SEC in 1986 & 1987.

Belle had a daughter with a woman in 2000 that produced a daughter. In 2005, Belle married Melissa Lynn Galus and they have two daughters.

Baseball Career

The Cleveland Indians drafted in the second round of the 1987 MLB draft. In 1,539 games over 12 seasons, Belle posted a .295 batting average with 974 runs, 369 doubles, 21 triples, 381 home runs, 1239 RBI, 88 stolen bases, 683 bases on balls, .369 on-base percentage and .564 slugging percentage. Defensively, he recorded a .976 fielding percentage playing the outfield. His career was cut short due to having osteoarthritis in his hips which caused Belle to retire much earlier than he should have.

Achievements:

- 3-Time AL RBI leader (1993, 1995-tied with Mo Vaughn, 1996).
- 2-Time AL slugging percentage leader (1995, 1998).
- 5-time Silver Slugger (1993, 1994, 1995, 1996, 1998)
- 5-Time All-Star (1993, 1994, 1995, 1996, 1997).
- AL leader in total bases (1994, 1995, 1998) & 1-Time AL home run leader (1995)

Hall of Fame

Belles was eligible for Hall of Fame in 2006 but in 2007, he received 3.5% and was dropped. Belle was eligible for the 2023 Game Era ballet with the results unavailable.

Analysis

Belles 104.050 Hall of Fame Point Total should get him elected by the BBWAA but due to the Character Clause, his statistics should be in the Hall without a plaque.

A Fan's Perspective

Belle, Albert

Left Fielder Potential Hall of Fame Inductee

Positions		Born :	August 25, 1966	Height:	6'1"	USC	185	cm
Left Fielder		From:	Shreveport, LA	Weight:	190	lbs.	85	Kg.
		Bats:	Right	Debut:	July 15, 1989			
		Throws:	Right	Last Game:	October 1, 2000			

Year	Age	Tm	Lg	G	PA	AB	R	H	2B	3B	HR	RBI	SB	CS	BB	SO	BA	OBP	SLG	OPS	TB	HBP	Awards
1989	22	CLE	AL	62	234	218	22	49	8	4	7	37	2	2	12	55	0.225	0.269	0.394	0.664	86	2	
1990	23	CLE	AL	9	25	23	1	4	0	0	1	3	0	0	1	6	0.174	0.208	0.304	0.513	7	0	
1991	24	CLE	AL	123	496	461	60	130	31	2	28	95	3	1	25	99	0.282	0.323	0.540	0.863	249	5	
1992	25	CLE	AL	153	651	585	81	152	23	1	34	112	8	2	52	128	0.260	0.320	0.477	0.797	279	4	MVP-23
1993	26	CLE	AL	159	693	594	93	172	36	3	38	129	23	12	76	96	0.290	0.370	0.552	0.922	328	8	AS,MVP-7,SS
1994	27	CLE	AL	106	480	412	90	147	35	2	36	101	9	6	58	71	0.357	0.438	0.714	1.152	294	5	AS,MVP-3,SS
1995	28	CLE	AL	143	631	546	121	173	52	1	50	126	5	2	73	80	0.317	0.401	0.690	1.091	377	6	AS,MVP-2,SS
1996	29	CLE	AL	158	715	602	124	187	38	3	48	148	11	0	99	87	0.311	0.410	0.623	1.033	375	7	AS,MVP-3,SS
1997	30	CHW	AL	161	701	634	90	174	45	1	30	116	4	4	53	105	0.274	0.332	0.491	0.823	311	6	AS
1998	31	CHW	AL	163	706	609	113	200	48	2	49	152	6	4	81	84	0.328	0.399	0.655	1.055	399	1	MVP-8,SS
1999	32	BAL	AL	161	722	610	108	181	36	1	37	117	17	3	101	82	0.297	0.400	0.541	0.941	330	7	
2000	33	BAL	AL	141	622	559	71	157	37	1	23	103	0	5	52	68	0.281	0.342	0.474	0.817	265	4	
162 Game Avg.				162	703	616	103	182	41	2	40	130	9	4	72	101	0.295	0.369	0.564	0.933	347	6	
CLE (8 yrs)				913	3925	3441	592	1014	223	16	242	751	61	25	396	622	0.295	0.369	0.580	0.949	1995	37	
BAL (2 yrs)				302	1344	1169	179	338	73	2	60	220	17	8	153	150	0.289	0.374	0.509	0.882	595	11	
CHW (2 yrs)				324	1407	1243	203	374	93	3	79	268	10	8	134	189	0.301	0.366	0.571	0.937	710	7	
12 Yrs				1539	6676	5853	974	1726	389	21	381	1239	88	41	683	961	0.295	0.369	0.564	0.933	3300	55	**Career Pts.**
				3.000	0.000	0.000	3.750	2.000	0.000	0.000	8.000	6.750	1.000	0.000	2.000	0.000	5.500	4.500	11.750	10.500	4.500	0.000	**63.250**

Post Seasonal Play

Year	Age	Tm	Lg	G	PA	AB	R	H	2B	3B	HR	RBI	SB	CS	BB	SO	BA	OBP	SLG	OPS	TB	HBP	
1995	28	CLE	ALDS	3	15	11	3	3	1	0	1	3	0	0	4	3	0.273	0.467	0.636	1.103	7	0	
1995	28	CLE	ALCS	5	22	18	1	4	1	0	1	1	0	0	3	5	0.222	0.364	0.444	0.808	8	1	
1996	29	CLE	ALDS	4	18	15	2	3	0	0	2	6	1	0	3	2	0.200	0.333	0.600	0.933	9	0	
				12	55	44	6	10	2	0	4	10	1	0	10	10	0.227	0.382	0.545	0.937	24	1	**Post Seaon Pts.**
				0.400	0.000	0.000	0.250	0.250	0.000	0.000	0.400	0.400	0.250	0.000	0.400	0.000	0.000	1.000	1.200	1.000	0.400	0.000	**5.950**

World Series Play

Year	Age	Tm	Lg	G	PA	AB	R	H	2B	3B	HR	RBI	SB	CS	BB	SO	BA	OBP	SLG	OPS	TB	HBP	
1995	28	CLE	WS	6	24	17	4	4	0	0	2	4	0	1	7	5	0.235	0.458	0.588	1.047	10	0	
				6	24	17	4	4	0	0	2	4	0	1	7	5	0.235	0.458	0.588	1.047	10	0	**World Series Pts.**
				0.400	0.000	0.000	0.250	0.250	0.000	0.000	0.400	0.250	0.000	0.000	0.400	0.000	0.250	2.000	1.200	1.200	0.250	0.000	**6.850**

Yearly Points Leading the League

Category	Times	Points	Total	Category	Times	Points	Total	Categ	Times	Points	Total		Hall of Fame Points	
MVP	0	7	0	B.A.	0	3	0	T. B.	3	2	6	Career Points		63.250
Rookie of Yea	0	5	0	Runs	1	2	2	B.O.B.	0	2	0	Post Season Points		5.950
Triple Crown	0	5	0	H.R.'s	1	3	3	OBP%	0	2	0	World Series Points		6.850
Golden Glove	0	3	0	R.B.I's	3	3	9	SLG %	2	2	4	Career Add-On Points		28.000
All-Star	0	2	0	Hits	0	2	0	OBPS%	1	2	2	Writers Association Pts.		0.000
Games	1	2	2	S.B.	0	2	0	Totals			12	Military/Lifetime Achievement		0.000
Totals			2	Totals			14	Grand Total Add-On Points			28	Grand Total HOF Points		104.050

Foster, George

Personal Life

George Arthur Foster (born December 1, 1948) in Tuscaloosa, Alabama, to George and Regina (Beale) Foster. He has an older brother, John, and an older sister, Mamie.

Foster married Shelia Roberts on November 3, 1977, with the couple having two daughters, Shawna, and Starr.

Baseball Career

The Giants drafted Foster in the third round by the Giants in 1968, he advanced through their system and in 1971 Foster made the Giants' roster but was traded to the Reds Foster. In 1975, the Reds installed Foster as the regular left fielder. Foster compiled a .274 batting average,1,925 hits, 986 runs, 348 home runs, 1,239 RBI, and a .984 fielding percentage in the outfield. In 23 post-season games, he hit .289, 11 runs, 3 home runs, 12 runs batted in.

Achievements

- 5-time NL All-Star (1976-1979 & 1981)
- 5-Times received VP votes (1976, 1977 (Winning the award), 1978, 1979 & 1981).
- Two-Time World Series Champion 1975 & 1976.
- NL Silver Slugger Award Winner (1981) & NL Slugging Percentage Leader (1977)
- NL OPS Leader, NL Runs Scored Leader, & NL Total Bases Leader (1977).
- 2-time NL Home Runs Leader (1977 & 1978) & 3-time NL RBI Leader (1976 - 1978).
- 20-Home Run Seasons: 10 (1975-1981 & 1983-1985)
- 100 RBI Seasons: 3 (1976, 1977 & 1978) & 100 Runs Scored Seasons: 1 (1977)

Hall of Fame

Foster became eligible in 1989 and dropped off after receiving only 4.1% of the vote in 1995. Foster is eligible via the Classic Baseball Era Committee in 2025.

Summary Analysis

Fosters 98.950 Hall of Fame Score indicates he should be elected by the BBWAA.

A Fan's Perspective

Foster, George **Left Fielder Potential Hall of Fame Inductee**

Positions	Born:	December 1, 1948	Height:	6' 1" USC 185 cm
Left Fielder	From:	Tuscaloosa, AL	Weight:	180 lbs. 81 Kg.
	Bats:	Right	Debut:	September 10, 1969
	Throws:	Right	Last Game:	September 6, 1986

Year	Age	Tm	Lg	G	PA	AB	R	H	2B	3B	HR	RBI	SB	CS	BB	SO	BA	OBP	SLG	OPS	TB	HBP	Awards
1969	20	SFG	NL	9	5	5	1	2	0	0	0	1	0	0	0	1	0.400	0.400	0.400	0.800	2	0	
1970	21	SFG	NL	9	21	19	2	6	1	1	1	4	0	0	2	5	0.316	0.381	0.632	1.013	12	0	
1971	22	TOT	NL	140	514	473	50	114	23	4	13	58	7	7	29	120	0.241	0.292	0.389	0.681	184	7	
1971	22	SFG	NL	36	112	105	11	28	5	0	3	8	0	1	6	27	0.267	0.304	0.400	0.704	42	0	
1971	22	CIN	NL	104	402	368	39	86	18	4	10	50	7	6	23	93	0.234	0.289	0.386	0.675	142	7	
1972	23	CIN	NL	59	152	145	15	29	4	1	2	12	2	1	5	44	0.200	0.230	0.283	0.513	41	1	
1973	24	CIN	NL	17	43	39	6	11	3	0	4	5	0	1	4	7	0.282	0.349	0.667	1.016	26	0	
1974	25	CIN	NL	106	314	276	31	73	18	0	7	41	3	2	30	52	0.264	0.343	0.408	0.749	112	4	
1975	26	CIN	NL	134	511	463	71	139	24	4	23	78	2	1	40	73	0.300	0.356	0.518	0.875	240	3	
1976	27	CIN	NL	144	627	562	86	172	21	9	29	121	17	3	52	89	0.306	0.364	0.530	0.894	298	4	AS,MVP-2
1977	28	CIN	NL	158	689	615	124	197	31	2	52	149	8	4	61	107	0.320	0.382	0.631	1.013	388	5	AS,MVP-1
1978	29	CIN	NL	158	687	604	97	170	26	7	40	120	4	4	70	138	0.281	0.360	0.546	0.906	330	7	AS,MVP-6
1979	30	CIN	NL	121	505	440	68	133	18	3	30	98	0	2	58	105	0.302	0.386	0.561	0.948	247	3	AS,MVP-12
1980	31	CIN	NL	144	608	528	79	144	21	5	25	93	1	0	75	99	0.273	0.362	0.473	0.835	250	1	
1981	32	CIN	NL	108	472	414	64	122	23	2	22	90	4	0	51	75	0.295	0.373	0.519	0.892	215	3	AS,MVP-3,SS
1982	33	NYM	NL	151	608	550	64	136	23	2	13	70	1	1	50	123	0.247	0.309	0.367	0.676	202	2	
1983	34	NYM	NL	157	647	601	74	145	19	2	28	90	1	1	38	111	0.241	0.289	0.419	0.708	252	4	
1984	35	NYM	NL	146	595	553	67	149	22	1	24	86	2	2	30	122	0.269	0.311	0.443	0.754	245	6	
1985	36	NYM	NL	129	504	452	57	119	24	1	21	77	0	1	46	87	0.263	0.331	0.460	0.792	208	2	
1986	37	TOT	MLB	87	310	284	30	64	6	3	14	42	1	1	24	61	0.225	0.284	0.415	0.699	118	0	
1986	37	NYM	NL	72	256	233	28	53	6	1	13	38	1	1	21	53	0.227	0.289	0.429	0.718	100	0	
1986	37	CHW	AL	15	54	51	2	11	0	2	1	4	0	0	3	8	0.216	0.259	0.353	0.612	18	0	
162 Game Avg.				162	640	575	81	158	25	4	29	102	4	3	55	116	0.274	0.338	0.480	0.818	278	4	
CIN (11 yrs)				1253	5010	4454	680	1276	207	37	244	861	46	24	470	882	0.286	0.356	0.514	0.870	2289	36	
NYM (5 yrs)				655	2610	2389	290	602	94	7	99	361	5	6	185	496	0.252	0.307	0.422	0.728	1007	14	
SFG (3 yrs)				54	138	129	14	36	6	1	4	13	0	1	8	33	0.279	0.319	0.434	0.753	56	0	
CHW (1 yr)				15	54	51	2	11	0	2	1	4	0	0	3	8	0.216	0.259	0.353	0.612	18	0	
NL (18 yrs)				1962	7758	6972	984	1914	307	45	347	1235	51	31	663	1411	0.275	0.359	0.485	0.82	3352	52	
AL (1 yr)				15	54	51	2	11	0	2	1	4	0	0	3	8	0.216	0.259	0.353	0.612	18	0	
18 Yrs				1977	7812	7023	986	1925	307	47	348	1239	51	31	666	1419	0.274	0.338	0.480	0.818	3370	52	**Career Pts.**
				5.500	0.000	0.000	3.750	2.500	0.000	0.000	6.750	6.750	0.500	0.000	1.500	0.000	3.000	2.500	4.500	5.500	4.500	0.000	**47.250**

Post Season Pts.

Year	Age	Tm	Lg	G	PA	AB	R	H	2B	3B	HR	RBI	SB	CS	BB	SO	BA	OBP	SLG	OPS	TB	HBP	
1972	23	CIN	NLCS	1	0	0	1	0	0	0	0	0	0	0	0	0	0.000	0.000	0.000	0.000	0	0	
1975	26	CIN	NLCS	3	12	11	3	4	0	0	0	1	0	1	1	2	0.364	0.417	0.364	0.780	4	0	
1976	27	CIN	NLCS	3	13	12	2	2	0	0	2	4	0	0	0	4	0.167	0.154	0.667	0.821	8	0	
1979	30	CIN	NLCS	3	14	10	1	2	0	0	1	2	0	0	4	3	0.200	0.429	0.500	0.929	5	0	
				10	39	33	7	8	0	0	3	6	1	0	5	9	0.242	0.333	0.515	0.848	17	0	**Post Season Pts.**
				0.250	0.000	0.000	0.250	0.250	0.000	0.000	0.400	0.400	0.250	0.000	0.250	0.000	0.250	0.400	1.000	0.600	0.250	0.000	**4.550**

World Series Play

Year	Age	Tm	Lg	G	PA	AB	R	H	2B	3B	HR	RBI	SB	CS	BB	SO	BA	OBP	SLG	OPS	TB	HBP	
1973	23	CIN	WS	2	0	0	0	0	0	0	0	0	0	0	0	0	0.000	0.000	0.000	0.000	0	0.000	
1975	26	CIN	WS	7	30	29	1	8	1	0	0	2	1	1	1	1	0.276	0.300	0.310	0.610	9	0.000	
1976	27	CIN	WS	4	16	14	3	6	1	0	0	4	0	2	2	3	0.429	0.500	0.500	1.000	7	0.000	
				13	46	43	4	14	2	0	0	6	1	3	3	4	0.326	0.370	0.372	0.742	16	0.000	**World Series Pts.**
				0.400	0.000	0.000	0.250	0.600	0.000	0.000	0.000	0.400	0.250	0.000	0.250	0.000	1.400	0.600	0.000	0.400	0.600	0.000	**5.150**

Yearly Points Leading the League

Category	Times	Points	Total
MVP	1	7	7
Rookie of Year	0	5	0
Triple Crown	0	5	0
Golden Glove	0	3	0
All-Star	5	2	10
Games	0	2	0
Totals			17

Category	Times	Points	Total
B.A.	0	3	0
Runs	1	2	2
H.R.'s	2	3	6
R.B.I's	3	3	9
Hits	0	2	0
S.B.	0	2	0
Totals			17

Categ	Times	Points	Total
T.B.	1	2	2
B.O.B.	0	2	0
OBP%	1	2	2
SLG %	1	2	2
OBPS%	1	2	2
Totals			8
Grand Total Add-On Points	42		

Hall of Fame Points	
Career Points	47.250
Post Season Points	4.550
World Series Points	5.150
Career Add-On Points	42.000
Writers Association Pts.	0.000
Military/Lifetime Achievement	0.000
Grand Total HOF Points	98.950

Holliday, Matt

Personal Life

Matthew Thomas Holliday (born January 15, 1980) to Tom & Kathy Holliday and raised in Stillwater, Oklahoma with older brother, Josh. grew up playing sports. At Stillwater High School, Holliday played both baseball and earned All-American honors in Both.

Holliday married Leslee Ann Smith December 30, 2000. The couple have four children: Jackson, Ethan, Gracy, and Reed.

Baseball Career

The Rockies selected him in the seventh round of the 1998 Major League Baseball draft. The Rockies assigned him to the Arizona League and he played in their system until he made his major league debut on April 16, 2004 and retired in 2018. For his career, he played 1903 games, had 316 home runs, and a .299/.379/.510 batting line.

Achievements:

- Led N.L. in hits 2007 and in RBIs 2007
- Led N.L. in Batting Average 2007 in Total Bases 2007
- 7-Times All-Star (2006, 2007, 2008, 2010, 2011, 2012 & 2015).
- 8-Times received MVP Votes (2006 – 2009, 2010, 2012, 2013 & 2014).
- 4-Times Silver Slugger (2006, 2007, 2008 &,2010).
- 5-Times 100 plus Runs Batted in (2006, 2007. 2009, 2010 & 2012).
- 4-Times 100 plus Scored (2006, 2007, 2008 & 2013).
- 10-Times 20 Plus home runs (2006 – 2014, and 2016).
- 1-Time World Series Winner with the Cardinals in 2011.

Hall of Fame

Holliday will appear on the Baseball Hall of Fame Ballet for the first time in 2024.

Summary Analysis

Holliday had a 100.150 Hall of Fame Point total and should be elected by the BBWAA.

Left Fielder Potential Hall of Fame Inductee

Holliday, Matt

Positions	Born :	January 15, 1980	Height: 6' 4" USC 193 cm
Left Fielder	From:	Stillwater, OK	Weight: 240 lbs. 108 kg
	Bats:	Right	Debut: April 16, 2004
	Throws:	Right	Last Game: October 1, 2018

Year	Age	Tm	Lg	G	PA	AB	R	H	2B	3B	HR	RBI	SB	CS	BB	SO	BA	OBP	SLG	OPS	TB	HSP	Awards
2004	24	COL	NL	121	439	400	65	116	31	3	14	57	3	3	31	86	0.290	0.349	0.488	0.837	195	6	RoY-5
2005	25	COL	NL	125	526	479	68	147	24	7	19	87	14	3	36	79	0.307	0.361	0.505	0.866	242	7	
2006	26	COL	NL	155	667	602	119	196	45	5	34	114	10	5	47	110	0.326	0.387	0.586	0.973	353	15	AS,MVP-15,SS
2007	27	COL	NL	158	713	636	120	216	50	6	36	137	11	4	63	126	0.340	0.405	0.607	1.012	386	10	AS,MVP-2,SS
2008	28	COL	NL	139	623	539	107	173	38	2	25	88	28	2	74	104	0.321	0.409	0.538	0.947	290	8	AS,MVP-18,SS
2009	29	TOT	MLB	156	670	581	94	182	39	3	24	109	14	7	72	101	0.313	0.394	0.515	0.909	299	10	MVP-16
2009	29	OAK	AL	93	400	346	52	99	23	1	11	54	12	3	46	58	0.286	0.378	0.454	0.831	157	6	
2009	29	STL	NL	63	270	235	42	83	16	2	13	55	2	4	26	43	0.353	0.419	0.604	1.023	142	4	
2010	30	STL	NL	158	675	596	95	188	45	1	28	103	9	5	69	93	0.312	0.390	0.532	0.922	317	8	AS,MVP-12,SS
2011	31	STL	NL	124	516	446	83	132	36	0	22	75	2	1	60	93	0.296	0.388	0.525	0.912	234	8	AS
2012	32	STL	NL	157	688	599	95	177	36	2	27	102	4	4	75	132	0.295	0.379	0.497	0.877	298	9	AS,MVP-11
2013	33	STL	NL	141	602	520	103	156	31	1	22	94	6	1	69	86	0.300	0.389	0.490	0.879	255	9	MVP-23
2014	34	STL	NL	156	667	574	83	156	37	0	20	90	4	1	74	100	0.272	0.370	0.441	0.811	253	17	MVP-14
2015	35	STL	NL	73	277	229	24	64	16	1	4	35	2	1	39	49	0.279	0.394	0.410	0.804	94	6	AS
2016	36	STL	NL	110	426	382	48	94	20	1	20	62	0	0	85	71	0.246	0.322	0.461	0.782	176	0	
2017	37	NYY	AL	105	427	373	50	86	18	0	19	64	1	0	46	114	0.231	0.316	0.432	0.748	161	3	
2018	38	COL	NL	25	65	53	3	15	2	0	2	1	0	0	12	38	0.281	0.415	0.434	0.849	23	0	
162 Game Avg.				162	679	597	98	178	40	3	27	104	9	3	68	116	0.299	0.379	0.510	0.889	304	11	
STL (8 yrs)				982	4121	3581	573	1048	237	8	156	616	29	17	447	667	0.293	0.380	0.494	0.874	1769	69	
COL (6 yrs)				723	3033	2709	482	863	190	23	130	486	66	17	283	523	0.319	0.387	0.550	0.936	1489	46	
NYY (1 yr)				105	427	373	50	86	18	0	19	64	1	0	46	114	0.231	0.316	0.432	0.748	161	3	
OAK (1 yr)				93	400	346	52	99	23	1	11	54	12	3	46	58	0.286	0.378	0.454	0.831	157	6	
NL (14 yrs)				1705	7154	6290	1055	1911	427	31	286	1102	95	34	710	1190	0.304	0.382	0.518	0.900	3258	115	
AL (2 yrs)				198	827	719	102	185	41	1	30	118	13	3	92	172	0.257	0.346	0.442	0.788	318	9	
15 Yrs				1903	7981	7009	1157	2096	468	32	336	1220	108	37	802	1362	0.299	0.379	0.510	0.889	3576	124	Career Pts.
				5.500	0.000	0.000	5.500	3.750	0.000	0.000	5.500	6.750	1.000	0.000	2.500	0.000	6.750	5.500	6.750	8.000	5.500	0.000	63.000

Post Season Play

Year	Age	Tm	Lg	G	PA	AB	R	H	2B	3B	HR	RBI	SB	CS	BB	SO	BA	OBP	SLG	OPS	TB	HSP
2007	27	COL	NLDS	3	13	13	2	3	0	0	2	3	0	0	0	3	0.231	0.231	0.692	0.923	9	0
2007	27	COL	NLCS	4	17	15	3	5	0	0	2	4	0	0	1	6	0.333	0.412	0.733	1.145	11	1
2009	29	STL	NLDS	3	13	12	1	2	0	0	1	1	0	0	0	2	0.167	0.231	0.417	0.647	5	1
2011	31	STL	NLDS	4	10	9	2	2	0	0	0	0	0	0	0	3	0.222	0.300	0.222	0.522	2	1
2011	31	STL	NLCS	6	26	23	6	10	2	0	1	5	0	1	3	7	0.435	0.500	0.652	1.152	15	0
2012	32	STL	NLWC	1	4	3	2	2	0	0	1	1	0	0	0	0	0.667	0.750	1.667	2.417	5	1
2012	32	STL	NLDS	5	24	21	2	4	1	0	0	4	0	0	2	1	0.190	0.292	0.238	0.530	5	1
2012	32	STL	NLCS	6	26	25	1	5	0	0	0	2	1	0	0	4	0.200	0.231	0.200	0.431	5	1
2013	33	STL	NLDS	5	21	20	4	6	1	0	1	2	0	0	1	2	0.300	0.333	0.500	0.833	10	0
2013	33	STL	NLCS	6	25	25	2	5	2	0	1	3	0	0	0	4	0.200	0.200	0.400	0.600	10	0
2014	34	STL	NLDS	4	16	15	3	4	0	0	1	3	0	0	1	5	0.267	0.313	0.867	0.779	7	0
2014	34	STL	NLCS	5	22	22	2	5	1	0	0	0	0	0	0	5	0.227	0.227	0.273	0.500	6	0
2015	35	STL	NLDS	4	17	16	2	2	0	0	0	1	0	0	1	3	0.125	0.176	0.125	0.301	2	0
2017	37	NYY	NLCS					Did not play in series														
2017	37	NYY	ALDS					Did not play in series														
2017	37	NYY	ALCS	1	3	3	0	0	0	0	0	0	0	0	0	0	0.000	0.000	0.000	0.000	0	0
2018	38	COL	NLCS	1	3	3	0	1	1	0	0	0	0	0	0	2	0.333	0.333	0.667	1.000	2	0
2018	38	COL	NLDS	3	6	5	0	1	0	0	0	0	0	0	1	2	0.200	0.333	0.200	0.533	1	0
				61	246	230	32	57	8	0	10	29	1	1	10	50	0.248	0.397	0.412	0.709	95	6	Post Season Pts.
				1.400	0.000	0.000	0.800	1.000	0.000	0.000	1.000	1.200	0.250	0.000	0.800	0.000	0.250	0.000	0.400	0.400	1.000	0.000	8.500

World Series Play

Year	Age	Tm	Lg	G	PA	AB	R	H	2B	3B	HR	RBI	SB	CS	BB	SO	BA	OBP	SLG	OPS	TB	HSP
2007	27	COL	WS	4	17	17	1	5	0	0	1	3	0	0	0	3	0.294	0.294	0.471	0.765	8	0
2011	31	STL	WS	6	26	19	5	3	1	0	0	0	0	0	7	4	0.158	0.385	0.211	0.595	4	0
2013	33	STL	WS	6	25	24	4	6	1	1	2	5	0	0	1	5	0.25	0.28	0.625	0.905	15	0
				16	68	60	10	14	2	1	3	8	0	0	8	12	0.233	0.324	0.450	0.774	27	0	World Season Pts.
				0.6	0.000	0.000	0.600	0.600	0.000	0.000	0.400	0.400	0.000	0.000	0.400	0.000	0.750	0.000	0.000	0.400	1.000	0.000	4.650

Yearly Points Leading the League

Category	Times	Points	Total
MVP	0	7	0
Rookie of Year	0	5	0
Triple Crown	0	5	0
Golden Glove	0	3	0
All-Star	7	2	14
Games	0	2	0
Totals			14

Category	Times	Points	Total
B.A.	1	3	3
Runs	0	2	0
H.R.'s	0	3	0
R.B.I's	1	3	3
Hits	1	2	2
S.B.	0	2	0
Totals			8

Catego	Times	Points	Total
T.B.	1	2	2
B.O.B.	0	2	0
OBP%	0	2	0
SLG %	0	2	0
OBPS%	0	2	0
Totals			2
Grand Total Add-On Points			24

Hall of Fame Points	
Career Points	63.000
Post Season Points	8.500
World Series Points	4.650
Career Add-On Points	24.000
Writers Association Pts.	0.000
Military/Lifetime Achievement	0.000
Grand Total HOF Points	100.15

The Baseball Hall of Fame

Statistical Review of Potential Center Fielders for the Hall of Fame

Player	Years Played	Career Pts.	Post Season Pts.	World Series Pts.	Add-On Pts.	Mil/LT Pts.	Total HOF Pts.	Needed HOF Votes	Comments
Players Needing to be Inducted									
Beltran, Carlos	20	87.250	15.800	2.450	22.000	0.000	134.500	0	Inducted
Jones, Andrew	17	55.500	10.200	5.550	48.000	0.000	119.250	0	Inducted
Lofton, Kenny	17	64.500	11.750	5.100	36.000	0.000	117.350	0	Inducted
Lynn, Fred	17	51.250	9.850	3.700	55.000	0.000	119.800	0	Inducted
Murphy, Dale	18	53.280	1.375	0.000	58.000	0.000	112.655	0	Inducted
Williams, Bernie	16	63.500	17.000	8.050	25.000	0.000	113.550	0	Inducted
Players Needing to be Voted into the Hall of Fame by the BBWAA									
Damon, Johnny	18	71.500	9.390	7.500	8.000	0.000	96.390	14	Need Voting
Edmonds, Jim	17	64.000	12.450	1.500	32.000	0.000	109.950	1	Need Voting
Finley, Steve	19	62.000	5.300	3.850	23.000	0.000	94.150	16	Need Voting
Hunter, Tori	19	60.250	7.200	0.000	37.000	0.000	104.450	6	Need Voting
Players Not Meeting the Statistical Requirements									
Burkes, Ellis	18	58.750	3.750	0.000	14.000	0.000	76.500	N/A	DMF
Butler, Brett	17	53.250	1.750	2.650	12.000	0.000	69.650	N/A	DMR
Cedano, Cesar	17	39.500	1.900	1.250	23.000	0.000	65.650	N/A	DMR
Dimaggio, Dominic	11	33.000	0.000	2.000	22.000	0.000	69.000	N/A	DMR
McGhee, Willie	18	39.250	4.450	7.050	29.000	0.000	79.750	N/A	DMR
Murcer, Bobby	17	41.250	0.750	0.500	17.000	8.000	67.500	N/A	DMF
Van Haltren, George	19	44.000	0.000	0.000	22.000	0.000	66.000	N/A	DMR

Hall of Fame Statistical Requirements:

All Players achieving the total of 110.000, or greater, Total Hall of Fame Points, shall be Inducted after five (5) years of retirement. This provision can be waived due to the death by a 75% vote of the 25 Panel BBWAA's. Individuals receiving less than the required 110.000 Hall of Fame Points are eligible for Election after five (5) years of retirement. A 25 person BBWAA will determine the Players that will be Inducted and vote on the Players needing to be elected. An example of those needing to be elected are as follows: Player "A" has a total of 95 Hall of Fame Points and will need 15 of the (25) BBWAA votes to be Elected in the following year.

Center Fielders Needing to be Inducted.

- **Carlos Beltran**
- **Andruw Jones**
- **Kenny Lofton**
- **Fred Lynn**
- **Dale Murphy**
- **Bernie Williams**

110.000 Hall of Fame Statistical Induction Criteria

Beltran, Carlos

Personal Life

Carlos Iván Beltrán (Spanish pronunciation) was born on April 24,1977, in Manati, Puerto Rico to Wilfredo, and Carmen. Carlos has three siblings an elder brother. Nino, and twin sisters Marie Liz and Liz Marie. In his youth, Beltrán excelled in many sports, and graduated from Fernando Callejo High School in 1995.

Beltrán married his wife Jessica Lugo on November 6, 1999. The couple have two daughters Ivana and Kiara along with one son Evan.

Baseball Career

The Kansas City Royals selected Beltrán in the second round of the draft and assigned him to the Rookie-level Gulf Coast League. He taught himself to hit left-handed, with advice from New York Yankees outfielder Bernie Williams and Royals coach Kevin Long. Beltran continued moving up the system until he made his major league debut on September 14, 1998. In 1999, Beltran won the job as the Royals' starting center fielder and leadoff hitter. He began hitting for power and was moved to the #3 slot in the batting order. Beltrán won the American League Rookie of the Year Award batting .293 with 22 home runs, 108 runs batted in and 27 stolen bases in 156 games played

From 1998 through 2005, Beltran played 1036 games, 699 runs scored, 1140 hits, 162 home runs, 699 runs-batted-in, 209 stolen bases, and a.282 batting average with a .356 on-base-percentage, .493 slugging percentage and an OPS of .849.

In January 2010, Beltrán had surgery on his knee and expected to miss 8–12 weeks. The Mets stated that the surgery was done without their consent, and the team expressed their disappointment with Beltrán's failure to inform the team of his injury and consent. In 2013, Beltrán played in 145 games with a .296 average, 24 HR's, and 84 RBI. He played in his 2,000th game and selected to his third straight All-Star Game. In October, Beltrán was the recipient of the Roberto Clemente Award. In the 2013 National League Division Series against the Pirates, Beltrán had 4 hits in 18 at-bats, hitting 2 home runs and 6 RBI in the series. In game 1 of the 2013 National League Championship Series against the Dodgers, Beltrán hit a double at the bottom of the 3rd inning to tie the game 2–2. At the bottom of the 13th inning, Beltrán hit a walk-off single off of Kenley Jansen, giving the Cardinals a 3–2 victory. For the NLCS, Beltrán had 6 hits and 6 RBI in 21 at-bats. The Cardinals won the series 4–2, and Beltrán advanced to the first World Series in his career. In Game 1 of the 2013 World Series against the Red Sox, Beltrán injured his ribs and despite the injury, Beltrán would play in all 6 games of the series, batting .294 with 5 hits and 3 RBI as the Cardinals fell to the Red Sox.

From 2006 through 2013, Beltran played 1028 games, 647 runs scored, 1088 hits, 196 home runs, 680 runs-batted-in, 99 stolen bases, and a.285 batting average with a .356 on-base-percentage, .513 slugging percentage and an OPS of .869.

Beltrán filed for free agency after the World Series and on December 6, 2013, Beltrán agreed to a three-year, deal to join the New York Yankees. On May 15, he placed on the 15-day disabled list on May 15, 2014, and activated on June 5, 2014. Beltran was used primarily as a designated hitter for the remainder of the season as he was limited to 109 games. Beltrán batted .233 with 15 home runs and 49 RBI. In 2014, due to a variety of injuries, Beltrán had a .233 average in 109 games, with 15 homers and 49 RBI. In 2015, he played 133 games, bouncing back to .276 with 34 doubles and 19 homers, driving in 67 runs. In 2015, Beltrán ended the regular season with 19 home runs, 67 RBIs and a .276 average in 133 games.

On December 3, 2016, Beltrán signed a one-year, contract to return to the Houston Astros for the 2017 season. The Astros won 101 games and clinched the AL West division title and faced the Boston Red Sox in the best-of-five ALDS. In Game 4 on October 9, Beltrán hit a ninth-inning RBI double that proved to be the deciding run in a 5–4 victory that clinched the ALDS for the Astros. The Astros advanced to the World Series and opposed the Los Angeles Dodgers. During the series, Beltrán registered three plate appearances over three games, going 0–3. The Astros defeated the Dodgers in seven games, making Beltrán a World Series champion. Beltrán announced his retirement from playing on November 13, 2017.

In 2,586 games over 20 seasons, Beltrán posted a .279 batting average with 1,582 runs, 435 home runs, 1,587 RBI, 312 stolen bases, 1,084 bases on balls, .350 on-base percentage and .486 slugging percentage. He finished his career with a .986 fielding percentage. In 65 postseason games, Beltrán batted .307 (66-for-215) with 45 runs, 15 doubles, 16 home runs, 42 RBI, 11 stolen bases and 37 walks. He broke the 1.000 OPS mark in four different playoff series. Beltrán also had a 100% stolen base percentage (11-for-11) during the playoffs, which are the most stolen bases without being caught.

Achievements:

- 1999 AL Rookie of the Year Award & 3-time NL Gold Glove Winner (2006-2008).
- 9-time All-Star (2004-2007, 2009, 2011-2013 & 2016)
- 2-time NL Silver Slugger Award Winner (2006 & 2007)
- 20-Home Run Seasons: 12 (1999, 2001-2004, 2006-2008, 2011-2013 & 2016)
- 4-Times 30-plus Home Run Seasons: (2004, 2006 (40), 2007 & 2012).
- 100 RBI Seasons: 8 (1999, 2001-2004 & 2006-2008)
- 100 Runs Scored Seasons: 7 (1999, 2001-2004, 2006 & 2008)
- 8-Time Received MVP Votes (2003, 2004, 2006, 2007, 2011 & 2012)
- Won one World Series with the Houston Astros in 2017

Hall of Fame

In 2023 Beltran became eligible and had 181 votes (46.5%) out of 297 ballots cast by the Baseball Writers' Association of America. He is eligible for election by the BBWAA in 2024.

Summary Analysis

Carlos Beltran's has 134.500 Statistical Hall of Fame Points and is over the Induction Score of 110.000. He is arguably one of the ten best center fielders in the history of baseball and needs to be enshrined the next time he is on the ballot.

Beltran, Carlos

Centerfield Potential Hall of Fame Inductee

Positions	**Born :**	April 24, 1977	**Heigh**	6' 1"	**USC**	185	cm
Outfielder	**From:**	Manati, Puerto Rico	**Weigl**	215	**lbs.**	97	**Kg.**
	Bats:	Both	**Debut:**	September 14, 1998			
	Throws:	Right	**Last Game:**	October 1, 2017			

Year	Age	Tm	Lg	G	PA	AB	R	H	2B	3B	HR	RBI	SB	CS	BB	SO	BA	OBP	SLG	OPS	TB	HBP	Awards
1998	21	KCR	AL	14	63	58	12	16	5	3	0	7	3	0	3	12	0.276	0.317	0.466	0.783	27	1	
1999	22	KCR	AL	156	723	663	112	194	27	7	22	108	27	8	46	123	0.293	0.337	0.454	0.791	301	4	RoY-1
2000	23	KCR	AL	98	413	372	49	92	15	4	7	44	13	0	35	69	0.247	0.309	0.366	0.675	136	0	
2001	24	KCR	AL	155	680	617	106	189	32	12	24	101	31	1	52	120	0.306	0.362	0.514	0.876	317	5	
2002	25	KCR	AL	162	722	637	114	174	44	7	29	105	35	7	71	135	0.273	0.346	0.501	0.847	319	4	
2003	26	KCR	AL	141	602	521	102	160	14	10	26	100	41	4	72	81	0.307	0.389	0.522	0.911	272	2	MVP-9
2004	27	TOT	MLB	159	708	599	121	160	36	9	38	104	42	3	92	101	0.267	0.367	0.548	0.915	328	7	AS,MVP-12
2004	27	KCR	AL	69	309	266	51	74	19	2	15	51	14	3	37	44	0.278	0.367	0.534	0.901	142	2	
2004	27	HOU	NL	90	399	333	70	86	17	7	23	53	28	0	55	57	0.258	0.368	0.559	0.926	186	5	
2005	28	NYM	NL	151	650	582	83	155	34	2	16	78	17	6	56	96	0.266	0.330	0.414	0.744	241	2	AS
2006	29	NYM	NL	140	617	510	127	140	38	1	41	116	18	3	95	99	0.275	0.388	0.594	0.982	303	4	AS,MVP-4,GG,SS
2007	30	NYM	NL	144	636	554	93	153	33	3	33	112	23	2	69	111	0.276	0.353	0.525	0.878	291	2	AS,MVP-20,GG,SS
2008	31	NYM	NL	161	706	606	116	172	40	5	27	112	25	3	92	96	0.284	0.376	0.500	0.876	303	1	MVP-21,GG
2009	32	NYM	NL	81	357	308	50	100	22	1	10	48	11	1	47	43	0.325	0.415	0.500	0.915	154	1	AS
2010	33	NYM	NL	64	255	220	21	56	11	3	7	27	3	1	30	39	0.255	0.341	0.427	0.768	94	1	
2011	34	TOT	NL	142	598	520	78	156	39	6	22	84	4	2	71	88	0.300	0.385	0.525	0.910	273	3	AS,MVP-20
2011	34	NYM	NL	98	419	353	61	102	30	2	15	66	3	0	60	61	0.289	0.391	0.513	0.904	181	2	
2011	34	SFG	NL	44	179	167	17	54	9	4	7	18	1	2	11	27	0.323	0.369	0.551	0.920	92	1	
2012	35	STL	NL	151	619	547	83	147	26	1	32	97	13	6	65	124	0.269	0.346	0.495	0.842	271	2	AS,MVP-26
2013	36	STL	NL	145	600	554	79	164	30	3	24	84	2	1	38	90	0.296	0.339	0.491	0.830	272	1	AS
2014	37	NYY	AL	109	449	403	46	94	23	0	15	49	3	1	37	80	0.233	0.301	0.402	0.703	162	4	
2015	38	NYY	AL	133	531	478	57	132	34	1	19	67	0	0	45	85	0.276	0.337	0.471	0.808	225	2	
2016	39	TOT	AL	151	593	552	73	163	33	0	29	93	1	0	35	101	0.295	0.337	0.513	0.850	283	2	AS
2016	39	NYY	AL	99	387	359	50	109	21	0	22	64	0	0	22	70	0.304	0.344	0.546	0.890	196	2	
2016	39	TEX	AL	52	206	193	23	54	12	0	7	29	1	0	13	31	0.280	0.325	0.451	0.776	87	0	
2017	40	HOU	AL	129	509	467	60	108	29	0	14	51	0	0	33	102	0.231	0.283	0.383	0.666	179	3	
162 Game Avg.				162	691	612	99	171	35	5	27	99	20	3	68	112	0.279	0.350	0.486	0.837	298	3	
KCR (7 yrs)				795	3512	3134	546	899	156	45	123	516	164	23	316	584	0.287	0.352	0.483	0.835	1514	18	
NYM (7 yrs)				839	3640	3133	551	878	208	17	149	559	100	16	449	545	0.280	0.369	0.500	0.869	1567	13	
NYY (3 yrs)				341	1367	1240	153	335	78	1	56	180	3	1	104	235	0.270	0.327	0.470	0.797	583	8	
STL (2 yrs)				296	1219	1101	162	311	56	4	56	181	15	7	103	214	0.282	0.343	0.493	0.836	543	3	
HOU (2 yrs)				219	908	800	130	194	46	7	37	104	28	0	88	159	0.243	0.320	0.456	0.776	365	8	
TEX (1 yr)				52	206	193	23	54	12	0	7	29	1	0	13	31	0.280	0.325	0.451	0.776	87	0	
SFG (1 yr)				44	179	167	17	54	9	4	7	18	1	2	11	27	0.323	0.369	0.551	0.920	92	1	
AL (11 yrs)				1317	5594	5034	782	1396	275	46	200	776	168	24	466	952	0.277	0.338	0.469	0.808	2363	29	
NL (10 yrs)				1269	5437	4734	800	1329	290	32	235	811	144	25	618	843	0.281	0.363	0.504	0.867	2388	22	
20 Yrs				2586	11031	9768	1582	2725	565	78	435	1587	312	49	1084	1795	0.279	0.350	0.486	0.837	4751	51	Career Pts.
				11.750	0.000	0.000	11.750	8.000	0.000	0.000	9.250	11.750	3.000	0.000	4.500	0.000	3.750	3.000	4.500	5.500	10.500	0.000	87.25

Post Season Play

Year	Age	Tm	Lg	G	PA	AB	R	H	2B	3B	HR	RBI	SB	CS	BB	SO	BA	OBP	SLG	OPS	TB	HBP	
2004	27	HOU	NLDS	5	24	22	9	10	2	0	4	9	2	0	1	4	0.455	0.500	1.091	1.591	24	1	
2004	27	HOU	NLCS	7	32	24	12	10	1	0	4	5	4	0	8	4	0.417	0.563	0.958	1.521	23	0	
2006	29	NYM	NLDS	3	14	9	2	2	0	0	0	1	1	0	5	2	0.222	0.500	0.222	0.722	2	0	
2006	29	NYM	NLCS	7	31	27	8	8	1	0	3	4	1	0	4	3	0.296	0.387	0.667	1.054	18	0	
2012	35	STL	NLCS	1	4	4	1	1	0	0	0	0	0	0	0	1	0.250	0.250	0.250	0.500	1	0	
2012	35	STL	NLDS	5	24	18	5	8	3	0	2	4	1	0	5	1	0.444	0.542	0.944	1.486	17	0	
2012	35	STL	NLCS	6	22	20	2	6	3	0	1	2	2	0	2	3	0.300	0.364	0.600	0.964	12	0	
2013	36	STL	NLDS	5	21	18	3	4	1	0	2	6	0	0	3	1	0.222	0.333	0.611	0.944	11	0	
2013	36	STL	NLCS	6	26	21	2	6	2	1	0	6	0	0	5	3	0.286	0.423	0.476	0.899	10	0	
2015	38	NYY	ALWC	1	4	4	0	1	0	0	0	0	0	0	0	2	0.250	0.250	0.250	0.500	1	0	
2016	39	TEX	ALDS	3	12	11	0	2	0	0	0	1	0	0	1	1	0.182	0.250	0.182	0.432	2	0	
2017	40	HOU	ALDS	3	6	5	0	2	1	0	0	1	0	0	1	1	0.400	0.500	0.600	1.100	3	0	
2017	40	HOU	ALCS	4	12	12	0	1	1	0	0	0	0	0	0	4	0.083	0.083	0.167	0.250	2	0	
				56	232	195	44	61	15	1	16	39	11	0	35	30	0.313	0.420	0.646	1.066	126	1	Post Season Pts:
				1.200	0.000	0.000	1.200	1.000	0.000	0.000	1.600	1.600	1.200	0.000	1.400	0.000	0.800	1.600	1.800	1.200	1.200	0.000	15.800

World Series Play

Year	Age	Tm	Lg	G	PA	AB	R	H	2B	3B	HR	RBI	SB	CS	BB	SO	BA	OBP	SLG	OPS	TB	HBP	
2013	36	STL	WS	6	21	17	1	5	0	0	0	3	0	0	2	2	0.294	0.400	0.294	0.694	5	1	
2017	40	HOU	WS	3	3	3	0	0	0	0	0	0	0	0	0	1	0.000	0.000	0.000	0.000	0	0	
				9	24	20	1	5	0	0	0	3	0	0	2	3	0.250	0.348	0.350	0.598	5	1	World Series Pts.
				0.400	0.000	0.000	0.250	0.250	0.000	0.000	0.000	0.250	0.000	0.000	0.250	0.000	0.400	0.400	0.000	0.000	0.250	0	2.45

Yearly Points Leading the League

Category	Times	Points	Total
MVP	0	7	0
Rookie of Yea	0	5	0
Triple Crown	0	5	0
Golden Glove	3	3	9
All-Star	9	2	18
Games	1	2	2
Totals			29

Category	Times	Points	Total
B.A.	0	3	0
Runs	0	2	0
H.R.'s	0	3	0
R.B.I's	0	3	0
Hits	0	2	0
S.B.	0	2	0
Totals			0

Categor	Times	Points	Total
T. B.	0	2	0
B.O.B.	0	2	0
OBP%	0	2	0
SLG %	0	2	0
OBPS%	0	2	0
Totals			0
Total Add-On Pts			29

Hall of Fame Points	
Career Points	87.250
Post Season Points	15.800
World Series Points	2.450
Career Add-On Points	29.000
Writers Association Pts.	0.000
Military/Lifetime Achievement	0.000
Grand Total HOF Points	134.500

Jones, Andruw "The Curacao Kid"

Personal Life

Andruw Rudolf Jones was born April 23, 1977 in the capital city of Williamstad of Curaçao, Willemstad, Netherlands Antilles to Henry Jones. No information about his mother, or siblings, was found. Jones's father, was a baseball player in Curacao noted for his speed and he helped teach his son the game. By age 11, Jones was on a team that traveled to Japan to play in a tournament. Jones was signed by Atlanta Braves and could handle any position on the field, but switched to the outfield.

Jones married Nicole Derick in 2002 in Marietta, GA. They are the parents of two sons, Druw and Andrean Jones, as well as a daughter Madison. Jones also has a son, Joshua, born in 2005, from an extra marital affair with Mélissa Vaillancourt.

Baseball Career

Andruw Jones signed with the Atlanta Braves organization as a free agent in 1993 at the age of 16. He hit .277/.340/.512 for the 1995 Macon Braves as a 18-year-old in full-season ball. He hit 25 home runs, 41 doubles and 5 triples, scored 104 runs and drove in 100, 70 walks and stole 56 bases. He led Atlanta farmhands in steals and runs. He tied for third in the affiliated minors in runs, was 5th in total bases (275) and led in extra-base hits and he won their Minor League Player of the Year Award. Jones added to his prospect stock in 1996, leading Braves minor leaguers in runs (115), total bases (290) and average (.339). *Baseball America* named him the best batting prospect and best defensive outfielder in the Carolina League. He was again named Baseball America's Minor League Player of the Year and promoted to the Braves at the end of 1996 and finished the season batting .217 with five home runs and 13 RBIs with the parent club. Jones was then selected to the Braves' postseason roster for the National League Championship Series against the Cardinals and batted .222 with a home run and 3 RBIs. The Braves won the Series and advanced to the World Series. In Game 1 of the 1996 World Series on October 20, 1996, Jones was able to demonstrate his talents on the national stage. He connected for two home runs to left field on his first two at bats as the Braves routed the New York Yankees 12–1. Jones became the youngest player ever to homer in the World Series at the age of 19 years, 180 days, breaking Mickey Mantle's record of 20 years, 362 days Jones became the Braves' everyday right fielder in 1997 and finished his rookie season with a .231 batting average, 18 home runs, and 70 runs batted in. Jones also showed his speed by stealing 20 bases. and finished 5th in Rookie of the Year voting. In 1998, he moved to center field and won his first of ten straight Gold Glove Awards. In the 1998 National League Division Series, Jones went 0 for 9 but did draw 3 walks. The Braves won the series against the Cubs and lost in the 1998 NLCS against the San Diego Padres, Jones batted .273 with a home run and two RBIs. Jones went on to hit .271 with 31 home runs and 90 runs batted in and stole 27 bases. From 1998 to 1999, he continued to increase his offensive production, and in 2000, Jones batted .303 with 36 home runs and 104 runs batted in (RBIs), making the All-Star team. He had a breakout season with his bat in 2000 with career highs up until that point in batting average (.303), home runs (36), and RBIs (104). Jones struggled in the N.L.D.S, against the Cardinals as the Braves lost the series.

From 1998 to 2007, Jones won 10 consecutive Gold Gloves. His 10 Gold Gloves for an outfielder ranks him in a tie for third for most Gold Gloves won by an outfielder. Jones is also one of five center fielders to record at least 400 putouts in a season six times. After the 2007 season, Jones signed with the Los Angeles Dodgers to a two-year deal. However, Jones struggled with the Dodgers, batting just .158 with three home runs and 14 RBIs. Jones ended his career with a .254 Batting Average, 434 Home Runs, 1289 Runs-Batted-In, .337 On-Base%, .486 SLG%, and an OBPS% of .823 His home run total was tied for 40th on the all-time home run list when he ended his career. However, Jones' weakness was hitting against breaking balls and hitting for good average. Only once in his career did Jones bat .300 or better (he batted .303 in 2000), Jones was also known for his speed early in his career which earned him the last playoff spot on the Braves' roster in 1996. Jones stole 20 or more bases from 1997 to 2000. However, his speed declined, and he never stole over 10 after 2001.

Jones' defensive prowess in center field and power at the plate during his peak helped put him in the conversation with some of the best we've seen at the position. His defense led to 10 Gold Glove Awards. He crushed 434 career home runs, including an MLB-leading 51 in 2005. From 1998-2006, he hit 319 of those homers while slugging .513. His years after playing in Atlanta, from 2008-12 with the Dodgers, Rangers, White Sox and Yankees, represented a steep drop-off when he slugged .424 and hit .210, with 66 homers in 435 games over those later years.

The Baseball Hall of Fame

Jones played 17 seasons in Major League Baseball with the Atlanta Braves, then the Los Angeles Dodgers, Texas Rangers, Chicago White Sox, and New York Yankees. Jones was a noted defensive specialist won Gold Glove Award every year from 1998 through 2007.

Achievements:

- 5-time NL All-Star (2000, 2002, 2003, 2005 & 2006).
- 10-time NL Gold Glove Winner (1998-2007).
- 5-Time received MVP Votes (2000, 2002, 2003, 2005 & 2006).
- Silver Slugger Award Winner (2005) & 20-Home Run Seasons: 10 (1998-2007).
- 30-Home Run Seasons: 7 (1998, 2000-2003, 2005 & 2006).
- 40-Home Run Seasons: 2 (2005 (51 HR's) & 2006).
- 5-Times stole 20 plus baes in a year (1997, 1998, 1999, 2000.
- 100 RBI Seasons: 5 (2000, 2001, 2003, 2005(Led League) & 2006).
- 100 Runs Scored Seasons: 4 (2000, 2001, 2003 & 2006).

Hall of Fame

Jones first appeared in 2018 on the BBWAA balloting when he received 7.3% of the vote. His support has increased to 58.1% in his 6th year of eligibility in the 2023 ballot.

Summary Analysis

Andruw Jones Statistical Hall of Fame Points is 119.250 and should have been inducted when eligible. He is one of four players to have won 10 Gold Gloves with 400 career home runs. Andruw Jones is a Hall of Famer.

A Fan's Perspective

Jones, Andruw — Center Fielder Potential Hall of Fame Inductee

Positions		Born:	April 23, 1977	April 23, 1977	Height:	6' 1" USC 185 cm
Centerfielder		From:	October 3, 2012	Willemstad, Curacao	Weight:	225 lbs. 102 Kg.
		Bats:	Right	Right	Debut:	August 15, 1990
		Throws:	Right	Right	Last Game:	October 3, 2012

Year	Age	Tm	Lg	G	D	AB	R	H	2B	3B	HR	RBI	SB	CS	BB	SO	BA	OBP	SLG	OPS	TB	HBP	Awards
1996	19	ATL	NL	31	113	106	11	23	7	1	5	13	3	0	7	29	0.217	0.265	0.443	0.709	47	0	
1997	20	ATL	NL	153	467	399	60	92	18	1	18	70	20	11	56	107	0.231	0.329	0.416	0.745	166	4	RoY-5
1998	21	ATL	NL	159	631	582	89	158	33	8	31	90	27	4	40	129	0.271	0.321	0.515	0.836	300	4	GG
1999	22	ATL	NL	162	679	592	97	163	35	5	26	84	24	12	76	103	0.275	0.365	0.483	0.848	286	9	GG
2000	23	ATL	NL	161	729	656	122	199	36	6	36	104	21	6	59	100	0.303	0.366	0.541	0.907	355	9	8,GG
2001	24	ATL	NL	161	693	625	104	157	25	2	34	104	11	4	56	142	0.251	0.312	0.461	0.772	288	3	GG
2002	25	ATL	NL	154	659	560	91	148	34	0	35	94	8	3	83	135	0.264	0.366	0.513	0.878	287	10	16,GG
2003	26	ATL	NL	156	659	595	101	165	28	2	36	116	4	3	53	125	0.277	0.338	0.513	0.851	305	5	13,GG
2004	27	ATL	NL	154	646	570	85	149	34	4	29	91	6	6	71	147	0.261	0.345	0.488	0.833	278	3	GG
2005	28	ATL	NL	160	672	586	95	154	24	3	51	128	5	3	64	112	0.263	0.347	0.575	0.922	337	15	2,GG,SS
2006	29	ATL	NL	156	669	565	107	148	29	0	41	129	4	1	81	127	0.262	0.363	0.531	0.894	300	13	11,GG
2007	30	ATL	NL	154	659	572	83	127	27	2	26	94	5	2	70	138	0.222	0.311	0.413	0.724	236	8	GG
2008	31	LAD	NL	75	238	209	21	33	8	1	3	14	0	1	27	76	0.158	0.256	0.249	0.505	52	1	
2009	32	TEX	AL	82	331	281	43	60	18	0	17	43	5	1	45	72	0.214	0.323	0.459	0.782	129	2	
2010	33	CHW	AL	107	328	278	41	64	12	1	19	48	9	2	45	73	0.23	0.341	0.486	0.827	135	3	
2011	34	NYY	AL	77	222	190	27	47	8	0	13	33	0	0	29	62	0.247	0.356	0.495	0.851	94	3	
2012	35	NYY	AL	94	269	233	27	46	7	0	14	34	0	0	28	71	0.197	0.294	0.408	0.701	95	5	
162 Game Avg.				162	639	561	89	143	28	3	32	95	11	4	66	129	0.254	0.337	0.486	0.823	272	7	
ATL (12 yrs)				1761	7276	6408	1045	1683	330	34	368	1117	138	55	717	1394	0.263	0.342	0.497	0.839	3185	83	
NYY (2 yrs)				171	491	423	54	93	15	0	27	67	0	0	57	133	0.220	0.322	0.447	0.769	189	8	
TEX (1 yr)				82	331	281	43	60	18	0	17	43	5	1	45	72	0.214	0.323	0.459	0.782	129	2	
LAD (1 yr)				75	238	209	21	33	8	1	3	14	0	1	27	76	0.158	0.256	0.249	0.505	52	1	
CHW (1 yr)				107	328	278	41	64	12	1	19	48	9	2	45	73	0.230	0.341	0.486	0.827	135	3	
NL (13 yrs)				1836	7514	6617	1066	1716	338	35	371	1131	138	56	744	1470	0.259	0.339	0.489	0.828	3237	84	
AL (4 yrs)				360	1150	982	138	217	45	1	63	158	14	3	147	278	0.221	0.328	0.461	0.789	453	13	
17 Yrs				2196	8664	7599	1204	1933	383	36	434	1289	152	59	891	1748	0.254	0.337	0.486	0.823	3690	97	Career Pts.
				8.000	0.000	0.000	5.500	2.500	0.000	0.000	9.250	6.750	1.500	0.000	3.000	0.000	1.500	2.000	4.500	5.500	5.500	0.000	55.500

Post Season Play

Year	Age	Tm	Lg	G	PA	AB	R	H	2B	3B	HR	RBI	SB	CS	BB	SO	BA	OBP	SLG	OPS	TB	HBP	
1996	19	ATL	NLDS	3	1	0	0	0	0	0	0	0	0	0	1	0	0.000	1.000	0.000	0.000	0	0	
1996	19	ATL	NLCS	5	12	9	3	2	0	0	1	3	0	0	3	2	0.222	0.417	0.556	0.972	5	0	
1997	20	ATL	NLDS	3	6	5	1	0	0	0	0	1	0	0	1	1	0.000	0.167	0.000	0.167	0	0	
1997	20	ATL	NLCS	5	10	9	0	4	0	0	0	1	0	0	1	1	0.444	0.5	0.444	0.944	4	0	
1998	21	ATL	NLDS	3	13	9	2	0	0	0	0	1	2	0	3	2	0.000	0.231	0.000	0.231	0	0	
1998	21	ATL	NLCS	6	24	22	3	6	0	0	1	2	1	1	1	4	0.273	0.292	0.409	0.701	9	0	
1999	22	ATL	NLDS	4	19	18	1	4	1	0	0	2	0	0	1	3	0.222	0.263	0.278	0.541	5	0	
1999	22	ATL	NLCS	6	28	23	5	5	0	0	0	1	0	1	4	4	0.217	0.333	0.217	0.551	5	0	
2000	23	ATL	NLDS	3	13	9	3	1	0	0	1	1	0	1	4	1	0.111	0.385	0.444	0.829	4	0	
2001	24	ATL	NLDS	3	12	12	2	6	0	0	1	1	0	0	0	3	0.500	0.500	0.750	1.250	9	0	
2001	24	ATL	NLCS	5	18	17	4	3	0	0	1	1	0	0	1	5	0.176	0.222	0.353	0.575	6	0	
2002	25	ATL	NLDS	5	21	19	4	6	1	0	0	2	0	0	2	3	0.316	0.381	0.368	0.749	7	0	
2003	26	ATL	NLDS	5	21	17	1	1	0	0	0	1	0	0	4	7	0.059	0.238	0.059	0.297	1	0	
2004	27	ATL	NLDS	5	21	19	4	10	2	0	2	5	1	0	2	3	0.526	0.571	0.947	1.519	18	0	
2005	28	ATL	NLDS	4	21	17	5	8	3	0	1	5	0	0	2	3	0.471	0.524	0.824	1.347	14	1	
2011	34	NYY	AL	1	1	0	0	0	0	0	0	1	0	0	0	0	0.000	0.000	0.000	0.000	0	0	
				66	241	205	38	56	7	0	8	28	4	3	30	41	0.273	0.366	0.424	0.790	87	1	Post Season Pts.
				1.400	0.000	0.000	1.000	1.000	0.000	0.000	0.800	1.200	0.400	0.000	1.200	0.000	0.400	0.800	0.400	0.600	1.000	0.000	10.200

World Series Play

Year	Age	Tm	Lg	G	PA	AB	R	H	2B	3B	HR	RBI	SB	CS	BB	SO	BA	OBP	SLG	OPS	TB	HBP	
1996	19	ATL	WS	6	24	20	4	8	1	0	2	6	1	2	3	6	0.400	0.500	0.750	1.250	15	1	
1999	22	ATL	WS	4	14	13	1	1	0	0	0	0	0	0	1	3	0.077	0.143	0.077	0.220	1	0	
				10	38	33	5	9	1	0	2	6	1	2	4	9	0.273	0.368	0.485	0.853	16	1	World Series Pts.
				0.400	0.000	0.000	0.400	0.400	0.000	0.000	0.400	0.400	0.250	0.000	0.250	0.000	0.800	0.600	0.250	0.800	0.600	0.000	5.550

Yearly Points Leading the League

Category	Times	Points	Total
MVP	0	7	0
Rookie of Year	0	5	0
Triple Crown	0	5	0
Golden Glove	10	3	30
All-Star	5	2	10
Games	1	2	2
Totals			42

Category	Times	Points	Total
B.A.	0	3	0
Runs	0	2	0
H.R.'s	1	3	3
R.B.I's	1	3	3
Hits	0	2	0
S.B.	0	2	0
Totals			6

Catego	Times	Points	Total
T.B.	0	2	0
B.O.B.	0	2	0
OBP%	0	2	0
SLG %	0	2	0
OBPS%	0	2	0
Totals			0
Grand Total Add-On Points		48	

Hall of Fame Points

Career Points	55.500
Post Season Points	10.200
World Series Points	5.550
Career Add-On Points	48.000
Writers Association Pts.	0.000
Military/Lifetime Achievement	0.000
Grand Total HOF Points	119.250

Lofton, Kenny

Personal Life

Kenneth Lofton was born May 31, 1967, to his mother Annie, while she was in high school, His mother moved to Alabama after she graduated and lost contact with Lofton during his childhood. He was raised by his widowed grandmother, Rosie Person, in East Chicago, Indiana, and attended Washington High School in East Chicago. He played on the school's baseball team and also was an all-state basketball player.

Lofton attended the University of Arizona on a basketball. He did not join the school's baseball team until his junior year with Lofton decided to try out for the baseball team during his junior year. He played in just five baseball games and recorded only one official at-bat while at Arizona, but his speed and potential were recognized by scouts.

Baseball Career

The Astros selected Lofton in the 17th round of the 1988 MLB draft. Lofton struggled early in career in the Astros' farm system. After spring training in 1991, he went directly to Triple-A of the Pacific Coast League. His 168 hits led the league. He hit .308 with 30 steals, and Lofton made the league's All-Star team. On September 14, 1991, the Astros promoted Lofton to the majors where he hit .203 in 20 games for the remainder of the Astros' regular season. Lofton was traded during the off-season to the Cleveland Indians.

During his first season with Cleveland, in 1992, Lofton finished second in Rookie of the Year voting and hit .285. His 66 stolen bases broke the all-time record for an AL rookie and started a five-year run as league champion. Indians first base coach Dave Nelson helped Lofton refine his base running technique and learn how to be successful with bunting. Over his career, Lofton became one of the best bunters in baseball history. After one season with Cleveland, Lofton agreed to a four-year contract. Lofton became a star in the 1993 expansion year when he hit .325, scored 116 runs, , 70 stolen bases (which led MLB) and won a Gold Glove. In 1994, Lofton led the league in hits with 160, had a .349 batting average, won a Gold Glove, finished 2nd in runs with105, selected to his first career All-Star Game, had an on-base percentage of .412.

The 1995 season he hit .310 and led the AL in triples with 13. In the American League Championship Series against the Mariners, he batted.458 in six games and dashed home from second base on a passed ball in the final game of the ALCS in Seattle. In the World Series loss to the Braves, Lofton hit only .200. The 1996 season he batted .317 with 210 hits, 132 runs scored, 75 stolen bases, and won his 4th Golden Glove in a row. However, in March of 1997 he was traded to the Braves and hit .333 for Atlanta.

Following the 1997 season, he returned to the Cleveland Indians when he signed a three-year, contract. In 1998, Lofton hit .282, 87 walks, and 64 RBIs His average bounced back to .301 in 1999 along with 110 runs and 25 stolen bases. In 2000, Lofton had career highs in home runs with 15, runs batted in with 73, recording 30 stolen bases and 107 runs scored but his batting average declined to .278. Lofton tied an A. L. record by scoring in an 18th straight game, matching Red Rolfe's achievement in 1939 for the Yankees. The Indians returned in 2001 after winning the AL Central with a 91–71 record. Cleveland lost their match-up with the Mariners in the 2001 ALDS.

In 2002, Lofton signed a one-year contract with the Chicago White Sox. He appeared in 93 games with the White Sox and was traded to the San Francisco Giants of the NL. In the Giants' match-up with the Cardinals in the 2002 NLCS, Lofton delivered a key hit to help the Giants win their first pennant since 1989. The Giants held a five-run lead in the seventh inning of game six of the World Series against the Anaheim Angels, but eight outs away from winning the World Series, the Angels rallied to win 6–5. The Angels took game seven the following night, with Lofton flying out to end that game and the World Series, the second time Lofton lost a World Series.

The Pittsburgh Pirates signed Lofton to a one-year, contract to begin the 2003 season. With the Pirates, he hit .277 and stole 18 bases before being traded to the Chicago Cubs. In 56 regular-season appearances with the Cubs, Lofton stole 12 bases and hit 327. Lofton and the Cubs won the NL Central division and beat the Atlanta Braves three games to two in the 2003 NLDS. Lofton's .323 against the Marlins led the Cubs' starting line-up, as did his 31 at-bats, and he had the team's only stolen base of the seven-game series, which the Cubs lost in seven games.

On December 23, 2003, the New York Yankees signed him to a two-year contract. New York finished the regular season with an AL-best record, 101–61. To begin the postseason, the Yankees defeated the Minnesota Twins, three games to one, in the 2004 ALDS. In the 2004 ALCS against the Boston Red Sox, the Yankees the Yankees went up in the series three games to none before becoming the first team in MLB history to lose a series after holding a 3–0 series lead. With the Phillies in 2005, Lofton hit .335 in 110 appearances. He also recorded 22 stolen bases.

On December 12, 2006, the Texas Rangers signed Lofton to a one-year contract. In 84 games with the Rangers, he hit .303 with 16 doubles. Lofton became a free agent at the end of the season but did not sign with an MLB team. During his career, Lofton played for Houston, Cleveland, Atlanta, Chicago White Sox, Chicago Cubs, New York Yankees, Philadelphia, Los Angeles Dodgers, and Texas Rangers.

Achievements:

- 6-time All-Star (1994-1999) 5-time AL Stolen Bases Leader (1992-1996).
- 4-time AL Gold Glove Winner (1993-1996) & AL Hits Leader (1994).
- 6-Times 100 plus Runs Scored (1993, 1994, 1996 & 1998-2000)
- 6 – Time 50 plus Stolen Bases Seasons (1992-1996 & 1998)
- Holds the all-time postseason stolen base record with 34.

Hall of Fame

Lofton was eligible for the Hall of Fame in 2013 but received only 3.2% of the vote and dropped from the ballot. The Contemporary Baseball Era ballot is voting again in 2025.

Summary Analysis

Kenny Lofton's Statistical Hall of Fame Points are 117.350. Lofton is an underrated player whose career is Cooperstown-worthy.

Lofton, Kenny — Center Fielder — Potential Hall of Fame Inductee

Positions	Centerfielder	**Born:** May 31, 1967	**Height:** 6'0" UBC 183 cm
		From: East Chicago, IN	**Weight:** 180 lbs. 81 Kg
		Bats: Left	**Debut:** September 14, 1991
		Throws: Left	**Last Game:** September 29, 2007

Year	Age	Tm	Lg	G	O	AB	R	H	2B	3B	HR	RBI	SB	CS	BB	SO	BA	OBP	SLG	OPS	TB	HBP	Awards
1991	24	HOU	NL	20	79	74	9	15	1	0	0	0	2	1	5	19	0.203	0.253	0.216	0.469	16	0	
1992	25	CLE	AL	148	651	576	96	164	15	8	5	42	66	12	68	54	0.285	0.362	0.365	0.728	210	2	RoY-2
1993	26	CLE	AL	148	657	569	116	185	28	8	1	42	70	14	81	83	0.325	0.408	0.408	0.815	232	1	MVP-15,GG
1994	27	CLE	AL	112	513	459	105	160	32	9	12	57	60	12	52	56	0.349	0.412	0.536	0.948	246	3	AS,MVP-4,GG
1995	28	CLE	AL	118	529	481	93	149	22	13	7	53	34	15	40	49	0.310	0.362	0.453	0.815	218	1	AS,GG
1996	29	CLE	AL	154	738	662	132	210	35	4	14	67	75	17	61	82	0.317	0.372	0.446	0.817	395	0	AS,MVP-11,GG
1997	30	ATL	NL	122	564	493	90	164	20	6	5	48	17	20	64	83	0.333	0.409	0.428	0.837	211	2	AS,MVP-26
1998	31	CLE	AL	154	688	600	101	169	31	6	12	64	54	10	87	80	0.282	0.371	0.413	0.785	248	3	AS
1999	32	CLE	AL	120	581	465	110	140	28	6	7	39	25	6	79	84	0.301	0.405	0.432	0.838	201	6	AS
2000	33	CLE	AL	137	640	548	107	151	23	5	15	73	30	7	79	72	0.278	0.369	0.422	0.791	229	4	
2001	34	CLE	AL	153	576	517	91	135	21	4	14	66	16	8	47	69	0.261	0.322	0.398	0.721	206	2	
2002	35	TOT	MLB	139	611	532	98	139	30	9	11	51	29	11	72	73	0.261	0.350	0.414	0.763	220	1	
2002	35	CHW	AL	93	406	352	68	91	20	6	8	42	22	8	49	51	0.259	0.348	0.418	0.766	147	0	
2002	35	SFG	NL	46	205	180	30	48	10	3	3	9	7	3	23	22	0.267	0.353	0.406	0.758	73	1	
2003	36	TOT	NL	140	610	547	97	162	32	8	12	46	30	9	46	51	0.296	0.352	0.450	0.801	246	4	
2003	36	PIT	NL	84	374	330	58	94	19	4	9	26	18	5	28	29	0.277	0.333	0.437	0.770	148	2	
2003	36	CHC	NL	56	236	208	39	68	13	4	3	20	12	4	18	22	0.327	0.381	0.471	0.852	98	2	
2004	37	NYY	AL	83	313	276	51	76	14	7	3	18	7	3	31	27	0.275	0.346	0.395	0.741	109	1	
2005	38	PHI	NL	110	406	367	67	123	15	5	2	36	22	3	32	41	0.335	0.392	0.420	0.811	154	2	
2006	39	LAD	NL	129	522	469	79	141	15	12	3	41	32	9	45	42	0.301	0.360	0.403	0.763	189	0	
2007	40	TOT	AL	136	559	490	86	145	25	6	7	38	23	7	56	51	0.296	0.367	0.414	0.782	203	2	
2007	40	TEX	AL	84	365	317	62	96	16	3	7	23	21	4	30	28	0.303	0.380	0.458	0.818	139	2	
2007	40	CLE	AL	52	196	173	24	49	9	3	0	15	2	3	17	23	0.283	0.344	0.370	0.714	64	0	
162-Game Avg.				163	711	626	118	187	30	8	10	69	48	12	79	78	0.299	0.372	0.413	0.794	264	2	
CLE (10 yrs)				1276	5767	5045	975	1512	244	66	87	518	432	104	611	852	0.300	0.375	0.428	0.800	2149	20	
PIT (1 yr)				84	374	330	58	94	19	4	9	26	18	5	28	29	0.277	0.333	0.437	0.770	148	2	
SFG (1 yr)				46	205	180	30	48	10	3	3	9	7	3	23	22	0.267	0.353	0.406	0.758	73	1	
PHI (1 yr)				110	406	367	67	123	15	5	2	36	22	3	32	41	0.335	0.392	0.420	0.811	154	3	
ATL (1 yr)				122	564	493	90	164	20	6	5	48	27	20	64	83	0.333	0.409	0.428	0.837	211	2	
TEX (1 yr)				84	365	317	62	96	16	3	7	23	21	4	30	28	0.303	0.380	0.458	0.818	139	2	
LAD (1 yr)				129	522	469	79	141	15	12	3	41	32	9	45	42	0.301	0.360	0.403	0.763	189	0	
CHC (1 yr)				56	236	208	39	68	13	4	3	20	12	4	18	22	0.327	0.381	0.471	0.852	98	2	
NYY (1 yr)				83	313	276	51	76	10	7	3	18	7	3	31	27	0.275	0.346	0.395	0.741	109	1	
HOU (1 yr)				20	79	74	9	15	1	0	0	0	2	1	5	19	0.203	0.253	0.216	0.469	16	0	
CHW (1 yr)				93	406	352	68	91	20	6	8	42	22	8	49	51	0.259	0.348	0.418	0.766	147	0	
AL (12 yrs)				1536	6849	5990	1156	1775	290	82	105	601	502	119	730	758	0.296	0.372	0.425	0.797	2544	23	
NL (6 yrs)				567	2386	2130	372	653	93	34	25	180	120	41	215	258	0.307	0.375	0.417	0.789	889	9	
17 Yrs				2103	9235	8120	1528	2428	383	116	130	781	622	160	945	1016	0.299	0.372	0.423	0.794	3433	32	**Career Pts.**
				6.750	0.000	0.000	12.500	5.500	0.000	0.000	2.000	2.500	9.250	0.000	9.750	0.000	6.750	4.500	2.000	4.500	4.500	0.000	64.500

Post Season Play

Year	Age	Tm	Lg	G	PA	AB	R	H	2B	3B	HR	RBI	SB	CS	BB	SO	BA	OBP	SLG	OPS	TB	HBP	
1995	28	CLE	ALDS	3	15	13	1	2	0	0	0	0	0	0	1	3	0.154	0.267	0.154	0.421	2	1	
1995	28	CLE	ALCS	6	29	24	4	11	0	2	0	3	5	0	4	6	0.458	0.517	0.625	1.142	15	0	
1996	29	CLE	ALDS	4	21	18	3	3	0	0	0	1	5	0	2	3	0.167	0.250	0.167	0.417	3	0	
1997	30	ATL	NLDS	3	14	13	2	2	1	0	0	0	0	2	1	3	0.154	0.214	0.231	0.445	3	0	
1997	30	ATL	NLCS	6	28	27	3	5	0	1	0	1	1	1	1	7	0.185	0.214	0.259	0.474	7	0	
1998	31	CLE	ALDS	4	17	16	3	6	1	0	2	4	2	0	1	1	0.375	0.412	0.813	1.224	13	0	
1998	31	CLE	ALCS	6	28	27	2	5	1	0	1	3	1	0	1	7	0.185	0.214	0.333	0.548	9	0	
1999	32	CLE	ALDS	5	21	16	5	2	1	0	0	1	2	0	5	6	0.125	0.333	0.188	0.521	3	0	
2001	34	CLE	ALDS	5	23	19	2	2	0	0	1	3	0	0	4	5	0.105	0.217	0.263	0.481	2	0	
2002	35	SFG	NLDS	5	26	20	5	7	1	0	0	2	1	0	3	3	0.350	0.391	0.400	0.791	8	0	
2002	35	SFG	NLCS	5	24	21	4	5	0	0	1	2	1	0	2	4	0.238	0.333	0.381	0.714	8	1	
2003	36	CHC	NLDS	5	23	21	1	6	1	0	0	1	3	1	2	2	0.286	0.348	0.333	0.681	7	0	
2003	36	CHC	NLCS	7	35	31	8	10	1	0	0	3	1	0	3	4	0.323	0.382	0.355	0.737	11	0	
2004	37	NYY	ALDS	1	4	4	0	1	0	0	0	1	0	0	0	1	0.250	0.250	0.250	0.5	1	0	
2004	37	NYY	ALCS	3	12	10	1	3	0	0	1	2	1	0	2	3	0.300	0.417	0.600	1.017	6	0	
2006	39	LAD	NLDS	3	13	13	0	1	0	0	0	0	0	0	0	4	0.077	0.077	0.077	0.154	1	0	
2007	40	CLE	ALDS	4	18	16	2	6	1	0	0	4	1	1	2	2	0.375	0.444	0.438	0.882	7	0	
2007	40	CLE	ALCS	7	28	27	2	6	2	0	1	2	1	0	1	8	0.222	0.250	0.407	0.657	11	0	
				82	376	336	52	83	10	3	7	82	25	5	38	65	0.247	0.314	0.333	0.647	120	2	**Post Season Pts.**
				1.800	0.000	0.000	1.000	1.400	0.000	0.000	0.800	1.400	2.000	0.000	1.400	0.000	0.250	0.250	0.000	0.250	1.200	0.000	11.750

World Series Play

Year	Age	Tm	Lg	G	PA	AB	R	H	2B	3B	HR	RBI	SB	CS	BB	SO	BA	OBP	SLG	OPS	TB	HBP	
1995	28	CLE	WS	6	28	25	6	5	1	0	0	0	6	1	3	1	0.200	0.286	0.240	0.526	6	0	
2002	35	SFG	WS	7	34	31	7	9	1	1	0	2	3	0	2	2	0.290	0.333	0.387	0.720	12	0	
				13	62	56	13	14	2	1	0	2	9	1	5	3	0.250	0.311	0.321	0.632	18	0	**World Series Pts.**
				0.400	0.000	0.000	0.800	0.600	0.000	0.000	0.000	0.250	1.400	0.000	0.400	0.000	0.400	0.000	0.000	0.250	0.600	0.000	5.100

Yearly Points Leading the League

Category	Times	Points	Total	Category	Times	Points	Total	Category	Times	Points	Total
MVP	0	7	0	B.A.	0	3	0	T.B.	0	3	0
Rookie of Year	0	5	0	Runs	0	3	0	B.O.B.	0	3	0
Triple Crown	0	5	0	H.R.'s	0	3	0	OBP%	0	3	0
Golden Glove	4	3	12	R.B.I's	0	3	0	SLG %	0	3	0
All-Star	6	2	12	Hits	1	2	2	OBPS%	0	3	0
Games	0	3	0	S.B.	5	2	10	Totals			0
Totals			24	Totals			12	Grand Total Add-On Points			36

Hall of Fame Points	
Career Points	64.500
Post Season Points	11.750
World Series Points	5.100
Career Add-On Points	36.000
Writers Association Pts.	0.000
Military/Lifetime Achievement	0.000
Grand Total HOF Points	117.350

Lynn, Fred

Personal Life

Fredric Michael Lynn was born on February 3, 1952, in Chicago to Fred and Marie Lynn. When he was one-year-old his family moved to Southern California. He was an only child, and after his parents' divorce in 1965 he lived with his father.

Lynn played for the USC varsity as a freshman, sophomore, and junior and the team enjoyed three years of amazing success 1971-1973, winning the NCAA Baseball Championship each season. Fred played in 158 games, batting .320 in his career (159-for-497). He added 28 home runs and 111 RBIs in that span.

Lynn married Diane May Minkle in February 1974 and they had son, Jason and daughter, Jennifer. Fred and Dee Dee later divorced. In 1986. Lynn married Natalia Selby with Fred being the proud grandfather of three Tyler, Hayden, and Carter.

Baseball Career

In 1973 Lynn, the Red Sox took him with the 41st overall pick. Lynn reported to Double-A Bristol of the Eastern League, where he hit .259 in 53 games. But the Red Sox were impressed enough to call him up to Triple-A Pawtucket for the playoffs, where he helped the team win the International League's Governors Cup. Then in 1974, Lynn hit .282 with 21 homers and 68 RBI for Pawtucket and was called up to Boston and made his major league debut on September 5, 1974. He appeared in 15 games through the end of the season, batting 18-for-43 (.419) with 10 RBI in 15 games.

Lynn earned the Opening Day start in center in 1975 and hit safely in 10 of his first 13 games in April, his batting average never dropped below .323 after May as Lynn regularly made spectacular plays in center as the Red Sox shocked the pundits by winning the American League East. On June 18 against the Tigers, Lynn became just the eighth player in AL/NL history with at least 10 RBI in one game when he had five hits, including a triple and three home runs, in a 15-1 win over the Tigers. Lynn had an outstanding 1975 season; in 145 games, he batted .331, 21 home runs, and 105 RBIs. He led the A.L. in doubles, runs scored, and slugging percentage, finished second in batting and won a Gold Glove Award for his defensive play. Lynn won both the Most Valuable

A Fan's Perspective

Player Award and Rookie of the Year Award, becoming the first player to win both in the same season. In the playoffs, Lynn hit .364 with three RBI as the Red Sox swept Oakland in the ALCS. That set the stage for the 1975 World Series, which re-energized the sport thanks to a fantastic seven games between the Red Sox and the Reds. In the 1975 World Series, which Boston lost in seven games to the Cincinnati Reds, Lynn batted 7-for-25 (.280) with a home run and five RBIs.

In 1979 won the AL batting title with a .333 average and selected to the All-Star team. On May 13, 1980, he hit for the cycle and in seven seasons with the Red Sox, Lynn batted .308 with 124 home runs and 521 RBIs in 828 games played. After 1979 when he hit 39 homers, Lynn never hit more than 25 in a season again. Lynn settled in for 20, or 25, homers every season for seven straight years in his 30s. It should have been a big highlight in a Hall of Fame career, but instead it's a footnote.

In January 1981, Lynn was traded to the Angels and was limited to 76 games in his first year with the Angels due to a knee injury. For the season, he batted just .219 with five home runs and 31 RBIs. He played three more seasons with the Angels, batting .299 in 138 games during 1982, .272 in 117 games in 1983, and .271 in 142 games in 1984. In 1982, Lynn and the Angels won the AL West division and made the playoffs, but lost to the Milwaukee Brewers in 5 games. Even so, Lynn was selected as MVP of the ALCS, becoming the first payer from a losing team to be so honored. Lynn batted an astounding .611 (11 hits in 18 at-bats), with a home run and 5 RBI's. Lynn was an All-Star his first three seasons with the Angels and in his four seasons with, and appeared in 473 games, batting .271 with 71 home runs and 270 RBIs.

In his 17-year career, Lynn batted .283 with 1,111 RBIs, 1,960 hits, 1,063 runs, 306 home runs, 388 doubles, 43 triples, and 72 stolen bases in 1969 games. From 1982 to 1988, he had seven consecutive seasons of hitting more than twenty home runs (his totals were 21-22-23-23-23-23-25). His 306 career home runs place him, through the end of the 2017 seasons, in 13th place among center fielders. Defensively, Lynn recorded a career .988 fielding percentage at centerfield, his primary position. In 15 career postseason games, Lynn batted 22-for-54 (.407) with two home runs and 13 RBIs. In All-Star Games, Lynn hit four home runs and ten RBIs, including the first (and to date, only) grand slam in All-Star Game history, which he hit in the 1983 game. His four home runs in All-Star Games is second only to Stan Musial with six.

The Baseball Hall of Fame

He played for 17 years in the major leagues for 5 teams. Boston Red Sox (1974-1980), California Angels (1981-1984), Baltimore Orioles (1985-1988), Detroit Tigers (1988-1989), and San Diego Padres (1990). Fred ran into an outfield wall one year, then he broke his elbow when he collided with a teammate in the outfield. He pulled a hamstring here and stubbed a toe there. Down the stretch in 1988, Lynn hit seven home runs for the Tigers and became a popular player in the Motor City. Three of his home runs were game winners, and though the Tigers ended up losing the division by one game, his efforts were appreciated. The Tigers brought him back in 1989 and Lynn smacked 11 home runs as a lefthanded designated hitter.

Achievements:

- American League Rookie of the Year -1975
- 4-Times received MVP Votes (1975 Won, 1978, 1979 & 198.),
- 4-Times Golden Glove Winner (1975, 1978, 1979 & 1980)
- 9-Time All-Star (1975 through 1983) & 2-Times 100 plus Runs (1975 & 1979).
- 2-Times led A.L. in Slugging% (1975 & 1979).
- 10-Times 20 plus home runs (1975, 1978, 1979, 1982 – 1988).

Hall of Fame Candidacy

Lynn was on the ballot in 1996 receiving 5.5 percent of the vote by the BBWAA. He went below 5 percent the next year and was dropped. He's yet to appear on a Veterans Committee ballot.

Summary Analysis

Fred Lynn Statistical Hall of Fame Points of 119.800 is over the Induction Score of 110.000 and he should have been inducted when eligible.

Lynn, Fred — Center Field Potential Hall of Fame Inductee

Positions	Centerfielder	**Born:** February 3, 1952	**Height:** 6' 1" USC 185 cm
		From: Chicago, IL	**Weight:** 185 lbs. 83 Kg.
		Bats: Left	**Debut:** September 5, 1974
		Throws: Left	**Last Game:** October 3, 1990

Year	Age	Tm	Lg	G	D	AB	R	H	2B	3B	HR	RBI	SB	CS	BB	SO	BA	OBP	SLG	OPS	TB	HBP	Awards
1974	22	BOS	AL	15	51	43	5	18	2	2	2	10	0	0	6	6	0.419	0.490	0.698	1.188	30	1	
1975	23	BOS	AL	145	605	528	103	175	47	7	21	105	10	5	62	90	0.381	0.401	0.566	0.967	299	3	1,GG
1976	24	BOS	AL	132	566	507	76	159	32	8	10	65	14	9	48	67	0.314	0.367	0.467	0.835	237	1	AS
1977	25	BOS	AL	129	564	497	81	129	29	5	18	76	2	3	51	68	0.260	0.327	0.447	0.774	222	3	AS
1978	26	BOS	AL	150	627	541	75	161	33	3	22	82	3	6	75	50	0.298	0.380	0.492	0.872	266	1	AS,MVP-25,GG
1979	27	BOS	AL	147	622	531	116	177	42	1	39	122	2	2	82	79	0.333	0.423	0.637	1.059	338	4	AS,MVP-4,GG
1980	28	BOS	AL	110	478	415	67	125	32	3	12	61	12	0	58	39	0.301	0.383	0.480	0.862	199	0	AS,MVP-24,GG
1981	29	CAL	AL	76	302	256	28	56	8	1	5	31	1	2	38	42	0.219	0.322	0.316	0.639	81	3	AS
1982	30	CAL	AL	138	545	472	89	141	38	1	21	86	7	8	58	72	0.299	0.374	0.517	0.891	244	3	AS
1983	31	CAL	AL	117	500	437	56	119	20	3	22	74	2	2	55	83	0.272	0.352	0.483	0.835	211	2	AS
1984	32	CAL	AL	142	600	517	84	140	28	4	23	79	3	2	77	97	0.271	0.366	0.474	0.840	245	2	
1985	33	BAL	AL	124	508	448	59	118	12	1	23	68	7	3	53	100	0.263	0.339	0.449	0.787	201	1	
1986	34	BAL	AL	112	456	397	67	114	13	1	23	67	2	2	53	59	0.287	0.371	0.499	0.869	198	2	
1987	35	BAL	AL	111	438	396	49	100	24	0	23	60	3	7	39	72	0.253	0.320	0.487	0.807	193	1	
1988	36	TOT	AL	114	432	391	46	96	14	1	25	56	2	2	33	82	0.246	0.302	0.478	0.780	187	1	
1988	36	BAL	AL	87	334	301	37	76	13	1	18	37	2	2	28	66	0.252	0.312	0.482	0.794	145	0	
1988	36	DET	AL	27	98	90	9	20	1	0	7	19	0	0	5	16	0.222	0.265	0.467	0.732	42	1	
1989	37	DET	AL	117	406	353	44	85	11	1	11	46	1	1	47	71	0.241	0.328	0.371	0.699	131	1	
1990	38	SDP	NL	90	223	196	18	47	3	1	6	23	2	0	22	44	0.240	0.315	0.357	0.672	70	1	
162 Game Avg.				162	652	570	87	161	32	4	25	91	6	4	71	92	0.283	0.360	0.484	0.845	276	2	
BOS (7 yrs)				828	3513	3062	523	944	217	29	124	521	43	25	382	394	0.308	0.383	0.520	0.902	1591	13	
CAL (4 yrs)				473	1947	1682	257	456	94	9	71	270	12	14	228	294	0.271	0.358	0.464	0.822	781	10	
BAL (4 yrs)				434	1736	1542	212	408	62	3	87	232	14	14	173	297	0.265	0.337	0.478	0.815	737	4	
DET (2 yrs)				144	504	443	53	105	12	1	18	65	1	1	52	87	0.237	0.315	0.391	0.706	173	2	
SDP (1 yr)				90	223	196	18	47	3	1	6	23	2	0	22	44	0.240	0.315	0.357	0.672	70	1	
AL (16 yrs)				1879	7700	6729	1045	1913	385	42	300	1088	70	54	835	1072	0.284	0.362	0.488	0.850	3282	29	
NL (1 yr)				90	223	196	18	47	3	1	6	23	2	0	22	44	0.24	0.315	0.357	0.672	70	1	
17 Yrs				1969	7923	6925	1063	1960	388	43	306	1111	72	54	857	1116	0.283	0.360	0.484	0.845	3352	30	Career Pts.
				5.500	0.000	0.000	4.500	3.000	0.000	0.000	5.500	4.500	1.000	0.000	3.000	0.000	3.750	3.750	4.500	6.750	5.500	0.000	51.250

Post Season Play

Year	Age	Tm	Lg	G	PA	AB	R	H	2B	3B	HR	RBI	SB	CS	BB	SO	BA	OBP	SLG	OPS	TB	HBP	
1975	23	BOS	ALCS	3	12	11	1	4	1	0	0	3	0	0	0	0	0.364	0.364	0.455	0.818	5	0	
1982	30	CAL	ALCS	5	20	18	4	11	2	0	1	5	0	0	2	3	0.611	0.65	0.889	1.539	16	0	
				8	32	29	5	15	3	0	1	8	0	0	2	3	0.517	0.548	0.724	1.273	21	0	Post Season Pts.
				0.250	0.000	0.000	0.250	0.400	0.000	0.000	0.250	0.400	0.000	0.000	0.250	0.000	2.000	2.000	2.000	1.800	0.250	0.000	9.850

World Series Points

Year	Age	Tm	Lg	G	PA	AB	R	H	2B	3B	HR	RBI	SB	CS	BB	SO	BA	OBP	SLG	OPS	TB	HBP	
1975	23	BOS	WS	7	29	25	3	7	1	0	1	5	0	0	3	5	0.280	0.345	0.440	0.785	11	0	
				7	29	25	3	7	1	0	1	5	0	0	3	5	0.280	0.345	0.440	0.785	11	0	World Series Pts.
				0.250	0.000	0.000	0.250	0.250	0.000	0.000	0.250	0.400	0.000	0.000	0.250	0.000	0.800	0.250	0.000	0.600	0.400	0.000	3.700

Yearly Points Leading the League

Category	Times	Points	Total	Category	Times	Total	Categ	Times	Points	Total
MVP	1	7	7	B.A.	1	3	3	T.B.	0	2	0
Rookie of Year	1	5	5	Runs	1	2	2	B.O.B.	0	2	0
Triple Crown	0	5	0	H.R.'s	0	3	0	OBP%	1	2	2
Golden Glove	4	3	12	R.B.I's	0	3	0	SLG %	2	2	4
All-Star	9	2	18	Hits	0	2	0	OBPS%	1	2	2
Games	0	2	0	S.B.	0	2	0	Totals			8
Totals			42	Totals			5	Grand Total Add-On Points			55

Hall of Fame Points	
Career Points	51.250
Post Season Points	9.850
World Series Points	3.700
Career Add-On Points	55.000
Writers Association Pts.	0.000
Military/Lifetime Achievement	0.000
Grand Total HOF Points	119.800

Murphy, Dale

Personal Life

Dale Bryan Murphy was born in Portland, Oregon, on March 12, 1956, to parents Charles and Betty with a sister, Sue. Murphy played American Legion Baseball and attended Woodrow Wilson High School.

Murphy married Nancy Thomas on October 27, 1979. The couple having eight children: sons Chad, Travis, Shawn, Tyson, Taylor, Jake, McKay and daughter Madison.

Baseball Career

The Atlanta Braves selected Murphy as the 5th pick of the June draft in 1974 Murphy began the 1976 season with Savannah of the AA Southern League and hit .267 with 12 homers and 55 RBIs. In 1977 he was promoted to Richmond of the AAA International League. Murphy made his major league debut on September 13, going 2 for 4 with two R.B.I.s. In 17 starts as a catcher, he threw out nine of 21 would-be base stealers.

He returned to Richmond for the 1977 season because he had developed a throwing problem from his catcher's position. Some of his throws would bounce in front of the pitching mound; some would go in all directions around the infield, or sail into the outfield. Rarely did he hit the spot he was trying to throw to. "It'll come around," said Murphy. "It's got to be in my head and not physical. It's been discouraging but something I've got to forget." Offensively it was a breakout year. Murphy batted .305 to go with 22 home runs and a league-leading 90 RBIs. Once again, the Braves called Murphy up in September where he appeared in only eighteen games with 2 home runs, 14 runs batted in with a .316 batting average.

In 1978, when Atlanta departed spring training and headed north, Dale Murphy was with them, but the team moved him to first base. Manager Bobby Cox said, "Give Murphy 500 at-bats this season and he'll hit 25 homers minimum in the National League," said Cox. Murphy posted 530 at-bats and homered 23 times, sharing the team lead. Murphy was the league leader in strikeouts, whiffing 145 times. On the defensive side, the Braves found that their prized prospect had a hard time throwing from the first base position as well. He led the league with 20 errors.

A Fan's Perspective

In May of 1979, Murphy was dealing with a sore left knee and underwent arthroscopic surgery to remove the cartilage. Murphy did not return to full-time duty until July 19. Murphy switched to the outfield in 1980, a move that would help initiate a decade of highly productive play in the National League. Beginning in left field, he soon switched to center field, the position at which he would find his greatest success. By 1982, the most decorated year of Murphy's career, the former catcher had transformed himself into an All-Star MVP outfielder who appeared in each of Atlanta's 162 games. His turnaround as a fielder was equally stark. In 1978, Murphy led all National League first basemen in errors. In 1982, spending time at each of the three outfield positions, he won the first of five consecutive Gold Gloves, as well as the first MVP award.

Playing in the decade before the Braves began their dominance of the National League East, Murphy also made his only postseason appearance in 1982. Although he performed well, the eventual World Series-champion St. Louis Cardinals eliminated the Braves in the 1982 National League Championship Series. The league's most valuable player failed to translate his regular season preeminence into October success, hitting safely only three times and scoring one run. Murphy rebounded from the postseason sweep with another MVP award in 1983. This time period ultimately proved the high-water era of Murphy's career.

During the 1980s, Murphy led the National League in games, at bats, runs, hits, extra base hits, RBIs, runs created, total bases, and plate appearances. His 308 home runs during the decade is second only to Mike Schmidt's 313. He also accomplished a 30–30 (30 home runs with 30 stolen bases) season in 1983. Murphy played in 740 consecutive games, at the time the 11th longest such streak in baseball history. His jersey number ("3") was retired by the Atlanta Braves on June 13, 1994, in his honor as opposed to that of even Babe Ruth, who wore Boston Braves number 3 during the partial season with which his career concluded. On the morning of May 27, 1993, he announced his retirement from baseball at age 37. Murphy finished his career with 398 home runs, 1,266 RBI, and a .265 lifetime batting average. The Veterans Committee advocating his election and praising him for meeting the voting criteria: ability, integrity, sportsmanship, character, and contributions to the team(s) on which the player played. 2010s. During an 18-year career in Major League Baseball (MLB) from 1976 to 1993, he played for the Atlanta Braves, Philadelphia Phillies, and Colorado Rockies.

The Baseball Hall of Fame

Achievements

- Lou Gehrig Memorial Award (1985) & Roberto Clemente Award (1988).
- 7-Time All-Star (1980, 1982 – 1987).
- 4-Times led the N.L. in Games played (1982, 1983, 1984 & 1985).
- 5-Times received MVP Votes (1980, 1982 Won) & 1983 Won - 1987).
- 5-time NL Gold Glove Winner (1982-1986).
- 4-time NL Silver Slugger Award Winner (1982-1985).
- 2-time NL Slugging Percentage Leader (1983 & 1984) & NL OPS Leader (1983).
- NL Runs Scored Leader (1985) & NL Total Bases Leader (1984).
- 2-time NL Home Runs Leader (1984 & 1985).
- 2-time NL RBI Leader (1982 & 1983) & NL Bases on Balls Leader (1985).
- 20-Home Run Seasons: 12 (1978-1980 & 1982-1990).
- 30-Home Run Seasons: 6 (1980, 1982-1985 & 1987 (40HR's)).
- 100 RBI Seasons: 5 (1982-1985 & 1987).
- 100 Runs Scored Seasons: 4 (1982, 1983, 1985 & 1987).

Hall of Fame

Dale Murphy appeared on the Hall of Fame Ballot in 1999 and averaged 13.6% over the first twelve years of voting. January 9, 2013, in his final appearance, Murphy secured 18.9% of the vote.

Summary Analysis

Murphy's Statistical Hall of Fame Points of 112.655 is over the Induction Score of 110.000. He should have been inducted when eligible and DESERVES to be placed in the Hall of Fame so he can enjoy being considered one of the best of all time.

Murphy, Dale

Positions
Catcher
Outfielder
First Base

Center Fielder Potential Hall of Fame Inductee

Born:	March 12, 1956	**Height:**	6' 4"	**USC** 193 cm
From:	Portland, OR	**Weight:**	210 lbs.	95 Kg.
Bats:	Right	**Debut:**	September 13, 1976	
Throws:	Right	**Last Game:**	May 21, 1993	

Year	Age	Tm	Lg	G	D	AB	R	H	2B	3B	HR	RBI	SB	CS	BB	SO	BA	OBP	SLG	OPS	TB	HBP	Awards
1976	20	ATL	NL	19	72	65	3	17	6	0	0	9	0	0	7	9	0.262	0.333	0.354	0.687	23	0	
1977	21	ATL	NL	18	76	76	5	24	8	1	2	14	0	1	0	8	0.316	0.316	0.526	0.842	40	0	
1978	22	ATL	NL	151	583	530	66	120	14	3	23	79	11	7	42	145	0.226	0.284	0.394	0.679	209	3	
1979	23	ATL	NL	104	429	384	53	106	7	2	21	57	6	1	38	67	0.276	0.34	0.469	0.809	180	2	
1980	24	ATL	NL	156	634	569	98	160	27	2	33	89	9	6	59	133	0.281	0.349	0.51	0.858	290	1	AS,MVP-12
1981	25	ATL	NL	104	416	369	43	91	12	1	13	50	14	5	44	72	0.247	0.325	0.39	0.716	144	0	
1982	26	ATL	NL	162	698	598	113	168	23	2	36	109	23	11	93	134	0.281	0.378	0.507	0.885	303	3	AS,MVP-1,GG,SS
1983	27	ATL	NL	162	687	589	131	178	24	4	36	121	30	4	90	110	0.302	0.393	0.54	0.933	318	2	AS,MVP-1,GG,SS
1984	28	ATL	NL	162	691	607	94	176	32	8	36	100	19	7	79	134	0.29	0.372	0.547	0.919	332	2	AS,MVP-9,GG,SS
1985	29	ATL	NL	162	712	616	118	185	32	2	37	111	10	3	90	141	0.3	0.388	0.539	0.927	332	1	AS,MVP-7,GG,SS
1986	30	ATL	NL	160	692	614	89	163	29	7	29	83	7	7	75	141	0.265	0.347	0.477	0.824	293	2	AS,MVP-21,GG
1987	31	ATL	NL	159	693	566	115	167	27	1	44	105	16	6	115	136	0.295	0.417	0.58	0.997	328	7	AS,MVP-11
1988	32	ATL	NL	156	671	592	77	134	35	4	24	77	3	5	74	125	0.226	0.313	0.421	0.734	249	2	
1989	33	ATL	NL	154	647	574	60	131	16	0	20	84	3	2	65	142	0.228	0.306	0.361	0.667	207	2	
1990	34	TOT	NL	154	629	563	60	138	23	1	24	83	9	3	61	130	0.245	0.318	0.417	0.735	235	1	
1990	34	ATL	NL	97	394	349	38	81	14	0	17	55	9	2	41	84	0.232	0.312	0.418	0.731	146	1	
1990	34	PHI	NL	57	235	214	22	57	9	1	7	28	0	1	20	46	0.266	0.328	0.416	0.744	89	0	
1991	35	PHI	NL	153	599	544	66	137	33	1	18	81	1	0	48	93	0.252	0.309	0.415	0.724	226	0	
1992	36	PHI	NL	18	63	62	5	10	1	0	2	7	0	0	1	13	0.161	0.175	0.274	0.449	17	0	
1993	37	COL	NL	26	49	42	1	6	1	0	0	7	0	0	5	15	0.143	0.224	0.167	0.391	7	0	
162 Game Avg.				162	672	592	89	157	26	3	30	94	12	5	73	130	0.265	0.346	0.469	0.815	277	2	
ATL (15 yrs)				1926	8095	7098	1103	1901	306	37	371	1143	160	67	912	1581	0.268	0.351	0.478	0.829	3394	28	
PHI (3 yrs)				228	897	820	93	204	43	2	27	116	1	1	69	152	0.249	0.304	0.405	0.709	332	0	
COL (1 yr)				26	49	42	1	6	1	0	0	7	0	0	5	15	0.143	0.224	0.167	0.391	7	0	
18 Yrs				2180	9041	7960	1197	2111	350	39	398	1266	161	68	986	1748	0.265	0.346	0.469	0.815	3733	28	**Career Pts.**
				6.500	0.000	0.000	5.750	3.000	0.000	0.000	6.500	7.500	1.000	0.000	3.750	0.000	1.000	2.250	3.750	6.500	5.750	0.000	**53.250**

Post Season Play

Year	Age	Tm	Lg	G	PA	AB	R	H	2B	3B	HR	RBI	SB	CS	BB	SO	BA	OBP	SLG	OPS	TB	HBP	
1982	26	ATL	N.L-CS	3	11	11	1	3	0	0	0	0	1	1	0	2	0.273	0.273	0.273	0.545	3	0	
				3	11	11	1	3	0	0	0	0	1	1	0	2	0.273	0.273	0.273	0.545	3	0	**Post Season Pts.**
				0.200	0.000	0.000	0.200	0.200	0.000	0.000	0.000	0.000	0.200	0.000	0.000	0.000	0.575	0.000	0.000	0.000	0.000	0.000	**1.375**

World Series Play

Year	Age	Tm	Lg	G	PA	AB	R	H	2B	3B	HR	RBI	SB	CS	BB	SO	BA	OBP	SLG	OPS	TB	HBP	
				0	0	0	0	0	0	0	0	0	0	0	0	0	0	0	0	0	0	0	**World Series Pts.**
				0.000	0.000	0.000	0.000	0.000	0.000	0.000	0.000	0.000	0.000	0.000	0.000	0.000	0.000	0.000	0.000	0.000	0.000	0.000	**0.000**

Yearly Points Leading the League

Category	Times	Points	Total	Category	Times	Points	Total	Categ	Times	Points	Total	Hall of Fame Points	
MVP	2	7	14	B.A.	0	3	0	T.B.	1	2	2	Career Points	53.250
Rookie of Year	0	5	0	Runs	1	2	2	B.O.B.	1	2	2	Post Season Points	1.375
Triple Crown	0	5	0	H.R.'s	1	3	3	OBP%	0	2	0	World Series Points	0.000
Golden Glove	0	3	0	R.B.J's	2	3	6	SLG %	2	2	4	Career Add-On Points	57.000
All-Star	7	2	14	Hits	0	2	0	OBP%	1	2	2	Writers Association Pts.	0.000
Games	4	2	8	S.B.	0	2	0	Totals			10	Military/Lifetime Achievement	0.000
Totals			36	Totals			11	Grand Total Add-On Points		57		Grand Total HOF Points	111.625

Williams, Bernie

Personal Life

Bernabé Williams Figueroa Jr. was born to Bernabé Williams Sr., and Rufina Figueroa. The Williams family lived in the Bronx until Bernie was one year old, when they moved to Puerto Rico. Growing up, Williams played classical guitar as well as baseball.

On February 23, 1990, he married Waleska Ortega. The couple have three children, Bernie Jr., Beatriz, and Bianca. In 1999, they purchased a home in Armonk, New York.

Baseball Career

Williams began his minor-league career in 1986 and was strictly a right-handed hitter. Williams's breakout season came in 1988, when he hit.335 in 92 games for Prince William in the Class-A Carolina League. He was promoted to the Columbus Clippers of the Triple-A International League at the start of the 1989 campaign, but after hitting just .216 in 50 games, he was demoted to Double-A. He inquired Buck Showalter, his manager at both Fort Lauderdale and Albany-Colonie, to practice switch hitting. During the following two campaigns, Williams established himself at Columbus, respectively hitting .294 in 78 games and .306 in 95 games. Within two months of the 1991 season, Williams' major-league debut came on July 7 against the Baltimore Orioles as the starting center fielder and was the Yankees starting center fielder for the remainder of the season, playing in 85 games, batting .238 with 3 home runs and 34 RBIs. His big-league high point was a five-hit game against the Cleveland Indians on October 5.

In 1992 Williams was back in Columbus but he also spent part of the season with the Yankees. He started off in the Bronx but was returned to the Clippers on April 15 after appearing in two games. Williams was recalled on July 31, appeared in 60 games, and hit .281 with 5 home runs and 26 RBIs. Williams played left field in four games and right field in four but was shifted to center field on August 7. From then on, he appeared in every game and played every inning for the rest of the season, his 1992 highlights included a 10-game hitting streak and a four-hit game on September 12.

The 1993 campaign was extra special for Williams: His minor-league apprenticeship was completed, and he spent the entire season with the Yankees as the starting center fielder. However, the easily exasperated Yankees owner, was putting pressure on general manager Gene Michael to trade

A Fan's Perspective

Williams. Williams appeared in 139 games and hit a respectable .268, with 12 home runs and 68 RBIs. The following season, Williams' batting average improved to .289 (with 12 home runs and 57 RBIs) in 108 games. He returned to the leadoff spot for 28 games, during which he hit .362, but also batted sixth, seventh, and eighth. In 1995, Steinbrenner again considered trading Williams but the Yankees kept Williams, who hit 18 home runs and led the team in runs, hits, total bases and stolen bases. Williams continued his hot hitting into the postseason, leading the Yankees with a .429 batting average in the against the Seattle Mariners.

After continuing to improve in 1996, Williams again showcased his skills in the postseason. He batted .467 in the ALDS against Texas and played a sparkling center field. He picked up where he left off in the ALCS against Baltimore, belting an 11th-inning walk-off homer in Game 1. Ending with a .474 ALCS average and two homers, he was named the ALCS MVP. Williams collected just four hits in the 1996 World Series but his clutch homer in the eighth inning of Game 3 helped spark the team's comeback from a 2-0 series deficit to capture the team's first championship since 1978.

Despite his success, following the 1997 season, Williams again was the subject of trade rumors but Yankees general manager Bob Watson refused trade offers from the Tigers and Cubs keeping Williams a Yankee. It was a good thing for the Yankees as he hit 21 home runs, 100 runs batted in, and had a batting average of .328. During the 1998 season, the Yankees went 114–48 to set a then-American League regular-season record, Williams finished with a .339 average, becoming the first player to win a batting title, Gold Glove award, and World Series ring in the same year.

In 1999, Williams recorded 200+ hits for the first time in his career and won his third straight Gold Glove Award. He finished third in the American League in batting average (.342), third in hits (202), fourth in on-base percentage (.435), fifth in bases on balls (100), and seventh in runs scored (116). The following year, he once again won a Gold Glove Award and set career highs with 30 home runs and 121 runs batted in. Williams followed up in 2000 by hitting .307 in 141 games and setting career highs with 30 home runs and 121 RBIs. In the three-postseason series, against Oakland, Seattle, and the Mets, Williams hit .279 with two home runs and five RBIs. Williams maintained his solid play in 2001, appearing in 146 games and hitting .307 with 26 home runs and 94 RBIs. His 38 doubles were a career high, and he was an American League All-Star.

$$\text{The Baseball Hall of Fame}$$

In 2002, Williams appeared in 154 games and finished third in the AL batting race with a .333 average and hit 19 home runs and drove in 102 runs and he was 5-for-15 in four postseason games. His average began to decline starting in 2003 and continued until 2005. Williams wanted to return for 2006 but offered only a minor-league contract and compete for a roster spot. He refused the invitation.

Achievements

- 5-time AL All-Star (1997-2001) & 4-time AL Gold Glove Winner (1997-2000),
- AL Silver Slugger Award Winner (2002) & AL Batting Average Leader (1998).
- 20-Home Run Seasons: 7 (1996-2001 & 2004)
- 1- 30-Home Run Seasons: (2000) & 2-200 Hits Seasons: (1999 & 2002).
- 5-Time 100 RBI Seasons: (1996, 1997, 1999, 2000 & 2002)
- 8-Times 100 Runs Scored Seasons: (1996-2002 & 2004)
- Won four World Series with the New York Yankees (1996, 1998, 1999 & 2000).
- Holds the career postseason record for runs batted in 80.

Hall of Fame

Williams first year of eligibility for the Hall of Fame was in 2012, Williams received for 9.6 %. However, he fell to 3.3% in 2013 and was dropped from the ballot.

Summary Analysis

Williams' Statistical Hall of Fame Points of 113.550 is over the Induction Score of 110.000 and should have been inducted when he became eligible instead of being removed after two years but deserves to be by the BBWAA.

A Fan's Perspective

Williams, Bernie
Positions — Center Fielder

Center Field Potential Hall of Fame Inductee

Born:	September 13, 1968	Height:	6'2" USC 188 cm
From:	San Juan, Puerto Rico	Weight:	180 lbs. 81 Kg.
Throws:	Right	Debut:	July 7, 1991
Bats	Both	Last Game:	October 1, 2006

Year	Age	Tm	Lg	G	PA	AB	R	H	2B	3B	HR	RBI	SB	CS	BB	SO	BA	OBP	SLG	OPS	TB	HBP	Awards
1991	22	NYY	AL	85	374	320	43	76	19	4	3	34	10	5	48	57	0.238	0.336	0.350	0.686	112	1	
1992	23	NYY	AL	62	293	261	39	73	14	2	5	26	7	6	29	36	0.280	0.354	0.406	0.760	106	1	
1993	24	NYY	AL	139	628	567	67	152	31	4	12	68	9	9	53	106	0.268	0.333	0.400	0.734	227	4	
1994	25	NYY	AL	108	475	408	80	118	29	1	12	57	16	9	61	54	0.289	0.384	0.453	0.837	185	3	
1995	26	NYY	AL	144	648	563	93	173	29	9	18	82	8	6	75	98	0.307	0.392	0.487	0.878	274	5	
1996	27	NYY	AL	143	641	551	108	168	26	7	29	102	17	4	82	72	0.305	0.391	0.535	0.926	295	0	MVP-17
1997	28	NYY	AL	129	591	509	107	167	35	6	21	100	15	8	73	80	0.328	0.408	0.544	0.952	277	1	AS,MVP-17,GG
1998	29	NYY	AL	128	578	499	101	169	30	5	26	97	15	9	74	81	0.339	0.422	0.575	0.997	287	1	AS,MVP-7,GG
1999	30	NYY	AL	158	697	591	116	202	28	6	25	115	9	10	100	95	0.342	0.435	0.536	0.971	317	1	AS,MVP-11,GG
2000	31	NYY	AL	141	618	537	108	165	37	6	30	121	13	5	71	84	0.307	0.391	0.566	0.957	304	5	AS,MVP-13,GG
2001	32	NYY	AL	146	633	540	102	166	38	0	26	94	11	5	78	67	0.307	0.395	0.522	0.917	282	6	AS
2002	33	NYY	AL	154	699	612	102	204	37	2	19	102	8	4	83	97	0.333	0.415	0.493	0.908	302	3	MVP-10,SS
2003	34	NYY	AL	119	521	445	77	117	19	1	15	64	5	0	71	61	0.263	0.367	0.411	0.778	183	3	
2004	35	NYY	AL	148	651	561	105	147	29	1	22	70	1	5	85	96	0.262	0.360	0.435	0.795	244	2	
2005	36	NYY	AL	141	546	485	53	121	19	1	12	64	1	2	53	75	0.249	0.321	0.367	0.688	178	1	
2006	37	NYY	AL	131	462	420	65	118	29	0	12	61	2	0	33	53	0.281	0.332	0.436	0.768	183	2	
162 Game Avg.				162	706	614	107	182	35	4	22	98	11	7	83	95	0.297	0.381	0.477	0.858	293	3	
16 Yrs				2076	9053	7869	1366	2336	449	55	287	1257	347	87	1069	1212	0.297	0.381	0.477	0.858	3756	39	Career Pts.
				6.750	0.000	0.000	8.000	4.500	0.000	0.000	4.500	6.750	1.500	0.000	4.500	0.000	5.500	5.500	3.750	6.750	5.500	0.000	63.500

Post Season Play

Year	Age	Tm	Lg	G	PA	AB	R	H	2B	3B	HR	RBI	SB	CS	BB	SO	BA	OBP	SLG	OPS	TB	HBP
1995	26	NYY	S	5	28	21	8	9	2	0	2	5	1	0	7	3	0.429	0.429	0.571	0.810	17	0
1996	27	NYY	S	4	18	15	5	7	0	0	3	5	1	1	2	1	0.467	0.467	0.500	1.067	16	0
1996	27	NYY	S	5	24	19	6	9	3	0	2	6	1	0	5	4	0.474	0.474	0.583	0.947	18	0
1997	28	NYY	S	5	22	17	3	2	1	0	0	1	0	0	4	3	0.118	0.118	0.318	0.176	3	1
1998	29	NYY	S	3	12	11	0	0	0	0	0	0	0	0	1	4	0.000	0.000	0.083	0.000	0	0
1998	29	NYY	S	6	28	21	4	8	1	0	0	5	1	1	7	4	0.381	0.381	0.536	0.429	9	0
1999	30	NYY	S	3	13	11	2	4	1	0	1	6	0	0	1	2	0.364	0.364	0.462	0.727	8	1
1999	30	NYY	S	5	22	20	3	5	1	0	1	2	1	0	2	5	0.250	0.250	0.318	0.450	9	0
2000	31	NYY	S	5	22	20	3	5	3	0	0	1	0	1	1	4	0.250	0.250	0.273	0.400	8	0
2000	31	NYY	S	6	27	23	5	10	1	0	1	3	1	0	2	3	0.435	0.435	0.481	0.609	14	1
2001	32	NYY	S	5	21	18	4	4	3	0	0	5	0	1	3	3	0.222	0.222	0.333	0.389	7	0
2001	32	NYY	S	5	22	17	4	4	0	0	3	5	0	1	5	4	0.235	0.235	0.409	0.765	13	0
2002	33	NYY	S	4	18	15	4	5	1	0	1	3	0	0	3	2	0.333	0.333	0.444	0.600	9	0
2003	34	NYY	S	4	18	15	3	6	2	0	0	3	0	0	2	2	0.400	0.400	0.444	0.533	8	0
2003	34	NYY	S	7	30	26	5	5	1	0	0	2	0	0	4	3	0.192	0.192	0.300	0.231	6	0
2004	35	NYY	S	4	19	18	7	5	1	0	1	3	0	0	1	2	0.278	0.278	0.316	0.500	9	0
2004	35	NYY	S	7	36	36	4	11	3	0	2	10	0	0	0	5	0.306	0.306	0.306	0.556	20	0
2005	36	NYY	S	5	21	19	2	4	2	0	0	1	0	0	1	3	0.211	0.211	0.238	0.316	6	0
2006	37	NYY	S	1	3	3	0	0	0	0	0	0	0	0	0	1	0.000	0.000	0.000	0.000	0	0
				89	404	345	67	103	26	0	17	66	6	5	51	59	0.299	0.393	0.522	0.915	180	3	Post Season Pts.
				1.800	0.000	0.000	1.800	1.600	0.000	0.000	1.800	2.000	0.600	0.000	2.000	0.000	0.600	1.200	1.000	0.800	1.800	0.000	17.000

World Series Play

Year	Age	Tm	Lg	G	PA	AB	R	H	2B	3B	HR	RBI	SB	CS	BB	SO	BA	OBP	SLG	OPS	TB	HBP
1996	27	NYY	WS	6	27	24	3	4	0	0	1	4	1	0	3	6	0.167	0.259	0.292	0.551	7	0
1998	29	NYY	WS	4	18	16	2	1	0	0	1	3	0	0	2	5	0.063	0.167	0.250	0.417	4	0
1999	30	NYY	WS	4	17	13	2	3	0	0	0	0	1	0	4	2	0.231	0.412	0.231	0.643	3	0
2000	31	NYY	WS	5	23	18	2	2	0	0	1	1	0	0	5	5	0.111	0.304	0.278	0.582	5	0
2001	32	NYY	WS	7	28	24	2	5	1	0	0	1	0	0	4	6	0.208	0.321	0.250	0.571	6	0
2003	34	NYY	WS	6	28	25	5	10	2	0	2	5	0	0	2	2	0.400	0.429	0.720	1.149	18	0
				32	141	120	16	25	3	0	5	14	2	0	20	26	0.208	0.321	0.358	0.679	43	0	World Series Pts.
				1.200	0.000	0.000	1.000	0.800	0.000	0.000	1.000	0.800	0.400	0.000	1.000	0.000	0.000	0.000	0.000	0.250	1.600	0.000	8.050

Yearly Points Leading the League

Category	Times	Point	Total	Category	Times	Points	Total	Category	Times	Points	Total
MVP	0	7	0	B.A.	1	3	3	T.B.	0	2	0
Rookie of Ye	0	5	0	Runs	0	2	0	B.O.B.	0	2	0
Triple Crown	0	5	0	H.R.'s	0	3	0	OBP%	0	2	0
Golden Glov	4	3	12	R.B.J's	0	3	0	SLG %	0	2	0
All-Star	5	2	10	Hits	0	2	0	OBPS%	0	2	0
Games	0	2	0	S.B.	0	2	0	Totals	0		0
Totals	9		22	Totals	1		3	Grand Total Add-On Points			25

Hall of Fame Points

Career Points	63.500
Post Season Points	17.000
World Series Points	8.050
Career Add-On Points	25.000
Writers Association Pts.	0.000
Military/Lifetime Achievement	0.000
Grand Total HOF Points	113.550

Damon, Johnny

Personal Life

Johnny David Damon (born November 5, 1973) in Fort Riley, Kansas to Yome and Jimmy Damon. The Damon family settled in Orlando, Florida and he attended Dr. Phillips High School where he was rated the top high school prospect his senior year.

Damon married Angela Vannice, in 1992, and divorced in 2002. The couple had a son and a daughter together. Damon married Michelle Mangan in 2004 and they have six children together: five daughters and a son.

Baseball Career

Damon was selected by the Kansas City Royals 35th overall of the 1992 MLB draft. From 1992 through 1995, Damon rose through the Royals system and made his debut on August 12,1995. He played for Kansas City, Oakland, Boston, New York, Detroit, Tampa Bay, and Cleveland. Damon played in 2490 games, had 2769 hits, 1668 runs, 235 HR's, 1139 R.B.I's,408 S.B., and a .284 batting average over his 18-year career".

Achievements:

- 2-time All-Star (2002 & 2005) & 1-Time Runs Scored Leader (2000).
- 1-Time Stolen Bases Leader & 1-Time 200 Hit Season: (2000).
- 3-Times 20-Home Run Seasons: (2004, 2006 & 2009).
- 10-Time 100 plus Runs Scored Seasons (1998-2006 & 2009).
- 4-Times received MVP Votes (2000, 2004, 2005 & 2006).
- 2-Time World Series Winner: (Red Sox 2004 & Yankees 2009).

Hall of Fame

Damon received 1.9% vote for the 2018 Hall of Fame Election and was dropped off the ballot. He will be eligible again at a to-be determined date in the future.

Summary Analysis

Johnny Damon's Hall of Fame Points is 96.390 and should be voted in by the BBWAA.69

Damon, Johnny — Center Fielder Potential Hall of Fame Inductee

Positions: Outfielder
Born: November 5, 1973
From: Fort Riley, KS
Bats: Left
Throws: Left
Height: 6'2" USG 188 cm
Weight: 206 lbs. 92 Kg.
Debut: August 17, 1995
Last Game: August 1, 2012

Year	Age	Tm	Lg	G	PA	AB	R	H	2B	3B	HR	RBI	SB	CS	BB	SO	BA	OBP	SLG	OPS	TB	HBP	Awards
1995	21	KCR	AL	47	206	188	32	53	11	5	3	23	7	0	12	22	0.282	0.324	0.441	0.765	83	1	
1996	22	KCR	AL	145	566	517	61	140	22	5	6	50	25	5	31	64	0.271	0.313	0.368	0.680	190	3	
1997	23	KCR	AL	146	524	472	70	130	12	8	8	48	16	10	42	70	0.275	0.338	0.386	0.723	182	3	
1998	24	KCR	AL	161	710	642	104	178	30	10	18	66	26	12	58	84	0.277	0.339	0.439	0.779	282	4	
1999	25	KCR	AL	145	660	583	101	179	39	9	14	77	36	6	67	50	0.307	0.379	0.477	0.856	278	3	
2000	26	KCR	AL	159	741	655	136	214	42	10	16	88	46	9	65	60	0.327	0.382	0.495	0.877	324	1	MVP-19
2001	27	OAK	AL	155	719	644	108	165	34	4	9	49	27	12	61	70	0.256	0.324	0.363	0.687	234	5	
2002	28	BOS	AL	154	702	623	118	178	34	11	14	63	31	6	65	70	0.286	0.356	0.443	0.799	276	6	AS
2003	29	BOS	AL	145	690	608	103	166	12	6	12	67	30	6	68	74	0.273	0.345	0.405	0.750	246	2	
2004	30	BOS	AL	150	702	621	123	189	35	6	20	94	19	8	76	71	0.304	0.380	0.477	0.857	296	2	MVP-16
2005	31	BOS	AL	148	688	624	117	197	35	6	10	75	18	1	53	69	0.316	0.366	0.439	0.805	274	2	AS,MVP-13
2006	32	NYY	AL	149	671	593	115	169	35	5	24	80	25	10	67	85	0.285	0.359	0.482	0.841	286	4	MVP-15
2007	33	NYY	AL	141	605	533	93	144	27	2	12	63	27	3	66	79	0.270	0.351	0.396	0.747	211	1	
2008	34	NYY	AL	143	623	555	95	168	27	5	17	71	29	8	64	82	0.303	0.375	0.461	0.836	256	1	
2009	35	NYY	AL	143	626	550	107	155	36	3	24	82	12	0	71	98	0.282	0.365	0.489	0.854	269	2	
2010	36	DET	AL	145	613	539	81	146	36	5	8	51	11	1	69	90	0.271	0.355	0.401	0.756	216	2	
2011	37	TBR	AL	150	647	582	79	152	29	7	16	73	19	6	51	92	0.261	0.326	0.418	0.743	243	7	
2012	38	CLE	AL	64	224	207	25	46	6	2	4	19	4	0	17	27	0.222	0.281	0.329	0.610	68	0	
162 Game Avg.				162	710	633	109	180	34	7	15	74	27	7	65	82	0.284	0.352	0.433	0.785	274	3	
KCR (6 yrs)				803	3407	3057	504	894	156	47	65	352	156	42	275	350	0.292	0.351	0.438	0.789	1339	15	
NYY (4 yrs)				576	2525	2231	410	636	125	15	77	296	93	21	268	344	0.285	0.363	0.458	0.821	1022	9	
BOS (4 yrs)				597	2782	2476	461	730	136	29	56	299	98	21	262	284	0.295	0.362	0.441	0.803	1092	12	
TBR (1 yr)				150	647	582	79	152	29	7	16	73	19	6	51	92	0.261	0.326	0.418	0.743	243	7	
CLE (1 yr)				64	224	207	25	46	6	2	4	19	4	0	17	27	0.222	0.281	0.329	0.610	68	0	
DET (1 yr)				145	613	539	81	146	36	5	8	51	11	1	69	90	0.271	0.355	0.401	0.756	216	2	
OAK (1 yr)				155	719	644	108	165	34	4	9	49	27	12	61	70	0.256	0.324	0.363	0.687	234	5	
18 Yrs				2490	10917	9736	1668	2769	522	109	235	1139	408	103	1003	1257	0.284	0.352	0.433	0.785	4214	50	Career Pts.
				10.500	0.000	0.000	13.000	9.250	0.000	0.000	3.750	5.500	4.500	0.000	3.750	0.000	3.750	3.000	2.000	4.500	8.000	0.000	71.500

Post Season Play

Year	Age	Tm	Lg	G	PA	AB	R	H	2B	3B	HR	RBI	SB	CS	BB	SO	BA	OBP	SLG	OPS	TB	HBP	
2001	27	OAK	ALDS	5	23	22	3	9	2	1	0	0	2	0	1	1	0.409	0.435	0.591	1.026	13	1	
2003	29	BOS	ALDS	5	22	19	2	6	2	0	1	3	2	0	2	1	0.316	0.409	0.579	0.988	11	0	
2003	29	BOS	ALCS	5	23	20	1	4	1	0	0	1	1	0	3	3	0.200	0.304	0.250	0.554	5	0	
2004	30	BOS	ALDS	3	16	15	4	7	1	0	0	0	3	0	1	2	0.467	0.500	0.533	1.033	8	0	
2004	30	BOS	ALCS	7	37	35	5	6	0	0	2	7	2	1	2	8	0.171	0.216	0.343	0.559	12	0	
2005	31	BOS	ALDS	3	14	13	2	3	1	0	0	0	0	0	1	4	0.231	0.286	0.308	0.593	4	0	
2006	32	NYY	ALDS	4	18	17	3	4	0	0	1	3	0	0	1	2	0.235	0.278	0.412	0.690	7	0	
2007	33	NYY	ALDS	4	19	18	2	5	0	0	2	5	0	0	1	5	0.278	0.316	0.611	0.927	11	0	
2009	35	NYY	ALDS	3	13	12	0	1	0	0	0	0	0	0	1	4	0.083	0.154	0.083	0.237	1	0	
2009	35	NYY	ALCS	6	31	30	4	9	1	0	2	5	0	0	1	2	0.300	0.323	0.533	0.856	16	0	
2011	37	TBR	ALDS	4	17	17	3	4	0	0	1	3	0	0	0	4	0.235	0.235	0.412	0.647	7	0	
				49	233	218	29	58	8	1	9	27	10	1	14	36	0.266	0.310	0.436	0.746	95	1	Post Season Pts.
				1.200	0.000	0.000	0.800	1.000	0.000	0.000	1.000	1.000	1.200	0.000	0.600	0.000	0.400	0.250	0.540	0.400	1.000	0.000	9.390

World Series Play

Year	Age	Tm	Lg	G	PA	AB	R	H	2B	3B	HR	RBI	SB	CS	BB	SO	BA	OBP	SLG	OPS	TB	HBP	
2004	30	BOS	WS	4	21	21	4	6	2	1	1	2	0	0	0	1	0.286	0.286	0.619	0.905	13	0	
2009	35	NYY	WS	6	25	22	6	8	2	0	0	4	3	0	3	3	0.364	0.440	0.455	0.895	10	0	
				10	46	43	10	14	4	1	1	6	3	0	3	4	0.326	0.370	0.535	0.904	23	0	World Series Pts.
				0.400	0.000	0.000	0.600	0.600	0.000	0.000	0.250	0.400	0.600	0.000	0.250	0.000	1.400	0.600	0.800	0.800	0.800	0.000	7.500

Yearly Points Leading the League

Category	Times	Points	Total
MVP	0	7	0
Rookie of Year	0	5	0
Triple Crown	0	5	0
Golden Glove	0	3	0
All-Star	2	2	4
Games	0	2	0
Totals			4

Category	Times	Points	Total
B.A.	0	3	0
Runs	1	2	2
H.R.'s	0	3	0
R.B.I's	0	3	0
Hits	0	2	0
S.B.	1	2	2
Totals			4

Categ	Times	Points	Total
T.B.	0	2	0
B.O.B.	0	2	0
OBP%	0	2	0
SLG%	0	2	0
OBPS%	0	2	0
Totals	0		0
Grand Total Add-On Points			8

Hall of Fame Points	
Career Points	71.5000
Post Season Points	9.3900
World Series Points	7.5000
Career Add-On Points	8.0000
Writers Association Pts.	0.0000
Military/Lifetime Achievement	0.0000
Grand Total HOF Points	96.3900

Edmonds, James "Jimmy Baseball"

Personal Life

James Patrick Edmonds was born June 27, 1970 in Fullerton, California. His parents divorced when he was a child and had joint custody. He attended Diamond Bar High School in Diamond Bar, in eastern Los Angeles County.

Edmonds has been married four times. He has 4 daughters and 3 sons from the unions. Edmonds married his fourth wife Kortnie O'Connor in 2022.

Baseball Career

Edmonds was selected in the seventh round of the 1988 Major League Baseball draft by the California Angels and played in the minors until 1993 when the Angels promoted Edmonds to the majors for the first time. He made his MLB debut on September 9, and played for the California/Anaheim Angels, St. Louis Cardinals, San Diego Padres, Chicago Cubs, Milwaukee Brewers, and Cincinnati Reds of Major League Baseball from 1993 to 2010.

- 8-time Gold Glove Winner (1997/AL, 1998/AL & 2000-2005/NL)
- 20-Home Run Seasons: 11 (1995-1998, 2000-2005 & 2008)
- 30-Home Run Seasons: 5 (1995, 2000 (40), 2001, 2003 & 2004 (40).
- 100 RBI Seasons: 4 (1995, 2000, 2001 & 2004)
- 100 Runs Scored Seasons: 4 (1995, 1998, 2000 & 2004)
- Won a World Series with the St. Louis Cardinals in 2006

Hall of Fame Candidacy

Edmonds was eligible for the Baseball Hall of Fame in 2015 and received just 2.5% of the vote and fell off of the ballot. He is next eligible in 2029.

Summary Analysis

Jim Edmonds Statistical Hall of Fame Points of 109.750 and should be elected when eligible. His career achievements are Hall of Fame worthy.

A Fan's Perspective

Edmonds, Jim — Center Fielder Potential Hall of Fame Inductee

Positions: Centerfielder
Bats: Left
Throw Left

Born: June 27, 1970
From: Fullerton, CA
Debut: September 9, 1993
Last Game: September 21, 2010

Height: 6'1" USC 185 cm
Weight: 190 lbs. 86 Kg.

Year	Age	Tm	Lg	G	D	AB	R	H	2B	3B	HR	RBI	SB	CS	BB	SO	BA	OBP	SLG	OPS	TB	HBP	Awards
1993	23	CAL	AL	18	63	61	5	15	4	1	0	4	0	2	2	16	0.246	0.270	0.344	0.614	21	0	
1994	24	CAL	AL	94	323	289	35	79	13	1	5	37	4	2	30	72	0.273	0.343	0.377	0.720	109	1	RoY-8
1995	25	CAL	AL	141	620	558	120	162	30	4	33	107	1	4	51	130	0.290	0.352	0.536	0.888	299	5	AS,MVP-14
1996	26	CAL	AL	114	483	431	73	131	28	3	27	66	4	0	46	101	0.304	0.375	0.571	0.946	246	4	
1997	27	ANA	AL	133	571	502	82	146	27	0	26	80	5	7	60	80	0.291	0.368	0.500	0.868	251	4	GG
1998	28	ANA	AL	154	659	599	115	184	42	1	25	91	7	5	57	114	0.307	0.368	0.506	0.874	303	1	GG
1999	29	ANA	AL	55	233	204	34	51	17	2	5	23	5	4	28	45	0.258	0.339	0.426	0.766	87	0	
2000	30	STL	NL	152	643	525	129	155	25	0	42	108	10	3	103	167	0.295	0.411	0.583	0.994	306	6	AS,MVP-4,GG
2001	31	STL	NL	150	600	500	95	152	38	1	30	110	5	5	93	136	0.304	0.410	0.564	0.974	282	4	GG
2002	32	STL	NL	144	576	476	96	148	31	3	28	83	4	3	86	134	0.311	0.420	0.561	0.981	267	8	MVP-17,GG
2003	33	STL	NL	137	531	447	89	123	32	2	39	89	1	3	77	127	0.275	0.385	0.617	1.002	276	4	AS,MVP-27,GG
2004	34	STL	NL	153	612	498	102	150	38	3	42	111	8	3	101	150	0.301	0.418	0.643	1.061	320	5	MVP-5,GG,SS
2005	35	STL	NL	142	567	467	88	123	37	1	29	89	5	5	91	139	0.263	0.385	0.533	0.918	249	4	AS,MVP-26,GG
2006	36	STL	NL	110	408	350	52	90	18	0	19	70	4	0	53	101	0.257	0.350	0.471	0.822	165	0	
2007	37	STL	NL	117	411	365	39	92	15	1	12	53	0	2	41	75	0.252	0.325	0.403	0.728	147	0	
2008	38	TOT	NL	111	401	340	53	80	19	2	20	55	2	2	55	82	0.235	0.343	0.479	0.822	163	2	
2008	38	SDP	NL	26	103	90	6	16	2	0	1	6	2	1	10	24	0.178	0.265	0.233	0.498	21	1	
2008	38	CHC	NL	85	298	250	47	64	17	2	19	49	0	1	45	58	0.256	0.369	0.568	0.937	142	1	
2010	40	TOT	NL	86	272	246	44	68	23	0	11	23	2	0	24	60	0.276	0.342	0.504	0.846	124	1	
2010	40	MIL	NL	73	240	217	38	62	21	0	8	20	2	0	21	53	0.286	0.350	0.493	0.843	107	1	
2010	40	CIN	NL	13	32	29	6	6	2	0	3	3	0	0	3	7	0.207	0.281	0.586	0.867	17	1	
162 Game Avg.				162	643	552	101	157	35	2	32	97	5	4	80	139	0.284	0.376	0.527	0.904	291	0	
STL (11 yrs)				1305	4358	3638	690	1033	234	11	243	713	37	24	645	1029	0.285	0.393	0.555	0.947	2012	31	
ANA (7 yrs)				709	2951	2644	464	768	161	12	121	408	26	24	274	558	0.290	0.359	0.498	0.856	1316	15	
SDP (1 yr)				26	103	90	8	16	2	0	1	6	2	1	10	24	0.178	0.265	0.233	0.498	21	1	
CIN (1 yr)				13	32	29	6	6	2	0	3	3	0	0	3	7	0.207	0.281	0.586	0.867	17	0	
CHC (1 yr)				85	298	250	47	64	17	2	19	49	0	1	45	58	0.256	0.369	0.568	0.937	142	1	
MIL (1 yr)				73	240	217	38	62	21	0	8	20	2	0	21	53	0.286	0.350	0.493	0.843	107	1	
NL (10 yrs)				1300	5029	4214	787	1181	276	13	272	791	41	26	724	1171	0.280	0.386	0.546	0.932	2299	34	
AL (7 yrs)				709	2951	2644	464	768	161	12	121	408	26	24	274	558	0.290	0.359	0.498	0.856	1316	15	
17 Yrs				2011	7980	6858	1251	1949	437	25	393	1199	67	50	998	1729	0.284	0.376	0.527	0.903	3615	49	Career Points
				5.500	0.000	0.000	6.750	1.500	0.000	0.000	8.000	5.500	1.000	0.000	3.750	0.000	3.750	5.500	8.000	9.250	5.500	0	64.000

Post Season Play

Year	Age	Tm	Lg	G	D	AB	R	H	2B	3B	HR	RBI	SB	CS	BB	SO	BA	OBP	SLG	OPS	TB	HBP	
2000	30	STL	NL	5	15	14	5	8	4	0	2	7	1	0	1	2	0.571	1.286	1.286	1.886	18	0	
2000	30	STL	NL	5	23	22	1	5	1	0	1	5	0	0	1	9	0.227	0.409	0.409	0.670	9	0	
2001	31	STL	NL	5	20	17	3	4	1	0	2	3	0	0	3	6	0.235	0.647	0.647	0.897	11	0	
2002	32	STL	NL	3	13	11	1	3	0	0	1	2	0	1	2	4	0.273	0.545	0.545	0.930	6	0	
2002	32	STL	NL	5	22	20	2	8	2	0	1	4	0	0	2	5	0.400	0.650	0.650	1.105	13	0	
2004	34	STL	NL	4	18	15	1	4	0	0	1	2	0	1	1	9	0.267	0.467	0.467	0.779	7	1	
2004	34	STL	NL	7	28	24	2	7	3	0	2	7	0	0	2	6	0.292	0.625	0.625	0.982	15	0	
2005	35	STL	NL	3	13	11	5	4	2	0	1	1	0	0	2	2	0.364	0.818	0.818	1.280	9	0	
2005	35	STL	NL	6	24	19	2	4	1	0	0	0	1	0	5	5	0.211	0.263	0.263	0.638	5	0	
2006	36	STL	NL	4	16	13	2	4	0	0	0	2	0	0	2	3	0.308	0.308	0.308	0.745	4	0	
2006	36	STL	NL	7	27	22	5	5	0	0	2	4	0	0	5	8	0.227	0.500	0.500	0.870	11	1	
2008	38	CHC	NL	3	10	10	1	2	1	0	0	1	0	0	0	2	0.200	0.200	0.300	0.500	3	0	
				55	227	198	30	58	14	0	13	38	2	2	26	58	0.293	0.375	0.561	0.936	111	2	Post Season Pts.
				1.200	0.000	0.000	0.800	1.000	0.000	0.000	1.400	1.600	0.250	0.000	1.200	0.000	0.600	1.000	1.200	1.000	1.200	0.000	12.458

World Series Play

Year	Age	Tm	Lg	G	D	AB	R	H	2B	3B	HR	RBI	SB	CS	BB	SO	BA	OBP	SLG	OPS	TB	HBP	
2004	34	STL	NL	4	16	15	2	1	0	0	0	0	0	0	1	8	0.067	0.067	0.067	0.192	1	0	
2006	36	STL	NL	5	20	17	1	4	2	0	0	4	0	0	3	8	0.235	0.353	0.353	0.702	8	0	
				9	36	32	3	5	2	0	0	4	0	0	4	14	0.156	0.250	0.219	0.469	7	0	World Series Pts.
				0.400	0.000	0.000	0.250	0.250	0.000	0.000	0.000	0.250	0.000	0.000	0.250	0.000	0.000	0.000	0.000	0.000	0.250	0.000	1.500

Yearly Points Leading the League

Category	Times	Points	Total	Category	Times	Points	Total	Categs	Times	Points	Total
MVP	0	7	0	B.A.	0	3	0	T.B.	0	2	0
Rookie of Year	0	5	0	Runs	0	2	0	B.O.B.	0	2	0
Triple Crown	0	5	0	H.R.'s	0	3	0	OBP%	0	2	0
Golden Glove	8	3	24	R.B.I's	0	3	0	SLG%	0	2	0
All-Star	4	2	8	Hits	0	2	0	OBPS%	0	2	0
Games	0	2	0	S.B.	0	2	0	Totals			0
Totals			32	Totals			0	Grand Total Add-On Points			32

Hall of Fame Points

Career Points	64.000
Post Season Points	12.450
World Series Points	1.500
Career Add-On Points	32.000
Writers Association Pts.	0.000
Military/Lifetime Achievement	0.000
Grand Total HOF Points	109.950

Finley, Steve

Personal Life

Steven Allen Finley was born March 12, 1965, in Union City, Tennessee to Howard and no information is available on his mother, or siblings. He attended Paducah Tilghman High School and Southern Illinois University, where he earned a degree in physiology.

Finley was married to Amy Jantzen from 992 to 2008. They had 5 children Franchesca, Reed, Austin, Blake, and Sophia. Finley married Meaghan Hunt in 2012.

Baseball Career

In 1987, he was selected by the Baltimore Orioles in the 13th round of the draft, and did sign. For his 19-year career, Finley played in 2583 games, had 2548 hits. 304 home runs, 1167 runs batted in, 320 stolen bases, .271 batting average, .332 OBP, .442 SLG%, and an OPS of .775. Finley is one of only two players in major league history to hit 300, or more home runs, 425 doubles, 100 triples, and steal 300 plus bases. He played for Baltimore, Houston, San Diego, and Arizona.

Achievements

- 2-time NL All-Star (1997 & 2000) & 1 Time 100 RBI Seasons: (1999).
- 5-time NL Gold Glove Winner (1995, 1996, 1999, 2000 & 2004)
- 20, or more Home Run Seasons: 7 (1996, 1997, 1999, 2000 & 2002-2004)
- 100 Runs Scored Seasons: 5 (1995-1997, 1999 & 2000)
- Won a World Series with the Arizona Diamondbacks in 2001

Hall of Fame

He was eligible for the Hall of Fame in 2013 but received only four votes and was dropped from the ballot. He will be eligible at a to-be determined date in the future.

Summary Analysis

Steve Finley's Statistical Hall of Fame Points are 94.150 and should be voted on by the BBWAA for election.

A Fan's Perspective

Finley, Steve
Positions: Centerfielder

Center Fielder Potential Hall of Fame Inductee

Born:	March 12, 1965	Height:	6' 2" USC 188 cm
From:	Union City, TN	Weight:	175 lbs. 79 Kg
Bats:	Left	Debut:	April 3, 1989
Throws:	Left	Last Game:	June 3, 2007

Year	Age	Tm	Lg	G	PA	AB	R	H	2B	3B	HR	RBI	SB	CS	BB	SO	BA	OBP	SLG	OPS	TB	HBP	Awards
1989	24	BAL	AL	81	241	217	35	54	5	2	2	25	17	3	15	30	0.249	0.298	0.318	0.616	69	1	
1990	25	BAL	AL	142	513	464	46	119	16	4	3	37	22	9	32	53	0.256	0.304	0.328	0.632	153	1	
1991	26	HOU	NL	159	656	596	84	170	28	10	8	54	34	18	42	65	0.285	0.331	0.406	0.737	242	2	
1992	27	HOU	NL	162	686	607	84	177	29	13	5	55	44	9	58	63	0.292	0.355	0.407	0.762	247	3	
1993	28	HOU	NL	142	585	545	69	145	15	13	8	44	19	6	28	65	0.266	0.304	0.385	0.689	210	3	
1994	29	HOU	NL	94	417	373	64	103	16	5	11	33	13	7	28	52	0.276	0.329	0.434	0.764	162	2	
1995	30	SDP	NL	139	630	562	104	167	23	8	10	44	36	12	59	62	0.297	0.366	0.420	0.786	236	3	GG
1996	31	SDP	NL	161	721	655	126	195	45	9	30	95	22	8	56	87	0.298	0.354	0.531	0.885	348	4	MVP-10,GG
1997	32	SDP	NL	143	615	560	101	146	26	5	28	92	15	3	43	82	0.261	0.313	0.475	0.788	266	3	AS
1998	33	SDP	NL	159	674	619	92	154	40	6	14	67	12	3	45	103	0.249	0.301	0.401	0.702	248	3	
1999	34	ARI	NL	156	663	590	100	156	32	10	34	103	8	4	63	94	0.264	0.336	0.525	0.861	310	3	GG
2000	35	ARI	NL	152	623	539	100	151	27	5	35	96	12	6	65	87	0.280	0.361	0.544	0.904	293	8	AS,GG
2001	36	ARI	NL	140	548	495	66	136	27	4	14	73	11	7	47	67	0.275	0.337	0.430	0.767	213	1	
2002	37	ARI	NL	150	577	505	82	145	24	4	25	89	16	4	65	73	0.287	0.370	0.499	0.869	252	3	
2003	38	ARI	NL	147	582	516	82	148	24	10	22	70	15	8	57	94	0.287	0.363	0.500	0.863	258	6	MVP-14,GG
2004	39	TOT	NL	162	706	628	92	170	38	1	36	94	9	7	61	82	0.271	0.333	0.490	0.823	308	1	
2004	39	ARI	NL	104	456	404	61	111	16	1	23	48	8	4	40	52	0.275	0.338	0.490	0.828	198	1	
2004	39	LAD	NL	58	250	224	31	59	12	0	13	46	1	3	21	30	0.263	0.324	0.491	0.815	110	0	
2005	40	LAA	AL	112	440	406	41	90	20	1	12	54	8	4	26	71	0.222	0.273	0.374	0.645	152	3	
2006	41	SFG	NL	139	481	426	66	105	21	12	6	40	7	0	46	55	0.246	0.320	0.394	0.714	168	2	
2007	42	COL	NL	43	102	94	9	17	3	0	1	2	0	0	8	4	0.181	0.245	0.245	0.490	23	0	
162 Game Avg.				162	656	589	91	160	28	8	19	73	20	7	53	81	0.271	0.332	0.442	0.775	261	3	
ARI (6 yrs)				849	3449	3049	491	847	150	34	153	479	70	33	337	467	0.278	0.351	0.500	0.851	1524	22	
SDP (4 yrs)				602	2640	2396	423	662	134	28	82	298	85	26	203	344	0.276	0.334	0.458	0.792	1098	13	
HOU (4 yrs)				557	2344	2121	301	595	88	41	32	186	110	40	156	245	0.281	0.331	0.406	0.737	861	10	
BAL (2 yrs)				223	754	681	81	173	21	6	5	62	39	12	47	83	0.254	0.302	0.325	0.627	221	3	
COL (1 yr)				43	102	94	9	17	3	0	1	2	0	0	8	4	0.181	0.245	0.245	0.490	23	0	
SFG (1 yr)				139	481	426	66	105	21	12	6	40	7	0	46	55	0.246	0.320	0.394	0.714	168	2	
LAD (1 yr)				58	250	224	31	59	12	0	13	46	1	3	21	30	0.263	0.324	0.491	0.815	110	0	
LAA (1 yr)				112	440	406	41	90	20	1	12	54	8	4	26	71	0.222	0.271	0.374	0.645	152	3	
NL (16 yrs)				2248	9266	8310	1321	2285	408	115	287	1051	273	102	771	1145	0.275	0.338	0.455	0.793	3764	47	
AL (3 yrs)				335	1194	1087	122	263	41	9	17	116	47	16	73	154	0.242	0.291	0.343	0.634	373	6	
19 Yrs				2583	10460	9397	1443	2548	449	124	304	1167	320	118	844	1299	0.271	0.332	0.442	0.775	4157	53	Career Pts.
				11.750	0.000	0.000	9.250	6.750	0.000	0.000	4.500	5.500	3.000	0.000	2.500	0.000	2.500	1.000	2.500	3.750	8.000	0	62.000

Post Season Play

Year	Age	Tm	Lg	G	PA	AB	R	H	2B	3B	HR	RBI	SB	CS	BB	SO	BA	OBP	SLG	OPS	TB	HBP	
1996	31	SDP	NLDS	3	13	12	0	1	0	0	0	1	1	0	0	4	0.083	0.154	0.083	0.237	1	1	
1998	33	SDP	NLDS	4	11	10	2	1	1	0	0	1	0	0	1	4	0.100	0.182	0.200	0.382	2	0	
1998	33	SDP	NLCS	6	27	21	3	7	1	0	0	2	1	0	6	2	0.333	0.481	0.381	0.862	8	0	
1999	34	ARI	NLDS	4	16	13	0	5	1	0	0	5	0	0	3	1	0.385	0.500	0.462	0.962	6	0	
2001	36	ARI	NLDS	5	19	19	1	8	1	0	0	2	0	0	0	2	0.421	0.421	0.474	0.895	9	0	
2001	36	ARI	NLCS	5	17	14	1	4	1	0	0	4	1	0	3	1	0.286	0.412	0.357	0.769	5	0	
2002	37	ARI	NLDS	3	12	9	1	2	0	0	0	1	1	0	2	2	0.222	0.333	0.222	0.556	2	0	
2004	39	LAD	NLDS	4	17	16	0	2	1	0	0	2	0	0	1	0	0.125	0.176	0.188	0.364	3	0	
2005	40	LAA	ALDS	5	16	11	2	1	1	0	0	1	0	0	1	4	0.091	0.167	0.162	0.348	2	0	
2005	40	LAA	ALCS	3	9	9	1	2	0	0	0	0	0	0	0	2	0.222	0.222	0.222	0.444	2	0	
				42	157	134	11	33	7	0	0	19	4	0	17	22	0.246	0.331	0.299	0.630	40	1	Post Season Pts.
				1.000	0.000	0.000	0.400	0.600	0.000	0.000	0.000	0.800	0.400	0.000	0.800	0.000	0.250	0.400	0.000	0.250	0.400	0.000	5.300

World Series Play

Year	Age	Tm	Lg	G	PA	AB	R	H	2B	3B	HR	RBI	SB	CS	BB	SO	BA	OBP	SLG	OPS	TB	HBP	
1998	33	SDP	WS	3	12	12	0	1	1	0	0	0	1	0	0	2	0.083	0.083	0.167	0.25	2	0	
2001	36	ARI	WS	7	23	19	5	7	0	0	1	2	0	1	4	5	0.368	0.478	0.526	1.005	10	0	
				10	35	31	5	8	1	0	1	2	1	1	4	7	0.258	0.343	0.387	0.730	12	0	World Series Pts.
				0.400	0.000	0.000	0.400	0.400	0.000	0.000	0.250	0.250	0.250	0.000	0.250	0.000	0.600	0.250	0.000	0.400	0.400	0.000	3.850

Yearly Points Leading the League

Category	Times	Points	Total
MVP	0	7	0
Rookie of Year	0	5	0
Triple Crown	0	5	0
Golden Glove	5	3	15
All-Star	1	2	4
Games	3	2	4
Totals			23

Category	Times	Points	Total
B.A.	0	3	0
Runs	0	3	0
H.R.'s	0	3	0
R.B.I's	0	3	0
Hits	0	2	0
S.B.	0	2	0
Totals			0

Categor	Times	Points	Total
T.B.	0	2	0
B.O.B.	0	2	0
OBP%	0	2	0
SLG %	0	2	0
OBPS%	0	2	0
Totals			0
Grand Total Add-On Points			23

Hall of Fame Points	
Career Points	62.000
Post Season Points	5.300
World Series Points	3.850
Career Add-On Points	23.000
Writers Association Pts.	0.000
Military/Lifetime Achievement	0.000
Grand Total HOF Points	94.150

Hunter, Torii

Personal Life

Torii Kedar Hunter was born July 18, 1975, in Pine Bluffs, Arkansas to Shirley and Theotis Hunter. He has three brothers and attended Pine Bluff High School where he excelled in baseball, football, basketball, and track and received All-State honors for his junior and senior years.

Hunter married Katrina Hall on November 22, 1996, with the couple having two sons Torii Jr., Cameron, and Darius McClinton-Hunter. In addition, he has a son, Monshadrik, from outside of marriage.

Baseball Career

The Twins selected Hunter with the 20th overall pick in the 1993 draft. From 1993 through 1998, Hunter rose the ranks of the Twins farm system and made his debut in 1997. He became a mainstay of the Minnesota Twins for nine consecutive seasons. His overall statistics were 2,452 hits, 1,296 runs, 1,391 RBIs, 353 HRs, 195 SBs, and 498 doubles.

Achievements

- 5-time AL All-Star (2002, 2007, 2009, 2010 & 2013).
- 9-time AL Gold Glove (2001-2009) & 2-time Silver Slugger (2009 & 2013).
- 5-Times received Most Valuable Player Votes (2001, 2002, 2004, 2007 & 2013).
- 20, or more Home Run Seasons: 11 (2001-2004, 2006-2011 & 2015).
- 100 RBI Seasons: 2 (2003 & 2007),

Hall of Fame Candidacy

Hunter became eligible in 2021 and received 9.5% of the vote and continues to make the 5% minimum threshold in 2022 and 2023 and remains on the ballot.

Summary Analysis

Hunters Statistical Hall of Fame Points are 104.450. He should be voted on by the BBWAA for election and deserves to be elected into the Baseball Hall of Fame.

A Fan's Perspective

Hunter, Tori — **Center Fielder Potential Hall of Fame Inductee**

Positions	Centerfielder		
Born:	July 18, 1975	Height:	6'2" — USC 188 cm
From:	Pine Bluff, AR	Weight:	220 lbs. — 99 Kg.
Bats:	Right	Debut:	August 22, 1997
Throws:	Right	Last Game:	October 3, 2015

Year	Age	Tm	Lg	G	D	AB	R	H	2B	3B	HR	RBI	SB	CS	BB	SO	BA	OBP	SLG	OPS	TB	HBP	Awards
1997	21	MIN	AL	1	0	0	0	0	0	0	0	0	0	0	0	0	0.000	0.000	0.000	0.000	0	0	
1998	22	MIN	AL	6	19	17	0	4	1	0	0	2	0	1	2	6	0.235	0.316	0.294	0.610	5	0	
1999	23	MIN	AL	135	422	384	52	98	17	2	9	35	10	6	26	72	0.255	0.309	0.380	0.689	146	6	
2000	24	MIN	AL	99	358	336	44	94	14	7	5	44	4	3	18	68	0.280	0.318	0.408	0.726	137	3	
2001	25	MIN	AL	148	603	564	82	147	32	5	27	92	9	6	29	125	0.261	0.306	0.479	0.784	270	8	MVP-21,GG
2002	26	MIN	AL	148	604	561	85	162	37	4	29	94	23	8	35	118	0.289	0.334	0.524	0.859	294	5	AS,MVP-6,GG
2003	27	MIN	AL	154	642	581	83	145	31	4	26	102	6	7	50	106	0.250	0.312	0.451	0.762	262	5	GG
2004	28	MIN	AL	138	569	520	79	141	37	0	23	81	21	7	40	101	0.271	0.330	0.475	0.805	247	7	MVP-21,GG
2005	29	MIN	AL	98	416	372	63	100	24	1	14	56	23	7	34	65	0.269	0.337	0.452	0.788	168	6	GG
2006	30	MIN	AL	147	611	557	86	155	21	2	31	98	12	6	45	108	0.278	0.336	0.490	0.826	273	5	GG
2007	31	MIN	AL	160	650	600	94	172	45	1	28	107	18	9	40	101	0.287	0.334	0.505	0.839	303	5	AS,MVP-15,GG
2008	32	LAA	AL	146	608	551	85	153	37	2	21	78	19	5	50	108	0.278	0.344	0.466	0.810	257	6	GG
2009	33	LAA	AL	119	506	451	74	135	26	1	22	90	18	4	47	92	0.299	0.366	0.508	0.873	229	3	AS,GG,SS
2010	34	LAA	AL	152	646	573	76	161	36	0	23	90	9	12	61	106	0.281	0.354	0.464	0.819	266	7	AS
2011	35	LAA	AL	156	649	580	80	152	24	2	23	82	5	7	62	125	0.262	0.336	0.429	0.765	249	4	
2012	36	LAA	AL	140	584	534	81	167	24	1	16	92	9	1	38	133	0.313	0.365	0.451	0.817	241	8	
2013	37	DET	AL	144	652	606	90	184	37	5	17	84	3	2	26	113	0.304	0.334	0.465	0.800	282	7	AS,MVP-19,SS
2014	38	DET	AL	142	586	549	71	157	33	2	17	83	4	3	23	89	0.286	0.319	0.446	0.765	245	7	
2015	39	MIN	AL	139	567	521	67	125	22	0	22	81	2	5	35	105	0.240	0.293	0.409	0.702	213	6	
162 Game Avg.				162	662	605	89	167	34	3	24	95	13	7	45	119	0.277	0.331	0.461	0.793	279	7	
MIN (12 yrs)				1373	5461	5013	739	1343	281	26	214	792	128	65	354	975	0.268	0.321	0.462	0.783	2318	55	
LAA (5 yrs)				713	2993	2689	396	768	147	6	105	432	60	29	258	564	0.286	0.352	0.462	0.814	1242	28	
DET (2 yrs)				286	1238	1155	161	341	70	7	34	167	7	5	49	202	0.295	0.327	0.456	0.783	527	14	
19 Yrs				2372	9692	8857	1296	2452	498	39	353	1391	195	99	661	1741	0.277	0.331	0.461	0.793	4087	97	**Career Pts.**
				9.250	0.000	0.000	6.750	5.500	0.000	0.000	6.750	9.250	2.000	0.000	1.500	0.000	3.000	2.000	3.000	4.500	6.750	0.000	**60.250**

Post Season Play

Year	Age	Tm	Lg	G	PA	AB	R	H	2B	3B	HR	RBI	SB	CS	BB	SO	BA	OBP	SLG	OPS	TB	HBP	
2002	26	MIN	ALDS	5	21	20	4	6	4	0	0	2	0	0	1	4	0.300	0.333	0.500	0.833	10	0	
2002	26	MIN	ALCS	5	20	18	2	3	2	0	0	0	0	0	1	3	0.167	0.211	0.278	0.488	5	0	
2003	27	MIN	ALDS	4	16	14	3	6	0	1	1	2	0	0	2	2	0.429	0.500	0.786	1.286	11	0	
2004	28	MIN	ALDS	4	19	17	5	6	1	0	1	2	2	0	1	1	0.353	0.368	0.588	0.957	10	0	
2006	30	MIN	ALDS	3	12	11	1	3	1	0	1	2	0	0	0	1	0.273	0.273	0.636	0.909	7	0	
2008	32	LAA	ALDS	4	19	18	0	7	0	0	0	5	0	0	1	3	0.389	0.421	0.389	0.810	7	0	
2009	33	LAA	ALDS	3	13	10	2	2	1	0	1	3	0	0	2	1	0.200	0.385	0.600	0.985	6	1	
2009	33	LAA	ALCS	6	28	23	2	7	1	0	0	2	1	1	5	4	0.304	0.429	0.348	0.776	8	0	
2013	37	DET	ALDS	5	21	19	3	3	0	0	0	0	0	1	1	6	0.158	0.238	0.158	0.396	3	1	
2013	37	DET	ALCS	6	27	26	2	6	2	0	0	2	0	0	1	5	0.231	0.259	0.308	0.567	8	0	
2014	38	DET	ALDS	3	12	10	2	2	0	0	0	0	0	0	2	2	0.200	0.333	0.200	0.533	2	0	
				48	208	186	26	51	12	1	4	20	3	2	17	32	0.274	0.340	0.414	0.754	77	2	**Post Season Pts.**
				1.000	0.000	0.000	0.800	0.800	0.000	0.000	0.400	0.400	0.400	0.000	0.800	0.000	0.400	0.600	0.400	0.400	0.800	0.000	**7.200**

World Series Play

Year	Age	Tm	Lg	G	PA	AB	R	H	2B	3B	HR	RBI	SB	CS	BB	SO	BA	OBP	SLG	OPS	TB	HBP	
None				0	0	0	0	0	0	0	0	0	0	0	0	0	0	0	0	0	0	0	**World Saeries Pts.**
				0.000	0.000	0.000	0.000	0.000	0.000	0.000	0.000	0.000	0.000	0.000	0.000	0.000	0.000	0.000	0.000	0.000	0.000	0.000	**0.000**

Yearly Points Leading the League

Category	Times	Points	Total	Category	Times	Points	Total	Category	Times	Points	Total
MVP	0	7	0	B.A.	0	3	0	T.B.	0	2	0
Rookie of Yea	0	5	0	Runs	0	2	0	B.O.B.	0	2	0
Triple Crown	0	5	0	H.R.'s	0	3	0	OBP%	0	2	0
Golden Glove	9	3	27	R.B.I's	0	3	0	SLG %	0	2	0
All-Star	5	2	10	Hits	0	2	0	OBPS%	0	2	0
Games	0	2	0	S.B.	0	2	0	Totals			0
Totals			37	Totals			0	Grand Total Add-On Points			37

Hall of Fame Points	
Career Points	60.250
Post Season Points	7.200
World Series Points	0.000
Career Add-On Points	37.000
Writers Association Pts.	0.000
Military/Lifetime Achievement	0.000
Grand Total HOF Points	104.450

The Baseball Hall of Fame

Statistical Review of Potential Right Fielders for the Hall of Fame

Player	Years Played	Career Pts.	Post Season Pts.	World Series Pts.	Add-On Pts.	Mil/LT Pts.	Total HOF Pts.	Needed HOF Votes	Comments
Players Needing to be Inducted									
Evans, Dwight	20	78.250	2.050	8.800	53.000	0.000	142.100	0	Inducted
Parker, Dave	19	63.000	1.850	3.200	53.000	0.000	121.050	0	Inducted
Sheffield, Gary	12	106.750	7.550	6.200	22.000	0.000	142.500	0	Inducted
Suziki, Ichiro	19	74.500	7.450	0.000	85.000	0.000	166.950	0	Inducted
Players Needing to be Voted into the Hall of Fame by the BBWAA									
Abreau, Bobby	18	79.700	6.500	0.000	11.000	0.000	97.200	13	Need Voting
Staub, Rusty	23	66.500	6.450	6.250	16.000	0.000	95.200	15	Inducted
Players Not Meeting the Statistical Requirements									
Batista, Jose	15	42.250	6.650	0.000	18.000	0.000	66.900	N/A	DMF
Bonds, Bobby	14	50.750	1.500	0.000	18.000	0.000	70.250	N/A	DMR
Colavito, Rocky	14	48.000	0.000	0.000	36.000	0.000	84.000	N/A	DMR
Green, Shawn	15	50.000	6.150	0.000	11.000	0.000	67.150	N/A	DMR
Maris, Roger	12	30.750	0.000	8.050	46.000	0.000	84.800	N/A	DMR
Ordonez, Magglio	15	54.500	4.400	0.600	17.000	0.000	76.500	N/A	DMF
Singleton, Ken	15	51.000	2.610	2.675	10.000	0.000	66.285	N/A	DMR
Smith, Reggie	17	51.225	4.225	7.000	21.000	0.000	83.450	N/A	DMR
Tiernan, Mike	13	53.250	0.000	10.400	20.000	0.000	73.650	N/A	DMR

Hall of Fame Statistical Requirements:

All Players achieving the total of 110.000, or greater, Total Hall of Fame Points, shall be Inducted after five (5) years of retirement. This provision can be waived due to the death by a 75% vote of the 25 Panel BBWAA's. Individuals receiving less than the required 110.000 Hall of Fame Points are eligible for Election after five (5) years of retirement. A 25 person BBWAA will determine the Players that will be Inducted and vote on the Players needing to be elected. An example of those needing to be elected are as follows: Player "A" has a total of 95 Hall of Fame Points and will need 15 of the (25) BBWAA votes to be Elected in the following year.

Right Fielders Needing to be Inducted.

1. **Dwight Evans**
2. **Dave Parker**
3. **Gary Sheffield**
4. **Ichiro Suzuki**

110.000 Hall of Fame Statistical Induction Criteria

Evans, Dwight "Dewey"

Personal Life

Dwight Michael "Dewey" Evans (born November 3, 1951) in Santa Monica, California to Marie and Duff Evans. Dwight attended Granada Hills High School in the tenth grade, he transferred to Chatsworth High School where he made the team his junior year but made All-Valley in the San Fernando Valley League and graduated in 1969. He won the league MVP award his senior year and found himself being scouted.

Evans married Susan Severson on September 12, 1970, with the couple having three children, Timothy, Kirstin, and Justin. Their youngest child, Justin, died in April 2019 at age 42 of complication from neurofibromatosis. Their son Timothy died ten months later from complications of the same disease.

Baseball Career

The Red Sox selected Evans in the fifth round of the 1969 amateur draft with the 107th overall pick. Evans was assigned to the Jamestown, NY farm club and played in Boston's minor league system from 1969 until he made his major league debut on September 16, 1972. Early in his major league career, Evans was primarily a defensive standout with a modest bat. In the second half of his career, he became a powerful hitter. In 1973, the Sox gave him number 24 and wore it for the rest of his career.

Evans was the Red Sox regular right fielder starting in 1973, a role he would have until 1987. In 1973 he batted .223 with 10 home runs and 32 RBIs, and in 1974 he batted .281 with 10 home runs and 70 RBIs. In 1975, the Red Sox won the AL East and then swept the Oakland Athletics in the 1975 ALCS. Evans batted 1-for-10 against Oakland, being held to a double in the first game. In the 1975 World Series against the Cincinnati Reds, Evans batted 7-for-24 (.292) with a home run and five RBIs. In the historic sixth game, with the score tied 6–6 in the 11th inning, Evans made a spectacular catch of a drive hit by Reds second baseman Joe Morgan; Evans then threw to first base to complete an inning-ending double play. Carlton Fisk hit his famous in the 12th inning to win the game for the Red Sox, 7–6, forcing a seventh game, which was won the next day by the Reds.

<h1 style="text-align:center">A Fan's Perspective</h1>

From 1976 through 1980, Evans batted an overall .260 with 94 home runs and 279 RBIs; he was limited to 73 games in 1977 by a knee injury; in each of the other years he appeared in at least 146 games. He was named an All-Star in 1978; he would be an All-Star twice during his career. In 1981, despite the strike-shortened season, Evans had his best all-around year. He paced the league in total bases 215, OPS .937, walks 85, and tied for the home run title with 22. He also ranked second in runs scored (84) and on-base percentage (.415), and third in slugging percentage (.522). He added a .296 batting average with 71 RBIs, was an All-Star for the second time, and received his first Silver Slugger Award.

From 1982 through 1985, Evans batted an overall .274 with 115 home runs and 338 RBIs; in both 1982 and 1984 he played in every Red Sox game. On June 28, 1984, he hit for the cycle, in a 9–6 extra-innings win over the Seattle Mariners. In 1986, Evans hit a home run on opening day, April 7, on the first pitch of the MLB season, as Boston and the Detroit Tigers were playing the first game. His home run eclipsed the mark held by the Bump Wills, who hit the second pitch for a home run on April 5, 1982.

Achievements

- 3-Times All-Star (1978, 1981, 1987)
- 4-Times Top-10 finishes in AL MVP Awards (1981–82, 1987–88)
- 1-Time Led league in On-base percentage (1982)
- 1-Time Led league in OPS (1981 and 1984)
- 8-Time AL Gold Glove Winner (1976, 1978, 1979 & 1981-1985)
- 2-Times AL Silver Slugger Award Winner (1981 & 1987).
- 2-Time AL OPS Leader (1981 & 1984)
- 1-Time AL Runs Scored Leader (1984).
- 1-Time AL Total Bases Leader (1981)
- 1-Time AL Home Run Leader (1981).
- 3-Times AL Bases on Balls Leader (1981, 1985 & 1987).
- 11-Times 20-HR Seasons: (1978, 1979 & 1981-1989)
- 30-HR Seasons: 3 (1982, 1984 & 1987).
- 100 RBI Seasons: 4 (1984, 1987, 1988 & 1989)

- 1-Time AL On-Base Percentage Leader (1982).
- 100 Runs Scored Seasons: 4 (1982, 1984, 1985 & 1987).

Evans was one of the finest defensive right fielders of his time, winning eight Gold Glove Awards (1976, 1978, 1979 & 1981-1985) despite playing in Fenway Park, one the toughest right fields in the majors. His throwing arm was among the best in baseball during his prime. Evans played for 20 seasons and became a power hitter the second half of his career. He was known for hitting home runs from the leadoff spot, having a high OBP and being a clutch hitter. He was considered a great defensive right fielder during most of his peak with a very strong arm. Very patient at the plate, he would have been very successful as a modern type of player.

Dwight Evans played in the 1975 and 1986 World Series, where he was a combined .300 hitter in all 14 of those games, hitting 3 homers and driving in 14 runs. During the 1975 World Series, he made a fantastic catch in Fenway Park that for many years was replayed as a highlight before other televised Red Sox games. He started.

Hall of Fame

Dwight Evans became eligible for the BBWAA ballot of the Baseball Hall of Fame in 1997 when he received 5.9%. In 1998 he received 10.45, and in 1999 he received 3.6% and was dropped from the ballot. Evans was included as a Modern Baseball Era finalist in the 2020 balloting and again fell short of being elected in 2021.

Summary Analysis

Dwight Evans' Statistical Hall of Fame Point Total of 142.100. Evans should have been inducted as soon as he became eligible instead of being taken off the ballot. Over 26 years after he first appeared on the ballot, Dwight Evans not being in the Hall of Fame proves that many individuals are not elected because the BBWAA's is more of a "popularity contest judge" than an impartial sector for selecting the best individuals.

A Fan's Perspective

Evans, Dwight — Right Fielder Potential Hall of Fame Inductee

Positions: Right Fielder, First Baseman

Born :	November 3, 1951	Height: 6'2" USC 188 cm
From:	Santa Monica, CA	Weight: 180 lbs. 81 Kg.
Bats:	Right	Debut: September 16, 1972
Throws:	Right	Last Game: October 6, 1991

Year	Age	Tm	Lg	G	D	AB	R	H	2B	3B	HR	RBI	SB	CS	BB	SO	BA	OBP	SLG	OPS	TB	HBP	Awards
1972	20	BOS	AL	18	64	57	2	15	3	1	1	6	0	0	7	13	0.263	0.344	0.404	0.747	23	0	
1973	21	BOS	AL	119	328	282	46	63	13	1	10	32	5	0	40	52	0.223	0.32	0.383	0.703	108	1	
1974	22	BOS	AL	133	514	463	60	130	19	8	10	70	4	4	38	77	0.281	0.335	0.421	0.756	195	2	
1975	23	BOS	AL	128	470	412	61	113	24	6	13	56	3	4	47	60	0.274	0.353	0.456	0.809	188	4	
1976	24	BOS	AL	146	571	501	61	121	34	5	17	62	6	7	57	92	0.242	0.324	0.431	0.755	216	6	GG
1977	25	BOS	AL	73	265	230	39	66	9	2	14	36	4	2	28	58	0.287	0.363	0.526	0.889	121	0	
1978	26	BOS	AL	147	572	497	75	123	24	2	24	63	8	5	65	119	0.247	0.336	0.449	0.784	223	2	AS,GG
1979	27	BOS	AL	152	563	489	69	134	24	1	21	58	6	9	69	76	0.274	0.364	0.456	0.82	223	1	GG
1980	28	BOS	AL	148	542	463	72	123	37	5	18	60	3	1	64	96	0.266	0.358	0.484	0.842	224	5	
1981	29	BOS	AL	108	504	412	84	122	19	4	22	71	3	2	85	85	0.296	0.415	0.522	0.937	215	1	AS,MVP-3,GG,SS
1982	30	BOS	AL	162	727	609	122	178	37	7	32	98	3	2	112	125	0.292	0.402	0.534	0.936	325	1	MVP-7,GG
1983	31	BOS	AL	126	544	470	74	112	19	4	22	58	3	0	70	97	0.238	0.338	0.436	0.774	205	2	GG
1984	32	BOS	AL	162	738	630	121	186	37	8	32	104	3	1	96	115	0.295	0.388	0.532	0.92	335	4	MVP-11,GG
1985	33	BOS	AL	159	744	617	110	162	29	1	29	78	7	2	114	105	0.263	0.378	0.454	0.832	280	5	GG
1986	34	BOS	AL	152	640	529	86	137	33	2	26	97	3	3	97	117	0.259	0.376	0.476	0.853	252	6	
1987	35	BOS	AL	154	657	541	109	165	37	2	34	123	4	6	106	98	0.305	0.417	0.569	0.986	308	3	AS,MVP-4,SS
1988	36	BOS	AL	149	645	559	96	164	31	7	21	111	5	1	76	99	0.293	0.375	0.487	0.861	272	1	MVP-9
1989	37	BOS	AL	146	630	520	82	148	27	3	20	100	3	3	99	84	0.285	0.397	0.463	0.861	241	3	
1990	38	BOS	AL	123	522	445	66	111	18	3	13	63	3	4	67	73	0.249	0.349	0.391	0.74	174	4	
1991	39	BAL	AL	101	329	270	35	73	9	1	6	38	2	3	54	54	0.27	0.393	0.378	0.771	102	2	
162 Game Avg.				162	657	559	91	152	30	5	24	86	5	4	86	105	0.272	0.37	0.47	0.84	263	3	
BOS (19 yrs)				2505	10240	8726	1435	2373	474	72	379	1346	76	56	1337	1643	0.272	0.369	0.473	0.842	4128	2	
BAL (1 yr)				101	329	270	35	73	9	1	6	38	2	3	54	54	0.27	0.393	0.378	0.771	102	51	
20 Yrs				2606	10569	8996	1470	2446	483	73	385	1384	78	59	1391	1697	0.272	0.370	0.470	0.840	4230	53	Career Pts.
				11.750	0.000	0.000	9.250	5.500	0.000	0.000	8.000	8.000	1.000	0.000	9.250	0.000	2.500	4.500	3.750	6.750	8.000	0.000	78.250

Post Season Play

Year	Age	Tm	Lg	G	PA	AB	R	H	2B	3B	HR	RBI	SB	CS	BB	SO	BA	OBP	SLG	OPS	TB	HBP	
1975	23	BOS	ALCS	3	11	10	1	1	1	0	0	0	0	0	1	2	0.100	0.182	0.200	0.382	2	0	
1986	34	BOS	ALCS	7	31	28	2	6	1	0	1	4	0	0	3	3	0.214	0.290	0.357	0.647	10	0	
1988	36	BOS	ALCS	4	15	12	1	2	1	0	0	1	0	0	3	5	0.167	0.333	0.250	0.583	3	0	
1990	38	BOS	ALCS	4	14	13	0	3	1	0	0	0	0	0	1	3	0.231	0.286	0.308	0.593	4	0	
				18	71	63	4	12	4	0	1	5	0	0	8	13	0.190	0.282	0.302	0.583	19	0	Post Season Pts.
				0.400	0.000	0.000	0.250	0.250	0.000	0.000	0.250	0.250	0.000	0.000	0.400	0.000	0.000	0.000	0.000	0.000	0.250	0.000	2.050

World Series Play

Year	Age	Tm	Lg	G	PA	AB	R	H	2B	3B	HR	RBI	SB	CS	BB	SO	BA	OBP	SLG	OPS	TB	HBP	
1975	23	BOS	AL	7	29	24	3	7	1	1	1	5	0	1	3	4	0.292	0.393	0.542	0.935	13	1	
1986	34	BOS	AL	7	30	26	4	8	2	0	2	9	0	0	4	3	0.308	0.400	0.615	1.015	16	0	
				14	59	50	7	15	3	1	3	14	0	1	7	7	0.300	0.397	0.580	0.977	29	1	World SeriesPts.
				0.600	0.000	0.000	0.400	0.600	0.000	0.000	0.600	0.800	0.000	0.000	0.400	0.000	1.000	1.200	1.200	1.000	1.000	0.000	8.800

Yearly Points Leading the League

Category	Times	Points	Total	Category	Times	Points	Total	Category	Times	Points	Total
MVP	0	7	0	B.A.	0	3	0	T.B.	1	2	2
Rookie of Year	0	5	0	Runs	1	2	2	B.O.B.	3	2	6
Triple Crown	0	5	0	H.R.'s	1	3	3	OBP%	1	2	2
Golden Glove	8	3	24	R.B.I's	0	3	0	SLG %	0	2	0
All-Star	3	2	6	Hits	0	2	0	OBPS%	2	2	4
Games	2	2	4	S.B.	0	2	0	Totals			14
Totals			34	Totals			5	Grand Total Add-On Points			53

Hall of Fame Points	
Career Points	78.250
Post Season Points	2.050
World Series Points	8.800
Career Add-On Points	53.00
Writers Association Pts.	0.000
Military/Lifetime Achievement	0.000
Grand Total HOF Points	142.100

Parker, Dave "The Cobra"

Personal Life

David Gene Parker was born on June 9, 1951, in Grenada, Mississippi, one of six children of Richard and Dannie Mae Parker. He attended Courter Tech High School.

Dave Parker was married to a woman named Stella Miller, but no information available. Dave Parker married Kellye Crockett in 1984with the couple having six children.

Baseball Career

The Pirates drafted Parker in the 14th round in 1970. The team converted him from catcher to the outfield for the Pirates' team in 1970. In 1972 he earned player-of-the-year honors at Salem (Virginia) in the Class A-Carolina League. In 1973 the Pirates promoted Parker to Charleston (West Virginia) of the Triple-A International League, where he got off to a blazing start. On July 10, Parker was called up and made his major-league debut as the Pirates' right fielder and leadoff hitter.

Coming up at age 22 in 1973, Parker played his first eleven years with the Pittsburgh Pirates. In the five-year period from 1975 to 1979, he always hit over .300, winning batting titles in 1977 and 1978. He led the National League in slugging in 1975 and 1978, and was first in doubles in 1977. In MVP voting, he won the award in 1978, and was 3rd in both 1975 and 1977. He also had a very good year in 1979, the "We Are Family" year in Pittsburgh, he hit .310 with 45 doubles, 25 home runs, and 109 runs scored. He was second in the National League in total bases that year.

During his years in Pittsburgh, the Pirates won the division three times, and finished second three times. Parker won three Gold Gloves for his fielding from 1977 to 1979. Parker became the first player ever to earn a million-dollar salary. After this early peak, things went downhill. In the early 1980s, however, Parker's hitting suffered due to injuries, weight problems and his increasing cocaine use. He became one of the central figures in a drug scandal that spread through the major leagues. Parker missed over 20 games in 1980 and his batting average dipped below .300 for the first time since 1974. He started putting on weight and became surly, enduring some well-publicized confrontations with fans, including an incident when one fan threw a battery at him while Parker was standing in the outfield. In 1981, with the Pirates slipping into the second division, he hit .258 in 67 games. It was more of the same in 1982, as he hit .270 with only 6 home runs in 73 games, missing half the season to various injuries. Fans were openly questioning his desire to play by this point, and everyone was wondering what had happened to his considerable hitting talent, as he was only 31. It would later be revealed in the 1985 Pittsburgh drug trials that he had become a habitual drug user during that period, and the habit was affecting his overall health, his personal life, and his performance.

Parker started bouncing back in 1983 when he was finally healthy and played 144 games, hitting .279 as the Pirates were in contention for the first time in years. He became a free agent after the season and signed with the Cincinnati Reds. In Cincinnati, he returned to the form that made him an All-Star in Pittsburgh. In 1985, he enjoyed his best season since he won the 1978 MVP with a .312 batting average and 34 home runs; he also led the National League with 125 RBIs, 42 doubles, 80 extra-base hits and 350 total bases. In 1986, Parker was among several players who testified against a dealer in the Pittsburgh drug trials. Named as "regular users", Parker and six other players were suspended for the following season. The sentences were commuted, however, in exchange for donating ten percent of their base salaries to drug-related community service, submitting to random drug testing, and contributing 100 hours of drug-related community service.

After the 1987 season, Cincinnati traded Parker to the Oakland Athletics. In Oakland, Parker was able to extend his career by spending most of his time as a designated hitter. He hit just .257 with 12 homers in 377 at-bats in 1988 and .264 with 22 homers in 553 at-bats in 1989, his veteran leadership was a significant factor in the A's consecutive World Series appearances which included a second World Series title for Parker in 1989. Parker signed with the Milwaukee Brewers for the 1990 season and had a solid year as the Brewers' DH with a .289 average and 21 home runs in 610 at-bats. Milwaukee opted for youth however, at the end of the year and traded the aging Parker to the Angels. Parker's last season was 1991. He played for the California Angels until late in the season before being released. The Toronto Blue Jays then signed him as insurance for the pennant race, and Parker hit .333 in limited action. Parker retired at the end of the season.

Achievements:

- 7-time All-Star (1977, 1979-1981, 1985, 1986 & 1990)
- 9-times received MVP votes: (1975-Won 78,1979, 1985, 1986, 1989 & 1990).
- 3-time NL Gold Glove Winner (1977-1979)
- 3-time Silver Slugger Award Winner (1985/OF-NL, 1986/OF-NL & 1990/DH-AL)

The Baseball Hall of Fame

- 2-time NL Batting Average Leader (1977 & 1978)
- 2-time NL Slugging Percentage Leader (1975 & 1978)
- NL OPS Leader (1978) & NL Hits Leader (1977)
- 3-time NL Total Bases Leader (1978, 1985 & 1986)
- NL RBI Leader (1985) & 200 Hits Seasons: 1 (1977)
- 20-Home Run Seasons: 9 (1975, 1977-1979, 1985-1987, 1989 & 1990)
- 30-Home Run Seasons: 3 (1978, 1985 & 1986)
- 100 RBI Seasons: 4 (1975, 1978, 1985 & 1986)
- 100 Runs Scored Seasons: 3 (1977, 1978 & 1979)
- Won two World Series with the Pirates in 1979 and the Athletics in 1989

Parker's career achievements include a lifetime batting average of .290, a solid defensive outfielder. In terms of career totals, he ranks 69th in games played, 54th in at-bats, 67th in hits (with 2,712), 56th in total bases, 45th in doubles (with 526), tied for 102nd in home runs (with 339), 58th in RBI (with 1,493), and 56th in extra-base hits.

Hall of Fame

Dave Parker's Hall of Fame voting peaked at 25% of the vote in 1998 and his 15-year BBWAA eligibility was exhausted in the 2011 election when he received only 15.3%.

Summary Analysis

Parker's Statistical Hall of Fame Points is 121.050 and he should have been inducted when eligible. By any measure, Dave Paker should be in the Hall of Fame.

Parker, Dave — Right Fielder Potential Hall of Fame Inductee

Positions	Right Fielder
Born:	June 9, 1951
From:	Grenada, MS
Bats:	Left
Throws:	Left
Height:	6' 5" USC 196 cm
Weight:	230 lbs. 104 Kg.
Debut:	July 12, 1973
Last Game:	October 2, 1991

Year	Age	Tm	Lg	G	D	AB	R	H	2B	3B	HR	RBI	SB	CS	BB	SO	BA	OBP	SLG	OPS	TB	HBP	Awards
1973	22	PIT	NL	54	144	139	17	40	9	1	4	14	1	1	2	27	0.288	0.308	0.453	0.761	63	2	
1974	23	PIT	NL	73	233	220	27	62	10	3	4	29	3	3	10	53	0.282	0.322	0.409	0.731	90	3	
1975	24	PIT	NL	148	602	558	75	172	35	10	25	101	8	6	38	89	0.308	0.357	0.541	0.898	302	5	MVP-3
1976	25	PIT	NL	138	573	537	82	168	28	10	13	90	19	7	30	80	0.313	0.349	0.475	0.824	255	2	MVP-20
1977	26	PIT	NL	159	706	637	107	215	44	8	21	88	17	19	58	107	0.338	0.397	0.531	0.927	338	7	AS,MVP-3,GG
1978	27	PIT	NL	148	642	581	102	194	32	12	30	117	20	7	57	92	0.334	0.394	0.585	0.979	340	2	MVP-1,GG
1979	28	PIT	NL	158	707	622	109	193	45	7	25	94	20	4	67	101	0.310	0.380	0.526	0.906	327	9	AS,MVP-10,GG
1980	29	PIT	NL	139	550	518	71	153	31	1	17	79	10	7	25	69	0.295	0.327	0.458	0.785	237	2	AS
1981	30	PIT	NL	67	254	240	29	62	14	3	9	48	6	2	9	25	0.258	0.287	0.454	0.742	109	2	AS
1982	31	PIT	NL	73	270	244	41	66	19	3	6	29	7	5	22	45	0.270	0.330	0.447	0.776	109	1	
1983	32	PIT	NL	144	586	552	68	154	29	4	12	69	12	9	28	89	0.279	0.311	0.411	0.722	227	0	
1984	33	CIN	NL	156	655	607	73	173	28	0	16	94	11	10	41	89	0.285	0.328	0.410	0.738	249	1	
1985	34	CIN	NL	160	694	635	88	198	42	4	34	125	5	13	52	80	0.312	0.365	0.551	0.916	350	3	AS,MVP-2,SS
1986	35	CIN	NL	162	700	637	89	174	31	3	31	116	1	6	56	126	0.273	0.330	0.477	0.807	304	1	AS,MVP-5,SS
1987	36	CIN	NL	153	647	589	77	149	28	0	26	97	7	3	44	104	0.253	0.311	0.433	0.744	255	8	
1988	37	OAK	AL	101	411	377	43	97	18	1	12	55	0	1	32	70	0.257	0.314	0.406	0.720	153	0	
1989	38	OAK	AL	144	600	553	56	146	27	0	22	97	0	0	38	81	0.264	0.308	0.432	0.741	239	1	MVP-11
1990	39	MIL	AL	157	669	610	71	176	30	3	21	92	4	7	41	102	0.289	0.330	0.451	0.781	275	4	AS,MVP-16,SS
1991	40	TOT	AL	132	541	502	47	120	26	2	11	59	3	3	33	98	0.239	0.288	0.365	0.653	183	3	
1991	40	CAL	AL	119	501	466	45	108	22	2	11	56	3	2	29	91	0.232	0.279	0.358	0.638	167	3	
1991	40	TOR	AL	13	40	36	2	12	4	0	0	3	0	1	4	7	0.333	0.400	0.444	0.844	16	0	
162				162	669	615	84	178	35	5	22	98	10	7	45	101	0.290	0.339	0.471	0.810	289	11	
PIT				1301	5267	4848	728	1479	296	62	166	758	123	70	346	777	0.305	0.353	0.494	0.848	2397	35	
CIN (4				631	2696	2468	327	694	129	7	107	432	24	32	193	399	0.281	0.334	0.469	0.803	1158	13	
OAK				245	1011	930	99	243	45	1	34	152	0	1	70	161	0.261	0.311	0.422	0.732	392	1	
CAL (1				119	501	466	45	108	22	2	11	56	3	2	29	91	0.232	0.279	0.358	0.638	167	3	
TOR				13	40	36	2	12	4	0	0	3	0	1	4	7	0.333	0.400	0.444	0.844	16	0	
MIL (1				157	669	610	71	176	30	3	21	92	4	7	41	102	0.289	0.330	0.451	0.781	275	4	
NL				1932	7963	7316	1055	2173	425	69	273	1190	147	102	539	1176	0.297	0.347	0.486	0.833	3555	48	
AL (4				534	2221	2042	217	539	101	6	66	303	7	11	144	361	0.264	0.311	0.418	0.727	850	8	
19 Yrs				2466	10184	9358	1272	2712	526	75	339	1493	154	113	683	1537	0.290	0.339	0.471	0.810	4405	56	**Career Pts.**
				8.500	0.000	0.000	6.500	7.500	0.000	0.000	5.750	10.500	1.000	0.000	1.000	0.000	3.750	1.500	3.750	5.750	7.500	0.000	**63.000**

Post Season Play

Year	Age	Tm	Lg	G	PA	AB	R	H	2B	3B	HR	RBI	SB	CS	BB	SO	BA	OBP	SLG	OPS	TB	HBP	
1974	23	PIT	NLCS	3	8	8	0	1	0	0	0	0	0	0	0	1	0.125	0.125	0.125	0.250	1	0	
1975	24	PIT	NLCS	3	12	10	2	0	0	0	0	0	0	0	1	3	0.000	0.167	0.000	0.167	0	1	
1979	28	PIT	NLCS	3	15	12	2	4	0	0	0	2	1	0	2	3	0.333	0.400	0.333	0.733	4	0	
1988	37	OAK	ALCS	3	12	12	1	3	1	0	0	0	0	0	0	4	0.250	0.250	0.333	0.583	4	0	
1989	38	OAK	ALCS	4	16	16	2	3	0	0	2	3	0	0	0	0	0.188	0.188	0.563	0.750	9	0	
				16	63	58	7	11	1	0	2	5	1	0	3	11	0.196	0.230	0.310	0.540	18	1	**Post Season Pts.**
				0.325	0.000	0.000	0.200	0.200	0.000	0.000	0.325	0.200	0.200	0.000	0.200	0.000	0.000	0.000	0.000	0.000	0.200	0.000	**1.850**

World Season Play

Year	Age	Tm	Lg	G	PA	AB	R	H	2B	3B	HR	RBI	SB	CS	BB	SO	BA	OBP	SLG	OPS	TB	HBP	
1979	28	PIT	WS	7	33	29	2	10	3	0	0	4	0	1	2	7	0.345	0.394	0.448	0.842	13	1	
1988	37	OAK	WS	4	17	15	0	3	0	0	0	0	0	0	2	4	0.200	0.294	0.200	0.494	3	0	
1989	38	OAK	WS	3	9	9	2	2	1	0	1	2	0	0	0	2	0.222	0.222	0.667	0.889	6	0	
				14	59	53	4	15	4	0	1	6	0	1	4	13	0.283	0.339	0.415	0.754	22	1	**World Series Pts.**
				0.450	0.000	0.000	0.200	0.450	0.000	0.000	0.200	0.325	0.000	0.000	0.000	0.000	0.575	0.000	0.000	0.200	0.800	0.000	**3.200**

Yearly Points Leading the League

Category	Times	Points	Total
MVP	1	7	7
Rookie of Yea	0	5	0
Triple Crown	0	5	0
Golden Glove	3	3	9
All-Star	7	2	14
Games	1	2	2
Totals			32

Category	Times	Points	Total
B.A.	2	3	6
Runs	0	3	0
H.R.'s	0	3	0
R.B.J's	1	3	3
Hits	1	2	2
S.B.	0	2	0
Totals			11

Category	Times	Points	Total
T.B.	3	2	6
B.O.B.	0	2	0
OBP%	0	2	0
SLG%	2	2	4
OBPS%	1	2	0
Totals			10
Grand Total Add-On Points			53

Hall of Fame Points	
Career Points	63.000
Post Season Points	1.850
World Series Points	3.200
Career Add-On Points	53.00
Writers Association Pts.	0.000
Military/Lifetime Achievement	0.000
Grand Total HOF Points	121.050

Sheffield, Gary

Personal Life

Gary Antonian Sheffield (born November 18, 1968) was born in Tampa, Florida and raised by his mother Betty Jones and step-father Harold Jones. When Sheffield was eleven, his Belmont Heights Little League All-Stars made it to the finals of the 1980 Little League World Series losing to Taiwan 4–3.

Sheffield married Deleon Richards, on February 5th, 2000 and together they have three sons Jaden, Noah, and Christian. In addition, Sheffield has four other children from previous relationships, Gary Jr., Ebony, Garret, and Carissa.

Baseball Career

The Milwaukee Brewers drafted Sheffield with the sixth pick of the 1986 MLB draft. In his third season, 1988, he went from Double-A to the majors. In 134 games for the El Paso Diablos and Denver, he batted .327 with 28 homers and 118 RBIs and played in 24 games for the Brewers, with 3 home runs, 12 runs batted in, and a .238 batting average. Sheffield was with the Brewers at the start of the 1989 season, but was mired in a deep slump, led the Brewers in errors, and was sent back to Denver. While there, doctors discovered a broken bone in his foot. Sheffield had complained of discomfort since mid-May, but at the time it was diagnosed as a bone bruise. Overall, he hit .247, with five homers and 32 RBIs in 95 games. Although Sheffield didn't show much power, in 1990, he kept his batting average above .300 through late August before a slump reduced his final mark to .294 with an OPS34 of .771. An injured shoulder, which would plague his entire career, ended his season on September 12. In 1991, Sheffield's season was a washout due to a jammed left shoulder and irritated wrist tendon. He played only 32 games after April 30, the last on July 24.

On March 26, 1992, the Brewers traded Sheffield to the San Diego Padres where Sheffield was given a clean slate by Padres' manager Greg Riddoch. Sheffield nearly won the Triple Crown, leading the National League with a career-high batting average of .330 and finishing third in home runs and fifth in RBIs. Sheffield also won *The Sporting News*'s National League Comeback Player of the Year Award and, for the first time, made the All-Star Team and won a Silver Slugger Award. After Sheffield's great year, the Padres traded Sheffield to the Florida Marlins on June 24, 1993.

Although Sheffield had an above-average season, all his offensive statistics declined from 1992.

Nevertheless, unlike the Padres, the Marlins were not afraid to give him a huge payday. In late September,

A Fan's Perspective

they signed him to a four-year contract, making him the highest-paid third baseman in baseball. Despite playing only 87 games in '94 due to his left shoulder, and the players' strike, Sheffield drove in 78 runs, a pace of 145 in 162 games. In 1995, Sheffield was again hampered by injury. On June 10, he tore a ligament in his left thumb and thought to be out for the season, but he returned and hit .343 with 10 homers and 27 RBIs in September. Although he played just 63 games, he batted .324, 16 home runs, 46 runs batted in and a 1.054 OPS.

Sheffield started the 1996 season by tying the then-major-league record with 11 home runs in April and continued his hot hitting throughout the summer. Injury-free, he played a career-high 161 games, and led the NL in OBP (on-base percentage) (.465), OPS (1.090), and OPS+56 (189) – all of which would remain career highs. His 42 homers ranked second, and he was walked 142 times (19 intentional). After helping the Florida Marlins win the 1997 World Series, he was traded to the Dodgers as part of the Marlins' fire sale. He hit .302 with 22 home runs and 85 runs batted in.

From 1999 through 2001, Sheffield hit .312, 113 home runs, 310 runs batted in. From 2002 through 2005, Sheffield played two years each with the Braves and Yankees, hitting .304, 134 home runs, 460 batted in, and the teams making the playoffs each year. In 2006, Sheffield had a great start, batting .341 with 18 RBIs in the first 22 games, but injured his left wrist, underwent surgery, and appeared in just 39 contests.
During the off-season, the Yankees dealt Sheffield to the Tigers.

On December 13, 2007, Sheffield was Implicated in the Mitchell Report. Sheffield states that he had no knowledge of the cream containing steroids and no reason to assume so at the time and a look at his numbers showed no improvement after the incident. In 2007 and 2008, Sheffield combined to hit 44 home runs and 132 runs batted in for the Detroit Tigers to finish 2008 season with 499 career home runs. However, Sheffield was released towards the end of spring training in 2009, and was picked up by the New York Mets. Sheffield hit his 500th major league home run for the Mets at Citi Field on April 17th He was the first player to hit his 500th home run as a New York Met.

Achievements:

- 9-time All-Star (1992, 1993, 1996, 1998-2000 & 2003-2005).
- 5-time Silver Slugger Award Winner: (1992,1996, 2003, 2004,& 2005).
- Led National League in batting average (.330).

The Baseball Hall of Fame

- Led National League in on-base percentage (.465) and OPS (1.090) in 1996.
- NL Batting Average Leader (1992) & NL Total Bases Leader (1992).
- NL On-Base Percentage Leader (1996) & NL OPS Leader (1996).
- 20-Home Run Seasons: 14 (1992-1994, 1996-2005 & 2007).
- 30-Home Run Seasons: 8 (1992, 1996, 1999-2001 & 2003-2005).
- 40-Home Run Seasons: 2 (1996 & 2000).
- 100 RBI Seasons: 8 (1992, 1996, 1999-2001 & 2003-2005).
- 100 Runs Scored Seasons: 7 (1996, 1999, 2000, 2003-2005 & 2007).

Won a World Series with the Florida Marlins in 1997.

- First player to hit at least 25 home runs for 6 different teams.
- 25th player in MLB history to reach 500 home runs.

Sheffield played for the Milwaukee Brewers, San Diego Padres, Florida Marlins, Los Angeles Dodgers, Atlanta Braves, New York Yankees, Detroit Tigers, and the New York Mets. Sheffield ranked second among all active players in walks (1,475), third in runs (1,636), fourth in RBIs (1,676), fifth in hits (2,689) and home runs (509), and sixth in hit by pitches (135). He is the only player in history to record 100 RBIs in a season for five different teams. Despite his high home run total, Sheffield only topped 80 strikeouts twice in 22 seasons.

Hall of Fame

Sheffield appeared on balloting for the National Baseball Hall of Fame since 2015, when he received 11.7% of the vote. His support increased to 55% in 2023, his ninth appearance. He has one year left on the BBWAA ballot before he is dropped off.

Summary Analysis

Gary Sheffield's Hall of Fame Statistics are 142.00 and considerably higher than the 110.00 Induction Criteria. He should be elected to the Baseball Hall of Fame.

A Fan's Perspective

Sheffield, Gary — Right Fielder Potential Hall of Fame Inductee

Positions	Rightfielder / Third Base / Shortstop
Born	November 18, 1968
From	Tampa, FLA
Bats	Both
Throws	Right
Height	5' 11" USC 180 cm
Weight	190 lbs. 86 Kg.
Debut	September 1, 1988
Last Game	September 30, 2009

Year	Age	Tm	Lg	G	PA	AB	R	H	2B	3B	HR	RBI	SB	CS	BB	SO	BA	OBP	SLG	OPS	TB	HBP	
1988	19	MIL	AL	24	89	80	12	19	1	0	4	12	3	1	7	7	0.238	0.295	0.400	0.695	32	0	
1989	20	MIL	AL	95	405	368	34	91	18	0	5	32	10	6	27	33	0.247	0.303	0.337	0.640	124	4	
1990	21	MIL	AL	125	547	487	67	143	30	1	10	67	25	10	44	41	0.294	0.350	0.421	0.771	205	3	
1991	22	MIL	AL	50	203	175	25	34	12	2	2	22	5	5	19	15	0.194	0.277	0.320	0.597	56	3	
1992	23	SDP	NL	146	618	557	87	184	34	3	33	100	5	6	48	40	0.330	0.385	0.580	0.965	323	6	AS,MVP-3,SS
1993	24	TOT	NL	140	557	494	67	145	20	5	20	73	17	5	47	64	0.284	0.361	0.476	0.837	235	9	AS
1993	24	SDP	NL	68	282	258	34	76	12	2	10	36	5	1	18	30	0.295	0.344	0.473	0.817	122	3	
1993	24	FLA	NL	72	275	236	33	69	8	3	10	37	12	4	29	34	0.292	0.378	0.479	0.857	113	6	
1994	25	FLA	NL	87	384	322	61	89	16	1	27	78	12	6	51	50	0.276	0.380	0.584	0.964	188	6	
1995	26	FLA	NL	63	274	213	46	69	8	0	16	46	19	4	55	45	0.324	0.467	0.587	1.054	125	4	
1996	27	FLA	NL	161	677	519	118	163	33	1	42	120	16	9	142	66	0.314	0.465	0.624	1.090	324	10	AS,MVP-6,SS
1997	28	FLA	NL	135	582	444	86	111	22	1	21	71	11	7	121	79	0.250	0.424	0.446	0.870	198	15	
1998	29	TOT	NL	130	549	437	73	132	27	2	22	85	22	7	95	46	0.302	0.428	0.524	0.952	229	8	AS
1998	29	FLA	NL	40	166	136	21	37	11	1	8	28	4	2	26	16	0.272	0.392	0.500	0.892	68	2	
1998	29	LAD	NL	90	383	303	52	95	16	1	16	57	18	5	69	30	0.316	0.444	0.535	0.979	161	6	
1999	30	LAD	NL	152	663	549	103	165	20	0	34	101	11	5	101	64	0.301	0.407	0.523	0.930	287	4	AS
2000	31	LAD	NL	141	612	501	105	163	24	3	43	109	4	6	101	71	0.325	0.438	0.643	1.081	322	4	AS,MVP-9
2001	32	LAD	NL	143	618	515	98	160	28	2	36	100	10	4	94	67	0.311	0.417	0.583	1.000	300	4	
2002	33	ATL	NL	135	579	492	82	151	26	0	25	84	12	2	72	53	0.307	0.404	0.512	0.916	252	11	MVP-17
2003	34	ATL	NL	155	678	576	126	190	37	2	39	132	18	4	86	55	0.330	0.419	0.604	1.023	348	8	AS,MVP-3,SS
2004	35	NYY	AL	154	684	573	117	166	30	1	36	121	5	6	92	85	0.290	0.393	0.534	0.927	306	11	AS,MVP-2,SS
2005	36	NYY	AL	154	675	584	104	170	27	0	34	123	10	2	78	76	0.291	0.379	0.512	0.891	299	8	AS,MVP-8,SS
2006	37	NYY	AL	39	186	151	22	45	5	0	6	25	5	1	13	16	0.298	0.355	0.450	0.806	68	1	
2007	38	DET	AL	133	593	494	107	131	20	1	25	75	22	5	84	71	0.265	0.378	0.462	0.839	228	9	
2008	39	DET	AL	114	482	418	52	94	16	0	19	57	9	2	58	87	0.225	0.326	0.400	0.725	167	5	
2009	40	NYM	NL	100	312	268	44	74	13	2	10	43	2	1	40	46	0.276	0.372	0.451	0.823	121	2	
162 Game Avg.				162	688	580	103	169	29	2	32	105	16	7	93	74	0.292	0.393	0.514	0.907	298	8	
FLA (6 yrs)				558	2358	1870	365	538	98	7	122	380	74	32	424	290	0.288	0.426	0.543	0.970	1016	43	
LAD (4 yrs)				526	2276	1866	358	583	88	6	129	367	43	20	355	232	0.312	0.424	0.573	0.998	1070	18	
MIL (4 yrs)				294	1244	1110	138	287	61	3	21	133	43	21	97	96	0.239	0.319	0.376	0.695	417	10	
NYY (3 yrs)				347	1525	1308	243	381	62	1	76	269	20	9	183	175	0.291	0.383	0.515	0.897	673	20	
ATL (2 yrs)				290	1257	1068	208	341	63	2	64	216	30	6	158	108	0.319	0.412	0.562	0.974	600	19	
SDP (2 yrs)				214	900	815	121	260	46	5	43	136	10	7	66	70	0.319	0.372	0.546	0.918	445	9	
DET (2 yrs)				247	1075	912	159	225	36	1	44	132	31	7	142	154	0.247	0.354	0.433	0.788	395	14	
NYM (1 yr)				100	312	268	44	74	13	2	10	43	2	1	40	46	0.276	0.372	0.451	0.823	121	2	
NL (13 yrs)				1688	7103	5887	1096	1796	308	22	368	1142	159	66	1053	746	0.305	0.414	0.552	0.960	3252	91	
AL (9 yrs)				888	3844	3330	540	893	159	5	141	534	94	38	422	425	0.268	0.354	0.446	0.800	1485	44	
22 Yrs				2576	10947	9217	1636	2689	467	27	509	1676	253	104	1475	1171	0.292	0.393	0.514	0.907	4737	135	**Career Pts.**
				11.750	0.000	0.000	11.750	8.000	0.000	0.000	11.750	13.000	2.500	0.000	9.250	0.000	5.500	6.750	6.750	9.250	10.500	0.000	**106.750**

Post Season Play

Year	Age	Tm	Lg	G	PA	AB	R	H	2B	3B	HR	RBI	SB	CS	BB	SO	BA	OBP	SLG	OPS	TB	HBP	
1997	28	FLA	NLDS	3	14	9	3	5	1	0	1	1	1	0	5	0	0.556	0.714	1	1.714	9	0	
1997	28	FLA	NLCS	6	24	17	6	4	0	0	1	1	0	0	7	3	0.235	0.458	0.412	0.87	7	0	
2002	33	ATL	NLDS	5	23	16	3	1	0	0	1	1	1	0	7	3	0.063	0.348	0.25	0.598	4	0	
2003	34	ATL	NLDS	4	17	14	0	2	0	0	0	1	0	0	2	0	0.143	0.294	0.143	0.437	2	1	
2004	35	NYY	ALDS	4	21	18	2	4	1	0	1	2	0	1	3	1	0.222	0.333	0.444	0.778	8	0	
2004	35	NYY	ALCS	7	36	30	7	10	3	0	1	5	0	0	6	8	0.333	0.444	0.533	0.978	16	0	
2005	36	NYY	ALDS	5	22	21	1	6	0	0	0	2	0	0	1	2	0.286	0.318	0.286	0.604	6	0	
2006	37	NYY	ALDS	3	12	12	1	1	0	0	0	1	0	0	0	4	0.083	0.083	0.083	0.167	1	0	
				37	169	137	23	33	5	0	5	14	1	1	31	21	0.241	0.379	0.397	0.776	53	1	**Post Season Pts.**
				0.800	0.000	0.000	0.600	0.600	0.000	0.000	0.600	0.600	0.250	0.000	1.400	0.000	0.250	1.000	0.250	0.600	0.600	0.000	**7.550**

World Series Play

Year	Age	Tm	Lg	G	PA	AB	R	H	2B	3B	HR	RBI	SB	CS	BB	SO	BA	OBP	SLG	OPS	TB	HBP	
1997	28	FLA	WS	7	33	24	4	7	1	0	1	5	0	0	8	5	0.292	0.485	0.458	0.943	11	1	
				7	33	24	4	7	1	0	1	5	0	0	8	5	0.292	0.485	0.458	0.943	11	1	**World Series Pts.**
				0.250	0.000	0.000	0.250	0.250	0.000	0.000	0.250	0.400	0.000	0.000	0.400	0.000	1.000	2.000	0.000	1.000	0.400	0.000	**6.200**

Yearly Points Leading the League

Category	Times	Points	Total
MVP	0	7	0
Rookie of Year	0	5	0
Triple Crown	0	6	0
Golden Glove	0	3	0
All-Star	9	2	18
Games	0	2	0
Totals			18

Category	Times	Points	Total
B.A.	0	3	0
Runs	0	2	0
H.R.'s	0	3	0
R.B.I's	0	3	0
Hits	0	2	0
S.B.	0	2	0
Totals			0

Categor	Times	Points	Total
T.B.	0	2	0
B.O.B.	1	2	2
OBP%	1	2	2
SLG %	0	2	0
OBPS%	0	2	0
Totals			4
Grand Total Add-On Points		22	

Hall of Fame Points	
Career Points	106.750
Post Season Points	7.550
World Series Points	6.200
Career Add-On Points	22.00
Writers Association Pts.	0.000
Military/Lifetime Achievement	0.000
Grand Total HOF Points	142.5

Suzuki, Ichiro

Personal Life

Ichiro Suzuki was born October 22, 1973 in Toyoyama, a small town just outside Negoya, Nobuyuki Suzuki and Yoshie Suzuki. He has an elder brother, Kazuyasu. At the age of seven, Suzuki joined his first baseball team and asked his father to teach him to be a better player. The two began a daily routine, which included throwing 50 pitches, fielding 50 infield balls and 50 outfield balls, and hitting 500 pitches. As a little leaguer, Suzuki had the word "concentration" written on his glove. By age 12, he had dedicated himself to pursuing a career in professional baseball, and their training sessions were no longer for leisure, and less enjoyable.

When Suzuki joined his high-school baseball team, his father told the coach, "No matter how good Ichiro is, don't ever praise him. We have to make him spiritually strong." When he was ready to enter high school, Suzuki was selected by a school with a prestigious baseball program, Nagoya's *Aikodai Meiden* High School. Suzuki was primarily used as a pitcher instead of as an outfielder, owing to his exceptionally strong arm. His cumulative high-school batting average was .505, with 19 home runs. He built strength and stamina by hurling car tires and hitting Wiffle balls with a heavy shovel, among other regimens. These exercises helped develop his wrists and hips, adding power and endurance to his thin frame.

Ichiro married Fukushima Yumiko on 3 December 1999, in Santa Monica, California. The couple do not have any children and reside in Issaquah, Washington.

Baseball Career

Despite his outstanding numbers in high school, Suzuki was not drafted until the fourth round of the NPB draft in November 1991, because many teams were discouraged by his small size of 5 ft 9+½ in and 124 pounds. When Orin changed managers in 1994, Ichiro began to play every day. Leading off for the for most of the season, his 210 hits marked the first time anyone exceeded 200 hits in the circuit's 130-game season. He batted .385 and scored 111 runs. His reward for this stellar offense was the Most Valuable Player award in the Pacific League. In addition, he won the first of seven consecutive Gold Gloves (in Japan) for his defensive expertise. He played the first nine years of his career with the Orix Blue Wave of Nippon Professional Baseball (NPB), and the next 12 years with the Seattle Mariners of Major League Baseball (MLB) Ichiro made his Nippon Professional Baseball debut with the Blue Wave at age 18 in 1992. But the manager of the team had doubts about his future in baseball because of his small size and unorthodox hitting technique, so he spent most of his first two seasons in the minor leagues. As part of his development, Orix sent Suzuki to play in the Hawaii Winter Baseball League after the 1993 Japanese season. Playing for the Hilo Stars of the four-city circuit, Ichiro led the team to a 28-20 record and a first-place finish. League owner Duane Kurisu said Suzuki's play stood out even then. He exclaimed, "Ichiro, man. His name would keep popping up throughout. It was from Day 1. One day I was with some farm directors, they said you have to look at this kid. Here was this small guy hitting bombs. This was the first inkling of who Ichiro was as he was hitting things beyond these warehouses that were over 450 feet away."

In his first ten seasons in the major leagues (2001-2010), Ichiro had a .331 average with 90 HR's and 558 RBI and 2244 hits in the majors. Ichiro displayed excellent defense in both right field and center field with the Mariners, displayed a great arm and overall defensive ability. Ichiro won a total of 10 Gold Gloves in the majors and selected to 10 All-Star squads after switching countries. Also, Ichiro holds the record with the most hits in his first five years, breaking the previous record held by Paul Waner.

During Ichiro's 14 years with Seattle, he played in 1861 games, had 7907 at bats, 1181 runs, 2542 hits, 99 home runs, 633 runs-batted-in, 438 stolen bases, a .321 batting average, and a .791 OPS. In addition, all of Ichiro's league leading statistics were acquired playing for the Mariner's. They were all achieved prior to Ichiro turning 38 years of age. The last eight years Ichiro played he was a shell of his prior 20 years in Major League Baseball spent over two continents. He never was able to showcase his talents in a World Series and on March 20, 2019, the Mariners opened the MLB season at the Tokyo Dome and Suzuki started the game in right field. The next night, the Mariners again played the Athletics at the Tokyo Dome and Suzuki played in his final professional game. He went 0–4 at the plate and in the bottom of the eighth inning walked off the field to applause. Later in the day, Suzuki officially announced his retirement.

Suzuki's final Major League statistics had him appearing in 2653 games, 1420 runs, 3089 hits, 117 home runs, 780 runs-batted-in, 509 stolen bases, .311 batting average, and an OPS of .860. In addition, Suzuki is the only left-handed hitter in Major League history with at least 2,000 plate appearances against left-handed pitching to have better results hitting off left-handed pitchers than right-handed pitchers.

Achievements:

- 10-Times All-Star: (2001 - 2010).
- 3-Times Silver Slugger Award Winner: (2001, 2007 & 2009).
- 2-Times Led American League in batting average: (2001, 2004).
- 7-Times Led American League in hits: (2001, 2004, & 2006 - 2010).
- 10 Times - 200-Hit Seasons: (2001 - 2010) – All-Time Record.
- 10 Times Golden Glove Winner: (2001 - 2010).
- 2001 Rookie of the Year Winner.
- 9-Times received MVP Votes (2001-Winner, 2002-2004, & 2006-2010).
- Major League record of hits in a season – 2004 (262 hits).
- World Record for most professional hits, 4,367 (3089 in MLB & 1,278 in Japan).

Hall of Fame

Ichiro Suzuki will be eligible for election into the Baseball Hall of Fame in 2025. In the analysis by this writer, he should be an undisputed first ballot electee.

Summary Analysis

Ichiro Suzuki's Statistical 166.950 Hall of Fame Points listed in this book fare exceeds the Induction Total of 110.000. Suzuki is another excellent case for the elimination of the BBWAA voting process as he should be Indicted immediately following the five-year mandatory waiting period before being placed on the ballot for the Hall of Fame.

Suziki, Ichiro — **Right Field Potential Hall of Fame Inductee**

Positions: Rightfielder	Born: October 22, 1973
Bats: Left	From: Nichi Kasug ai-gun, Ja
Throws: Right	Height: 5' 11" USC 180 cm
	Weight: 175 lbs. 79 Kg
	Debut: April 2, 2001
	Last Game: March 21, 2019

Year	Age	Tm	Lg	G	PA	AB	R	H	2B	3B	HR	RBI	SB	CS	BB	SO	BA	OBP	SLG	OPS	TB	HBP	Awards
2001	27	SEA	AL	157	738	692	127	242	34	8	8	69	56	14	30	53	0.35	0.381	0.457	0.838	316	8	AS,MVP-
2002	28	SEA	AL	157	738	647	111	208	27	8	8	51	31	15	68	62	'0.321	0.388	0.425	0.813	275	5	AS,MVP-
2003	29	SEA	AL	159	725	679	111	212	29	8	13	62	34	8	36	69	0.312	0.352	0.436	0.788	296	6	AS,MVP-
2004	30	SEA	AL	161	762	704	101	262	24	5	8	60	36	11	49	63	0.372	0.414	0.455	0.869	320	4	AS,MVP-
2005	31	SEA	AL	162	739	679	111	206	21	12	15	68	33	8	48	66	0.303	0.350	0.436	0.786	296	4	AS,GG
2006	32	SEA	AL	161	752	695	110	224	20	9	9	49	45	2	49	71	0.322	0.370	0.416	0.786	289	5	AS,MVP-
2007	33	SEA	AL	161	736	678	111	238	22	7	6	68	37	8	49	77	0.351	0.396	0.431	0.827	292	3	AS,MVP-
2008	34	SEA	AL	162	749	686	103	213	20	7	6	42	43	4	51	65	0.31	0.361	0.386	0.747	265	5	AS,MVP-
2009	35	SEA	AL	146	678	639	88	225	31	4	11	46	26	9	32	71	0.352	0.386	0.465	0.851	297	4	AS,MVP-
2010	36	SEA	AL	162	732	680	74	214	30	3	6	43	42	9	45	86	0.315	0.359	0.394	0.754	268	3	AS,MVP-
2011	37	SEA	AL	161	721	677	80	184	22	3	5	47	40	7	39	69	0.272	0.310	0.335	0.645	227	0	
2012	38	TOT	AL	162	663	629	77	178	28	6	9	55	29	7	22	61	0.283	0.307	0.390	0.696	245	2	
2012	38	SEA	AL	95	423	402	49	105	15	5	4	28	15	2	17	40	0.261	0.288	0.353	0.642	142	0	
2012	38	NYY	AL	67	240	227	28	73	13	1	5	27	14	5	5	21	0.322	0.340	0.454	0.794	103	2	
2013	39	NYY	AL	150	555	520	57	136	15	3	7	35	20	4	26	63	0.262	0.297	0.342	0.639	178	1	
2014	40	NYY	AL	143	385	359	42	102	13	2	1	22	15	3	21	68	0.284	0.324	0.340	0.664	122	1	
2015	41	MIA	NL	153	438	398	45	91	5	6	1	21	11	5	31	51	0.229	0.282	0.279	0.561	111	0	
2016	42	MIA	NL	143	365	327	48	95	15	5	1	22	10	3	30	42	0.291	0.354	0.376	0.730	123	3	
2017	43	MIA	NL	136	215	196	19	50	6	0	3	20	1	1	17	35	0.255	0.318	0.332	0.649	65	1	
2018	44	SEA	AL	15	47	44	5	9	0	0	0	0	0	0	3	7	0.205	0.255	0.205	0.460	9	0	
2019	45	SEA	AL	2	6	5	0	0	0	0	0	0	0	0	1	1	0	0.167	0.000	0.167	0	0	
162 Game Avg.				162	655	607	87	189	22	6	7	48	31	7	40	66	0.311	0.355	0.402	0.757	244		3
SEA (14 yrs)				1861	8536	7907	1181	2542	295	79	99	633	438	97	517	800	0.321	0.365	0.416	0.781	3292	47	
NYY (3 yrs)				360	1180	1106	127	311	41	6	13	84	49	12	52	152	0.281	0.324	0.364	0.679	403	4	
MIA (3 yrs)				432	1018	921	112	236	26	11	5	63	22	8	78	128	0.256	0.315	0.325	0.64	299	4	
AL (16 yrs)				2221	9716	9013	1308	2853	336	85	112	717	487	109	569	952	0.317	0.359	0.41	0.769	3695	51	
NL (3 yrs)				432	1018	921	112	236	26	11	5	63	22	8	78	128	0.256	0.315	0.325	0.64	299	4	
19 Yrs				2653	10734	9934	1420	3089	362	96	117	780	509	117	647	1080	0.311	0.355	0.402	0.757	3994	55	Career Pts.
				11.750	0.000	0.000	9.250	11.750	0.000	0.000	1.500	2.500	6.750	0.000	1.500	0.000	8.000	3.000	8.000	3.750	6.750	0.000	74.500

Post Season Play

Year	Age	Tm	Lg	G	PA	AB	R	H	2B	3B	HR	RBI	SB	CS	BB	SO	BA	OBP	SLG	OPS	TB	HBP	
2001	27	Sea	ALDS	5	21	21	20	12	1	0	0	2	1	2	1	0	0.600	0.619	0.650	1.269	13	0	
2001	27	Sea	ALCS	5	22	22	18	4	1	0	0	1	2	0	4	4	0.222	0.364	0.278	0.641	5	0	
2012	38	NY	ALDS	5	25	25	23	5	2	0	0	3	1	1	1	3	0.217	0.250	0.304	0.554	7	0	
2012	38	NY	ALCS	4	18	18	17	8	0	0	1	2	0	0	1	2	0.353	0.389	0.529	0.918	9	0	
				19	86	86	78	29	4	0	1	8	4	3	7	9	0.311	0.424	0.436	0.860	34	0	Post Season Pts.
				0.400	0.000	0.000	0.400	0.600	0.000	0.000	0.250	0.400	0.400	0.000	0.400	0.000	1.400	1.600	0.400	0.800	0.400	0.000	7.450

World Series Play

Year	Age	Tm	Lg	G	PA	AB	R	H	2B	3B	HR	RBI	SB	CS	BB	SO	BA	OBP	SLG	OPS	TB	HBP	
				0	0	0	0	0	0	0	0	0	0	0	0	0	0	0	0	0	0	0	
None				0	0	0	0	0	0	0	0	0	0	0	0	0	0	0	0	0	0	0	World Series Pts.
				0.000	0.000	0.000	0.000	0.000	0.000	0.000	0.000	0.000	0.000	0.000	0.000	0.000	0.000	0.000	0.000	0.000	0.000	0.000	0.000

Yearly Points Leading the League

Category	Times	Points	Total
MVP	1	7	0
Rookie of Year	1	5	5
Triple Crown	0	5	0
Golden Glove	10	3	30
All-Star	10	2	20
Games	4	2	8
Totals			63

Category	Times	Points	Total
B.A.	2	3	6
Runs	0	2	0
H.R.'s	0	3	0
R.B.I's	0	3	0
Hits	7	2	14
S.B.	1	2	2
Totals			22

Categor	Times	Points	Total
T. B.	0	2	0
B.O.B.	0	2	0
OBP%	0	2	0
SLG %	0	2	0
OBPS%	0	2	0
Totals	0	0	0
Grand Total Add-On Points			85

Hall of Fame Points	
Career Points	74.500
Post Season Points	7.450
World Series Points	0.000
Career Add-On Points	85.000
Writers Association Pts.	0.000
Military/Lifetime Achievement	0.000
Grand Total HOF Points	166.950

Abreu, Bobby "El Comedulce"

Personal Life

Bob Kelly Abreu was born in Maracay, Aragua, Venezuela on March 11, 1974. Abreu is a very private individual as this writer was unable to find any information about his parents, siblings, marriages, or children.

Baseball Career

At the age of 16, he was signed by the Houston Astros in 1990. He moved up the minors until 1997 when he played in 59 games with Houston, Abreu was left unprotected in the 1997 MLB Expansion Draft and was selected by Tampa Bay, only to be dealt hours later to the Phillies. Over the next 14 seasons, nobody in baseball played more games than Abreu with him finishing his career with a .291/.395/.475 slash line. He led the majors with 1,396 walks from 1998-2011 and ranks 20th on the all-time list. In 2,425 games over 18 seasons, Abreu had a .291 batting average, 1,453 runs, 288 home runs, 1,363 RBI, 400 stolen bases, and 1,476 bases on balls..

Achievements:

- 2-time NL All-Star (2004 & 2005) & NL Gold Glove Winner (2005).
- 20-Home Run Seasons: 9 (1999-2005, 2008 & 2010).
- 30-Home Run Seasons: 2 (2001 & 2004) & NL Silver Slugger Award Winner (2004).
- 100 Runs Scored Seasons: 8 (1999-2002, 2004, 2005, 2007 & 2008).
- 100 RBI Seasons: 8 (2001 & 2003-2009).
- 7-Times received MVP Votes: (1999, 2001, 2003, 2004, 2005, 2007 & 2009).

Hall of Fame

Bobby Abreu became eligible for the Hall of Fame in 2020 and received 5.5% of the vote. He has been on the ballot five times and received 15.4% of the vote in 2023.

Summary Analysis

Bobby Abreu's Hall of Fame Points are 97.200. Only three individuals have reached base more times and he should be voted in by the BBWAA.

Bobby Abreu — Right Fielder Potential Hall of Fame Inductee

Positions		Born :	March 11, 1974	Height:	6'0"	USC	183	cm
Right Fielder		From:	Maracay, Venezuela	Weight:	200	lbs.	99	Kg.
Centerfield		Bats:	Left	Debut:	September 1, 1996			
		Throws:	Right	Last Game:	September 28, 2014			

Year	Age	Tm	Lg	G	PA	AB	R	H	2B	3B	HR	RBI	SB	CS	BB	SO	BA	OBP	SLG	OPS	TB	HBP	Awards
1996	22	HOU	NL	15	24	22	1	5	1	0	0	1	0	0	2	3	0.227	0.292	0.273	0.564	6	0	
1997	23	HOU	NL	59	210	188	22	47	10	2	3	26	7	2	21	48	0.250	0.329	0.372	0.701	70	1	
1998	24	PHI	NL	151	589	497	68	155	29	6	17	74	19	10	84	133	0.312	0.409	0.497	0.906	247	0	
1999	25	PHI	NL	152	662	546	118	183	35	11	20	93	27	9	109	113	0.335	0.446	0.549	0.995	300	3	MVP-23
2000	26	PHI	NL	154	680	576	103	182	42	10	25	79	28	8	100	116	0.316	0.416	0.554	0.970	319	1	
2001	27	PHI	NL	162	704	588	118	170	48	4	31	110	36	14	106	137	0.289	0.393	0.543	0.936	319	1	MVP-16
2002	28	PHI	NL	157	685	572	102	176	50	6	20	85	31	12	104	117	0.308	0.413	0.521	0.934	298	3	
2003	29	PHI	NL	158	695	577	99	173	35	1	20	101	22	9	109	126	0.300	0.409	0.468	0.877	270	2	MVP-27
2004	30	PHI	NL	159	713	574	118	173	47	1	30	105	40	5	127	116	0.301	0.428	0.544	0.971	312	5	AS,MVP-23,SS
2005	31	PHI	NL	162	719	588	104	168	37	1	24	102	31	9	117	134	0.286	0.405	0.474	0.879	279	6	AS,MVP-14,GG
2006	32	TOT	MLB	156	686	548	98	163	41	2	15	107	30	6	124	138	0.297	0.424	0.462	0.886	253	3	
2006	32	PHI	NL	98	438	339	61	94	25	2	8	65	20	4	91	86	0.277	0.427	0.434	0.861	147	2	
2006	32	NYY	AL	58	248	209	37	69	16	0	7	42	10	2	33	52	0.330	0.419	0.507	0.926	106	1	
2007	33	NYY	AL	158	699	605	123	171	40	5	16	101	25	8	84	115	0.283	0.369	0.445	0.814	269	3	MVP-17
2008	34	NYY	AL	156	684	609	100	180	39	4	20	100	22	11	73	109	0.296	0.371	0.471	0.843	287	1	
2009	35	LAA	AL	152	667	563	96	165	29	3	15	103	30	8	94	113	0.293	0.390	0.435	0.825	245	1	MVP-12
2010	36	LAA	AL	154	667	573	88	146	41	1	20	78	24	10	87	132	0.255	0.352	0.435	0.787	249	2	
2011	37	LAA	AL	142	585	502	54	127	30	1	8	60	21	5	78	113	0.253	0.353	0.365	0.717	183	1	
2012	38	TOT	MLB	100	257	219	29	53	11	1	3	24	6	2	37	56	0.242	0.350	0.342	0.693	75	0	
2012	38	LAA	AL	8	27	24	1	5	3	0	0	5	0	0	2	5	0.208	0.259	0.333	0.593	8	0	
2012	38	LAD	NL	92	230	195	28	48	8	1	3	19	6	2	35	51	0.246	0.361	0.344	0.704	67	0	
2014	40	NYM	NL	78	155	133	12	33	9	0	1	14	1	0	20	21	0.248	0.342	0.338	0.680	45	0	
18 Yrs				2425	10081	8480	1453	2470	574	59	288	1363	400	128	1476	1840	0.291	0.395	0.475	0.870	4025	33	Career Pts.
				#####	0.000	0.000	9.250	6.750	0.000	0.000	0.450	8.000	4.500	0.000	9.250	0.000	4.500	8.000	3.750	8.000	6.750	0.000	79.700

Post Seasonal Play

Year	Age	Tm	Lg	G	PA	AB	R	H	2B	3B	HR	RBI	SB	CS	BB	SO	BA	OBP	SLG	OPS	TB	HBP	
1997	23	HOU	NL-DS	3	3	3	0	1	0	0	0	0	1	0	0	2	0.333	0.333	0.333	0.667	1	0	
2006	32	NYY	AL-DS	4	17	15	2	5	1	0	0	4	0	0	2	2	0.333	0.412	0.4	0.812	6	0	
2007	33	NYY	AL-DS	4	17	15	1	4	1	0	1	2	1	0	2	3	0.267	0.353	0.533	0.886	8	0	
2009	35	LAA	AL-DS	3	13	9	4	5	2	0	0	1	0	1	4	0	0.556	0.692	0.778	1.47	10	0	
2009	35	LAA	AL-CS	6	29	25	2	4	2	0	0	2	0	0	4	8	0.16	0.276	0.24	0.516	6	0	
				20	79	67	9	19	6	0	1	9	2	1	12	15	0.284	0.392	0.463	0.855	31	0	Post Season Pts.
				0.400	0.000	0.000	0.400	0.400	0.000	0.000	0.250	0.400	0.250	0.000	0.600	0.000	0.600	1.200	0.600	0.800	0.600	0	6.500

World Series Play

Year	Age	Tm	Lg	G	PA	AB	R	H	2B	3B	HR	RBI	SB	CS	BB	SO	BA	OBP	SLG	OPS	TB	HBP	
None Played In				0	0	0	0	0	0	0	0	0	0	0	0	0	0	0	0	0	0	0	0	World Series Pts.
				0.000	0.000	0.000	0.000	0.000	0.000	0.000	0.000	0.000	0.000	0.000	0.000	0.000	0.000	0.000	0.000	0.000	0.000	0.000		0.000

Yearly Points Leading the League

Category	Times	Points	Total	Category	Times	Points	Total	Categ	Times	Points	Total
MVP	0	7	0	B.A.	0	3	0	T.B.	0	2	0
Rookie of Year	0	5	0	Runs	0	2	0	B.O.B.	0	2	0
Triple Crown	0	5	0	H.R.'s	0	3	0	OBP%	0	2	0
Golden Glove	1	3	3	R.B.I's	0	3	0	SLG %	0	2	0
All-Star	2	2	4	Hits	0	2	0	OBPS%	0	2	0
Games	2	2	4	S.B.	0	2	0	Totals			0
Totals			11	Totals			0	Grand Total Add-On Points			11

Hall of Fame Points	
Career Points	79.700
Post Season Points	6.500
World Series Points	0.000
Career Add-On Points	11.000
Writers Association Pts.	0.000
Military/Lifetime Achievement	0.000
Grand Total HOF Points	97.200

Staub, Rusty "Le Grand Orange"

Personal Life

Daniel Joseph "Rusty" Staub was born on April 1, 1944, in New Orleans, LA. to Ray Staub and Alma Morton. Staub and his older brother, Chuck, played at Jesuit High School and they won the 1960 American Legion national championship.

In 1985, Staub founded the New York Police and Fire Widows' and Children's Benefit Fund. Staub was never married or had children.

Baseball Career

Staub was signed as a bonus baby by the Houston Colt .45's at the age of 17 in 1961. He batted .299 in the Arizona Fall League in 1961 and dominated the Class-B Carolina League in 1962 which earned a trip to the big club in 1963. In his first season, he played regularly, but hit only .220. Staub finished his career playing 2951 games, 2716 hits, 1189 runs, 292 HR's, 1466 R.B. I's, .279 B.A, .362 OBP, and an OPS of .793.

Achievements

- 6-time All-Star: (1967-1971 & 1976).
- 7-Times received MVP votes: (1966, 1967, 1969, 1971, 1972, 1975 & 1978).
- 2-Times led the N.L. in games played: (1971 & 1976).
- 4-Times 20-Home Run Seasons: (1969, 1970 - 30, 1977 & 1978).
- 3-Times 100 RBI Seasons: (1975, 1977 & 1978)
- 4-Times batted over .300 (1967, 1969, 1971, & 1980)

Hall of Fame

Staub was on the Hall of Fame ballot from 1991 to 1997 and received more than 7.9%, and was dropped off the ballot after receiving 3.8% in 1997.

Summary Analysis

Rusty Staub had a Hall of Fame Point Total of 99.450. He was a great ambassador and a role model that should be rewarded by the BBWAA.

A Fan's Perspective

Staub, Rusty — Right Field Potential Hall of Fame Inductee

Positions: Rightfielder, First Baseman

Born:	April 1, 1944
Died:	March 29, 2018
From:	New Orleans, LA
Bats:	Left
Throws:	Right

Height:	6'2" — USC 188 cm
Weight:	190 lbs. — 86 Kg.
Debut:	April 9, 1963
Last Game:	October 6, 1985

Year	Age	Tm	Lg	G	PA	AB	R	H	2B	3B	HR	RBI	SB	CS	BB	SO	BA	OBP	SLG	OPS	TB	HBP	Awards
1963	19	HOU	NL	150	585	513	43	115	17	4	6	45	0	0	59	58	0.224	0.309	0.308	0.617	158	5	
1964	20	HOU	NL	89	320	292	26	63	10	2	8	35	1	1	21	31	0.216	0.272	0.346	0.618	101	3	
1965	21	HOU	NL	131	470	410	43	105	20	1	14	63	3	0	52	57	0.256	0.339	0.412	0.751	169	2	
1966	22	HOU	NL	153	628	554	60	155	28	3	13	81	2	1	58	61	0.280	0.345	0.412	0.756	228	1	MVP-22
1967	23	HOU	NL	149	621	546	71	182	44	1	10	74	0	4	60	47	0.333	0.398	0.473	0.871	258	3	AS,MVP-16
1968	24	HOU	NL	161	682	591	54	172	37	1	6	72	2	0	73	57	0.291	0.373	0.387	0.761	229	7	AS
1969	25	MON	NL	158	673	549	89	166	26	5	29	79	3	4	110	61	0.302	0.426	0.526	0.952	289	9	AS,MVP-36
1970	26	MON	NL	160	699	569	98	156	23	7	30	94	12	11	112	93	0.274	0.394	0.497	0.891	283	3	AS
1971	27	MON	NL	162	690	599	94	186	34	6	19	97	9	5	74	42	0.311	0.392	0.482	0.874	289	9	AS,MVP-19
1972	28	NYM	NL	66	278	239	32	70	11	0	9	38	0	1	31	13	0.293	0.372	0.452	0.824	108	2	MVP-25
1973	29	NYM	NL	152	666	585	77	163	36	1	15	76	1	1	74	52	0.279	0.361	0.421	0.781	246	3	
1974	30	NYM	NL	151	649	561	65	145	22	2	19	78	2	1	77	39	0.258	0.347	0.406	0.754	228	3	
1975	31	NYM	NL	155	670	574	93	162	30	4	19	105	2	0	77	55	0.282	0.371	0.448	0.818	257	9	MVP-14
1976	32	DET	AL	161	690	589	73	176	28	3	15	96	3	1	83	49	0.299	0.386	0.433	0.818	255	7	AS
1977	33	DET	AL	158	695	623	84	173	34	3	22	101	1	1	59	47	0.278	0.336	0.448	0.784	279	1	
1978	34	DET	AL	162	734	642	75	175	30	1	24	121	3	1	76	35	0.273	0.347	0.435	0.782	279	3	MVP-5
1979	35	TOT	MLB	106	389	332	41	81	15	1	12	54	1	0	46	28	0.244	0.340	0.404	0.744	134	5	
1979	35	DET	AL	68	288	246	32	58	12	1	9	40	1	0	32	18	0.236	0.331	0.402	0.733	99	5	
1979	35	MON	NL	38	101	86	9	23	3	0	3	14	0	0	14	10	0.267	0.366	0.407	0.773	35	0	
1980	36	TEX	AL	109	388	340	42	102	23	2	9	55	1	1	39	18	0.300	0.370	0.459	0.828	156	2	
1981	37	NYM	NL	70	186	161	9	51	9	0	5	21	1	0	22	12	0.317	0.398	0.466	0.864	75	1	
1982	38	NYM	NL	112	250	219	11	53	9	0	3	27	0	0	24	10	0.242	0.309	0.324	0.633	71	0	
1983	39	NYM	NL	104	132	115	5	34	6	0	3	28	0	0	14	10	0.296	0.371	0.426	0.797	49	1	
1984	40	NYM	NL	78	79	72	2	19	4	0	1	18	0	0	4	9	0.264	0.291	0.361	0.652	26	0	
1985	41	NYM	NL	54	55	45	2	12	3	0	1	8	0	0	10	4	0.267	0.400	0.400	0.800	18	0	
162 Game Avg.				162	616	534	65	149	27	3	16	80	3	2	69	49	0.279	0.362	0.431	0.793	230	16	
NYM (9 yrs)				942	2965	2571	396	709	130	7	75	399	6	3	333	204	0.276	0.358	0.419	0.778	1078	82	
HOU (6 yrs)				833	3306	2906	297	792	156	12	57	370	8	6	323	311	0.273	0.346	0.393	0.740	1143	72	
MON (4 yrs)				518	2163	1803	290	531	86	18	81	284	24	20	310	206	0.295	0.402	0.497	0.899	896	44	
DET (4 yrs)				549	2407	2100	264	582	104	8	70	358	8	3	250	149	0.277	0.353	0.434	0.787	912	83	
TEX (1 yr)				109	388	340	42	102	23	2	9	55	1	1	39	18	0.300	0.370	0.459	0.828	156	16	
NL (19 yrs)				2293	8434	7280	883	2032	372	37	213	1053	38	29	966	721	0.279	0.365	0.428	0.793	3117	198	
AL (5 yrs)				658	2795	2440	306	684	127	10	79	413	9	4	289	167	0.28	0.355	0.438	0.793	1068	99	
23 Yrs				2951	11229	9720	1189	2716	499	47	292	1466	47	33	1255	888	0.279	0.362	0.431	0.793	4185	297	**Career Pts.**
				14.250	0.000	0.000	5.500	8.000	0.000	0.000	4.500	9.250	0.500	0.000	6.750	0.000	3.750	3.750	2.000	4.500	8.000	0.000	**70.750**

Post Season Play

Year	Age	Tm	Lg	G	PA	AB	R	H	2B	3B	HR	RBI	SB	CS	BB	SO	BA	OBP	SLG	OPS	TB	HBP	
1973	29	NYM	NLCS	4	18	15	4	3	0	0	3	5	0	0	3	2	0.200	0.333	0.800	1.133	12	0	
				4	18	15	4	3	0	0	3	5	0	0	3	2	0.200	0.333	0.800	1.133	12	0	**Post Season Pts.**
				0.200	0.000	0.000	0.200	0.200	0.000	0.000	0.450	0.200	0.000	0.000	0.200	0.000	0.000	0.000	2.500	2.500	0.000	0.000	**6.450**

World Series Play

Year	Age	Tm	Lg	G	PA	AB	R	H	2B	3B	HR	RBI	SB	CS	BB	SO	BA	OBP	SLG	OPS	TB	HBP	
1973	29	NYM	WS	7	28	26	1	11	2	0	1	6	0	0	2	2	0.423	0.464	0.615	1.08	16	0	
				7	28	26	1	11	2	0	1	6	0	0	2	2	0.423	0.464	0.615	1.08	16	0	**World Series Pts.**
				0.200	0.000	0.000	0.200	0.325	0.000	0.000	0.200	0.325	0.000	0.000	0.000	0.000	2.500	0.000	0.000	2.500	0.000	0.000	**6.250**

Yearly Points Leading the League

Category	Times	Points	Total	Category	Times	Points	Total	Categ.	Times	Points	Total
MVP	0	7	0	B.A.	0	3	0	T.B.	0	3	0
Rookie of Year	0	5	0	Runs	0	2	0	B.O.B.	0	2	0
Triple Crown	0	5	0	H.R.'s	0	3	0	OBP%	0	2	0
Golden Glove	0	3	0	R.B.I's	0	3	0	SLG %	0	2	0
All-Star	6	2	12	Hits	0	2	0	OBPS%	0	2	0
Games	2	2	4	S.B.	0	2	0	Totals			0
Totals			16	Totals			0	Grand Total Add-On Points		16	

Hall of Fame Points	
Career Points	70.750
Post Season Points	6.450
World Series Points	6.250
Career Add-On Points	16.000
Writers Association Pts.	0.000
Military/Lifetime Achievement	0.000
Grand Total HOF Points	99.450

The Baseball Hall of Fame

Statistical Review of Potential Left-Handed Pitchers for the Hall of Fame

Player	Years Played	Career Pts.	Post Season Pts.	World Series Pts.	Add-On Pts.	Mil/LT Pts.	Total HOF Pts.	Needed HOF Votes	Comments
Players Needing to be Inducted									
Guidry, Ron	14	59.250	4.000	6.500	52.000	0.000	121.750	0	Inducted
John, Tommy	26	90.750	6.850	5.700	16.000	20.000	139.300	0	Inducted
Sabathia, CC	19	71.000	9.300	2.400	33.000	0.000	115.700	0	Inducted
Santana, Johan	12	55.750	4.050	0.000	52.0002	0.000	111.800	0	Inducted
Players Needing to be Voted into the Hall of Fame by the BBWAA									
Blue, Vida	17	66.500	5.250	4.300	29.000	0.000	105.050	5	Need Voting
Buehrle, Mark	16	53.250	4.300	1.750	32.000	0.000	91.550	19	Need Voting
Cuellar, Mike	15	61.250	5.450	6.000	24.000	0.000	96.700	14	Need Voting
Franco, John	21	73.000	5.450	2.150	18.000	0.000	98.600	12	Need Voting
Koosman, Jerry	19	71.250	2.200	6.500	4.000	10.000	93.950	17	Need Voting
Lee, Cliff	13	47.750	9.800	4.300	31.000	0.000	92.850	18	Need Voting
Lester, John	16	56.250	10.050	8.600	16.000	0.000	90.900	20	Need Voting
Lolich, Mickey	16	72.500	4.400	7.800	19.000	0.000	103.700	7	Need Voting
Lyle, Sparky	16	62.750	6.350	2.450	23.000	0.000	94.550	16	Need Voting
Pettite, Andy	18	61.500	11.050	6.600	15.000	0.000	94.150	16	Need Voting
Valenzuela, Fernando	16	49.750	8.250	2.150	34.000	0.000	94.150	16	Need Voting
Vaughn, Hippo	13	63.000	0.000	6.550	26.000	0.000	95.550	15	Need Voting
Wagner, Billy	16	85.500	3.450	0.000	18.000	0.000	106.950	4	Need Voting
Players Not Meeting the Statistical Requirements									
Buffington, Charlie	11	76.250	0.000	0.000	2.000	0.000	78.250	N/A	DMR
Hamels, Cole	15	54.000	9.850	2.200	12.000	0.000	78.050	N/A	DMR
Key, Jimmy	15	53.000	4.450	5.450	20.000	0.000	82.900	N/A	DMR
Langston, Mark	16	45.250	1.250	0.500	35.000	0.000	82.000	N/A	DMR
McDowell, Sam	15	48.500	0.000	0.000	29.000	0.000	77.500	N/A	DMR
McGraw, Tug	19	53.250	7.850	5.100	4.000	0.000	70.200	N/A	DMF
McNally, Dave	14	59.000	6.250	8.950	15.000	0.000	89.200	N/A	DMF
Myers, Randy	14	47.500	9.250	2.250	17.000	0.000	76.000	N/A	DMR
Moyer, Jamie	25	66.750	8.000	1.650	4.000	0.000	80.400	N/A	DMR
Osteen, Claude	18	59.750	0.000	6.050	6.000	0.000	71.800	N/A	DMF
Pierce, Billy	18	66.750	0.000	5.350	14.000	0.000	86.100	N/A	DMF
Tanana, Frank	21	71.750	2.1250	0.000	13.000	0.000	86.000	N/A	DMF
Viola, Frank	15	43.750	1.250	4.500	22.000	0.000	71.500	N/A	DMR
Wood, Wilbur	17	53.750	0.000	0.000	30.000	0.000	83.750	N/A	DMR

Hall of Fame Statistical Requirements:

All Players achieving the total of 110.000, or greater, Total Hall of Fame Points, shall be Inducted after five (5) years of retirement. This provision can be waived due to the death by a 75% vote of the 25 Panel BBWAA's. Individuals receiving less than the required 110.000 Hall of Fame Points are eligible for Election after five (5) years of retirement. A 25 person BBWAA will determine the Players that will be Inducted and vote on the Players needing to be elected. An example of those needing to be elected are as follows: Player "A" has a total of 95 Hall of Fame Points and will need 15 of the (25) BBWAA votes to be Elected in the following year.

Left-Handed Pitchers Needing to be Inducted.

1. Ron Guidry
2. Tommy John
3. C.C. Sabathia
4. Johan Santana

110.000 Hall of Fame Statistical Induction Criteria

Guidry, Ron ("Louisiana Lightning" & "Gator")

Personal Life

Ronald Ames Guidry was born August 28, 1950 in Lafayette, Louisiana to Mary Grace Broussard and Roland Guidry. He has a younger brother, Travis, who was born 17 years after Guidry, and is mentally challenged.

Guidry excelled as a two-sport (baseball, track, and field) star at Northside High School in Lafayette. He chose to stay close to home and accepted a baseball scholarship from the University of Southwestern Louisiana. He was a combined 12–5 with a 2.03 earned run average and 137 strikeouts in 1969 and 1970 and threw up to 95 miles per hour.

Guidry enlisted into the National Guard in 1971 and was active through 1977. He married Bonnie Rutledge, September 23, 1972, with the couple having three children: two daughters, Jamie and Danielle, and a son, Brandon.

Baseball Career

The Yankees selected him in the third round of the free agent draft on June 8, 1971. In his first four years in the minor leagues, he did not distinguish himself as a future starter with the Yankees, or as a reliever. In 1974, Guidry was moved to the pen and the results were disastrous. In spite of his poor showing, Guidry was promoted to AAA which provided a glimpse of the big leagues. Bobby Cox was the manager of the club and someone Guidry admired. Cox made Guidry his closer, and he racked up 14 saves to go with a 6-5 record and a 2.90 ERA in 42 games. He earned a promotion to the Yankees, with Guidry making his major league debut on July 27, 1975.

After one relief appearance for New York on May 20, 1976, Guidry was left idling in the Yankee bullpen for 47 consecutive games. On July 6, he was sent back to the AAA International League and ready to quit the game. He balked at his demotion, packed up his car and headed home to Louisiana with Bonnie. On the drive home, Bonnie asked him, "Are you sure you want to give up on everything you've been working toward for the last 10 years? You've never quit on anything you thought you could do in your life. Don't quit on your own. Let the Yankees tell you you're no good before you quit."

A Fan's Perspective

Guidry began 1977 as a relief pitcher but was moved into the Yankees starting rotation after an emergency start on April 30. In the longest outing Guidry, he helped the Yankees beat the Seattle Mariners 3–0. Guidry finished the season with a 16–7record. His emergence as a starter made him one of the Yankees' biggest surprises helped lead the them to a World Series championship.

In 1978, Guidry posted a career year that has been one of the all-time best seasons by a Yankees pitcher. Against the California Angels on June 17, he struck out a Yankee-record 18 batters. For the season, Guidry went 25–3, setting the all-time mark for winning percentage by a pitcher with at least twenty wins. He led the league with a 1.74 ERA, an .893 winning percentage, nine shutouts, and 248 strikeouts. Guidry's success in 1978 was due in large part to his mastery of the slider. His 248 strikeouts set a Yankees' franchise record for most strikeouts by a pitcher in a single season. Guidry's 25th win of the 1978 regular season came in the Yankees' 5–4 win over the Boston Red Sox in a one-game playoff and determined the American League East division winner. The Yankees won the World Series over the Los Angeles Dodgers and Guidry won the 1978 American League Cy Young Award unanimously.

The Yankees finished in fourth place with tragedy striking the team on August 2, when Thurman Munson was killed while piloting his Cessna jet. Despite the loss of his batterymate, Guidry posted an 18-8 record and led the AL with a 2.78 ERA. Guidry showed his leadership abilities when he volunteered to go to the bullpen to help the team where needed," said Guidry. "There's nothing else on my mind."

Through August 18, 1980, Guidry posted a 12-9 record with a 3.71 ERA. He had lost three straight losses when he went back to the bullpen. In eight relief appearances, covering 18 1/3 innings, Guidry was 1-1 with a 1.96 ERA. For the year he was 17-10. 3.56 ERA, and the Yankees won the AL East. They were matched with Kansas City in the LCS and ousted in five games. Guidry made one start, losing Game One, 7-2.

Known as an excellent fielder, Guidry won a Gold Glove each year from 1982 through 1986. In 1984, On August 7, 1984, Guidry struck out three batters on nine pitches in the ninth inning of a 7–0 win over the Chicago White Sox becoming the eighth American League pitcher and the 27th pitcher in major-league history to accomplish an immaculate inning. However, Guidry had a losing season of 10 wins, 11 loses, ERA

The Baseball Hall of Fame

of 4.69. The 1984 season was a tough one as he landed on the disabled list with a rib injury. He finished 10-11 with an ERA of 4.51.

In 1985, Guidry bounced back and led the American League with 22 wins, winning percentage of .786, ERA of 3.27 and was named co-captain of the Yankees Guidry posted a losing record of 16 wins and 23 losses from 1986 through 1989 and was sent down to the International League when he made the decision to retire from baseball.

Overall, Guidry was 170-91 with a 3.29 ERA over 14 seasons and 2,392 innings pitched. He struck out 1,778 batters while walking 633 and won 3 World Series games.

Notable Achievements:

- 4-time AL All-Star (1978, 1979, 1982 & 1983) & Roberto Clemente award 1984.
- AL Cy Young Award Winner (1978) & 5-time AL Gold Glove Winner (1982-1986).
- 2 time AL ERA Leader (1978 & 1979) & 2-time AL Wins Leader (1978 & 1985).
- 2-time AL Winning Percentage Leader (1978 & 1985).
- AL Complete Games Leader (1983) & AL Shutouts Leader (1978).
- 6 - 15 Win Seasons (1977-1980, 1983 & 1985).
- 2 - 200 Strikeouts Seasons (1978 & 1979.
- 3 - 20 Win Seasons (1978, 1983 & 1985) & 1 - 25 Win Season 1 (1978).
- 7-Times Pitched Seasons 200 or more Innings (1977-1980, 1982, 1983 & 1985).
- Two-Time World Series Champion with the New York Yankees (1977 & 1978)
- All-Time Season Winning percentage (minimum 20 wins), .893, 1978.

Hall of Fame Candidacy

Ron Guidry was eligible for the Hall of Fame voting by the BBWAA in 1994. His highest percentage was 9% in 2000 and removed after ten years in 2003.

Summary Analysis

Ron Guidry's Hall of Fame Point Total is 121.750. Guidry should have been Inducted, yet 35 years after his retirement, he still has not been enshrined in Cooperstown.

A Fan's Perspective

Guidry, Ron — Pitcher - Left Handed Potential Hall of Fame Inductee

Positions		**Born:** August 28, 1950	**Height:** 5'11" USC 10 cm
Pitcher		**From:** Lafeyette, LA	**Weight:** 181 lbs. 173 Kg.
		Bats: Left	**Debut** July 27, 1975
		Throws: Left	**Last Game:** September 27, 1988

Year	Age	Tm	Lg	W	L	Pct%	ERA	G	GS	GF	CG	SHO	SV	IP	H	R	ER	BB	SO	BF	WHIP	Awards
1975	24	NYY	AL	0	1	0.000	3.45	10	1	6	0	0	0	15.2	15	6	6	9	15	69	1.532	
1976	25	NYY	AL	0	0	0.000	5.63	7	0	1	0	0	0	16	20	12	10	4	12	72	1.500	
1977	26	NYY	AL	16	7	0.696	2.82	31	25	4	9	5	1	210.2	174	72	66	65	176	850	1.134	CYA-7,MVP-18
1978	27	NYY	AL	25	3	0.893	1.74	35	35	0	16	9	0	273.2	187	61	53	72	248	1057	0.946	AS,CYA-1,MVP-2
1979	28	NYY	AL	18	8	0.692	2.78	33	30	3	15	2	2	236.1	203	83	73	71	201	946	1.159	AS,CYA-3,MVP-26
1980	29	NYY	AL	17	10	0.630	3.56	37	29	4	5	3	1	219.2	215	97	87	80	166	929	1.343	
1981	30	NYY	AL	11	5	0.688	2.76	23	21	1	0	0	0	127	100	41	39	26	104	497	0.992	CYA-7
1982	31	NYY	AL	14	8	0.636	3.81	34	33	0	6	1	0	222	216	104	94	69	162	935	1.284	AS,GG
1983	32	NYY	AL	21	9	0.700	3.42	31	31	0	21	3	0	250.1	232	99	95	60	156	1024	1.166	AS,CYA-5,MVP-
1984	33	NYY	AL	10	11	0.476	4.51	29	28	1	5	1	0	195.2	223	102	98	44	127	841	1.365	GG
1985	34	NYY	AL	22	6	0.786	3.27	34	33	0	11	2	0	259	243	104	94	42	143	1033	1.100	CYA-2,MVP-15,GG
1986	35	NYY	AL	9	12	0.429	3.98	30	30	0	5	0	0	192.1	202	94	85	38	140	809	1.248	GG
1987	36	NYY	AL	5	8	0.385	3.67	22	17	2	2	0	0	117.2	111	50	48	38	96	493	1.266	
1988	37	NYY	AL	2	3	0.400	4.18	12	10	1	0	0	0	56	57	28	26	15	32	239	1.286	
162 Game Avg.				17	9	0.651	3.29	36	32	2	9	3	0	235	216	94	86	62	175	964	1.184	
14 Yrs				170	91	0.651	3.29	368	323	23	95	26	4	2392	2198	953	874	633	1778	9794	1.184	**Career Pts.**
				5.500	0.000	14.250	7.500	2.500	4.500	0.500	2.000	3.000	0.000	4.500	0.000	0.000	0.000	0.000	4.500	0.000	10.500	59.250

Post Seasonal Play

Year	Age	Team	Series	W	L	PCT	ERA	G	GS	GF	CG	SHO	SV	IP	H	R	ER	BB	SO	BF	WHIP	
1977	26	NYY	ALCS	1	0	1.000	3.97	2	2	0	1	0	0	11.1	9	5	5	3	8	45	1.059	
1978	27	NYY	ALCS	1	0	1.000	1.13	1	1	0	0	0	0	8	7	1	1	1	7	30	1.000	
1980	29	NYY	ALCS	0	1	0.000	12.00	1	1	0	0	0	0	3	5	4	4	4	2	17	3.000	
1981	30	NYY	ALDS	0	0	0.000	5.40	2	2	0	0	0	0	8.1	11	5	5	3	8	39	1.680	
1981	30	NYY	ALCS	0	0	0.000	0.00	0	0	0	0	0	0	0	0	0	0	0	0	0	0.000	
				2	1	0.667	4.403	6	6	0	1	0	0	30.2	32	15	15	11	25	131	1.402	**Post Series Pts.**
				0.250	0.000	0.250	0.250	0.600	0.600	0.000	0.250	0.000	0.000	0.600	0.000	0.000	0.000	0.000	0.800	0.000	0.600	4.000

World Series Play

Year	Age	Team	Series	W	L	PCT	ERA	G	GS	GF	CG	SHO	SV	IP	H	R	ER	BB	SO	BF	WHIP	
1976	25	NYY	AL	Did	Not	Pitch	in	Series														
1977	26	NYY	AL	0	0	0.000	2.00	1	1	0	1	0	0	9	4	2	2	3	7	33	0.778	
1978	27	NYY	AL	1	0	1.000	1.00	1	1	0	1	0	0	9	8	1	1	7	4	39	1.667	
1981	30	NYY	AL	1	1	0.500	1.93	2	2	0	0	0	0	14	8	3	3	4	15	53	0.857	
				2	1	0.667	1.69	4	4	0	2	0	0	32	20	6	6	14	26	125	1.063	**World Series Pts.**
				0.400	0.000	0.250	1.800	0.250	0.400	0.000	0.400	0.000	0.000	0.600	0.000	0.000	0.000	0.000	0.800	0.000	1.600	6.500

Yearly Points Leading the League

Category	Times	Points	Total		Category	Times	Points	Total		Categor	Times	Points	Total		Hall of Fame Points	
MVP	0	7	0		Saves	0	3	0		SHO	1	2	2		Career Points	59.250
ROY	0	5	0		ERA	2	3	6		WinPct	2	2	4		Post Season Points	4.000
Cy Young	1	5	5		S.O.'s	0	2	0		Innings	0	2	0		World Series Points	6.500
Golden Glove	5	3	15		Games	0	2	0		WHIP	2	2	4		Career Add-On Points	52.000
All-Star	4	2	8		G.S.	0	2	0		GF	0	2	0		Writers Association Pts.	0.000
Wins	2	3	6		C.G.	1	2	2		Totals			10		Military/Lifetime Achievement	0.000
Totals			34		Totals			8		Grand Total Add-On Points			52		Grand Total HOF Points	121.750

Thomas (Tommy) Edward John Jr.

Personal life

Thomas Edward John Jr. was born May 22, 1943, in Terre Haute, Indiana, to Thomas Edward John and Ruth. He had a sister Marilyn, born in 1937, who Tommy believed could have sung professionally. The family was raised in the Protestant faith and very active in the church and community. Both parents were very supportive of Tommy and his sister and did whatever was needed to help them succeed.

As a youth, he often played sandlot ball with other kids, either at Spencer F. Ball Park or Woodrow Wilson field. Arley Andrews, a former minor league pitcher and a friend of his father, taught John to throw a curveball, which would be John's main pitch. John was an outstanding baseball and basketball player at Gerstmeyer High School in Terre Haute, Indiana and had a 28–2 record as a pitcher. Tommy Athletics did not get in the way of his schoolwork, as John graduated as Gerstmeyer's 1961 valedictorian. School faculty forbade John from delivering a valedictory address because of his stutter which he eventually overcame.

On July 13, 1970, Tommy married the former Sally Simmons and became proud parents of four children: Tamara, Tommy III, Travis, and Taylor.

Baseball Career

Several colleges recruited John as a basketball player, but John had caught the eye of Cleveland Indians' scout Johnny Schulte. So after graduating in 1961, he signed with the Indians and was assigned to Dubuque in the Class D League where he had a 10–4 record in 1961 but had some trouble with the Charleston Indians of the Class A Eastern League in 1962. "I was rearing back on every pitch and firing with all my strength at the strike zone," he said. "As a result, I kept getting behind in the ball-and-strike count, often running it to three balls and no strikes, so I just had to put my fastball right over the plate and get it creamed." This led to a lot of walks, but player-coach Steve Jankowski worked with him, suggesting that John throw less hard so that he would have more control. The alterations helped John get called up to the Class AAA Jacksonville Suns of the International League during the year, and John won two games for them with the playoffs. He started 1963 with Jacksonville, got sent down to Charleston, went 9–2 with a 1.61 ERA for the West

A Fan's Perspective

Virginian Indians, and got called up to the major leagues in September at the age of 20 on September 6, 1963, John started what would become a 26-year major league career, allowing one unearned run in one inning of a 7–2 loss to the Washington Senators. He was used as a reliever at first, but finished the year with three starts. Though his record was 0–2, his earned run average (ERA) was 2.21.

In his first start of 1964, John threw a shutout against the Baltimore Orioles for his first major league win in the second game of a double header. He won two of his first three games but then lost eight decisions in a row and got sent to the AAA Pacific Coast League in July. Indians' pitching coach Early Wynn had been trying to get John to throw a slider, but John altered his grip, affecting his control. He returned to throwing just a fastball and a curveball in the minors and was called up for a few games in September by the Indians. After the season, he was sent to the Chicago White Sox as part of a three-way trade between Cleveland, Chicago, and the Kansas City Athletics. The 1965 season produced a 14–7 record, a 3.09 ERA, 126 strikeouts, 58 walks, and 162 hits allowed in 183+$\frac{2}{3}$ innings. By 1966, manager Eddie Stinky made John his Opening Day starter. 1972 John pitched in 38 games, he had a 13–16 record, a 3.61 ERA, three shutouts, 131 strikeouts, 58 walks, and 244 hits in 229+$\frac{1}{3}$ innings pitched. John was traded to the Los Angeles Dodgers for Dick Allen at the Winter Meetings.

John finally had a team that could score runs and not lose leads when he was relieved.
From 1972 until his injury July 17th his record was 40-15 when the course of his career, and many others would change. With the Dodgers leading 4–0 in the third inning, John tried to throw a sinking fastball when he felt the "strangest sensation he had ever known happened,". With his career in doubt, John decided to allow Dr. Jobe to attempt a revolutionary surgical operation. This operation, now known as Tommy John surgery, replaced the ligament in the elbow of John's pitching arm with a tendon from his right forearm. John was the first baseball pitcher to have it done on his elbow, and he and Dr. Jobe put together a procedure to bring Tommy back pitching. Not only did he come back, but came back on the same trajectory he was on before the injury occurred.
John pitched his first game after surgery on April 16, 1976, and became one of the Majors' most consistent pitchers, winning 164 games over the next 14 seasons. In fact, John notched more wins after the surgery than he had pre-surgery. John finished his career 288–231, a 3.34 ERA, 2,245 strikeouts, 1,259 walks, and in 4,710+$\frac{1}{3}$ innings pitched. After pitching for 26 years, he ranked among baseball's all-time leaders in wins (26th), innings pitched games started (700, eighth), shutouts (46, 26th),

Achievements

3-Times 20 or more wins in a season: (1977, 1979 & 1980).

2-Times Led the National League in Winning Percentage: (1973 & 1974).

3-Times Led League in Shutouts: (1966, 1967, & 1980).

4-Times All-Star: (1968, 1978-1980).

3-Times Received Cy Young Votes: (1977-1980).

2-Times Received Most Valuable Player Votes: (1977 & 1979).

13-Times 200 or more Innings Pitched: (1966, 1969 – 1971, 1973, 1976-1983).

188 career no decisions, an all-time MLB record among starting pitchers

Hall of Fame

John first appeared on the Baseball Hall of Fame ballot in 1995 and earned 21.3% of the vote, but not enough for election. John never received more than 31.7% of the vote in 2009, his final year of eligibility for election on the main ballot. John appeared on the Expansion Era Committee ballots for the 2011, 2014, 2017 elections and was a finalist for the 2020 Modern Baseball Era ballot but was not one of the inductees. He becomes eligible by the Modern Era Subcommittee of the Veterans Committee in 2024.

Summary Analysis

Tommy John's Hall of Fame Point Total is 138.300 which is well over the Induction Criteria of 110.000. John should have been Inducted, yet 35 years after his retirement, he still has not been enshrined in Cooperstown. This needs to be corrected.

A Fan's Perspective

John, Tommy

Positions: Pitcher

Pitcher - Left Handed Potential Hall of Fame Inductee

Born:	May 22, 1943	Height:	6'3" USC 180 cm
From:	Terre Haute, IN	Weight:	180 lbs. 81 Kg.
Bats:	Left	Debut:	September 6, 1963
Throws:	Left	Last Game:	May 25, 1989

Year	Age	Tm	Lg	W	L	W-L%	ERA	G	GS	GF	CG	SHO	SV	IP	H	R	ER	BB	SO	BF	WHIP	Awards
1963	20	CLE	AL	0	2	0	2.21	6	3	1	0	0	0	20.1	23	10	5	6	9	91	1.426	
1964	21	CLE	AL	2	9	0.182	3.91	25	14	0	2	1	0	94.1	97	53	41	35	65	412	1.399	
1965	22	CHW	AL	14	7	0.667	3.09	39	27	4	6	1	2	183.2	162	67	61	58	126	752	1.198	
1966	23	CHW	AL	14	11	0.56	2.62	34	33	0	10	5	0	223	195	76	65	57	138	904	1.13	
1967	24	CHW	AL	10	13	0.435	2.47	31	29	1	9	6	0	178.1	143	62	49	47	110	715	1.065	
1968	25	CHW	AL	10	5	0.667	1.98	25	25	0	5	1	0	177.1	135	45	39	49	117	705	1.038	AS
1969	26	CHW	AL	9	11	0.45	3.25	33	33	0	6	2	0	232.1	230	91	84	90	128	984	1.377	
1970	27	CHW	AL	12	17	0.414	3.27	37	37	0	10	3	0	268.1	253	117	98	101	138	1133	1.314	
1971	28	CHW	AL	13	16	0.448	3.61	38	35	0	10	3	0	229.1	244	115	92	58	131	975	1.317	
1972	29	LAD	NL	11	5	0.688	2.89	29	29	0	4	1	0	186.2	172	68	60	40	117	766	1.136	
1973	30	LAD	NL	16	7	0.696	3.1	36	31	3	4	2	0	218	202	88	75	50	116	888	1.156	
1974	31	LAD	NL	13	3	0.813	2.59	22	22	0	5	3	0	153	133	51	44	42	78	616	1.144	
1975							Did not play in major or minor leagues (Did Not Play)															
1976	33	LAD	NL	10	10	0.5	3.09	31	31	0	8	2	0	207	207	76	71	61	81	866	1.30	
1977	34	LAD	NL	20	7	0.741	2.78	31	31	0	11	3	0	220.1	225	82	68	50	123	906	1.25	CYA-2,MVP-12
1978	35	LAD	NL	17	10	0.63	3.3	33	30	3	7	0	1	213	230	95	78	53	124	912	1.33	AS,CYA-8
1979	36	NYY	AL	21	9	0.7	2.96	37	36	1	17	3	0	276.1	268	109	91	65	111	1116	1.21	AS,CYA-2,MVP-22
1980	37	NYY	AL	22	9	0.71	3.43	36	36	0	16	6	0	265.1	270	115	101	56	78	1089	1.23	AS,CYA-4
1981	38	NYY	AL	9	8	0.529	2.63	20	20	0	7	0	0	140.1	135	50	41	39	50	580	1.24	
1982	39	TOT	AL	14	12	0.538	3.69	37	33	2	10	2	0	221.2	239	102	91	39	68	918	1.25	
1982	39	NYY	AL	10	10	0.5	3.66	30	26	2	9	2	0	186.2	190	84	76	34	54	766	1.20	
1982	39	CAL	AL	4	2	0.667	3.86	7	7	0	1	0	0	35	49	18	15	5	14	152	1.54	
1983	40	CAL	AL	11	13	0.458	4.33	34	34	0	3	0	0	234.2	287	126	113	49	65	1010	1.43	
1984	41	CAL	AL	7	13	0.35	4.52	32	29	1	4	1	0	181.1	223	97	91	56	47	797	1.54	
1985	42	TOT	AL	4	10	0.286	5.53	23	17	2	0	0	0	86.1	117	59	53	28	25	397	1.68	
1985	42	CAL	AL	2	4	0.333	4.7	12	6	2	0	0	0	38.1	51	22	20	15	17	176	1.72	
1985	42	OAK	AL	2	6	0.25	6.19	11	11	0	0	0	0	48	66	37	35	13	8	221	1.65	
1986	43	NYY	AL	5	3	0.625	2.93	13	10	2	1	0	0	70.2	73	27	23	15	28	290	1.25	
1987	44	NYY	AL	13	6	0.684	4.03	33	33	0	3	1	0	187.2	212	95	84	47	63	802	1.38	
1988	45	NYY	AL	9	8	0.529	4.49	35	32	2	0	0	0	176.1	221	96	88	46	61	776	1.514	
1989	46	NYY	AL	2	7	0.222	5.8	10	10	0	0	0	0	63.2	87	45	41	22	18	290	1.712	
162 Game Avg.				13	11	0.555	3.34	35	33	1	8	2	0	219	223	94	81	59	105	917	1.283	
NYY (8 yrs)				91	60	0.603	3.59	234	203	7	53	13	0	1367	1456	621	545	324	483	5709	1.302	
CHW (7 yrs)				82	80	0.506	2.95	237	219	5	56	21	2	1493	1363	573	490	460	888	6168	1.22	
LAD (6 yrs)				87	42	0.674	2.97	182	174	6	37	11	1	1198	1169	460	396	296	649	4956	1.223	
CAL (4 yrs)				24	32	0.429	4.4	85	76	3	14	1	0	489.1	610	263	239	125	143	2135	1.503	
CLE (2 yrs)				2	11	0.154	3.61	31	17	1	2	1	0	114.2	120	63	46	41	74	503	1.404	
OAK (1 yr)				2	6	0.25	6.19	11	11	0	0	0	0	48	66	37	35	13	8	221	1.646	
AL (30 yrs)				201	189	0.515	3.47	578	526	16	125	35	2	3512	3614	1557	1359	963	1599	14736	1.303	
NL (6 yrs)				87	42	0.674	2.97	182	174	6	37	11	1	1198	1169	480	396	296	649	4956	1.223	
26 Yrs				288	231	0.555	3.34	760	700	22	162	46	3	4710	4783	2017	1749	1259	2245	19692	1.283	Career Pts.
				11.000	0.000	5.500	7.500	0.250	15.500	0.500	3.750	6.750	0.000	15.500	0.000	0.000	0.000	0.000	6.750	0.000	6.750	90.750

Post Seasonal Play

Year	Age	Tm		W	L	PCT	ERA	G	GS	GF	CG	SHO	SV	IP	H	R	ER	BB	SO	BF	WHIP	
1977	34	LAD	NLCS	1	0	1.000	0.660	2	2	0	1	0	0	13.2	11	5	1	5	11	60	1.171	
1978	35	LAD	NLCS	1	0	1.000	0.000	1	1	0	1	1	0	9	4	0	0	2	4	30	0.667	
1980	37	NYY	ALCS	0	0	0.000	2.700	1	1	0	0	0	0	6.2	8	2	2	1	3	28	1.350	
1981	38	NYY	ALDS	0	1	0.000	6.430	1	1	0	0	0	0	7	8	5	5	2	0	29	1.429	
1981	38	NYY	ALCS	1	0	1.000	1.500	1	1	0	0	0	0	6	6	1	1	1	3	24	1.167	
1982	39	CAL	ALCS	1	1	0.500	5.110	2	2	0	1	0	0	12.1	11	9	7	6	6	54	1.378	
Totals				4	2	0.667	2.683	8	8	0	3	1	0	53.5	48	22	16	17	27	225	1.211	Post Season Pts.
				0.400	0.000	0.250	1.200	0.400	0.800	0.000	0.600	0.400	0.000	1.000	0.000	0.000	0.000	0.000	0.600	0.000	1.200	6.650

World Series Play

Year	Age	Team	Series	W	L	PCT	ERA	G	GS	GF	CG	SHO	SV	IP	H	R	ER	BB	SO	BF	WHIP	
1977	34	LAD	NL	0	1	0.000	6.000	1	1	0	0	0	0	6	9	5	4	3	7	30	2.000	
1978	35	LAD	NL	1	0	1.000	3.070	2	2	0	0	0	0	14.2	14	8	5	4	6	61	1.227	
1981	38	NYY	AL	1	0	1.000	0.690	3	2	1	0	0	0	13	11	1	1	0	8	51	0.846	
Totals				2	1	0.667	2.711	6	5	1	0	0	0	33.2	34	14	10	7	21	142	1.218	World Series Pts.
				0.400	0.000	0.250	1.200	0.600	0.500	0.250	0.000	0.000	0.000	0.600	0.000	0.000	0.000	0.000	0.600	0.000	1.200	5.700

Yearly Points Leading the League

Category	Times	Points	Total		Category	Times	Points	Total		Category	Times	Points	Total
MVP	0	7	0		Saves	0	2	0		SHO	2	2	4
ROY	0	5	0		ERA	0	2	0		WinPct	2	2	4
Cy Young	0	5	0		S.O.'s	0	2	0		Innings	0	2	0
Golden Glove	0	3	0		Games	0	2	0		WHIP	0	2	0
All-Star	4	2	8		G.S.	0	2	0		GF	0	2	0
Wins	0	2	0		C.G.	0	2	0		Totals			8
Totals			8		Totals			0		Grand Total Add-On Points			16

Hall of Fame Points	
Career Points	90.750
Post Season Points	6.850
World Series Points	5.700
Career Add-On Points	16.000
Writers Association Pts.	0.000
Military/Lifetime Achievement	20.000
Grand Total HOF Points	138.300

Sabathia, Carsten (C.C.)

Personal Life

Charles Carsten Sabathia Jr. was born July 21, 1980, to Charles Sabathia Sr. and Margie Lanier. CC attended Vallejo High and starred on the basketball team. On the baseball diamond, the southpaw played first base, left field, and pitched. He had a 6-0 record and 0.87 ERA as a senior, allowing 20 hits in 67 innings and striking out 107.

CC married his wife Amber on June 9, 2003. They have four children, Carsten Charles III (Little C), daughter Jaden, and son Carter.

Baseball Career

Sabathia was drafted by the Indians in June of 1998, as the 20th overall of the amateur draft. Sabathia went to minor league baseball at 17 years old was a participant in the 2000 Futures Game. Sabathia made his major league debut in 2001 winning 17 games, losing 5, pitched in 33 games, 180.1 innings, 171 strikeouts, a 4.39 Earned Run Average, and finished 2nd in the Rookie of the Year balloting. Sabathia finished 10th in the league with 149 strikeouts in 2002, and 10th in ERA at 3.60 in 2003. He also represented the club in the 2003 All-Star Game. 2004 his win total dropped to 11, ERA increased to 4.12 but he still represented the club in the All-Star game. In 2005, the hard-throwing lefty won 15 and ranked seventh in the AL with 161 strikeouts. In 2006, Sabathia I finished the season with a 3.22 ERA, 172 strikeouts, a 1.17 WHIP, and 6 complete games. His record for the season was 12-11.

Sabathia made his third All-Star team in 2007, posted a 12-3 record in the first half of the season, and finished the season with new career bests in wins (19), ERA (3.21), innings (241), strikeouts (209), WHIP (1.14), and Sabathia was awarded the American League Cy Young Award for 2007.

In 2008, Sabathia was 6-8 with a 3.83 ERA for the Indians and was traded to the Milwaukee Brewers on July 7th for four players. Sabathia made his first start for the Brewers on July 8, 2008, getting credit for a 7-3 win. In his next game for Milwaukee, he threw a complete game win and became the first pitcher in over 30 years to post complete game wins in two consecutive games. He began his time with Milwaukee 9-0 with a 1.43 ERA; the 9th win was a one-hitter against the Pirates in which he fanned 11. Sabathia went 11-2 with a 1.65 ERA for the Brewers and was a key reason they made it to the playoffs.

After the 2008 season, Sabathia signed a contract with the New York Yankees for seven years. It was the largest contract for a pitcher in MLB history at the time. Sabathia finished the 2009 season 19–8 with a 3.37 ERA and 1.15 WHIP across 34 starts. He struck out 197 batters in 230 innings against 67 walks, gave up 197 hits and threw two complete games. Sabathia was particularly dominant after the All-Star break, going 11–2 in 15 starts, striking out 102 batters in 101+$\frac{2}{3}$ innings and posting a 2.74 ERA. The Yankees finished the regular season with a 103–59 record.

Sabathia earned his first career postseason victory with the Yankees in the first game of the 2009 ALDS against the Minnesota Twins. Sabathia also won the A.L.C.S. Most Valuable Player Award; in two starts against the Los Angeles Angels of Anaheim, he went 2–0 with a 1.13 ERA in 16 innings, throwing eight innings of one-run ball in both of his starts. The Yankees beat the Angels in six games to advance to their first World Series since 2003. Despite failing to pick up a win in either of his World Series starts, Sabathia was effective, posting a 3.29 ERA in 13+$\frac{2}{3}$ innings to help lead the Yankees to a series win in six games. The World Series championship was the first of Sabathia's career. In five postseason starts, Sabathia went 3–1 with a 1.98 ERA in 36+$\frac{1}{3}$ innings.

In 2010, Sabathia earned his fourth All-Star selection, and his first as a Yankee. He ended the season with 21 wins, the most in the major leagues, against 7 losses. In 237+$\frac{2}{3}$ innings pitched, Sabathia posted a 3.18 ERA and 1.19 WHIP, struck out 197 batters, two complete games, and held opponents to a .239 batting average. In 2011, Sabathia was the opening day starter for the Yankees for the third year in a row. Sabathia was named to his fifth career All-Star game and across 33 starts in 2011, Sabathia had a 19–8 record, a 3.00 ERA, and a 1.23 WHIP. Across 237+$\frac{1}{3}$ innings, he struck out 230 batters against 61 walks, held batters to a .255 batting average, threw three complete games, and posted 22 quality starts. His 230 strikeouts marked the third-highest number of strikeouts in a single season in franchise history. The Yankees won the AL East, however, Sabathia struggled in the ALDS, posting a 6.23 ERA in 8+ 2/3 3 innings in three appearances as the Yankees were defeated by the Detroit Tigers.

The Baseball Hall of Fame

Sabathia signed a contract extension with the Yankees for 2011. Despite only making 28 starts in the 2012 season, Sabathia reached the 200+ innings pitched for the sixth consecutive year. Alongside a record of 15 wins and 6 losses with a 3.38 ERA and a 1.14 WHIP, Sabathia pitched 200 innings, struck out 197, 44 walks, two complete games, and held batters to a .238 average. In the 2012 ALDS, Sabathia dominated, winning both the first and fifth games against the Baltimore Orioles. He finished his tenure with the Yankees with 134 wins against 88 losses (a .604 winning percentage) in 307 games (306 starts), a 3.81 ERA, 1.272 WHIP, and 1,700 strikeouts in 1,918 innings pitched. His record for 19 years was 561 games, 251 wins, 161 losses, .609 PCT, 3.74 ERA, 38 CG, 12 S.O., 3577.1 Innings, and 3,093 Strike-outs.

Achievements:

- 6-time AL All-Star (2003, 2004, 2007 & 2010-2012).
- 5-Times received Cy Young Award Votes - Winner (2007).
- 2-time AL Wins Leader (2009 & 2010) & 1-Time AL Innings Pitched Leader (2007).
- 2-time League Complete Games Leader (2006/AL & 2008/NL).
- 3-time League Shutouts Leader (2006/AL, 2008/AL & 2008/NL).
- 15 Wins Seasons: 8 (2001, 2005 & 2007-2012) & 1 Time 20 Wins Season (2010).
- 8-Times 200 Innings Pitched Seasons (2002 & 2007-2013).
- 3-Times 200 Strikeouts Seasons (2007, 2008 & 2011) & 3,000 strikeout club.
- 1 – Time World Series winner with the New York Yankees in 2009.

Hall of Fame

CC Sabathia will be eligible for the Baseball Hall of Fame vote in 2025 by the BBWAA.

Summary Analysis

CC Sabathia's Hall of Fame Point Total is 115.700 which exceeds the Induction total of 110.000. Sabathia should be inducted/elected in his first year of eligibility.

A Fan's Perspective

Sabbathia, C. C.
Positions
Pitcher

Pitcher – Left Handed Potential Hall of Fame Inductee

Born :	July 21, 1980	Height:	6' 6" USC 198 cm
From:	Vallejo, CA	Weight:	306 lbs. 136 Kg.
Bats:	Left	Debut	April 8, 2001
Throws:	Left	Last Game:	September 24, 2019

Year	Age	Tm	Lg	W	L	PCT	ERA	G	GS	GF	CG	SHO	SV	IP	H	R	ER	BB	SO	BF	WHIP	Awards
2001	20	CLE	AL	17	5	0.773	4.390	33	33	0	0	0	0	180.1	149	93	88	95	171	763	1.353	RoY-2
2002	21	CLE	AL	13	11	0.542	4.370	33	33	0	2	0	0	210	198	109	102	88	149	891	1.362	
2003	22	CLE	AL	13	9	0.591	3.600	30	30	0	2	1	0	197.2	190	85	79	66	141	832	1.295	AS
2004	23	CLE	AL	11	10	0.524	4.120	30	30	0	1	1	0	188	176	90	86	72	139	787	1.319	AS
2005	24	CLE	AL	15	10	0.600	4.030	31	31	0	1	0	0	196.2	185	92	88	62	161	823	1.256	
2006	25	CLE	AL	12	11	0.522	3.220	28	28	0	6	2	0	192.2	182	83	69	44	172	802	1.173	
2007	26	CLE	AL	19	7	0.731	3.210	34	34	0	4	1	0	241	238	94	86	37	209	975	1.141	AS,CYA-1,MVP-14
2008	27	TOT	MLB	17	10	0.630	2.700	35	35	0	10	5	0	253	223	85	76	59	251	1023	1.115	CYA-5,MVP-6
2008	27	CLE	AL	6	8	0.429	3.830	18	18	0	3	2	0	122.1	117	54	52	34	123	507	1.234	
2008	27	MIL	NL	11	2	0.846	1.650	17	17	0	7	3	0	130.2	106	31	24	25	128	516	1.003	
2009	28	NYY	AL	19	8	0.704	3.370	34	34	0	2	1	0	230	197	96	86	67	197	938	1.148	CYA-4,MVP-21
2010	29	NYY	AL	21	7	0.750	3.180	34	34	0	2	0	0	237.2	209	92	84	74	197	970	1.191	AS,CYA-3,MVP-13
2011	30	NYY	AL	19	8	0.704	3.000	33	33	0	3	1	0	237.1	230	87	79	61	230	985	1.226	AS,CYA-4,MVP-14
2012	31	NYY	AL	15	6	0.714	3.380	28	28	0	2	0	0	200	184	89	75	44	197	833	1.140	AS
2013	32	NYY	AL	14	13	0.519	4.780	32	32	0	2	0	0	211	224	122	112	65	175	908	1.370	
2014	33	NYY	AL	3	4	0.429	5.280	8	8	0	0	0	0	46	58	31	27	10	48	209	1.478	
2015	34	NYY	AL	6	10	0.375	4.730	29	29	0	1	0	0	167.1	188	92	88	50	137	726	1.422	
2016	35	NYY	AL	9	12	0.429	3.910	30	30	0	0	0	0	179.2	172	83	78	65	152	768	1.319	
2017	36	NYY	AL	14	5	0.737	3.690	27	27	0	0	0	0	148.2	139	64	61	50	120	623	1.271	
2018	37	NYY	AL	9	7	0.563	3.650	29	29	0	0	0	0	153	150	72	62	51	140	665	1.314	
2019	38	NYY	AL	5	8	0.385	4.950	23	22	0	0	0	0	107.1	112	64	59	39	107	468	1.407	
162 Game Avg.				15	10	0.609	3.740	34	34	0	2	1	0	217	206	98	90	67	188	909	1.259	
NYY (11 yrs)				134	88	0.604	3.810	307	306	0	12	2	0	1918	1863	892	811	576	1700	8093	1.272	
CLE (8 yrs)				106	71	0.599	3.830	237	237	0	18	7	0	1528.2	1435	700	650	498	1265	6380	1.265	
MIL (1 yr)				11	2	0.846	1.650	17	17	0	7	3	0	130.2	106	31	24	25	128	516	1.003	
AL (18 yrs)				240	159	0.602	3.810	544	543	0	31	9	0	3446.2	3298	1592	1461	1074	2965	14473	1.268	
NL (1 yr)				11	2	0.846	1.650	17	17	0	7	3	0	130.2	106	31	24	25	128	516	1.003	
19 Yrs				351	161	0.609	3.74	563	560	0	38	12	0	3577.1	3404	1623	1485	1099	3093	14989	1.259	Career Pts.
				10.500	0.000	10.500	3.750	5.500	10.500	0.000	1.000	1.500	0.000	10.500	0.000	0.000	0.000	0.000	10.500	0.000	6.750	71.000

Post Seasonal Play

Year	Age	Team	Series	W	L	PCT	ERA	G	GS	GF	CG	SHO	SV	IP	H	R	ER	BB	SO	BF	WHIP	
2001	20	CLE	ALDS	1	0	1.000	3.000	1	1	0	0	0	0	6	6	2	2	5	5	28	1.833	
2007	26	CLE	ALDS	1	0	1.000	5.400	1	1	0	0	0	0	5	4	3	3	6	5	24	2.000	
2007	26	CLE	ALCS	0	2	0.000	10.450	2	2	0	0	0	0	10.1	17	12	12	7	9	53	2.323	
2008	27	MIL	NLDS	0	1	0.000	12.270	1	1	0	0	0	0	3.2	6	5	5	4	5	21	2.727	
2009	28	NYY	ALDS	1	0	1.000	1.350	1	1	0	0	0	0	6.2	8	2	1	0	8	28	1.200	
2009	28	NYY	ALCS	2	0	1.000	1.130	2	2	0	0	0	0	16	9	2	2	3	12	59	0.750	
2010	29	NYY	ALDS	1	0	1.000	4.500	1	1	0	0	0	0	6	5	4	3	3	5	27	1.333	
2010	29	NYY	ALCS	1	0	1.000	6.300	2	2	0	0	0	0	10	17	7	7	4	10	48	2.100	
2011	30	NYY	ALDS	0	0	0.000	6.230	3	3	0	0	0	0	8.2	10	6	6	8	11	41	2.077	
2012	31	NYY	ALDS	2	0	1.000	1.530	2	2	0	1	0	0	17.2	12	3	3	3	16	67	0.849	
2012	31	NYY	ALCS	0	1	0.000	12.270	1	1	0	0	0	0	3.2	11	6	5	2	3	25	3.545	
2017	36	NYY	ALWC	0	0	0.000	0.000	0	0	0	0	0	0	0	0	0	0	0	0	0	0.000	
2017	36	NYY	ALDS	0	0	0.000	3.720	2	2	0	0	0	0	9.2	8	6	4	3	14	42	1.138	
2017	36	NYY	ALCS	1	1	0.500	0.980	2	2	0	0	0	0	9.1	8	1	1	7	5	44	1.607	
2018	37	NYY	ALWC	0	0	0.000	0.000	0	0	0	0	0	0	0	0	0	0	0	0	0	0.000	
2018	37	NYY	ALDS	0	1	0.000	9.000	1	1	0	0	0	0	3	5	3	3	2	1	17	2.333	
2019	38	NYY	ALDS	0	0	0.000	0.000	0	0	0	0	0	0	0	0	0	0	0	0	0	0.000	
2019	38	NYY	ALCS	0	0	0.000	0.000	2	0	0	0	0	0	1	0	0	0	0	0	5	0.000	
				10	6	0.625	4.54	24	21	0	1	0	0	113.4	126	62	57	57	109	529	1.619	Post Season Pts.
				1.000	0.000	0.000	0.250	2.000	2.000	0.000	0.250	0.000	0.000	1.800	0.000	0.000	0.000	0.000	2.000	0.000	0.000	9.300

World Series Play

Year	Age	Team	Series	W	L	W-L%	ERA	G	GS	GF	CG	SHO	SV	IP	H	R	ER	BB	SO	BF	WHIP	
2009	28	NYY	AL	0	1	0.000	3.29	2	2	0	0	0	0	13.2	11	5	5	6	12	57	1.244	
				0	1	0.000	3.29	2	2	0	0	0	0	13.2	11	5	5	6	12	57	1.244	World Series Pts.
				0.000	0.000	0.000	0.250	0.250	0.250	0.000	0.000	0.000	0.000	0.250	0.000	0.000	0.000	0.000	0.400	0.000	1.000	2.400

Yearly Points Leading the League

Category	Times	Points	Total		Category	Times	Points	Total		Category	Times	Points	Total
MVP	0	7	0		Saves	0	3	0		SHO	1	2	2
ROY	0	5	0		ERA	0	3	0		WinPct	0	2	0
Cy Young	1	5	5		S.O.'s	0	2	0		Innings	1	2	2
Golden Glove	0	3	0		Games	2	2	4		WHIP	0	2	0
All-Star	6	2	12		G.S.	0	2	0		GF	0	2	0
Wins	2	3	6		C.G.	1	2	2		Totals			4
Totals			23		Totals			6		Grand Total Add-On Points			33

Hall of Fame Points	
Career Points	71.000
Post Season Points	9.300
World Series Points	2.400
Career Add-On Points	33.000
Writers Association Pts.	0.000
Military/Lifetime Achievement	0.000
Grand Total HOF Points	115.700

Santana, Johan

Personal Life

Johan Alexander Santana was born on March 13, 1979 to Jesus, and (no information available on his mother). Santana is the second of five children and grew up in the remote town of Tovar, located in the Merida province of Venezuela.

He married Yasmile Garcia in 1998 with the couple having daughters, Jasmine and Jasmily, and a son Johan Jr.

Baseball Career

The Astros signed Santana in 1997 and he worked his way through their system until 1999, when the Astros felt he was still years away and they exposed the young lefty in the 1999 Rule V Draft. The Minnesota Twins had the first selection and wanted Johan even though they had to keep him on the major league roster for a year. From 2000 - 2002 seasons, Santana pitched in 72 games, 18 starts for a total of 239.00 innings. He compiled 11 wins, 9 losses, 229 strikeouts, and a 4.58 earned run average.

The Twins entered 2003 Santana being more valuable as a rally-killer out of the bullpen until July, when the club decided to give Santana a shot as a starter and his impact arm helped to keep the Twins ahead. His biggest victory came on September 10th, when Johan shut down the White Sox and the Twins never looked back. Johan wound up at 12-3, with a 3.07 ERA and 169 strikeouts in 159 innings. Santana was a perfect 8-0 down the stretch and was Minnesota's ace heading into the postseason. The only glitch in Johan's season was a balky hamstring forcing him to leave the mound.

For the 2004 campaign, Santana had a fantastic August as he allowed just 10 earned runs with 52 strikeouts in 43.1 innings. He had 6 victories for the month and he went on to win six more in September, with a 0.45 ERA and 52 strikeouts for the second consecutive month. After wrapping up the AL Central, the Twins headed east to face the Yankees with Santana pitching Game One. He delivered a 2-0 victory with seven scoreless innings. When Minnesota dropped the next two, Santana was forced to take the hill on short rest in Game Four. Santana departed with a 4-1 lead, but the Yankees rallied for four runs in the eighth inning and beat Minnesota. Santana 2004 line in the playoffs was pitching 12 innings over two games, with a win and a 0.75 ERA. Santana ended the second half with a 13-0 record, a 1.18 ERA and a .154 opponents' batting average. For the year, Santana was awarded the Cy Young Award.

In 2005, he went 16-7, 2.87 in 33 starts and led the American League in strikeouts for the second consecutive season with 238. While his ERA was second in the A.L., he pitched 2 shutouts that season and was named to the All-Star team for the first time that year. In 2006, he was the best pitcher in the American League, leading the circuit with 19 wins, part of a 19-6 record, a 2.77 ERA and 275 strikeouts. He was the unanimous winner of the Cy Young Award and named to the All-Star team once again. The Twins reached the postseason again, and he was given the starting assignment in Game 1 of the ALDS against the Oakland Athletics on October 3rd. He pitched very well, allowing only 2 runs in 8 innings, while striking out 8 and walking only one batter, but left trailing, 2-1, as Barry Zito had done even better. A pair of relievers allowed another run in the 9th, and Johan and the Twins lost, 3-2, on their way to being swept in three games.

Santana struck out 17 in a 1-0 win on August 19, 2007, to set a new Minnesota Twins single-game record. His record fell to 15-13, as his ERA rose by half a run, to 3.33. He struck out 235 batters but snapped his streak of three consecutive seasons leading the league in that category. Santana was to become a free agent after the next season so the team decided to trade him on February 2, 2008 to the New York Mets. His first season in New York was very much in line with his best years in Minnesota. He went 16-7, with a National League-leading 2.53 ERA. He made 34 starts and pitched 234 1/3 innings. His strikeout total still topped 200 for the 5th straight year.

Santana struggled with injuries over the next few years as the Mets fans often referred to Santana as a complete bust. In 2009, Santana was limited to 25 starts as had health issues for the first time. He still was very good, finishing 13-9, 3.13, but the missed time meant that his usually sparkling numbers were down. He pitched only 166 2/3 innings and struck out only 146 batters. Santana was still outstanding, but the sense began to grow in New York that he was not contributing enough to justify his large salary.

His health problems continued in 2010, as he finished at 11-9. Santana missed the entire 2011 season with a shoulder problem. In 2012, on May 26th, he shut out the San Diego Padres needing fewer than 100 pitches. On June 1st, he pitched the first no-hitter in history of the New York Mets,

The Baseball Hall of Fame

shutting out the St. Louis Cardinals, 8-0. On July 21st, he sprained his right ankle and came back on August 11th, but was hit hard in his next two starts with the Mets deciding to shut him down for the rest of the season. He ended the year with a record of 6-9, 4.85 in 21 starts. The Mets were hoping to have Santana back for Opening Day in 2013 but on, an MRI showed that he had re-torn the capsule and would have surgery, missing the season. The Mets declined to pick up Santana's option for 2014, making him a free agent. On March 4th, 2014 the Baltimore Orioles signed him to a one- deal but suffered an injury on June 6th, as he tore his Achilles tendon. Santana never officially retired.

Achievements:

- 4-time All-Star (2005-2007 & 2009) & 1-Time Gold Glove Winner (2007).
- 3-time League ERA Leader (2004/AL, 2006/AL & 2008/NL).
- 1-Time AL Wins Leader (2006) & 1-Time AL Winning Percentage Leader (2003).
- 2-time League Innings Pitched Leader (2006/AL & 2008/NL).
- 3-time Strikeouts Leader (2004-2006).
- 15 Wins Seasons: 5 (2004-2008) & 1 - 20 Wins Seasons (2004).
- 5-Times 200 Innings Pitched Seasons (2004-2008).
- 2006 - Won the Triple Crown in wins (19), strikeouts (245), and ERA (2.77).
- 6-Times Received Cy Young Votes (2003-2008 & Won in 2004 & 2006).
- 3-Time Received MVP Votes Award (2004, 2006 & 2008).

Hall of Fame

He became eligible for induction in the Hall of Fame in the 2018 Hall of Fame Election but received just 10 votes and dropped off the ballot.

Summary Analysis

Johan Santana's Hall of Fame Point Total of 111.80 listed in this book is over the 110.000 Induction total. Santana should eventually be elected to the Hall of Fame.

A Fan's Perspective

Santana, Johan   **Pitcher - Left Handed Potential Hall of Fame Inductee**

Positions		
Pitcher		

Born :	March 13, 1979	**Height:**	6'0"	**USC** 183 cm
From:	Tovar, Venezuela	**Weight:**	210 lbs.	95 Kg.
Bats:	Left	**Debut**	April 3, 2000	
Throws:	Left	**Last Game:**	August 17, 2012	

Year	Age	Tm	Lg	W	L	PCT	ERA	G	GS	GF	CG	SHO	SV	IP	H	R	ER	BB	SO	BF	WHIP	Awards
2000	21	MIN	AL	2	3	0.400	6.49	30	5	9	0	0	0	86	102	64	62	54	64	398	1.814	
2001	22	MIN	AL	1	0	1.000	4.74	15	4	5	0	0	0	43.2	50	25	23	16	28	195	1.511	
2002	23	MIN	AL	8	6	0.571	2.99	27	14	2	0	0	1	108.1	84	41	36	49	137	452	1.228	
2003	24	MIN	AL	12	3	0.800	3.07	45	18	7	0	0	0	158.1	127	56	54	47	169	644	1.099	CYA-7
2004	25	MIN	AL	20	6	0.769	2.61	34	34	0	1	1	0	228	156	70	66	54	265	881	0.921	CYA-1,MVP-6
2005	26	MIN	AL	16	7	0.696	2.87	33	33	0	3	2	0	231.2	180	77	74	45	238	910	0.971	AS,CYA-3
2006	27	MIN	AL	19	6	0.760	2.77	34	34	0	1	0	0	233.2	186	79	72	47	245	923	0.997	AS,CYA-1,MVP-7
2007	28	MIN	AL	15	13	0.536	3.33	33	33	0	1	1	0	219	183	88	81	52	235	878	1.073	AS,CYA-5,GG
2008	29	NYM	NL	16	7	0.696	2.53	34	34	0	3	2	0	234.1	206	74	66	63	206	964	1.148	CYA-3,MVP-14
2009	30	NYM	NL	13	9	0.591	3.13	25	25	0	0	0	0	166.2	156	67	58	46	146	701	1.212	AS
2010	31	NYM	NL	11	9	0.550	2.98	29	29	0	4	2	0	199	179	67	66	55	144	817	1.176	
2012	33	NYM	NL	6	9	0.400	4.85	21	21	0	2	2	0	117	117	65	63	39	111	499	1.333	
162 Game Avg.				15	8	0.641	3.20	38	30	2	2	1	0	214	182	82	76	60	210	872	1.132	
MIN (8 yrs)				93	44	0.679	3.22	251	175	23	6	4	1	1308	1068	500	468	364	1381	5281	1.094	
NYM (4 yrs)				46	34	0.575	3.18	109	109	0	9	6	0	717	658	273	253	203	607	2981	1.201	
									0.2													
AL (8 yrs)				93	44	0.679	3.22	251	175	23	6	4	1	1308	1068	500	468	364	1381	5281	1.094	
NL (4 yrs)				46	34	0.575	3.18	109	109	0	9	6	0	717	658	273	253	203	607	2981	1.201	
12 Yrs				139	78	0.641	3.20	360	284	23	15	10	1	2025	1726	773	721	567	1988	8262	1.132	**Career Pts.**
				3.750	0.000	13.000	8.500	2.500	3.750	0.500	0.500	1.000	0.000	3.750	0.000	0.000	0.000	0.000	5.500	0.000	13.000	**55.750**

Post Seasonal Play

Year	Age	Team	Series	W	L	PCT	ERA	G	GS	GF	CG	SHO	SV	IP	H	R	ER	BB	SO	BF	WHIP	
2002	23	MIN	ALDS	0	0	0.000	6	2	0	0	0	0	0	3	3	2	2	2	2	14	1.667	
2002	23	MIN	ALCS	0	1	0.000	10.8	4	0	0	0	0	0	3.1	4	4	4	0	4	14	1.200	
2003	24	MIN	ALDS	0	1	0.000	7.04	2	2	0	0	0	0	7.2	9	6	6	3	6	34	1.565	
2004	25	MIN	ALDS	1	0	1.000	0.75	2	2	0	0	0	0	12	14	1	1	4	12	51	1.500	
2006	27	MIN	ALDS	0	1	0.000	2.25	1	1	0	0	0	0	8	5	2	2	1	8	30	0.750	
				1	3	0.333	3.97	11	5	0	0	0	0	33.3	35	15	15	10	32	143	1.324	**Career Pts.**
				0.250	0.000	0.000	0.400	0.600	0.600	0.000	0.000	0.000	0.000	0.600	0.000	0.000	0.000	0.000	0.800	0.000	0.800	**4.050**

World Series Play

Year	Age	Team	Series	W	L	PCT	ERA	G	GS	GF	CG	SHO	SV	IP	H	R	ER	BB	SO	BF	WHIP	
None				0	0	0	0	0	0	0	0	0	0	0	0	0	0	0	0	0	0	**World Series Pts.**
				0.000	0.000	0.000	0.000	0.000	0.000	0.000	0.000	0.000	0.000	0.000	0.000	0.000	0.000	0.000	0.000	0.000	0.000	**0.000**

Yearly Points Leading the League

Category	Times	Points	Total	Category	Times	Points	Total	Categor	Times	Points	Total
MVP	0	7	0	Saves	0	3	0	SHO	0	2	0
ROY	0	5	0	ERA	3	3	9	WinPct	0	2	0
Cy Young	2	5	10	S.O.'s	3	2	6	Innings	2	2	4
Golden Glove	0	3	0	Games	0	2	0	WHIP	4	2	8
All-Star	4	2	8	G.S.	2	2	4	GF	0	2	0
Wins	1	3	3	C.G.	0	2	0	Totals			12
Totals			21	Totals			19	Grand Total Add-On Points		52	

Hall of Fame Points	
Career Points	55.750
Post Season Points	4.050
World Series Points	0.000
Career Add-On Points	52.000
Writers Association Pts.	0.000
Military/Lifetime Achievement	0.000
Grand Total HOF Points	111.800

The Baseball Hall of Fame

Blue, Vida

Personal Life

Vida Rochelle Blue, Jr. was born on July 28, 1949, to Vida Blue Sr. and Sallie Blue in Mansfield, Louisiana. He was the eldest of six children born and attended DeSoto High.

Blue married Peggy Shannon on September 24, 1989, and divorced in 1996. The couple had twin daughters, Sallie and Evelyn and Blue has a son, Derrick from a previous relationship along with two other daughters, Alexis and Valerie.

Baseball Career

Blue was selected by the Kansas City Athletics in the second round of the 1967 draft. From 1967. Blue rose through their system and debuted against the White Sox July, 20, 1970. He pitched a one-hitter against the Kansas City Royals, giving up a single with two outs in the eighth inning and followed it with a no hitter against the Minnesota Twins on September 21. Blue's 1971 season was dominant as he had a 24-8 record, a 1.82 ERA, 301 S.O's, 24 CG, 8 S.O.'s and won the MVP Award and Cy Young Award. Overall, Blue won 209 games, lost 161, a 3.27 ERA, 2,175 strikeouts,143 complete games, and 37 shutouts. He played with the A's, Giants, and Royals.

Achievements:

- 3-Time 20-win seasons (1971, 1973 & 1975).
- 5-Times received Cy Young Votes (1971 (won award), 1973, 1975, 1976 & 1978).
- 1-Time ERA Title, Led AL in Shutouts, & 1-Time Led AL in WHIP: (1971).
- 4-Times received MVP Votes (1971, 1973, 1976, & 1978)
- 6-Times All-Star (1971, 1975, 1977, 1978, 1980 & 1981)

Hall of Fame

In 1992, Blue was eligible for the Baseball Hall of Fame. He received little support in the years he was considered and was removed from the ballot in 1995.

Summary Analysis

Vida Blues Hall of Fame Point Total is 105.050. He had a drug conviction and was suspended for the 1984 season and this case needs to be voted on by the BBWAA.

Blue, Vida
Positions: Pitcher

Pitcher - Left Handed Potential Hall of Fame Inductee

Born:	July 28, 1949		Height:	6' 0" USC 183 cm	
From:	Mansfield, LA		Weight:	190 lbs. 85 Kg.	
Died:	May 6, 2023		Debut	July 20, 1969	
Bats:	Both		Last Game:	October 2, 1986	
Throws:	Left				

Year	Age	Tm	Lg	W	L	W-L%	ERA	G	GS	GF	CG	SHO	SV	IP	H	R	ER	BB	S.O.	BF	WHIP	Awards
1969	19	OAK	AL	1	1	0.5	6.64	12	4	1	0	0	1	42	49	34	31	18	24	191	1.595	
1970	20	OAK	AL	2	0	1	2.09	6	6	0	2	2	0	38.2	20	12	9	12	35	147	0.828	
1971	21	OAK	AL	24	8	0.75	1.82	39	39	0	24	8	0	312	209	73	63	88	301	1207	0.952	AS,CYA-1,MVP-1
1972	22	OAK	AL	6	10	0.375	2.8	25	23	0	5	4	0	151	117	55	47	48	111	606	1.093	
1973	23	OAK	AL	20	9	0.69	3.28	37	37	0	13	4	0	263.2	214	108	96	105	158	1083	1.21	CYA-7,MVP-29
1974	24	OAK	AL	17	15	0.531	3.25	40	40	0	12	1	0	282.1	246	118	102	98	174	1159	1.218	
1975	25	OAK	AL	22	11	0.667	3.01	39	38	1	13	2	1	278	243	103	93	99	189	1153	1.23	AS,CYA-6
1976	26	OAK	AL	18	13	0.581	2.35	37	37	0	20	6	0	298.1	268	90	78	63	166	1205	1.109	CYA-6,MVP-20
1977	27	OAK	AL	14	19	0.424	3.83	38	38	0	16	1	0	279.2	284	138	119	86	157	1184	1.323	AS
1978	28	SFG	NL	18	10	0.643	2.79	35	35	0	9	4	0	258	233	87	80	70	171	1042	1.174	AS,CYA-3,MVP-12
1979	29	SFG	NL	14	14	0.5	5.01	34	34	0	10	0	0	237	246	143	132	111	138	1041	1.506	
1980	30	SFG	NL	14	10	0.583	2.97	31	31	0	10	3	0	224	202	79	74	61	129	914	1.174	AS
1981	31	SFG	NL	8	6	0.571	2.45	18	18	0	1	0	0	124.2	97	40	34	54	63	513	1.211	AS
1982	32	KCR	AL	13	12	0.52	3.78	31	31	0	6	2	0	181	163	80	76	80	103	773	1.343	
1983	33	KCR	AL	0	5	0	6.01	19	14	4	1	0	0	85.1	96	62	57	35	53	382	1.535	
1985	35	SFG	NL	8	8	0.5	4.47	33	20	5	1	0	0	131	115	70	65	80	103	574	1.489	
1986	36	SFG	NL	10	10	0.5	3.27	28	28	0	0	0	0	156.2	137	65	57	77	100	663	1.366	
162 Game Avg.				15	11	0.565	3.27	35	33	1	10	3	0	233	205	95	85	83	152	965	1.233	
OAK (9 yrs)				124	86	0.59	2.95	273	262	2	105	28	2	1945	1650	731	638	617	1315	7935	1.165	
SFG (6 yrs)				72	58	0.554	3.52	179	166	5	31	7	0	1131	1030	484	442	453	704	4747	1.311	
KCR (2 yrs)				13	17	0.433	4.49	50	45	4	7	2	0	266.1	259	142	133	115	156	1155	1.404	
AL (11 yrs)				137	103	0.571	3.14	323	307	6	112	30	2	2212	1909	873	771	732	1471	9090	1.194	
NL (6 yrs)				72	58	0.554	3.52	179	166	5	31	7	0	1131	1030	484	442	453	704	4747	1.311	
17 Yrs				209	161	0.565	3.27	502	473	11	143	37	2	3543	2939	1357	1213	1185	2175	13837	1.233	Career Pts. 66.500
				8.000	0.000	6.750	8.500	4.500	8.000	0.500	3.000	4.500	0.000	9.250	0.000	0.000	0.000	0.000	5.500	0.000	8.000	

Post Seasonal Play

Year	Age	Tm	Lg	W	L	W-L%	ERA	G	GS	GF	CG	SHO	SV	IP	H	R	ER	BB	SO	BF	WHIP	
1971	21	OAK	ALCS	0	1	0.000	6.43	1	1	0	0	0	0	7	7	5	5	2	8	29	1.286	
1972	22	OAK	ALCS	0	0	0.000	0.00	4	0	1	0	0	1	5.1	4	0	0	1	5	22	0.938	
1973	23	OAK	ALCS	0	1	0.000	10.29	2	2	0	0	0	0	7	8	8	8	5	3	33	1.857	
1974	24	OAK	ALCS	1	0	1.000	0.00	1	1	0	1	1	0	9	2	0	0	0	7	30	0.222	
1975	25	OAK	ALCS	0	0	0.000	9.00	1	1	0	0	0	0	3	6	3	3	0	2	14	2.000	
				1	2	0.333	4.60	9	5	1	1	1	1	31.1	27	16	16	8	25	128	1.117	Post Season Pts. 5.250
				0.250	0.000	0.000	0.250	0.400	0.600	0.250	0.250	0.400	0.250	0.600	0.000	0.000	0.000	0.000	0.600	0.000	1.400	

World Series Play

Year	Age	Tm	Lg	W	L	W-L%	ERA	G	GS	GF	CG	SHO	SV	IP	H	R	ER	BB	SO	BF	WHIP	
1972	22	OAK	AL	0	1	0.000	4.15	4	1	1	0	0	1	8.2	8	4	4	5	5	38	1.500	
1973	23	OAK	AL	0	1	0.000	4.91	2	2	0	0	0	0	11	10	6	6	3	8	48	1.182	
1974	24	OAK	AL	0	1	0.000	3.29	2	2	0	0	0	0	13.2	10	5	5	7	9	56	1.244	
				0	3	0.000	4.05	8	5	1	0	0	1	33.1	28	15	15	15	22	142	1.290	World Series Pts. 4.300
				0.000	0.000	0.000	0.400	0.800	0.600	0.250	0.000	0.000	0.250	0.600	0.000	0.000	0.000	0.000	0.600	0.000	0.800	

Yearly Points Leading the League

Category	Times	Points	Total	Category	Times	Points	Total	Category	Times	Points	Total	Hall of Fame Points	
MVP	1	7	7	Saves	0	3	0	SHO	1	2	2	Career Points	66.500
ROY	0	5	0	ERA	1	3	3	WinPct	0	2	0	Post Season Points	5.250
Cy Young	1	5	5	S.O.'s	0	2	0	Innings	0	2	0	World Series Points	4.300
Golden Glove	0	3	0	Games	0	2	0	WHIP	0	2	0	Career Add-On Points	29.000
All-Star	6	2	12	G.S.	0	2	0	GF	0	2	0	Writers Association Pts.	0.000
Wins	0	3	0	C.G.	0	2	0	Totals			2	Military/Lifetime Achievement	0.000
Totals			24	Totals			3	Grand Total Add-On Points		29		Grand Total HOF Points	105.050

Buehrle, Mark

Personal Life

Mark Buehrle was born March 23, 1979 in St. Charles, Missouri, to Pat & John Buehrle Mark was the third of four children. Buehrle has older brothers, Mike and Jason and a younger sister Amay. Buehrle went to Francis Howell North High School.

Buehrle married his wife, Jamie Streck, in December of 2005 and the couple have a son (born July 26, 2007) and a daughter (born March 3, 2009).

Baseball Career

In 1998, Mark was drafted by the Chicago White Sox, in the 38th round of the draft. He signed the following May and began his career in 1999 with the White Sox' and joined the White Sox roster in 2000. He was there for twelve seasons and threw 200-plus innings while making 30-plus starts over 14 consecutive seasons, with season ERAs ranging from 3.12 in 2005 to 4.99 Buehrle retired with a 214-160 record and 3.81 ERA over 3283 1/3 innings.

Achievements

- 5-time All-Star (2002, 2005, 2006, 2009 & 2014).
- 4-time Gold Glove Winner (2009-2011 & 2012).
- 2-time Innings Pitched Leader (2004 & 2005) & Complete Games Leader (2015)
- 15 Wins Seasons: 6 (2001, 2002, 2004, 2005, 2008 & 2015)
- 14 - 200 Innings Pitched Seasons: 14 (2001-2014) & Won a World Series in 2005.
- Pitched the 18th perfect game in history, on July 23, 2009.

Hall of Fame

Mark Buehrle was eligible for the Hall of Fame in 2021 and received 11%. However, he fell to 5.8% in 2022, 10.8% in 2023 and has six years left on the BBWAA ballot.

Summary Analysis

Mark Buehrle's Hall of Fame Point Total is 91.550. He needs to be voted in before his BBWAA time is up and continue being a great Ambassador to the game.

Buehrle, Mark Pitcher Left - Handed Potential Hall of Fame Inductee

Positions		Born:	March 23, 1979	Height:	6' 2"	USC	188	cm
Pitcher		From:	St. Charles, MO	Weight:	240	lbs.	108	Kg.
		Bats:	Left	Debut	July 16, 2000			
		Throws:	Left	Last Game:	October 12, 2015			

Year	Age	Tm	Lg	W	L	W-L%	ERA	G	GS	GF	CG	SHO	SV	IP	H	R	ER	BB	S.O.	BF	WHIP	Awards
2000	21	CHW	AL	4	1	0.800	4.210	28	3	6	0	0	0	51.1	55	27	24	19	37	225	1.442	
2001	22	CHW	AL	16	8	0.667	3.290	32	32	0	4	2	0	221.1	188	89	81	48	126	885	1.066	
2002	23	CHW	AL	19	12	0.613	3.580	34	34	0	5	2	0	239	236	102	95	61	134	984	1.243	AS
2003	24	CHW	AL	14	14	0.500	4.140	35	35	0	2	0	0	230.1	250	124	106	61	119	978	1.35	
2004	25	CHW	AL	16	10	0.615	3.890	35	35	0	4	1	0	245.1	257	119	106	51	165	1016	1.255	
2005	26	CHW	AL	16	8	0.667	3.120	33	33	0	3	1	0	236.2	240	99	82	40	149	971	1.183	AS,CYA-5
2006	27	CHW	AL	12	13	0.480	4.990	32	32	0	1	0	0	204	247	124	113	48	98	876	1.446	AS
2007	28	CHW	AL	10	9	0.526	3.630	30	30	0	3	1	0	201	208	86	81	45	115	835	1.259	
2008	29	CHW	AL	15	12	0.556	3.790	34	34	0	1	0	0	218.2	240	106	92	52	140	918	1.335	
2009	30	CHW	AL	13	10	0.565	3.840	33	33	0	1	1	0	213.1	222	97	91	45	105	874	1.252	AS,GG
2010	31	CHW	AL	13	13	0.500	4.280	33	33	0	3	0	0	210.1	246	105	100	49	99	897	1.403	GG
2011	32	CHW	AL	13	9	0.591	3.590	31	31	0	0	0	0	205.1	221	93	82	45	109	858	1.295	GG
2012	33	MIA	NL	13	13	0.500	3.740	31	31	0	1	0	0	202.1	197	88	84	40	125	828	1.171	GG
2013	34	TOR	AL	12	10	0.545	4.150	33	33	0	1	1	0	203.2	223	100	94	51	139	876	1.345	
2014	35	TOR	AL	13	10	0.565	3.390	32	32	0	0	0	0	202	228	83	76	46	119	857	1.356	AS
2015	36	TOR	AL	15	8	0.652	3.810	32	32	0	4	1	0	198.2	214	100	84	33	91	827	1.243	
162 Game Avg.				14	11	0.572	3.810	35	33	0	2	1	0	221	234	104	94	49	126	922	1.281	
CHW (12 yrs)				161	119	0.575	3.830	390	365	6	27	8	0	2476	2610	1171	1053	564	1396	10317	1.282	
TOR (3 yrs)				40	28	0.588	3.780	97	97	0	5	2	0	604.1	665	283	254	130	349	2560	1.315	
MIA (1 yr)				13	13	0.500	3.740	31	31	0	1	0	0	202.1	197	88	84	40	125	828	1.171	
AL (15 yrs)				201	147	0.578	3.82	487	462	6	32	10	0	3081	3275	1454	1307	694	1745	12877	1.288	
NL (1 yr)				13	13	0.5	3.74	31	31	0	1	0	0	202.1	197	88	84	40	125	828	1.171	
16 Yrs				214	160	0.572	3.81	518	493	6	33	10	0	3283	3473	1542	1391	734	1870	13705	1.281	Career Pts.
				8.000	0.000	6.750	3.000	4.500	9.250	0.000	1.000	0.500	0.000	9.250	0.000	0.000	0.000	0.000	4.500	0.000	6.750	53.500

Post Seasonal Play

Year	Age	Tm	Lg	W	L	PCT.	ERA	G	GS	GF	CG	SHO	SV	IP	H	R	ER	BB	SO	BF	WHIP	
2000	21	CHW	ALDS	0	0	0.000	0.00	1	0	1	0	0	0	0.1	2	0	0	0	1	3	6.000	
2005	26	CHW	ALDS	1	0	1.000	5.14	1	1	0	0	0	0	7	8	4	4	1	2	30	1.286	
2005	26	CHW	ALCS	1	0	1.000	1.00	1	1	0	1	0	0	9	5	1	1	0	4	32	0.556	
2008	29	CHW	ALDS	0	1	0.000	6.43	1	1	0	0	0	0	7	10	5	5	0	3	30	1.429	
				2	1	0.667	3.86	4	3	1	1	0	0	23.1	25	10	10	1	10	95	1.114	Post Season Pts.
				0.250	0.000	0.250	0.250	0.400	0.400	0.250	0.250	0.000	0.000	0.600	0.000	0.000	0.000	0.000	0.250	0.000	1.400	4.300

World Series Play

Year	Age	Tm	Lg	W	L	PCT.	ERA	G	GS	GF	CG	SHO	SV	IP	H	R	ER	BB	SO	BF	WHIP	
2005	26	CHW	AL	0	0	0.000	4.91	2	1	1	0	0	1	7.1	7	4	4	0	6	29	0.955	
				0	0	0.000	4.91	2	1	1	0	0	1	7.1	7	4	4	0	6	29	0.955	World Series Pts.
				0.000	0.000	0.000	0.000	0.250	0.250	0.250	0.000	0.000	0.250	0.250	0.000	0.000	0.000	0.000	0.250	0.000	0.250	1.750

Yearly Points Leading the League

Category	Times	Points	Total	Category	Times	Points	Total	Categor	Times	Points	Total	Hall of Fame Points	
MVP	0	7	0	Saves	0	3	0	SHO	0	2	0	Career Points	53.500
ROY	0	5	0	ERA	0	3	0	WinPc	0	2	0	Post Season Points	4.300
Cy Young	0	5	0	S.O.'s	0	2	0	Inning	2	2	4	World Series Points	1.750
Golden Glove	4	3	12	Games	0	2	0	WHIP	1	2	2	Career Add-On Points	32.000
All-Star	5	2	10	G.S.	2	2	4	GF	0	2	0	Writers Association Pts.	0.000
Wins	0	3	0	C.G.	0	2	0	Totals			6	Military/Lifetime Achievement	0.000
Totals			22	Totals			4	Grand Total Add-On Points			32	Grand Total HOF Points	91.550

The Baseball Hall of Fame

Miguel "Mike" Angel Cuellar Santana

Personal Life

Miguel "Mike" Angel Cuellar Santana was born on May 8, 1937, in Santa Clara, Las Villas province, Cuba. His family, including four boys. Not much information was found about Cuellar's personal life except he was married and divorced and then remarried.

Baseball Career

Cuellar was signed by the Cincinnati Reds in 1957 and worked in the minors until 1959, when he was ineffective in two relief appearances and returned to Havana. From 1960, Cuellar played in the minor leagues 1964 when he started to throw a screwball. The St. Louis Cardinals called him up in June 1964, and he got into 32 games. Cuellar was traded on June 15, 1965, to the Houston Astros and spent the rest of 1965 with the Astros. Cuellar started using his screwball the majority of the time and given a chance to start. After the 1968 season, he was traded to the Baltimore Orioles. He soon became a dominant pitcher as he pitched in 264 games, won 139, lost 79, threw 1920 Innings with an Earned Run Average of 3.08 until 1974. Cuellar's career ended in 1977.

Achievements:

- 4-Times 20 or more game winner (1969, 1970, 1971, & 1974)
- 3-Times received Cy Young Votes (1969 (Winning the Award), 1970, 1974).
- 4-Time All-Star (1967,1970, 1971, & 1974).
- 1-Time led AL in Wins (24 in 1970) & 2-Times led AL in Winning PCT (1970 & 1974).

Hall of Fame

Mike Cuellar was on the ballot in 1983 and did not receive a vote and was taken off for future ballots. Cuellar needs to have his career revisited by The Classic Baseball Era.

Summary Analysis

Mike Cuellar's Hall of Fame Point Total is 96.700. From 1969 to '74, he was one of the best in Baseball, a role model, and class that should be elected by the BB WAA.

Pitcher - Left Handed Potential Hall of Fame Inductee

Cuellar, Mike

Positions		Born :	May 8, 1937	Height:	6'1" USC	185	cm
Pitcher		From:	Las Villas, Cuba	Weight:	185 lbs.	81	Kg.
		Died:	April 2, 2010	Debut	April 18, 1959		
		Bats:	Left	Last Game:	May 3, 1977		
		Throws:	Left				

Year	Age	Tm	Lg	W	L	PCT	ERA	G	GS	GF	CG	SHO	SV	IP	H	R	ER	BB	SO	BF	WHIP	Awards
1959	22	CIN	NL	0	0	0.000	15.75	2	0	0	0	0	0	4	7	8	7	4	5	24	2.75	
1964	27	STL	NL	5	5	0.500	4.5	32	7	6	1	0	4	72	80	43	36	33	56	320	1.569	
1965	28	HOU	NL	1	4	0.200	3.54	25	4	11	0	0	2	56	55	24	22	21	46	238	1.357	
1966	29	HOU	NL	12	10	0.545	2.22	38	28	6	11	1	2	227.1	193	79	56	52	175	913	1.078	
1967	30	HOU	NL	16	11	0.593	3.03	36	32	3	16	3	1	246.1	233	99	83	63	203	1021	1.202	AS
1968	31	HOU	NL	8	11	0.421	2.74	28	24	3	11	2	1	170.2	152	60	52	45	133	700	1.154	
1969	32	BAL	AL	23	11	0.676	2.38	39	39	0	18	5	0	290.2	213	91	77	79	182	1137	1.005	CYA-1,MVP-8
1970	33	BAL	AL	24	8	0.750	3.48	40	40	0	21	4	0	297.2	273	126	115	69	190	1214	1.149	AS,CYA-4,MVP-11
1971	34	BAL	AL	20	9	0.690	3.08	38	38	0	21	4	0	292.1	250	111	100	78	124	1166	1.122	AS,MVP-24
1972	35	BAL	AL	18	12	0.600	2.57	35	35	0	17	4	0	248.1	197	78	71	71	132	989	1.079	
1973	36	BAL	AL	18	13	0.581	3.27	38	38	0	17	2	0	267	265	120	97	84	148	1127	1.307	
1974	37	BAL	AL	22	10	0.688	3.11	38	38	0	20	5	0	289.1	253	106	93	86	106	1111	1.258	AS,CYA-6,MVP-10
1975	38	BAL	AL	14	12	0.538	3.66	36	36	0	17	5	0	256	228	112	104	84	105	1034	1.223	
1976	39	BAL	AL	4	13	0.235	4.96	26	19	4	2	1	1	107	128	63	59	50	32	490	1.673	
1977	40	CAL	AL	0	1	0.000	18.9	2	1	0	0	0	0	3.1	9	7	7	3	3	21	3.600	
162 Game Avg.				15	11	0.587	3.34	37	31	3	14	3	1	230	207	92	80	67	133	940	1.197	
BAL (8 yrs)				143	88	0.619	3.18	290	283	4	133	30	1	2028	1809	810	716	601	1011	8268	1.188	
HOU (4 yrs)				37	36	0.507	2.74	127	88	23	38	6	6	700.1	633	262	213	181	557	2872	1.162	
STL (1 yr)				5	5	0.5	4.5	32	7	6	1	0	4	72	80	43	36	33	56	320	1.569	
CAL (1 yr)				0	1	0	18.9	2	1	0	0	0	0	3.1	9	7	7	3	3	21	3.6	
CIN (1 yr)				0	0		15.75	2	0	0	0	0	0	4	7	8	7	4	5	24	2.75	
AL (9 yrs)				143	89	0.616	3.2	292	284	4	133	30	1	2031	1818	817	723	604	1014	8289	1.192	
NL (6 yrs)				42	41	0.506	2.97	161	95	29	39	6	10	776.1	720	313	256	218	618	3216	1.208	
15 Yrs				185	130	0.587	3.14	453	379	33	172	36	11	2808	2538	1130	979	822	1632	11505	1.197	Career Pts.
				6.750	0.000	8.000	9.500	3.750	5.500	0.500	3.750	4.500	0.500	6.750	0.000	0.000	0.000	0.000	2.500	0.300	9.250	61.250

Post Seasonal Play

Year	Age	Team	Series	W	L	PCT	ERA	G	GS	GF	CG	SHO	SV	IP	H	R	ER	BB	SO	BF	WHIP	
1969	32	BAL	ALCS	0	0	0.000	2.25	1	1	0	0	0	0	8	3	3	2	1	7	27	0.500	
1970	33	BAL	ALCS	0	0	0.000	12.46	1	1	0	0	0	0	4.1	10	6	6	1	2	25	2.538	
1971	34	BAL	ALCS	1	0	1.000	1.00	1	1	0	1	0	0	9	6	1	1	1	2	33	0.778	
1973	36	BAL	ALCS	0	1	0.000	1.80	1	1	0	1	0	0	10	4	2	2	3	11	37	0.700	
1974	37	BAL	ALCS	1	1	0.500	2.84	2	2	0	0	0	0	12.2	9	4	4	13	6	60	1.737	
None				2	2	0.500	3.07	6	6	0	2	0	0	44	32	16	15	19	28	182	1.159	Post Season Pts.
				0.250	0.000	0.000	2.000	0.400	0.600	0.000	0.400	0.000	0.000	0.800	0.000	0.000	0.000	0.000	0.600	0.000	1.400	5.450

World Series Play

Year	Age	Team	Series	W	L	PCT	ERA	G	GS	GF	CG	SHO	SV	IP	H	R	ER	BB	SO	BF	WHIP	
1964	27	STL	WS	0	0	0.000	0	0	0	0	0	0	0	0	0	0	0	0	0	0	0.000	
1969	32	BAL	WS	1	0	1.000	1.13	2	2	0	1	0	0	16	13	2	2	1	4	61	1.063	
1970	33	BAL	WS	1	0	1.000	3.18	2	2	0	1	0	0	11.1	10	7	4	1	2	46	1.059	
1971	34	BAL	WS	0	2	0.000	3.86	2	2	0	0	0	0	14	11	7	6	2	6	60	1.214	
				2	2	0.500	2.61	6	6	0	2	0	0	41.1	34	16	12	12	28	167	1.113	World Series Pts.
				0.400	0.000	0.000	1.200	0.600	0.600	0.000	0.400	0.000	0.000	0.600	0.000	0.000	0.000	0.000	0.800	0.000	1.400	6.000

Yearly Points Leading the League

Category	Times	Points	Total
MVP	0	7	0
ROY	0	5	0
Cy Young	1	5	5
Golden Glove	0	3	0
All-Star	4	2	8
Wins	1	3	3
Totals			16

Category	Times	Points	Total
Saves	0	3	0
ERA	0	3	0
S.O.'s	0	2	0
Games	0	2	0
G.S.	1	2	2
C.G.	1	2	2
Totals			4

Categor	Times	Points	Total
SHO	0	2	0
WinPct	2	2	4
Innings	0	2	0
WHIP	0	2	0
GF	0	2	0
Totals			4
Grand Total Add-On Points		24	

Hall of Fame Points	
Career Points	61.250
Post Season Points	5.450
World Series Points	6.000
Career Add-On Points	24.000
Writers Association Pts.	0.000
Military/Lifetime Achievement	0.000
Grand Total HOF Points	96.700

Franco, John

Personal Life

John Anthony Franco was born September 17,1960 to Jim Franco Sr, and Mary Starace. Franco graduated from Lafayette High School in Brooklyn and St. John's University in Queens, where he pitched two no-hitters in his freshman year.

John married Rose Morrone, in 1987 and the couple have three children, Nicole, John James (J.J.), and Ella. J.J. Franco,

Baseball Career

In 1981, Franco was selected by the Los Angeles Dodgers in the 5th round of the amateur draft. From 1981 through 1983, Franco was used as a starter before being traded to the Cincinnati Reds on May 9, 1983. The Reds converted Franco into a reliever and he debuted on April 24, 1984. On December 6, 1989, Cincinnati traded him to the Mets where he remained until the end of the 2004 season. Injuries caused Franco to miss the 2002 baseball season, but he recovered from the surgery and returned in June 2003. Franco's 1,119 career games pitched is a National League record and ranks fourth in major league history. His 424 career saves ranks fifth all-time in major league history and a Postseason record: 2-0, one save, 1.88 ERA in 15 postseason appearances He retired in July 1975.

Achievements:

- 4-Times NL All-Star (1986, 1987, 1989 & 1990).
- 3-Times NL Saves Leader & Reliever of the Year Award Winner (1988, 1990 & 1994).
- 8-Times 30+ Saves Seasons: (1987-1991, 1994, 1997 & 1998).

Hall of Fame Candidacy

Franco was eligible for the in 2011 but failed to gain 5% of the votes and was dropped.

Summary Analysis

John Franco's Hall of Fame Point Total is 98.600. Statistically, Franco is one of the best closers of all time, pitched throughout the steroid era, and should be elected.

Franco, John   Pitcher - Left Handed Potential Hall of Fame Inductee

Position	Born:	September 17, 1960	Height:	5' 10" USC 178 cm
Pitcher	From:	Brooklyn NY	Weight:	170 lbs. 77 Kg.
	Bats:	Left	Debut:	April 24, 1984
	Throws:	Left	Last Game:	July 1, 2005

Year	Age	Tm	Lg	W	L	W-L%	ERA	G	GS	GF	CG	SHO	SV	IP	H	R	ER	BB	SO	BF	WHIP	Awards
1984	23	CIN	NL	6	2	0.750	2.610	54	0	30	0	0	4	79.1	74	28	23	36	55	335	1.387	
1985	24	CIN	NL	12	3	0.800	2.180	67	0	33	0	0	12	99	83	27	24	40	61	407	1.242	
1986	25	CIN	NL	6	6	0.500	2.940	74	0	52	0	0	29	101	90	40	33	44	84	429	1.327	AS
1987	26	CIN	NL	8	5	0.615	2.520	68	0	60	0	0	32	82	76	26	23	27	61	344	1.256	AS
1988	27	CIN	NL	6	6	0.500	1.570	70	0	61	0	0	39	86	60	18	15	27	46	336	1.012	MVP-12
1989	28	CIN	NL	4	8	0.333	3.120	60	0	50	0	0	32	80.2	77	35	28	36	60	345	1.401	AS
1990	29	NYM	NL	5	3	0.625	2.530	55	0	48	0	0	33	67.2	66	22	19	21	56	287	1.286	AS
1991	30	NYM	NL	5	9	0.357	2.930	52	0	48	0	0	30	55.1	61	27	18	18	45	247	1.428	
1992	31	NYM	NL	6	2	0.750	1.640	31	0	30	0	0	15	33	24	6	6	11	20	128	1.061	
1993	32	NYM	NL	4	3	0.571	5.200	35	0	30	0	0	10	36.1	46	24	21	19	29	172	1.789	
1994	33	NYM	NL	1	4	0.200	2.700	47	0	43	0	0	30	50	47	20	15	19	42	216	1.320	CYA-7,MVP-20
1995	34	NYM	NL	5	3	0.625	2.440	48	0	41	0	0	29	51.2	48	17	14	17	41	213	1.258	
1996	35	NYM	NL	4	3	0.571	1.830	51	0	44	0	0	28	54	54	15	11	21	48	235	1.389	
1997	36	NYM	NL	5	3	0.625	2.550	59	0	53	0	0	36	60	49	18	17	20	53	244	1.150	
1998	37	NYM	NL	0	8	0.000	3.620	61	0	54	0	0	38	64.2	66	28	26	29	59	289	1.469	
1999	38	NYM	NL	0	2	0.000	2.880	46	0	34	0	0	19	40.2	40	14	13	19	41	182	1.451	
2000	39	NYM	NL	5	4	0.556	3.400	62	0	14	0	0	4	55.2	46	24	21	26	56	239	1.293	
2001	40	NYM	NL	6	2	0.750	4.050	58	0	16	0	0	2	53.1	55	25	24	19	50	232	1.388	
2002											Did not play in major or minor leagues (injured)											
2003	42	NYM	NL	0	3	0.000	2.620	38	0	13	0	0	2	34.1	35	11	10	13	16	148	1.398	
2004	43	NYM	NL	2	7	0.222	5.280	52	0	16	0	0	0	46	46	28	27	24	36	207	1.522	
2005	44	HOU	NL	0	1	0.000	7.200	31	0	4	0	0	0	15	23	13	12	9	16	77	2.133	
162 Game Avg.				5	5	0.508	2.890	68	0	47	0	0	26	76	71	28	24	30	59	323	1.333	
NYM (14 yrs)				48	56	0.462	3.100	695	0	484	0	0	276	702.2	683	279	242	276	592	3039	1.365	
CIN (6 yrs)				42	30	0.583	2.490	393	0	286	0	0	148	528	460	174	146	210	367	2196	1.269	
21 Yrs				90	87	0.508	2.89	1119	0	774	0	0	424	1245	1166	466	400	495	975	5312	1.333	Career Pts.
				2.50	0.00	3.00	11.50	18.25	0.00	14.25	0.00	0.00	15.50	1.50	0.00	0.00	0.00	0.00	2.00	0.00	4.50	73.00

Post Seasonal Play

Year	Age	Tm		W	L	PCT	ERA	G	GS	GF	CG	SHO	SV	IP	H	R	ER	BB	SO	BF	WHIP	
1999	38	NYM	NLDS	1	0	1.000	0.00	3	0	2	0	0	0	3.2	1	0	0	0	2	11	0.273	
1999	38	NYM	NLCS	0	0	0.000	3.38	3	0	0	0	0	0	2.2	3	1	1	1	3	12	1.500	
2000	39	NYM	NLDS	0	0	0.000	0.00	2	0	1	0	0	1	2	1	0	0	0	2	7	0.500	
2000	39	NYM	NLCS	0	0	0.000	6.75	3	0	0	0	0	0	2.2	3	2	2	2	2	13	1.875	
				1	0	1.000	2.450	11	0	3	0	0	1	11	8	3	3	3	9	43	1.000	Post Season Pts.
				0.250	0.000	0.250	1.400	0.600	0.000	0.450	0.000	0.000	0.250	0.400	0.000	0.000	0.000	0.000	0.250	0.000	1.600	5.450

World Series Play

Year	Age	Team	Series	W	L	PCT	ERA	G	GS	GF	CG	SHO	SV	IP	H	R	ER	BB	SO	BF	WHIP	
2000	39	NYM	WS	1	0	1.000	0.000	4	0	1	0	0	0	3.1	3	0	0	0	1	11	0.900	
				1	0	1.000	0.000	4	0	1	0	0	0	3.1	3	0	0	0	1	11	0.900	World Series Pts.
				0.250	0.000	0.250	0.250	0.400	0.000	0.250	0.000	0.000	0.000	0.250	0.000	0.000	0.000	0.000	0.250	0.000	0.250	2.150

Yearly Points Leading the League

Category	Times	Points	Total		Category	Times	Points	Total		Categc	Times	Points	Total
MVP	0	7	0		Saves	3	2	6		SHO	0	2	0
ROY	0	5	0		ERA	0	2	0		WinPc	0	2	0
Cy Young	0	5	0		S.O.'s	0	2	0		Inning	0	2	0
Golden Glove	0	3	0		Games	0	2	0		WHIP	0	2	0
All-Star	4	2	8		G.S.	0	2	0		GF	2	2	4
Wins	0	2	0		C.G.	0	2	0		Totals			4
Totals			8		Totals			6		Grand Total Add-On Points			18

Hall of Fame Points	
Career Points	73.000
Post Season Points	5.450
World Series Points	2.150
Career Add-On Points	18.000
Writers Association Pts.	0.000
Military Points/Special	0.000
Grand Total HOF Points	98.600

Koosman, Jerry "Kooz"

Personal Life

Jerome Martin Koosman was born December 23, 1942, to Martin & Lydia Koosman in Appleton, Minnesota. He has two brothers, Elton and Orville, and a sister, Violet.

Jerry married LaVonne Sorum on February 11, 1967. They have a daughter Danielle and sons Shawn and Michael. The couple divorced in 2003.

Baseball Career

Koosman signed with the Mets on August 27, 1964, and played in the minors until he made his debut late in 1967. In 1968, Koosman won 19 games and followed that up with a 17-win season in 1969, one that finished with a 2-0 record in the World Series. Jerry Koosman retired after 19 games in 1985 with a career record of 222-209, 140 CG, 33 SO's, and 2,556 strikeouts. His career ERA was 3.36.

Achievements:

- 2-Times received MVP Votes: (1968 & 1969 & 2-Times Received Cy Young Votes: (1976 & 1979).
- 2-Times won 20+ Games in a season: (1976 & 1979).
- 200 Innings Pitched Seasons: 12 (1968-1970, 1973-1980 & 1984).
- 200 Strikeouts Seasons: 1 (1976) 2-Times an All-Star: (1968 & 1969).
- Won a World Series with the New York Mets in 1969.

Hall of Fame

Koosman was on the ballot in 1991 receiving 0.9% and being removed from future voting. Koosman's only path to the is the Eras Committee.

Summary Analysis

Koosman's 93.950 Hall of Fame Point Total is enough where the BBWAA should explore his candidacy again.

Pitcher - Left Handed Potential Hall of Fame Inductee

Koosman, Jerry

Positions	Pitcher		
Born:	December 23, 1942	Height:	6' 2" USC 180 cm
From:	Appleton, MN	Weight:	205 lbs. 92 Kg.
Bats:	Right	Debut	April 14, 1967
Throws:	Left	Last Game:	August 21, 1985

Year	Age	Tm	Lg	W	L	PCT	ERA	G	GS	GF	CG	SHO	SV	IP	H	R	ER	BB	SO	BF	WHIP	Awards
1967	24	NYM	NL	0	2	0.000	6.04	9	3	1	0	0	0	22.1	22	17	15	19	11	105	1.836	
1968	25	NYM	NL	19	12	0.613	2.08	35	34	0	17	7	0	263.2	221	72	61	69	178	1058	1.100	AS,MVP-13,RoY-2
1969	26	NYM	NL	17	9	0.654	2.28	32	32	0	16	6	0	241	187	66	61	68	180	957	1.058	AS,MVP-23
1970	27	NYM	NL	12	7	0.632	3.14	30	29	0	5	1	0	212	189	87	74	71	118	884	1.226	
1971	28	NYM	NL	6	11	0.353	3.04	26	24	0	4	0	0	165.2	160	66	56	51	96	694	1.274	
1972	29	NYM	NL	11	12	0.478	4.14	34	24	5	4	1	1	163	155	81	75	52	147	692	1.270	
1973	30	NYM	NL	14	15	0.483	2.84	35	35	0	12	3	0	263	234	93	83	76	156	1071	1.179	
1974	31	NYM	NL	15	11	0.577	3.36	35	35	0	13	0	0	265	258	113	99	85	188	1118	1.294	
1975	32	NYM	NL	14	13	0.519	3.42	36	34	2	11	4	2	239.2	234	106	91	98	173	1018	1.385	
1976	33	NYM	NL	21	10	0.677	2.69	34	32	0	17	3	0	247.1	205	81	74	66	200	994	1.096	CYA-2,MVP-14
1977	34	NYM	NL	8	20	0.286	3.49	32	32	0	6	1	0	226.2	195	102	88	81	192	940	1.218	
1978	35	NYM	NL	3	15	0.167	3.75	38	32	6	3	0	2	235.1	221	110	98	84	160	986	1.296	
1979	36	MIN	AL	20	13	0.606	3.38	37	36	0	10	2	0	263.2	268	108	99	83	157	1101	1.331	CYA-6
1980	37	MIN	AL	16	13	0.552	4.03	38	34	2	8	0	2	243.1	252	119	109	69	149	1022	1.319	
1981	38	TOT	AL	4	13	0.235	4.01	27	16	9	3	1	5	121.1	125	59	54	41	76	517	1.368	
1981	38	MIN	AL	3	9	0.250	4.2	19	13	5	2	1	5	94.1	98	49	44	34	55	404	1.399	
1981	38	CHW	AL	1	4	0.200	3.33	8	3	4	1	0	0	27	27	10	10	7	21	113	1.259	
1982	39	CHW	AL	11	7	0.611	3.84	42	19	12	3	1	3	173.1	194	81	74	38	88	726	1.338	
1983	40	CHW	AL	11	7	0.611	4.77	37	24	6	2	1	2	169.2	176	96	90	53	90	730	1.350	
1984	41	PHI	NL	14	15	0.483	3.25	36	34	0	3	1	0	224	232	95	81	60	137	950	1.304	
1985	42	PHI	NL	6	4	0.600	4.62	19	18	0	3	1	0	99.1	107	56	51	34	60	433	1.419	
162 Game Avg.				13	12	0.515	3.36	37	31	3	8	2	1	229	217	96	86	72	153	955	1.259	
NYM (12 yrs)				140	137	0.505	3.09	376	346	14	108	26	5	2544	2281	994	875	820	1799	10517	1.219	
MIN (3 yrs)				39	35	0.527	3.77	94	83	7	20	3	7	601.1	618	276	252	186	361	2527	1.337	
CHW (3 yrs)				23	18	0.561	4.23	87	46	22	6	2	5	370	397	187	174	98	199	1569	1.338	
PHI (2 yrs)				20	19	0.513	3.67	55	52	0	6	2	0	323.1	339	151	132	94	197	1383	1.339	
NL (14 yrs)				160	156	0.506	3.16	431	398	14	114	28	5	2868	2620	1145	1007	914	1996	11900	1.232	
AL (5 yrs)				62	53	0.539	3.95	181	129	29	26	5	12	971.1	1015	463	426	284	560	4096	1.337	
19 Yrs				222	209	0.515	3.36	612	527	43	140	33	17	3839	3635	1608	1433	1198	2556	15996	1.259	**Career Pts.**
				9.250	0.000	3.000	7.500	6.750	10.500	0.500	3.000	3.750	0.500	11.750	0.000	0.000	0.000	0.000	8.000	0.000	6.750	**71.250**

Post Seasonal Play

Year	Age	Team	Series	W	L	PCT	ERA	G	GS	GF	CG	SHO	SV	IP	H	R	ER	BB	SO	BF	WHIP	
1969	26	NY	NLCS	0	0	0.000	11.57	1	1	0	0	0	0	4.2	7	6	6	4	5	24	2.357	
1973	30	NY	NLCS	1	0	1.000	2.00	1	1	0	1	0	0	9	8	2	2	0	9	35	0.889	
1983	40	Chi	ALCS	0	0	0.000	54.00	1	0	0	0	0	0	0.1	1	3	2	2	0	4	9.000	
				1	0	1.000	6.752	3	2	0	1	0	0	13.3	16	11	10	6	14	63	1.618	**Post Season Pts.**
				0.250	0.000	0.250	0.000	0.250	0.250	0.000	0.250	0.000	0.000	0.400	0.000	0.000	0.000	0.000	0.400	0.000	0.000	**2.050**

World Series Play

Year	Age	Team	Series	W	L	PCT	ERA	G	GS	GF	CG	SHO	SV	IP	H	R	ER	BB	SO	BF	WHIP	
1969	26	NY	NL	2	0	1.000	2.04	2	2	0	1	0	0	17.2	7	4	4	4	9	64	0.623	
1973	30	NY	NL	1	0	1.000	3.12	2	2	0	0	0	0	8.2	9	3	3	7	8	41	1.846	
				3	0	1.000	2.46	4	4	0	1	0	0	25.4	16	7	7	11	17	105	1.055	**World Series Pts.**
				0.600	0.000	1.000	1.400	0.400	0.400	0.000	0.250	0.000	0.000	0.400	0.000	0.000	0.000	0.000	0.600	0.000	1.600	**6.650**

Yearly Points Leading the League

Category	Times	Points	Total
MVP	0	7	0
ROY	0	5	0
Cy Young	0	5	0
Golden Glove	0	3	0
All-Star	2	2	4
Wins	0	3	0
Totals			4

Category	Times	Points	Total
Saves	0	3	0
ERA	0	3	0
S.O.'s	0	2	0
Games	0	2	0
G.S.	0	2	0
C.G.	0	2	0
Totals			0

Catego	Times	Points	Total
SHO	0	2	0
WinPct	0	2	0
Innings	0	2	0
WHIP	0	2	0
GF	0	2	0
Totals			0
Grand Total Add-On Points			4

Hall of Fame Points	
Career Points	71.250
Post Season Points	2.050
World Series Points	6.650
Career Add-On Points	4.000
Writers Association Pts.	0.000
Military/Lifetime Achievement	10.000
Grand Total HOF Points	93.950

Lee, Cliff

Personal Life

Clifton Phifer Lee was born on August 30, 1978, in Benton, Arkansas, to Steve and Sharon Lee. Cliff played football and basketball in high In 2000, Lee accepted a scholarship offer to play baseball for Arkansas.

Lee married Kristen in 2000 with the couple having a son Jaxon, and a daughter Maci. Jaxon was detected with infant leukemia, but he beat the odds and is doing well.

Baseball Career

Cliff Lee signed with the Montreal Expos after being selected in the fourth round, of the 2000 MLB Draft. He moved up in their system but was traded to Cleveland in June of 1972 and called-up for 2 big league starts. In 2003, he started in the minors but was recalled on June 30th. He earned his first big league win and became a member of the Indians rotation in 2004. In 2008, Lee won the Cy Young Award and was 22-3. Lee had a 143–91 record, 3.52 ERA and struck out 1,824 batters when he retired.

Achievements:

- 4-Time All-Star: (2008, 2010, 2011 & 2013) & AL Cy Young Award 2008
- 1-Time AL ERA Leader: (2008) & 1-Time AL Wins Leader: (2008).
- 2-Time AL Winning Percentage Leader: (2005 & 2008).
- 2-Time League Shutouts Leader: (2008/AL & 2011/NL).
- 3-Time 15 Wins Seasons: (2005, 2008 & 2011) & 20 Wins Seasons: 1 (2008).
- 8-Time 200 Innings Pitched Seasons: (2005, 2006 & 2008-2013).
- 3-200 Strikeouts Seasons: (2011-2013).

Hall of Fame Candidacy

Lee was on the 2020 ballot for the National Baseball Hall of Fame but fell short of the 5-percent threshold and removed. His candidacy can be considered at some future date.

Summary Analysis

Cliff Lee's 92.850 Hall of Fame Point total. This is a call for the BBWAA to make.

Lee, Cliff
Positions: Pitcher

Pitcher - Left Handed Potential Hall of Fame Inductee

Born :	August 30, 1978	Height:	6'3" USC 190 cm
From:	Benton, AZ	Weight:	205 lbs. 92 Kg.
Bats:	Left	Debut	September 15, 2002
Throws:	Left	Last Game:	July 31, 2914

Year	Age	Tm	Lg	W	L	PCT	ERA	G	GS	GF	CG	SHO	SV	IP	H	R	ER	BB	SO	BF	WHIP	Awards
2002	23	CLE	AL	0	1	0.00	1.74	2	2	0	0	0	0	10.1	6	2	2	8	6	44	1.355	
2003	24	CLE	AL	3	3	0.50	3.61	9	9	0	0	0	0	52.1	41	28	21	20	44	210	1.166	
2004	25	CLE	AL	14	8	0.64	5.43	33	33	0	0	0	0	179	188	113	108	81	161	802	1.503	
2005	26	CLE	AL	18	5	0.78	3.79	32	32	0	1	0	0	202	194	91	85	52	143	838	1.218	CYA-4
2006	27	CLE	AL	14	11	0.56	4.40	33	33	0	1	0	0	200.2	224	114	98	58	129	882	1.405	
2007	28	CLE	AL	5	8	0.39	6.29	20	16	1	1	0	0	97.1	112	73	68	36	66	443	1.521	
2008	29	CLE	AL	22	3	0.88	2.54	31	31	0	4	2	0	223.1	214	68	63	34	170	891	1.110	AS,CYA-1,MVP-12
2009	30	TOT	MLB	14	13	0.52	3.22	34	34	0	6	2	0	231.2	245	88	83	43	181	969	1.243	
2009	30	CLE	AL	7	9	0.44	3.14	22	22	0	3	1	0	152	165	53	53	33	107	641	1.303	
2009	30	PHI	NL	7	4	0.64	3.39	12	12	0	3	1	0	79.2	80	35	30	10	74	328	1.130	
2010	31	TOT	AL	12	9	0.57	3.18	28	28	0	7	1	0	212.1	195	84	75	18	185	843	1.003	AS,CYA-7
2010	31	SEA	AL	8	3	0.73	2.34	13	13	0	5	1	0	103.2	92	31	27	6	89	408	0.945	
2010	31	TEX	AL	4	6	0.40	3.98	15	15	0	2	0	0	108.2	103	53	48	12	96	435	1.058	
2011	32	PHI	NL	17	8	0.68	2.40	32	32	0	6	6	0	232.2	197	66	62	42	238	920	1.027	AS,CYA-3,MVP-15
2012	33	PHI	NL	6	9	0.40	3.16	30	30	0	0	0	0	211	207	79	74	28	207	847	1.114	
2013	34	PHI	NL	14	8	0.64	2.87	31	31	0	2	1	0	222.2	193	77	71	32	222	876	1.010	AS,CYA-6
2014	35	PHI	NL	4	5	0.44	3.65	13	13	0	1	0	0	81.1	100	40	33	12	72	352	1.377	
	162 Game Avg.			15	9	0.61	3.52	34	34	0	3	1	0	225	221	96	88	48	190	930	1.196	
	CLE (8 yrs)			83	48	0.63	4.01	182	178	1	10	3	0	1117	1144	542	498	322	826	4751	1.312	
	PHI (5 yrs)			48	34	0.59	2.94	118	118	0	12	8	0	827.1	777	297	270	124	813	3323	1.089	
	TEX (1 yr)			4	6	0.40	3.98	15	15	0	2	0	0	108.2	103	53	48	12	96	435	1.058	
	SEA (1 yr)			8	3	0.727	2.34	13	13	0	5	1	0	103.2	92	31	27	6	89	408	0.945	
	AL (9 yrs)			95	57	0.625	3.88	210	206	1	17	4	0	1329	1339	626	573	340	1011	5594	1.263	
	NL (5 yrs)			48	34	0.585	2.94	118	118	0	12	8	0	827.1	777	297	270	124	813	3323	1.089	
	13 Yrs			143	91	0.611	3.52	328	324	1	29	12	0	2156	2116	923	843	464	1824	8917	1.196	Career Pts.
				4.500	0.000	10.500	5.750	2.500	4.500	0.000	1.000	1.500	0.000	3.750	0.000	0.000	0.000	0.000	4.500	0.000	9.250	47.750

Post Seasonal Play

Year	Age	Team	Series	W	L	PCT	ERA	G	GS	GF	CG	SHO	SV	IP	H	R	ER	BB	SO	BF	WHIP	
2009	30	PHI	NLDS	1	0	1.000	1.10	2	2	0	1	0	0	16.1	11	4	2	3	10	62	0.857	
2009	30	PHI	NLCS	1	0	1.000	0.00	1	1	0	0	0	0	8	3	0	0	0	10	26	0.375	
2010	31	TEX	ALDS	2	0	1.000	1.13	2	2	0	1	0	0	16	11	2	2	0	21	60	0.688	
2010	31	TEX	ALCS	1	0	1.000	0.00	1	1	0	0	0	0	8	2	0	0	1	13	27	0.375	
2011	32	PHI	NLDS	0	1	0.000	7.50	1	1	0	0	0	0	6	12	5	5	2	9	31	2.333	
				5	1	0.833	1.49	7	7	0	2	0	0	54.1	39	11	9	6	63	206	0.828	Post Season Pts.
				0.600	0.000	1.400	1.800	0.400	0.800	0.000	0.400	0.000	0.000	1.000	0.000	0.000	0.000	0.000	1.400	0.000	2.000	9.8

World Series Play

Year	Age	Team	Series	W	L	PCT	ERA	G	GS	GF	CG	SHO	SV	IP	H	R	ER	BB	SO	BF	WHIP	
2009	30	PHI	NL	2	0	1.000	2.81	2	2	0	1	0	0	16	13	6	5	3	13	63	1.000	
2010	31	TEX	AL	0	2	0.000	6.94	2	2	0	0	0	0	11.2	14	10	9	1	13	51	1.286	
				2	2	0.500	4.55	4	4	0	1	0	0	27.2	27	16	14	4	26	114	1.120	World Series Pts.
				0.400	0.000	0.000	0.250	0.400	0.400	0.000	0.250	0.000	0.000	0.400	0.000	0.000	0.000	0.000	0.800	0.000	1.400	4.300

Yearly Points Leading the League

Category	Times	Points	Total	Category	Times	Points	Total	Category	Times	Points	Total
MVP	0	7	0	Saves	0	3	0	SHO	2	2	4
ROY	0	5	0	ERA	1	3	3	WinPct	2	2	4
Cy Young	1	5	5	S.O.'s	0	2	0	Innings	0	2	0
Golden Glove	0	3	0	Games	0	2	0	WHIP	1	2	2
All-Star	4	2	8	G.S.	0	2	0	GF	0	2	0
Wins	1	3	3	C.G.	1	2	2	Totals			10
Totals			16	Totals			5	Grand Total Add-On Points			31

Hall of Fame Points	
Career Points	47.750
Post Season Points	9.800
World Series Points	4.300
Career Add-On Points	31.000
Writers Association Pts.	0.000
Military/lifetime Achieveme	0.000
Grand Total HOF Points	92.850

Lester, Jon

Personal Life

Jonathan Tyler Lester was born January 7, 1984, in Tacoma, Washington to John and Kathie Lester. Lester attended Bellarmine Preparatory School in Tacoma, Washington.

On January 9, 2009, Lester married Farrah Stone Johnson. Together, they have two sons, Hudson and Walker, and a daughter Cy Elizabeth.

Baseball Career

Lester was selected in the second round of the 2002 amateur draft by Boston. He moved up in their system. In 2006, he made his big league debut June 2006. He went 7-2 with a 4.76 ERA in 15 starts with the club but was sidelined late in the season when he was diagnosed as having lymphoma. After successful chemotherapy treatment, Lester went on to pitch for the Red Sox until he was traded in 2014. On January 12, 2022, Lester announced his retirement after 16 major league seasons. With the Red Sox, Athletics, Cubs, Nationals and Cardinals. His record was 200 wins, lost 117, 3.66 ERA, 2740.0 Innings Pitched, 2488 strikeouts, and a 1.278 EWHIP for his career.

Achievements

- 5-time All-Star (2010, 2011, 2014, 2016 & 2018) & 1-Time AL Shutouts Leader (2008).
- 4-Times Received Cy Young Votes (2010, 2014, 2016 & 2018).
- 1-Time Led NL in Wins (2018) & 1-Time NL Winning Percentage Leader (2016).
- 15 Wins Seasons: 8 (2008-2011, 2013, 2014, 2016 & 2018).
- 200 Innings Pitched Seasons: 8 (2008-2010 & 2012-2016).
- 200 Strikeouts Seasons: 4 (2009, 2010, 2014 & 2015).
- Won three World Series: (Boston Red Sox (2007 & 2013) & Chicago Cubs (2016).

Hall of Fame

Jon Lester will be eligible to be voted into the Hall of fame by the BBWAA in 2027.

Analysis

Jon Lester's has a Hall of Fame Point Total of 90.900. In 26 playoff appearances (22 starts) he posted a 2.51 ERA, including a 1.77 ERA in six Fall Classic games (five starts). Lester should be elected to the Hall of Fame by the BBWAA in the future.

Lester, Jon
Positions: Pitcher

Born:	January 7, 1984
From:	Tacoma, WA
Bats:	Left
Throws:	Left

Pitcher - Left Handed Potential Hall of Fame Inductee

Height:	6' 4"	193 cm
Weight:	249 lbs	112 Kg
Debut	June 10, 2006	
Last Game:	October 2, 2021	

Year	Age	Tm	Lg	W	L	PCT	ERA	G	GS	GF	CG	SHO	SV	IP	H	R	ER	BB	SO	BF	WHIP	Awards
2006	22	BOS	AL	7	2	0.778	4.760	15	15	0	0	0	0	81.1	91	43	43	43	60	387	1.648	
2007	23	BOS	AL	4	0	1.000	4.570	12	11	0	0	0	0	63	61	33	32	31	50	275	1.460	
2008	24	BOS	AL	16	6	0.727	3.210	33	33	0	2	2	0	210.1	202	78	75	66	152	874	1.274	
2009	25	BOS	AL	15	8	0.652	3.410	32	32	0	2	0	0	203.1	186	80	77	64	225	843	1.230	
2010	26	BOS	AL	19	9	0.679	3.250	32	32	0	2	0	0	208	167	81	75	83	225	861	1.202	AS,CYA-4
2011	27	BOS	AL	15	9	0.625	3.470	31	31	0	0	0	0	191.2	166	77	74	75	182	790	1.257	AS
2012	28	BOS	AL	9	14	0.391	4.820	33	33	0	3	0	0	205.1	216	117	110	68	166	878	1.383	
2013	29	BOS	AL	15	8	0.652	3.750	33	33	0	1	1	0	213.1	209	94	89	67	177	903	1.294	
2014	30	TOT	AL	16	11	0.593	2.460	32	32	0	1	1	0	219.2	184	76	60	48	220	885	1.102	AS,CYA-4
2014	30	BOS	AL	10	7	0.588	2.520	21	21	0	0	0	0	143	129	52	40	32	149	580	1.119	
2014	30	OAK	AL	6	4	0.600	2.350	11	11	0	1	1	0	76.2	86	24	20	16	71	305	1.070	
2015	31	CHC	NL	11	12	0.478	3.340	32	32	0	1	0	0	205	183	83	76	47	207	828	1.122	
2016	32	CHC	NL	19	5	0.792	2.440	32	32	0	2	0	0	202.2	154	57	55	52	197	796	1.016	AS,CYA-2
2017	33	CHC	NL	13	8	0.619	4.330	32	32	0	1	0	0	180.2	179	101	87	60	180	763	1.323	
2018	34	CHC	NL	18	6	0.750	3.320	32	32	0	0	0	0	181.2	174	75	67	64	149	761	1.310	AS,CYA-9
2019	35	CHC	NL	13	10	0.565	4.460	31	31	0	0	0	0	171.2	205	101	83	52	165	754	1.497	
2020	36	CHC	NL	3	3	0.500	5.160	12	12	0	0	0	0	61	64	35	35	17	42	265	1.328	
2021	37	TOT	NL	7	6	0.538	4.710	28	28	0	0	0	0	141.1	159	84	74	55	91	627	1.514	
2021	37	WSN	NL	3	5	0.375	5.030	16	16	0	0	0	0	75.1	91	50	42	28	51	342	1.589	
2021	37	STL	NL	4	1	0.800	4.360	12	12	0	0	0	0	66	68	34	32	26	40	385	1.424	
162 Game Avg.				15	9	0.631	3.860	34	34	0	1	0	0	206	197	91	84	67	187	885	1.378	
BOS (9 yrs)				110	63	0.636	3.640	242	341	0	10	3	0	1319	1436	655	615	529	1366	6378	1.287	
CHC (6 yrs)				77	44	0.636	3.640	171	171	0	4	0	0	1002	959	452	405	292	940	4177	1.246	
STL (1 yr)				4	1	0.800	4.360	12	12	0	0	0	0	66	68	34	32	26	40	385	1.424	
OAK (1 yr)				6	4	0.600	2.350	11	11	0	1	1	0	76.2	86	24	20	16	71	305	1.070	
WSN (1 yr)				3	5	0.375	5.030	16	16	0	0	0	0	75.1	81	50	42	29	51	342	1.589	
AL (9 yrs)				116	67	0.634	3.580	353	352	0	11	4	0	1596	1491	679	635	545	1437	6683	1.276	
NL (7 yrs)				84	50	0.627	3.770	199	199	0	4	0	0	1144	1118	536	479	347	1031	4804	1.261	
16 Yrs				200	117	0.631	3.66	452	431	0	15	4	0	2740	2610	1215	1114	892	2468	11487	1.278	**Career Pts.**
				6.750	0.000	11.750	4.750	3.750	8.000	0.000	0.500	0.500	0.000	3.500	0.000	0.000	0.000	0.000	8.000	0.000	6.750	56.250

Post Seasonal Play

Year	Age	Team	Series	W	L	PCT	ERA	G	GS	GF	CG	SHO	SV	IP	H	R	ER	BB	SO	BF	WHIP	
2007	23	BOS	ALDS	0	0	0.000	0.000	0	0	0	0	0	0	0	0	0	0	0	0	0	0.000	
2007	23	BOS	ALCS	0	0	0.000	4.910	2	0	1	0	0	0	3.2	3	2	2	1	5	15	1.091	
2008	24	BOS	ALDS	1	0	1.000	0.000	2	2	0	0	0	0	14	10	1	0	3	11	56	0.829	
2008	24	BOS	ALCS	0	2	0.000	4.970	2	2	0	0	0	0	12.3	14	8	7	3	15	53	1.263	
2008	25	BOS	ALDS	0	1	0.000	4.500	1	1	0	0	0	0	6	4	3	3	4	5	28	1.333	
2013	29	BOS	ALDS	1	0	1.000	2.350	1	1	0	0	0	0	7.2	3	2	2	3	7	29	0.783	
2013	29	BOS	ALCS	1	1	0.500	2.310	2	2	0	0	0	0	11.2	13	3	3	4	7	51	1.457	
2014	30	OAK	ALWC	0	0	0.000	7.360	1	1	0	0	0	0	7.1	8	6	6	2	5	31	1.364	
2015	31	CHC	NLWC	0	0	0.000	0.000	0	0	0	0	0	0	0	0	0	0	0	0	0	0.000	
2015	31	CHC	NLDS	0	1	0.000	3.680	1	1	0	0	0	0	7.1	5	3	3	1	9	28	0.818	
2015	31	CHC	NLCS	0	1	0.000	5.400	1	1	0	0	0	0	8.1	8	6	4	1	5	28	1.250	
2016	32	CHC	NLDS	1	0	1.000	0.000	1	1	0	0	0	0	8	5	0	0	0	5	27	0.625	
2016 MVP	32	CHC	NLCS	1	0	1.000	1.380	3	3	0	0	0	0	13	9	2	2	2	9	49	0.846	
2017	33	CHC	NLDS	0	0	0.000	1.800	2	1	0	0	0	0	9.2	3	2	2	3	8	34	0.621	
2017	33	CHC	NLCS	0	0	0.000	1.930	1	1	0	0	0	0	4.2	3	1	1	5	2	21	1.714	
2018	34	CHC	NLWC	0	0	0.000	1.500	1	1	0	0	0	0	6	4	1	1	1	3	25	0.833	
				5	6	0.455	2.75	20	17	2	0	0	0	114.6	92	38	36	32	99	473	1.08	**Post Season Pts.**
				0.600	0.000	3.000	1.200	0.800	1.800	0.250	0.000	0.000	0.000	1.800	0.000	0.000	0.000	0.000	2.000	0.000	1.600	10.050

World Series Play

Year	Age	Team	Series	W	L	PCT	ERA	G	GS	GF	CG	SHO	SV	IP	H	R	ER	BB	SO	BF	WHIP	
2007	23	BOS	AL	1	0	1.000	0.000	1	1	0	0	0	0	5.2	3	0	0	3	3	23	1.059	
2013	29	BOS	AL	2	0	1.000	0.590	2	2	0	0	0	0	15.1	9	1	1	1	15	54	0.652	
2016	32	CHC	NL	1	1	0.500	3.680	3	2	0	0	0	0	14.2	15	7	6	4	16	60	1.159	
				4	1	0.800	1.770	6	5	0	0	0	0	35.2	27	8	7	8	34	137	0.923	**World Series Pts.**
				0.800	0.000	1.400	1.600	0.600	0.600	0.000	0.000	0.000	0.000	3.600	0.000	0.000	0.000	0.000	1.000	0.000	2.000	8.000

Yearly Points Leading the League

Category	Times	Points	Total	Category	Times	Points	Total	Category	Times	Points	Total
MVP	0	7	0	Saves	0	3	0	SHO	0	3	0
ROY	0	5	0	ERA	1	5	5	WinPct	0	2	0
Cy Young	0	5	0	S.O.'s	0	3	0	Innings	0	2	0
Golden Glove	0	3	0	Games	0	1	0	WHIP	0	2	0
All-Star	5	2	10	G.S.	0	2	0	GF	0	2	0
Wins	1	3	3	C.G.	0	2	0	Totals			0
Totals			13	Totals			5	Grand Total Add-On Points			18

Hall of Fame Points	
Career Points	56.250
Post Season Points	10.050
World Series Points	8.000
Career Add-On Points	16.300
Writers Association Pts.	0.000
Militar Military Points	0.000
Grand Total HOF Points	90.500

Lolich, Mickey

Personal Life

Michael Stephen Lolich was born September 12, 1940 in Portland, Oregon to Steven Lolich and Margarite Greblo. Lolich attended Lincoln High School in Portland and posted a record of 19 wins against 5 losses for the school team in 1958

In 1962, Lolich married Joyce Feenor, on November 21, from Hollywood, Florida. They have three daughters, Kimberly Ann, Jody Joanne, and Stacy Michelle.

Baseball Career

Lolich was signed by the Detroit Tigers on June 30, 1958. His career began in 1959, as he moved up through their system. He made his debut on May 12, 1963. In a 16-year major league career, Lolich played in 586 games, accumulating a 217–191 win–loss record along with a 3.44 earned run average. He struck out 2,832, threw 41 shutouts, 195 complete games, and 496 games started. Lolich retired in 1979.

Achievements:

- Led the A.L. in wins & Games Started (1971).
- Led the A.L. in shutouts (1967) & led the A.L. in Innings Pitched (1971).
- Led the A.L. in Strikeouts (1971) & 3-times All-Star (1969, 1971 & 1972).
- 2-Time 20 Game Winner (1971 & 1972) & led the A.L. in Complete Games (1971).
- 8-Times 15 Wins Seasons: (1964, 1965, 1968, 1969 & 1971-1974).
- 12-Times 200 Innings Pitched Seasons: (1964-1975 with 300 Innings (1971-1974).
- 7-Times 200 Strikeouts Seasons:(1965 & 1969-1974) & Won a World Series 1968.

Hall of Fame

Lolich was on the ballot from 1985 to 2000 and was removed after 15 years in 2000. In 2003, 2005, and 2007 Lolich was on the final ballot by the Veterans but wasn't elected.

Summary Analysis

Mickey Lolich's Hall of Fame Point total is 103.700. Lolich was consistent and durable throughout his career and shined in the World Series. He needs to be elected.

Lolich, Mickey **Pitcher - Left Handed Potential Hall of Fame Inductee**

Positions	Born :	September 12, 1940	Height:	6' 1"	USC 185	cm
Pitcher	From:	Portland, OR	Weight:	170	lbs. 77	Kg.
	Bats:	Both	Debut	May 12, 1963		
	Throws:	Left	Last Game:	September 23, 1979		

Year	Age	Tm	Lg	W	L	PCT	ERA	G	GS	GF	CG	SHO	SV	IP	H	R	ER	BB	SO	SO	WHIP	Awards
1963	22	DET	AL	5	9	0.357	3.55	33	18	5	4	0	0	144.1	145	64	57	56	103	620	1.393	
1964	23	DET	AL	18	9	0.667	3.26	44	33	5	12	6	2	232	196	88	84	64	192	949	1.121	
1965	24	DET	AL	15	9	0.625	3.44	43	37	5	7	3	3	243.2	216	103	93	72	226	1015	1.182	
1966	25	DET	AL	14	14	0.500	4.77	40	33	4	5	1	2	203.2	204	119	108	83	173	894	1.409	
1967	26	DET	AL	14	13	0.519	3.04	31	30	1	11	6	0	204	165	71	69	56	174	820	1.083	MVP-23
1968	27	DET	AL	17	9	0.654	3.19	39	32	4	8	4	1	220	178	84	78	65	197	905	1.105	
1969	28	DET	AL	19	11	0.633	3.14	37	36	1	15	1	1	280.2	214	111	98	122	271	1172	1.197	AS
1970	29	DET	AL	14	19	0.424	3.80	40	39	0	13	3	0	272.2	272	125	115	109	230	1181	1.397	
1971	30	DET	AL	25	14	0.641	2.92	45	45	0	29	4	0	376	336	133	122	92	308	1538	1.138	AS,CYA-2,MVP-5
1972	31	DET	AL	22	14	0.611	2.50	41	41	0	23	4	0	327.1	282	100	91	74	250	1321	1.088	AS,CYA-3,MVP-10
1973	32	DET	AL	16	15	0.516	3.82	42	42	0	17	3	0	308.2	315	143	131	79	214	1286	1.276	
1974	33	DET	AL	16	21	0.432	4.15	41	41	0	27	3	0	308	310	155	142	78	202	1263	1.26	
1975	34	DET	AL	12	18	0.400	3.78	32	32	0	19	1	0	240.2	260	119	101	64	139	1016	1.346	
1976	35	NYM	NL	8	13	0.381	3.22	31	30	1	5	2	0	192.2	184	83	69	52	120	797	1.225	
1979	38	SDP	NL	0	2	0.000	4.74	27	5	7	0	0	0	49.1	59	33	26	22	20	223	1.642	
162 Game Avg.				14	12	0.532	3.44	37	31	3	12	3	1	229	212	97	87	69	178	951	1.227	
DET (13 yrs)				207	175	0.542	3.45	508	459	25	190	39	9	3361	3093	1415	1289	1014	2679	13980	1.222	
SDP (2 yrs)				2	3	0.4	3.43	47	7	14	0	0	1	84	89	39	32	33	33	363	1.452	
NYM (1 yr)				8	13	0.381	3.22	31	30	1	5	2	0	192.2	184	83	69	52	120	797	1.225	
AL (13 yrs)				207	175	0.542	3.45	508	459	25	190	39	9	3361	3093	1415	1289	1014	2679	13980	1.222	
NL (3 yrs)				10	16	0.385	3.29	78	37	15	5	2	1	276.2	273	122	101	85	153	1160	1.294	
16 Yrs				217	191	0.532	3.44	586	496	40	195	41	10	3638	3366	1537	1390	1099	2832	15140	1.227	Career Pts.
				8.000	0.000	4.500	6.500	5.500	9.250	0.500	4.500	5.500	0.500	10.500	0.000	0.000	0.000	0.000	9.250	0.000	8.000	72.500

Post Seasonal Play

Year	Age	Team	Series	W	L	PCT	ERA	G	GS	GF	CG	SHO	SV	IP	H	R	ER	BB	SO	BF	WHIP	
1972	31	Det	ALCS	0	1	0.000	1.42	2	2	0	0	0	0	19	14	3	1	5	10	76	1.000	
				0	1	0.000	1.42	2	2	0	0	0	0	19	14	3	1	5	10	76	1.000	Post Season Pts.
				0.000	0.000	0.000	1.800	0.200	0.200	0.000	0.000	0.000	0.000	0.325	0.000	0.000	0.000	0.000	0.200	0.000	1.675	4.400

World Series Play

Year	Age	Team	Series	W	L	PCT	ERA	G	GS	GF	CG	SHO	SV	IP	H	R	ER	BB	SO	BF	WHIP	
1968	28	Det	WS	3	0	1.000	1.67	3	3	0	3	0	0	27	20	5	5	6	21	164	0.978	
				3	0	1.000	1.67	3	3	0	3	0	0	27	20	5	5	6	21	164	0.978	World Series Pts.
				0.600	0.000	1.000	1.800	0.400	0.400	0.000	0.600	0.000	0.000	0.400	0.000	0.000	0.000	0.000	0.600	0.000	2.000	7.800

Yearly Points Leading the League

Category	Times	Points	Total	Category	Times	Points	Total	Categ	Times	Points	Total	Hall of Fame Points	
MVP	0	7	0	Saves	0	3	0	SHO	1	2	2	Career Points	72.500
ROY	0	5	0	ERA	0	3	0	WinPc	0	2	0	Post Season Points	4.400
Cy Young	0	5	0	S.O.'s	1	2	2	Inning	1	2	2	World Series Points	7.800
Golden Glove	0	3	0	Games	0	2	0	WHIP	0	2	0	Career Add-On Points	19.000
All-Star	3	2	6	G.S.	1	2	2	GF	0	2	0	Writers Association Pts.	0.000
Wins	1	3	3	C.G.	1	2	2	Totals			4	Military/Lifetime Achievement	0.000
Totals			9	Totals			6	Grand Total Add-On Points		19		Grand Total HOF Points	103.700

Lyle, Albert "Sparky"

Personal Life

Albert Walter "Sparky" Lyle was born in DuBois, Pennsylvania on July 22, 1944. No information on his parents was found. He attended Reynoldsville High School.

Lyle married Mary Fontaine Massey on May 2, 1977. They have three boys but unable to find any information on them.

Baseball Career

Lyle was selected by the Boston Red Sox in the draft on November 30, 1964. He progressed up the Red Sox farm system as a relief pitcher, called up to Boston on June 24, 1967. He registered 64 saves during the next four years, serving as the team's closer from 1969 to 1971. From 1972 through 1978, Lyle established himself as the Yankees' bullpen ace. He helped lead the Yankees to three straight pennants from 1976-1978 and World Series titles in 1977 and 1978. After the '78 World Series, Lyle was traded to the Texas Rangers. He pitched in 680 games, had a won/loss record of 79-57, 210 saves, 1074 innings, and 1074 innings with an earned run average of 2.57.

Achievements:

- 1- Time Led in games pitched: (1977) & 2-Times Led in games finished (1972/1977).
- 2-Times Led A.L. in saves (1972 & 1976) & 3-Times All-Star (1973, 1976 & 1977).
- 2-Times received Cy Young Votes: (1972 & 1977 (Winning the Award).
- 4-Times received Most Valuable Player Votes (1972, 1974. 1976 & 1977)

Hall of Fame

Sparky Lyle was on the Hall of Fame Ballot from 1988 through and was dropped off futures ballots in 1991.

Summary Analysis

Sparky Lyle's Hall of Fame Point total is 92.550. He was a very good pitcher and a trailblazer for relief pitchers. He needs to be voted into the Baseball Hall of Fame.

A Fan's Perspective

Lyle, Sparky — **Pitcher - Left Handed Potential Hall of Fame Inductee**

Positions: Pitcher

Born:	July 22, 1944	Height:	6' 1" USC 185 cm
From:	Du Bois, PA	Weight:	182 lbs. 82 Kg.
Bats:	Left	Debut:	July 4, 1967
Throws:	Left	Last Game:	September 27, 1982

Year	Age	Tm	Lg	W	L	PCT	ERA	G	GS	GF	CG	SHO	SV	IP	H	R	ER	BB	SO	BF	WHIP	Awards
1967	22	BOS	AL	1	2	0.333	2.28	27	0	11	0	0	5	43.1	33	13	11	14	42	173	1.085	
1968	23	BOS	AL	6	1	0.857	2.74	49	0	29	0	0	11	65.2	67	25	20	14	52	274	1.234	
1969	24	BOS	AL	8	3	0.727	2.54	71	0	44	0	0	17	102.2	91	33	29	48	93	439	1.354	
1970	25	BOS	AL	1	7	0.125	3.88	63	0	40	0	0	20	67.1	62	37	29	34	51	297	1.426	
1971	26	BOS	AL	6	4	0.600	2.75	50	0	36	0	0	16	52.1	41	16	16	23	37	209	1.223	
1972	27	NYY	AL	9	5	0.643	1.92	59	0	56	0	0	35	107.2	84	25	23	29	75	427	1.050	CYA-7,MVP-3
1973	28	NYY	AL	5	9	0.357	2.51	51	0	45	0	0	27	82.1	66	30	23	18	63	330	1.020	AS
1974	29	NYY	AL	9	3	0.750	1.66	66	0	59	0	0	15	114	93	30	21	43	89	469	1.193	MVP-25
1975	30	NYY	AL	5	7	0.417	3.12	49	0	37	0	0	6	89.1	94	34	31	36	65	387	1.455	
1976	31	NYY	AL	7	8	0.467	2.26	64	0	58	0	0	23	103.2	82	33	26	42	61	420	1.196	AS,MVP-22
1977	32	NYY	AL	13	5	0.722	2.17	72	0	60	0	0	26	137	131	41	33	33	68	554	1.197	AS,CYA-1,MVP-6
1978	33	NYY	AL	9	3	0.750	3.47	59	0	33	0	0	9	111.2	116	46	43	33	33	470	1.334	
1979	34	TEX	AL	5	8	0.385	3.13	67	0	53	0	0	13	95	78	37	33	28	48	384	1.116	
1980	35	TOT	MLB	3	2	0.600	4.28	59	0	37	0	0	10	94.2	108	52	45	34	49	412	1.500	
1980	35	TEX	AL	3	2	0.600	4.69	49	0	32	0	0	8	80.2	97	47	42	28	43	353	1.550	
1980	35	PHI	NL	0	0	0.000	1.93	10	0	5	0	0	2	14	11	5	3	6	6	59	1.214	
1981	36	PHI	NL	9	6	0.600	4.44	48	0	19	0	0	2	75	85	40	37	33	29	332	1.573	
1982	37	TOT	MLB	3	3	0.500	4.62	45	0	17	0	0	3	48.2	61	27	25	19	18	217	1.644	
1982	37	PHI	NL	3	3	0.500	5.15	34	0	11	0	0	2	36.2	50	23	21	12	12	167	1.691	
1982	37	CHW	AL	0	0	0.000	3.00	11	0	6	0	0	1	12	0.2	4	4	7	6	50	1.500	
162 Game Avg.				7	6	0.566	2.88	68	0	48	0	0	18	105	98	39	34	36	66	438	1.275	
NYY (7 yrs)				57	40	0.588	2.41	420	0	348	0	0	141	745.2	666	239	200	234	454	3057	1.207	
BOS (5 yrs)				22	17	0.564	2.85	260	0	160	0	0	69	331.1	294	124	105	133	275	1392	1.289	
PHI (3 yrs)				12	9	0.571	4.37	92	0	35	0	0	6	125.2	146	68	61	51	47	558	1.568	
TEX (2 yrs)				8	10	0.444	3.84	116	0	85	0	0	21	175.2	175	84	75	56	91	737	1.315	
CHW (1 yr)				0	0	0.000	3.00	11	0	6	0	0	1	12	11	4	4	7	6	50	1.500	
AL (13 yrs)				87	67	0.565	2.73	807	0	599	0	0	232	1264	1146	451	384	430	826	5236	1.246	
NL (3 yrs)				12	9	0.571	4.37	92	0	35	0	0	6	125.2	146	68	61	51	47	558	1.568	
16 Yrs				99	76	0.566	2.88	899	0	634	0	0	238	1390	1292	519	445	481	873	5794	1.275	**Career Pts.**
				2.500	0.000	6.750	12.500	13.000	0.000	10.500	0.000	0.000	6.750	2.000	0.000	0.000	0.000	0.000	2.000	0.000	6.750	**62.750**

Post Season Pts.

Year	Age	Team	Series	W	L	PCT	ERA	G	GS	GF	CG	SHO	SV	IP	H	R	ER	BB	SO	BF	WHIP	
1976	31	NYY	ALCS	0	0	0.000	0.000	1	0	1	0	0	1	1	0	0	0	1	0	4	1.000	
1977	32	NYY	ALCS	2	0	1.000	0.960	4	0	4	0	0	0	9.1	7	1	1	0	3	32	0.750	
1978	33	NYY	ALCS	0	0	0.000	13.500	1	0	1	0	0	0	1.1	3	2	2	0	0	7	2.250	
				2	0	1.000	1.690	6	0	6	0	0	1	11.2	10	3	3	1	9	43	0.938	**Post Season Pts.**
				0.250	0.000	0.400	1.800	0.400	0.000	0.600	0.000	0.000	0.250	0.400	0.000	0.000	0.000	0.000	0.250	0.000	2.000	**6.350**

World Series Play

Year	Age	Team	Series	W	L	PCT	ERA	G	GS	GF	CG	SHO	SV	IP	H	R	ER	BB	SO	BF	WHIP	
1976	31	NYY	WS	0	0	0.000	0.000	2	0	2	0	0	0	2.2	1	0	0	0	3	10	0.375	
1977	32	NYY	WS	1	0	1.000	1.930	2	0	2	0	0	0	4.2	2	1	1	0	2	16	0.429	
1978	33	NYY	WS	0	0	0.000	0.000	0	0	0	0	0	0	0	0	0	0	0	0	0	0.000	
				1	0	1.000	1.230	4	0	4	0	0	0	6.4	3	1	1	0	5	26	0.481	**World Series Pts.**
				0.250	0.000	0.400	0.250	0.400	0.000	0.400	0.000	0.000	0.000	0.250	0.000	0.000	0.000	0.000	0.250	0.000	0.250	**2.450**

Yearly Points Leading the League

Category	Times	Points	Total
MVP	0	7	0
ROY	0	5	0
Cy Young	1	5	5
Golden Glove	0	3	0
All-Star	3	2	6
Wins	0	3	0
Totals			11

Category	Times	Points	Total
Saves	2	3	6
ERA	0	3	0
S.O.'s	0	2	0
Games	1	2	2
G.S.	1	2	0
C.G.	0	2	0
Totals			8

Category	Times	Points	Total
SHO	0	2	0
WinPct	0	2	0
Innings	0	2	0
WHIP	0	2	0
GF	2	2	4
Totals			4
Grand Total Add-On Points			23

Hall of Fame Points

Career Points	62.750
Post Season Points	6.350
World Series Points	2.450
Career Add-On Points	23.000
Writers Association Pts.	0.000
Military/Lifetime Achievement	0.000
Grand Total HOF Points	94.550

Pettitte, Andy

Personal Life

Andrew Eugene Pettitte was born June 15, 1972, born to Tommy Pettitte and JoAnn Martello. He has a younger sister Robin and attended Deer Park High School.

Pettitte married Laura Dunn in 1992 with the couple having four children, Josh, Jared, Lexy, and Luke.

Baseball Career

The Yankees selected Pettitte in the 22nd round of the 1990 Major League Baseball draft and moved up the Yankees until called up to the majors in 1995. Pettitte would finish his career with a 256-153 record, 3.85 ERA, 531 Games, 3316 Innings, 2448 Strikeouts, and a Career postseason: 19-11, 3.81 ERA in 276.2 IP.

Achievements:

- 2-Times won 20 games (1996 & 2003).
- 13 Times won 14 games or more (1996 – 2001, 2003, 2005 – 2009).
- 3-Times led in games started (A.L. 1997& 2007 & 2006).
- 3-time All-Star (2006, 2001, 2010) & 2-Times received MVP Votes (1996 & 2005).
- 5 times in the top 6 of Cy Young Award voting (1996, 1997, 2000, 2003, & 2005).
- 8-World Series appearances with the Yankees (1996, 1998, 1999-2001, 2003, & 2009)
- Won 5 Championships & 1-World Series with the Houston Astros (2005).

Hall of Fame

Petites first appeared on the ballot in 2019 receiving just 9.9% of the vote on the BBWAA ballot. In his five years on the ballot, his best was 17.0 in 2023.

Summary Analysis

Andy Pettitte's Hall of Fame Point total is 94.150. After being identified as using HGH, Pettitte admitted to being injected with the substance that wasn't banned at the time and that he believed that he was taking to recover more quickly from an elbow injury. Pettitte should be elected to the baseball Hall of Fame.

Pettite, Andy — Pitcher - Left Handed Potential Hall of Fame Inductee

Positions: Pitcher	Born: June 15, 1972
Bats: Left	From: Baton Rouge, LA
Throws: Left	Debut: April 29, 1995
	Last Game: September 23, 2013
Height: 6'5" / 196 cm	Weight: 235 lbs / 106 Kg

Year	Age	Tm	Lg	W	L	PCT	ERA	G	GS	GF	CG	SHO	SV	IP	H	R	ER	BB	SO	BF	WHIP	Awards
1995	23	NYY	AL	12	9	0.571	4.170	31	28	1	3	0	0	175	183	86	81	63	114	745	1.406	RoY-3
1996	24	NYY	AL	21	8	0.724	3.870	35	34	1	2	0	0	221	229	105	95	72	162	929	1.362	AS,CYA-2,MVP-14
1997	25	NYY	AL	18	7	0.720	2.880	35	35	0	4	1	0	240.1	233	86	77	65	166	966	1.240	CYA-5
1998	26	NYY	AL	16	11	0.593	4.240	33	32	0	5	0	0	216.1	226	110	102	87	146	932	1.467	
1999	27	NYY	AL	14	11	0.560	4.700	31	31	0	0	0	0	191.2	216	105	100	89	121	851	1.591	
2000	28	NYY	AL	19	9	0.679	4.350	32	32	0	3	1	0	204.2	219	111	99	80	125	903	1.461	CYA-4
2001	29	NYY	AL	15	10	0.600	3.990	31	31	0	2	0	0	200.2	224	103	89	41	164	858	1.321	AS
2002	30	NYY	AL	13	5	0.722	3.270	22	22	0	3	1	0	134.2	144	58	49	32	97	570	1.307	
2003	31	NYY	AL	21	8	0.724	4.020	33	33	0	1	0	0	208.1	227	109	93	50	180	896	1.330	CYA-6
2004	32	HOU	NL	6	4	0.600	3.900	15	15	0	0	0	0	83	71	37	36	31	79	346	1.229	
2005	33	HOU	NL	17	9	0.654	2.390	33	33	0	0	0	0	222.1	188	66	59	41	171	875	1.030	CYA-5,MVP-24
2006	34	HOU	NL	14	13	0.519	4.200	36	35	1	2	1	0	214.1	238	114	100	70	178	929	1.437	
2007	35	NYY	AL	15	9	0.625	4.050	36	34	0	0	0	0	215.1	238	106	97	89	141	916	1.426	
2008	36	NYY	AL	14	14	0.500	4.540	35	33	0	0	0	0	204	233	112	103	55	158	881	1.412	
2009	37	NYY	AL	14	8	0.636	4.160	32	32	0	0	0	0	194.2	193	101	90	76	148	834	1.382	
2010	38	NYY	AL	11	3	0.786	3.280	21	21	0	0	0	0	129	123	52	47	41	101	536	1.271	AS
2012	40	NYY	AL	5	4	0.556	2.870	12	12	0	0	0	0	75.1	65	26	24	11	68	303	1.143	
2012	40	NYY	AL	3	4	0.556	2.870	12	12	0	0	0	0	75.1	65	26	24	21	69	303	1.143	
2013	41	NYY	AL	11	11	0.500	3.740	30	30	0	1	0	0	185.1	198	85	77	48	138	784	1.327	
162 Games Avg.				17	10	0.626	3.850	34	34	0	2	0	0	214	223	102	82	67	158	910	1.351	
NYY (15 yrs)				219	127	0.633	3.940	447	438	2	24	3	0	2796	2951	1355	1223	889	2020	11924	1.373	
HOU (3 yrs)				37	26	0.587	3.380	84	83	1	2	1	0	519.1	497	217	195	142	428	2150	1.330	
AL (15 yrs)				219	127	0.633	3.940	447	438	2	24	3	0	2796	2951	1355	1223	889	2020	11924	1.373	
NL (3 yrs)				37	26	0.587	3.380	84	83	1	2	1	0	519.2	497	217	195	142	428	2150	1.23	
18 Yrs				256	159	0.626	3.85	531	521	3	26	4	0	3316	3448	1572	1418	1031	2448	14074	1.351	Career Pts.
				10.500	0.800	11.750	3.000	4.500	10.500	0.000	1.000	0.500	0.000	9.250	0.000	0.000	0.000	0.000	6.750	0.000	3.750	61.500

Post Seasonal Play

Year	Age	Team	Series	W	L	PCT	ERA	G	GS	GF	CG	SHO	SV	IP	H	R	ER	BB	SO	BF	WHIP	
1995	23	NYY	ALDS	0	0	0.000	5.14	1	1	0	0	0	0	7	8	4	4	3	0	30	1.714	
1996	24	NYY	ALDS	0	0	0.000	5.68	1	1	0	0	0	0	6.1	4	8	4	6	3	28	1.579	
1996	24	NYY	ALCS	1	0	1.000	3.60	2	2	0	0	0	0	15	10	6	5	7	7	60	1.000	
1997	25	NYY	ALDS	0	2	0.000	8.49	2	2	0	0	0	0	11.2	15	11	11	1	3	49	1.371	
1998	26	NYY	ALDS	1	0	1.000	1.29	1	1	0	0	0	0	7	5	1	1	0	8	24	0.429	
1998	26	NYY	ALCS	0	1	0.000	11.57	1	1	0	0	0	0	4.2	8	6	6	3	1	25	2.357	
1999	27	NYY	ALDS	1	0	1.000	1.23	1	1	0	0	0	0	7.1	7	1	1	0	5	29	0.955	
1999	27	NYY	ALCS	1	0	1.000	2.45	1	1	0	0	0	0	7.1	8	2	2	1	5	28	1.227	
2000	28	NYY	ALDS	1	0	1.000	3.97	2	2	0	0	0	0	11.1	15	5	5	3	7	51	1.588	
2000	28	NYY	ALCS	1	0	1.000	2.70	1	1	0	0	0	0	6.2	9	2	2	1	2	28	1.500	
2001	29	NYY	ALDS	0	1	0.000	1.42	1	1	0	0	0	0	6.1	7	1	1	2	4	28	1.421	
2001	29	NYY	ALCS	2	0	1.000	2.51	2	2	0	0	0	0	14.1	11	4	4	2	8	54	0.907	
2002	30	NYY	ALDS	0	0	0.000	12.00	1	1	0	0	0	0	3	8	4	4	0	1	17	2.667	
2003	31	NYY	ALDS	1	0	1.000	1.29	1	1	0	0	0	0	7	4	1	1	3	10	29	1.000	
2003	31	NYY	ALCS	1	0	1.000	4.63	2	2	0	0	0	0	11.2	17	8	6	4	10	54	1.800	
2005	33	HOU	NLDS	1	0	1.000	3.64	1	1	0	0	0	0	7	4	3	3	2	6	26	0.857	
2005	33	HOU	NLCS	0	1	0.000	5.11	2	2	0	0	0	0	12.1	15	7	7	4	6	55	1.541	
2007	35	NYY	ALDS	0	0	0.000	0.00	1	1	0	0	0	0	6.1	7	0	0	3	5	25	1.421	
2009	37	NYY	ALDS	1	0	1.000	1.42	1	1	0	0	0	0	6.1	3	1	1	1	7	23	0.632	
2009	37	NYY	ALCS	1	0	1.000	2.84	2	2	0	0	0	0	12.2	14	4	4	2	8	49	1.263	
2010	38	NYY	ALDS	1	0	1.000	2.57	1	1	0	0	0	0	7	5	2	2	1	4	28	0.857	
2010	38	NYY	ALCS	0	1	0.000	2.57	1	1	0	0	0	0	7	5	2	2	0	5	26	0.714	
2012	40	NYY	ALDS	0	1	0.000	3.86	1	1	0	0	0	0	7	7	3	3	1	5	30	1.143	
2012	40	NYY	ALCS	0	0	0.000	2.70	1	1	0	0	0	0	6.2	7	2	2	3	5	29	1.500	
				14	7	0.667	3.80	31	31	0	0	0	0	194.1	202	82	83	50	127	823	1.297	Post Season Pts.
				1.400	0.000	0.250	0.600	2.000	2.000	0.000	0.000	0.000	0.000	2.000	0.000	0.000	0.000	0.000	2.000	0.000	0.800	11.050

World Series Play

Year	Age	Team	Series	W	L	W-L%	ERA	G	GS	GF	CG	SHO	SV	IP	H	R	ER	BB	SO	BF	WHIP	
1996	24	NYY	WS	1	1	0.500	5.91	2	2	0	0	0	0	10.2	11	7	7	4	5	45	1.406	
1998	26	NYY	WS	1	0	1.000	0.00	1	1	0	0	0	0	7.1	5	0	0	3	4	29	1.091	
1999	27	NYY	WS	0	0	0.000	12.27	1	1	0	0	0	0	3.2	10	5	5	1	3	21	3.000	
2000	28	NYY	WS	0	0	0.000	1.98	2	2	0	0	0	0	13.2	16	3	3	4	9	90	1.463	
2001	29	NYY	WS	0	2	0.000	10.00	2	2	0	0	0	0	9	12	10	10	2	9	40	1.556	
2003	31	NYY	WS	1	1	0.500	0.57	2	2	0	0	0	0	15.2	12	3	1	4	14	60	1.021	
2005	33	HOU	WS	0	0	0.000	3.00	1	1	0	0	0	0	6	4	2	2	0	4	25	1.333	
2009	37	NYY	WS	2	0	1.000	3.60	2	2	0	0	0	0	11.1	8	7	7	7	10	51	1.457	
				5	4	0.555	4.18	13	13	0	0	0	0	75.1	83	37	35	26	58	334	1.447	World Series Pts.
				1.000	0.000	0.000	0.400	1.200	1.200	0.000	0.000	0.000	0.000	1.000	0.000	0.000	0.000	0.000	1.400	0.000	0.400	8.600

Yearly Points Leading the League

Category	Times	Points	Total
MVP	0	7	0
ROY	0	5	0
Cy Young	0	5	0
Golden Glove	0	3	0
All-Star	3	2	6
Wins	1	3	3
Totals			9

Category	Times	Points	Total
Saves	0	5	0
ERA	0	3	0
S.O.'s	0	2	0
Games	0	2	0
G.S.	3	2	6
C.G.	0	2	0
Totals			6

Career	Times	Points	Total
SHO	0	2	0
WhnPc	0	2	0
Inning	0	2	0
WHIP	0	2	0
GF	0	2	0
Totals			0
Grand Total Add-On Points		15	

Hall of Fame Points	
Career Points	61.500
Post Season Points	11.050
World Series Points	6.600
Career Add-On Points	15.000
Writers Association Pts.	0.000
Military/Lifetime Achievement	0.000
Grand Total HOF Points	94.150

Valenzuela, Fernando "El Toro"

Personal Life

Fernando Valenzuela Anguamea was born November 1, 1960 in Etchohuaquila, in the state of Sonora, Mexico to Avelino and María. He has 5 sisters and 6 brothers.

In 1981, Valenzuela married Linda Burgos, and the couple have four children. Sons, Fernando, Jr., & Ricardo and daughters Maria Fernanda and Linda, Ricardo.

Baseball Career

Valenzuela was signed by the Dodgers on July 6, 1979, and called up to the Dodgers bullpen in 1980. He helped the Dodgers tie with the Astros and in 1981, He won his first eight starts and finished 13–7 and had a 2.48 ERA becoming the only, player to win both Cy Young and Rookie of the Year awards in the same season. Valenzuela retired from baseball after the 1997 season with a final record of 173–153 and a 3.54 ERA.

Achievements:

- 1981 NL Rookie of the Year Award &15 Wins Seasons: 4 (1982, 1983, 1985 & 1986).
- 6-time NL All-Star: (1981-1986) & 1981 NL Cy Young Award Winner.
- NL Gold Glove Winner (1986) & NL Wins Leader (1986)
- NL Innings Pitched Leader (1981) & NL Strikeouts Leader (1981)
- 3-time NL Complete Games Leader (1981, 1986 & 1987)
- 20 Wins Seasons: 1 (1986) & 200 Strikeouts Seasons: 3 (1984-1986)
- 200 Innings Pitched Seasons: 7 (1982-1987 & 1990)
- Won 2 World Series with the Los Angeles Dodgers in 1981 and 1988.

Hall of Fame

Fernando Valenzuela first appeared on the Hall of Fame ballot in 2004. He only received 19 votes for 3.8% and was removed from future voting by the BBWAA

Summary Analysis

Fernando Valenzuela's Hall of Fame Point total is 94.150. When looking at Valenzuela's career overall, he does not have the numbers for induction.

Pitcher - Left Handed Potential Hall of Fame Inductee

Valenzuela, Fernando

Positions		Born:	November 1, 1980	Height:	5' 11" USC 180 cm
Pitcher		From:	Navaijo, Mexico	Weight:	180 lbs. 81 Kg.
		Bats:	Left	Debut	September 15, 1980
		Throws:	Left	Last Game:	July 14, 1997

Year	Age	Tm	Lg	W	L	PCT	ERA	G	GS	GF	CG	SHO	SV	IP	H	R	ER	BB	SO	BF	WHIP	Awards
1980	19	LAD	NL	2	0	1.000	0.00	10	0	4	0	0	1	17.2	8	2	0	5	16	66	0.736	
1981	20	LAD	NL	13	7	0.650	2.48	25	25	0	11	8	0	192.1	140	55	53	61	180	758	1.045	AS,CYA-1,MVP-
1982	21	LAD	NL	19	13	0.594	2.87	37	37	0	18	4	0	285	247	105	91	83	199	1156	1.158	AS,CYA-3,MVP-21
1983	22	LAD	NL	15	10	0.600	3.75	35	35	0	9	4	0	257	245	122	107	99	189	1094	1.339	AS,SS
1984	23	LAD	NL	12	17	0.414	3.03	34	34	0	12	2	0	261	218	109	88	106	240	1078	1.241	AS
1985	24	LAD	NL	17	10	0.630	2.45	35	35	0	14	5	0	272.1	211	92	74	101	208	1109	1.146	AS,CYA-5,MVP-23
1986	25	LAD	NL	21	11	0.656	3.14	34	34	0	20	3	0	269.1	226	104	94	85	242	1102	1.155	19,GG
1987	26	LAD	NL	14	14	0.500	3.98	34	34	0	12	1	0	251	254	120	111	124	190	1116	1.506	
1988	27	LAD	NL	5	8	0.385	4.24	23	22	1	3	0	1	142.1	142	71	67	76	64	626	1.532	
1989	28	LAD	NL	10	13	0.435	3.43	31	31	0	3	0	0	196.2	185	89	75	98	116	852	1.439	
1990	29	LAD	NL	13	13	0.500	4.59	33	33	0	5	2	0	204	223	112	104	77	115	900	1.471	
1991	30	CAL	AL	0	2	0.000	12.15	2	2	0	0	0	0	6.2	14	10	9	3	5	36	2.550	
1992											Did not play in major or minor leagues (Mexico)											
1993	32	BAL	AL	8	10	0.444	4.940	32	31	0	5	2	0	178.2	179	104	98	79	78	768	1.444	
1994	33	PHI	NL	1	2	0.333	3.000	8	7	0	0	0	0	45	42	16	15	7	19	182	1.089	
1995	34	SDP	NL	8	3	0.727	4.980	29	15	5	0	0	0	90.1	101	53	50	34	57	395	1.494	
1996	35	SDP	NL	13	8	0.619	3.620	33	31	0	0	0	0	171.2	177	78	69	67	95	741	1.421	
1997	36	TOT	NL	2	12	0.143	4.960	18	18	0	1	0	0	89	106	61	49	46	61	419	1.708	
1997	36	SDP	NL	2	8	0.200	4.750	13	13	0	1	0	0	66.1	84	42	35	32	51	313	1.749	
1997	36	STL	NL	0	4	0.000	5.560	5	5	0	0	0	0	22.2	22	19	14	14	10	106	1.588	
162 Game Avg.				13	12	0.531	3.540	35	33	1	9	2	0	227	211	101	89	89	161	961	1.320	
LAD (11 yrs)				141	116	0.549	3.310	331	320	5	107	29	2	2348	2099	981	864	915	1759	9857	1.283	
SDP (3 yrs)				23	19	0.548	4.220	75	59	5	1	0	0	328.1	362	173	154	133	203	1449	1.508	
PHI (1 yr)				1	2	0.333	3.000	8	7	0	0	0	0	45	42	16	15	7	19	182	1.089	
STL (1 yr)				0	4	0.000	5.560	5	5	0	0	0	0	22.2	22	19	14	14	10	106	1.588	
CAL (1 yr)				0	2	0.000	12.150	2	2	0	0	0	0	6.2	14	10	9	3	5	36	2.550	
BAL (1 yr)				8	10	0.444	4.940	32	31	0	5	2	0	178.2	179	104	98	79	78	768	1.444	
NL (15 yrs)				165	141	0.539	3.430	419	391	10	108	29	2	2744	2525	1189	1047	1069	1991	11594	1.309	
AL (2 yrs)				8	12	0.400	5.200	34	33	0	5	2	0	185.1	193	114	107	82	83	804	1.484	
17 Yrs				173	153	0.531	3.54	453	424	10	113	31	2	2930	2718	1303	1154	1151	2074	12398	1.320	Post Season Pts.
				5.500	0.000	4.500	5.750	3.750	6.750	0.500	2.500	3.750	0.000	6.750	0.000	0.000	0.000	0.000	5.500	0.000	4.500	49.750

Post Seasonal Play

Year	Age	Team	Series	W	L	PCT.	ERA	G	GS	GF	CG	SHO	SV	IP	H	R	ER	BB	SO	BF	WHIP	
1981	20	LAD	NLCS	1	0	1.000	1.06	2	2	0	1	0	0	17	10	2	2	3	10	62	0.765	
1981	20	LAD	NLCS	1	1	0.500	2.45	2	2	0	0	0	0	14.2	10	4	4	5	10	57	1.023	
1983	22	LAD	NLCS	1	0	1.000	1.13	1	1	0	0	0	0	8	7	1	1	4	5	33	1.375	
1985	24	LAD	NLCS	1	0	1.000	1.88	2	2	0	0	0	0	14.1	11	3	3	10	13	63	1.465	
1996	35	SDP	NLDS	0	0	0.000	0.00	1	0	0	0	0	0	0.2	0	0	0	2	0	4	3.000	
				4	1	0.800	1.68	8	7	0	1	0	0	53.5	38	10	10	24	38	219	1.159	Post Season Pts.
				0.400	0.000	1.000	1.800	0.800	0.800	0.000	0.250	0.000	0.000	1.000	0.000	0.000	0.000	0.000	0.800	0.000	1.400	8.250

World Series Play

Year	Age	Team	Series	W	L	PCT	ERA	G	GS	GF	CG	SHO	SV	IP	H	R	ER	BB	SO	BF	WHIP	
1981	20	LAD	NL	1	0	1	4.00	1	1	0	1	0	0	9	9	4	4	7	6	40	1.778	
				1	0	1	4.00	1	1	0	1	0	0	9	9	4	4	7	6	40	1.778	World Series Pts.
				0.250	0.000	0.250	0.400	0.250	0.250	0.000	0.250	0.000	0.000	0.250	0.000	0.000	0.000	0.000	0.250	0.000	0.000	2.150

Yearly Points Leading the League

Category	Times	Points	Total	Category	Times	Points	Total	Category	Times	Points	Total
MVP	0	7	0	Saves	0	3	0	SHO	1	2	2
ROY	0	5	0	ERA	0	3	0	WinPct	0	2	0
Cy Young	1	5	5	S.O.'s	1	2	2	Innings	1	2	2
Golden Glove	0	3	0	Games	0	2	0	WHIP	0	2	0
All-Star	6	2	12	G.S.	1	2	2	GF	0	2	0
Wins	1	3	3	C.G.	3	2	6	Totals			4
Totals			20	Totals			10	Grand Total Add-On Points			34

Hall of Fame Points	
Career Points	49.750
Post Season Points	8.250
World Series Points	2.150
Career Add-On Points	34.000
Writers Association Pts.	0.000
Military/Lifetime Achievement	0.000
Grand Total HOF Points	94.150

Vaughn, James's "Hippo"

Personal Life

James Leslie "Hippo" Vaughn was born in Weatherford, Texas, April 9, 1888 as one of eight children *to* Josephine and Thomas Vaughn.

Vaughn married Edna Coburn DeBold on February 11, 1916. No information was found on whether the couple had any children.

Baseball Career

Hippo Vaughn began his career with the New York Highlanders in 1908 and traded to the Washington Senators 1912. On May 2, 1917, was the losing pitcher in baseball's only double no-hitter facing the Cincinnati Reds. From 1914 to 1920, Vaughn was the best lefty in the National League. In 1921, he went 3–11 with a 6.01 ERA on July 9 and was suspended. The Cubs attempted to reinstate him but commissioner Landis barred him for having signed a contract with a semi-pro team in Wisconsin, finding it to be a violation of his contract with the Cubs. Vaughn finished with 178 wins, 390 games, and a 2.49 ERA. He pitched in the minor and semi-pro leagues with a record of 223–145.

Achievements:

- NL Pitcher's Triple Crown (1918), NL ERA Leader (1918), NL Wins Leader (1918)
- 2-time NL Innings Pitched Leader & Strikeouts Leader (1918 & 1919)
- NL Shutouts Leader (1918) & 15 Wins Seasons: 7 (1914-1920)
- 5-Times 20 Wins Seasons: (1914, 1915 & 1917-1919).
- 8-Times 200 Innings Pitched Seasons: (1910 & 1914-1920) w/300 IP (1919 & 1920).

Hall of Fame

No indication that Hippo Vaughn was ever brought up for a vote by the BBWAA.

Summary Analysis

James's "Hippo" Vaughn's Hall of Fame Point total is 97.050. The decision is ultimately up to the Baseball Hall of Fame's selection committee. Landis' suspension of Vaughn from 2021 to 2031 was the reason his MLB career was cut short.

Pitcher - Left Handed Potential Hall of Fame Inductee

Vaughn, Hippo

Positions
Pitcher

Born:	April 9, 1888	Height:	6'4" USC 193 cm
Died:	May 29, 1966	Weight:	215 lbs. 97 Kg.
From:	Weatherford, TX	Debut	June 6, 1982
Bats:	Both	Last Game:	May 6, 1996
Throws:	Left		

Year	Age	Tm	Lg	W	L	PCT	ERA	G	GS	GF	CG	SHO	SV	IP	H	R	ER	BB	SO	BF	WHIP	Awards
1908	20	NYY	AL	0	0	0.000	3.860	2	0	1	0	0	0	2.1	1	1	1	4	2	10	2.14	
1910	22	NYY	AL	13	11	0.542	1.830	30	25	3	18	5	1	221.2	190	76	45	58	107	869	1.12	
1911	23	NYY	AL	8	10	0.444	4.390	26	19	3	10	0	0	145.2	158	92	71	54	74	618	1.46	
1912	24	TOT	AL	6	11	0.353	3.880	27	18	7	9	1	0	144	141	81	62	80	95	631	1.54	
1912	24	NYY	AL	2	8	0.200	5.140	15	10	3	5	1	0	63	66	48	36	37	46	288	1.64	
1912	24	WSH	AL	4	3	0.571	2.890	12	8	4	4	0	0	81	75	33	26	43	49	343	1.46	
1913	25	CHC	NL	5	1	0.833	1.450	7	6	1	5	2	0	56	37	13	9	27	36	235	1.14	
1914	26	CHC	NL	21	13	0.618	2.050	42	35	6	23	4	1	293.2	236	119	67	109	165	1209	1.18	
1915	27	CHC	NL	20	12	0.625	2.870	41	34	6	18	4	1	269.2	240	105	86	77	148	1123	1.18	
1916	28	CHC	NL	17	15	0.531	2.200	44	35	9	21	4	1	294	269	94	72	67	144	1191	1.14	
1917	29	CHC	NL	23	13	0.639	2.010	41	38	2	27	5	0	295.2	255	97	66	91	195	1216	1.17	
1918	30	CHC	NL	22	10	0.688	1.740	35	33	2	27	8	0	290.1	216	75	56	76	148	1146	1.01	
1919	31	CHC	NL	21	14	0.600	1.790	38	37	1	25	4	1	306.2	264	83	61	62	141	1224	1.05	
1920	32	CHC	NL	19	16	0.543	2.540	40	38	2	24	4	0	301	301	113	85	81	131	1255	1.27	
1921	33	CHC	NL	3	11	0.214	6.010	17	14	2	7	0	0	109.1	153	90	73	31	30	500	1.68	
162 Game Avg.				17	13	0.565	2.490	37	31	4	20	4	0	257	232	98	71	77	133	1057	1.20	
CHC (9 yrs)				151	105	0.590	2.330	305	270	31	177	35	4	2216	1971	789	575	621	1138	9097	1.17	
NYY (4 yrs)				23	29	0.442	3.180	73	54	10	33	6	1	432.2	415	217	153	153	229	1785	1.31	
WSH (1 yr)				4	3	0.571	2.89	12	8	4	4	0	0	81	75	33	26	43	49	343	1.46	
NL (9 yrs)				151	105	0.590	2.33	305	270	31	177	35	4	2216	1971	789	575	621	1138	9097	1.17	
AL (4 yrs)				27	32	0.458	3.14	85	62	14	37	6	1	513.2	490	250	179	196	278	2128	1.335	
13 Yrs				178	137	0.565	2.49	390	332	45	214	41	5	2730	2461	1039	754	817	1416	11225	1.201	Career Pts.
				5.500	0.000	6.750	15.000	3.000	4.500	0.500	5.500	5.500	0.500	5.500	0.000	0.000	0.000	0.000	3.000	0.000	9.250	64.500

Post Seasonal Play

Year	Age	Team	Series	W	L	PCT.	ERA	G	GS	GF	CG	SHO	SV	IP	H	R	ER	BB	SO	BF	WHIP	
None				0	0	0.000	0	0	0	0	0	0	0	0	0	0	0	0	0	0	0	
				0	0	0.000	0	0	0	0	0	0	0	0	0	0	0	0	0	0	0	Post Season Pts.
				0.000	0.000	0.000	0.000	0.000	0.000	0.000	0.000	0.000	0.000	0.000	0.000	0.000	0.000	0.000	0.000	0.000	0.000	0.000

World Series Play

Year	Age	Team	Series	W	L	PCT.	ERA	G	GS	GF	CG	SHO	SV	IP	H	R	ER	BB	SO	BF	WHIP	
1918	30	Chi	NL	1	2	0.333	1.00	3	3	0	3	1	0	27	17	3	3	5	17	97	1.034	
				1	2	0.333	1.00	3	3	0	3	1	0	27	17	3	3	5	17	97	1.034	World Series Pts.
				0.250	0.000	0.000	2.0000	0.250	0.400	0.000	0.600	0.250	0.000	0.400	0.000	0.000	0.000	0.000	0.600	0.000	1.800	6.550

Yearly Points Leading the League

Category	Times	Points	Total	Category	Times	Points	Total	Category	Times	Points	Total	Hall of Fame Points	
MVP	0	7	0	Saves	0	3	0	SHO	1	2	2	Career Points	64.500
ROY	0	5	0	ERA	1	3	3	WinPct	0	2	0	Post Season Points	0.000
Cy Young	0	5	0	S.O.'s	2	2	4	Innings	2	2	4	World Series Points	6.550
Golden Glove	0	3	0	Games	0	2	0	WHIP	1	2	2	Career Add-On Points	26.000
All-Star	0	2	0	G.S.	2	2	4	GF	0	2	0	Writers Association Pts.	0.000
Wins	1	3	3	C.G.	2	2	4	Totals			8	Military/Lifetime Achievement	0.000
Totals			3	Totals			15	Grand Total Add-On Points		26		Grand Total HOF Points	97.050

Wagner, William "Billy the Kid"

Personal Life

William Edward "Billy" Wagner was born July 25, 1971, to Bill "Hotrod" Wagner and Yvonne Hall in Marion, Virginia. He has a sister Chastity, born in 1974.

Wagner's life took a positive turn at 14, when he moved in with his aunt, uncle, and cousins, who lived in the Tannersville/Tazewell area. In his senior year, he had a breakout season compiling a 7-1 pitching record with 116 strikeouts in 46 innings and a 1.52 ERA. Wagner followed his cousin to College where his coach had him concentrate on baseball. Wagner led the nation, averaging 19.1 strikeouts per nine innings.

Wagner married Sarah Quesenberry in December 1995. The couple have four children Will, Jeremy, Olivia, and Kason.

Baseball Career

The Houston Astros drafted him with the 12th pick in the first round of the 1993 draft. Wagner began his career in the minors with the Astros adding him to their 40-man roster in September 1995 after he learned his wife's parents were brutally murdered. Wagner left to be with his family and when he returned, made his MLB debut on September 13, 1995. Wagner played 16 seasons in (MLB) pitching for the Houston, Philadelphia, New York Mets, Boston, and Atlanta. Wagner is one of eight relief pitchers to accumulate 400, or more saves. His 1999 season, in which he struck out 124 hitters in 74 innings with a 1.57 ERA, remains one of the best single-season performances. He retired in 2010 with a career WHIP under 1.000, the best since 1910.

Hall of Fame:

Billy Wager has been on the BBWAA ballot since 2016 with his highest total of votes being 68.1% in 2023, He has two more chances to be elected this way.

Summary Analysis

Billy Wagner's Hall of Fame Point Total is 106.950. There is no reason Wagner has had to go through 8 different elections. The BBWAA should vote Wagner in.

Pitcher - Left Handed Potential Hall of Fame Inductee

Wagner, Billy

Positions	Pitcher	Born:	July 25, 1971
		From:	Marion, VA
		Bats:	Left
		Throws:	Left

Height:	5' 10" USC 178 cm
Weight:	180 lbs. 81 Kg.
Debut:	September 13, 1995
Last Game:	October 3, 2010

Year	Age	Team	Lg	W	L	PCT	ERA	G	GS	GF	CG	SHO	SV	IP	H	R	ER	BB	SO	BF	WHIP	
1995	23	HOU	NL	0	0	0.000	0.00	1	0	0	0	0	0	0.1	0	0	0	0	0	1	0.000	
1996	24	HOU	NL	2	2	0.500	2.44	37	0	20	0	0	9	51.2	28	15	14	30	67	212	1.123	
1997	25	HOU	NL	7	8	0.467	2.85	62	0	49	0	0	23	66.1	49	23	21	30	106	277	1.191	
1998	26	HOU	NL	4	3	0.571	2.70	58	0	50	0	0	30	60	46	19	18	25	97	247	1.183	
1999	27	HOU	NL	4	1	0.800	1.57	66	0	55	0	0	39	74.2	35	14	13	23	124	286	0.777	AS,CYA-4,MVP-16
2000	28	HOU	NL	2	4	0.333	6.18	28	0	19	0	0	6	27.2	28	19	19	18	28	129	1.663	
2001	29	HOU	NL	2	5	0.286	2.73	64	0	58	0	0	39	62.2	44	19	19	20	79	251	1.021	AS
2002	30	HOU	NL	4	2	0.667	2.52	70	0	61	0	0	35	75	51	21	21	22	88	289	0.973	
2003	31	HOU	NL	1	4	0.200	1.78	78	0	67	0	0	44	86	52	18	17	23	105	335	0.872	AS,MVP-23
2004	32	PHI	NL	4	0	1.000	2.42	45	0	38	0	0	21	48.1	31	16	13	6	59	182	0.766	
2005	33	PHI	NL	4	3	0.571	1.51	75	0	70	0	0	38	77.2	45	17	13	20	87	297	0.837	AS
2006	34	NYM	NL	3	2	0.600	2.24	70	0	59	0	0	40	72.1	59	22	18	21	94	297	1.106	CYA-6
2007	35	NYM	NL	2	2	0.500	2.63	66	0	57	0	0	34	68.1	55	22	20	22	80	282	1.127	AS
2008	36	NYM	NL	0	1	0.000	2.30	45	0	34	0	0	27	47	32	17	12	10	52	184	0.894	AS
2009	37	TOT	MLB	1	1	0.500	1.72	17	0	2	0	0	0	15.2	8	5	3	8	26	63	1.021	
2009	37	NYM	NL	0	0	0.000	0.00	2	0	0	0	0	0	2	0	0	0	1	4	7	0.500	
2009	37	BOS	AL	1	1	0.500	1.98	15	0	2	0	0	0	13.2	8	5	3	7	22	56	1.098	
2010	38	ATL	NL	7	2	0.778	1.43	71	0	64	0	0	37	69.1	38	14	11	22	104	268	0.865	AS
162 Game Avg.				4	3	0.540	2.31	68	0	56	0	0	34	72	48	21	18	24	95	287	0.998	
HOU (9 yrs)				26	29	0.473	2.53	464	0	379	0	0	225	504.1	333	149	142	191	694	2027	1.039	
NYM (4 yrs)				5	5	0.500	2.37	183	0	150	0	0	101	189.2	146	61	50	54	230	770	1.054	
PHI (2 yrs)				8	3	0.727	1.86	120	0	108	0	0	59	126	76	33	26	26	146	479	0.810	
ATL (1 yr)				7	2	0.778	1.43	71	0	64	0	0	37	69.1	38	14	11	22	104	268	0.865	
BOS (1 yr)				1	1	0.500	1.98	15	0	2	0	0	0	13.2	8	5	3	7	22	56	1.098	
NL (18 yrs)				46	39	0.541	2.32	838	0	701	0	0	422	889.1	593	257	229	293	1174	3544	0.996	
AL (1 yr)				1	1	0.541	1.98	15	0	2	0	0	0	13.2	8	5	3	7	22	56	1.098	
16 Yrs				47	40	0.540	2.31	855	0	703	0	0	422	903	601	262	232	300	1196	3600	0.998	**Career Pts.**
				1.500	0.000	4.500	17.500	11.750	0.000	13.000	0.000	0.000	15.500	1.000	0.000	0.000	0.000	0.000	2.500	0.000	18.250	**85.500**

Post Seasonal Play

Year	Age	Team	Series	W	L	PCT	ERA	G	GS	GF	CG	SHO	SV	IP	H	R	ER	BB	SO	BF	WHIP	
1997	25	HOU	NLDS	0	0	0.000	18.00	1	0	1	0	0	0	1	3	2	2	0	2	6	3	
1998	26	HOU	NLDS	1	0	1.000	18.00	1	0	1	0	0	0	1	4	2	2	0	1	7	4	
1999	27	HOU	NLDS	0	0	0.000	0.00	1	0	1	0	0	0	1	0	0	0	0	1	3	0	
2001	29	HOU	NLDS	0	0	0.000	5.40	2	0	1	0	0	0	1.2	1	1	1	0	3	7	0.6	
2006	34	NYM	NLDS	0	0	0.000	3.00	3	0	3	0	0	2	3	3	1	1	0	4	12	1	
2006	34	NYM	NLCS	0	1	0.000	16.88	3	0	2	0	0	1	2.2	7	5	5	1	0	16	3	
2008	37	BOS	ALDS	0	0	0.000	18.00	2	0	0	0	0	0	1	2	2	2	1	2	6	3	
2010	38	ATL	NLDS	0	0	0.000	0.00	1	0	0	0	0	0	0.1	1	0	0	0	0	2	3	
				1	1	0.500	10.03	14	0	9	0	0	3	11.2	21	13	13	2	13	59	1.971	**Post Season Pts.**
				0.250	0.000	0.000	0.000	0.800	0.000	1.000	0.000	0.000	0.600	0.400	0.000	0.000	0.000	0.000	0.400	0.000	0.000	**3.450**

World Series Play

Year	Age	Team	Series	W	L	W-L%	ERA	G	GS	GF	CG	SHO	SV	IP	H	R	ER	BB	SO	BF	WHIP	
None				0	0	0	0	0	0	0	0	0	0	0	0	0	0	0	0	0	0	
				0	0	0	0	0	0	0	0	0	0	0	0	0	0	0	0	0	0	**World Series Pts.**
				0.000	0.000	0.000	0.000	0.000	0.000	0.000	0.000	0.000	0.000	0.000	0.000	0.000	0.000	0.000	0.000	0.000	0.000	**0.000**

Yearly Points Leading the League

Category	Times	Points	Total
MVP	0	7	0
ROY	0	5	0
Cy Young	0	5	0
Golden Glove	0	3	0
All-Star	7	2	14
Wins	0	3	0
Totals			14

Category	Times	Points	Total
Saves	0	3	0
ERA	0	3	0
S.O.'s	0	2	0
Games	0	2	0
G.S.	0	2	0
C.G.	0	2	0
Totals			0

Categ	Times	Points	Total
SHO	0	2	0
WinPc	0	2	0
Inning	0	2	0
WHIP	0	2	0
GF	1	2	4
Totals			4
Grand Total Add-On Points		18	

Hall of Fame Points	
Career Points	85.500
Post Season Points	3.450
World Series Points	0.000
Career Add-On Points	18.000
Writers Association Pts.	0.000
Military/Lifetime Achievemen	0.000
Grand Total HOF Points	106.950

The Baseball Hall of Fame

Statistical Review of Potential Right-Handed Pitchers for the Hall of Fame

Player	Years Played	Career Pts.	Post Season Pts.	World Series Pts.	Add-On Pts.	Mil/LT Pts.	Total HOF Pts.	Needed HOF Votes	Comments
Players Needing to be Inducted									
Mathews, Bobby	16	98.250	0.000	0.000	20.000	0.000	118.250	0	Inducted
McCormick, Jim	10	101.500	6.800	0.000	26.000	0.000	134.300	0	Inducted
Mullane, Tony	13	93.750	0.000	0.000	28.000	0.000	121.750	0	Inducted
Rodriguez, Francisco	16	75.750	6.250	1.900	29.000	0.000	112.850	0	Inducted
Schilling, Curt	20	73.00	12.200	9.500	46.200	0.000	140.700	0	Inducted
Walters, Bucky	16	56.000	0.000	6.150	59.000	0.000	121.150	0	Inducted
Players Needing to be Voted into the Hall of Fame by the BBWAA									
Adams, Babe	19	72.500	0.000	6.100	14.000	0.000	94.600	16	Need Voting
Bridges, Tommy	16	52.490	0.000	7.800	24.000	0.000	90.290	20	Need Voting
Brown, Kevin	19	65.500	7.600	1.800	30.000	0.000	104.900	6	Need Voting
Caruthers, Bob	9	76.250	11.500	0.000	16.000	0.000	103.750	7	Need Voting
Cone, David	17	59.750	7.000	5.600	25.000	0.000	97.350	13	Need Voting
Derringer, Paul	15	66.000	0.000	6.250	26.000	0.000	98.250	12	Need Voting
Gooden, Dwight	16	58.250	4.050	0.950	34.000	0.000	97.250	13	Need Voting
Hershiser, Orel	18	60.250	11.300	6.050	27.000	0.000	104.600	6	Need Voting
Leever, Sam	13	78.500	0.000	1.250	12.000	0.000	91.750	18	Need Voting
Martinez, Dennis	23	70.500	5.900	1.550	24.000	0.000	101.950	9	Need Voting
Mays, Carl	15	73.000	0.000	8.750	22.000	0.000	103.750	7	Need Voting
Nathan, Joe	16	78.750	2.500	0.000	14.000	0.000	95.250	15	Need Voting
Newcombe, Don	12	49.750	0.000	2.100	38.000	0.000	97.850	13	Need Voting
Papelbon, Jonathon	12	73.000	8.500	2.050	14.000	0.000	97.550	13	Need Voting
Quesenberry, Dan	11	57.985	4.800	3.350	35.000	0.000	101.135	9	Need Voting
Saberhagen, Brett	16	55.750	3.050	5.950	31.000	0.000	95.750	15	Need Voting
Tiant, Luis	19	76.250	2.3275	4.000	18.000	0.000	100.525	10	Need Voting
Warneke, Lon	15	61.250	0.000	5.550	24.000	0.000	96.800	14	Need Voting
Welch, Bob	17	66.500	4.300	2.100	18.000	0.000	90.900	20	Need Voting
Wood, Howard	14	80.500	0.000	7.000	16.000	0.000	103.500	7	Need Voting

<u>Hall of Fame Statistical Requirements:</u>

All Players achieving the total of 110.000, or greater, Total Hall of Fame Points, shall be Inducted after five (5) years of retirement. This provision can be waived due to the death by a 75% vote of the 25 Panel BBWAA's. Individuals receiving less than the required 110.000 Hall of Fame Points are eligible for Election after five (5) years of retirement. A 25 person BBWAA will determine the Players that will be Inducted and vote on the Players needing to be elected. An example of those needing to be elected are as follows: Player "A" has a total of 95 Hall of Fame Points and will need 15 of the (25) BBWAA votes to be Elected in the following year.

Right-Handed Pitchers Needing to be Inducted.

1. Bobby Matthews
2. Jim McCormick
3. Tony Mullane
4. Francisco Rodriguez
5. Curt Schilling
6. Bucky Walters

110.000 Hall of Fame Statistical Induction Criteria

The Baseball Hall of Fame

Mathews, Bobby "Little Bobby"

Personal Life:

Bobby Mathews was born on November 21, 1851, in Baltimore, Maryland, the only son of Irish natives John and Mary Mathews. At the age of 16, Mathews, a right-hander, joined the junior team of the Maryland's of Baltimore in 1868. Mathews, who never married, moved around the East Coast from job to job.

Baseball Career

In late July 1870, the Marylands embarked on a Western tour that took them to Washington, D.C., Indianapolis, Cincinnati, Rockford, and Chicago, among other stops. It wasn't a successful tour by any means. Of the four league games they played, the Marylands won only one. The Marylands then left for Pittsburgh but soon the Kekiongas reached out and poached the Baltimore club for Mathews and Carey

Fort Wayne's Opening Day roster in 1871 included five Maryland club players: On that day, May 4, Mathews, just 19 years old, pitched and won the first game in National Association history – some might call it the first major-league game. It was one of the cleanest, most competitive baseball games any fan had seen to that point. Mathews allowed only five hits and struck out six in the 2-0 shutout. It was the lowest-scoring game anyone could ever remember. The game was still in its genesis in 1871. It was played barehanded, and the style of pitching was underhanded from 45 feet. The previous winter, standout catcher Nat Hicks had gone to Baltimore to work with Mathews and he developed a curveball.

The Pastimes reorganized administratively again in 1872, now calling themselves the Lord Baltimore's. From the previous year, Mathews, Carey, and Hall were retained as the ballclub joined the National Association. The team adopted a colorful black, white, and bright yellow uniform, which led some to call them the Baltimore Canaries. In September, Mathews re-signed with Baltimore, but didn't rejoin the team the following spring. Instead, Mathews took his batterymate, Dick Higham, to New York. The Mutuals were run as a cooperative, but Mathews and first baseman Joe Start were guaranteed salaries to assure their continued loyalty to the club. Mathews started all but one game for New York in 1873, amassing a 29-23 record. On July 3 he tossed a two-hitter against

Washington in a rain-shortened six-inning contest. Though generally complimentary, he wrote, "Unfortunately, Mathews' name was brought up a number of times in connection with some of the New York Mutuals scandals." The scandals involved the pitcher's time with the Mutuals, a club with a long history of suspicious play.

The Mutuals finished second to Boston in the National Association in 1874. Mathews, starting every game for the team, placed second in the league in wins with a 42-22 record and also placed second in ERA.

Mathews was the first to introduce a slow raise as far back as 1872. He was one of the few to master the various deliveries as the rules of the game changed over the years: underhand, side-arm, and overhand. Mathews relied a great deal on psychology, intellect, and confusion, strong pitching weapons. He pitched with his head as well as with his arm, and that explains why he lasted so many years. There never stood in the box a cooler and nervier man than Matthews. In a tight place he had no equal, as there never has been a pitcher as good a strategist he was.

It's thought that Candy Cummings and Bobby Mathews were the only two professionals to have mastered the curveball through the 1873 season. Mathews said he learned the curve by watching Cummings efforts to identify himself as the originator of the curveball, said, "The first man to get the curve after myself was Bobby Mathews of Baltimore, and never claimed to have invented the curve, but always told all who asked that he learned it off me." Mathews started all but one of New York's 71 games in 1875.

Mathews' 131 wins in the National Association rank third behind Al Spalding of Boston (205) and Dick McBride of Philadelphia (149), quite a feat considering that the latter two played for stronger clubs while Mathews' nines were typically weak with the bat. Over the final four National Association seasons, Mathews amassed more than 2,050 innings on the mound. He was the career National Association leader in strikeouts and strikeouts per nine innings. Mathews remained with the Mutuals as the club moved into the upstart National League in 1876. It was a poor club, though. He started all but one of the team's games, accruing 516 innings and a 21-34 record.

Mathews pitching record can be broken down into three sections as the game of Baseball evolved, teams and leagues game became more stable, rules changed, and eventually chaos and unruliness

The Baseball Hall of Fame

was gradually being replaced by organization and eliminating/reducing gambling and improving player's character.

League	W	L	PCT	ERA	G	GS	GF	CG	SV	IP	H	R	ER	BB	SO	BF	WHIP
NL(5 yrs)	60	75	.444	2.910	151	143	8	125	3	1244	1516	850	403	121	322	5533	1.315
AA(5 yrs)	106	61	.635	3.060	172	172	0	164	0	1489	1492	903	507	215	877	6056	1.146
NA(5 Yrs)	131	112	.539	2.690	255	253	4	236	0	2221	2593	1739	663	196	329	10108	1.255
15 Years	**297**	**248**	**.550**	**2.860**	**578**	**568**	**12**	**525**	**3**	**4956**	**5601**	**3497**	**1573**	**532**	**1528**	**21997**	**1.237**

Achievements

- 1-time NA Innings Pitched Leader (1875) & NA Complete Games Leader (1875)
- 2-time NA St.O. Leader (1872 & 1873) & 2-time NA Shutouts Leader (1871 & 1874)
- 20 Wins Seasons: 8 (1872-1876 & 1883-1885)
- 30 Wins Seasons: 4 (1874 & 1883-1885) & 40 Wins Seasons: 1 (1874)
- 200 Innings Pitched Seasons: 9 (1872-1876 & 1882-1885)
- 300 Innings Pitched Seasons: 8 (1872-1876 & 1883-1885)
- 400 Innings Pitched Seasons: 7 (1872-1876, 1884 & 1885)
- 200 Strikeouts Seasons: 3 (1883-1885)

Hall of Fame

When the Hall of Fame came into existence in 1936, Mathews was forgotten. He is the first pitcher between 1871 and 1887, won 297 games, and has never received a vote.

Summary Analysis

Bobby Mathews Hall of Fame Point Total is 118.250 and was forgotten as one of the top pitchers of the early professional players between 1871 and 1887. Mathews' career had many negatives with gambling and his "careless habits" which most would assume meant drinking and poor conditioning. He needs to be added to the "Character Clause" violator section without a plaque so the true history of Baseball can be viewed by all.

Pitcher Right Handed Potential Hall of Fame Inductee

Mathews, Bobby

Position	Born:	November 21, 1851	Height:	5' 5"	USC 165	cm
Pitcher	Died:	April 17, 1898	Weight:	140 lbs.	63	Kg.
	From:	Baltimore, MD	Debut:	May 4, 1871		
	Bats:	Right	Last Game:	October 10, 1887		
	Throws:	Right				

Year	Age	Tm	Lg	W	L	PCT	ERA	G	GS	GF	CG	SHO	SV	IP	H	R	ER	BB	SO	BF	WHIP	Awards
1871	19	KEK	NA	6	11	0.353	5.170	19	19	0	19	1	0	169	261	243	97	21	17	876	1.669	
1872	20	BAL	NA	25	18	0.581	3.190	49	47	4	39	0	0	406	480	356	144	52	57	1922	1.310	
1873	21	NYU	NA	29	23	0.558	2.580	52	52	0	47	2	0	443	489	348	127	62	79	2008	1.244	
1874	22	NYU	NA	42	22	0.656	1.900	65	65	0	62	4	0	578	652	371	122	41	101	2543	1.199	
1875	23	NYU	NA	29	38	0.433	2.490	70	70	0	69	3	0	625.2	711	421	173	20	75	2759	1.168	
1876	24	NYU	NL	21	34	0.382	2.860	56	56	0	55	2	0	516	693	395	164	24	37	2327	1.390	
1877	25	CIN	NL	3	12	0.200	4.040	15	15	0	13	0	0	129.1	208	132	58	17	9	631	1.740	
1879	27	PRO	NL	12	6	0.667	2.290	27	25	2	15	1	1	189	194	85	48	26	90	779	1.164	
1881	29	TOT	NL	5	8	0.385	3.020	19	15	4	11	1	2	125.1	143	92	42	32	33	576	1.396	
1881	29	PRO	NL	4	8	0.333	3.170	14	14	0	10	1	0	102.1	121	81	36	21	28	473	1.388	
1881	29	BSN	NL	1	0	1.000	2.350	5	1	4	1	0	2	23	22	11	6	11	5	103	1.435	
1882	30	BSN	NL	19	15	0.559	2.870	34	32	2	31	0	0	285	278	151	91	22	153	1220	1.053	
1883	31	PHA	AA	30	13	0.698	2.460	44	44	0	41	1	0	381	396	224	104	31	203	1609	1.121	
1884	32	PHA	AA	30	18	0.625	3.320	49	49	0	48	3	0	430.2	401	238	159	49	286	1788	1.045	
1885	33	PHA	AA	30	17	0.638	2.430	48	48	0	46	2	0	422.1	394	229	114	57	286	1766	1.068	
1886	34	PHA	AA	13	9	0.591	3.960	24	24	0	22	0	0	197.2	226	148	87	53	93	913	1.411	
1887	35	PHA	AA	3	4	0.429	6.670	7	7	0	7	0	0	58	75	64	43	25	9	280	1.724	
162 Game Avg.				18	15	0.545	2.860	34	34	1	31	1	0	294	332	208	93	32	91	1305	1.237	
PHA (5 yrs)				106	61	0.635	3.060	172	172	0	164	6	0	1489	1492	903	507	215	877	6356	1.146	
NYU (3 yrs)				100	83	0.546	2.310	187	187	0	178	9	0	1646	1852	1140	422	123	255	7310	1.199	
PRO (2 yrs)				16	14	0.533	2.590	41	39	2	25	2	1	291.1	315	166	84	47	118	1252	1.243	
BSN (2 yrs)				20	15	0.571	2.830	39	33	6	32	0	2	308	300	162	97	33	158	1323	1.081	
CIN (1 yr)				3	12	0.200	4.040	15	15	0	13	0	0	129.1	208	132	58	17	9	631	1.740	
KEK (1 yr)				6	11	0.353	5.170	19	19	0	19	1	0	169	261	243	97	21	17	876	1.669	
NYU (1 yr)				21	34	0.382	2.860	56	56	0	55	2	0	516	693	395	164	24	37	2327	1.390	
BAL (1 yr)				25	18	0.581	3.190	49	47	4	39	0	0	406	480	356	144	52	57	1922	1.310	
NL (5 yrs)				60	75	0.444	2.910	151	143	8	125	4	3	1244	1516	855	403	121	322	5533	1.315	
AA (5 yrs)				106	61	0.635	3.060	172	172	0	164	6	0	1489	1492	903	507	215	877	6356	1.146	
NA (5 yrs)				131	112	0.539	2.690	255	253	4	236	10	0	2221	2593	1739	663	196	329	10108	1.255	
15 Yrs				297	248	0.545	2.86	578	568	12	525	20	3	4956	5601	3497	1573	532	1528	21997	1.237	Career Pts.
				13.000	0.000	4.50	12.50	5.500	11.750	0.500	20.000	2.000	0.000	16.750	0.000	0.000	0.000	0.000	3.750	0.000	8.000	98.250

Post Seasonal Play

Year	Age	Team	Series	W	L	PCT	ERA	G	GS	GF	CG	SHO	SV	IP	H	R	ER	BB	SO	BF	WHIP	
None				0	0	0	0	0	0	0	0	0	0	0	0	0	0	0	0	0	0	Post Season Pts.
				0.000	0.000	0.000	0.000	0.000	0.000	0.000	0.000	0.000	0.000	0.000	0.000	0.000	0.000	0.000	0.000	0.000	0.000	0.000

World Series Play

Year	Age	Team	Series	W	L	PCT	ERA	G	GS	GF	CG	SHO	SV	IP	H	R	ER	BB	SO	BF	WHIP	
				0	0	0	0	0	0	0	0	0	0	0	0	0	0	0	0	0	0	World Series
				0.000	0.000	0.000	0.000	0.000	0.000	0.000	0.000	0.000	0.000	0.000	0.000	0.000	0.000	0.000	0.000	0.000	0.000	0.000

Yearly Points Leading the League

Category	Times	Points	Total	Category	Times	Points	Total	Category	Times	Points	Total	Hall of Fame Points	
MVP	0	7	0	Saves	2	2	4	SHO	2	2	4	Career Points	98.250
ROY	0	5	0	ERA	0	2	0	WinPct	0	2	0	Post Season Points	0.000
y Young	0	5	0	S.O.'s	3	2	6	Innings	1	2	2	World Series Points	0.000
den Glove	0	3	0	Games	0	2	0	WHIP	0	2	0	Career Add-On Points	20.000
All-Star	0	2	0	G.S.	1	2	2	GF	0	2	0	Writers Association Pts.	0.000
Wins	0	2	0	C.G.	1	2	2	Totals	0		6	Military Points	0.000
Totals			0	Totals			14	Grand Total Add-On Points		20		Grand Total HOF Points	118.250

McCormick "Jimsy"

Personal Life

James McCormick born November 3,1856 – died March 10, 1918, was the son of James McCormick and Rosa Lawry. They were born in Ireland but moved to Scotland. Called "Jimsy" by friends was born in Glasgow.

McCormick's married his wife, Jennie, (date unknown). She became ill with consumption (tuberculosis) and died on August 21, 1888, leaving a son, James, and daughter, Franci which Jim raised on his own.

Baseball Career

As a teenager, McCormick played with future Hall of Famer Mike "King" Kelly and future major leaguers Blondie Purcell, Edward "The Only" Nolan, and John "Kick" Kelly, on a team called the Keystones. McCormick debuted in pro ball in the International Association in 1877, playing for Columbus. That league/year is considered to be the first minor league season. He had a 6-6 record over 135 innings, completing all 13 of his starts. We know that he allowed 3.87 runs per nine innings.

The Buckeyes recruited McCormick and he made his Major League debut for the 1878 Indianapolis Blues, a one-year National League franchise that finished in fifth place (out of six teams). He went just 5-8 that year, which makes his final career win total over a short career that much more impressive. Despite the losing record, he had a 1.69 ERA and a 1.22 WHIP in 117 innings. He completed 12 of his 14 starts. McCormick weathered injuries to make 14 starts and post a 5-8 record. On July 11, in a game against Boston, he broke a small bone in his forearm and was sidelined all of August. Indianapolis lost money in 1878 and failed to make the final payroll. McCormick reportedly lost $300 in salary. He led the NL in losses with 40 in 1879 but led the league in wins with 45 the following year. He led the NL in wins again in 1882, with 36, and led the league in ERA in 1883, matching his 1.84 ERA with a 28-12 record.

When they disbanded in September, he was picked up by the Indianapolis Blues. Indianapolis joined the National League in 1878 and McCormick's first major-league appearance was on June 20. The Blues dropped the game by a 7-4 score. He then joined the Cleveland Blues as a player and manager in 1879. He lost a league-leading 40 games in his first year with Cleveland, but the next summer, he won a league-high 45, posted a 1.85 ERA, and paced the NL with 72 complete games as his club came in third. He then joined the 1879 Cleveland Blues, which was a team that finished last in hitting. He started 60 of the team's 82 games, completing all but one start. Despite a 2.42 ERA, 197 strikeouts and a 1.20 WHIP in 546.1 innings, he finished with a 20-40 record. He actually tied for the league lead in losses that year, putting up a mark that has only been topped three times in baseball history (all in the 1880's).

McCormick's 1880 season is one of the best pitching seasons ever, and he did it while doubling as the Blues manager. He posted a 1.85 ERA and a 1.00 WHIP, while winning a National League leading 45 games. He completed 72 of 74 starts, while leading the National League with 657.2 innings pitched. His totals that year for starts, complete games and innings all rank him among the top four all-time for single seasons. He had 260 strikeouts, which ranks as his second-best season in that category.

With added support, McCormick fashioned a 45-28 (the team record was 47-37) mark in 657⅔innings. He led the league in wins, complete games, and innings pitched, and finished fifth in ERA and second in strikeouts. McCormick went 26-30, 2.45 over 526 innings in 1881, with a 1.08 WHIP and 178 strikeouts. He completed 57 starts, which led the league. The other two starters for Cleveland that season combined for a 10-18 record. He had a 36-30, 2.37 record, 200 strikeouts and a 1.10 WHIP over 595.2 innings in 1882. He led the league in wins, innings, games pitched, started (67) and complete games (65), which was his third straight season leading the league in games pitched.

McCormick went 28-12, 1.84 over 342 innings in 1883, with 145 strikeouts and a 1.11 WHIP. He had the best winning percentage and ERA in the league. In 1884, McCormick pitched 42 games for the Spiders, but then jumped mid-season to the Cincinnati Outlaw Reds of the Union Association for $2,500. He received a $1,000 bonus for switching leagues mid-season, but UA only lasted one year. He didn't debut until August 10th, but he ended up dominating over 24 starts. He went 21-3, 1.54 in 210 innings for Cincinnati. He had seven shutouts in the Union Association, giving him a total of ten shutouts for the season. He finished the year with 40 wins, a career high 343 strikeouts and a 1.05 WHIP over 569 innings pitched. He won 40 games between the two clubs and paced UA with a 1.54

ERA. The circuit folded, however, after the season, and he had to pay a $1,000 fine to return to the NL.

McCormick joined Providence in he was used only four times in 10 weeks. He had a 1-3 mark when Cap Anson contacted the Grays about his services. The White Stockings needed a partner to team with John Clarkson. McCormick proved to be the perfect partner for Clarkson, who fashioned a 53-16 record. McCormick was 20-4 with an ERA of 2.43. The White Stockings won the pennant and faced the American Association champions from St. Louis in the postseason. The seven-game series ended in a tie, three wins for each squad and a tie game. McCormick posted a 3-2 mark in the series and earned a lifelong fan in manager Cap Anson. He began 1985 with the Providence Grays but was sold to the Chicago White Stockings in early July. He would throw 5 complete games in that fall's World Series against the St. Louis Browns of the American Association. After the 1886 championship, club President Albert G. Spalding sold several of his best-known players, mainly for drinking during the season. He sent McCormick to Pittsburgh just before the 1887 season.

Hall of Fame

No information was found indicating if McCormick was ever voted on by the BBWAA for the Hall of Fame.

Summary Analysis

His final career record stands at 265-214, 2.43 in 4,275.2 innings, with 485 starts and 466 complete games. He had 1,704 strikeouts, a 1.13 WHIP and 33 career shutouts. His 76.0 career WAR as a pitcher is the 29th best mark in baseball history. Jim left Baseball behind after his wife, Jemmie, died on August 21, 1888, leaving a son and daughter for Jim to raise. A man like Jim, who prioritized raising his children over playing Baseball should not be denied his rightful spot in the Hall of Fame simply because her ONLY played 10 years, which by the way is the minimum required.

Pitcher Right Handed Potential Hall of Fame Inductee

McCormick, Jim

Position	Born :	November 3, 1856	Height:	5' 10" USC 178 cm
Pitcher	Died:	March 10, 1918	Weight:	215 lbs. 97 Kg.
Putfield	From:	Glascow, United Kingdon	Debut:	May 20, 1878
	Bats:	Right	Last Game:	October 7, 1887
	Throws:	Right		

Year	Age	Tm	Lg	W	L	PCT	ERA	G	GS	GF	CG	SHO	SV	IP	H	R	ER	BB	SO	BF	WHIP	Awards
1878	21	IND	NL	5	8	0.385	1.69	14	14	0	12	1	0	117	128	47	22	15	36	490	1.222	
1879	22	CLV	NL	20	40	0.333	2.42	62	60	1	59	3	0	546.1	582	308	147	74	197	2325	1.201	
1880	23	CLV	NL	45	28	0.616	1.85	74	74	0	72	7	0	657.2	585	274	135	75	260	2669	1.004	
1881	24	CLV	NL	26	30	0.464	2.45	59	58	1	57	2	0	526	484	267	143	84	178	2145	1.080	
1882	25	CLV	NL	36	30	0.545	2.37	68	67	1	65	4	0	595.2	550	274	157	103	200	2412	1.096	
1883	26	CLV	NL	28	12	0.700	1.84	43	41	2	36	1	1	342	316	151	70	65	145	1421	1.314	
1884	27	TOT	MLB	40	25	0.615	2.37	66	65	2	63	10	0	569	508	263	150	89	343	2336	1.049	
1884	27	CLV	NL	19	22	0.463	2.86	42	41	2	39	3	0	359	357	206	114	75	182	1518	1.203	
1884	27	COR	UA	21	3	0.875	1.54	24	24	0	24	7	0	210	151	57	36	14	161	818	0.786	
1885	28	TOT	NL	21	7	0.750	2.43	28	28	0	28	3	0	252	221	129	68	60	96	1038	1.115	
1885	28	PRO	NL	1	3	0.250	2.43	4	4	0	4	0	0	37	34	26	10	20	8	165	1.459	
1885	28	CHC	NL	20	4	0.833	2.43	24	24	0	24	3	0	215	187	103	58	40	88	873	1.056	
1886	29	CHC	NL	31	11	0.738	2.82	42	42	0	38	2	0	347.2	341	165	109	100	172	1449	1.268	
1887	30	PIT	NL	13	23	0.361	4.30	36	36	0	36	0	0	322.1	377	217	154	84	77	1417	1.430	
162 Game Avg.				18	15	0.553	2.43	34	34	0	32	2	0	298	285	146	80	52	119	1232	1.132	
CLV (6 yrs)				174	162	0.518	2.28	348	341	7	328	20	1	3026.2	2874	1480	766	476	1162	12490	1.107	
CHC (2 yrs)				51	15	0.773	2.67	66	66	0	62	5	0	562.2	528	268	167	140	260	2322	1.187	
PRO (1 yr)				1	3	0.250	2.43	4	4	0	4	0	0	37	34	26	10	20	8	165	1.459	
PIT (1 yr)				13	23	0.361	4.30	36	36	0	36	0	0	322.1	377	217	154	84	77	1417	1.430	
COR (1 yr)				21	3	0.875	1.54	24	24	0	24	7	0	210	151	57	36	14	161	818	0.786	
IND (1 yr)				5	8	0.385	1.69	14	14	0	12	1	0	117	128	47	22	15	36	490	1.222	
NL (10 yrs)				244	211	0.536	2.48	468	461	7	442	26	1	4065.2	3941	2038	1119	735	1543	16884	1.150	
UA (1 yr)				21	3	0.875	1.54	24	24	0	24	7	0	210	151	57	36	14	161	818	0.786	
10 Yrs				265	214	0.553	2.43	492	485	7	466	33	1	4275.2	4092	2095	1155	749	1704	17702	1.132	Career Pts.
				11.750	0.000	5.500	17.500	4.500	9.250	0.000	18.250	3.750	0.000	14.250	0.000	0.000	0.000	0.000	3.750	0.000	13.000	101.500

Post Seasonal Play

Year	Age	Team	Series	W	L	PCT	ERA	G	GS	GF	CG	SHO	SV	IP	H	R	ER	BB	SO	BF	WHIP	
1885	28	Chi	WS	3	2	0.600	2.00	5	5	0	5	0	0	36	27	22	8	6	19	0	0.917	
1886	29	Chi	WS	0	1	0.000	6.75	1	1	0	1	0	0	8	13	12	6	2	4	0	1.875	
				3	3	5.000	2.86	6	6	0	6	0	0	44	40	34	14	8	23	0	1.091	Post Season Pts.
				0.400	0.000	0.000	1.200	0.400	0.600	0.000	1.200	0.000	0.000	0.800	0.000	0.000	0.000	0.000	0.600	0.000	1.600	6.800

World Series Play

Year	Age	Team	Series	W	L	W-L%	ERA	G	GS	GF	CG	SHO	SV	IP	H	R	ER	BB	IBB	SO	HBP	WHIP	
None				0	0	0	0	0	0	0	0	0	0	0	0	0	0	0	0	0	0		World Series Pts.
				0.000	0.000	0.000	0.000	0.000	0.000	0.000	0.000	0.000	0.000	0.000	0.000	0.000	0.000	0.000	0.000	0.000	0.000		0.000

Yearly Points Leading the League

Category	Times	Points	Total	Category	Times	Points	Total	Catego	Times	Points	Total	Hall of Fame Points	
MVP	0	7	0	Saves	0	2	0	SHO	0	2	0	Career Points	101.500
ROY	0	5	0	ERA	2	2	4	WinPct	1	2	2	Post Season Points	6.800
Cy Young	0	5	0	S.O.'s	0	2	0	Innings	2	2	4	World Series Points	0.000
Golden Glove	0	3	0	Games	0	2	0	WHIP	1	2	2	Career Add-On Points	26.000
All-Star	0	2	0	G.S.	2	2	4	GF	0	2	0	Writers Association Pts.	0.000
Wins	2	2	4	C.G.	3	2	6	Totals			8	Military Points	0.000
Totals			4	Totals			14	Grand Total Add-On Points			26	Grand Total HOF Points	134.300

Mullane, Tony "Count" or "Apollo of the Box"

Personal Life

Anthony John Mullane was born January 30, 1859, in County Cork, Ireland to Dennis Mullane and Elizabeth Behan. He had two brothers, John, Sam, and a sister, Nora.

Mullane married a woman named Barbara in 1886 and records show she filed for divorce in 1996 with the couple having a daughter, Ina, and a son that died in July 1891.

Baseball Career

Mullane signed a professional contract in 1876 with the Geneva, Ohio, team and between 1876 and 1880, drifted from club to club in eastern. Mullane began his professional baseball career in Ohio, where he played for a number of local teams during the 1880 season. Early in the 1881 season, Mullane played for Akron again, against other amateur teams in Ohio as well as National League teams that would play Akron when they were playing near Cleveland, which had a National League franchise. Mullane pitched for at least seven teams during his 13-season career. He is best known as an ambidextrous pitcher who could throw left- and right-handed. Mullane suffered an injury to his right arm and managed to teach himself to throw left-handed. He resumed throwing right-handed once the injury healed, and even alternated throwing right-handed and left-handed in the same game, which was easy for him since he did not wear a glove. Mullane faced the batter with both hands on the ball, and then would use either one to throw a pitch.

In 1882, Mullane joined the Louisville Eclipse, where he started 55 of the team's 80 games. He compiled a record of 30–24 with a 1.88 earned run average, the first of five consecutive 30-win seasons. On September 11, he pitched a no-hitter against the Cincinnati Red Stockings and recorded 35 victories with the 1883 St. Louis Browns. Tony Mullane was one of the very few ambidextrous pitchers in the history of the game. In a game in July 1882, he pitched with both hands, though not at the same time. He might have done this on other occasions, but the July incident is the most widely documented one. A handsome man, Mullane was nicknamed "The Apollo of the Box." Teams would often schedule Mullane on "Ladies' Day" promotions to drum up business.

In 1884, the Browns sold him to the Toledo Blue Stockings, with whom he won a career-high 36 games. Mullane is also known for his racism and his catcher in 1884 was sometimes Moses

A Fan's Perspective

Fleetwood Walker, one of the first black men to play in Major League Baseball. Mullane admitted to purposefully mixing up Walker by throwing pitches the catcher hadn't called for. In addition, Mullane stated Walker "was the best catcher I ever worked with, but I disliked a Negro and whenever I had to pitch to him, I used to pitch anything I wanted without looking at his signals. In 1884, Mullane won 36 games for the Toledo Blue Stockings. In 1884, Mullane signed with Cincinnati. For this action, the American Association suspended him for the 1885 season. Following the suspension, Mullane joined the Cincinnati Red Stockings for the 1986 season and remained there the next seven and a half years, over which he won 163 games.

After being reserved again by Cincinnati, and signed for the 1887 season, Mullane was suspended without pay in May and placed on their reserve list. If he had merely been released, he could have been claimed by another club. Later, Mullane was reinstated by the Red Stockings and despite the disrupted season, he won 31 games and lost 17. In 1888, he posted a 26-16 record, increased his strikeout total to 186 from 97 the previous year and reduced his ERA to 2.84 from 3.24; he also umpired in three games. But by 1889 Mullane appeared to be on the decline as a pitcher. His record dropped to 11-9 in only 33 appearances as a pitcher; he also played 34 games as a third baseman, outfielder, and first baseman and batted .296, a career high, a slugging percentage of .418, and 24 stolen bases in 196 at-bats.

In 1890 Cincinnati moved to the National League, Mullane played outfield, third base, shortstop, and first base while pitching in 25 games. He came back strong on the mound in the second half of the season, posting a 12-10 record with a 2.24 ERA. After an 1891 season when he won 23 games but lost 26 and saw his ERA rise by a full run to 3.23, the pressure was on Mullane to produce better statistics in 1892 or risk not pitching regularly again, especially since he was an active participant in dissension that had riddled the Cincinnati team. Perhaps contributing to that dismal season was the fact that Mullane's son had died in July and that Mullane had played injured.

The 1893 season brought several rules changes, most notably the moving of the pitcher's mound an additional five feet from home plate. Mullane began the season a mediocre 6–6, and was traded to the Baltimore Orioles on June 16. He staggered to an 18–25 record with the Orioles in a little more than one full season over 1893 and 1894.. Mullane retired after the 1894 season with a record of 284–220 and a 3.05 ERA over a 13-year career. A fine hitter as well as a great pitcher, Mullane played over 250 games at other positions and his 661 career hits are tops among pitchers. Mullane is 2nd all-time in wins among pitchers not enshrined in the Hall of Fame who are eligible.

Achievements:

- AA Winning Percentage Leader (1883) & AA Games Pitched Leader (1882).
- 5-time League Saves Leader (1883/AA, 1888/AA, 1889/AA, 1893/94 NL).
- AA Strikeouts Leader (1882) & 2-time AA Shutouts Leader (1884 & 1887).
- 20 Wins Seasons: 8 (1882-1884, 1886-1888, 1891 & 1892).
- 30 Wins Seasons: 5 (1882-1884, 1886 & 1887).
- 200 Innings Pitched Seasons: 11 (1882-1884 & 1886-1893).
- 300 Innings Pitched Seasons: 8 (1882-1884, 1886-1888, 1891 & 1893).
- 400 Innings Pitched Seasons: 6 (1882-1884, 1886, 1887 & 1891).
- 500 Innings Pitched Seasons: 2 (1884 & 1886).
- 200 Strikeouts Seasons: 2 (1884 & 1886) & 300 Strikeouts Seasons: 1 (1884).

Hall of Fame

Mullane's name was on the 2013 Hall of Fame ballot in which the Veterans Committee examined candidates from the pre-integration era. However, due to his many Character Clause Violations, he wasn't really considered and did not get elected.

Summary Analysis

Tony Mullane's Hall of Fame Point Total is 121.750. His problems marred the legacy of a sporting great whose statistics are worthy of being displayed in the Hall of Fame, but his character will prevent him from ever having a plaque.

Pitcher - Right Handed Potential Hall of Fame Inductee

Mullane. Tony

Position		Born :	January 30, 1859	Height:	5' 10"	USC	178	cm
Pitcher		Died:	April 25, 1944	Weight:	165.	lbs.	74	Kg.
		From:	Cork, Ireland	Debut:	August 27, 1881			
		Bats:	Both	Last Game:	July 26, 1894			
		Throws:	Right					

Year	Age	Tm	Lg	W	L	PCT	ERA	G	GS	GF	CG	SHO	SV	IP	H	R	ER	BB	SO	SO	WHIP	Awards
1881	22	DTN	NL	1	4	0.200	4.91	5	5	0	5	0	0	44	55	42	24	37	7	199	1.636	
1882	23	LOU	AA	30	24	0.556	1.88	55	55	0	51	5	0	460.1	418	212	96	78	170	1927	1.077	
1883	24	STL	AA	35	15	0.700	2.19	53	49	4	49	3	1	460.2	372	222	112	74	191	1875	0.968	
1884	25	TOL	AA	36	26	0.581	2.52	67	65	2	64	7	0	567	481	276	159	89	325	2364	1.005	
1985	26											Did Not Play.										
1886	27	CIN	AA	33	27	0.550	3.7	63	56	7	55	1	0	529.2	501	315	218	166	250	2258	1.259	
1887	28	CIN	AA	31	17	0.646	3.24	48	48	1	47	6	0	416.1	414	234	150	121	97	1763	1.285	
1888	29	CIN	AA	26	16	0.619	2.84	44	42	2	41	4	1	380.1	341	194	120	75	186	1580	1.094	
1889	30	CIN	AA	11	9	0.550	2.99	33	24	9	17	0	5	220	218	133	73	89	112	972	1.395	
1890	31	CIN	NL	12	10	0.545	2.24	25	21	4	21	0	1	209	175	101	52	96	91	899	1.297	
1891	32	CIN	NL	23	26	0.469	3.23	51	47	4	42	1	0	426.1	380	250	153	187	124	1870	1.353	
1892	33	CIN	NL	21	13	0.618	2.59	37	34	3	30	3	1	295	222	131	85	127	109	1246	1.183	
1893	34	TOT	NL	18	22	0.450	4.44	49	39	10	34	0	2	367	407	261	181	189	95	1698	1.624	
1893	34	CIN	NL	6	6	0.500	4.41	15	13	2	11	0	1	122.1	130	84	60	65	24	566	1.594	
1893	34	BLN	NL	12	16	0.429	4.45	34	26	8	23	0	1	244.2	277	177	121	124	71	1132	1.639	
1894	35	TOT	NL	7	11	0.389	6.59	25	19	6	12	0	4	155.2	201	152	114	100	46	756	1.934	
1894	35	BLN	NL	6	9	0.400	6.31	21	15	6	9	0	4	122.2	155	117	86	90	43	605	1.997	
1894	35	CLV	NL	1	2	0.333	7.64	4	4	0	3	0	0	33	46	35	28	10	3	151	1.697	
162 Game Avg.				18	14	0.563	3.05	38	32	3	30	2	1	291	269	162	99	90	116	1246	1.237	
CIN (8 yrs)				163	124	0.568	3.15	316	285	32	264	15	9	2599	2391	1442	911	926	993	11154	1.276	
BLN (2 yrs)				18	25	0.419	5.07	55	41	14	32	0	5	367.1	432	294	207	214	114	1737	1.759	
LOU (1 yr)				30	24	0.556	1.88	55	55	0	51	5		460.1	418	212	96	78	170	1927	1.077	
TOL (1 yr)				36	26	0.581	2.52	67	65	2	64	7	0	567	481	276	159	89	325	2364	1.005	
STL (1 yr)				35	15	0.700	2.19	53	49	4	49	3	1	460.2	372	222	112	74	191	1875	0.968	
CLV (1 yr)				1	2	0.333	7.64	4	4	0	3	0	0	33	46	35	28	10	3	151	1.697	
DTN (1 yr)				1	4	0.200	4.91	5	5	0	5	0	0	44	55	42	24	17	7	199	1.636	
NL (6 yrs)				82	86	0.488	3.66	192	165	27	144	4	8	1497	1450	937	609	716	472	6668	1.447	
AA (7 yrs)				202	134	0.601	2.75	363	339	25	324	26	7	3034.1	2745	1586	928	692	1331	12739	1.133	
13 Yrs				284	220	0.563	3.05	555	504	52	468	30	15	4531.1	4195	2523	1537	1408	1803	19407	1.237	Post Season Pts.
				13.000	0.000	6.750	10.500	3.500	9.250	1.000	18.250	3.000	0.500	15.500	0.000	0.000	0.000	0.000	4.500	0.000	8.000	93.750

Post Season Play

Year	Age	Team	Series	W	L	PCT	ERA	G	GS	GF	CG	SHO	SV	IP	H	R	ER	BB	SO	BF	WHIP	
None				0	0	0	0	0	0	0	0	0	0	0	0	0	0	0	0	0	0	Career Pts.
				0.000	0.000	0.000	0.000	0.000	0.000	0.000	0.000	0.000	0.000	0.000	0.000	0.000	0.000	0.000	0.000	0.000	0.000	0.000

World Series Play

Year	Age	Team	Series	W	L	PCT	ERA	G	GS	GF	CG	SHO	SV	IP	H	R	ER	BB	SO	BF	WHIP	
None				0	0	0	0	0	0	0	0	0	0	0	0	0	0	0	0	0	0	World Series Pts.
				0.000	0.000	0.000	0.000	0.000	0.000	0.000	0.000	0.000	0.000	0.000	0.000	0.000	0.000	0.000	0.000	0.000	0.000	0.000

Yearly Points Leading the League

Category	Times	Points	Total	Category	Times	Points	Total	Categ.	Times	Points	Total	Hall of Fame Points	
MVP	0	7	0	Saves	5	2	10	SHO	2	2	4	Career Points	93.750
ROY	0	5	0	ERA	0	2	0	WinPc	1	2	2	Post Season Points	0.000
Cy Young	0	5	0	S.O.'s	1	2	2	Inning:	0	2	0	World Series Points	0.000
Golden Glove	0	3	0	Games	1	2	2	WHIP	0	2	0	Career Add-On Points	28.000
All-Star	0	2	0	G.S.	1	2	2	GF	3	2	6	Writers Association Pts.	0.000
Wins	0	2	0	C.G.	0	2	0	Totals			12	Military Points	0.000
Totals			0	Totals			16	Grand Total Add-On Points		28		Grand Total HOF Points	121.750

Rodriguez Sr., Francisco "K-Rod or Frankie"

Personal Life

Francisco José Rodríguez, Sr. was born January 7, 1982, and keeps his personal life private. He pitched for Venezuela at the 1998 Pan-American Youth.

Rodriguez has 9 children with the mother's information not found. In addition, no records of marriage have been made available.

Baseball Career

Rodriguez was signed as an undrafted free agent by the Anaheim Angels in 1998 and pitched in the minors until 2002, when he came up for 5 games, pitching 5 2/3 innings, without giving up a run. He burst onto the national scene with a highly successful postseason run that saw him win five games while striking out 28 batters in 17 2/3 innings. Controversially, he was included on the postseason roster by the vagueness in roster rules that allowed an injury replacement for any player on the 40-man roster:

In 2003, Rodríguez was used as set-up man appearing in 59 games, finishing 23, 2 saves, 3.03 ERA, and a record of 8-3. In 2004, he began to rack up saves, with 12 in 69 games, posting an ERA of 1.82. He was named to the All-Star team. In 2005, Rodríguez recorded 45 saves to lead the league, and in 2006, his league-leading 47 put him on the way to winning the Rolaids Relief Award. He had another good season in 2007, going 5-2, 2.41 with 40 saves as the Angels won their division. He had another good season in 2007, going 5-2, 2.41 with 40 saves as the Angels won their division. In 2008, he began to rack up saves at an unseen rate, as the Angels were winning a lot of close games. He was already closing in on 40 saves by the All-Star Game, to which he was selected, and he set a new major league mark when he notched his 58th save of the season against the Seattle Mariners on September 13. He ended the season with 62, along with a 2.24 ERA, and earned a second Rolaids Relief Award. After his record-setting season, Rodríguez signed a 3-year, deal with the New York Mets.

After a so-so season in 2009, in which he went 3-6, 3.71 with 35 saves, he ran into trouble off the field in mid-2010, when he punched the father of his girlfriend in the face several times in front of witnesses at Citi Field, following a Mets loss to the Colorado Rockies on August 11. He was arrested and placed on the restricted list. He returned to action three days later, after issuing a brief apology, but on August 16 the team announced that Rodríguez had torn a ligament in his thumb during the altercation, ending his season. On December 3, Rodríguez pleaded guilty to attempted assault and was sentenced to take anger management classes to avoid jail time; he also pleaded guilty to disorderly conduct charges for harassing his girlfriend, but he still faced a civil lawsuit from his victim for the injuries he suffered. On the field, he went 4-2, 2.20 with 25 saves in 53 games and 67 strikeouts in 57 1/3rd innings of work.

Rodriguez showed up in spring training in February 2011, expressing regret and remorse for his actions the previous year. He was back in the closer's role and pitched fairly well over the season's first half, going 2-2 with 23 saves and 3.16 ERA. But with the Mets unlikely to mount a serious challenge for a playoff spot, the team faced a dilemma: Rodriguez already had 34 games finished by the All-Star break, and his contract included a vesting option if he reached a total of 55 this season. Not wanting to back themselves into such a huge financial commitment, the Mets traded him to the Milwaukee Brewers on July 12th in return for two players to be named later.

In Milwaukee, he was to become the set-up man for their closer and pitched 31 games for the Brewers down the stretch, without recording a single save. He gave Milwaukee everything they were looking for, going 4-0 with a 1.86 ERA and 33 Ks over 29 innings during that time. He pitched two scoreless innings in the NLDS and gave up a run in three innings in the NLCS. After the season, Rodriguez was a free agent, and re-signed with Milwaukee for a year, but was far from happy with the turn of events. He pitched fairly well in the first half of the season until July 17th, when Rodriguez would be given the closer's role. Rodriguez was 2-4, 3.67 with 1 save and 39 Ks in 41 2/3 innings when the change was made. In his first game as closer on July 18th. Rodriguez finished the season with a disappointing record of 2-7, 4.38 and only 3 saves in 78 outings.

Rodriguez was back with the Brewers in 2013 and pitched in some high-leverage situations as his record stood at 1-1, 1.09 ERA and 10 saves in 25 appearances. After being traded to Baltimore on July 23rd, he was 2-1, 4.50 ERA, 23 games and did not pick up any saves. In a surprising move, Rodriguez signed back with the Brewers for one year as spring training was getting under way on February 7, 2014. He injured his foot when he stepped on a cactus the day before he was to make his first appearance. Despite the injury, he finished with 44 saves, a 5-5 record and a 3.04 ERA.

In 2015, he was one of the few bright lights on the Brewers team as he went 1-3, 2.21 and added another 38 saves. On November 18th, he was sent to the Detroit Tigers and on May 24, 2016, Francisco earned the 400th save of his career when he was pitching well for his new team, converting 14 straight save opportunities after being charged with a blown save on Opening Day. He was only the sixth pitcher in MLB history to reach the 400-save mark and was the active leader in the category. He went 3-4, 3.24 in 61 games with 44 saves. He lost his effectiveness at the start of the 2017 season as his record stood at 1-4, 8.49, and had 4 blown saves. On May 9th, he was released on June 23rd but Rodriguez tried making it back to the big leagues without success. He played in MLB for the Angels, Mets, Orioles, Brewers and Tigers.

Achievements:

- 6-time All-Star (2004, 2007-2009, 2014 & 2015).
- 2-time AL Rolaids Relief Award Winner (2006 & 2008).
- 3-time AL Saves Leader (2005, 2006 & 2008)
- 30 Saves Seasons: 8 (2005-2009 & 2014-2016).
- 40 Saves Seasons: 6 (2005-2008, 2014 & 2016) & 60 Saves Seasons (2008).
- Won a World Series with the Anaheim Angels in 2002.

Hall of Fame

He first became eligible for the Hall of Fame in 2023. He received 10.8% of the vote, he had a long way to go in the election into the Baseball Hall of Fame.

Summary Analysis

Rodriguez's Hall of Fame Point Total is 112.850. The BBWAA needs to review the Character Clause Violations during Rodriguez's career. Here is where legal woes would count against him with Rodriguez's statistics going into the Hall of Fame.

Pitcher Right Handed Potential Hall of Fame Inductee

Rodriguez, Francisco

Positions	Pitcher	Born:	January 7, 1982	
		From:	Caracas, Venezuela	
		Bats:	Right	
		Throws:	Right	

Height: 6'0" — USC 183 cm
Weight: 195 lbs. — 88 Kg.
Debut: September 18, 2002
Last Game: June 22, 2017

Year	Age	Tm	Lg	W	L	PCT	ERA	G	GS	GF	CG	SHO	SV	IP	H	R	ER	BB	SO	SO	WHIP	Awards
2002	20	ANA	AL	0	0	0.000	0.00	5	0	4	0	0	0	5.2	3	0	0	2	13	21	0.882	
2003	21	ANA	AL	8	3	0.727	3.03	59	0	23	0	0	2	86	50	30	29	35	95	334	0.988	
2004	22	ANA	AL	4	1	0.800	1.82	69	0	29	0	0	12	84	51	21	17	33	123	335	1.000	AS,CYA-4
2005	23	LAA	AL	2	5	0.286	2.67	66	0	58	0	0	45	67.1	45	20	20	32	91	279	1.144	
2006	24	LAA	AL	2	3	0.400	1.73	60	0	58	0	0	47	73	52	16	14	28	98	296	1.096	CYA-4
2007	25	LAA	AL	5	2	0.714	2.81	64	0	56	0	0	40	67.1	50	22	21	34	90	285	1.248	AS
2008	26	LAA	AL	2	3	0.400	2.24	76	0	69	0	0	62	68.1	54	21	17	34	77	288	1.288	AS,CYA-3,MVP-6
2009	27	NYM	NL	3	6	0.333	3.71	70	0	66	0	0	35	68	51	34	28	38	73	295	1.305	AS
2010	28	NYM	NL	4	2	0.667	2.20	53	0	46	0	0	25	57.1	45	14	14	21	67	236	1.151	
2011	29	TOT	NL	6	2	0.750	2.64	73	0	36	0	0	23	71.2	67	22	21	26	79	307	1.298	
2011	29	NYM	NL	2	2	0.500	3.16	42	0	34	0	0	23	42.2	44	15	15	16	46	187	1.406	
2011	29	MIL	NL	4	0	1.000	1.86	31	0	2	0	0	0	29	23	7	6	10	33	120	1.136	
2012	30	MIL	NL	2	7	0.222	4.38	78	0	13	0	0	3	72	65	37	35	31	72	305	1.333	
2013	31	TOT	MLB	3	2	0.600	2.70	48	0	23	0	0	10	46.2	42	14	14	14	54	193	1.200	
2013	31	MIL	NL	1	1	0.500	1.09	25	0	18	0	0	10	24.2	17	3	3	9	26	97	1.054	
2013	31	BAL	AL	2	1	0.667	4.50	23	0	5	0	0	0	22	25	11	11	5	28	96	1.364	
2014	32	MIL	NL	5	5	0.500	3.04	69	0	66	0	0	44	68	49	23	23	18	73	268	0.985	AS
2015	33	MIL	NL	1	3	0.250	2.21	60	0	55	0	0	38	57	38	15	14	11	62	216	0.860	AS
2016	34	DET	AL	3	4	0.429	3.24	61	0	55	0	0	44	58.1	45	24	21	21	52	235	1.131	
2017	35	DET	AL	2	5	0.286	7.82	28	0	20	0	0	7	25.1	31	23	22	11	23	118	1.658	
162 Game Avg.				4	4	0.495	2.86	68	0	49	0	0	31	70	53	24	22	28	82	288	1.155	
LAA (7 yrs)				23	17	0.575	2.35	408	0	297	0	0	208	451.2	305	130	118	198	587	1838	1.114	
MIL (5 yrs)				13	16	0.448	2.91	263	0	154	0	0	95	250.2	192	85	81	79	266	1006	1.081	
NYM (3 yrs)				9	10	0.474	3.05	165	0	146	0	0	83	168	140	63	57	75	186	718	1.280	
DET (2 yrs)				5	9	0.357	4.63	89	0	75	0	0	51	83.2	76	47	43	32	75	353	1.291	
BAL (1 yr)				2	1	0.667	4.5	23	0	5	0	0	0	22	25	11	11	5	28	96	1.364	
AL (10 yrs)				30	27	0.526	2.78	520	0	377	0	0	259	557.1	406	188	172	235	690	2287	1.150	
NL (7 yrs)				22	26	0.458	2.97	428	0	300	0	0	178	418.2	332	148	138	154	452	1724	1.161	
16 Yrs				52	53	0.495	2.86	948	0	677	0	0	437	976	738	336	310	389	1142	4011	1.155	Career Pts.
Points				1.500	0.000	2.500	12.500	14.250	0.000	11.750	0.000	0.000	16.750	1.000	0.000	0.000	0.000	0.000	2.500	0.000	13.000	75.750

Post Seasonal Play

Year	Age	Team	Series	W	L	PCT	ERA	G	GS	GF	CG	SHO	SV	IP	H	R	ER	BB	SO	BF	WHIP	
2002	20	ANA	ALDS	2	0	1.000	3.18	3	0	0	0	0	0	5.2	2	2	2	2	8	21	0.706	
2002	20	ANA	ALCS	2	0	1.000	0.00	4	0	0	0	0	0	4.1	2	0	0	2	7	17	0.923	
2004	22	ANA	ALDS	0	2	0.000	3.86	2	0	0	0	0	0	4.2	4	2	2	3	5	22	1.500	
2005	23	LAA	ALDS	0	0	0.000	2.70	3	0	3	0	0	2	3.1	5	1	1	0	2	14	1.500	
2005	23	LAA	ALCS	0	0	0.000	0.00	2	0	2	0	0	1	2.1	2	2	0	3	3	12	2.143	
2007	25	LAA	ALDS	0	0	0.000	54.00	1	0	1	0	0	0	0.1	1	2	2	1	1	3	6.000	
2008	26	LAA	ALDS	0	1	0.000	7.71	2	0	1	0	0	0	2.1	5	2	2	2	2	13	3.000	
2011	29	MIL	NLDS	0	0	0.000	0.00	2	0	0	0	0	0	2	2	0	0	3	4	11	2.500	
2011	29	MIL	NLCS	0	0	0.000	3.00	3	0	0	0	0	0	3	3	1	1	1	4	13	1.333	
Totals				4	3	0.571	3.21	22	0	7	0	0	3	28	26	12	10	17	36	126	1.536	Post Season Pts.
Points				0.400	0.000	0.000	1.000	2.000	0.000	0.800	0.000	0.000	0.600	0.600	0.000	0.000	0.000	0.000	0.800	0.000	0.000	6.200

World Series Play

Year	Age	Team	Series	W	L	PCT	ERA	G	GS	GF	CG	SHO	SV	IP	H	R	ER	BB	SO	BF	WHIP	
2002	20	ANA	WS	1	1	0.500	2.08	4	0	1	0	0	0	8.2	6	3	2	1	13	32	0.808	
Totals				1	1	0.500	2.08	4	0	1	0	0	0	8.2	6	3	2	1	13	32	0.808	World Series Pts.
Points				0.250	0.000	0.000	0.250	0.250	0.000	0.250	0.000	0.000	0.000	0.250	0.000	0.000	0.000	0.000	0.400	0.000	0.250	1.900

Yearly Points Leading the League

Category	Times	Points	Total
MVP	0	7	0
ROY	0	5	0
Cy Young	0	5	0
Golden Glove	0	3	0
All-Star	6	2	12
Wins	0	3	0
Totals			12

Category	Times	Points	Total
Saves	3	3	9
ERA	0	3	0
S.O.'s	0	2	0
Games	1	2	2
G.S.	0	2	0
C.G.	0	2	0
Totals			11

Categ	Times	Points	Total
SHO	0	2	0
WinPc	0	3	0
Inning	0	2	0
WHIP	0	2	0
GF	3	2	6
Totals			6
Grand Total Add-On Points		29	

Hall of Fame Points	
Career Points	75.750
Post Season Points	6.200
World Series Points	1.900
Career Add-On Points	29.000
Writers Association Pts.	0.000
Military/Lifetime Achievement	0.000
Grand Total HOF Points	112.850

Schilling, Curt

Personal Life

Curtis Montague Schilling was born on November 14, 1966, as the middle child to Cliff Schilling and Mary Schilling. Curt's father was a Pirates fan, and the first baseball game Curt ever attended was Roberto Clemente's last."

Schilling attended Shadow Mountain High School in Phoenix, Arizona. He didn't make the varsity until his senior year and once out of high school he enrolled at Yavapai Junior College in Prescott, Arizona in 1986. During his time, his team made it to the Junior College World Series.

Schilling married Shonda Michelle Brewer on November 7, 1992. They have four children, son Gehring, daughter Gabriella, son Grant, and son Garrison. Schilling became a born-again Christian, an evangelical in 1997.

Baseball Career

In 1986, Schilling began his professional career in the Boston Red Sox farm system as a second-round pick. He was traded to the Baltimore Orioles and called up to the big leagues in time to make his first appearance on September 7, 1988. Schilling was a September pitcher again in 1989. He began the 1990 season with Rochester again but was brought up near the end of Jume and got his first extended taste of major-league pitching, working exclusively in relief, working 46 innings in 35 games, with an excellent 2.54 ERA. He earned his first save and win in 1990 by not allowing a run in the last $2+\frac{1}{3}$ innings of a 6–2 victory over Minnesota which was his first Orioles appearance of the year on June 29. The win came when he pitched two shutout innings in a 7–5 win over Kansas City on July 11 finishing the season with a 1–2 record and a 2.54 ERA.

Playing On January 10, 1991, he was traded to the Houston Astros and given regular work. Schilling worked 56 games in relief in 1991, with a 3-5 record and a 3.82 ERA. Just before the 1992 season began, he was traded to the Philadelphia Phillies on April 2. With the Phillies, Schilling settled in and 1992 was one of the best with a 2.35 earned-run average and a league-leading WHIP of 0.990. With 26 starts, Schilling won 14 games, losing 11 for a sixth-place team. He threw 10 complete games.

A Fan's Perspective

The 1993 Phillies went all the way to the World Series. Schilling (16-7) and Tommy Greene (16-4) tied for the team lead in wins. Schilling was named MVP of the NLCS against Atlanta. In the World Series, against the Toronto Blue Jays, he was tagged for seven runs (six earned) in Game One, and bore the loss. In Game Five, when a Jays win would have given them the championship, Schilling threw a five-hit, 2-0 shutout. Toronto won Game Six and the Series.

Schilling had a rough year in 1994 after starting the 1994 season with a poor spring training and then going 0-7 made it clear that something was wrong. His earned-run average climbed to 5.40 through May 16, after which he didn't pitch for two months because of surgery to remove bone spurs on his right elbow. Then the player strike brought about an end to the season. In 1995 he suffered a torn labrum and after July 18 needed season-ending surgery. He came back on May 14, 1996, with seven innings of no-run ball and was clearly back on track and Schilling started 26 games and led the league with eight complete games. His won-lost record reflected the team; he was 9-10, but he pitched with a 3.19 ERA, ranking him seventh.

In 1997, he led the league with 319 strikeouts, had a record of 17-11 (2.97). He struck out an even 300 opponents in 1998 and led the majors with 15 complete games. In both 1998 and 1999, Schilling won 15 games. From July 23, 1999, when he had to leave a game due to right biceps and shoulder issues, to September 3, he appeared in only one game, giving up eight runs.

In 2000 there was a change of scenery. Schilling had a middling 6-6 (3.91) record as the trade deadline approached; on July 23, the Arizona Diamondbacks traded four players to the Phillies so they could add Schilling to their rotation. Schilling more or less continued as he had been, 5-6 with a 3.69 ERA the remainder of the season. But in 2001 the Diamondbacks got everything they had been hoping for, and maybe more. Schilling had a dominant 22-6 season, with a 2.93 earned-run average, leading the league in wins and coming in second only to teammate Randy Johnson in ERA.

Come the postseason, Schilling shone. He threw a three-hit shutout in Game One of the Division Series against the Cardinals. He won the clinching Game Five with a 2-1 complete game. In the League Championship Series, he pitched once, again throwing a complete game and again giving up just one run. This put Schilling in position to start Game One of the World Series against the New York Yankees. He allowed three hits and one run in seven innings, winning the game and improving his record to 4-0 in the 2001 postseason. At this point he had a 0.79 ERA. He started two more games in the World Series, Game Four (again seven innings, three hits, one run) and Game Seven (7⅓ innings, with six hits and two runs.) Both Games Four and Seven were closely contested games, the Yankees winning Game Four in the 10th inning and the Diamondbacks winning Game Seven with two runs in the bottom of the ninth.

Schilling's final record in the 2001 postseason was 4-0 (1.12) and he was named co-MVP of the World Series with Randy Johnson. Johnson had been 21-6 in the regular season, and was 5-1 (1.52) in the postseason, 3-0 in the World Series itself, winning Game Seven when he threw the final inning and a third in hitless relief. 2002, was similar to 2001. Schilling won one more game and lost one more, for a still very enviable 23-7. His ERA nudged up to 3.23, a figure most pitchers could only aspire to get down to. His 0.968 WHIP led the league and was the best of his career. Schilling placed second in Cy Young voting. When it came to the postseason, he couldn't have pitched much better. He gave up one run in seven innings of Game Two of the Division Series against St. Louis, but the Cardinals swept the series. 2003 Schilling's had an appendectomy and on May 30, he was struck twice on his right hand by batted balls and broke the hand. He battled through the season and emerged with a 2.95 ERA but a record of 8-9. On a November 28, 2003, deal, Boston traded four players for Schilling.

In 2004, Schilling led the American League with 21 wins and worked to a 3.26 ERA. Schilling finished second in the Cy Young voting. The Red Sox and Yankees met again in the ALCS. Schilling won Game One in the Division Series against the Angels, but at a cost that appeared evident when it happened; he seemed to come up lame after making a play by the first-base line in the seventh inning. "I felt the tendon tear," he said later. The Red Sox swept, so Schilling wasn't called on again until the ALCS. From the start it was clear he was hit hard as he gave up six runs in three innings and it looked probable that his season was done as the Yankees took the first three games with the third one a 19-8 beat down in Boston. No team in history had ever come back from a three-games-to-none deficit and won a playoff series. But this year's Red Sox team was tough. Dave Roberts stole a base; the Red Sox tied Game Four in the bottom of the ninth. In the bottom of the 12th, David Ortiz won it on a walk off homer. In Game Five, Ortiz won another one in extras, a walk off single in the bottom of the 14th. The two teams traveled to Yankee Stadium to play Game Six, and Schilling had a medical procedure done on his damaged ankle to temporarily stitch his tendons back into place. There was some seepage of blood from the procedure but the 4-2 win was built on Schilling's seven innings of one-run, four-hit pitching. The Red Sox won Game Seven, a game that wasn't even close, over a now-demoralized New York team. The Red Sox had won four in a row, and went on to make those eight consecutive wins, sweeping St. Louis in the World Series. Schilling pitched Game Two, at Fenway Park, allowing an unearned run on four hits in six innings, again pitching on a sutured ankle, one that Dr, Morgan said could not have been rigged up for a third time. He got the win.

In 2006 Schilling reached 3,000 strikeouts on August 30 in Oakland and finished the year with a 15–7 record and 198 strikeouts, with a respectable 3.97 ERA. On May 27, he earned his 200th career win, the 104th major league pitcher to accomplish the feat On August 30, Schilling collected his 3,000th strikeout. Schilling has the highest ratio of strikeouts to walks of any pitcher with at least 3,000 strikeouts and is one of four pitchers to reach the 3,000-K milestone before reaching 1,000 career walks.

On June 7 Schilling threw 8⅔ innings of no-hit ball against Oakland, only to yield a single. He was 9-8 for the season (3.87). and he went out with glory, winning one game each in the Division Series (Game Three in Anaheim, seven innings, no runs), Game Six in the League Championship Series against Cleveland (seven innings, two runs), and Game Two in the World Series against the Colorado Rockies (5⅓ innings, one run). There had also been an unsuccessful start but a no-decision in ALCS Game Two and his last work from a major-league mound was his win in game two of the World Series. Schilling signed to come back for one last year in 2008, but was physically unable to perform, so his final year on the mound was 2007. On March 23, 2009, Schilling officially announced his retirement from professional baseball after 20 seasons. Schilling ended his career with a 216–146 record, 3.46 ERA, 3116 strikeouts, 711 walks.

Accomplishments

- 3-Times 300 strikeouts in one season (1996, 1997, 2002) & 3,000 strikeout club (2006)
- 4-Times NL complete games leader (1996, 1998, 2000, 2001)
- 3-Times NL games started leader (1997, 1998, 2001)
- 2-Times NL innings pitched leader (1998, 2001)
- 2-Times NL strikeout leader (1998, 2001) & 2-Times MLB wins leader (2001, 2004).

The Baseball Hall of Fame

Schillings postseason record is 11-2, and holds a few distinctions such as: No one with 10 or more postseason decisions has a better winning percentage (.846), he won World Series games with three different franchises; the Phillies, Diamondbacks, and Red Sox. With Randy Johnson, he was co-MVP of the 2001 World Series. When pitching for the Red Sox, he won game in each of the three rounds of the playoffs in 2004 and again in 2007. Overall Schilling has struck out 120 and walked 25 in postseason play.

Hall of Fame

Curt Schilling became eligible for election to the National Baseball Hall of Fame with the 2013 ballot. He 71.1% of the votes in the 2021 balloting but once again falling short of the 75% election threshold and is now off the BBWAA balloting.

Summary Analysis

Curt Schillings Hall of Fame Point Total is 140.700 which is considerably over the 110.000 Induction criteria. He should have been automatically. In no way SHOULD Schilling's political views, religious beliefs, or any variation of his first amendment rights have anything to do with the BBWAA voting him into the Hall of Fame. This is a total disgrace and needs to be corrected so Schilling can enjoy his status as being one of the best of all time.

A Fan's Perspective

Pitchers Right Handed Potential Hall of Fame Inductee

Schilling, Curt

Positions		Born:	November, 14, 1966	Height:	6' 5"	USC	196	cm
Pitcher		From:	Anchorage, AK	Weight:	205	lbs.	92	Kg.
		Bats:	Right	Debut:	September 7, 1988			
		Throws:	Right	Last Game:	September 25,2007			

Year	Age	Tm	Lg	W	L	PCT	ERA	G	GS	GF	CG	SHO	SV	IP	H	R	ER	BB	SO	BF	WHIP	Awards
1988	21	BAL	AL	0	3	0	9.82	4	4	0	0	0	0	14.2	22	19	16	10	4	76	2.182	
1989	22	BAL	AL	0	1	0	6.23	5	1	0	0	0	0	8.2	10	6	6	3	6	38	1.5	
1990	23	BAL	AL	1	2	0.333	2.54	35	0	16	0	0	3	46	38	13	13	19	32	191	1.239	
1991	24	HOU	NL	3	5	0.375	3.81	56	0	34	0	0	8	75.2	79	35	32	39	71	336	1.559	
1992	25	PHI	NL	14	11	0.56	2.35	42	26	10	10	4	2	226.1	165	67	59	59	147	895	0.99	
1993	26	PHI	NL	16	7	0.696	4.02	34	34	0	7	2	0	235.1	234	114	105	57	186	982	1.237	
1994	27	PHI	NL	2	8	0.2	4.48	13	13	0	1	0	0	82.1	87	42	41	28	58	360	1.397	
1995	28	PHI	NL	7	5	0.583	3.57	17	17	0	1	0	0	116	96	52	46	26	114	473	1.052	
1996	29	PHI	NL	9	10	0.474	3.19	26	26	0	8	2	0	183.1	149	69	65	50	182	732	1.085	
1997	30	PHI	NL	17	11	0.607	2.97	35	35	0	7	2	0	254.1	208	96	84	58	319	1009	1.046	AS,CYA-4,MVP-14
1998	31	PHI	NL	15	14	0.517	3.25	35	35	0	15	2	0	268.2	236	101	97	61	300	1089	1.105	AS
1999	32	PHI	NL	15	6	0.714	3.54	24	24	0	8	1	0	180.1	159	74	71	44	152	735	1.126	AS
2000	33	TOT	NL	11	12	0.478	3.81	29	29	0	8	2	0	210.1	204	90	89	45	168	862	1.184	
2000	33	PHI	NL	6	6	0.5	3.91	16	16	0	4	1	0	112.2	110	49	49	32	96	474	1.26	
2000	33	ARI	NL	5	6	0.455	3.69	13	13	0	4	1	0	97.2	94	41	40	13	72	388	1.096	
2001	34	ARI	NL	22	6	0.786	2.98	35	35	0	6	1	0	256.2	237	86	85	39	293	1021	1.075	AS,CYA-2,MVP-10
2002	35	ARI	NL	23	7	0.767	3.23	36	35	0	5	1	0	259.1	218	95	93	33	316	1017	0.968	AS,CYA-2,MVP-10
2003	36	ARI	NL	8	9	0.471	2.95	24	24	0	3	2	0	168	144	58	55	32	194	673	1.048	
2004	37	BOS	AL	21	6	0.778	3.26	32	32	0	3	0	0	226.2	206	84	82	35	203	910	1.063	AS,CYA-2,MVP-11
2005	38	BOS	AL	8	8	0.5	5.69	32	11	21	0	0	9	93.1	121	59	59	22	87	418	1.532	
2006	39	BOS	AL	15	7	0.682	3.97	31	31	0	0	0	0	204	220	90	90	28	183	834	1.216	
2007	40	BOS	AL	9	8	0.529	3.87	24	24	0	1	1	0	151	165	68	65	23	101	633	1.245	
162 Game Avg.				15	10	0.597	3.46	38	30	5	6	1	1	221	203	89	85	48	211	899	1.137	
PHI (9 yrs)				101	78	0.564	3.35	242	226	10	61	14	2	1659	1444	664	617	415	1554	6749	1.12	
ARI (4 yrs)				58	28	0.674	3.14	108	107	0	18	5	0	781.2	693	280	273	117	875	3099	1.036	
BOS (4 yrs)				53	29	0.646	3.95	119	98	21	4	1	9	675	712	301	296	108	574	2795	1.215	
BAL (3 yrs)				1	6	0.143	4.54	44	5	16	0	0	3	69.1	70	38	35	32	42	305	1.471	
HOU (1 yr)				3	5	0.375	3.81	56	0	34	0	0	8	75.2	79	35	32	39	71	336	1.559	
NL (13 yrs)				162	111	0.593	3.30	406	333	44	79	19	10	2516	2216	979	922	571	2500	10184	1.107	
AL (7 yrs)				54	35	0.607	4.00	163	103	37	4	1	12	744.1	782	339	331	140	616	3100	1.239	
20 Yrs				216	146	0.597	3.46	569	436	81	83	20	22	3261	2998	1318	1253	711	3116	13284	1.137	**Career Pts.**
				8.000	0.000	9.250	6.500	5.500	6.750	1.000	2.000	2.000	0.500	9.250	0.000	0.000	0.000	0.000	10.500	0.000	11.750	73.000

Post Season Play

Year	Age	Team	Series	W	L	PCT	ERA	G	GS	GF	CG	SHO	SV	IP	H	R	ER	BB	SO	BF	WHIP	
1993	26 PHI		NLCS	0	0	0.000	1.69	2	2	0	0	0	0	16	11	4	3	5	19	63	1.000	
2001	34 ARI		NLDS	2	0	1.000	0.50	2	2	0	2	1	0	18	9	1	1	2	18	67	0.611	
2001	34 ARI		NLCS	1	0	1.000	1.00	1	1	0	1	0	0	9	4	1	1	2	12	32	0.667	
2002	35 ARI		NLDS	0	0	0.000	1.29	1	1	0	0	0	0	7	7	1	1	1	7	30	1.143	
2004	37 BOS		ALDS	1	0	1.000	2.70	1	1	0	0	0	0	6.2	9	3	2	2	4	32	1.650	
2004	37 BOS		ALCS	1	1	0.500	6.30	2	2	0	0	0	0	10	10	7	7	2	5	42	1.200	
2007	40 BOS		ALDS	1	0	1.000	0.00	1	1	0	0	0	0	7	6	0	0	1	4	27	1.000	
2007	40 BOS		ALCS	1	0	1.000	5.40	2	2	0	0	0	0	11.2	15	7	7	0	8	48	1.286	
				7	1	0.875	2.35	12	12	0	3	1	0	84.4	71	24	22	15	77	341	1.019	**Post Game Pts.**
				0.800	0.000	1.800	1.400	1.200	1.200	0.000	0.600	0.400	0.000	1.400	0.000	0.000	0.000	0.000	1.600	0.000	1.800	12.200

World Series Play

Year	Age	Team	Series	W	L	PCT	ERA	G	GS	GF	CG	SHO	SV	IP	H	R	ER	BB	SO	BF	WHIP	
1993	26 PHI		WS	1	1	0.500	3.52	2	2	0	1	1	0	15.1	13	7	6	5	9	61	1.174	
2001	34 ARI		WS	1	0	1.000	1.69	3	3	0	0	0	0	21.1	12	4	4	2	26	77	0.656	
2004	37 BOS		WS	1	0	1.000	0.00	1	1	0	0	0	0	6	4	1	0	1	4	24	0.833	
2007	40 BOS		WS	1	0	1.000	1.69	1	1	0	0	0	0	5.1	4	1	1	2	4	22	1.125	
				4	1	0.800	2.06	7	7	0	1	1	0	48	33	13	11	10	43	184	0.896	**World Series Pts.**
				0.800	0.000	1.400	1.600	0.400	0.800	0.000	0.250	0.250	0.000	0.800	0.000	0.000	0.000	0.000	1.200	0.008	2.000	9.500

Yearly Points Leading the League

Category	Times	Points	Total	Category	Times	Points	Total	Categor	Times	Points	Total
MVP	0	7	0	Saves	0	3	0	SHO	0	2	0
ROY	0	5	0	ERA	0	3	0	WinPct	1	2	2
Cy Young	0	5	0	S.O.'s	2	2	4	Innings	2	2	4
Golden Glove	0	3	0	Games	0	2	0	WHIP	2	2	4
All-Star	6	2	12	G.S.	3	2	6	GF	0	2	0
Wins	2	3	6	C.G.	4	2	8	Totals			10
Totals			18	Totals			18	Grand Total Add-On Points		46	

Hall of Fame Points		
Career Points		73.000
Post Season Points		12.200
World Series Points		9.500
Career Add-On Points		46.000
Writers Association Pts.		0.000
Military/Lifetime Achievement		0.000
Grand Total HOF Points		140.700

Walters, William "Bucky"

Personal Life

William Henry "Bucky" Walters was born April 19, 1909, the oldest of seven children of Mildred and William Henry Walters Sr. Bucky married Jane Caroline Yoast (date not found) with the couple having a son (name unknown) and a daughter Carolyn Jane.

Baseball Career

Walters began his baseball career in 1929 as a pitcher and infielder. Walters made his major-league debut with the Boston Braves on September 18, 1931, hitting .211 in 9 games. He spent most of 1932 with Montreal, and was called up to the Braves again, but hit only .187 in 22 games. As a result, he was sold to the San Francisco Missions. Walters hit .376 in 91 games with the Missions in 1933 was purchased by the Red Sox, finishing the season and starting 1934 with them. Walters broke his thumb that season, did not hit well and was sold to the Philadelphia Phillies on June 14, 1934 at 25 years old, that he converted to pitching. Walters made his mound debut September 24 against the Brooklyn Dodgers. He got his first MLB start six days later against the Braves, and allowed one unearned run in five innings. Then, in 1935, Walters pitched in 24 games, with 22 starts, and notched nine victories. He became a sinker-ball specialist, and after winning 14 games and leading the National League with 34 starts in 1937, and was traded to the Cincinnati Reds on June 13, 1938.

For an eight-year period before, during, and after World War II, Bucky Walters was the premier pitcher in the National League and one of the best in the major leagues. Over the years from 1939 to 1946, Walters led the majors in wins (141), innings pitched (2,030), complete games (178), support-neutral wins (146), and, among those with 1,000 or more innings pitched, in ERA. In addition, he led National League pitchers in starts and fewest hits allowed per 9 innings (7.96) and ranked second in the league in baserunners allowed per 9 innings (11.06), shutouts (28), and winning percentage (.610) and fourth in strikeouts.

His most productive season came in 1939, when he won the Triple Crown with 27 victories, a 2.29 ERA, and 137 strikeouts. For his performance, Walters garnered Most Valuable Player honors, the second of three straight Cincinnati players to win the award. Having led the Cincinnati Reds to the pennant along with pitching mate Paul Derringer (25-7), Walters was voted the Most Valuable Player in the National League, receiving three-quarters of the first-place votes. He also batted .325

in 120 at-bats. A panel of distinguished sports writers voted him the major league "All Around Player" of the year, ahead of AL MVP Joe DiMaggio. When the Yankees swept the Reds in four games In the 1939 World Series, Walters started and lost Game 2 and was the loser in relief of the final game. Nevertheless, in the 1940 Series, facing Detroit, Walters gave the National League its first Series game victory since 1937 with a three-hitter in Game 2. Four days later, he pitched a five-hit shutout in Game 6. In Game 7, the Reds won the second world championship of their modern (post-1900) history.

In 1940, Walters helped the Reds win a second straight National League pennant, again leading NL pitchers in wins, ERA, complete games and innings pitched. In the following year, 1940, Walters again led the majors in ERA (2.48) and the National League in Wins (22), innings pitched, complete games, and opponents' batting average (again .220), and played a key role in leading the Reds to their first World Series victory since 1919, four games to three over the Detroit Tigers. He pitched two complete-game wins in the Series, yielding three runs on three hits in Game Two and shutting out the Tigers on five hits in the sixth game when the Reds were down three games to two. He also homered and drove in two runs in that elimination-game win.

In 1941, Walters had a record of 19-15 with a 2.83 ERA, 27 complete games, 202 innings, 129 strikeouts. Walter's performance fell off somewhat during the war years of 1942 and 1943. He won 15 games each year despite injuring his leg during spring training in 1943 and dealing with a troubled appendix. After an appendectomy, he returned in 1944 and enjoyed another golden year reminiscent of his prewar years. He led the league in wins with 23, losing only 8 and trailing a teammate for the ERA lead by two hundredths of a run. On May 14, he pitched a perfect game through 7 2/3 innings, until Connie Ryan singled, finishing with a one-hit shutout victory. On July 31, 1945, Walters hurt his arm in St. Louis and pitched in only two more games that season. He won only 10 games in 1945 and 10 in the postwar season of 1946, though still with low ERAs of 2.68 and 2.56. In 1947 his ERA soared to 5.75 and as he won 8 and lost 8. Though he pitched in seven games in 1948 and one in 1950. he was unable to add to his total of 198. Fittingly, his last win came on Bucky Walters Night at Cincinnati's Crosley Field, on September 9, 1947. He responded with a 2-0, four-hit shutout.

The Baseball Hall of Fame

Achievements

- 2-Pitched on National League Pennant Winners: (Cincinnati 1939 & 1940).
- 1-Pitched on National League World Series Winners: (Cincinnati 1940),
- 2-Times led the National League in ERA: (1939, & 1940).
- 3-Times led the National League in Complete Games: (1939, 1940 & 1941).
- 1-Time led the National League in Shutouts (1936):
- 3-Times led the National League in Innings Pitched: (1939, 1940 & 1941).
- 1-Time led the National League in Strikeouts: (1939).
- 2-Times led the National League in Strikeouts: (1939 & 1940).
- 6-Times National League All-Star: (1937, 1939-1942 & 1944).
- 5-Times received Most Valuable Player Votes: (1939-1942, 1943 & 1944).

Over the course of his 19-year big-league career, he played for the Boston Braves, Boston Red Sox, Philadelphia Phillies, and Cincinnati Reds. He pitched 42 shutouts, a 198–160 won–lost record, 1,107 strikeouts and a 3.30 ERA in 3,104⅔ innings, 428 appearances, 242 complete games.

Hall of Fame

From 1950 through 1970, Walters had little support in the BBWAA elections for the National Baseball Hall of Fame. In August 2008, he was considered by the Veterans Committee and again in 2013 Veterans Committee but failed to be elected.

Summary Analysis

Walters Hall of Fame Statistical Point Total is 121.150 which covers the pitching portion of his career. Walters should have been elected years ago as an all-around position-player, pitcher, coach, and manager. He needs to be elected into the Hall of Fame.

Pitcher Right Handed Potential Hall of Fame Inductee

Walters, Bucky

Positions	Born :	April 19, 1909	Height: 6' 1" cm 185
Pitcher	Died:	April 20, 1991	Weight: 180 Kg. 81
	From:	Abington, PA	Debut:
	Bats:	Right	Last Game:
	Throws:	Right	

Year	Age	Tm	Lg	W	L	PCT	ERA	G	GS	GF	CG	SHO	SV	IP	H	R	ER	BB	SO	BF	WHIP	Awards
1934	25	PHI	NL	0	0	0.000	1.29	2	1	1	0	0	0	7	8	3	1	2	7	30	1.429	
1935	26	PHI	NL	9	9	0.500	4.17	24	22	2	8	2	0	151	168	86	70	68	40	666	1.563	
1936	27	PHI	NL	11	21	0.344	4.26	40	33	3	15	4	0	258	284	146	122	115	66	1159	1.547	
1937	28	PHI	NL	14	15	0.483	4.75	37	34	1	15	3	0	246.1	292	148	130	86	87	1094	1.535	AS
1938	29	TOT	NL	15	14	0.517	4.2	39	34	3	20	3	1	251	259	134	117	108	93	1111	1.462	
1938	29	PHI	NL	4	8	0.333	5.23	12	12	0	9	1	0	82.2	91	53	48	42	28	376	1.609	
1938	29	CIN	NL	11	6	0.647	3.69	27	22	3	11	2	1	168.1	168	81	69	66	65	735	1.390	
1939	30	CIN	NL	27	11	0.711	2.29	39	36	2	31	2	0	319	250	98	81	109	137	1283	1.125	AS,MVP-1
1940	31	CIN	NL	22	10	0.688	2.48	36	36	0	29	3	0	305	241	95	84	92	115	1207	1.092	AS,MVP-3
1941	32	CIN	NL	19	15	0.559	2.83	37	35	2	27	5	2	302	292	108	95	88	129	1252	1.258	AS,MVP-28
1942	33	CIN	NL	15	14	0.517	2.66	34	32	1	21	2	0	253.2	223	101	75	73	109	1054	1.167	AS
1943	34	CIN	NL	15	15	0.500	3.54	34	34	0	21	5	0	246.1	244	105	97	109	80	1054	1.433	MVP-32
1944	35	CIN	NL	23	8	0.742	2.4	34	32	2	27	6	1	285	233	92	76	87	77	1162	1.123	AS,MVP-5
1945	36	CIN	NL	10	10	0.500	2.68	22	22	0	12	3	0	168	166	62	50	51	45	706	1.292	
1946	37	CIN	NL	10	7	0.588	2.56	22	22	0	10	2	0	151.1	146	55	43	64	60	636	1.388	
1947	38	CIN	NL	8	8	0.500	5.75	20	20	0	5	2	0	122	137	83	78	49	43	550	1.525	
1948	39	CIN	NL	0	3	0.000	4.63	7	5	1	1	0	0	35	42	25	18	18	19	157	1.714	
1950	41	BSN	NL	0	0	0.000	4.5	1	0	0	0	0	0	4	5	2	2	2	0	19	1.750	
162 Game Avg.				16	13	0.553	3.3	35	33	1	20	3	0	256	246	111	94	92	91	1082	1.324	
CIN (11 yrs)				160	107	0.599	2.93	312	296	11	195	32	4	2355	2142	905	766	806	879	9796	1.251	
PHI (5 yrs)				38	53	0.418	4.48	115	102	7	47	10	0	745	843	436	371	313	228	3325	1.552	
BSN (1 yr)				0	0	0.000	4.50	1	0	0	0	0	0	4	5	2	2	2	0	19	1.750	
16 Yrs				198	160	0.553	3.30	428	398	18	242	42	4	3104	2990	1343	1139	1121	1107	13140	1.324	Career Pts.
				6.750	0.000	5.500	7.500	3.000	5.500	0.500	6.750	5.500	0.000	8.000	0.000	0.000	0.000	0.000	2.500	0.000	4.500	56.000

Post Seasonal Play

Year	Age	Team	Series	W	L	PCT	ERA	G	GS	GF	CG	SHO	SV	IP	H	R	ER	BB	SO	BF	WHIP	
None				0	0	0	0	0	0	0	0	0	0	0	0	0	0	0	0	0	0	Post Season Pts.
				0.000	0.000	0.000	0.000	0.000	0.000	0.000	0.000	0.000	0.000	0.000	0.000	0.000	0.000	0.000	0.000	0.000	0.000	0.000

World Series Play

Year	Age	Team	Series	W	L	PCT	ERA	G	GS	GF	CG	SHO	SV	IP	H	R	ER	BB	SO	BF	WHIP	
1939	30	Cin	WS	0	2	0.000	4.91	2	1	1	1	0	0	11	13	9	6	1	6	47	1.273	
1940	31	Cin	WS	2	0	1.000	1.50	2	2	0	2	1	0	18	8	3	3	6	6	66	0.778	
				2	2	0.500	2.79	4	3	1	3	1	0	29	21	12	9	7	12	108	0.966	World Series Pts.
				0.400	0.000	0.000	1.200	0.250	0.400	0.250	0.600	0.250	0.000	0.400	0.000	0.000	0.000	0.000	0.400	0.000	2.000	6.150

Yearly Points Leading the League

Category	Times	Points	Total	Category	Times	Points	Total	Category	Times	Points	Total
MVP	1	7	7	Saves	1	3	3	SHO	0	2	0
ROY	0	5	0	ERA	2	3	6	WinPct	0	2	0
Cy Young	0	5	0	S.O.'s	1	2	2	Innings	3	2	6
Golden Glove	0	3	0	Games	0	2	0	WHIP	2	2	4
All-Star	6	2	12	G.S.	2	2	4	GF	0	2	0
Wins	3	3	9	C.G.	3	2	6	Totals			10
Totals			28	Totals			21	Grand Total Add-On Points			59

Hall of Fame Points	
Career Points	56.000
Post Season Points	0.000
World Series Points	6.150
Career Add-On Points	59.000
Writers Association Pts.	0.000
Military/Lifetime Achievement	0.000
Grand Total HOF Points	121.150

Adams, Charles "Babe"

Personal Life

Charles Benjamin "Babe" Adams (May 18, 1882 – July 27, 1968) was born as the eight child in Tipton, Indiana to Nancy Jane Tower and Samuel Adams.

Adams was married March 2, 1909, to Blanche Wright. They had daughters, Mary Elizabeth, born June 16, 1916, and Virginia Lee, born June 21, 1918.

Baseball Career

Addams signed to play in the Missouri Valley League in 1905. After small parts with the St. Louis Cardinals in 1906 and Pirates in 1907, his contract was sold to the Pirates. In 1909, he joined the Pittsburgh staff and posted a 12-3 record with a 1.11 ERA as the Pirates won the pennant. In the World Series, Adams won three complete game victories. Adams became the first rookie in World Series history to start and win Game 7 as the Pirates won their first championship. In 1910, he became a full-time starter in finishing 18-9, 2.24. His big league career ended in August 1926, when he was released by the Pirates. Adams ended his career at 194-140, 2.76 over 19 seasons.

Achievements:

- NL Winning Percentage Leader (1921) & NL Shutouts Leader (1920)
- 15 Wins Seasons: 5 (1910, 1911, 1913, 1919 & 1920)
- 20 Wins Seasons: 2 (1911 & 1913) & 300 Innings (1913).
- 200 Innings Pitched Seasons: 7 (1910, 1911, 1913-1915, 1919 & 1920)
- Won two World Series with the Pittsburgh Pirates (1909 & 1925)

Hall of Fame Candidacy

Letters were written to get Adams on the Veteran Committee in 2015 without success.

Summary Analysis

Babe Adams Hall of Fame Point Total is 94.600. Noted for his outstanding control, his career average of 1.29 walks per 9 innings pitched was the second lowest of the 20th century. Adams career should be voted on by the Veteran Committee Ballot.

Pitcher Right Handed Potential Hall of Fame Inductee

Adams, Babe

Position	Pitcher

Born :	May 18, 1882		Height:	5' 11" USC	180 cm
Died:	July 27, 1968		Weight:	185 lbs.	83 Kg.
From:	Tipton, IN		Debut:	April 18,1906	
Bats:	Left		Last Game:	August 11, 1926	
Throws:	Right				

Year	Age	Tm	Lg	W	L	W-L%	ERA	G	GS	GF	CG	SHO	SV	IP	H	R	ER	BB	S.O.	BF	WHIP	Awards
1906	24	STL	NL	0	1	0	13.5	1	1	0	0	0	0	4	9	8	6	2	0	21	2.75	
1907	25	PIT	NL	0	2	0	6.95	4	3	1	1	0	0	22	40	25	17	3	11	104	1.955	
1909	27	PIT	NL	12	3	0.8	1.11	25	12	11	7	3	2	130	88	25	16	23	65	475	0.854	
1910	28	PIT	NL	18	9	0.667	2.24	34	30	3	16	3	0	245	217	95	61	60	101	971	1.131	
1911	29	PIT	NL	22	12	0.647	2.33	40	37	2	24	6	0	293.1	253	97	76	42	133	1117	1.006	MVP-27
1912	30	PIT	NL	11	8	0.579	2.91	28	20	5	11	2	0	170.1	169	73	55	35	63	704	1.198	
1913	31	PIT	NL	21	10	0.677	2.15	43	37	5	24	4	0	313.2	271	94	75	49	144	1227	1.02	MVP-22
1914	32	PIT	NL	13	16	0.448	2.51	40	35	4	19	3	1	283	253	97	79	39	91	1116	1.032	
1915	33	PIT	NL	14	14	0.5	2.87	40	30	8	17	2	2	245	229	90	78	34	62	969	1.073	
1916	34	PIT	NL	2	9	0.182	5.72	16	10	5	4	1	0	72.1	91	51	46	12	22	314	1.424	
1918	36	PIT	NL	1	1	0.5	1.19	3	3	0	2	0	0	22.2	15	4	3	4	6	82	0.838	
1919	37	PIT	NL	17	10	0.63	1.98	34	29	5	23	6	1	263.1	213	66	58	23	92	1017	0.896	
1920	38	PIT	NL	17	13	0.567	2.16	35	33	2	18	8	2	263	240	83	63	18	84	1035	0.981	
1921	39	PIT	NL	14	5	0.737	2.64	25	20	3	11	2	0	160	155	57	47	18	55	646	1.081	
1922	40	PIT	NL	8	11	0.421	3.57	27	19	4	12	4	1	171.1	191	77	68	15	39	707	1.202	
1923	41	PIT	NL	13	7	0.65	4.42	26	22	3	11	0	1	158.2	196	83	78	25	38	676	1.393	
1924	42	PIT	NL	3	1	0.75	1.13	9	3	3	2	0	0	39.2	31	9	5	3	5	154	0.857	
1925	43	PIT	NL	6	5	0.545	5.42	33	10	12	3	0	3	101.1	129	67	61	17	18	448	1.441	
1926	44	PIT	NL	2	3	0.4	6.14	19	0	14	0	0	3	36.2	51	32	25	8	7	164	1.609	
162 Game Avg.				16	11	0.581	2.76	39	29	7	17	4	1	244	231	92	75	35	84	972	1.092	
PIT (18 yrs)				194	139	0.583	2.74	481	353	90	205	44	16	2991	2832	1125	911	428	1036	11926	1.09	
STL (1 yr)				0	1	0	13.50	1	1	0	0	0	0	4	9	8	6	2	0	21	2.75	
19 Yrs				194	140	0.581	2.76	482	354	90	205	44	16	2995	2841	1133	917	430	1036	11947	1.092	Career Pts.
				6.750	0.000	8.000	13.500	3.750	4.500	1.000	5.500	5.500	0.500	6.750	0.000	0.000	0.000	0.000	2.500	0.000	14.250	72.500

Post Seasonal Play

Year	Age	Tm	Lg	W	L	W-L%	ERA	G	GS	GF	CG	SHO	SV	IP	H	R	ER	BB	SO	BF	WHIP	
				0	0	0	0	0	0	0	0	0	0	0	0	0	0	0	0	0	0	Post Season Pts.
				0.000	0.000	0.000	0.000	0.000	0.000	0.000	0.000	0.000	0.000	0.000	0.000	0.000	0.000	0.000	0.000	0.000	0.000	0.000

World Series Play

Year	Age	Tm	Lg	W	L	W-L%	ERA	G	GS	GF	CG	SHO	SV	IP	H	R	ER	BB	SO	BF	WHIP	
1909	27	PIT	WS	3	0	1.000	1.33	3	3	0	3	1	0	27	18	5	4	6	11	106	0.889	
1925	43	PIT	WS	0	0	0.000	0.00	1	0	1	0	0	0	1	2	0	0	0	0	5	2	
2 Yrs (2 Series)				3	0	1.000	1.29	4	3	1	3	1	0	28	20	5	4	6	11	111	0.929	World Series Pts.
				0.600	0.000	1.000	1.800	0.400	0.400	0.250	0.600	0.250	0.000	0.400	0.000	0.000	0.000	0.000	0.400	0.000	2.000	8.100

Yearly Points Leading the League

Category	Times	Points	Total	Category	Times	Points	Total	Categ.	Times	Points	Total
MVP	0	7	0	Saves	0	2	0	SHO	1	2	2
ROY	0	5	0	ERA	0	2	0	PCT1	1	2	2
Cy Young	0	5	0	S.O.'s	0	2	0	Innings	0	2	0
Golden Glove	0	3	0	Games	0	2	0	WHIP	5	2	10
All-Star	0	2	0	G.S.	0	2	0	GF	0	2	0
Wins	0	2	0	C.G.	0	2	0	Totals			14
Totals			0	Totals			0	Grand Total Add-On Points			14

Hall of Fame Points

Career Points	72.500
Post Season Points	0.000
World Series Points	8.100
Career Add-On Points	14.000
Writers Association Pts.	0.000
Military Points	0.000
Grand Total HOF Points	94.600

Bridges, Thomas "Tommy"

Personal Life

Thomas Jefferson Davis Bridges was born on December 28, 1906, as the only child to Joseph Bridges and Florence Davis in Gordonsville, Tennessee.

Bridges married Carolyn Jellicorse in 1930. Carolyn gave birth to daughter Evelyn, the couple's only child in 1935. Bridges married another woman in 1950 but no information was available about her.

Baseball

A Tigers scout signed Bridges to his first contract in 1929 and pitched in the minors until he joined the Tigers in 1930. His first outing came on August 13 against the New York Yankees in the Bronx. Bridges was one of the best pitchers in baseball from 1931 until 1943, when he entered the Army. He was a member of the Tigers 1945 World Series championship team, his fourth Series, making a relief appearance in Game 6. He finished his career with a 4-1 record, in 7 games, 46 innings, 4 complete games, and an earned run average of 3.52 for the World Series. Bridges' career with the Tigers was 194–138 with a 3.57 ERA.

Achievements

- 3-Times won 20 or more games: (1934-1936) & 1-Time Led the A.L. in Wins (936).
- 2-Times Led A.L. in Games Started: (1934 & 1936).
- 6-Times All-Star: (1934-1937, 1939 & 1940).
- 3-Times Received MVP Votes: (1935, 1936 & 1939).

Hall of Fame Candidacy

Tommy Bridges last year on the BBWAA ballot was 1966 when he received 16 votes for 5.3 %. He needs to be added to the Classic Baseball Era ballot.

Summary Analysis

Tommy Bridges Hall of Fame Point Total in this book is 90.290 which is lower than the Induction Criteria of 110.000. Due to his military service after having the two lowest ERAs of his career, it is assumed the two years he missed would have made his career numbers even better. He should be a Hall of Famer.

Pitcher Right Handed Potential Hall of Fame Inductee

Bridges, Tommy

Position	Pitcher		
Born:	December 28, 1906	Height:	5' 10" USC 178 cm
Died:	April 19, 1968	Weight:	155 lbs. 70 Kg.
From:	Gordonsville, TN	Debut:	August 13, 1930
Bats:	Right	Last Game:	July 20, 1946
Throws:	Right		

Year	Age	Tm	Lg	W	L	PCT	ERA	G	GS	GF	CG	SHO	SV	IP	H	R	ER	BB	S.O.	BF	WHIP	Awards
1930	23	DET	AL	3	2	0.600	4.06	8	5	2	2	0	0	37.2	28	18	17	23	17	158	1.354	
1931	24	DET	AL	8	16	0.333	4.99	35	23	8	8	2	0	173	187	120	96	108	105	809	1.676	
1932	25	DET	AL	14	12	0.538	3.36	34	26	7	10	4	1	201	174	95	75	119	108	881	1.458	
1933	26	DET	AL	14	12	0.538	3.09	33	28	4	17	2	2	233	192	102	80	110	120	984	1.296	
1934	27	DET	AL	22	11	0.667	3.67	36	35	1	23	3	1	275	249	117	112	104	151	1153	1.284	AS
1935	28	DET	AL	21	10	0.677	3.51	36	34	1	23	4	1	274.1	277	129	107	113	163	1195	1.422	AS,MVP-11
1936	29	DET	AL	23	11	0.676	3.60	39	38	1	26	5	0	294.2	289	141	118	115	175	1272	1.371	AS,MVP-9
1937	30	DET	AL	15	12	0.556	4.07	34	31	2	18	3	0	245.1	267	129	111	91	138	1076	1.459	AS
1938	31	DET	AL	13	9	0.591	4.59	25	20	4	13	0	1	151	171	83	77	58	101	665	1.517	
1939	32	DET	AL	17	7	0.708	3.50	29	26	2	16	2	2	198	186	87	77	61	129	840	1.247	AS,MVP-22
1940	33	DET	AL	12	9	0.571	3.37	29	28	1	12	2	0	197.2	171	89	74	88	133	843	1.31	AS
1941	34	DET	AL	9	12	0.429	3.41	25	22	2	10	1	0	147.2	128	66	56	70	90	630	1.341	
1942	35	DET	AL	9	7	0.563	2.74	23	22	1	11	2	1	174	164	66	53	61	97	742	1.293	
1943	36	DET	AL	12	7	0.632	2.39	25	22	3	11	3	0	191.2	159	57	51	61	124	774	1.148	
1944										Did not play in major or minor leagues (Military Service)											
1945	38	DET	AL	1	0	1.00	3.27	4	1	2	0	0	0	11	14	6	4	2	8	48	1.455	
1946	39	DET	AL	1	1	0.50	5.91	9	1	6	0	0	1	21.1	24	16	14	8	17	95	1.500	
162 Game Avg.				17	12	0.58	3.57	37	31	4	17	3	1	245	231	114	97	103	145	1052	1.368	

16 Yrs	W	L	PCT	ERA	G	GS	GF	CG	SHO	SV	IP	H	R	ER	BB	S.O.	BF	WHIP	Career Pts.
	194	138	0.584	3.57	424	362	47	200	33	10	2826	2675	1321	1122	1192	1674	12165	1.368	
	6.750	0.000	8.000	5.750	3.000	5.500	0.500	4.500	3.750	0.500	6.750	0.000	0.000	0.000	0.000	3.750	0.000	3.740	52.490

Post Seasonal Play

Year	Age	Tm	Lg	W	L	PCT.	ERA	G	GS	GF	CG	SHO	SV	IP	H	R	ER	BB	SO	BF	WHIP	Post Season Pts.
				0	0	0	0	0	0	0	0	0	0	0	0	0	0	0	0	0	0	
				0.000	0.000	0.000	0.000	0.000	0.000	0.000	0.000	0.000	0.000	0.000	0.000	0.000	0.000	0.000	0.000	0.000	0.000	0.000

World Series Play

Year	Age	Tm	Lg	W	L	PCT.	ERA	G	GS	GF	CG	SHO	SV	IP	H	R	ER	BB	SO	BF	WHIP	World Series Pts.
1934	27	DET	WS	1	1	0.500	3.63	3	2	0	1	0	0	17.1	21	9	7	1	12	75	1.269	
1935	28	DET	WS	2	0	1.000	2.50	2	2	0	2	0	0	18	18	6	5	4	9	74	1.222	
1940	33	DET	WS	1	0	1.000	3.00	1	1	0	1	0	0	9	10	4	3	1	5	38	1.222	
1945	38	DET	WS	0	0	0.000	16.20	1	0	0	0	0	0	1.2	3	3	3	3	1	10	3.600	
	4	1	0.800	3.52	7	5	0	4	0	0	46	52	22	18	9	27	197	1.326	
	0.800	0.000	1.400	0.800	0.800	0.800	0.000	0.800	0.000	0.000	0.800	0.000	0.000	0.000	0.000	0.800	0.000	0.800	7.800

Yearly Points Leading the League

Category	Times	Points	Total	Category	Times	Points	Total	Categor	Times	Points	Total	Hall of Fame Points	
MVP	0	7	0	Saves	0	2	0	SHO	1	2	2	Career Points	52.490
ROY	0	5	0	ERA	0	2	0	WinPc	0	2	0	Post Season Points	0.000
Cy Young	0	5	0	S.O.'s	2	2	4	Inning	0	2	0	World Series Points	7.800
Golden Glove	0	3	0	Games	0	2	0	WHIP	0	2	0	Career Add-On Points	24.000
All-Star	6	2	12	G.S.	2	2	4	GF	0	2	0	Writers Association Pts.	0.000
Wins	1	2	2	C.G.	0	2	0	Totals			2	Military Points	6.000
Totals			14	Totals			8	Grand Total Add-On Points		24		Grand Total HOF Points	90.290

Brown, Kevin "Brownie"

Personal Life

James Kevin Brown was born March 14, 1965, in Milledgeville, Georgia. No information was available during the research process about Browns parents, or siblings. Brown played three years of college baseball at Georgia Tech for their baseball team and was named a first team All-American.

Brown married his wife, Candace, in 1987 with the couple having four sons: Ridge, Grayson, Dawson, and Maclain.

Baseball Career

The Texas Rangers selected Brown 4th in the first round of the 1986 draft. From 1989 when he secured a spot in the Texas rotation, through 2005, he was perceived to have a lack of loyalty by moving from team to team while at his peak. Brown finished his career with a 211-144, 3.28 ERA, 486 games, 3256.1 innings, 2397 strikeouts, and a 1.222 EWHIP, over 19 years and threw a no-hitter against the San Francisco Giants

Achievements

- 6-time All-Star (1992, 1996-1998, 2000 & 2003)
- 2-time NL ERA Leader (1996 & 2000) & NL Shutouts Leader (1996).
- AL Wins Leader (1992) & AL innings Pitched Leader (1992)
- 15 Wins Seasons: 6 (1992, 1993 & 1996-1999) & 20 Wins Seasons: 1 (1992)
- 200 Innings Pitched Seasons: 9 (1991-1993, 1996-2000 & 2003)
- 200 Strikeouts Seasons: 4 (1997-2000) & Won a World Series with Florida (1997).

Hall of Fame

Kevin Brown was eligible for the Hall of Fame BBWAA Ballot in 2011. He received 12 votes for 2.1% and was removed from further Hall of Fame voting by the BBWAA.

Summary Analysis

Kevin Browns Hall of Fame Point Total is 104.900. Brown was a pitcher who had the rare talent of relying both on movement and velocity. He needs to be elected.

A Fan's Perspective

Pitcher Right Handed Potential Hall of Fame Inductee

Brown, Kevin

Position	Pitcher	Born:	March 14, '965
		From:	Milledgeville, GA
		Bats:	Right
		Throws:	Right

Height:	6' 4"	USC 193 cm
Weight:	195 lbs.	88 Kg.
Debut:	September 30, 1986	
Last Game:	July 23, 2005	

Year	Age	Tm	Lg	W	L	PCT	ERA	G	GS	GF	CG	SHO	SV	IP	H	R	ER	BB	SO	BF	WHIP	Awards
1986	21	TEX	AL	1	0	1.000	3.6	1	1	0	0	0	0	5	6	2	2	0	4	19	1.200	
1988	23	TEX	AL	1	1	0.500	4.24	4	4	0	1	0	0	23.1	33	15	11	8	12	110	1.757	
1989	24	TEX	AL	12	9	0.571	3.35	28	28	0	7	0	0	191	167	81	71	70	104	798	1.241	RoY-6
1990	25	TEX	AL	12	10	0.545	3.60	26	26	0	6	2	0	180	175	84	72	60	88	757	1.306	
1991	26	TEX	AL	9	12	0.429	4.40	33	33	0	0	0	0	210.2	233	116	103	90	96	934	1.533	
1992	27	TEX	AL	21	11	0.656	3.32	35	35	0	11	1	0	265.2	262	117	98	76	173	1108	1.272	AS,CYA-6
1993	28	TEX	AL	15	12	0.556	3.59	34	34	0	12	3	0	233	228	105	93	74	142	1001	1.296	
1994	29	TEX	AL	7	9	0.438	4.82	26	25	1	3	0	0	170	218	109	91	50	123	760	1.576	
1995	30	BAL	AL	10	9	0.526	3.60	26	26	0	3	1	0	172.1	155	73	69	48	117	706	1.178	
1996	31	FLA	NL	17	11	0.607	1.89	32	32	0	5	3	0	233	187	60	49	33	159	906	0.944	AS,CYA-2,MVP-22
1997	32	FLA	NL	16	8	0.667	2.69	33	33	0	6	2	0	237.1	214	77	71	66	205	976	1.180	AS
1998	33	SDP	NL	18	7	0.720	2.38	36	35	0	7	3	0	257	225	77	68	49	257	1032	1.066	AS,CYA-3,MVP-16
1999	34	LAD	NL	18	9	0.667	3.00	35	35	0	5	1	0	252.1	210	99	84	59	221	1018	1.066	CYA-6
2000	35	LAD	NL	13	6	0.684	2.58	33	33	0	5	1	0	230	181	76	66	47	216	921	0.991	AS,CYA-6
2001	36	LAD	NL	10	4	0.714	2.65	20	19	0	1	0	0	115.2	94	41	34	38	104	465	1.141	
2002	37	LAD	NL	3	4	0.429	4.81	17	10	0	0	0	0	63.2	68	36	34	23	58	278	1.429	
2003	38	LAD	NL	14	9	0.609	2.39	32	32	0	0	0	0	211	184	67	56	56	185	856	1.137	AS
2004	39	NYY	AL	10	6	0.625	4.09	22	22	0	0	0	0	132	132	65	60	35	83	551	1.265	
2005	40	NYY	AL	4	7	0.364	6.50	13	13	0	0	0	0	73.1	107	57	53	19	50	346	1.718	
162 Game Avg.				15	10	0.594	3.28	34	34	0	5	1	0	230	218	96	84	64	169	957	1.222	
TEX (8 yrs)				78	64	0.549	3.81	187	186	1	40	6	0	1278	1322	629	541	428	742	5487	1.369	
LAD (5 yrs)				58	32	0.644	2.83	137	129	0	11	2	0	872.2	737	319	274	223	784	3538	1.100	
NYY (2 yrs)				14	13	0.519	4.95	35	35	0	0	0	0	205.1	239	122	113	54	133	897	1.427	
FLA (2 yrs)				33	19	0.635	2.30	65	65	0	11	5	0	470.1	401	137	120	99	364	1882	1.063	
SDP (1 yr)				18	7	0.72	2.38	36	35	0	7	3	0	257	225	77	68	49	257	1032	1.066	
BAL (1 yr)				10	9	0.526	3.60	26	26	0	3	1	0	172.1	155	73	69	48	117	706	1.178	
AL (11 yrs)				102	86	0.543	3.93	248	247	1	43	7	0	1656	1716	824	723	530	992	7090	1.356	
NL (8 yrs)				109	58	0.653	2.6	238	229	0	29	10	0	1600	1363	533	462	371	1405	6452	1.084	
19 Yrs				211	144	0.594	3.28	486	476	1	72	17	0	3256	3079	1357	1185	901	2397	13542	1.222	Career Pts.
				8.000	0.000	9.250	8.500	4.500	7.500	0.000	1.500	2.000	0.000	9.250	0.000	0.000	0.000	0.000	5.750	0.000	9.250	65.500

Post Seasonal Play

Year	Age	Team	Series	W	L	PCT.	ERA	G	GS	GF	CG	SHO	SV	IP	H	R	ER	BB	SO	BF	WHIP	
1997	32	FLA	NLDS	0	0	0.000	1.29	1	1	0	0	0	0	7	4	1	1	0	5	24	0.571	
1997	32	FLA	NLCS	2	0	1.000	4.20	2	2	0	1	0	0	15	16	7	7	5	13	66	1.400	
1998	33	SDP	NLDS	1	0	1.000	0.61	2	2	0	0	0	0	14.2	5	1	1	7	21	56	0.818	
1998	33	SDP	NLCS	1	1	0.500	2.61	2	1	0	1	1	0	10.1	5	3	3	4	12	39	0.871	
2004	39	NYY	ALDS	1	0	1.000	1.50	1	1	0	0	0	0	6	8	1	1	0	1	23	1.333	
2004	39	NYY	ALCS	0	1	0.000	21.60	2	2	0	0	0	0	3.1	9	9	8	4	2	22	3.900	
				5	2	0.714	3.39	10	9	0	2	1	0	55.4	47	22	21	20	52	230	1.358	Post Season Pts.
				0.600	0.000	1.200	0.800	0.400	1.000	0.000	0.400	0.400	0.000	1.000	0.000	0.000	0.000	0.000	1.200	0.000	0.600	7.600

World Series Play

Year	Age	Team	Series	W	L	PCT.	ERA	G	GS	GF	CG	SHO	SV	IP	H	R	ER	BB	SO	BF	WHIP	
1997	32	FLA	WS	0	2	0	8.18	2	2	0	0	0	0	11	15	10	10	5	6	48	1.818	
1998	33	SDP	WS	0	1	0	4.40	2	2	0	0	0	0	14.1	14	7	7	6	13	62	1.395	
				0	3	0	6.04	4	4	0	0	0	0	25.1	29	17	17	11	19	110	1.579	World Series Pts.
				0.000	0.000	0.000	0.000	0.400	0.400	0.000	0.000	0.000	0.000	0.400	0.000	0.000	0.000	0.000	0.600	0.000	0.000	1.800

Yearly Points Leading the League

Category	Times	Points	Total
MVP	0	7	0
ROY	0	5	0
Cy Young	0	5	0
Golden Glove	0	3	0
All-Star	6	2	12
Wins	1	2	2
Totals			14

Category	Times	Points	Total
Saves	0	2	0
ERA	2	2	4
S.O.'s	0	2	0
Games	0	2	0
G.S.	3	2	6
C.G.	0	2	0
Totals			10

Categ	Times	Points	Total
SHO	0	2	0
WinPc	0	2	0
Inning	1	2	2
WHIP	2	2	4
GF	0	2	0
Totals			6
Grand Total Add-On Points		30	

Half of Fame Points	
Career Points	65.500
Post Season Points	7.600
World Series Points	1.800
Career Add-On Points	30.000
Writers Association Pts.	0.000
Military Points	0.000
Grand Total HOF Points	104.900

Caruthers, Bob "Parisian Bob"

Personal Life

Robert Lee Caruthers (January 5, 1864 – August 5, 1911), was born in Memphis, Tennessee, the son of Flora McNeil and John Caruthers. He had two older brothers and a younger sister.

Before the start of the 1888 baseball season Caruthers married Mary "Mamie" Danks. The couple had two children who could not be identified during the research.

Baseball Career

Caruthers debuted in the Major Leagues in September 1884 as a call up for the St. Louis Browns. Charles Comiskey, liked what he saw, and made Caruthers the Browns' top starter for 1885. He led the league in ERA 2.07, wins 40, and winning % .755 and led the Browns to their first AA pennant. In 1893 he got into a handful of games - 1 with the Chicago Colts and 13 with the Cincinnati Reds - before being sent to the minors. In his ten major-league seasons, Caruthers pitched in 340 games and was 218-99 while batting .282/.391/.400 in 705 total games, had 2465 AB's, 29 home runs, 359 runs batted in, 359 runs batted in, 152 stolen bases, .282 batting average, .391 OBP %, .400 SLG%, and a .791 OPS. He was a 19th century star who excelled as possibly the greatest two-way player in the history of the majors.

Achievements

- AA ERA Leader (1885) & 2-time AA Wins Leader (1885 & 1889)
- 3-time Winning % Leader (1885, 1887 & 1889) & 400 Innings Seasons: 2 (1885 & 1889
- AA Shutouts Leader (1889) & AA OPS Leader (1886)
- 20 Wins Seasons: 6 (1885-1890) & 30 Wins Seasons: 3 (1885, 1886 & 1889)
- 40 Wins Seasons: 2 (1885 & 1889) & 200-300 Innings Pitched Seasons: 6 (1885-1890)
- 100 Runs Scored Seasons: 1 (1887) & AA On-Base Percentage Leader (1886).

Hall of Fame

Bob Caruthers was one of the best pitchers of his era, yet never inducted because the HOF said he didn't meet the 10-year minimum requirement. He needs to be on the Veteran's ballot.

Summary Analysis

Bob Caruthers Hall of Fame Point Total in is 103.750. Caruthers is considered to be one of the most deserving candidates for the Baseball Hall of Fame. He needs to be INDUCTED.

Pitcher Right Handed Potential Hall of Fame Inductee

Carruthers, Bob

Position		Born :	January, 5, 1864	Height:	5' 7" USC 170 cm
Pitcher		Died:	August 5, 1911	Weight:	138 lbs. 62 Kg.
		From:	Memohis, TN	Debut:	September 7, 1864
		Bats:	Left	Last Game:	May 19, 1893
		Throws:	Right		

Year	Age	Tm	Lg	W	L	PCT	ERA	G	GS	GF	CG	SHO	SV	IP	H	R	ER	BB	SO	BF	WHIP	Awards
1884	20	STL	AA	7	2	0.778	2.61	13	7	6	7	0	0	82.2	61	34	24	15	58	341	0.919	
1885	21	STL	AA	40	13	0.755	2.07	53	53	0	53	6	0	482.1	430	196	111	57	190	1948	1.01	
1886	22	STL	AA	30	14	0.682	2.32	44	43	1	42	2	0	387.1	323	164	100	86	166	1581	1.056	
1887	23	STL	AA	29	9	0.763	3.3	39	39	0	39	2	0	341	337	185	125	61	74	1442	1.167	
1888	24	BRO	AA	29	15	0.659	2.39	44	43	1	42	4	0	391.2	337	176	104	53	140	1569	0.996	
1889	25	BRO	AA	40	11	0.784	3.13	56	50	6	46	7	1	445	444	215	155	104	118	1880	1.231	
1890	26	BRO	NL	23	11	0.676	3.09	37	33	4	30	1	0	300	292	163	103	87	64	1281	1.263	
1891	27	BRO	NL	18	14	0.563	3.12	38	32	6	29	2	1	297	323	185	103	107	69	1331	1.448	
1892	28	STL	NL	2	10	0.167	5.84	16	10	5	10	0	1	101.2	131	75	66	27	21	469	1.554	
162 Game Avg.				23	10	0.688	2.83	36	32	3	31	3	0	296	280	146	93	62	94	1239	1.158	
STL (5 yrs)				108	48	0.692	2.75	165	152	12	151	10	1	1395	1282	654	426	246	509	5781	1.095	
BRO (4 yrs)				110	51	0.683	2.92	175	158	17	147	14	2	1433	1396	739	465	351	391	6061	1.219	
AA (6 yrs)				175	64	0.732	2.62	249	235	14	229	21	1	2130	1932	970	619	376	746	8761	1.084	
NL (3 yrs)				43	35	0.551	3.5	91	75	15	69	3	2	698.2	746	423	272	221	154	3081	1.384	
9 Yrs				218	99	0.688	2.83	340	310	29	298	24	3	2828	2678	1393	891	597	900	11842	1.158	Career Pts.
				8.000	0.000	16.750	12.500	2.500	3.750	0.500	9.250	2.500	0.000	6.750	0.000	0.000	0.000	0.000	2.000	0.000	11.750	76.250

Post Seasonal Play

Year	Age	Team	Series	W	L	PCT.	ERA	G	GS	GF	CG	SHO	SV	IP	H	R	ER	BB	SO	BF	WHIP	
1885	21	STL	WS	1	1	0.5	2.42	3	3	0	3	0	0	26	25	18	7	4	16		1.115	
1886	22	STL	WS	2	1	0.667	2.42	3	3	0	3	1	0	26	18	14	7	6	12		0.923	
1887	23	STL	WS	4	4	0.5	2.15	8	8	0	8	0	0	71	64	29	17	12	19		1.07	
1889	25	BRO	WS	0	2	0	3.75	4	2	2	2	0	1	24	28	19	10	6	6		1.417	
				7	8	0.467	2.51	18	16	2	16	1	1	147	135	80	41	28	53		1.109	Post Season Pts.
				0.800	0.000	0.000	1.400	0.800	1.600	0.250	2.000	0.400	0.250	2.000	0.000	0.000	0.000	0.000	1.200	0.000	0.800	11.500

World Series Play

Year	Age	Team	Series	W	L	PCT.	ERA	G	GS	GF	CG	SHO	SV	IP	H	R	ER	BB	SO	BF	WHIP	
				0	0	0	0	0	0	0	0	0	0	0	0	0	0	0	0	0	0	World Series Pts.
				0.000	0.000	0.000	0.000	0.000	0.000	0.000	0.000	0.000	0.000	0.000	0.000	0.000	0.000	0.000	0.000	0.000	0.000	0.000

Yearly Points Leading the League

Category	Times	Points	Total	Category	Times	Points	Total	Categor	Times	Points	Total
MVP	0	7	0	Saves	0	2	0	SHO	1	2	2
ROY	0	5	0	ERA	1	2	2	WinPct	3	2	6
Cy Young	0	5	0	S.O.'s	0	2	0	Innings	0	2	0
Golden Glove	0	3	0	Games	0	2	0	WHIP	1	2	2
All-Star	0	2	0	G.S.	0	2	0	GF	0	2	0
Wins	2	2	4	C.G.	0	2	0	Totals			10
Totals			4	Totals			2	Grand Total Add-On Points			16

Hall of Fame Points	
Career Points	76.250
Post Season Points	11.500
World Series Points	0.000
Career Add-On Points	16.000
Writers Association Pts.	0.000
Military Points	0.000
Grand Total HOF Points	103.750

Cone, David

Personal Life

David Brian Cone was born January 2, 1963 in Kansas City, Missouri, the son of Joan Curran and Edwin Cone. He attended Rockhurst High School, a Jesuit school.

Cone married Lynn DiGioia on November 12, 1994. The couple have a son, Brian. They divorced in 2011.

Baseball Career

Cone was drafted by Kansas City in the third round of the draft. From 1986 to 2003, he had a record of 194-126, ERA of 3.46, 1.256 WHIP, and 2,668 strikeouts in 450 games. His 8–3 career In the postseason, he was 8-3, 21 games, 111 , ERA of 3.80.

Achievements

- 5 - time All-Star (1988, 1992, 1994, 1997 & 1999
- 5 -Times received Cy Young Votes (1988, 1994 (Won Award), 1995, 1998, & 1999).
- 2 -Times received Most Valuable Player Voyes (1988 & 1994)
- 1 - Time AL Wins Leader (1998) & 1 -Time NL Winning Percentage Leader (1988).
- 1 - Time AL Innings Pitched Leader (1995) & 1 -Time NL Shutouts Leader (1992.
- 2 - Time NL Strikeouts Leader (1990 & 1991)
- 5 - 15 Wins Seasons: (1988 (20), 1992, 1994, 1995 & 1998 (20)).
- 8 – Time 200 Innings Pitched Seasons: 8 (1988-1993, 1995 & 1998)
- 6 – Time 200 Strikeouts Seasons: 6 (1988, 1990-1992, 1997 & 1998)
- 5 – Time World Series Winner: (1992 with Toronto & ((1996, 1998-2000 Yankees).
- Cone pitched the sixteenth perfect game in baseball history in 1999.

Hall of Fame Candidacy

Cone was on the 2009 BBWAA Ballot, received 3.9% of the votes and removed.

Summary Analysis

David Cones Hall of Fame Point Total is 97.350. His career is worthy of the Hall of Fame and should eventually be elected.

Pitcher Right Handed Potential Hall of Fame Inductee

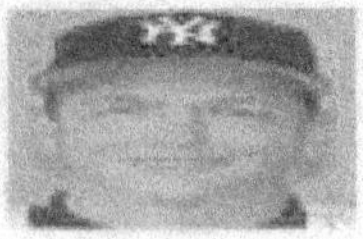

Cone, David
Position: Pitcher

Born:	January 2, 1963
From:	Kansas City, MO
Bats:	Left
Throws:	Right

Height:	6' 1"	USC 185 cm
Weight:	180 lbs.	81 Kg.
Debut:	June 8, 1986	
Last Game:	May 28, 2003	

Year	Age	Tm	Lg	W	L	Pct	ERA	G	GS	GF	CG	SHO	SV	IP	H	R	ER	BB	SO	BF	WHIP	Awards
1986	23	KCR	AL	0	0	0.000	5.560	11	0	5	0	0	0	22.2	29	14	14	13	21	108	1.853	
1987	24	NYM	NL	5	6	0.455	3.710	21	13	3	1	0	1	99.1	87	46	41	44	88	420	1.319	
1988	25	NYM	NL	20	3	0.870	2.220	35	28	0	8	4	0	231.1	178	67	57	40	213	936	1.115	AS,CYA-5,MVP-10
1989	26	NYM	NL	14	8	0.636	3.520	34	33	0	7	2	0	219.2	183	82	86	74	190	820	1.170	
1990	27	NYM	NL	14	10	0.583	3.230	31	30	1	6	2	0	211.2	177	84	76	65	233	840	1.148	
1991	28	NYM	NL	14	14	0.500	3.290	34	34	0	5	2	0	232.2	204	85	85	73	241	966	1.191	
1992	29	TOT	MLB	17	10	0.630	2.810	35	34	0	7	5	0	249.2	201	91	78	111	261	1055	1.250	AS
1992	29	NYM	NL	13	7	0.650	2.880	27	27	0	7	5	0	196.2	162	75	63	82	214	831	1.341	
1992	29	TOR	AL	4	3	0.571	2.550	8	7	0	0	0	0	53	39	16	15	29	47	224	1.283	
1993	30	KCR	AL	11	14	0.440	3.330	34	34	0	6	1	0	254	205	102	94	114	191	1060	1.256	
1994	31	KCR	AL	16	5	0.763	2.940	23	23	0	4	3	0	171.2	130	60	56	54	132	680	1.072	AS,CYA-1,MVP-9
1995	32	TOT	AL	18	8	0.682	3.570	30	30	0	6	2	0	229.1	195	99	91	88	191	954	1.234	CYA-4
1995	32	TOR	AL	9	6	0.600	3.380	17	17	0	5	2	0	130.1	113	53	48	41	102	537	1.182	
1995	32	NYY	AL	9	2	0.818	3.820	18	13	0	1	0	0	99	82	42	42	47	89	417	1.305	
1996	33	NYY	AL	7	2	0.778	2.880	11	11	0	1	0	0	72	50	25	23	34	71	295	1.167	
1997	34	NYY	AL	12	6	0.667	2.820	29	29	0	1	0	0	195	155	67	61	86	222	805	1.236	AS
1998	35	NYY	AL	20	7	0.741	3.550	31	31	0	3	0	0	207.2	186	89	82	59	209	866	1.180	CYA-4
1999	36	NYY	AL	12	9	0.571	3.440	31	31	0	1	1	0	193.1	164	84	74	90	177	827	1.314	AS,CYA-6
2000	37	NYY	AL	4	14	0.222	6.910	30	29	0	0	0	0	155	192	124	119	82	120	733	1.768	
2001	38	BOS	AL	9	7	0.563	4.310	25	25	0	0	0	0	135.2	148	74	65	57	115	614	1.511	
2003	40	NYM	NL	1	3	0.250	6.500	5	4	0	0	0	0	18	20	13	13	13	13	85	1.833	
162 Game Avg.				15	10	0.606	3.460	35	33	1	4	2	0	227	196	96	87	89	209	953	1.256	
NYM (7 yrs)				81	33	0.634	3.180	187	169	4	34	15	1	1209.1	1011	472	421	451	1172	5008	1.192	
NYY (6 yrs)				64	40	0.615	3.510	145	144	0	7	1	0	922	829	431	401	398	888	3843	1.881	
KCR (3 yrs)				27	19	0.587	3.290	68	57	3	10	4	0	448.1	364	176	164	181	344	1858	1.218	
TOR (2 yrs)				13	9	0.591	3.140	25	24	0	5	2	0	183.1	152	82	84	70	149	761	1.211	
BOS (1 yr)				9	7	0.563	4.310	25	25	0	0	0	0	135.2	148	74	65	57	115	614	1.511	
AL (11 yrs)				113	75	0.601	3.700	263	250	5	22	7	0	1689.1	1495	750	684	766	1496	7176	1.352	
NL (7 yrs)				81	51	0.614	3.130	187	169	4	34	15	1	1209.1	1011	472	421	451	1172	5008	1.192	
17 Yrs				194	128	0.606	3.48	450	419	9	56	22	1	2898.2	2506	1222	1115	1187	2668	13184	1.256	Career Pts.
				8.750	0.000	10.500	6.500	3.750	6.750	0.000	1.500	2.500	0.000	6.750	0.000	0.000	0.000	0.000	8.000	0.000	6.750	59.750

Post Seasonal Play

Year	Age	Team	Series	W	L	PCT	ERA	G	GS	GF	CG	SHO	SV	IP	H	R	ER	BB	SO	HBP	WHIP	
1988	25	NYM	NLCS	1	1	0.500	4.50	2	2	1	1	0	0	12	10	6	6	5	8	52	1.250	
1992	29	TOR	ALCS	1	1	0.500	3.00	2	2	0	0	0	0	13	11	7	4	2	9	51	1.308	
1995	32	NYY	ALDS	1	0	1.000	4.60	2	2	0	0	0	0	15.2	15	8	8	0	14	71	1.552	
1996	33	NYY	ALDS	0	1	0.000	9.00	1	1	0	0	0	0	6	8	8	6	2	8	27	1.667	
1996	33	NYY	ALCS	0	0	0.000	3.00	1	1	0	0	0	0	6	5	2	2	5	5	28	1.667	
1997	34	NYY	ALDS	0	0	0.000	16.20	1	1	0	0	0	0	3.1	7	6	6	2	2	20	2.700	
1998	35	NYY	ALDS	1	0	1.000	0.00	1	1	0	0	0	0	5.2	2	0	0	1	8	20	0.529	
1998	35	NYY	ALCS	1	0	1.000	4.15	2	2	0	0	0	0	13	12	6	6	4	13	56	1.385	
1999	36	NYY	ALDS											Did not pitch in series								
1999	36	NYY	ALCS	1	0	1.000	2.57	1	1	0	0	0	0	7	7	2	2	3	8	31	1.429	
2000	37	NYY	ALCS	0	0	0.000	0.00	1	0	1	0	0	0	1	0	0	0	3	0	3	0	
				6	3	0.667	4.41	15	13	2	1	0	0	81.2	77	43	40	38	75	358	1.408	Post Season Pts.
				0.500	0.000	0.250	0.250	0.600	1.400	0.250	0.250	0.000	0.000	1.400	0.000	0.000	0.000	0.000	1.600	0.000	0.400	7.000

World Series Play

Year	Age	Team	Series	W	L	PCT	ERA	G	GS	GF	CG	SHO	SV	IP	H	R	ER	BD	SO	BF	WHIP	
1992	29	TOR	WS	0	0	0.000	3.48	2	2	0	0	0	0	10.1	8	5	4	8	8	47	1.548	
1996	33	NYY	WS	1	0	1.000	1.90	1	1	0	0	0	0	6	4	3	1	4	3	24	1.333	
1998	35	NYY	WS	0	0	0.000	0.00	1	1	0	0	0	0	6	2	0	2	2	4	20	0.889	
1999	36	NYY	WS	1	0	1.000	0.00	1	1	0	0	0	0	7	1	0	0	5	4	26	0.857	
2000	37	NYY	WS	0	0	0.000	0.00	1	0	0	0	0	0	0.1	0	0	0	0	0	1	0.000	
				2	0	1.000	2.134	6	5	0	0	0	0	29.2	16	8	7	20	19	121	1.327	World Series Pts.
				0.400	0.000	0.600	1.400	3.000	0.600	0.000	0.000	0.000	0.000	0.400	0.000	0.000	0.000	0.000	0.600	0.000	1.000	5.890

Yearly Points Leading the League

Category	Times	Points	Total
MVP	0	7	0
ROY	0	5	0
Cy Young	1	5	5
Golden Glove	0	3	0
All-Star	5	2	10
Wins	1	3	3
Totals			37

Category	Times	Points	Total
Saves	0	2	0
ERA	0	2	0
S.O.'s	2	2	4
Games	0	2	0
G.S.	0	2	0
C.G.	0	2	0
Totals			4

Category	Times	Points	Total
SHO	0	2	0
WinPct	1	2	2
Innings	1	2	2
WHIP	0	2	0
GF	0	2	0
Totals			4
Grand Total Add-On Points		25	

Hall of Fame Points	
Career Points	59.750
Post Season Points	7.000
World Series Points	5.890
Career Add-On Points	25.000
Writers Association Pts.	0.000
Military Points	0.000
Grand Total HOF Points	97.308

Derringer, Paul "Oom Paul"

Personal Life

Samuel Paul Derringer was born in Springfield, Kentucky, on October 17, 1906, to Samuel P. Derringer and Lula Ellen Oneal. He had a brother Howard and was a catcher on his high school team at Springfield High. He was a three- letter man playing on the football & basketball teams.

He was married three times, the first being Sera Trent, in 1928 - 1936. Derringer married his second wife, Eloise Brownback1937-1944, with the couple having a daughter Lida Eloise. Derringer married, Mary Jane Stein, on September 3, 1944.

Baseball Career

Derringer debuted with the St. Louis Cardinals in 1931 and he retired after the 1945 season with a record of 223–212, 1507 strikeouts and a 3.46 ERA, 251 CG and 32 shutouts. Paul Derringer is a case of two men, a pitcher with exceptional control of his pitches and work on the mound, and a man with little control of himself anywhere else. He was hot tempered at times, but on the mound, he exhibited great control.

Achievements

- 2 - Times led the N.L. in Winning Pct. (1931 & 1939)
- 3 - Times led the N.L. in Games Started (1936, 1938, & 1940)
- 1 - Time led the N.L. in Complete Games & in Innings Pitched (1938).
- 4 – Time 20 games won (1935, 1938. 1939, & 1940)
- 6 – Times Received MVP Votes (1931, 1935, 1936, 1938, 1939, & 1940).
- 6 – Times All-Star (1935,1938, 1939, 1940, 1941 & 1942).

Hall of Fame

Research indicates that Paul Derringer has never been on the BBWAA ballot.

Summary Analysis

Paul Derringers Hall of Fame Point Total is 98.250. Derringer's Hall of Fame case should be decided by the Classic Baseball Era Committee.

Pitcher Right Handed Potential Hall of Fame Inductee

Derringer, Paul

Position		Born	October 17, 1906	Height:	6 3"	USC	190	cm
Pitcher		Died:	32098	Weight:	205	lbs.	92	Kg.
		From:	Springfield, KY	Debut:	April 16, 1931			
		Bats:	Right	Last Game:	September 27, 1945			
		Throws:	Right					

Year	Age	Tm	Lg	W	L	PCT.	ERA	G	GS	GF	CG	SHO	SV	IP	H	R	ER	BB	SO	BF	WHIP	Awards
1931	24	STL	NL	18	8	0.692	3.36	35	23	10	15	4	2	211.2	225	88	79	65	134	901	1.370	MVP-20
1932	25	STL	NL	11	14	0.440	4.05	39	30	4	14	1	0	233.1	296	133	105	67	78	1043	1.556	
1933	26	TOT	NL	7	27	0.206	3.30	36	33	3	17	2	1	248	264	117	91	60	89	1045	1.306	
1933	26	STL	NL	0	2	0.000	4.24	3	2	1	1	0	0	17	24	11	8	9	3	84	1.941	
1933	26	CIN	NL	7	25	0.219	3.23	33	31	2	16	2	1	231	240	106	83	51	86	961	1.260	
1934	27	CIN	NL	15	21	0.417	3.59	47	31	15	18	1	4	261	297	129	104	59	122	1128	1.364	
1935	28	CIN	NL	22	13	0.629	3.51	45	33	9	20	3	2	276.2	295	132	108	49	120	1153	1.243	AS,MVP-17
1936	29	CIN	NL	19	19	0.500	4.02	51	37	10	13	7	5	282.1	331	147	126	42	121	1207	1.321	MVP-11
1937	30	CIN	NL	10	14	0.417	4.04	43	26	12	12	1	1	222.2	240	112	100	55	94	963	1.325	
1938	31	CIN	NL	21	14	0.600	2.93	41	37	4	26	4	3	307	315	110	100	49	132	1263	1.186	AS,MVP-8
1939	32	CIN	NL	25	7	0.781	2.93	38	35	1	28	5	0	301	321	115	98	35	128	1245	1.183	AS,MVP-3
1940	33	CIN	NL	20	12	0.625	3.06	37	37	0	26	3	0	296.2	280	110	101	48	115	1205	1.106	AS,MVP-4
1941	34	CIN	NL	12	14	0.462	3.31	29	28	1	17	2	1	228.1	233	91	84	54	76	950	1.257	AS
1942	35	CIN	NL	10	11	0.476	3.06	29	27	0	13	1	0	208.2	203	83	71	49	68	872	1.208	AS
1943	36	CHC	NL	10	14	0.417	3.57	32	22	7	10	2	3	174	184	90	69	39	75	743	1.282	
1944	37	CHC	NL	7	13	0.350	4.15	42	16	17	7	0	3	180	205	96	83	39	69	772	1.356	
1945	38	CHC	NL	16	11	0.593	3.45	35	30	5	15	1	4	213.2	223	99	82	51	86	901	1.282	
162 Game Avg.				15	14	0.513	3.46	38	30	7	17	2	2	242	260	110	93	51	100	1022	1.282	
CIN (10 yrs)				161	150	0.518	3.36	393	322	54	189	24	17	2615.1	2755	1135	975	491	1062	10947	1.241	
STL (3 yrs)				29	24	0.547	3.74	77	55	15	30	5	2	462	545	232	192	141	215	2028	1.485	
CHC (3 yrs)				33	38	0.465	3.71	109	68	29	32	3	10	567.2	612	285	234	129	230	2416	1.305	
15 Yrs				223	212	0.513	3.46	579	445	98	251	32	29	3645	3912	1652	1401	761	1507	15391	1.282	Career Pts.
				9.250	0.000	3.000	5.500	5.500	8.000	1.000	8.000	3.750	1.000	10.500	0.000	0.000	0.000	0.000	3.750	0.000	5.750	66.000

Post Seasonal Play

Year	Age	Team	Series	W	L	W-L%	ERA	G	GS	GF	CG	SHO	SV	IP	H	R	ER	BB	SO	BF	WHIP	Post Season Pts.
None				0	0	0	0	0	0	0	0	0	0	0	0	0	0	0	0	0	0	
				0	0	0	0	0	0	0	0	0	0	0	0	0	0	0	0	0	0	0

World Series Play

Year	Age	Team	Series	W	L	W-L%	ERA	G	GS	GF	CG	SHO	SV	IP	H	R	ER	BB	SO	BF	WHIP	World Series Pts.
1931	24	STL	WS	0	2	0.000	4.26	3	2	1	0	0	0	12.2	14	10	6	7	14	59	1.658	
1939	32	CIN	WS	0	1	0.000	2.35	2	2	0	1	0	0	15.1	9	4	4	3	9	58	0.783	
1940	33	CIN	WS	2	1	0.667	2.79	3	3	0	2	0	0	19.1	17	8	6	10	6	84	1.397	
1945	38	CHC	WS	0	0	0.000	6.75	3	0	0	0	0	0	5.1	5	4	4	7	1	29	2.25	
				2	4	0.333	3.42	11	7	1	3	0	0	52.2	45	26	20	27	30	230	1.367	
				0.400	0.000	0.000	0.800	1.200	0.800	0.250	0.600	0.000	0.000	0.800	0.000	0.000	0.000	0.000	0.800	0.000	0.600	6.250

Yearly Points Leading the League

Category	Times	Points	Total	Category	Times	Points	Total	Category	Times	Points	Total
MVP	0	7	0	Saves	0	2	0	SHO	0	2	0
ROY	0	5	0	ERA	0	2	0	WinPct	1	2	2
Cy Young	0	5	0	S.O.'s	0	2	0	Innings	1	2	2
Golden Glove	0	3	0	Games	1	2	2	WHIP	0	2	0
All-Star	6	2	12	G.S.	3	2	6	GF	0	2	0
Wins	0	2	0	C.G.	1	2	2	Totals			4
Totals			12	Totals			10	Grand Total Add-On Points			26

Hall of Fame Points	
Career Points	66.000
Post Season Pts.	0.000
World Series Pts.	6.250
Career Add-On Pts.	26.000
Writers Association Pts.	0.000
Military Points	0.000
Grand Total HOF Points	98.250

The Baseball Hall of Fame

Gooden, Dwight "Doc or Dr, K"

Personal Life

Dwight Eugene Gooden was born November 16, 1964, in Tampa, Florida as the youngest of three children to Dan and Ella Gooden with a very troubled family life.

Gooden married Monica Harris in 1987 and divorced in 2004. Then he married Monique Moore in 2009. He has six children, Dwight Jr., Ashley, Ariel, Devin. Darren and Dylan.

Baseball Career

The Mets took Gooden as the fifth pick in the 1982 draft. He started out in the low minors but made the rare jump from High-A directly to the major leagues making his MLB debut in the 1984 season. He dominated the National League with a 17-9 record with a 2.60 ERA, averaging 11.4 strikeouts per nine innings and striking out 276 which earned him Rookie of the Year honors. In 1985 Gooden was even better ending the season 24-4, striking out 268 hitters in 276⅔ innings and finishing with an ERA of 1.53. All this would earn him the 1985 National League Cy Young Award. From 1984 through 1991, Gooden had some of the historical best statistics. He pitched in 238 games, had a W/L record of 132-53, 1713.2 innings, 1541 strikeouts, 2.391 earned run average, and a 1.152 WHIP. After the 1991 season, Gooden's demons got the best of him. Gooden retired in 2001 with a record of 194–112, 430 games, 2800.2 Innings, 2293 strike-outs, 3.51 ERA, a 1.256 WHIP, and an extreme "What If Tag" to a career derailed by drugs.

Hall of Fame

Gooden appeared on the 2006 Baseball Hall of Fame ballot named on only 3.3 percent. He was removed from future HOF consideration.

Summary Analysis

Dwight Gooden had a Hall of Fame Point Total of 97.250. Gooden is the perfect example of an individual that carried a troubled youth throughout life. Due many Character Clause violations, he should not have a plaque in the Hall of Fame, but his records should be enshrined.

Pitcher Right Handed Potential Hall of Fame Inductee

Gooden, Dwight

Position		Pitcher

Born :	November 16, 1964	
From:	Tampa, FLA	
Bats:	Right	
Throws:	Right	

Height:	6' 2" USC 188 cm	
Weight:	190 lbs. 86 Kg.	
Debut:	April 7, 1984	
Last Game:	September 29, 2000	

Year	Age	Tm	Lg	W	L	W-L%	ERA	G	GS	GF	CG	SHO	SV	IP	H	R	ER	BB	SO	BF	WHIP	Awards
1984	19	NYM	NL	17	9	0.654	2.60	31	31	0	7	3	0	218	161	72	63	73	276	879	1.073	AS,CYA-2,MVP-
1985	20	NYM	NL	24	4	0.857	1.53	35	35	0	16	8	0	276.2	198	51	47	69	268	1065	0.965	AS,CYA-1,MVP-4
1986	21	NYM	NL	17	6	0.739	2.84	33	33	0	12	2	0	250	197	92	79	80	200	1020	1.108	AS,CYA-7
1987	22	NYM	NL	15	7	0.682	3.21	25	25	0	7	3	0	179.2	162	68	64	53	148	730	1.197	CYA-5
1988	23	NYM	NL	18	9	0.667	3.19	34	34	0	10	3	0	248.1	242	98	88	57	175	1024	1.204	AS
1989	24	NYM	NL	9	4	0.692	2.89	19	17	1	0	0	1	118.1	93	42	38	47	101	497	1.183	
1990	25	NYM	NL	19	7	0.731	3.83	34	34	0	2	1	0	232.2	229	106	99	70	223	983	1.285	CYA-4,MVP-14
1991	26	NYM	NL	13	7	0.650	3.60	27	27	0	3	1	0	190	185	80	76	56	150	789	1.268	
1992	27	NYM	NL	10	13	0.435	3.67	31	31	0	3	0	0	206	197	93	84	70	145	863	1.296	SS
1993	28	NYM	NL	12	15	0.444	3.45	29	29	0	7	2	0	208.2	188	89	80	61	149	866	1.193	
1994	29	NYM	NL	3	4	0.429	6.31	7	7	0	0	0	0	41.1	46	32	29	15	40	182	1.476	
1995										Did not play in major or minor leagues (Did Not Play)												
1996	31	NYY	AL	11	7	0.611	5.01	29	29	0	1	1	0	170.2	169	101	95	88	126	756	1.506	
1997	32	NYY	AL	9	5	0.643	4.91	20	19	0	0	0	0	106.1	116	61	58	53	68	472	1.589	
1998	33	CLE	AL	8	6	0.571	3.76	23	23	0	0	0	0	134	135	59	56	51	83	580	1.388	
1999	34	CLE	AL	3	4	0.429	6.26	26	22	0	0	0	0	115	127	90	80	67	88	532	1.687	
2000	35	TOT	MLB	6	5	0.545	4.71	27	14	3	0	0	2	105	119	64	55	44	55	467	1.552	
2000	35	TOT	AL	6	5	0.545	4.54	26	13	3	0	0	2	101	113	60	51	41	54	447	1.525	
2000	35	HOU	NL	0	0	0.000	9.00	1	1	0	0	0	0	4	6	4	4	3	1	20	2.250	
2000	35	TBD	AL	2	3	0.400	6.63	8	8	0	0	0	0	36.2	47	32	27	20	23	173	1.827	
2000	35	NYY	AL	4	2	0.667	3.36	18	5	3	0	0	2	64.1	66	28	24	21	31	274	1.352	
162 Game Avg.				16	9	0.634	3.51	35	33	0	6	2	0	227	208	97	88	77	186	948	1.256	

	W	L	W-L%	ERA	G	GS	GF	CG	SHO	SV	IP	H	R	ER	BB	SO	BF	WHIP	
NYM (11 yrs)	157	85	0.649	3.10	305	303	1	67	23	1	2169.2	1898	823	747	651	1875	8898	1.175	
NYY (3 yrs)	24	14	0.632	4.67	67	53	3	1	1	2	341.1	351	190	177	162	223	1502	1.503	
CLE (2 yrs)	11	10	0.524	4.92	49	45	0	0	0	0	249	262	149	136	118	171	1112	1.526	
TBD (1 yr)	2	3	0.400	6.63	8	8	0	0	0	0	36.2	47	32	27	20	23	173	1.827	
HOU (1 yr)	0	0	0.000	9.00	1	1	0	0	0	0	4	6	4	4	3	1	20	2.250	
NL (12 yrs)	157	85	0.649	3.11	306	304	1	67	23	1	2173.2	1904	827	751	654	1876	8918	1.177	
AL (5 yrs)	37	27	0.578	4.88	124	106	3	1	1	2	627	660	371	340	300	417	2787	1.531	
16 Yrs	194	112	0.634	3.51	430	410	4	68	24	3	2800.2	2564	1198	1091	954	2293	11705	1.256	Career Pts.
	6.750	0.000	11.750	5.750	3.000	6.750	0.000	1.500	2.500	0.000	6.750	0.000	0.000	0.000	0.000	6.750	0.000	6.750	58.250

Post Season Play

Year	Age	Team	Series	W	L	W-L%	ERA	G	GS	GF	CG	SHO	SV	IP	H	R	ER	BB	SO	BF	WHIP	
1986	21	NYM	NLCS	0	1	0.000	1.06	2	0	0	0	0	0	17	16	2	2	5	9	68	1.235	
1988	23	NYM	NLCS	0	0	0.000	2.95	2	0	0	0	0	0	18.1	10	6	6	8	20	74	0.982	
1997	32	NYY	ALDS	0	0	0.000	1.59	1	0	0	0	0	0	5.2	5	1	1	3	5	25	1.412	
1998	33	CLE	ALDS	0	0	0.000	54.00	1	0	0	0	0	0	0.1	1	2	2	2	1	4	9.000	
1998	33	CLE	ALCS	0	1	0.000	5.79	1	0	0	0	0	0	4.2	3	3	3	3	3	20	1.286	
2000	35	NYY	ALDS	0	0	0.000	21.60	0	1	0	0	0	0	1.2	4	4	4	1	1	11	3.000	
2000	35	NYY	ALCS	0	0	0.000	0.00	0	0	0	0	0	0	2.1	1	0	0	0	1	8	0.429	
	0	2	0.000	3.24	7	7	1	0	0	0	50	40	18	18	22	40	210	1.600	Post Season Pts.
	0.000	0.000	0.000	0.800	0.400	0.800	0.250	0.000	0.000	0.000	1.000	0.000	0.000	0.000	0.000	0.800	0.000	0.000	4.050

World Series Play

Year	Age	Team	Series	W	L	W-L%	ERA	G	GS	GF	CG	SHO	SV	IP	H	R	ER	BB	SO	BF	WHIP	
1986	21	NYM	WS	0	2	0	8.00	2	2	0	0	0	0	9	17	10	8	4	9	50	2.333	
2000	35	NYY	WS	Did not pitch in series																		
	0	2	0.000	8.00	2	2	0	0	0	0	9	17	10	8	4	9	50	2.333	World Series Pts.
	0.000	0.000	0.000	0.000	0.250	0.250	0.000	0.000	0.000	0.000	0.200	0.000	0.000	0.000	0.000	0.250	0.000	0.000	0.950

Yearly Points Leading the League

Category	Times	Points	Total	Category	Times	Points	Total	Category	Times	Points	Total		Hall of Fame Points	
MVP	0	7	0	Saves	0	2	0	SHO	0	2	0		Career Points	58.250
ROV	1	5	5	ERA	1	2	2	WinPct	0	2	0		Post Season Points	4.050
Cy Young	1	5	5	S.O.'s	2	2	4	Innings	1	2	2		World Series Points	0.950
Golden Glove	0	3	0	Games	0	2	0	WHIP	1	2	2		Career Add-On Points	34.000
All-Star	5	2	10	G.S.	0	2	0	GF	0	2	0		Writers Association Pts	0.000
Wins	1	2	2	C.G.	1	2	2	Totals	0		4		Military Points	0.000
Totals			22	Totals			8	Grand Total Add-On Points			34		Grand Total HOF Points	97.250

Hershiser IV, Orel "Bulldog"

Personal Life

Orel Leonard Hershiser IV (born September 16, 1958) in Buffalo, New York, to Orel Leonard III and Mildred Hershiser. Hershiser married Jamie Byars from 1981-2005 and they have sons Quenton and Jordan. In 2010, he married Dana Deaver.

Baseball Career

Orel Hershiser signed as a 17th round pick in the 1979 draft by the Los Angeles Dodgers. Orel set a major league record by pitching 59 consecutive innings without allowing a run. Orel helped the Dodgers win the 1988 World Series and he won the NL Cy Young Award. Hershiser retired June 27, 2000, with a record of 204-150 won/loss, 510 games, 3130 innings, 3.48 earned run average, 2014 strikeouts, and a 1.26 WHIP. Orel had a post season record of 5-0, 16 games, 89 innings, 2.36 ERA, and 1.123 WHIP over nine series. His World Series record was 3 – 3 and a 4.07 ERA.

Achievements

- 3-time NL All-Star (1987-1989) & NL Cy Young Award Winner (1988).
- NL Gold Glove Winner (1988) & NL Wins Leader (1988).
- NL Winning Percentage Leader (1985) & NL Complete Games Leader (1988).
- 3-time NL Innings Pitched Leader (1987-1989) & Shutouts Leader (1984 & 1988).
- 15 Win Seasons: 6 (1985, 1987-1989, 1995 & 1996) & 20 Win Seasons: 1 (1988).
- 200 Innings Pitched Seasons: 9 (1985-1989, 1992, 1993, 1996 & 1998).
- Won a World Series with the Los Angeles Dodgers in 1988.

Hall of Fame

Orel Hershiser was on the ballot for the BBWAA starting in 2006 when he received 11.2%. He received only 4.4% in 2007 and was dropped from further BBWAA ballots.

Summary Analysis

Hershiser had a Hall of Fame Point Total of 104. His overall career and post season success shows Hershiser to be Hall of Fame worthy and needs to be voted in.

Pitcher - Right Handed Potential Hall of Fame Inductee

Hershiser, Orel

Position		Born:	September 16, 1958	Height:	6' 3"	USC	190	cm
Pitcher		From:	Buffalo, NY	Weight:	190	lbs.	86	Kg.
		Bats:	Right	Debut:	September 1, 1983			
		Throws:	Right	Last Game:	June 26, 2000			

Year	Age	Tm	Lg	W	L	PCT	ERA	G	GS	GF	CG	SHO	SV	IP	H	R	ER	BB	SO	BF	WHIP	Awards
1983	24	LAD	NL	0	0	0.000	3.38	8	0	4	0	0	1	8	7	6	3	6	5	37	1.625	
1984	25	LAD	NL	11	8	0.579	2.66	45	20	10	8	4	2	189.2	160	65	56	50	150	771	1.107	RoY-3
1985	26	LAD	NL	19	3	0.864	2.03	36	34	1	9	5	0	239.2	179	72	54	68	157	953	1.031	CYA-3,MVP-16
1986	27	LAD	NL	14	14	0.500	3.85	35	35	0	8	1	0	231.1	213	112	99	86	153	988	1.293	
1987	28	LAD	NL	16	16	0.500	3.06	37	35	2	10	1	1	264.2	247	105	90	74	190	1093	1.213	AS,CYA-4
1988	29	LAD	NL	23	8	0.742	2.26	35	34	1	15	8	1	267	208	73	67	73	178	1068	1.052	6,GG
1989	30	LAD	NL	15	15	0.500	2.31	35	33	0	8	4	0	256.2	226	75	66	77	178	1047	1.181	AS,CYA-4
1990	31	LAD	NL	1	1	0.500	4.26	4	4	0	0	0	0	25.1	26	12	12	4	16	106	1.184	
1991	32	LAD	NL	7	2	0.778	3.46	21	21	0	0	0	0	112	112	43	43	32	73	473	1.286	
1992	33	LAD	NL	10	15	0.400	3.67	33	33	0	1	0	0	210.2	23	101	86	69	130	910	1.320	
1993	34	LAD	NL	12	14	0.462	3.59	33	33	0	5	1	0	215.2	201	106	86	72	141	913	1.266	SS
1994	35	LAD	NL	6	6	0.500	3.79	21	21	0	1	0	0	135.1	146	67	57	42	72	575	1.389	
1995	36	CLE	AL	16	6	0.727	3.87	26	26	0	1	1	0	167.1	151	76	72	51	111	683	1.207	
1996	37	CLE	AL	15	9	0.625	4.24	33	33	0	1	0	0	206	238	115	97	58	125	908	1.437	
1997	38	CLE	AL	14	6	0.700	4.47	32	32	0	1	0	0	195.1	199	105	97	69	107	826	1.372	
1998	39	SFG	NL	11	10	0.524	4.41	34	34	0	0	0	0	202	200	105	99	85	126	887	1.411	
1999	40	NYM	NL	13	12	0.520	4.58	32	32	0	0	0	0	179	175	92	91	77	89	776	1.408	
2000	41	LAD	NL	1	5	0.167	13.14	10	6	1	0	0	0	24.2	42	36	36	14	13	136	2.270	
162 Game Avg.				14	10	0.576	3.48	36	32	1	5	2	0	218	205	95	84	70	140	916	1.261	
LAD (13 yrs)				135	107	0.558	3.12	353	309	19	65	24	5	2180	1976	873	755	667	1456	9070	1.212	
CLE (3 yrs)				45	21	0.682	4.21	91	91	0	3	1	0	568.2	588	296	266	178	343	2417	1.347	
NYM (1 yr)				13	12	0.520	4.58	32	32	0	0	0	0	179	175	92	91	77	89	776	1.408	
SFG (1 yr)				11	10	0.524	4.41	34	34	0	0	0	0	202	200	105	99	85	126	887	1.411	
NL (15 yrs)				159	129	0.552	3.32	419	375	19	65	24	5	2561	2351	1070	945	829	1671	10733	1.241	
AL (3 yrs)				45	21	0.682	4.21	91	91	0	3	1	0	568.2	588	296	266	178	343	2417	1.347	
18 Yrs				204	150	0.576	3.48	510	466	19	68	25	5	3130	2939	1366	1211	1007	2014	13150	1.261	**Career Pts.**
				8.000	0.000	8.000	6.500	4.500	8.000	0.500	1.500	2.500	0.500	8.000	0.000	0.000	0.000	0.000	5.500	0.000	6.750	**60.250**

Post Seasonal Play

Year	Age	Team	Series	W	L	PCT	ERA	G	GS	GF	CG	SHO	SV	IP	H	R	ER	BB	SO	BF	WHIP	
1985	26	LAD	NLCS	1	0	1.000	3.52	2	2	0	1	0	0	15	17	6	6	6	5	66	1.500	
1988	29	LAD	NLCS	1	0	1.000	1.09	4	3	1	1	1	1	24	18	5	3	7	15	98	1.014	
1995	36	CLE	ALDS	1	0	1.000	0.00	1	1	0	0	0	0	7	3	0	0	2	7	28	0.682	
1995	36	CLE	ALCS	2	0	1.000	1.29	2	2	0	0	0	0	14	9	3	2	3	15	57	0.857	
1996	37	CLE	ALDS	0	0	0.000	5.40	1	1	0	0	0	0	5	7	4	3	3	3	25	2.000	
1997	38	CLE	ALDS	0	0	0.000	3.97	2	2	0	0	0	0	11	14	5	5	2	4	49	1.412	
1997	38	CLE	ALCS	0	0	0.000	0.00	1	1	0	0	0	0	7	4	0	0	1	7	22	0.714	
1999	40	NYM	NLDS	0	0	0.000	0.00	1	0	1	0	0	0	1	0	0	0	0	1	3	0.000	
1999	40	NYM	NLCS	0	0	0.000	0.00	2	0	0	0	0	0	4	1	0	0	3	5	18	0.923	
				5	0	1.000	2.326	16	12	2	2	1	1	89	73	23	19	27	62	366	1.123	**Post Season Pts.**
				0.6	0.000	1.800	1.400	0.800	1.200	0.250	0.400	0.400	0.250	1.400	0.000	0.000	0.000	0.000	1.400	0.000	1.400	**11.3**

World Series Play

Year	Age	Team	Series	W	L	PCT	ERA	G	GS	GF	CG	SHO	SV	IP	H	R	ER	BB	SO	BF	WHIP	
1988	29	LAD	WS	2	0	1.000	1.00	2	2	0	2	1	0	18	7	2	2	6	17	66	0.722	
1995	36	CLE	WS	1	0	0.500	2.57	2	2	0	0	0	0	14	8	5	4	4	13	52	0.857	
1997	38	CLE	WS	0	2	0.000	11.70	2	2	0	0	0	0	10	15	13	13	6	5	49	2.100	
				3	3	0.500	4.07	6	6	0	2	1	0	42	30	20	19	16	35	167	1.095	**World Series Pts.**
				0.600	0.000	0.000	0.400	0.600	0.600	0.000	0.400	0.250	0.000	0.600	0.000	0.000	0.000	0.000	1.000	0.000	1.600	**6.050**

Yearly Points Leading the League

Category	Times	Points	Total	Category	Times	Points	Total	Categor	Times	Points	Total	Hall of Fame Points	
MVP	0	7	0	Saves	0	2	0	SHO	2	2	4	Career Points	60.250
ROY	0	5	0	ERA	0	2	0	WinPct	1	2	2	Post Season Points	11.300
Cy Young	1	5	5	S.O.'s	0	2	0	Innings	3	2	6	World Series Points	6.050
Golden Glove	0	3	0	Games	0	2	0	WHIP	0	2	0	Career Add-On Points	27.000
All-Star	3	2	6	G.S.	0	2	0	GF	0	2	0	Writers Association Pts.	0.000
Wins	1	2	2	C.G.	1	2	2	Totals			12	Military Points	0.000
Totals			13	Totals			2	Grand Total Add-On Points		27		Grand Total HOF Points	104.600

Leever, Sam "The Goshen Schoolmaster or Deacon"

Personal Life

Samuel Leever was born December 23, 1871 in Goshen, Ohio, the fourth of eight children, to Edward Leever and Ameredith Andelia. Leever married Margaret Leever in 1903 and the couple did not have any no children.

Baseball Career

Leever's first year in the Major Leagues was 1898 at age 26, making his debut on May 26. In 1901 and 1905 he led the league in winning percentage (14–5 and 20–5, respectively), as well as in 1903, when he had his best season, going 25–7 with a league-leading 2.06 ERA. In 1903 Leever led the Pirates to their third consecutive National League pennant. However he injured his shoulder and was ineffective in the World Series, as the Pirates were defeated by Boston. Leever played 13 years with the Pirates with Leever having a record of 179 – 94, Pitched in 338 games, 2441.1 innings. 2.45 earned run average, and a WHIP of 1.140. His lifetime ERA was 2.47, and he had a 194–100 record, 847 strikeouts, 39 shutouts, 241 complete games, 587 walks, 1.141 WHIP, 2,660.2 innings.

Achievements

- NL ERA Leader (1903) & NL Games Pitched Leader (1899).
- 3-time NL Winning % Leader (1901, 1903 & 1905) & NL Shutouts Leader (1903)
- NL Saves Leader (1899) & NL Innings Pitched Leader (1899).
- 15+ Wins Seasons: 4(1900, 1902, 1904, 1908) & 4-20 (1899, 1903, 1905, 1906).
- 200 Innings Pitched Seasons: 8 (1899 (300), 1900 & 1902-1907)

Hall of Fame

The only time Sam Leever was ever voted on for the Baseball Hall of Fame was ion 1937 when he received 1 vote and has not been voted on since.

Summary Analysis

Same Leever had a Hall of Fame Point Total of 91.750. Leever was a great pitcher in the early 1900's but has been forgotten. He should be inducted into the Hall of Fame.

Pitcher Right Handed Potential Hall of Fame Inductee

Leever, Sam
Position
Pitcher

Born :	December 23, 1871
Died:	May 19, 1953
From:	Goshen, OH
Bats:	Right
Throws:	Right

Height:	5' 10" USC	178 cm
Weight:	175 lbs.	79 Kg.
Debut:	May 26, 1898	
Last Game:	September 26, 1910	

Year	Age	Tm	Lg	W	L	PCT	ERA	G	GS	GF	CG	SHO	SV	IP	H	R	ER	BB	SO	BF	WHIP	Awards
1898	26	PIT	NL	1	0	1.000	2.45	5	3	2	2	0	0	33	26	10	9	5	15	127	0.939	
1899	27	PIT	NL	21	23	0.477	3.18	51	39	11	35	4	3	379	353	191	134	122	121	1564	1.253	
1900	28	PIT	NL	15	13	0.536	2.71	30	29	1	25	3	0	232.2	236	101	70	48	84	955	1.221	
1901	29	PIT	NL	14	5	0.737	2.86	21	20	1	18	2	0	176	182	82	56	39	82	733	1.256	
1902	30	PIT	NL	15	7	0.682	2.39	28	26	2	23	4	2	222	203	73	59	31	86	873	1.054	
1903	31	PIT	NL	25	7	0.781	2.06	36	34	2	30	7	1	284.1	255	98	65	60	90	1135	1.108	
1904	32	PIT	NL	18	11	0.621	2.17	34	32	2	26	1	0	253.1	224	85	61	54	63	1024	1.097	
1905	33	PIT	NL	20	5	0.800	2.70	33	29	3	20	3	1	229.2	199	94	69	54	81	928	1.102	
1906	34	PIT	NL	22	7	0.759	2.32	36	31	4	25	6	0	260.1	232	84	67	48	76	1007	1.076	
1907	35	PIT	NL	14	9	0.609	1.66	31	24	7	17	5	0	216.2	182	70	40	46	65	848	1.052	
1908	36	PIT	NL	15	7	0.682	2.10	38	20	14	14	4	2	192.2	179	60	45	41	28	764	1.142	
1909	37	PIT	NL	8	1	0.889	2.83	19	4	12	2	0	2	70	74	30	22	14	23	286	1.257	
1910	38	PIT	NL	6	5	0.545	2.76	26	8	14	4	0	2	111	104	45	34	25	33	432	1.162	
162 Game Avg.				19	10	0.660	2.47	38	30	7	24	4	1	263	242	101	72	58	84	1057	1.141	

13 Yrs	W	L	PCT	ERA	G	GS	GF	CG	SHO	SV	IP	H	R	ER	BB	SO	BF	WHIP	Career Pts.
	194	100	0.660	2.47	388	299	75	241	39	13	2660.2	2449	1023	731	587	847	10676	1.141	
	6.750	0.000	14.250	17.500	3.000	3.750	1.000	8.000	4.500	0.500	5.500	0.000	0.000	0.000	0.000	2.000	0.000	11.750	78.500

Post Seasonal Play

Year	Age	Team	Series	W	L	PCT	ERA	G	GS	GF	CG	SHO	SV	IP	H	R	ER	BB	SO	BF	WHIP	Post Season Pts.
None				0	0	0	0	0	0	0	0	0	0	0	0	0	0	0	0	0	0	
				0.000	0.000	0.000	0.000	0.000	0.000	0.000	0.000	0.000	0.000	0.000	0.000	0.000	0.000	0.000	0.000	0.000	0.000

World Series Play

Year	Age	Team	Series	W	L	PCT	ERA	G	GS	GF	CG	SHO	SV	IP	H	R	ER	BB	SO	BF	WHIP	World Series Pts.
1903	31	Pitts	WS	0	2	0.000	5.40	2	2	0	1	0	0	10	13	8	6	3	2	48	1.600	
1909	37	Pitts	WS	0	0	0.000	0.00	0	0	0	0	0	0	0	0	0	0	0	0	0	0.000	
				0	2	0.000	5.40	2	2	0	1	0	0	10	13	8	6	3	2	48	1.600	
				0.000	0.000	0.000	0.000	0.250	0.250	0.000	0.250	0.000	0.000	0.250	0.000	0.000	0.000	0.000	0.250	0.000	0.000	1.250

Yearly Points Leading the League

Category	Times	Points	Total	Category	Times	Points	Total	Categor	Times	Points	Total
MVP	0	7	0	Saves	0	2	0	SHO	0	2	0
ROY	0	5	0	ERA	1	2	2	WinPct	3	2	6
Cy Young	0	5	0	S.O.'s	1	2	0	Innings	1	2	2
Golden Glove	0	3	0	Games	0	2	0	WHIP	0	2	0
All-Star	0	2	0	G.S.	0	2	0	GF	1	2	2
Wins	0	2	0	C.G.	0	2	0	Totals			10
Totals			0	Totals			2	Grand Total Add-On Points			12

Hall of Fame Points	
Career Points	78.500
Post Season Points	0.000
World Series Points	1.250
Career Add-On Points	12.000
Writers Association Pts.	0.000
Military Points	0.000
Grand Total HOF Points	91.750

Martinez, Dennis "El Presidente"

Personal Life

José Dennis Martínez Ortiz was born May 14, 1955 in Granada, Nicaragua, the last of seven children to Edmundo and Emilia Martínez. Martinez married Luz Marina García on April 29,1 973. The couple have four children Dennis Jr., Erica, Gilberto, & Ricardo.

Baseball Career

Martinez signed with Baltimore on December 10, 1973, and made his debut in 1976. From 1977 through 1986 with the Orioles, Martinez had a won/loss record of 108-93, pitched in 319 games, 1775 innings and earned run average of 4.16. When Martinez retired in 1998, his final record was 245 wins, 692 games, 3999.2 IP, 2149 Strikeouts, 30 Shutouts, and an ERA of 3.70 with the bulk of his success with the Montreal Expos.

Achievements

- 4-time All-Star (1990–1992, 1995)
- 2-time Received Most Valuable Player Votes (1984 & 1991)
- 2-time Received Cy Young Votes(1981, 1991)
- Led league in complete games (1979 & 1991)
- Led league in wins (1981) & Led league in games started (1979).
- Led league in ERA (1991) & Led league in shutouts (1991)
- Led league in games started, innings pitched and batters faced (1979)
- 9-time pitched 220 or more innings in a season (1978–1979, 1982, 1988–1993)
- Pitched the 13th perfect game in baseball history with the Montreal Expos.

Hall of Fame

Dennis Martinez was on the Hall of Fame Ballot in 2004 and received 16 votes for 3.2% and was removed from the BBWAA panel.

Summary Analysis

Dennis Martinez's Hall of Fame Point total is 101.950. He had a long career with 15 winning seasons. He should get a chance for election by the Classic ERA Committee.

Pitcher Right Handed Potential Hall of Fame Inductee

Martinez, Dennis

Position	Born:	May 14, 1954	Height: 6' 1" USC 185 cm
Pitcher	From:	Granada, Nicaragua	Weight: 160 lbs. 72 Kg.
	Bats:	Right	Debut: September 14, 1976
	Throws:	Right	Last Game: September 27, 1998

Year	Age	Tm	Lg	W	L	PCT	ERA	G	GS	GF	CG	SHO	SV	IP	H	R	ER	BB	SO	BF	WHIP	Awards
1976	22	BAL	AL	1	2	0.333	2.60	4	2	1	1	0	0	27.2	23	8	8	8	18	106	1.120	
1977	23	BAL	AL	14	7	0.667	4.10	42	13	19	5	0	4	166.2	157	86	76	64	107	709	1.326	
1978	24	BAL	AL	16	11	0.593	3.52	40	38	0	15	2	0	276.1	257	121	108	93	142	1140	1.267	
1979	25	BAL	AL	15	16	0.484	3.66	40	39	0	18	3	0	292.1	279	129	119	78	132	1206	1.221	
1980	26	BAL	AL	6	4	0.600	3.97	25	12	8	2	0	1	99.2	103	44	44	44	42	428	1.475	
1981	27	BAL	AL	14	5	0.737	3.32	25	24	0	9	2	0	179	173	84	66	62	88	753	1.313	CYA-5,MVP-23
1982	28	BAL	AL	16	12	0.571	4.21	40	39	0	10	2	0	252	262	123	118	87	111	1093	1.385	
1983	29	BAL	AL	7	16	0.304	5.53	32	25	3	4	0	0	153	209	108	94	45	71	688	1.660	
1984	30	BAL	AL	6	9	0.400	5.02	34	20	4	2	0	0	141.2	145	81	79	37	77	599	1.285	
1985	31	BAL	AL	13	11	0.542	5.15	33	31	1	3	1	0	180	203	110	103	63	68	789	1.478	
1986	32	TOT	MLB	3	6	0.333	4.73	23	15	2	1	1	0	104.2	114	57	55	30	65	449	1.376	
1986	32	BAL	AL	0	0	0.000	6.75	4	0	1	0	0	0	6.2	11	5	5	2	2	33	1.950	
1986	32	MON	NL	3	6	0.333	4.59	19	15	1	1	1	0	98	103	52	50	28	63	416	1.337	
1987	33	MON	NL	11	4	0.733	3.30	22	22	0	2	1	0	144.2	133	59	53	40	84	599	1.196	
1988	34	MON	NL	15	13	0.536	2.72	34	34	0	9	2	0	235.1	215	94	71	55	120	968	1.147	
1989	35	MON	NL	16	7	0.696	3.18	34	33	1	5	2	0	232	227	88	82	49	142	950	1.190	
1990	36	MON	NL	10	11	0.476	2.95	32	32	0	7	2	0	226	191	80	74	49	156	908	1.062	AS
1991	37	MON	NL	14	11	0.560	2.39	31	31	0	9	5	0	222	187	70	59	62	123	905	1.122	AS,CYA-5,MVP-20
1992	38	MON	NL	16	11	0.593	2.47	32	32	0	6	0	0	226.1	172	75	62	60	147	900	1.025	AS
1993	39	MON	NL	15	9	0.625	3.85	35	34	1	2	0	1	224.2	211	110	96	64	138	945	1.224	
1994	40	CLE	AL	11	6	0.647	3.52	24	24	0	7	3	0	176.2	166	75	69	44	92	730	1.189	
1995	41	CLE	AL	12	5	0.706	3.08	28	28	0	3	2	0	187	174	71	64	46	99	771	1.176	AS
1996	42	CLE	AL	9	6	0.600	4.50	20	20	0	1	1	0	112	122	63	56	37	48	483	1.420	
1997	43	SEA	AL	1	5	0.167	7.71	9	9	0	0	0	0	49	65	46	42	29	17	239	1.918	
1998	44	ATL	NL	4	6	0.400	4.45	53	5	11	1	1	2	91	109	53	45	19	62	396	1.407	
162 Game Avg.				13	10	0.559	3.70	38	30	3	7	2	0	217	211	100	89	63	117	909	1.266	
BAL (11 yrs)				108	93	0.537	4.16	319	243	37	69	10	5	1775	1822	899	820	583	858	7544	1.355	
MON (8 yrs)				100	72	0.581	3.06	239	233	3	41	13	1	1609	1439	628	547	407	973	6591	1.147	
CLE (3 yrs)				32	17	0.653	3.58	72	72	0	11	6	0	475.2	462	209	189	127	239	1984	1.238	
ATL (1 yr)				4	6	0.400	4.45	53	5	11	1	1	2	91	109	53	45	19	62	396	1.407	
SEA (1 yr)				1	5	0.167	7.71	9	9	0	0	0	0	49	65	46	42	29	17	239	1.918	
AL (15 yrs)				141	115	0.551	4.11	400	324	37	80	16	5	2299	2349	1154	1051	739	1114	9767	1.343	
NL (9 yrs)				104	78	0.571	3.13	292	238	14	42	14	3	1700	1548	681	592	426	1035	6987	1.161	
23 Yrs				245	193	0.559	3.70	692	562	51	122	30	8	3999	3897	1835	1643	1165	2149	16754	1.266	Career Pts. 70.500
				10.500	0.000	5.500	3.750	8.000	11.750	1.000	2.500	3.000	0.500	11.750	0.000	0.000	0.000	0.000	5.500	0.000	6.750	0.250

Post Seasonal Play

Year	Age	Team	Series	W	L	PCT	ERA	G	GS	GF	CG	SHO	SV	IP	H	R	ER	BB	SO	BF	WHIP	
1979	25	BAL	ALCS	0	0	0.000	3.24	1	1	0	0	0	0	8.1	8	3	3	0	4	32	0.960	
1995	41	CLE	ALDS	0	0	0.000	3.00	1	1	0	0	0	0	8	5	2	2	0	2	23	0.833	
1995	41	CLE	ALCS	1	1	0.500	2.03	2	2	0	0	0	0	13.1	10	3	3	3	7	52	0.975	
1998	44	ATL	NLDS										Did not pitch in series									
1998	44	ATL	NLCS	1	0	1.000	0.000	4	0	0	0	0	0	3.1	1	0	0	1	0	12	0.600	
				2	1	0.667	2.322	8	4	0	0	0	0	31	24	8	8	3	25	119	0.871	Post Season Pts. 5.900
				0.250	0.000	0.250	1.400	0.400	0.400	0.000	0.000	0.000	0.000	0.600	0.000	0.000	0.000	0.000	0.600	0.000	2.000	

World Series Play

Year	Age	Team	Series	W	L	PCT	ERA	G	GS	GF	CG	SHO	SV	IP	H	R	ER	BB	SO	BF	WHIP	
1979	25	BAL	WS	0	0	0.000	18.00	2	1	1	0	0	0	2	6	4	4	0	0	10	3.000	
1983	29	BAL	WS										Did not pitch in series									
1995	41	CLE	WS	0	1	0.000	3.48	2	2	0	0	0	0	10.1	12	4	4	8	5	49	1.935	
				0	1	0.000	5.84	4	3	1	0	0	0	12.1	18	8	8	8	5	59	2.108	World Series Pts. 1.550
				0.000	0.000	0.000	0.000	0.250	0.400	0.250	0.000	0.000	0.000	0.400	0.000	0.000	0.000	0.000	0.250	0.000	0.000	

Yearly Points Leading the League

Category	Times	Points	Total		Category	Times	Points	Total		Category	Times	Points	Total
MVP	0	7	0		Saves	0	2	0		SHO	1	2	2
ROY	0	5	0		ERA	1	2	2		WinPct	1	2	2
Cy Young	0	5	0		S.O.'s	0	2	0		Innings	1	2	2
Golden Glove	0	3	0		Games	0	2	0		WHIP	0	2	0
All-Star	4	2	8		G.S.	1	2	2		GF	0	2	0
Wins	1	2	2		C.G.	2	2	4		Totals			6
Totals			10		Totals			8		Grand Total Add-On Points		24	

Hall of Fame Points	
Career Points	70.500
Post Season Points	5.900
World Series Points	1.550
Career Add-On Points	24.000
Writers Association Pts.	0.000
Military Points	0.000
Grand Total HOF Points	101.950

Mays, Carl "Sub"

Personal Life

Carl William Mays was born November 12, 1891, in Atterson, Kentucky, one of five sons born to Callie Louisa Mays and William Henry Mays. When Mays was 12, his father died and his mother moved the family to Kingfisher, Oklahoma, to live near her sister-in-law. Mays married Marjorie Fredricka Madden in 1915. They had two children, Carl Jr. and Elizabeth Jane, and were married until she passed away on February 13. 1934. Mays married his second wife, Ester Muriel Ugstad in 1939 and the couple never had any children.

Baseball Career

Mays made the Red Sox pitching staff in 1915, playing in 38 games. Mays had an unfortunate beaning of Ray Chapman occur in in a dark, overcast game on August 16, 1920. Many blamed Mays for the accident, with a few teams petitioning to have Mays banned from baseball. Over 15 seasons, his major league career ended with a record of 208 wins and 126 losses in 490 games. Mays had a 2.92 career run ERA against a league average of 3.48 during that era. He was in six World Series and played for the Red Sox, Yankees, Giants, and the Cincinnati Reds.

Achievements

- AL Wins Leader (1921), AL Winning % Leader (1921) & AL Games Pitched Leader (1921).
- 2-time AL Saves Leader (1915 & 1921) & AL Innings Pitched Leader (1921).
- 2-time League Complete Games Leader (1918/AL & 1926/NL).
- 2-time AL Shutouts Leader (1918 & 1920) & 15-Wins Seasons: 3 (1916. 1919, & 1926)
- 20 Wins Seasons: 5 (1917, 1918, 1920, 1921 & 1924),
- 200 Innings Pitched Seasons: 9 (1916-1922, 1924 & 1926) - 300 innings: (1920 & 1921).
- Won four World Series with Red Sox (1915, 1916 & 1918) and Yankees (1923).

Hall of Fame

No information was found indicating that Carl Mays inclusion into the Hall of Fame has ever been up for a vote. It appears he will be included in the 2025 *Classic Baseball Era vote.*

Summary Analysis

Carl Mays Hall of Fame Point total is 103.750. Mays is cited by many as one of the top 50 greatest pitchers of all time. Some cite the Chapman incident or surly disposition for not being elected, but that is no reason to exclude him from his place in the Hall of fame.

Pitcher Right Handed Potential Hall of Fame Inductee

Mays, Carl

Position	Pitcher	Born: November 12, 1891	Height: 5'11" USC 108 cm
		Died: April 4, 1971	Weight: 195 lbs. 88 Kg.
		From: Liberty, KY	Debut: April 15, 1915
		Bats: Left	Last Game: September 24, 1929
		Throws: Right	

Year	Age	Tm	Lg	W	L	PCT	ERA	G	GS	GF	CG	SHO	SV	IP	H	R	ER	BB	SO	BF	WHIP	Awards
1915	23	BOS	AL	6	5	0.545	2.60	38	6	27	2	0	7	131.2	119	54	38	21	65	514	1.063	
1916	24	BOS	AL	18	13	0.581	2.39	44	24	13	14	2	3	245	208	79	65	74	76	972	1.151	
1917	25	BOS	AL	22	9	0.710	1.74	35	33	2	27	2	0	289	230	81	56	74	91	1129	1.052	
1918	26	BOS	AL	21	13	0.618	2.21	35	33	1	30	8	0	293.1	230	94	72	81	114	1162	1.060	
1919	27	TOT	AL	14	14	0.500	2.10	34	29	4	26	3	2	266	227	91	62	77	107	1063	1.143	
1919	27	BOS	AL	5	11	0.313	2.47	21	16	4	14	2	2	146	131	57	40	40	53	576	1.171	
1919	27	NYY	AL	9	3	0.750	1.65	13	13	0	12	1	0	120	96	34	22	37	54	487	1.108	
1920	28	NYY	AL	26	11	0.703	3.06	45	37	8	26	6	3	312	310	127	106	84	92	1268	1.263	
1921	29	NYY	AL	27	9	0.750	3.05	49	38	10	30	1	7	336.2	332	145	114	76	70	1400	1.212	
1922	30	NYY	AL	13	14	0.481	3.60	34	29	4	21	1	1	240	257	111	96	50	41	988	1.279	
1923	31	NYY	AL	5	2	0.714	6.20	23	7	11	2	0	0	81.1	119	59	56	32	18	383	1.857	
1924	32	CIN	NL	20	9	0.690	3.15	37	27	10	15	2	0	226	238	97	79	36	63	940	1.212	
1925	33	CIN	NL	3	5	0.375	3.31	12	5	5	3	0	2	51.2	60	22	19	13	10	225	1.413	
1926	34	CIN	NL	19	12	0.613	3.14	39	33	2	24	3	1	281	286	112	98	53	58	1158	1.206	MVP-22
1927	35	CIN	NL	3	7	0.300	3.51	14	9	4	6	0	0	82	89	39	32	10	17	343	1.207	
1928	36	CIN	NL	4	1	0.800	3.88	14	7	4	4	1	1	62.2	67	33	27	22	10	269	1.420	
1929	37	NYG	NL	6	2	0.750	4.32	37	8	19	1	0	4	123	140	67	59	31	32	538	1.390	
162 Game Avg.				17	11	0.622	2.92	41	27	10	19	2	3	252	243	101	82	61	72	1031	1.207	
BOS (5 yrs)				72	51	0.585	2.21	173	112	47	87	14	12	1105	918	365	271	290	399	4353	1.093	
CIN (5 yrs)				49	34	0.590	3.26	116	81	25	52	6	4	703.1	740	303	255	134	158	2935	1.243	
NYY (5 yrs)				80	39	0.672	3.25	164	124	33	91	9	11	1090	1114	476	394	279	273	4526	1.278	
NYG (1 yr)				6	2	0.750	4.32	37	8	19	1	0	4	123	140	67	59	31	32	538	1.390	
AL (9 yrs)				152	90	0.628	2.73	337	236	80	178	23	23	2195	2032	841	665	569	672	8879	1.185	
NL (6 yrs)				55	36	0.604	3.42	153	89	44	53	6	8	826.1	880	370	314	165	190	3473	1.265	
15 Yrs				207	126	0.622	2.92	490	325	124	231	29	31	3021	2912	1211	979	734	862	12352	1.207	Career Pts.
				8.000	0.000	11.75	11.50	4.500	4.500	1.500	6.750	3.000	1.000	8.000	0.000	0.000	0.000	0.000	2.000	0.000	10.500	73.000

Post Seasonal Play

Year	Age	Team	Series	W	L	PCT	ERA	G	GS	GF	CG	SHO	SV	IP	H	R	ER	BB	SO	BF	WHIP	
None				0	0	0	0	0	0	0	0	0	0	0	0	0	0	0	0	0	0	Post Season Pts.
				0.000	0.000	0.000	0.000	0.000	0.000	0.000	0.000	0.000	0.000	0.000	0.000	0.000	0.000	0.000	0.000	0.000	0.000	0.000

World Series Play

Year	Age	Team	Series	W	L	PCT	ERA	G	GS	GF	CG	SHO	SV	IP	H	R	ER	BB	SO	BF	WHIP	
1915	23	BOS	WS					Did	Not	Play												
1916	24	BOS	WS	0	1	0.000	6.750	2	1	1	0	0	1	5.1	8	4	4	3	2	28	2.063	
1918	26	BOS	WS	2	0	1.000	1.000	2	2	0	2	0	0	18	10	2	2	3	5	63	0.722	
1921	29	NYY	WS	1	2	0.333	1.730	3	3	0	3	1	0	26	20	6	5	0	9	97	0.768	
1922	30	NYY	WS	0	1	0.000	4.500	1	1	0	0	0	0	8	9	4	4	2	1	33	1.375	
1923	31	NYY	WS					Did	Not	Play												
				3	4	0.429	2.35	8	7	1	5	1	1	57.1	47	16	15	8	17	221	0.959	World Series Pts.
				0.600	0.000	0.000	1.400	0.800	0.800	0.250	1.000	0.250	0.250	0.800	0.000	0.000	0.000	0.000	0.600	0.000	2.000	8.750

Yearly Points Leading the League

Category	Times	Points	Total	Category	Times	Points	Total	Categor	Times	Points	Total
MVP	0	7	0	Saves	2	2	4	SHO	2	2	4
ROY	0	5	0	ERA	0	3	0	WinPct	1	2	2
y Young	0	5	0	S.O.'s	0	2	0	Innings	1	2	2
lden Glove	0	3	0	Games	1	2	2	WHIP	0	2	0
All-Star	0	2	0	G.S.	0	2	0	GF	1	2	2
Wins	1	2	2	C.G.	2	2	4	Totals	1		10
Totals			2	Totals			10	Grand Total Add-On Points		22	

Hall of Fame Points	
Career Points	73.000
Post Season Points	0.000
World Series Points	8.750
Career Add-On Points	22.000
Writers Association Pts.	0.000
Military Points	0.000
Grand Total HOF Points	103.750

Nathan, Joe

Personal Life

Joseph Michael Nathan was born November 22, 1974, in Houston, to Mary and Rodney Nathan. Joe had an older sister, Michelle, and four stepsiblings. Nathan married Lisa Lemoncelli in 1997. Together, they have a son Cole, and a daughter Riley with Nathan divorcing his first wife in 2014. Nathan married Cristy Jones in 2018.

Baseball Career

Nathan was drafted in the sixth round (159th overall) of the 1995 MLB draft by the San Francisco Giants. He worked his way through the minor leagues and was promoted to the Giants on April 20,1999, He made MLB debut the next day, pitching seven shutout innings and winning his first major league decision. Nathan retired September 3, 2017, with 377 saves, a 2.87 ERA, and an 89.3% save percentage, the highest amongst all with at least 250 saves. He played 16 seasons in MLB for the San Francisco Giants, Minnesota Twins, Texas Rangers, Detroit Tigers, and Chicago Cubs.

Achievements

- 6-time All-Star (2004, 2005, 2008,2009, 2010 & 2012.
- 2 times in the top 6 of the Cy Young Award voting (2004, & 2005).
- 1-World Series appearance with the Houston Astros (2005).
- 2-Times received MVP Votes (1996 & 2005).
- 5-Times Had an E.R.A. under 2.00: (2004, 2006, 2007, 2008 & 2013).

Hall of Fame

Nathan was included on the ballot in 2022 and received 17 votes for 4.3%. He was taken off the ballot for future elections by the BBWWA.

Summary Analysis

Joe Nathan's Hall of Fame Point total listed is 97.50. His consideration hinges on a run of dominance in the mid-2000s. Nathan should be elected by one of the committees.

A Fan's Perspective

Pitcher Right Handed Potential Hall of Fame Inductee

Nathan, Joe

Positions	Pitcher

Born :	November 22, 1971	Height:	6 4"	USC	193	cm
From:	Houston, TX	Weight:	230	lbs.	104	Kg.
Bats:	Right	Debut:	Aprio 12, 1999			
Throws:	Right	Last Game:	September 27, 2016			

Year	Age	Tm	Lg	W	L	W-L%	ERA	G	GS	GF	CG	SHO	SV	IP	H	R	ER	BB	S.O.	BF	WHIP	Awards
1999	24	SFG	NL	7	4	0.636	4.180	19	14	2	0	0	1	90.1	84	45	42	46	54	395	1.439	
2000	25	SFG	NL	5	2	0.714	5.210	20	15	0	0	0	0	93.1	89	63	54	63	61	426	1.629	
								Did Not Play - Injures														
2002	27	SFG	NL	0	0	0.000	0.000	4	0	3	0	0	0	3.2	1	0	0	0	2	12	0.273	
2003	28	SFG	NL	12	4	0.750	2.960	78	0	9	0	0	0	79	51	26	26	33	83	316	1.063	
2004	29	MIN	AL	1	2	0.333	1.620	73	0	63	0	0	44	72.1	48	14	13	23	89	284	0.982	AS,CYA-4,MVP-12
2005	30	MIN	AL	7	4	0.636	2.700	69	0	58	0	0	43	70	46	22	21	22	94	276	0.971	AS
2006	31	MIN	AL	7	0	1.000	1.580	64	0	61	0	0	36	68.1	38	12	12	16	95	262	0.79	CYA-5,MVP-18
2007	32	MIN	AL	4	2	0.667	1.880	68	0	60	0	0	37	71.2	54	15	15	19	77	282	1.019	
2008	33	MIN	AL	1	2	0.333	1.330	68	0	57	0	0	39	67.2	43	13	10	18	74	261	0.901	AS
2009	34	MIN	AL	2	2	0.500	2.100	70	0	62	0	0	47	68.2	42	16	16	22	89	271	0.932	AS
								Did Not Play - Injures														
2011	36	MIN	AL	2	1	0.667	4.840	48	0	33	0	0	14	44.2	38	26	24	14	43	191	1.164	
2012	37	TEX	AL	3	5	0.375	2.800	66	0	62	0	0	37	64.1	55	23	20	13	78	257	1.057	AS
2013	38	TEX	AL	6	2	0.750	1.390	67	0	61	0	0	43	64.2	36	10	10	22	73	250	0.897	AS
2014	39	DET	AL	5	4	0.556	4.810	62	0	54	0	0	35	58	60	32	31	29	54	259	1.534	
2015	40	DET	AL	0	0	0.000	0.000	1	0	1	0	0	1	0.1	0	0	0	0	1	1	0	
2016	41	TOT	NL	2	0	1.000	0.000	10	0	1	0	0	0	6.1	5	0	0	4	9	28	1.421	
2016	41	CHC	NL	1	0	1.000	0.000	3	0	0	0	0	0	2	2	0	0	2	4	10	2	
2016	41	SFG	NL	1	0	1.000	0.000	7	0	1	0	0	0	4.1	3	0	0	2	5	18	1.154	
162 Game Avg.				5	3	0.653	2.87	66	2	49	0	0	31	77	58	26	24	29	81	314	1.12	
MIN (7 yrs)				24	13	0.649	2.16	460	0	394	0	0	260	463.1	309	118	111	134	561	1827	0.956	
SFG (5 yrs)				25	10	0.714	4.06	128	29	15	0	0	1	270.2	228	134	122	144	205	1167	1.374	
TEX (2 yrs)				9	7	0.563	2.09	133	0	123	0	0	80	129	91	33	30	35	151	507	0.977	
DET (2 yrs)				5	4	0.556	4.78	63	0	55	0	0	36	58.1	60	32	31	29	55	260	1.526	
CHC (1 yr)				1	0	1	0	3	0	0	0	0	0	2	2	0	0	2	4	10	2	
AL (11 yrs)				38	24	0.613	2.38	656	0	572	0	0	376	650.2	460	183	172	198	767	2594	1.011	
NL (5 yrs)				26	10	0.722	4.03	131	29	15	0	0	1	272.2	230	134	122	146	209	1177	1.379	
16 Yrs				64	34	0.653	2.87	787	29	587	0	0	377	923.1	690	317	294	344	976	3771	1.12	Career Pts.
				2.000	0.000	14.250	12.500	10.500	0.000	9.250	0.000	0.000	14.250	1.000	0.000	0.000	0.000	0.000	2.000	0.000	13.000	78.750

Post Season Play

Year	Age	Tm	Lg	W	L	W-L%	ERA	G	GS	GF	CG	SHO	SV	IP	H	R	ER	BB	SO	BF	WHIP	
2003	28	SFG	NLDS	0	1	0.000	81.00	2	0	0	0	0	0	0.1	4	3	3	1	1	6	15.00	
2004	29	MIN	ALDS	0	1	0.000	3.60	3	0	1	0	0	1	5	2	2	3	5	6	22	1.40	
2006	31	MIN	ALDS	0	0	0.000	0.00	1	0	1	0	0	0	0.2	1	0	0	0	1	3	1.50	
2009	34	MIN	ALDS	0	0	0.000	9.00	2	0	1	0	0	0	2	5	2	2	1	2	12	3.00	
2012	37	TEX	ALWC	0	0	0.000	18.00	1	0	1	0	0	0	1	2	2	2	1	1	6	3.00	
2014	39	DET	ALDS	0	0	0.000	0.00	1	0	1	0	0	0	1	0	0	0	0	3	3	0.00	
				0	2	0.000	8.10	10	0	5	0	0	1	10	14	9	9	8	12	52	2.20	Post Season Pts.
				0	0.000	0.000	0.000	1.000	0.000	0.600	0.000	0.000	0.250	0.250	0.000	0.000	0.000	0.000	0.400	0.000	0.000	2.500

World Series Play

Year	Age	Tm	Lg	W	L	W-L%	ERA	G	GS	GF	CG	SHO	SV	IP	H	R	ER	BB	SO	BF	WHIP	
None				0	0	0	0	0	0	0	0	0	0	0	0	0	0	0	0	0	0	World Series Pts.
				0	0	0	0	0	0	0	0	0	0	0	0	0	0	0	0	0	0	0.000

Yearly Points Leading the League

Category	Times	Points	Total
MVP	0	7	0
ROY	0	5	0
Cy Young	0	5	0
Golden Glove	0	3	0
All-Star	6	2	12
Wins	0	3	0
Totals			12

Category	Times	Points	Total
Saves	0	3	0
ERA	0	3	0
S.O.'s	0	2	0
Games	0	2	0
G.S.	0	2	0
C.G.	0	2	0
Totals			0

Catego	Times	Points	Total
SHO	0	2	0
WinPct	0	2	0
Innings	0	2	0
WHIP	0	2	0
GF	1	2	2
Totals			2
Grand Total Add-On Points			14

Hall of Fame Points	
Career Points	78.750
Post Season Points	2.500
World Series Points	0.000
Career Add-On Points	14.000
Writers Association Pts.	0.000
Military/Lifetime Achievement	0.000
Grand Total HOF Points	95.250

The Baseball Hall of Fame

Newcombe, Don "Newk"

Personal Life

Donald Newcombe was born June 14, 1926 in Madison, New Jersey, as the second of five children to Roland Newcombe and Sadie Sayers. He had three brothers & a sister. He was married three times: To Freddie Cross (1945-1960), Billie Roberts (1960-1994) and Karen Kroner (his death). He had 4 children: Don Jr. Brett, Greg, and Kellye.

Baseball Career

Newcombe played with Montreal in 1947 and 1948 before joining the Dodgers in 1949.

He went 17-8 in his first season and helped bring the Dodgers the pennant and won the Rookie of the League Award and is the only player to ever win the MVP Award, Cy Young Award, and Rookie of the Year Award. He won a World Series with the Dodgers in 1955 and retired in 1960 with a 149-90 record, 3.56 ERA, and a huge "What If".

Achievements

- NL Rookie of the Year Award (1949) & 4-time NL All-Star (1949-1951 & 1955).
- National League Most Valuable Player & Cy Young Winner (1956).
- 2-time NL Winning % Leader (1955 & 1956) & Wins Leader (1956.
- NL Strikeouts Leader (1951) & NL Shutouts Leader (1949).
- 15 Wins Seasons: 2 (1949 &1950) & 20 Wins Seasons: 3 (1951, 1955 & 1956).
- 200 Innings Pitched Seasons: 6 (1949-1951,1955, 1956 & 1959)

Hall of Fame

Newcombe exhausted his 15 years of eligibility with the BBWAA in 1980, peaking at 15.3% of the vote that year; he's eligible for enshrinement with the Veterans Committee.

Summary Analysis

Don Newcombe Hall of Fame Point total is 97.850. What would Newcombe's career numbers have been if he had pitched in the Major Leagues from 1946, including his military years, until he retired in 1960. Newcomb was a pioneer during one of the most critical times of the integration process. This failure by the BBWAA needs to be corrected so Don can take his place as one of the greats of all-time.

Pitcher Right Handed Potential Hall of Fame Inductee

Newcombe, Don

Positions	Born :	June 14, 1926
Pitcher	Died:	February 19, 2019
	From:	Madison, NJ
	Bats:	Left
	Throws:	Right

Height:	6' 4"	USC	193 cm
Weight:	220	lbs.	98 Kg.
Debut:	N.L. 1944		
Debut:	MLB: May 29, 1949		
Last Game:	October 1, 1960		

Year	Age	Tm	Lg	W	L	PCT	ERA	G	GS	GF	CG	SHO	SV	IP	H	R	ER	BB	S.O.	BF	WHIP	Awards
1944	18	NE	NN2	1	3	0.250	5.40	9	5	2	3	0	0	41.2	43	29	25	14	35	198	1.608	
1945	19	NE	NN2	3	3	0.500	2.60	7	6	1	6	0	0	55.1	43	23	16	16	33	231	1.066	
1949	23	BRO	NL	17	8	0.680	3.17	38	31	5	19	5	1	244.1	223	89	86	73	149	1005	1.211	AS,MVP-8,RoY-1
1950	24	BRO	NL	19	11	0.633	3.70	40	35	4	20	4	3	267.1	258	120	110	75	130	1101	1.246	AS,MVP-18
1951	25	BRO	NL	20	9	0.690	3.28	40	36	2	18	3	0	272	235	115	99	91	164	1125	1.199	AS,MVP-22
1952		Did not play in major or minor leagues (Military Service)																				
1953		Did not play in major or minor leagues (Military Service)																				
1954	28	BRO	NL	9	8	0.529	4.55	29	25	2	6	0	0	144.1	158	81	73	49	82	640	1.434	
1955	29	BRO	NL	20	5	0.800	3.20	34	31	1	17	1	0	233.2	222	103	83	38	143	943	1.113	AS,MVP-7
1956	30	BRO	NL	27	7	0.794	3.06	38	36	2	18	5	0	268	219	101	91	46	139	1052	0.989	CYA-1,MVP-1
1957	31	BRO	NL	11	12	0.478	3.49	28	28	0	12	4	0	198.2	199	86	77	33	90	815	1.168	
1958	32	TOT	NL	7	13	0.350	4.67	31	26	4	8	0	1	167.2	212	98	87	36	68	734	1.479	
1958	32	LAD	NL	0	6	0.000	7.86	11	6	2	1	0	0	34.1	53	37	30	8	18	163	1.777	
1958	32	CIN	NL	7	7	0.500	3.85	20	18	2	7	0	1	133.1	159	61	57	28	51	571	1.408	
1959	33	CIN	NL	13	8	0.619	3.16	30	29	1	17	2	1	222	216	87	78	27	100	899	1.095	
1960	34	TOT	MLB	6	9	0.400	4.48	36	17	13	1	0	1	136.2	160	76	68	22	63	577	1.332	
1960	34	CIN	NL	4	6	0.400	4.57	16	15	0	1	0	0	82.2	99	48	42	14	36	354	1.367	
1960	34	CLE	AL	2	3	0.400	4.33	20	2	13	0	0	1	54	61	28	26	8	27	223	1.278	
12 Yrs				153	96	0.614	3.57	360	305	37	145	24	7	2251.2	2188	1007	893	530	1187	9320	1.207	
162 Game Avg.				18	10	0.614	3.57	37	31	4	15	2	1	230	224	103	91	54	121	953	1.207	
LAD (8 yrs)				123	66	0.651	3.51	258	230	18	111	22	4	1662.2	1567	732	648	413	813	6844	1.191	
CIN (3 yrs)				24	21	0.533	3.64	66	62	3	25	2	2	438	474	198	177	89	189	1824	1.24	
NE (2 yrs)				4	6	0.400	3.80	16	11	3	9	0	0	97	86	51	41	40	58	429	1.289	
CLE (1 yr)				2	3	0.400	4.33	20	2	13	0	0	1	54	61	28	26	8	27	223	1.278	
NL (10 yrs)				147	87	0.628	3.54	324	292	21	136	24	6	2100.2	2041	928	826	482	1102	8668	1.201	
NN2 (2 yrs)				4	6	0.4	3.80	16	11	3	9	0	0	97	86	51	41	40	58	429	1.290	
AL (1 yr)				2	3	0.4	4.33	20	2	13	0	0	1	54	61	28	26	8	27	223	1.278	
12 Yrs				153	96	0.614	3.57	360	305	37	145	24	7	2251.2	2188	1007	893	530	1187	9320	1.207	Career Pts.
				4.5	0	10.500	5.75	2.5	3.75	0.5	3	2.5	0.5	4.5	0	0	0	0	2.5	0	9.250	49.750

Post Season Play

Year	Age	Tm	Lg	W	L	PCT	ERA	G	GS	GF	CG	SHO	SV	IP	H	R	ER	BB	SO	BF	WHIP	
None				0	0	0	0	0	0	0	0	0	0	0	0	0	0	0	0	0	0	Post Season Pts.
				0.000	0.000	0.000	0.000	0.000	0.000	0.000	0.000	0.000	0.000	0.000	0.000	0.000	0.000	0.000	0.000	0.000	0.000	0.000

World Season Play

Year	Age	Tm	Lg	W	L	PCT	ERA	G	GS	GF	CG	SHO	SV	IP	H	R	ER	BB	SO	BF	WHIP	
1949	23	BRO	NL	0	2	0	3.09	2	2	0	1	0	0	11.2	10	4	4	3	11	47	1.114	
1955	29	BRO	NL	0	1	0	9.53	1	1	0	0	0	0	5.2	8	6	6	2	4	25	1.765	
1956	30	BRO	NL	0	1	0	21.21	2	2	0	0	0	0	4.2	11	11	11	3	4	28	3	
				0	4	0	8.59	5	5	0	1	0	0	22	29	21	21	8	19	100	1.682	World Series Pts.
				0.000	0.000	0.000	0.000	0.250	0.600	0.000	0.250	0.000	0.000	0.400	0.000	0.000	0.000	0.000	0.600	0.000	0.000	2.100

Yearly Points Leading the League

Category	Times	Points	Total
MVP	1	7	7
RoY	1	5	5
Cy Young	1	5	5
Golden Glove	0	3	0
All-Star	4	2	8
Wins	1	3	3
Totals			28

Category	Times	Points	Total
Saves	0	3	0
ERA	0	3	0
S.O.'s	1	2	2
Games	0	2	0
G.S.	0	2	0
C.G.	0	2	0
Totals			2

Category	Times	Points	Total
SHO	0	2	0
WinPct	2	2	4
Innings	0	2	0
WHIP	2	2	4
GF	0	2	0
Totals			8

Hall of Fame Points	
Career Points	49.750
Post Season Points	0.000
World Series Points	2.100
Career Add-On Points	38.000
Writers Association Pts.	0.000
Military/Lifetime Achievement	8.000
Grand Total Add-On Points	38
Grand Total HOF Points	97.850

Papelbon, Jonathon

Personal Life

Jonathan Robert Papelbon was born November 23,1980, in Baton Rouge, LA. To John and Amy. He was the oldest of three sons, with twin brothers Jeremy and Josh, to John Papelbon married Ashley Jefferies on November 2. 2005, and the couple a daughter, Parker, and a son, Gunner.

Baseball Career

Papelbon was drafted by the Boston Red Sox in the fourth round making his debut in 2005. He helped win a World Series with the Boston Red Sox in 2007. In 2016, Papelbon was 2–4 with a 4.37 ERA and 19 saves for the Nationals but was released on August 13th. He did not find another team to complete the season, or give him a contract for 2017, making his retirement final. Papelbon was the closer from 2005 until 2016, with Boston, Philadelphia, Philadelphia and Washington with a 41-36 record, 2.44 ERA, 689 games, 725.2 Innings Pitched, 368 Saves, 808 strikeouts, and a 1.043 WHIP. He finished his career with 368 saves, the 9th highest lifetime total at the time.

Achievements

- 6-Time All-Star: (2006, 2007, 2008, 2009, 2012, 2015).
- MLB record for consecutive scoreless innings to start a postseason career (25).
- First pitcher to record 25 saves in each of his first ten full seasons: (2006 to 2015).
- Fastest pitcher in MLB history to reach 200 career saves.
- 8-Time 30 Saves Seasons: (2006-2012 & 2014) & 1-40 Saves Season: 1 (2008)

Hall of Fame

Papelbon was eligible for election to the Hall of Fame in 2022 but was dropped off the ballot after receiving just 1.3% of ballots.

Summary Analysis

Jonathon Papelbon 's Hall of Fame Point total is 97.50. His run of dominance in the mid-2000s to the mid-2010's that should eventually lead to the Hall of Fame.

Pitcher Right Handed Potential Hall of Fame Inductee

Papelbon, Jonathan

Positions		Born:	November 23, 1980	Height:	6'5	USC	196	cm
Pitcher		From:	Baton Rouge, LA	Weight:	230	lbs.	104	Kg.
		Bats:	Right	Debut:	July 31, 2005			
		Throws:	Right	Last Game:	August 6, 2016			

Year	Age	Tm	Lg	W	L	PCT	ERA	G	GS	GF	CG	SHO	SV	IP	H	R	ER	BB	SO	BF	WHIP	Awards
2005	24	BOS	AL	3	1	0.750	2.65	17	3	4	0	0	0	34	33	11	10	17	34	148	1.471	
2006	25	BOS	AL	4	2	0.667	0.92	59	0	49	0	0	35	68.1	40	8	7	13	75	257	0.776	AS,RoY-2
2007	26	BOS	AL	1	3	0.250	1.85	59	0	53	0	0	37	58.1	30	12	12	15	84	224	0.771	AS
2008	27	BOS	AL	5	4	0.556	2.34	67	0	62	0	0	41	69.1	58	24	18	8	77	273	0.952	AS
2009	28	BOS	AL	1	1	0.500	1.85	66	0	59	0	0	38	68	54	15	14	24	76	285	1.147	AS
2010	29	BOS	AL	5	7	0.417	3.90	65	0	53	0	0	37	67	57	34	29	28	76	287	1.269	
2011	30	BOS	AL	4	1	0.800	2.94	63	0	54	0	0	31	64.1	50	22	21	10	87	255	0.933	
2012	31	PHI	NL	5	6	0.455	2.44	70	0	64	0	0	38	70	56	22	19	18	92	284	1.057	AS
2013	32	PHI	NL	5	1	0.833	2.92	61	0	54	0	0	29	61.2	59	23	20	11	57	254	1.135	
2014	33	PHI	NL	2	3	0.400	2.04	66	0	52	0	0	39	66.1	45	15	15	15	63	259	0.905	
2015	34	TOT	NL	4	3	0.571	2.13	59	0	51	0	0	24	63.1	53	22	15	12	56	260	1.026	AS
2015	34	PHI	NL	2	1	0.667	1.59	37	0	34	0	0	17	39.2	31	9	7	8	40	161	0.983	
2015	34	WSN	NL	2	2	0.500	3.04	22	0	17	0	0	7	23.2	22	13	8	4	16	99	1.099	
2016	35	WSN	NL	2	4	0.333	4.37	37	0	30	0	0	19	35	37	18	17	14	31	152	1.457	
162 Game Avg.				4	4	0.532	2.44	68	0	57	0	0	36	71	56	22	19	18	79	289	1.043	
BOS (7 yrs)				23	19	0.548	2.33	396	3	334	0	0	219	429.1	322	126	111	115	509	1729	1.018	
PHI (4 yrs)				14	11	0.560	2.31	234	0	204	0	0	123	237.2	191	69	61	52	252	958	1.022	
WSN (2 yrs)				4	6	0.400	3.84	59	0	47	0	0	26	58.2	59	31	25	18	47	251	1.313	
NL (5 yrs)				18	17	0.514	2.61	293	0	251	0	0	149	296.1	250	100	86	70	299	1209	1.08	
AL (7 yrs)				23	19	0.548	2.33	396	3	334	0	0	219	429.1	322	126	111	115	509	1729	1.018	
12 Yrs				41	36	0.532	2.44	689	3	585	0	0	368	725.2	572	226	197	185	808	2938	1.043	Career Pts.
				1.5	0	4.500	17.50	8	0	9.25	0	0	13	0.5	0	0	0	0	2	0	16.75	73.000

Post Seasonal Play

Year	Age	Team	Series	W	L	PCT.	ERA	G	GS	GF	CG	SHO	SV	IP	H	R	ER	BB	SO	BF	WHIP	
2005	24	BOS	ALDS	0	0	0.000	0.000	2	0	1	0	0	0	4	2	0	0	0	2	14	0.500	
2007	26	BOS	ALDS	1	0	1.000	0.000	1	0	1	0	0	0	1.1	0	0	0	2	1	7	1.500	
2007	26	BOS	ALCS	0	0	0.000	0.000	3	0	2	0	0	1	5	3	0	0	2	3	20	1.000	
2008	27	BOS	ALDS	1	0	1.000	0.000	3	0	2	0	0	1	5	2	0	0	1	7	18	0.600	
2008	27	BOS	ALCS	0	0	0.000	0.000	4	0	2	0	0	2	5.1	1	0	0	1	6	17	0.375	
2009	28	BOS	ALDS	0	1	0.000	13.500	2	0	1	0	0	0	2	4	3	3	2	1	10	3.000	
				2	1	0.667	1.19	15	0	9	0	0	4	22.2	12	3	3	8	20	86	0.883	Post Season Pts.
				0.250	0.000	0.250	1.800	1.600	0.000	1.000	0.000	0.000	0.800	0.400	0.000	0.000	0.000	0.000	0.400	0.000	2.000	8.500

World Series Play

Year	Age	Team	Series	W	L	PCT.	ERA	G	GS	GF	CG	SHO	SV	IP	H	R	ER	BB	SO	BF	WHIP	
2007	26	BOS	WS	0	0	0.000	0	3	0	3	0	0	3	4.1	2	0	0	0	3	14	0.462	
				0	0	0.000	0	3	0	3	0	0	3	4.1	2	0	0	0	3	14	0.462	World Series Pts.
				0.000	0.000	0.000	0.250	0.250	0.000	0.400	0.000	0.000	0.400	0.250	0.000	0.000	0.000	0.000	0.250	0.000	0.250	2.050

Yearly Points Leading the League

Category	Times	Points	Total	Category	Times	Points	Total	Categor	Times	Points	Total
MVP	0	7	0	Saves	0	3	0	SHO	0	2	0
ROY	0	5	0	ERA	0	3	0	WinPct	0	2	0
Cy Young	0	5	0	S.O.'s	0	2	0	Innings	0	2	0
Golden Glove	0	3	0	Games	0	2	0	WHIP	0	2	0
All-Star	6	2	12	G.S.	0	2	0	GF	1	2	2
Wins	0	3	0	C.G.	0	2	0	Totals			2
Totals			12	Totals			0	Grand Total Add-On Points			14

Hall of Fame Points	
Career Points	73.000
Post Season Points	8.500
World Series Points	2.050
Career Add-On Points	14.000
Writers Association Pts.	0.000
Military/Lifetime Achievement	0.000
Grand Total HOF Points	97.550

Quisenberry, Dan "Quiz"

Personal Life

Daniel Raymond Quisenberry was born February 7, 1953 as the second son (older brother Marty) to John Quisenberry & Roberta Burmood in Santa Monica, California.

Quisenberry married Janie Howard on September 11, 1976, with the couple having a daughter, Alysia, and a son, David.

Baseball Career

Quisenberry signed as a free agent in 1975 with the Royals making major league debut July 8, 1979 against Chicago. Quisenberry baffled American League hitters and with his delivery style gathering more saves and reducing his E.R.A. consistently under 2.80. Dan was an integral part of two World Series teams (1980 and 1985) and set the major-league record for saves in a season (45 in '83). Quisenberry's last appearance came on April 23, 1990, with him retiring within a week. He pitched in 674 games, 244 saves, 1.175 WHIP, a 2.76 ERA, and 1,043⅓ innings averaging 1.4 walks per nine innings.

Achievements

- 3-Times led the A.L. in games pitched: (1980, 1983, 1984, & 1985).
- 4-Times led the A.L. in games finished: (1980, 1982. 1983 & 1985).
- 5-Times led the A.L. in games saved: (1980, 1982, 1983, 1984 & 1985).
- 5-Times received Most Valuable Player Votes (1980 & 1982-1985).
- 5-Times received Cy Young Award Votes (1980 & 1982-1985).

Hall of Fame

Dan Quisenberry was on the 1996 BBWAA balloting and received 3.8% of the votes, and was dropped from the ballot. In 2013, he was given a second look by the Expansion Era Committee but fell short of the votes needed from the 16-member panel.

Summary Analysis

Quisenberry career statistical points is 101.135. He helped revolutionize relief pitching, and his election would give Baseball someone who listened, learned, re-invented himself, and became one of the best. He should be elected by the BBWAA

Pitcher - Right Handed Potential Hall of Fame Inductee

Quisenberry, Dan

Positions		Born :	February 7, 1953	Height:	6' 2"	USC	188	cm
Pitcher		Died:	September 30, 1998	Weight:	170	lbs.	77	Kg.
		From:	Santa Monica, CA	Debut:	July 8, 1979			
		Bats:	Right	Last Game:	April 23, 1990			
		Throws:	Right					

Year	Age	Tm	Lg	W	L	PCT	ERA	G	GS	GF	CG	SHO	SV	IP	H	R	ER	BB	SO	BF	WHIP	Awards
1979	26	KCR	AL	3	2	0.600	3.15	32	0	21	0	0	5	40	42	16	14	7	13	163	1.225	
1980	27	KCR	AL	12	7	0.632	3.09	75	0	68	0	0	33	128.1	129	47	44	27	37	528	1.216	CYA-5,MVP-8
1981	28	KCR	AL	1	4	0.200	1.73	40	0	35	0	0	18	62.1	59	16	12	15	20	254	1.187	
1982	29	KCR	AL	9	7	0.563	2.57	72	0	68	0	0	35	136.2	126	43	39	12	46	529	1.010	AS,CYA-3,MVP-9
1983	30	KCR	AL	5	3	0.625	1.94	69	0	62	0	0	45	139	118	35	30	11	48	536	0.928	AS,CYA-2,MVP-6
1984	31	KCR	AL	6	3	0.667	2.64	72	0	67	0	0	44	129.1	121	39	38	12	41	506	1.028	AS,CYA-2,MVP-3
1985	32	KCR	AL	8	9	0.471	2.37	84	0	76	0	0	37	129	142	41	34	16	54	532	1.225	CYA-3,MVP-11
1986	33	KCR	AL	3	7	0.300	2.77	62	0	54	0	0	12	81.1	92	30	25	24	36	352	1.426	
1987	34	KCR	AL	4	1	0.800	2.76	47	0	39	0	0	8	49	58	15	15	10	17	215	1.388	
1988	35	TOT	MLB	2	1	0.667	5.12	53	0	26	0	0	1	63.1	86	37	36	11	28	278	1.532	
1988	35	KCR	AL	0	1	0.000	3.55	20	0	13	0	0	1	25.1	32	11	10	5	9	110	1.461	
1988	35	STL	NL	2	0	1.000	6.16	33	0	13	0	0	0	38	54	26	26	6	19	168	1.579	
1989	36	STL	NL	3	1	0.750	2.64	63	0	35	0	0	6	78.1	78	25	23	14	37	317	1.174	
1990	37	SFG	NL	0	1	0.000	13.5	5	0	2	0	0	0	6.2	13	12	10	3	2	37	2.400	
162 Game Avg.				6	5	0.549	2.76	68	0	56	0	0	25	105	107	36	32	16	38	428	1.175	
KCR (10 yrs)				51	44	0.537	2.55	573	0	503	0	0	238	920.1	919	293	261	139	321	3725	1.15	
STL (2 yrs)				5	1	0.833	3.79	96	0	48	0	0	6	116.1	132	51	49	20	56	485	1.307	
SFG (1 yr)				0	1	0	13.5	5	0	2	0	0	0	6.2	13	12	10	3	2	37	2.4	
AL (10 yrs)				51	44	0.537	2.55	573	0	503	0	0	238	920.1	919	293	261	139	321	3725	1.15	
NL (3 yrs)				5	2	0.714	4.32	101	0	50	0	0	6	123	145	63	59	23	58	522	1.366	
12 Yrs				56	46	0.549	2.76	674	0	553	0	0	244	1043	1064	356	320	162	379	4247	1.175	Career Pts.
				2.250	0.000	6.500	13.500	9.500	0.000	8.500	0.000	0.000	6.500	2.235	0.000	0.000	0.000	0.000	0.500	0.000	8.500	57.985

Post Seasonal Play

Year	Age	Team	Series	W	L	PCT	ERA	G	GS	GF	CG	SHO	SV	IP	H	R	ER	BB	SO	BF	WHIP	
1980	27	KCR	ALCS	1	0	1.000	0.00	2	0	2	0	0	1	4.2	4	1	0	2	1	18	1.285	
1981	28	KCR	ALDS	0	0	0.000	0.00	1	0	1	0	0	0	1	1	0	0	0	0	4	1.000	
1984	31	KCR	ALCS	0	1	0.000	3.00	1	0	1	0	0	0	3	2	2	1	1	1	13	1.000	
1985	32	KCR	ALCS	0	1	0.000	3.86	4	0	4	0	0	1	4.2	7	4	2	0	3	21	1.500	
				1	2	0.333	2.025	8	0	8	0	0	2	12.4	14	7	3	3	5	56	1.275	Post Season Pts.
				0.250	0.000	0.000	1.600	0.400	0.000	0.800	0.000	0.000	0.250	0.250	0.000	0.000	0.000	0.000	0.250	0.000	1.000	4.800

World Series Play

Year	Age	Team	Series	W	L	PCT	ERA	G	GS	GF	CG	SHO	SV	IP	H	R	ER	BB	SO	BF	WHIP	
1980	27	KCR	WS	1	2	0.333	5.23	6	0	6	0	0	1	10.1	10	6	6	3	0	43	1.258	
1985	32	KCR	WS	1	0	1.000	2.08	4	0	3	0	0	0	4.1	5	1	1	3	3	19	1.846	
				2	2	0.500	4.30	10	0	9	0	0	1	14.2	15	7	7	6	3	62	1.453	World Series Pts.
				0.400	0.000	0.000	0.400	0.400	0.000	1.000	0.000	0.000	0.250	0.250	0.000	0.000	0.000	0.000	0.250	0.000	0.400	3.350

Yearly Points Leading the League

Category	Times	Points	Total	Category	Times	Points	Total	Categ	Times	Points	Total	Hall of Fame Points	
MVP	0	7	0	Saves	5	3	15	SHO	0	2	0	Career Points	57.985
ROY	0	5	0	ERA	0	3	0	WinPc	0	2	0	Post Season Points	4.800
Cy Young	0	5	0	S.O.'s	0	2	0	Inning	0	2	0	World Series Points	3.350
Golden Glove	0	3	0	Games	3	2	6	WHIP	0	2	0	Career Add-On Points	35.000
All-Star	3	2	6	G.S.	0	2	0	GF	4	2	8	Writers Association Pts.	0.000
Wins	0	3	0	C.G.	0	2	0	Totals			8	Military/Lifetime Achievement	0.000
Totals			6	Totals			21	Grand Total Add-On Points		35		Grand Total HOF Points	101.135

Reynolds, Allie "Super Chief"

Personal Life

Allie Pierce Reynolds was born in Bethany, Oklahoma on February 10, 1917, to David C. Reynolds and Mary Brooks as the eldest of three sons

Reynolds married Dale Earleane Jones on July 7, 1935. The couple had two sons, Allie Dale & James David, and a daughter, Bobbye Kay.

Baseball Career

The Indians, who signed Reynolds as a free agent for a $1,000 signing bonus in 1938. During his five years with the Indians, he was primarily used as a starting pitcher. Reynolds became a Yankee on in 1946 and was a star of a Yankee team that won the first of five consecutive league championships. He played many important roles with the Yankees, his won/loss record was 131-60, averaging 212.5 innings, 16.4 wins, 12 complete games, and a 3.30 earned run average. In his MLB career, Reynolds had a 182–107 win–loss record, 3.30 earned run average, and 1,423 strikeouts. Reynolds was a six-time World Series champion (1947, 1949, 1950, 1951, 1952, 1953).

Achievements

- 1-Time Won 20 games & Led A.L. in Strileous: (Yankees 1952).
- 7-Times Won at least 15 games: (Indians 1945 & Yankees 1947 - 1952).
- 2-Time Led the American League in Strikeouts: (Indians 1943 & Yankees 1952).
- 6-Time an American League All-Star: (1945, 1949, 1950, 1952, 1953 & 1954).
- 5-Time received MVP Votes: (1947, 1949, 1951, 1952, & 1953.).

Hall of Fame

Reynolds was eligible in 1960 with his highest vote being 33.6% in the 15 years on the ballot. Reynolds was on ballots 4 times but never received the necessary twelve votes.

Summary Analysis

Allie Reynold had a Hall of Fame statistical points total of 86.400, This committee needs to look deep inside this man and the statistics he achieved.

Pitcher Right Handed Potential Hall of Fame Inductee

Reynolds, Allie

Positions		Born:	February 10, 1917		Height:	6' 0" USC	183	cm
Pitcher		Died:	December 26, 1994		Weight:	195 lbs.	88	Kg.
		From:	Bethany, OK		Debut:	September 17,1942		
		Bats:	Right		Last Game:	September 25,1954		
		Throws:	Right					

Year	Age	Tm	Lg	W	L	PCT	ERA	G	GS	GF	CG	SHO	SV	IP	H	R	ER	BB	SO	BF	WHIP	Awards
1942	25	CLE	AL	0	0	0.000	0.00	2	0	1	0	0	0	5	5	1	0	4	2	24	1.8000	
1943	26	CLE	AL	11	12	0.478	2.99	34	21	9	11	3	3	198.2	140	72	66	109	151	819	1.2530	
1944	27	CLE	AL	11	8	0.579	3.30	28	21	6	5	1	1	158	141	63	58	91	84	690	1.4680	
1945	28	CLE	AL	18	12	0.600	3.20	44	30	9	16	2	4	247.1	227	102	88	130	112	1074	1.4430	AS
1946	29	CLE	AL	11	15	0.423	3.88	31	28	2	9	3	0	183.1	180	93	79	108	107	815	1.5710	
1947	30	NYY	AL	19	8	0.704	3.20	34	30	3	17	4	2	241.2	207	94	86	123	129	1045	1.3660	MVP-15
1948	31	NYY	AL	16	7	0.696	3.77	39	31	5	11	1	3	236.1	240	108	99	111	101	1017	1.4850	
1949	32	NYY	AL	17	6	0.739	4.00	35	31	4	4	2	1	213.2	200	102	95	123	105	938	1.5120	AS,MVP-26
1950	33	NYY	AL	16	12	0.571	3.74	35	29	4	14	2	2	240.2	215	108	100	138	160	1045	1.4670	AS
1951	34	NYY	AL	17	8	0.680	3.05	40	26	11	16	7	6	221	171	84	75	100	126	913	1.2260	MVP-3
1952	35	NYY	AL	20	8	0.714	2.06	35	29	6	24	6	6	244.1	194	70	56	97	160	1000	1.1910	AS,MVP-2
1953	36	NYY	AL	13	7	0.650	3.41	41	15	23	5	1	13	145	140	64	55	61	86	627	1.3860	AS,MVP-12
1954	37	NYY	AL	13	4	0.765	3.32	36	18	14	5	4	7	157.1	133	65	58	66	100	653	1.2650	AS
162 Game Avg.				17	10	0.630	3.30	40	28	9	13	3	4	228	201	94	84	115	130	976	1.3860	
NYY (8 yrs)				131	60	0.686	3.30	295	209	70	96	27	40	1700	1500	695	624	819	967	7238	1.3640	
CLE (5 yrs)				51	47	0.520	3.31	139	100	27	41	9	8	792.1	693	331	291	442	456	3422	1.4320	
13 Yrs				182	107	0.630	3.30	434	309	97	137	36	48	2492.1	2193	1026	915	1261	1423	10660	1.3860	Career PTS.
				6.750	0.000	11.750	7.500	3.750	3.750	1.000	3.000	4.500	1.000	6.750	0.000	0.000	0.000	0.000	3.000	0.000	3.000	55.750

Post Season Play

Year	Age	Team	Series	W	L	PCT	ERA	G	GS	GF	CG	SHO	SV	IP	H	R	ER	BB	SO	BF	WHIP	
None				0	0	0	0	0	0	0	0	0	0	0	0	0	0	0	0	0	0	Post Season PTS.
				0.000	0.000	0.000	0.000	0.000	0.000	0.000	0.000	0.000	0.000	0.000	0.000	0.000	0.000	0.000	0.000	0.000	0.000	0.000

World Series Play

Year	Age	Team	Series	W	L	PCT	ERA	G	GS	GF	CG	SHO	SV	IP	H	R	ER	BB	SO	BF	WHIP	
1947	30	NYY	WS	1	0	1.000	4.76	2	2	0	1	0	0	11.1	15	7	6	3	6	49	1.588	
1949	32	NYY	WS	1	0	1.000	0	2	1	1	1	1	1	12.1	2	0	0	4	14	43	0.486	
1950	33	NYY	WS	1	0	1.000	0.87	2	1	1	1	0	1	10.1	7	1	1	4	7	40	1.065	
1951	34	NYY	WS	1	1	0.500	4.2	2	2	0	1	0	0	15	16	7	7	11	8	66	1.8	
1952	35	NYY	WS	2	1	0.667	1.77	4	2	1	1	1	1	20.1	12	4	4	6	18	74	0.885	
1953	36	NYY	WS	1	0	1.000	6.75	3	1	2	0	0	1	8	9	6	6	4	9	37	1.625	
6 Yrs				7	2	0.778	2.79	15	9	5	5	2	4	77.1	61	25	24	32	62	309	1.203	World Series PTS.
				1.400	0.000	1.200	1.200	0.600	1.000	0.450	0.800	0.400	0.400	1.200	0.000	0.000	0.000	0.000	1.600	0.000	1.400	11.650

Yearly Points Leading the League

Category	Times	Points	Total	Category	Times	Points	Total	Category	Times	Points	Total
MVP	0	7	0	Saves	0	3	0	SHO	0	2	0
ROY	0	5	0	ERA	1	3	3	WinPct	0	2	0
Cy Young	0	5	0	S.O.'s	2	2	4	Innings	0	2	0
Golden Glove	0	3	0	Games	0	2	0	WHIP	0	2	0
All-Star	6	2	12	G.S.	0	2	0	GF	0	2	0
Wins	0	3	0	C.G.	0	2	0	Totals			0
Totals			12	Totals			7	Grand Total Add-On Points			19

Hall of Fame Points	
Career Points	55.750
Post Season Points	0.000
World Series Points	11.650
Career Add-On Points	19.000
Writers Association Pts.	0.000
Military/Lifetime Achievement	0.000
Grand Total HOF Points	86.400

Saberhagen, Brett

Personal Life

Bret William Saberhagen was born April 11, 1964 in Chicago Heights, Illinois as the only child to Linda and Bob Saberhagen. His parents divorced when he was nine years old. He attended Grover Cleveland High School and starred in basketball, baseball football.

Saberhagen's was married to Janeane Inglett (1984-1994). The couple have three children son, Drew William, oldest daughter, Brittany, and second son, Dalton. Saberhagen married Kandace DeAngelo February 9, 2019, and has two stepsons, Aidan Stolz and Layton Stolz.

Baseball Career Saberhagen was drafted by the Kansas City Royals in the 19th round of the 1982 MLB raft. His minor-league career was brief as he made it to the majors in 1984 compiling a 10–11 record and a 3.48 ERA. The Royals made the postseason but lost to the Detroit Tigers in the SLCS. Saberhagen pitched well in his first postseason start, giving up two runs in eight innings. For his career, Saberhagen played for the Kansas City Royals, New York Mets, Colorado Rockies, and Boston Red Sox from 1984 through 1999, and a comeback in 2001. He led MLB in wins and earned run average in 1989, and threw a no-hitter in 1991. He had a career record of 167-117, 3.34 ERA in 399 games, with an ERA of 3.34, and a winning PCT. Of .588. He was known for his control, as he had the lowest walk rate in his league twice and he averaged just 1.8 BB/9 in his career.

Achievements

1-Time Led the American League in wins, winning %, & ERA: (1989).

1-Time Led the American League in complete games & Innings Pitched (1989).

2-Times Led the American League in WHIP: (1985 & 1989).

3-Time All-Star: (AL - 1987 &1989 and NL - 1994).

3-Times received Cy Young votes: (AL 1985 & 1989 (won award both years) & NL 1994

3-Times received MVP votes: (AL - 1985. 1989 (won award both years) & NL – 1994)

Hall of Fame

Saberhagen was on the 2007 BBWAA ballot for the Baseball Hall of Fame and inished with seven votes and removed. He is eligible under the Contemporary Baseball Era committee.

Summary Analysis

Brett Saberhagen has a career statistical points total of 95.750. He missed two full years due to injury. This is a case where the BBWAA could go either way on their vote.

First Baseman Potential Hall of Fame Inductee

Saberhagen, Brett

Positions	Pitcher		
Born:	April 11, 1974	Height:	6' 1" USC 185 cm
From:	Chicago Heights, IL	Weight:	160 lbs. 72 Kg.
Bats:	Right	Debut:	April 4, 1984
Throws:	Right	Last Game:	August 7, 2001

Year	Age	Tm	Lg	W	L	PCT	ERA	G	GS	GF	CG	SHO	SV	IP	H	R	ER	BB	SO	BF	WHIP	
1984	20	KCR	AL	10	11	0.476	3.48	38	18	9	2	1	1	157.2	138	71	61	36	73	634	1.104	
1985	21	KCR	AL	20	6	0.769	2.87	32	32	0	10	1	0	235.1	211	79	75	38	158	931	1.058	CYA-1,MVP-10
1986	22	KCR	AL	7	12	0.368	4.15	30	25	4	4	2	0	156	165	77	72	29	112	652	1.244	
1987	23	KCR	AL	18	10	0.643	3.36	33	33	0	15	4	0	257	246	99	96	53	163	1048	1.163	AS
1988	24	KCR	AL	14	16	0.467	3.8	35	35	0	9	0	0	260.2	271	122	110	59	171	1089	1.266	
1989	25	KCR	AL	23	6	0.793	2.16	36	35	0	12	4	0	262.1	209	74	63	43	193	1021	0.961	CYA-1,MVP-8,GG
1990	26	KCR	AL	5	9	0.357	3.27	20	20	0	5	0	0	135	146	52	49	28	87	561	1.289	AS
1991	27	KCR	AL	13	8	0.619	3.07	28	28	0	7	2	0	196.1	165	76	67	45	136	789	1.07	
1992	28	NYM	NL	3	5	0.375	3.5	17	15	0	1	1	0	97.2	84	39	38	27	81	397	1.137	
1993	29	NYM	NL	7	7	0.5	3.29	19	19	0	4	1	0	139.1	131	55	51	17	93	556	1.062	
1994	30	NYM	NL	14	4	0.778	2.74	24	24	0	4	0	0	177.1	169	58	54	13	143	696	1.026	AS,CYA-3,MVP-22
1995	31	TOT	NL	7	6	0.538	4.18	25	25	0	3	0	0	153	165	78	71	33	100	658	1.294	
1995	31	NYM	NL	5	5	0.5	3.35	16	16	0	3	0	0	110	105	45	41	20	71	452	1.136	
1995	31	COL	NL	2	1	0.667	6.28	9	9	0	0	0	0	43	60	33	30	13	29	206	1.698	
1996								Did not play in major or minor leagues (injured)														
1997	33	BOS	AL	0	1	0	6.58	6	6	0	0	0	0	26	30	20	19	10	14	120	1.538	
1998	34	BOS	AL	15	8	0.652	3.96	31	31	0	0	0	0	175	181	82	77	29	100	725	1.2	
1999	35	BOS	AL	10	6	0.625	2.95	22	22	0	0	0	0	119	122	43	39	11	81	480	1.118	
2001	37	BOS	AL	1	2	0.333	6	3	3	0	0	0	0	15	19	11	10	0	10	64	1.267	
162 Game Avg.				15	10	0.588	3.34	35	33	1	7	1	0	226	217	91	84	42	151	920	1.141	
KCR (8 yrs)				110	78	0.585	3.21	252	226	13	64	14	1	1660	1551	650	593	331	1093	6725	1.134	
NYM (4 yrs)				29	21	0.58	3.16	76	74	0	12	2	0	524.1	489	197	184	77	388	2101	1.079	
BOS (4 yrs)				26	17	0.605	3.9	62	62	0	0	0	0	335	352	156	145	50	205	1389	1.2	
COL (1 yr)				2	1	0.667	6.28	9	9	0	0	0	0	43	60	33	30	13	29	206	1.698	
AL (12 yrs)				136	95	0.589	3.33	314	288	13	64	14	1	1995	1903	806	738	381	1298	8114	1.145	
NL (4 yrs)				31	22	0.585	3.39	85	83	0	12	2	0	567.1	549	230	214	90	417	2307	1.126	
16 Yrs				167	117	0.588	3.34	399	371	13	76	16	1	2562	2452	1036	952	471	1715	10421	1.141	Career Pts.
				5.500	0.000	8.000	7.500	3.000	5.500	0.500	2.000	2.000	0.000	5.500	0.000	0.000	0.000	0.000	4.500	0.000	11.750	55.750

Post Seasonal Play

Year	Age	Team	Series	W	L	PCT	ERA	G	GS	GF	CG	SHO	SV	IP	H	R	ER	BB	SO	BF	WHIP	
1984	20	ALCS	ALCS	0	0	0.000	2.250	1	1	0	0	0	0	8	6	3	2	1	5	32	0.8750	
1985	21	ALCS	ALCS	0	0	0.000	6.140	2	2	0	0	0	0	7.1	12	5	5	2	6	35	1.9090	
1995	20	NLDS	NLDS	0	1	0.000	11.250	1	1	0	0	0	0	4	7	6	5	1	3	20	2.0000	
1998	21	ALDS	ALDS	0	1	0.000	3.860	1	1	0	0	0	0	7	4	3	3	1	7	26	0.7140	
1999	31	ALDS	ALDS	0	1	0.000	27.000	2	2	0	0	0	0	3.2	9	11	11	4	2	23	3.5450	
1999	34	ALCS	ALCS	0	1	0.000	1.500	1	1	0	0	0	0	6	5	3	1	1	5	25	1.0000	
				0	4	0.000	5.280	8	8	0	0	0	0	36	43	31	27	10	28	161	1.470	Post Season Pts.
				0.000	0.000	0.000	0.000	0.800	0.800	0.000	0.000	0.000	0.000	0.600	0.000	0.000	0.000	0.000	0.600	0.000	0.250	3.050

World Series Play

Year	Age	Team	Series	W	L	W-L%	ERA	G	GS	GF	CG	SHO	SV	IP	H	R	ER	BB	SO	BF	WHIP	
1985 MVP	21	KCR	WS	2	0	1.000	0.500	2	2	0	2	1	0	18	11	1	1	1	10	65	0.667	
			WS	2	0	1.000	0.500	2	2	0	2	1	0	18	11	1	1	1	10	65	0.667	World Series Pts.
				0.400	0.000	0.600	2.500	0.250	0.250	0.000	0.400	0.250	0.000	0.400	0.000	0.000	0.000	0.000	0.400	0.000	0.500	5.950

Yearly Points Leading the League

Category	Times	Points	Total	Category	Times	Points	Total	Category	Times	Points	Total
MVP	0	7	0	Saves	0	3	0	SHO	0	2	0
ROY	0	5	0	ERA	1	3	3	WinPct	1	2	2
Cy Young	2	5	10	S.O.'s	0	2	0	innings	1	2	2
Golden Glove	0	3	0	Games	0	2	0	WHIP	2	2	4
All-Star	3	2	6	G.S.	0	2	0	GF	0	2	0
Wins	1	2	2	C.G.	1	2	2	Totals			8
Totals			18	Totals			5	Grand Total Add-On Points			31

Hall of Fame Points	
Career Points	55.750
Post Season Points	3.050
World Series Points	5.950
Career Add-On Points	31.000
Writers Association Pts.	0.000
Military/Lifetime Achievement	0.000
Grand Total HOF Points	95.750

Tiant, Luis El Tiant

Personal Life

Luis Clemente Tiant Vega was born November 23, 1940 to Luis Tiant Sr. and Isabel Vega in Marianao, Cuba. Luis Jr. was an only child. Tiant married Maria Navarro in August 1961 with the couple having three children: Luis Jr., Isabel, and Daniel.

Baseball Career

At the end of the 1961 season, the Cleveland Indians purchased his contract and Tiant progressed through the Indians' In 1964, He had a 15–1 record at Triple-A when he was called in mid-July 1964. Tiant was 10-4 with a 2.83 ERA over 19 games and 127.0 innings pitched. Tiant was afflicted with a sore pitching arm in 1965, finishing 11-11, His ERAs in 1966 and 1967 were 2.79 and 2.74, respectively, more than adequate, but not enough to win more than 12 games each year. In 1968 Tiant became a star, finishing 21-9 and posting a league-leading 1.60 ERA. Luis also led the league with nine shutouts, including four in succession. From 1972 through 1979, Tiant was 134-82, in 283 games, 1897 innings, and a 3.64 earned run average. Overall, in parts of 19 seasons in the major leagues, Tiant compiled a 229–172 record with 2416 strikeouts, a 3.30 earned run average, 187 complete games, and 49 shutouts in 3486+⅓ innings.

Achievements

- 2-Times Led American League in Earned Run Average (ERA): (1968 & 1972).
- 2-Times Led American League in Shutouts: (1968 & 1974).
- 3-Times All-Star: (1968, 1974 & 1976) & 1-Time Led American League in WHIP: (1973).
- 3-Times Received Cy Young Award Votes: (1972, 1974 & 1976)
- 4-Times Received Most Valuable Player Votes (MVP): (1968, 1972, 1974 & 1976).

Hall of Fame

Tiant was on the Baseball Writers' Association of America from 1988 to 2002, and ERA in 2011, 2014, and 2017, falling short of the required votes for induction each time.

Summary Analysis

Luis Tiant had a statistical point Total of 100.525. His comeback, family reunion, and World Series heroics inspired a region, He needs to be elected by the Hall of Fame's ERA committee.

Pitcher Righ Handed Potential Hall of Fame Inductee

Tiant, Louis

Positions		Born :	November 23, 1940	Height:	6' 0"	USC	183	cm
Pitcher		From:	Marianao, Cuba	Weight:	180	lbs.	81	Kg.
		Bats:	Right	Debut:	July 19, 1964			
		Throws:	Right	Last Game:	September 4, 1982			

Year	Age	Tm	Lg	W	L	PCT	ERA	G	GS	GF	CG	SHO	SV	IP	H	R	ER	BB	IBB	SO	WHIP	Awards
1964	23	CLE	AL	10	4	0.714	2.83	19	16	3	9	3	1	127	94	41	40	47	105	512	1.110	
1965	24	CLE	AL	11	11	0.5	3.53	41	30	4	10	2	1	196.1	166	88	77	66	152	812	1.182	
1966	25	CLE	AL	12	11	0.522	2.79	46	16	22	7	5	8	155	121	50	48	50	145	628	1.103	
1967	26	CLE	AL	12	9	0.571	2.74	33	29	4	9	1	2	213.2	177	76	65	67	219	872	1.142	
1968	27	CLE	AL	21	9	0.7	1.6	34	32	0	19	9	0	258.1	152	53	46	73	264	987	0.871	AS,MVP-5
1969	28	CLE	AL	9	20	0.31	3.71	38	37	0	9	1	0	249.2	229	123	103	129	156	1091	1.434	
1970	29	MIN	AL	7	3	0.7	3.4	18	17	1	2	1	0	92.2	84	36	35	41	50	390	1.349	
1971	30	BOS	AL	1	7	0.125	4.85	21	10	4	1	0	0	72.1	73	42	39	32	59	321	1.452	
1972	31	BOS	AL	15	6	0.714	1.91	43	19	12	12	6	3	179	128	45	38	65	123	713	1.078	CYA-6,MVP-8
1973	32	BOS	AL	20	13	0.606	3.34	35	35	0	23	0	0	272	217	105	101	78	206	1096	1.085	
1974	33	BOS	AL	22	13	0.629	2.92	38	38	0	25	7	0	311.1	281	106	101	82	176	1266	1.166	AS,CYA-4,MVP-11
1975	34	BOS	AL	18	14	0.563	4.02	35	35	0	18	2	0	260	262	126	116	72	142	1080	1.285	
1976	35	BOS	AL	21	12	0.636	3.06	38	38	0	19	3	0	279	274	107	95	64	131	1136	1.211	AS,CYA-5,MVP-26
1977	36	BOS	AL	12	8	0.6	4.53	32	32	0	3	3	0	188.2	210	98	95	51	124	814	1.383	
1978	37	BOS	AL	13	8	0.619	3.31	32	31	1	12	5	0	212.1	185	80	78	57	114	863	1.140	
1979	38	NYY	AL	13	8	0.619	3.91	30	30	0	5	1	0	195.2	190	94	85	53	104	819	1.242	
1980	39	NYY	AL	8	9	0.471	4.89	25	25	0	3	0	0	136.1	139	79	74	50	84	588	1.386	
1981	40	PIT	NL	2	5	0.286	3.92	9	9	0	1	0	0	57.1	54	31	25	19	32	242	1.273	
1982	41	CAL	AL	2	2	0.5	5.76	6	5	0	0	0	0	29.2	39	20	19	8	30	135	1.584	
162 Game Avg.				15	11	0.571	3.3	37	31	3	12	3	1	224	198	90	82	71	155	924	1.199	
BOS (8 yrs)				122	81	0.601	3.36	274	238	17	113	26	3	1774	1630	709	663	501	1075	7289	1.201	
CLE (6 yrs)				75	64	0.54	2.84	211	160	33	63	21	12	1200	939	431	379	432	1041	4902	1.143	
NYY (2 yrs)				21	17	0.553	4.31	55	55	0	8	1	0	332	329	173	159	103	188	1407	1.301	
MIN (1 yr)				7	3	0.7	3.4	18	17	1	2	1	0	92.2	84	36	35	41	50	390	1.349	
PIT (1 yr)				2	5	0.286	3.92	9	9	0	1	0	0	57.1	54	31	25	19	32	242	1.273	
CAL (1 yr)				2	2	0.5	5.76	6	5	0	0	0	0	29.2	39	20	19	8	30	135	1.584	
AL (18 yrs)				227	167	0.576	3.29	564	475	51	186	49	15	3429	3021	1369	1255	1085	2384	14123	1.197	
NL (1 yr)				2	5	0.286	3.92	9	9	0	1	0	0	57.1	54	31	25	19	32	242	1.273	
19 Yrs				229	172	0.571	3.30	573	484	51	187	49	15	3486	3075	1400	1280	1104	2416	14365	1.199	Post Season Pts.
				9.25	0	6.75	7.5	5.5	9.25	1	4.5	6.75	0.5	9.25	0	0	0	0	6.75	0	9.25	76.250

Post Season Play

Year	Age	Team	Series	W	L	PCT	ERA	G	GS	GF	CG	SHO	SV	IP	H	R	ER	BB	SO	BF	WHIP	
1970	29	Min	ALCS	0	0	0.000	13.50	1	0	1	0	0	0	0.2	1	2	1	0	0	4	1.500	
1975	34	Bos	ALCS	1	0	1.000	0.00	1	1	0	1	0	0	9	3	1	0	3	8	35	0.667	
				1	0	1.000	0.93	2	1	1	1	0	0	9.2	4	3	1	3	8	39	0.724	Post Season Pts.
				0.250	0.000	0.250	0.250	0.025	0.250	0.250	0.250	0.000	0.000	0.250	0.000	0.000	0.000	0.000	0.250	0.250	0.250	2.525

World Series Play

Year	Age	Team	Series	W	L	W-L%	ERA	G	GS	GF	CG	SHO	SV	IP	H	R	ER	BB	SO	BF	WHIP	
1975	34	Bos	WS	2	0	1.000	3.60	3	3	0	2	1	0	25	25	10	10	8	12	107	1.320	
				2	0	1.000	3.60	3	3	0	2	1	0	25	25	10	10	8	12	107	1.320	World Series Pts.
				0.400	0.000	0.600	0.400	0.250	0.400	0.000	0.400	0.250	0.000	0.400	0.000	0.000	0.000	0.000	0.325	0.000	0.575	4.000

Yearly Points Leading the League

Category	Times	Points	Total
MVP	0	7	0
ROY	0	5	0
Cy Young	0	5	0
Golden Glove	0	3	0
All-Star	3	2	6
Wins	0	3	0
Totals			6

Category	Times	Points	Total
Saves	0	3	0
ERA	2	3	6
S.O.'s	0	2	0
Games	0	2	0
G.S.	0	2	0
C.G.	0	2	0
Totals			6

Categ	Times	Points	Total
SHO	2	2	4
WinPc	0	2	0
Inning	0	2	0
WHIP	1	2	2
GF	0	2	0
Totals			6
Grand Total Add-On Points		18	

Hall of Fame Points	
Career Points	76.250
Post Season Points	2.525
World Series Points	4.000
Career Add-On Points	18.000
Writers Association Pts.	0.000
Military/Lifetime Achievement	0.000
Grand Total HOF Points	100.775

The Baseball Hall of Fame

Warneke, Lon "The Arkansas Hummingbird"

Personal Life

Lonnie Warneke was born March 28,1909, as the fourth of five children to Louis W. ("Luke") Warneke and Martha Belle Scott in Owley, Arkansas. Warneke married Charlyne Shannon on February 12, 1933. The couple had a son and a daughter.

Baseball Career

Warneke was sold to the Cubs and reported to the Chicago Cubs spring training facilities and making the regular season roster but sent down to the minors for the next two years. In 1932, the team corrected a flaw in Warneke's pitching delivery. He gained control over his fastball and curveball. Warneke led the National League in wins (22), earned run average (2.37), shutouts (4), and winning percentage (.786), leading the Cubs to the National League Pennant. Warneke pitched 15 seasons in the MLB, winning 20+ games three times and accumulating 192 major league wins.

Achievements

- 5-time NL All-Star (1933, 1934, 1936, 1939 & 1941)
- NL ERA Leader, Wins Leader & Winning Percentage Leader (1932).
- NL Complete Games Leader (1933) & 2-time NL Shutouts Leader (1932 & 1936).
- 15 Wins Seasons: 5(1933, 1936, 1937, 1940, 1941) & (20 Wins 1932, 1934 & 1935).
- 200 Innings Pitched Seasons: 8 (1932-1937, 1940 & 1941)

Hall of Fame

Warneke has not been listed on any BBWAA Hall of Fame ballots, but he needs to be viewed closely by the Classic Baseball ERA Committee for possible election.

Summary Analysis

Lon Warnke's has 96.800 Career statistical Points. His peak (1932–1942) produced a 186-111 record and helped in the success of two Pennants for the Cubs. This is a case that should be decided by the Baseball Writers Association of America (BBWAA).

Pitcher Right Handed Potential Hall of Fame Inductee

Warneke, Lon

Positions: Pitcher

Born :	March 28, 1909	Height: 6'2" cm 188
Died:	June 23, 1976	Weight: 185 Kg. 83
From:	Mount Ida, AR	Debut: April 18, 1930
Bats:	Rightt	Last Game: September 29, 1945
Throws:	Rightt	

Year	Age	Tm	Lg	W	L	PCT	ERA	G	GS	GF	CG	SHO	SV	IP	H	R	ER	BB	SO	BF	WHIP	Awards
1930	21	CHC	NL	0	0	0.000	33.75	1	0	0	0	0	0	1.1	2	5	5	5	0	11	5.250	
1931	22	CHC	NL	2	4	0.333	3.22	20	7	7	3	0	0	64.1	67	33	23	37	27	299	1.617	
1932	23	CHC	NL	22	6	0.786	2.37	35	32	2	25	4	0	277.0	247	84	73	64	106	1117	1.123	MVP-2
1933	24	CHC	NL	18	13	0.581	2.00	36	34	1	26	4	1	287.1	262	83	64	75	133	1175	1.173	AS,MVP-20
1934	25	CHC	NL	22	10	0.688	3.21	43	35	7	23	3	3	291.1	273	116	104	66	143	1198	1.164	AS,MVP-13
1935	26	CHC	NL	20	13	0.606	3.06	42	30	11	20	1	4	261.2	257	102	89	50	120	1066	1.173	MVP-12
1936	27	CHC	NL	16	13	0.552	3.45	40	29	7	13	4	1	240.1	246	108	92	76	113	1024	1.340	AS
1937	28	STL	NL	18	11	0.621	4.53	36	33	1	18	2	0	238.2	280	139	120	69	87	1051	1.462	MVP-16
1938	29	STL	NL	13	8	0.619	3.97	31	26	3	12	4	0	197.0	199	102	87	64	89	855	1.335	MVP-30
1939	30	STL	NL	13	7	0.650	3.78	34	21	7	6	2	2	162.0	160	73	68	49	59	675	1.290	AS
1940	31	STL	NL	16	10	0.615	3.14	33	31	2	17	1	0	232.0	235	103	81	47	85	969	1.216	
1941	32	STL	NL	17	9	0.654	3.15	37	30	5	12	4	0	246.0	227	100	86	82	83	1014	1.256	AS,MVP-27
1942	33	TOT	NL	11	11	0.500	2.73	27	24	3	13	1	2	181.0	173	67	55	36	59	739	1.155	
1942	33	STL	NL	6	4	0.600	3.29	12	12	0	5	0	0	82.0	76	34	30	15	31	336	1.110	
1942	33	CHC	NL	5	7	0.417	2.27	15	12	3	8	1	2	99.0	97	33	25	21	28	403	1.192	
1943	34	CHC	NL	4	5	0.444	3.16	21	10	5	4	0	0	88.1	82	40	31	18	30	354	1.132	
1944											Did not play in major or minor leagues (Military Service)											
1945	36	CHC	NL	0	1	0.000	3.86	9	1	5	0	0	1	14	16	9	6	1	6	61	1.214	
162 Game Avg.				17	10	0.613	3.18	38	30	6	17	3	1	240	235	100	85	64	98	1002	1.245	
CHC (10 yrs)				109	72	0.602	2.84	262	190	48	122	17	12	1624	1549	613	512	413	706	6708	1.208	
STL (6 yrs)				83	49	0.629	3.67	183	153	18	70	13	2	1157	1177	551	472	326	434	4900	1.298	
15 Yrs				192	121	0.613	3.18	445	343	66	192	30	14	2782	2726	1164	984	739	1140	11608	1.245	Career Pts.
				6.750	0.000	10.500	9.500	3.750	4.500	1.000	4.500	3.000	0.500	6.750	0.000	0.000	0.000	0.000	2.500	0.000	8.000	61.250

Post Seasonal Play

Year	Age	Team	Series	W	L	PCT	ERA	G	GS	GF	CG	SHO	SV	IP	H	R	ER	BB	SO	BF	WHIP	
None																						
				0	0	0	0	0	0	0	0	0	0	0	0	0	0	0	0	0	0	Post Season Pts.
				0.000	0.000	0.000	0.000	0.000	0.000	0.000	0.000	0.000	0.000	0.000	0.000	0.000	0.000	0.000	0.000	0.000	0.000	0.000

World Series Play

Year	Age	Team	Series	W	L	PCT	ERA	G	GS	GF	CG	SHO	SV	IP	H	ER	ERA	BB	SO	BF	WHIP	
1932	23	Chi	WS	0	1	0.000	5.91	2	1	0	1	0	0	10.2	15	7	7	5	8	48	1.875	
1935	26	Chi	WS	2	0	1.000	0.54	3	2	0	1	1	0	16.2	9	1	1	4	5	62	0.780	
1945	36	Chi	WS	0	0	0.000	0.00	0	0	0	0	0	0	0	0	0	0	0	0	0	0.000	
				2	1	0.667	2.63	5	3	0	2	1	0	27.1	24	8	8	9	13	110	1.207	World Series Pts.
				0.400	0.000	0.250	1.200	0.250	0.400	0.000	0.400	0.250	0.000	0.800	0.000	0.000	0.000	0.000	0.400	0.000	1.200	5.550

Yearly Points Leading the League

Category	Times	Points	Total	Category	Times	Points	Total	Catego	Times	Points	Total
MVP	0	7	0	Saves	0	3	0	SHO	2	2	4
ROY	0	5	0	ERA	1	3	3	WinPct	1	2	2
Cy Young	0	5	0	S.O.'s	0	2	0	Innings	0	2	0
Golden Glove	0	3	0	Games	0	2	0	WHIP	0	2	0
All-Star	5	2	10	G.S.	0	2	0	GF	0	2	0
Wins	1	3	3	C.G.	1	2	2	Totals			6
Totals			13	Totals			5	Grand Total Add-On Points			24

Hall of Fame Points	
Career Points	61.250
Post Season Points	0.000
World Series Points	5.550
Career Add-On Points	24.000
Writers Association Pts.	0.000
Military/Lifetime Achievement	6.000
Grand Total HOF Points	96.800

The Baseball Hall of Fame

Welch, Robert "Bob"

Personal Life

Robert Lynn Welch was born November 3, 1956, in Detroit, Michigan to Robert Lynn Welch and Lorine Lunell. Bob and his older brother, Donnie, stayed active all year, by playing basketball in the driveway at home and hockey at a local rink

Welch married Mary Ellen January 19, 1984, with the couple having three children, sons Dylan & Riley, and a daughter named Kelly. The Welch's eventually divorced.

Baseball Career

The Dodgers selected Welch in the first round, 20th overall of the 1977 amateur draft and assigned him to the Class AA Texas League. He made his big-league debut on June 20, 1978, pitching, pitching two innings of scoreless relief. In a 17-year career, Welch compiled a 211–146 record, 1,969 strikeouts, a 3.47 ERA in 3,092 innings. Welch split his 17-year career between two teams: the Los Angeles Dodgers and the Oakland Athletics threw 61 complete games, tossed 28 shutouts, and 1,969 strikeouts.

Achievements

- 2-time All-Star (1980 & 1990) & NL Shutouts Leader (1987
- 3-Times received AL Cy Young Award Votes: (1983, 1987 & 1990-Won).
- AL Wins Leader & received MVP Votes: & AL Winning Percentage Leader (1990)
- 15 Wins Seasons: 6 (1982, 1983 & 1987-1990) & 25 Win Seasons:(1990).
- 200 Innings Pitched Seasons: 9 (1980, 1982, 1983 & 1986-1991);
- 2-Time World Series Champion: (Dodgers (1981) & Athletics (1989).

Hall of Fame

Bob Welch was on the BBWAA Ballot for the Hall of Fame in 2000 and received 1 vote for 0.2% and was dropped off for future election

Summary Analysis

Bob Welch had 90.900 career statistical points. The ERA Committee needs to review Welch's career and decide if he is Hall of Fame ready, or the Hall of Very Good.

Pitcher Right Handed Potential Hall of Fame Inductee

Welch, Bob

Positions
Pitcher

Born:	November 3, 1956	Height:	6'3"	cm	190
Died:	June 9, 2014	Weight:	190	Kg	86
From:	Detroit, MI	Debut:	June 20, 1978		
Bats:	Right	Last Game:	Augusat 11, 1994		
Throws:	Right				

Year	Age	Tm	Lg	W	L	PCT	ERA	G	GS	GF	CG	SHO	SV	IP	H	R	ER	BB	SO	BF	WHIP	Awards
1978	21	LAD	NL	7	4	0.636	2.02	23	13	6	4	3	3	111.1	92	28	25	26	66	439	1.060	
1979	22	LAD	NL	5	6	0.455	3.98	25	12	10	1	0	5	81.1	82	42	36	32	64	349	1.402	
1980	23	LAD	NL	14	9	0.609	3.29	32	32	0	3	2	0	213.2	190	85	78	79	141	889	1.259	AS
1981	24	LAD	NL	9	5	0.643	3.44	23	23	0	2	1	0	141.1	141	56	54	41	88	601	1.288	
1982	25	LAD	NL	16	11	0.593	3.36	36	36	0	9	3	0	235.2	199	94	88	81	176	965	1.188	
1983	26	LAD	NL	15	12	0.556	2.65	31	31	0	4	3	0	204	164	73	60	72	156	828	1.157	CYA-8
1984	27	LAD	NL	13	13	0.500	3.78	31	29	0	3	1	0	178.2	191	86	75	58	126	771	1.394	
1985	28	LAD	NL	14	4	0.778	2.31	23	23	0	8	3	0	167.1	141	49	43	35	96	675	1.052	
1986	29	LAD	NL	7	13	0.35	3.28	33	33	0	7	3	0	235.2	227	95	86	55	183	981	1.197	
1987	30	LAD	NL	15	9	0.625	3.22	35	35	0	6	4	0	251.2	204	94	90	86	196	1027	1.152	CYA-8
1988	31	OAK	AL	17	9	0.654	3.64	36	36	0	4	2	0	244.2	237	107	99	81	158	1034	1.300	
1989	32	OAK	AL	17	8	0.68	3	33	33	0	1	0	0	209.2	191	82	70	78	137	884	1.283	
1990	33	OAK	AL	27	6	0.818	2.95	35	35	0	2	2	0	238	214	90	78	77	127	979	1.223	AS,CYA-1,MVP-9
1991	34	OAK	AL	12	13	0.48	4.58	35	35	0	7	1	0	220	220	124	112	91	101	950	1.414	
1992	35	OAK	AL	11	7	0.611	3.27	20	20	0	0	0	0	123.2	114	47	45	43	47	513	1.270	
1993	36	OAK	AL	9	11	0.45	5.29	30	28	0	0	0	0	166.2	208	102	98	56	63	746	1.584	
1994	37	OAK	AL	3	6	0.333	7.08	25	8	4	0	0	0	68.2	79	56	54	43	44	325	1.777	
162 Game Avg.				15	10	0.591	3.47	36	32	1	4	2	1	217	203	92	84	73	138	910	1.270	
LAD (10 yrs)				115	86	0.572	3.14	292	267	16	47	23	8	1820	1631	702	635	565	1292	7525	1.206	
OAK (7 yrs)				96	60	0.615	3.94	214	195	4	14	5	0	1271	1263	608	556	469	677	5431	1.362	
NL (10 yrs)				115	86	0.572	3.14	292	267	16	47	23	8	1820	1631	702	635	565	1292	7525	1.206	
AL (7 yrs)				96	60	0.615	3.94	214	195	4	14	5	0	1271	1263	608	556	469	677	5431	1.362	
17 Yrs				211	146	0.591	3.47	506	462	20	61	28	8	3092	2894	1310	1191	1034	1969	12956	1.270	Career Pts.
				8	0	9.25	6.5	4.5	8	5	1.5	3	0.5	8	0	0	0	0	5.5	0	6.75	66.5

Post Seasonal Play

Year	Age	Team	Series	W	L	PCT	ERA	G	GS	GF	CG	SHO	SV	IP	H	R	ER	BB	SO	BF	WHIP	
1978	21	LAD	NLCS	1	0	1.000	2.08	1	0	1	0	0	0	4.1	2	1	1	0	5	16	0.462	
1981	24	LAD	NLDS	0	0	0.000	0	1	0	1	0	0	0	1	0	0	0	1	1	4	1.000	
1981	24	LAD	NLCS	0	0	0.000	5.4	3	0	1	0	0	1	1.2	2	1	1	0	2	7	1.200	
1983	26	LAD	NLCS	0	1	0.000	6.75	1	1	0	0	0	0	1.1	0	2	1	2	0	6	1.500	
1985	28	LAD	NLCS	0	1	0.000	6.75	1	1	0	0	0	0	2.2	5	4	2	6	2	18	4.125	
1988	31	OAK	ALCS	0	0	0.000	27	1	1	0	0	0	0	1.2	6	5	5	2	0	13	4.800	
1989	32	OAK	ALCS	1	0	1.000	3.38	1	1	0	0	0	0	5.2	8	2	2	1	4	27	1.588	
1990	33	OAK	ALCS	1	0	1.000	1.23	1	1	0	0	0	0	7.1	6	1	1	3	4	31	1.227	
1992	35	OAK	ALCS	0	0	0.000	2.57	1	1	0	0	0	0	7	7	2	2	1	7	29	1.143	
8 Years				3	2	0.600	4.505	11	6	3	0	0	1	30.1	36	18	15	16	25	151	1.716	Post Season Pts.
				0.400	0.000	0.000	0.250	1.200	0.600	0.400	0.000	0.000	0.250	0.500	0.000	0.000	0.000	0.000	0.600	0.000	0.000	4.300

World Series Play

Year	Age	Team	Series	W	L	PCT	ERA	G	GS	GF	CG	SHO	SV	IP	H	ER	ERA	BB	SO	BF	WHIP	
1978	21	LAD	WS	0	1	0.000	6.23	3	0	2	0	0	1	4.1	4	3	3	2	6	19	1.385	
1981	24	LAD	WS	0	0	0.000	inf	1	1	0	0	0	0	0	3	2	2	1	0	4	INF	
1988	31	OAK	WS	0	0	0.000	1.80	1	1	0	0	0	0	5	6	1	1	3	8	24	1.800	
1989	32	OAK	WS	Did not pitch in series																		
1990	33	OAK	WS	0	0	0.000	4.91	1	1	0	0	0	0	7.1	9	4	4	2	2	31	1.500	
				0	1	0.000	5.40	6	3	2	0	0	1	16.2	22	10	10	8	16	78	1.800	World Series Pts.
				0.000	0.000	0.000	0.000	0.400	0.400	0.250	0.000	0.000	0.250	0.400	0.000	0.000	0.000	0.000	0.400	0.000	0.000	2.100

Yearly Points Leading the League

Category	Times	Points	Total	Category	Times	Points	Total	Category	Times	Points	Total	Hall of Fame Points	
MVP	0	7	0	Saves	0	3	0	SHO	1	2	2	Career Points	66.500
ROY	0	5	0	ERA	0	3	0	WinPct	1	2	2	Post Season Points	4.300
Cy Young	1	5	5	S.O.'s	0	2	0	Innings	0	2	0	World Series Points	2.100
Golden Glove	0	3	0	Games	0	2	0	WHIP	0	2	0	Career Add-On Points	18.000
All-Star	2	2	4	G.S.	1	2	2	GF	0	2	0	Writers Association Pts.	0.000
Wins	1	3	3	C.G.	0	2	0	Totals			4	Military/Lifetime Achievement	0.000
Totals			12	Totals			2	Grand Total Add-On Points			18	Grand Total HOF Points	90.900

Wood, Howard "Smoky Joe" Wood

Personal Life

Howard Ellsworth Wood was born October 25, 1889, the second son of John and Rebecca Stevens Wood. Wood married Laura O'Shea on Dec. 20, 1913. They had three sons, Joe Jr., Stephen, Robert, and a daughter, Virginia.

Baseball

Wood played his first amateur baseball making his debut with the mostly-female "Bloomer Girls." After joining the Red Sox in 1908 at 18, Wood had his breakthrough season in 1911 in which he won 23 games, compiled an earned run average of 2.02, threw a no-hitter against the St. Louis Browns and struck out 15 batters in a single game. He earned the nickname "Smoky Joe" because of his blazing fastball. Wood's best season was in 1912, when he had an ERA of 1.91, 258 strikeouts, a record of 34 wins and only 5 losses. Wood's 34 victories rank as the sixth-highest total in major league history.

In 1012, Wood fell and broke his thumb, and pitched in pain for the following three seasons. Although he maintained a winning record and a low ERA, his appearances were limited, as he could no longer recover quickly from pitching a game. Wood sat out the 1916 season and most of the 1917 season, and ended his pitching career. Wood embarked on a second career as an outfielder. Wood finished in the top 10 in the American League in runs batted in 1918 and 1922. Wood finished his major league career after the 1922 season with a pitching record of 117–57 and an ERA of 2.03 and a lifetime batting average of .283.

Hall of Fame

Joe Wood appeared on the writers' Hall of Fame ballot 9 times from 1936-1951 but didn't receive the required votes. He need to be voted on again.

Summary Analysis

Wood had a combined Hall of Fame Total Point Total of 103.500 for pitching and as a position player. "Smokey Joe" belongs in the Baseball Hall of Fame.

Right Handed Pitcher Potential Hall of Fame Inductee

Wood., Joe "Smokey Joe"

Positions		Born:	October 25, 1889	Height:	5' 11" USC 180 cm
Pitcher		Died:	July 27, 1985	Weight:	180 lbs. 81 Kg.
		From:	Kansas City, MO	Debut:	August 24, 1908
		Bats:	Right	Last Game:	September 24, 1922
		Throws:	Right		

Pitching Statistics

Year	Age	Tm	Lg	W	L	W-L%	ERA	G	GS	GF	CG	SHO	SV	IP	H	R	ER	BB	SO	HBP	BF	WHIP	Awards
1908	18	BOS	AL	1	1	0.500	3.38	6	2	3	1	1	0	22.2	14	12	6	16	11	1	104	1.324	
1909	19	BOS	AL	11	7	0.611	3.18	24	19	3	13	4	0	160.2	121	51	39	48	88	6	629	1.071	
1910	20	BOS	AL	12	13	0.480	1.69	35	17	13	14	3	0	196.2	155	81	37	56	145	10	771	1.073	
1911	21	BOS	AL	23	17	0.575	2.02	44	33	11	25	5	3	275.2	226	113	62	76	231	11	1102	1.096	
1912	22	BOS	AL	34	5	0.872	1.91	43	38	6	35	10	1	344	267	104	73	82	258	12	1328	1.015	MVP-3
1913	23	BOS	AL	11	5	0.688	3.29	23	18	4	12	1	2	145.2	120	54	37	61	123	8	599	1.248	
1914	24	BOS	AL	10	3	0.769	2.62	18	14	4	11	1	0	113.1	94	38	33	34	67	0	444	1.129	
1915	25	BOS	AL	15	5	0.750	1.49	25	16	8	10	3	2	157.1	120	32	26	44	63	1	600	1.042	
1917	27	CLE	AL	0	1	0.000	3.45	5	1	3	0	0	1	15.2	17	7	6	7	2	0	62	1.532	
1919	29	CLE	AL	0	0	0.000	0.00	1	0	1	0	0	1	0.2	0	2	0	0	0	0	3	0.000	
1920	30	CLE	AL	0	0	0.000	22.50	1	0	1	0	0	0	2	4	3	5	2	1	0	11	3.000	
162 Game Avg.				22	10	0.672	2.03	40	38	10	21	5	3	255	202	88	58	75	276	5	1004	1.087	
BOS (8 yrs)				117	56	0.676	1.99	218	157	31	121	28	8	1416	1117	485	313	412	986	40	5577	1.080	
CLE (3 yrs)				0	1	0.000	5.40	7	1	5	0	0	2	18.1	21	12	11	8	3	0	76	1.632	
11 Yrs				117	57	0.672	2.03	225	158	36	121	28	10	1434	1138	497	324	421	989	40	5653	1.087	Career Pts.
				3.000	0.000	15.500	20.000	2.500	1.500	1.000	2.500	3.000	0.500	2.000	0.000	0.000	0.000	0.000	3.500	0.000	0.000	14.250	87.250

Post Season Play

Year	Age	Lg	Series	W	L	W-L%	ERA	G	GS	GF	CG	SHO	SV	IP	H	R	ER	BB	SO	HBP	BF	WHIP	
1912	22	AL	WS	3	1	0.75	4.50	4	3	1	2	0	0	22	27	11	11	3	21	1	93	1.364	
1915	25	AL	WS							Did not pitch in series													
1920	30	AL	WS							Did not pitch in series													
3 WS				3	1	0.750	4.50	4	3	1	2	0	0	22	27	11	11	3	21	1	93	1.364	World Series Pts.
				0.600	0.000	1.200	0.250	0.400	0.400	0.250	0.400	0.000	0.000	0.400	0.000	0.000	0.000	0.000	0.600	0.000	0.000	0.600	5.100

Yearly Points Leading the League

Category	Times	Points	Total		Category	Times	Points	Total		Category	Times	Points	Total
MVP	0	7	0		Saves	0	3	0		SHO	1	2	2
ROY	0	5	0		ERA	1	3	3		WinPct	2	2	4
Cy Young	0	5	0		S.O.'s	0	2	0		Innings	0	2	0
Golden Glove	0	3	0		Games	0	3	0		WHIP	0	2	0
All-Star	0	1	0		G.S.	1	2	2		GF	0	2	0
Wins	1	3	3		C.G.	1	2	2		Totals			6
Totals			3		Totals			7		Grand Total Add-On Points			16

Hall of Fame Points

Career Points	80.500
Post Season Points	0.000
World Series Points	7.000
Career Add-On Points	16.000
Writers Association Pts.	0.000
Military/Lifetime Achievement	0.000
Grand Total HOF Points	103.500

Hitting Statistics

Year	Age	Tm	Lg	G	PA	AB	R	H	2B	3B	HR	RBI	SB	CS	BB	SO	BA	OBP	SLG	OPS	TB	HBP	Awards
1908	18	BOS	AL	6	7	7	1	0	0	0	0	0	0	N/A	0	3	0.000	0.000	0.000	0.000	0	0	
1909	19	BOS	AL	24	80	55	4	9	0	1	0	3	0	N/A	2	6	0.164	0.207	0.200	0.407	11	1	
1910	20	BOS	AL	35	77	69	9	18	2	1	1	5	0	N/A	5	16	0.261	0.311	0.362	0.673	25	0	
1911	21	BOS	AL	44	106	89	15	23	4	2	3	11	3	N/A	10	23	0.261	0.343	0.420	0.764	37	1	
1912	22	BOS	AL	43	145	124	16	36	18	1	1	13	0	1	11	26	0.290	0.348	0.435	0.784	54	0	MVP-3
1913	23	BOS	AL	25	63	56	10	15	5	0	0	10	1	N/A	4	7	0.268	0.317	0.357	0.674	20	0	
1914	24	BOS	AL	31	48	43	2	6	1	0	0	1	1	0	3	14	0.140	0.213	0.163	0.376	7	1	
1915	25	BOS	AL	29	64	54	6	14	3	1	1	7	1	1	5	10	0.259	0.322	0.370	0.692	20	0	
1917	27	CLE	AL	10	0	6	1	0	0	0	0	0	0	N/A	0	3	0.000	0.000	0.000	0.000	0	0	
1918	28	CLE	AL	119	482	422	41	125	22	4	5	66	8	N/A	36	38	0.296	0.356	0.403	0.759	170	5	
1919	29	CLE	AL	72	235	192	30	49	10	6	0	27	3	N/A	32	21	0.255	0.367	0.370	0.737	71	2	
1920	30	CLE	AL	61	176	137	25	37	11	2	1	30	1	1	25	16	0.270	0.390	0.401	0.792	55	2	
1921	31	CLE	AL	66	234	194	32	71	16	5	4	60	2	0	25	17	0.366	0.438	0.562	1.000	109	0	
1922	32	CLE	AL	142	585	505	74	150	33	8	8	92	5	1	50	68	0.297	0.367	0.442	0.808	223	6	
162 Game Avg.				162	530	454	62	129	27	7	5	76	5	65	48	62	0.283	0.357	0.411	0.768	186	4	
BOS (8 yrs)				227	564	496	63	121	26	6	5	50	4	3	40	107	0.244	0.304	0.351	0.655	174	3	
CLE (6 yrs)				470	1718	1456	203	432	92	25	18	275	19	2	168	158	0.297	0.374	0.431	0.806	628	13	
14 Yrs				697	2282	1952	266	553	118	31	23	325	23	5	208	265	0.283	0.357	0.411	0.768	802	16	Career Pts.
				0.000	0.000	0.000	0.000	0.000	0.000	0.000	0.000	0.000	0.500	0.000	0.000	0.000	3.750	3.750	1.500	3.750	0.000	0.000	13.250

World Series Play

Year	Age	Tm	Series	G	PA	AB	R	H	2B	3B	HR	RBI	SB	CS	BB	SO	BA	OBP	SLG	OPS	TB	HBP	
1912	23	BOS	WS	4	8	7	1	2	0	0	0	1	0		1	0	0.286	0.375	0.286	0.661	2	0	
1915	25	BOS	WS						Did not play in series														
1920	30	CLE	WS	4	11	10	2	3	1	0	0	0	0	0	1	2	0.200	0.273	0.300	0.573	3	0	
3 WS				8	19	17	3	4	1	0	0	1	0	0	2	2	0.235	0.316	0.294	0.610	5	0	World Series Pts.
				0.400	0.000	0.000	0.250	0.250	0.000	0.000	0.000	0.250	0.000	0.000	0.250	0.000	0.250	0.000	0.000	0.000	0.250	0.000	3.900

Achievements

1	Times Most Valuable Player Votes	1912		1	Times Led League in Shutouts	1912
	Times Most Cy Young Award Votes				Times Led League in Games	
	Times Golden Glove Award				Times Led League in Games Started	
1	Times Led League in Wins	1912		1	Times Led League in Complete Games	1912
1	Times Led League in ERA	1915		2	Times Led League in Winning Percentage	1912 1915

<h1 align="center">The Baseball Hall of Fame</h1>

<h2 align="center">Statistical Review of Potential Player/Managers for the Hall of Fame</h2>

Player	Years Played	Years Managed	Years Coached	Career Points	P.S. & W.S. Pts.	Coaching Points	Manager Points	Military Points	HOF Points	Comments
Players Needing to be Inducted										
Baker, Dusty	19	25	N/A	40.000	13.700	0.000	141.500	0.000	184.200	Inducted
Bochy, Bruce	9	26	N/A	0.750	9.500	0.000	132.00	0.000	134.500	Inducted
Grim, Charlie	20	19	N/A	0.000	7.150	0.000	85.500	0.000	125.900	Inducted
Pinella, Lou	18	23	N/A	0.300	8.800	0.000	101.00	0.000	135.300	Inducted
Players Needing to be Voted into the Hall of Fame by the BBWAA										
Johnson, Dave	13	17	N/A	10.500	8.350	0.000	71.000	0.000	97.850	Voting
Leyland, Jim	0	19	N/A	0.000	0.000	0.000	97.000	0.000	Elected	2024
Martin, Billy	11	16	N/A	5.000	12.850	0.000	111.850	6.000	111.850	Voting
Murtaugh, Danny	9	15	N/A	5.00	8.000	0.000	101.000	8.000	101.000	Voting
Scioscia, Mike	11	19	N/A	6.500	5.500	0.000	105.000	0.000	105.000	Voting
Players Not Meeting the Statistical Requirements										
Alou, Felipe	17	19	N/A	36.500	4.700	0.000	33.500	0.000	72.600	DMR
Bauer, Hank	14	6	N/A	26.500	10.500	0.000	30.000	0.000	67.000	DMF
Gaston, Cito	11	12	N/A	6.000	0.000	0.000	54.500	0.000	60.500	DMR
Hargrove, Mike	12	16	N/A	28.750	0.000	0.000	55.000	0.000	83.750	DMR
Houk, Ralph	9	20	N/A	0.000	1.750	0.000	90.500	0.000	92.250	DMF
Howser, Dick	6	8	N/A	3.750	1.750	0.000	47.500	0.000	53.000	DMR
Girardi, Joe	15	14	N/A	7.000	8.750	0.000	80.000	0.000	90.750	DMR
Maddon, Joe	0	19	N/A	0.000	0.000	0.000	78.000	0.000	78.000	DMR
Manuel, Charlie	6	12	N/A	0.000	1.000	0.000	76.500	0.000	77.500	DMR
Mauch, Gene	9	26	N/A	3.000	0.000	4.000	78.500	0.000	85.500	DMF
Melvin, Bob	10	20	N/A	1.000	2.000	0.000	71.500	0.000	74.500	DMR
O'Neill, Steve	17	14	N/A	11.000	0.000	0.000	71.000	0.000	82.000	DMR
Showalter, Buck	0	22	N/A	0.000	0.000	0.000	94.000	0.000	94.000	DMR
Tanner, Chuck	8	10	N/A	6.500	0.000	0.000	57.500	0.000	64.000	DMF

<u>Hall of Fame Statistical Requirements:</u>

All Player/Managers achieving the total of 120.000, or greater, Total Hall of Fame Points, shall be Inducted after five (5) years of retirement. This provision can be waived due to the death by a 75% vote of the 25 Panel BBWAA's. Individuals receiving less than the required 120.000 Hall of Fame Points are eligible for Election after five (5) years of retirement. A 25 person BBWAA will determine the Players that will be Inducted and vote on the Players needing to be elected. An example of those needing to be elected are as follows: Player "A" has a total of 95 Hall of Fame Points and will need 25 of the (25) BBWAA votes to be Elected in the following year.

Player/Managers Needing to be Inducted.

- **Dusty Baker**
- **Bruce Bochy**
- **Charlie Grimm**
- **Lou Pinella**

110.000 Hall of Fame Statistical Induction Criteria

Jim Leyland – Elected by the BBWAA for 2024

Baker Jr., Johnny B (Dusty)

Personal Life

Johnnie B "Dusty" Baker Jr. was born June 15,1949 as the oldest of five children to Johnnie B. Baker Sr. and Christine. Baker grew up in Riverside, California.

Baker married Alice Lee Washington in the 1970's and they had a daughter, Natosha. The marriage ended in divorce (date not found) and Baker married his second wife, Melissa Esplana, in 1994. The two have a son Darren, born February 11, 1999.

Baseball Career

Baker was drafted by the Atlanta Braves in the 1967 amateur draft. Baker played in MLB for 19 seasons the majority with the Atlanta Braves and Los Angeles Dodgers. During his Dodgers tenure, he was a two-time All-Star, won two Silver Slugger Awards and a Gold Glove Award, and became the first NLCS MVP, which he received during the 1977 National League Championship Series. He also made three World Series appearances, winning in 1981.

Managerial Career

After retiring as a player, Baker served as the manager of the San Francisco Giants from 1993 to 2002, the Chicago Cubs from 2003 to 2006, the Cincinnati Reds from 2008 to 2013, the Washington Nationals from 2016 to 2017, and the Houston Astros from 2020 to 2023. Baker was named NL Manager of the Year three times with the Giants and won the 2022 World Series with the Astros. At age 73, he is the oldest manager to win a championship in the four major North American sports. He was the first MLB manager to reach the playoffs and win a division title with five different teams.

San Francisco Giants (1993 – 2002)

On December 16, 1992, Baker was hired to manage the San Francisco Giants. Baker would win the NL Manager of the Year award leading the team to a 103–59 record. However, it was not enough for a playoff berth. It was the second-best record in baseball that year behind the 104–58 Atlanta Braves and 31 games better than their 72–90 finish the previous season. The Giants missed the playoffs and he became the eighth and last manager to lead a team to 100 wins without making it to the postseason. Bakers Giants went on to win division titles in 1997, lost a tie-breaker game for the

Wild Card spot in 1998, Won a division title in 2000. In 2002, his Giants won 95 games and clinched the Wild Card by 3.5 games. In the 2002 National League Division Series, they faced the Atlanta Braves with the teams splitting the first four games before a pivotal Game 5 in Atlanta, which the Giants won 3–1 to deliver their first postseason series victory since 1989. The Giants faced the St. Louis Cardinals in the 2002 National League Championship Series. The Giants won the series in five games for their first pennant in thirteen years. They advanced to the World Series against the Anaheim Angels with the Giants losing the Championship in seven games. Despite Baker's success in San Francisco, the Giants did not renew his contract after the season, letting him leave to manage the Chicago Cubs.

Chicago Cubs (2003–2006)

On November 15, 2002, he was hired by the Chicago Cubs to a four-year deal to manage the team, Baker would make a major impact in his first season as manager for the Cubs in 2003. With the help of an impressive pitching staff and big gun batters such as Sammy Sosa and Moisés Alou, the Cubs claimed their first division title in fourteen years. Baker led the Cubs to victory over the Atlanta Braves in the National League Division Series. The Cubs lost to the Marlins in Game 7 at Wrigley Field on their way to winning the World Series over the New York Yankees.

In 2004, the team was involved in a heated wild card chase with the Houston Astros but fell out of contention near the season's end, losing six of their last eight games and missing the playoffs by three games. In 2005, the team finished the season with a 79–83 record, marking the first time in three years that the Cubs finished with a losing record. The Cubs performance continued to decline in 2006 as they fell to 66–96 and a month after the 2006 season ended, the Cubs declined to renew Baker's contract. Baker finished his tenure with a regular season record of 322 wins and 326.

Cincinnati Reds (2008-2013)

On October 13, 2007, Baker was hired as manager of the Reds. He was the first black manager in Cincinnati Reds history Baker and the Reds finished 74–88 and 78–84 in 2008 and 2009, In 2010, the Reds won the Central title. This championship led to their first playoff appearance in 15 years. However, the Reds were swept by the Philadelphia Phillies in the NLDS. Baker signed a two-year contract extension on October 4, 2010. The Reds won 97 games in 2012 to win the National League

Central for the second time in three seasons The Reds clinched the 2012 Central Division championship, their second in three years and Baker's fifth as a manager. In the 2012 National League Division Series, the Reds faced the San Francisco Giants. The Reds beat the Giants 5–2 and 9–0 in San Francisco to lead the series. Game 3 turned out to be a tight affair with the Reds on the wrong side and they tied the series with an 8–3 victory in Game 4. In Game 5, the Reds collapse became complete, as the Giants scored six runs in the fifth inning to win 6–4, making them the second team in NLDS history to blow a 2–0 series. On October 15, 2012, he signed a two-year contract extension as manager of the Reds.

In 2013, the Reds won ninety games, but it was only good enough for a third-place finish in the division, and a five-game losing streak closed out the regular season. As such, they were the second Wild Card team and faced the division rival Pittsburgh Pirates in Wild Card game. Baker was fired by the Reds three days after the game and finished his tenure with a regular season record of 509 wins and 463 losses and a post-season record of two wins and seven losses.

Washington Nationals (2016–2017)

On November 3, 2015, Baker was named the manager for the Washington Nationals for the 2016 season. The Nationals won the NL East in Baker's first season with 95 wins. However, the Nationals lost in the NLDS in five games against the Los Angeles Dodgers after losing Game 4 and Game 5. The following season, Baker led the Nationals to another NL East Championship. However, they lost the 2017 NLDS to the Chicago Cubs in five games making it the tenth time in fourteen years that a Baker-managed team had lost a "close-out" game with the opportunity to advance to the next round of the playoffs. On October 20, 2017, the Nationals announced that Baker and his entire coaching staff would not return in 2018.

Houston Astros

On January 29, Baker became the Astros manager with a contract for one year with a club option for a second year. On September 25, the Astros clinched a playoff spot as the sixth seed in the pandemic-shortened season. Baker became the first baseball manager to lead five teams to the postseason. The Astros lost to the Tampa Bay Rays in seven games. Baker's appearance in Game 7 was his ninth as manager, setting a new record for most appearances by a manager in a winner-take-all game, By winning the American League West division in 2021, Baker became the first manager in MLB to guide five different clubs to division titles. In the playoffs, the Astros played the Chicago White Sox in the American League Division Series and beat them.

The Astros faced the Red Sox in the ALCS for the AL pennant. On October 22, 2021, the Astros won Game 6 of the series to win the pennant. Baker became the ninth manager in major league history to win a pennant in both leagues but the Astros lost to Atlanta in six games. On November 5, 2021, Baker agreed to a one-year extension. On May 3, 2022, Baker earned his 2,000th win as manager with a 4–0 victory becoming the twelfth to reach the milestone. On September 19, the Astros clinched the AL West title, which is Baker's ninth division title as manager. On September 24, the Astros won their 100th of the season and made Baker the fourth manager to have 100-win seasons in both the American and National League.

In the 2022 postseason, the Astros went against the Seattle Mariners in the American League Division Series. The Astros rallied to win Game 1 and 2 before winning Game 3 in an eighteen-inning scoreless duel 1-0. It was Baker's the Astros a sixth straight appearance in the ALCS. In the 2022 ALCS against the New York Yankees, the Astros swept them, making them the third team to sweep the LDS and LCS since 1995. The Game 4 win clinched the fourth pennant in the last six seasons for the Astros and it was Baker's third pennant as a manager. It was his sixth postseason series victory with Houston, after having won three postseason matchups in his first 22 seasons. On November 3, Baker won his 50th postseason game as manager, becoming only the fourth in MLB history to do so. On November 5, the Astros defeated the Philadelphia Phillies, in Game 6 of the 2022 World Series, winning Baker his second World Series and first as a manager. At age 73, he is the oldest manager to win the World Series as Baker won his first World Series title 40 years after winning one as a player. Baker became the seventh person to win a World Series championship as both a player and a manager.

In 2023, Bakers Astros clinched the AL West on the final day of the season to mark the tenth division title won by a team managed by Baker. They beat the Minnesota Twins in the 2023 ALDS sending the Astros to the ALCS against the Texas Rangers where the Astros lost in seven games. Baker announced his retirement on October 25, 2023.

Achievements:

- First manager in major league history to lead five different teams to division titles[89]
- Ninth manager to win both an AL pennant and an NL pennant.[89]
- Oldest manager to appear in, and win, the World Series (2022)
- He was the 12th manager in MLB history to reach 2,000 wins and the first Black man to accomplish the feat.

Hall of Fame

Dusty Baker retired as a player in 1986 but became a manager in 1992. There is no record of Baker ever being voted on by the BBWAA for election into the Hall of Fame.

Summary Analysis

Dusty Baker has been in MLB since 1969. He is one of 11 managers who have accumulated at least 2,000 wins. Baker and Joe Torre are examples of individuals who should be Inducted once their cumulative Hall of Fame Points exceeded the 120 Induction Total for combined player /manager whether they were active managing, or not. Baker should have been enjoying the fruits of his labor for over 15 years.

Player-Manager Hall of Fame Criteria Points

Baker, Dusty
Position: Rightfielder

Born:	June 15, 1949
From:	Riverside, CA
Bats:	Right
Throws:	Right
Height:	6' 2" USC 188 cm
Weight:	183 lbs. 83 Kg.
Debut:	September 7, 1968
Final Game:	October 4, 1986

Playing Career

Years / Ages	G	PA	AB	R	H	2B	3B	HR	RBI	SB	CS	BB	SO	BA	OBP	SLG	OPS	TB	HBP	
Game Avg. (18 Yrs)	162	637	565	77	157	25	2	13	80	11	6	61	74	0.278	0.347	0.432	0.78	244	4	
	2039	8022	7117	964	1981	320	23	242	1013	137	73	762	928	0.278	0.347	0.432	0.78	3073	30	Career Pts.
	6.750	0.000	0.000	1.750	3.000	0.000	0.000	3.750	3.750	1.500	0.000	2.500	0.000	3.000	2.500	2.000	3.750	3.750	0.000	29.500

Post Season Points

Years: None

	G	PA	AB	R	H	2B	3B	HR	RBI	SB	CS	BB	SO	BA	OBP	SLG	OPS	TB	HBP	
	22	51	80	14	26	6	0	3	14	0	0	10	3	0.325	0.400	0.5125	0.913	41	0	Post Season Pts.
	0.600	3.000	0.000	0.400	0.600	0.000	0.000	0.400	0.600	0.000	0.000	0.400	0.000	1.000	1.200	1.000	0.800	0.400	0.000	7.400

World Series Points

Years: None

	G	PA	AB	R	H	2B	3B	HR	RBI	SB	CS	BB	SO	BA	OBP	SLG	OPS	TB	HBP	
	18	73	66	9	16	0	0	2	7	0	0	2	11	0.232	0.260	0.319	0.58	22	1	World Series Pts.
	0.600	0.000	0.000	0.600	1.000	0.000	0.000	0.400	0.400	0.000	0.000	0.250	0.000	0.250	0.000	0.000	0.000	0.800	1.000	5.300

Managerial Career

Rk	Year	Age	Team Managing	League	Won	Lost	Ties	PCT %	Games	Finish	PS Won	PS Lost	PS PCT %	WS Won	WS Lost	WS PCT %	Comments
1	1993	44	S. F. Giants	NL	103	59	0	0.636	162	2	0	0	0.000	0	0	0.000	Did Not Make Playoffs
2	1994	45	S. F. Giants	NL	55	60	0	0.478	115	2	0	0	0.000	0	0	0.000	Did Not Make Playoffs
3	1995	46	S. F. Giants	NL	67	77	0	0.465	144	4	0	0	0.000	0	0	0.000	Did Not Make Playoffs
4	1996	47	S. F. Giants	NL	68	94	0	0.420	162	4	0	0	0.000	0	0	0.000	Did Not Make Playoffs
5	1997	48	S. F. Giants	NL	90	72	0	0.556	162	1	0	3	0.000	0	0	0.000	Lost Division Series
6	1998	49	S. F. Giants	NL	89	74	0	0.546	163	2	0	0	0.000	0	0	0.000	Did Not Make Playoffs
7	1999	50	S. F. Giants	NL	86	76	0	0.531	162	2	0	0	0.000	0	0	0.000	Did Not Make Playoffs
8	2000	51	S. F. Giants	NL	97	65	0	0.599	162	1	1	3	0.000	0	0	0.000	Lost Division Series
9	2001	52	S. F. Giants	NL	90	72	0	0.556	162	2	0	0	0.000	0	0	0.000	Did Not Make Playoffs
10	2002	53	S. F. Giants	NL	95	66	1	0.590	162	2	7	3	0.000	3	4	0.000	Lost World Series
			SF Giants		840	715	1		1556		8	9	0.000	3	4	0.000	3 - Playoff Appearances
11	2003	54	Chicago	NL	88	74	0	0.543	162	1	6	6	0.500	0	0	0.000	Lost N.L. Championship Series
12	2004	55	Chicago	NL	89	73	0	0.549	162	3	0	0	0.000	0	0	0.000	Did Not Make Playoffs
13	2005	56	Chicago	NL	79	83	0	0.488	162	4	0	0	0.000	0	0	0.000	Did Not Make Playoffs
14	2006	57	Chicago	NL	66	96	0	0.407	162	6	0	0	0.000	0	0	0.000	Did Not Make Playoffs
			Chicago		322	326	0		648	14	6	6	0.500	0	0	0.000	1 - Playoff Appearance
15	2008	59	Cincinnati	NL	74	88	0	0.457	162	5	0	0	0.000	0	0	0.000	Did Not Make Playoffs
16	2009	60	Cincinnati	NL	78	84	0	0.481	162	4	0	0	0.000	0	0	0.000	Did Not Make Playoffs
17	2010	61	Cincinnati	NL	91	71	0	0.562	162	1	0	3	0.000	0	0	0.000	Lost Division Series
18	2011	62	Cincinnati	NL	79	83	0	0.488	162	3	0	0	0.000	0	0	0.000	Did Not Make Playoffs
19	2012	63	Cincinnati	NL	97	65	0	0.599	162	1	2	3	0.400	0	0	0.000	Lost Division Series
20	2013	64	Cincinnati	NL	90	72	0	0.556	162	1	0	1	0.000	0	0	0.000	Lost Wild Card Game
			Cincinnati		509	463	0		972		2	7	0.222	0	0	0.000	3 - Playoff Appearances
21	2016	67	Washington	NL	95	67	0	0.586	162	1	2	3	0.400	0	0	0.000	Lost Division Series
22	2017	68	Washington	NL	97	65	0	0.599	162	1	2	3	0.400	0	0	0.000	Lost Division Series
			Washington		192	132	0		324		4	6	0.400	0	0	0.000	2 - Playoff Appearances
23	2020	71	Houston	AL	29	31	0	0.483	60	2	8	5	0.615	0	0	0.000	Lost A.L. Championship Series
24	2021	72	Houston	AL	95	67	0	0.586	162	1	7	3	0.562	3	4	0.333	Lost World Series
25	2022	73	Houston	AL	106	56	0	0.654	162	1	7	0	0.846	4	2	0.667	World Series Champion
26	2023	74	Houston	AL	90	72	0	0.556	162	1							
			Houston		320	226	0	0.540	546		22	8	0.7333	6	6	0.500	4 - Playoff Appearances

Team		Seasons	League	Won	Lost	Ties	PCT %	Games	Finish	PS Won	PS Lost	PS PCT %	WS Won	WS Lost	WS PCT %	Comments
SF Giants		10 years	NL	840	715	1	0.497	1556	2.3	8	9	0.458	3	4	0.458	3 - Playoff Appearances
Chi. Cubs		4 years	NL	322	326	0	0.524	648	3.5	6	6	0.500	0	0	0.500	1 - Playoff Appearance
Cin. Reds		6 years	NL	509	463	0	0.593	972	2.8	2	7	0.222	0	0	0.222	3 - Playoff Appearances
Washington		2 years	NL	192	132	0	0.591	324	1	4	6	0.400	0	0	0.400	2 - Playoff Appearances
Houston		4 years	AL	230	154	0	0.540	472	1.3	22	14	0.667	6	6	0.667	4 - Playoff Appearances
				2093	1790	1		3881		47	42	0.526	9	10	0.53	13 - Playoff Appearances

Years	Total Full Sea.	Total Games	Total Won	Game Pct	Division Titles	League Titles	World Series	Winning Seasons	Season Pct	Total
26	25	3881	3093	0.540	0	3	1	17	0.731	Points
20.000	20.000	17.000	14.000	6.500	22.500	9.000	4.000	11.500	17.000	141.500

Combination Player / Managerial

Playing Career Points	29.500
Post Season Points	7.400
World Series Points	5.300
Writers Association Pts.	0.000
Military/Lifetime Achievement	0.000
Managerial Points	141.500
Grand Total HOF Points	**183.700**

Bochy, Bruce

Personal Life

Bruce Douglas Bochy was born April 16, 1955 in France (in Bussac-Forêt, Charente-Maritime), to Sgt. Major Gus & Melrose Bochy. He was the third of four children with the couple having sons Joe, Bruce, Mark and sister Terry.

Bochy married Kim Seib in 1978. They have two sons, Greg and Brett.

Playing Career

On June 3, 1975, he was drafted in the first round by the Houston Astros in the 1975 Supplemental Draft and decided to turn professional. During his playing career, Bochy was a catcher for the Houston Astros, New York Mets, and San Diego Padres.

Managerial Career

San Diego Padres (1995–2006)

After retiring as a player, Bochy was hired by Padres general manager Jack McKeon to manage in their minor league system. After four years of managing for their minor league teams, the San Diego Padres picked Bochy to be the team's third-base coach under new manager Jim Riggleman in 1993. Following the departure of Riggleman after the 1994 season, the Padres named Bochy as their new manager for the 1995 season. At age 39, Bochy became the youngest manager in the National League and helped the Padres improve from 47–70 in 1994 to 70–74 in his rookie year.

In 1996, his second season, Bochy led the Padres to a 91–71 record and their second National League West division title in franchise history, earning Bochy National League Manager of the Year and *Sporting News* National League Manager of the Year honors. In 1998, Bochy led the Padres to a franchise-best 98–64 record and the second National League pennant in Padres history, earning *Sporting News* Manager of the Year honors for the second time. The Padres were swept in four games in the 1998 World Series by the New York Yankees. After the World Series, the Padres dramatically cut payroll and suffered five straight losing seasons. In 2005 and 2006, Bochy led the Padres to consecutive NL West titles for the first time in franchise history, but they lost to the St. Louis Cardinals in the Division Series each year. Reliever Trevor Hoffman saved 457 games managed by Bochy, the most saves by one pitcher under one manager in Major League history. He finished his Padres career with a regular season record of 951–975 and a postseason record of 8–16. In twelve seasons under Bochy, the Padres had five winning seasons and won four NL West titles and one NL pennant. After the 2006 season, Padres CEO Sandy Alderson allowed Giants General Manager Brian Sabean to interview Bochy for his job opening.

San Francisco Giants (2007 to 2019)

Bochy left the Padres for the Giants after the 2006 season and agreed to a three-year contract to become the Giants' new manager on October 27, 2006. On August 8, 2007, he won his 1,000th game as manager in a 5–0 victory. After two seasons of 90+ losses in 2007 and 2008, the Giants rebounded to finish 88–74 in 2009 and remained in the playoff race into September. After the season, Bochy received a new two-year contract with an option for 2012.

In 2010, the Giants finished 92–70 and clinched their first NL West title since 2003 on the final day of the regular season against the Padres. Bochy's "bunch of castoffs and misfits" defeated the Atlanta Braves in the 2010 NLDS and the reigning 2-time National League champion Philadelphia Phillies in the NLCS. The Giants defeated the Texas Rangers in five games in the 2010 World Series, bringing the first World Series championship to San Francisco and the Giants' first title since 1954. Following the season, the Giants exercised Bochy's 2012 contract option. Bochy had managed in 2,574 games before earning his first World Series title, which established a record for most games managed to win a World Series that stood for 12 years. In 2011, the Giants finished 86–76 and missed the playoffs. After the season, the Giants extended Bochy's contract through 2013, with an option for 2014.

In 2012, the Giants clinched the NL West for the second time in three years against the Padres, finishing with a 94–68 record. In the postseason, the Giants fell behind the Cincinnati Reds 0–2 in the 2012 NLDS before winning three straight games to stave off elimination. In the NLCS, the Giants fell behind the St. Louis Cardinals three games to one, but again won three straight elimination games to clinch their second National League pennant in three seasons. The Giants swept the 2012 World Series against the Detroit Tigers in four games.

The Baseball Hall of Fame

Before the 2013 season, the Giants extended Bochy's contract through 2016. Bochy became the 21st manager with 1,500 wins on July 23, 2013. The Giants finished the season 76–86 and missed the playoffs in 2013. When Jim Leyland retired after the 2013 season, Bochy became MLB's active leader in wins with 1,530. In 2014, Bochy became the 19th manager to reach 1,600 wins on August 27, and also became the all-time NL Western Division leader in managerial wins since the installment of division play in 1969.

With an 88–74 record, the Giants made the 2014 postseason as the second wild-card team. During a low point of the regular season, Bochy told his players they had "champion blood", referring to the Giants' 2010 and 2012 championships. After defeating the Pittsburgh Pirates in the NL Wild Card Game, the Giants beat the heavily favored. Washington Nationals three games to one in the NLDS and the St. Louis Cardinals four games to one in the NLCS for their third NL pennant in five years. Bochy's "group of warriors" went on to defeat the Kansas City Royals to win the 2014 World Series, a series that went the full seven games. Bochy became the tenth manager in MLB history to win three championships, with the previous nine all inducted into the Hall of Fame.

On April 3, 2015, the Giants announced Bochy had signed a contract extension through the 2019 season. On June 10, 2015, Bochy recorded his 700th win as Giants manager, making him the fourth in history to win at least 700 games for two different teams, joining Sparky Anderson, Tony La Russa, and Jim Leyland. The milestone came on the same night that Chris Heston threw a no-hitter for the Giants, the fifth no-hitter by the Giants under Bochy (Jonathan Sánchez in 2009; Matt Cain's perfect game in 2012; and Tim Lincecum in 2013 and 2014). On September 27, 2015, Bochy became the 16th manager to record 1,700 wins. The Giants finished with an 84–78 record and missed the playoffs in 2015.

On June 26, 2016, Bochy recorded his 800th win as Giants manager. On June 30, Bochy became the first manager since 1976 to intentionally forfeit the designated hitter, allowing Madison Bumgarner to bat for himself against the Oakland Athletics. With an 87–75 record, the Giants made the 2016 postseason as the second wild-card team, clinching on the final day of the regular season. The Giants defeated the New York Mets 3–0 in the NL Wild Card Game, their 11th straight postseason series win, dating back to 2010. The Giants lost the 2016 NLDS in four games to the Chicago Cubs, their first postseason series loss under Bochy.

On April 9, 2017, at Petco Park, in a 5–3 win over the San Diego Padres, Bochy won his 840th game as Giants manager, tying Dusty Baker for the most wins in the West Coast portion of Giants history. The next day, in the Giants' home opener at AT&T Park and a 4–1 win over the Arizona Diamondbacks, Bochy surpassed Baker to become the all-time San Francisco Giants managerial wins leader. On May 3, 2017, Bochy became the 15th manager to reach 1,800 wins. On September 25 at Chase Field, in a 9–2 win over the Arizona Diamondbacks, Bochy won his 900th career game as manager of the San Francisco Giants, making him the first manager in Major League history to win 900 games with two different teams. In 2017, the Giants instead fell to 64–98, matching Bochy's worst record as a manager and the Giants' worst since 1985.

On February 18, 2019, Bochy announced he would retire following the conclusion of the 2019 season. On June 4 at Citi Field, in a 9–3 win over the New York Mets, Bochy won his 1,000th game as one and the first in San Francisco. On August 25, 2019, Bochy managed his 4,000th career game. He is only the eighth manager to manage 4,000 games. On September 18, 2019, Bochy won his 2,000th career game as a manager. He is the eleventh manager to win 2,000 games. Bochy finished his Giants managerial career with a regular season record of 1052–1054 and a postseason record of 36–17. In 13 seasons under Bochy, the Giants had seven winning seasons, four playoff appearances, and three NL pennants and World Series championships.

Texas Rangers (2023)

Bochy came out of retirement to manage the Rangers on October 21, 2022. On June 4, 2023, Bochy won his 2,041st career game, surpassing Walter Alston for 10th place on the all-time managerial wins list. On October 23, 2023, Bochy led the Texas Rangers past the Houston Astros to win Game 7 of the ALCS to clinch the franchise's third trip to the World Series. This also became the third different MLB franchise Bochy has led to the World Series. Bochy led the Rangers to the 2023 World Series title beating the Arizona Diamondbacks on November 1, 2023, in game 5 of the series, making him the fifth manager to have won a World Series with multiple teams, Bochy was the first to beat a team in the World Series and then manage that team to a title.

The Baseball Hall of Fame

Achievements:

- One of only three managers to win a World Series championship in both leagues
- Bochy is the 11th manager in MLB history to achieve 2,000 wins,
- Bochy was both the first foreign-born manager to reach the World Series (1998) and the first European-born manager to win the World Series (2010)
- He is the only manager in Major League history to win at least 900 games with two different teams.
- Bochy has six wins in winner-take-all postseason games as manager, the most in postseason history.

Hall of Fame

Bruce Bochy needs to be one of the eight candidates for Contemporary Baseball Era Committee consideration for the Class of 2025:

Summary Analysis

Bruce Bochy has a Hall of Fame Point total of 128.500 that exceeds the Induction Criteria of 120.000. One of only three managers to win a World Series championship in both leagues and just one of seven managers in baseball history to win four or more World Series. He should be Inducted the first year he is eligible.

Player-Manager Hall of Fame Criteria Points

Bochy, Bruce

Position: Catcher

Born :	April 16, 1955
From:	Landes de Bussac, France
Bats:	Right
Throws:	Right

Height:	6' 3"	USC 190	cm
Weight:	205	lbs. 92	Kg.
Debut:	July 19, 1978		
Final Game:	October 4, 1987		

Playing Career

Yea	Ages	G	PA	AB	R	H	2B	3B	HR	RBI	SB	CS	BB	SO	BA	OBP	SLG	OPS	TB	HBP	
162	162	162	399	363	34	87	17	1	12	42	0	1	30	80	0.239	0.298	0.388	0.685	141	1	
9 Yrs		358	881	802	75	192	37	2	26	93	1	2	67	177	0.239	0.298	0.388	0.685	311	2	Career Pts.
		0.000	0.000	0.000	0.000	0.000	0.000	0.000	0.000	0.000	0.000	0.000	0.000	0.000	0.000	0.000	0.000	0.000	0.000	0.000	0.000

Post Season Points

Yea	Ages	G	PA	AB	R	H	2B	3B	HR	RBI	SB	CS	BB	SO	BA	OBP	SLG	OPS	TB	HBP	
None		1	1	1	0	0	0	0	0	0	0	0	0	0	0	0	0	0	0	0	Post Season Pts.
		0.250	0.250	0.250	0.000	0.000	0.000	0.000	0.000	0.000	0.000	0.000	0.000	0.000	0.000	0.000	0.000	0.000	0.000	0.000	0.750

World Series Points

Yea	Ages	G	PA	AB	R	H	2B	3B	HR	RBI	SB	CS	BB	SO	BA	OBP	SLG	OPS	TB	HBP	
None		1	1	1	0	1	0	0	0	0	0	0	0	0	1.000	1.000	1.000	1.000	1.000	0	World Series Pts.
		0.250	0.000	0.000	0.000	0.250	0	0	0	0	0	0	0	0	0.250	0.250	0.250	0.250	0.250	0.000	1.750

Managerial Career

Rk	Year	Age	Team	League	Won	Lost	Ties	PCT %	Games	Finish	Won	Lost	%	Won	Lost	PCT %	Comments
					Regular Season						Post Season			World Series			
1	1995	40	S.D. Padres	N.L.	70	74	0	0.486	144	3	0	0	0.000	0	0	0.000	Did Not Make Playoffs
2	1996	41	S.D. Padres	N.L.	91	71	0	0.562	162	1	0	3	0.000	0	0	0.000	Lost Division Series
3	1997	42	S.D. Padres	N.L.	76	86	0	0.469	162	4	0	0	0.000	0	0	0.000	Did Not Make Playoffs
4	1998	43	S.D. Padres	N.L.	98	64	0	0.605	162	1	7	3	0.700	0	4	0.000	Lost in World Series
5	1999	44	S.D. Padres	N.L.	74	88	0	0.457	162	4	0	0	0.000	0	0	0.000	Did Not Make Playoffs
6	2000	45	S.D. Padres	N.L.	76	86	0	0.469	162	5	0	0	0.000	0	0	0.000	Did Not Make Playoffs
7	2001	46	S.D. Padres	N.L.	79	83	0	0.488	162	4	0	0	0.000	0	0	0.000	Did Not Make Playoffs
8	2002	47	S.D. Padres	N.L.	66	96	0	0.407	162	5	0	0	0.000	0	0	0.000	Did Not Make Playoffs
9	2003	48	S.D. Padres	N.L.	64	98	0	0.395	162	5	0	0	0.000	0	0	0.000	Did Not Make Playoffs
10	2004	49	S.D. Padres	N.L.	87	75	0	0.537	162	3	0	0	0.000	0	0	0.000	Did Not Make Playoffs
11	2005	50	S.D. Padres	N.L.	82	80	0	0.506	162	1	0	3	0.000	0	0	0.000	Lost Division Series
12	2006	51	S.D. Padres	N.L.	88	74	0	0.543	162	1	1	3	0.250	0	0	0.000	Lost Division Series
					951	975	0	0.494	1926		8	12	0.400	0	4	0.000	4 - Playoff Appearances

Rk	Year	Age	Team	League	Won	Lost	Ties	PCT %	Games	Finish	Won	Lost	PCT	Won	Lost	PCT %	Comments
					Regular Season						Post Season			World Series			
13	2007	52	S.F. Giants	N.L.	71	91	0	0.438	162	5	0	0	0.000	0	0	0.000	Did Not Make Playoffs
14	2008	53	S.F. Giants	N.L.	72	90	0	0.444	162	4	0	0	0.000	0	0	0.000	Did Not Make Playoffs
15	2009	54	S.F. Giants	N.L.	88	74	0	0.543	162	3	0	0	0.000	0	0	0.000	Did Not Make Playoffs
16	2010	55	S.F. Giants	N.L.	92	70	0	0.568	162	1	7	3	0.700	4	1	0.000	World Series Champion
17	2011	56	S.F. Giants	N.L.	86	76	0	0.531	162	2	0	0	0.000	0	0	0.000	Did Not Make Playoffs
18	2012	57	S.F. Giants	N.L.	94	68	0	0.58	162	1	7	5	0.583	4	0	0.000	World Series Champion
19	2013	58	S.F. Giants	N.L.	76	86	0	0.469	162	3	0	0	0.000	0	0	0.000	Did Not Make Playoffs
20	2014	59	S.F. Giants	N.L.	88	74	0	0.543	162	2	8	2	0.800	4	3	0.000	World Series Champion
21	2015	60	S.F. Giants	N.L.	84	78	0	0.519	162	2	0	0	0.000	0	0	0.000	Did Not Make Playoffs
22	2016	61	S.F. Giants	N.L.	87	75	0	0.537	162	2	0	0	0.000	0	0	0.000	Did Not Make Playoffs
23	2017	62	S.F. Giants	N.L.	64	98	0	0.395	162	5	0	0	0.000	0	0	0.000	Did Not Make Playoffs
24	2018	63	S.F. Giants	N.L.	73	89	0	0.451	162	4	0	0	0.000	0	0	0.000	Did Not Make Playoffs
25	2019	64	S.F. Giants	N.L.	77	85	0	0.475	162	3	0	0	0.000	0	0	0.000	Did Not Make Playoffs
			13 years		1052	1054	0	0.500	2106		22	10	0.688	12	4	0.750	3 - Playoff Appearances

Rk	Year	Age	Team	League	Won	Lost	Ties	PCT %	Games	Finish	Won	Lost	%	Won	Lost	PCT %	Comments
					Regular Season						Post Season			World Series			
26	2023	68	Texas	A.L.	90	72	0	0.556	162	2	9	3	0.750	4	1	0.800	World Series Champion
					90	72	0	0.556	162								1 - Playoff Appearances

Team	League	Won	Lost	Ties	PCT %	Games		Won	Lost	%	Won	Lost	PCT %	Comments
S.D. Padres	N.L.	951	975	0	0.494	1926		8	12	0.400	0	4	0.000	4 - Playoff Appearances
S.F. Giants	N.L.	1052	1054	0	0.500	2106		22	10	0.688	12	4	0.750	3 - Playoff Appearances & W
Texas	A.L.	90	72	0	0.556	162		9	3	0.750	4	1	0.800	1 - Playoff Appearances & W
		2093	2101	0	0.497	4194		39	25	0.577	16	9	0.600	8 - Playoff Appearances & 4 '

	Total Years	Total Full Sea	Total Games	Game Won	Pct	Division Titles	League Titles	World Series	Winning Seasons	Season Pct	Total
	26	26	4194	2093	0.497	6	5	4	13	0.500	Points
	20.000	20.000	14.000	14.000	1.500	15.000	15.000	16.000	9.000	1.500	126.000

Combination Player / Managerial

Playing Career Points	0.000
Post Season Points	0.750
World Series Points	1.750
Writers Association Pts.	0.000
Military/Lifetime Achievement	0.000
Managerial Points	126.000
Grand Total HOF Points	**128.500**

The Baseball Hall of Fame

Grimm, Charles "Jolly Charlie"

Personal Life

Charles John Grimm (August 28, 1898 – November 15, 1983) was born in St. Louis, Missouri, to *William S Grimm* and Emma A Vierheller. Grimm had an older brother sister Margaret, and a younger brother Albert. The only record found about Grimms personal life was that he married Marion Sayers in 1965.

Baseball Career

The 17-year-old Grimm signed with the Philadelphia Athletics on July 28, 1916. He appeared in his first major-league game on July 30, starting in left field. On September 1 Grimm had a memorable encounter: "Connie Mack sent me up to hit against Walter Johnson in Washington, but I wasn't at the plate long. I didn't even swing on one of the three strikes, and I still have the bat I carried to the plate that day. It's just like new. All I can tell you about Johnson is that I saw him raise his arm." Grimm batted .091 with two hits in 22 at-bats during 12 games with the 1916 Athletics, whose record of 36-117 (.235) was one of the worst ever. Grimm was sold by the Athletics to the Durham Bulls of the Class D North Carolina State League.

In 1919 Grimm was acquired by the Pittsburgh Pirates and played in 14 September games, with a .318 batting average. After batting .318 with the latter team, he stayed on with the team on a more permanent basis. As a first baseman, he played for the Pittsburgh Pirates but was traded to the Cubs in 1925 and worked mostly for the Cubs for the rest of his career Grimm is one of a select few to have played and managed in 2,000 games each. In 2,166 games over 20 seasons, spanning from 1916–1936, Grimm posted a .290 batting average, 908 runs, 394 doubles, 108 triples, 79 home runs, 1077 RBI, 57 stolen bases, 578 bases on balls, .341 on-base percentage and .397 slugging percentage. He finished his career with a .993 fielding percentage as a first baseman. In the 1929 and 1932 World Series, he hit .364 (12-for-33) with 4 runs, 2 doubles, 1 home run, 5 RBI and 3 walks.

Managerial Career

Chicago Cubs (1932–1938, 1944–1949)

A Fan's Perspective

On August 2, 1932, Rogers Hornsby was fired by the Cubs and Grimm was enlisted by the team to serve as player-manager. While serving as manager for the remaining 55 games, he rallied them to 37 wins that helped the team finish with a 90–64 record, finishing four games ahead of Pittsburgh for the National League pennant. In the 1932 World Series, they would be swept by the New York Yankees in four games. Grimm would retain the position of manager for the next seven seasons. In his first tenure as the Cubs manager, his teams would finish no worse than third place. In the two seasons after his first pennant, he led them to 86 wins each, which was good for third place.

The 1935 season proved superior for Grimm and Cubs, as he led them to their first 100-win season in 25 years, made most memorable by a 21-game winning streak in the month of September. In the World Series that year against the Detroit Tigers, they won the first game in Detroit before losing the next three. They rallied to win Game 5 at Wrigley Field, but the Tigers won a walk-off hit from Goose Goslin to win 4–3 and seal the Series. The Cubs went 87–67 for a third place finish the following year (which was Grimm's last as a player-manager), but they improved to 93–61 and second place the year after. 1938 was the last season of his first tenure as manager of the Cubs. The team was 45–36 when owner P. K. Wrigley moved Grimm to the broadcast booth and named catcher Gabby Hartnett as player-manager. As Grimm had done six years earlier, Hartnett led the Cubs to a dramatic comeback to win the pennant that season.

After a sluggish start to the 1944 season in which the team lost ten in a row, Grimm was hired to manage the club again. The team finished fourth in the standings with a 75–79 record (the fifth straight losing season for the team). However, Grimm led them to a dramatic improvement the following year, going 98–56 to win the league pennant for the first time since 1938. In the World Series that year, Grimm's team faced off against the Tigers once again. It was a hard-fought series, going down to the decisive seventh game at Wrigley Field. The Cubs were trounced 9–3, with six of the Tiger runs coming in the first two innings. It was the last pennant for the Cubs after 71 years. The Cubs went 82–71 the following year, finishing 3rd in the standings. It was the last time the team had a record of .500 until 1963. Grimm finished his last three seasons with a losing record (69–85, 64–90, 19–31) before resigning in 1949.

Milwaukee Braves

Grimm would soon become a major baseball figure in Milwaukee. He was hired by Bill Veeck, son of longtime Cubs president William Veeck Sr. to manage his Milwaukee Brewers, then the Cubs' top farm team, during World War II in 1941. He returned to the Brewers in 1951 when they were a farm team of the Boston Braves. He was highly successful as a manager during each term, winning the regular season American Association title in 1943 and 1951, and the playoff championship in 1951. On May 30, 1952, Grimm was promoted from Milwaukee to manager of the big-league Braves; he would prove to be the last skipper in the history of the Boston NL club. He went 51–67 (with two ties) as the Braves finished seventh place.

He then managed the Milwaukee Braves for their first three years after their move to Wisconsin in March 1953. The following year, the Braves went 92–62 (with three ties), finishing 13 games behind in second place to the Brooklyn Dodgers. It was the first time the Braves had won over 90 games since 1948. The next year, they regressed a bit as a team with an 89–65 record for a third-place finish (eight games back), but it was the first time that they had consecutive winning seasons since 1947–48. The next year, they went 85–69, finishing 13.5 games back of the Dodgers. The 1956 Grimm was dismissed after a 24–22 start to the season, replaced by Fred Haney. Grimms overall record with the Braves was 351 wins, 285 losses and 5 ties for a .560 winning %. He had 3 second place finishes and one third place.

He was brought out of retirement to direct the Cubs again in early 1960, but the team got off to a slow start, and owner P.K. Wrigley made the novel move of swapping Grimm with another former manager, Lou Boudreau, who was doing Cubs radiocasts at that time. Grimm had done play-by-play in the past, so he gave it one more go in 1960, before stepping back to the ranks of coaching and then front office duties. Grimm finished with a record of 1,287–1,067–12 while having a postseason record of 5–12. His 946 wins as a Cubs manager rank second behind Cap Anson. Serving as manager for nineteen seasons, Grimm won three pennants while finishing second three times and finishing 3rd four times; excluding his last brief run in 1960, he finished with a losing record as a manager just three times in a full season. Of the 26 managers, Grimm is one of eight to not be inducted into the National Baseball Hall of Fame. Grimm is one of 29 managers to win 1,000 games and three league pennants, although he is one of five not currently inducted into the National Baseball Hall of Fame and is one of six to not have won a World Series Baseball historian Bill James wrote, "One of the biggest surprises to me, when I ranked the managers, was how high up the lists Charlie Grimm was. He ranks about even with Al López, Whitey Herzog, Tony La Russa, and Frank, Chance, Not the 10 greatest managers in history, but the class right behind them."

Achievements

- NL Pennants: 3 (1932, 1935 & 1945) & 100 Wins Seasons as Manager: 1 (1935)
- 4-Times guided teams to 90, or more wins - (1935, 1937, 1945, & 1953).
- Managed 2344 games and played 2166 games.

Charlie Grimm was a man of many talents. Called "perhaps the best ever" defensive first baseman by Bill James,1 he led the National League in fielding percentage at the position seven times and finished in second place three times between 1920 and 1933 with the Pittsburgh Pirates and Chicago Cubs. He was a .290 hitter over his 20-year career, with nearly 2,300 hits and more than 1,000 RBIs. He managed the Cubs to three pennants, and as of 2014 no one except Cap Anson had won more games as the team's skipper. Grimm's career winning percentage of .547 was as of 2014 the 17th highest among managers with at least 1,000 wins.

Grimm was one of baseball's premier entertainers, and not just for his acrobatic play. He would serenade fans before games with his singing and banjo playing. "In the on-deck circle he might brandish two bats in imitation of a butcher sharpening his knives. He and [Cubs catcher Gabby] Hartnett liked to play 'burnout' in front of the fans, advancing up the line and firing the ball toward each other at closer and closer quarters. To the roars of the crowd, he might mimic an umpire's walk behind his back — an act that at least once earned him an ejection as a manager."
In 1930 Grimm led NL first basemen in fielding percentage for a fifth time (.995) while batting .289. He had one of his better years offensively in 1931, with a batting average of .331 and an on-base percentage of .393. On June 21 against the Brooklyn Robins, he went 5-for-5. He again topped the league in fielding percentage as a first baseman (.993). Grimm was eighth in the NL MVP voting. In Grimm's three stints as manager in Chicago, he had a record of 946-782. His career record during 19 seasons as manager was 1,287-1,067. He is one of the few men in the major leagues to both play in 2,000 games and manage 2,000 games.

Grimm compiled a batting average of .290 during his 20 years in the majors, most of which were spent with the Pittsburgh Pirates. He hit .345 for the Pirates in 1923 as a teammate of Pie Traynor, who hit .338 that year. With the Cubs in 1929, he hit .389 in the World Series. "I had fun playing baseball," wrote Grimm in his 1968 autobiography. "I tried to make it fun for my players after I became manager. I was 'Jolly Cholly' and I always thought a pat on the back, an encouraging word, or a wisecrack paid off a lot more than a brilliantly executed work of strategy."

Hall of Fame

Grimm was on the ballot twelve times from 1939 to 1962, but never received more than 9% of the vote. Charlie Grimm needs to be added to the Classic Baseball Era ballot with his entire career as a player and manager being reviewed together.

Summary Analysis

Charlie Grimms has a Hall of Fame Statistical Point Total of 125.900 for the "Proposed" new category of Player/Manager category. His total is higher than the proposed 120.000 Induction threshold and should be a benchmark for future Induction/Elections. Grimm had a 50-year career in Baseball as a player, coach, administrator, and manager and is one of the pillars that made this game great. This is one of the MAIN FAILINGS that has been illustrated in this book by not electing individuals like Grimm into the Hall of Fame. He could have enjoyed their celebrity and continue being a great Ambassador to the game he always had been. Grimm should have been elected to the Hall of Fame years ago and if the rules change, he should be INDUCTED now.

Player-Manager Hall of Fame Criteria Points

Grim, Charlie

Position: First Baseman

Born: August 28, 1898
Died: 15-Nov-83
From: St. Louis, MO
Bats: Left
Throw: Left

Height: 5'11" USC 180 cm
Weight: 173 lbs. 78 Kg.
Debut: July 30, 1916
Final Game: September 3, 1936

Playing Career

Yea	Ages	G	PA	AB	R	H	2B	3B	HR	RBI	SB	CS	BB	SO	BA	OBP	SLG	OPS	TB	HBP	
162 Game Av		162	654	592	68	172	29	8	6	81	4	4	43	91	0.290	0.341	0.397	0.738	235	2	Career Pts.
20 Years		2166	8750	7917	908	2299	394	108	79	1077	57	76	578	410	0.290	0.341	0.397	0.738	3146	31	
####		0.000		0.000	3.000	4.500	0.000	0.000	1.000	4.500	0.500	0.000	1.000	0.000	4.500	2.500	8.000	3.000	3.750	0.000	33.250

Post Season Points

Yea	Ages	G	PA	AB	R	H	2B	3B	HR	RBI	SB	CS	BB	SO	BA	OBP	SLG	OPS	TB	HBP	
None		0	0	0	0	0	0	0	0	0	0	0	0	0	0	0	0	0	0	0	Post Season Pts.
####		0.000		0.000	0.000	0.000	0.000	0.000	0.000	0.000	0.000	0.000	0.000	0.000	0.000	0.000	0.000	0.000	0.000	0.000	0.000

World Series Points

Yea	Ages	G	PA	AB	R	H	2B	3B	HR	RBI	SB	CS	BB	SO	BA	OBP	SLG	OPS	TB	HBP	
None		9	37	33	4	12	2	0	1	5	0	1	3	4	0.364	0.417	0.515	0.932	17	0	World Series Pts.
####		0.000		0.000	0.250	0.400	0	0	0.25	0.4	0	0	0.25	0	1.600	1.400	0.600	1.000	0.600	0.000	7.150

Managerial Career

Rk	Year	Age	Team	League	Won	Lost	Ties	PCT %	Games	Finish	Won	Lost	PCT %	Won	Lost	PCT %	Comments
					Regular Season						Post Season			World Series			
1	1932	33	Chicago Cubs	NL	37	18	0	0.673	55	1	0	0	0.000	0	4	0.000	Lost World Series
2	1933	34	Chicago Cubs	NL	86	68	0	0.558	154	3	0	0	0.000	0	0	0.000	Did Not Winn Pennant
3	1934	35	Chicago Cubs	NL	86	65	1	0.570	152	3	0	0	0.000	0	0	0.000	Did Not Winn Pennant
4	1935	36	Chicago Cubs	NL	100	54	0	0.649	154	1	0	0	0.000	2	4	0.333	Lost World Series
5	1936	37	Chicago Cubs	NL	87	67	0	0.565	154	3	0	0	0.000	0	0	0.000	Did Not Winn Pennant
6	1937	38	Chicago Cubs	NL	93	61	0	0.604	154	2	0	0	0.000	0	0	0.000	Did Not Winn Pennant
7	1938	39	Chicago Cubs	NL	45	36	0	0.556	81	1	0	0	0.000	0	0	0.000	Did Not Winn Pennant
					534	369			904	14	0	0	0.000	2	8	0.200	2 World Series Appearances

Rk	Year	Age	Team	League	Won	Lost	Ties	PCT %	Games	Finish	Won	Lost	PCT %	Won	Lost	PCT %	Comments
					Regular Season						Post Season			World Series			
8	1944	45	Chicago Cubs	NL	74	69	3	0.517	146	4	0	0	0.000	0	0	0.000	Did Not Winn Pennant
9	1945	46	Chicago Cubs	NL	98	56	1	0.636	155	1	0	0	0.000	3	4	0.429	Lost World Series
10	1946	47	Chicago Cubs	NL	82	71	2	0.536	155	3	0	0	0.000	0	0	0.000	Did Not Winn Pennant
11	1947	48	Chicago Cubs	NL	69	85	1	0.448	155	6	0	0	0.000	0	0	0.000	Did Not Winn Pennant
12	1948	49	Chicago Cubs	NL	64	90	1	0.416	155	8	0	0	0.000	0	0	0.000	Did Not Winn Pennant
13	1949	50	Chicago Cubs	NL	19	31	0	0.380	50	8	0	0	0.000	0	0	0.000	Did Not Winn Pennant
					406	402			816	30	0	0	0.000	3	4	0.429	1 World Series Appearances

Rk	Year	Age	Team	League	Won	Lost	Ties	PCT %	Games	Finish	Won	Lost	PCT %	Won	Lost	PCT %	Comments
					Regular Season						Post Season			World Series			
14	1952	53	Boston Braves	NL	61	67	2	0.432	130	7	0	0	0.000	0	0	0.000	Did Not Winn Pennant
15	1953	54	Milw. Braves	NL	92	62	3	0.597	157	2	0	0	0.000	0	0	0.000	Did Not Winn Pennant
16	1954	55	Milw. Braves	NL	89	65	0	0.578	154	3	0	0	0.000	0	0	0.000	Did Not Winn Pennant
17	1955	56	Milw. Braves	NL	85	69	0	0.552	154	2	0	0	0.000	0	0	0.000	Did Not Winn Pennant
18	1956	57	Milw. Braves	NL	24	22	0	0.522	46	2	0	0	0.000	0	0	0.000	Did Not Winn Pennant
					351	285	5		631		0	0	0.000	0	0	0.000	0 World Series Appearances

Rk	Year	Age	Team	League	Won	Lost	Ties	PCT %	Games	Finish	Won	Lost	PCT %	Won	Lost	PCT %	Comments
					Regular Season						Post Season			World Series			
19	1960	61	Chicago Cubs	NL	6	11	0	0.353	17	7	0	0	0.000	0	0	0.000	Did Not Winn Pennant
					6	11	0	0.353	17	7	0	0	0.000	0	0	0.000	0 World Series Appearances
	14		Chicago Cubs	N.L.	946	782	9	0.547	1728		0	0	0.000	5	12	0.294	3 World Series Appearances
	5		Mil. /Bos Braves	N.L.	341	285	5	0.545	626		0	0	0.000	0	0	0.000	0 World Series Appearances
	19				1287	1067	14	0.547	2344		0	0	0.000	5	12	0.294	3 World Series Appearances

Years	Total Full Sea.	Total Games	Won	Pct	Total Game Titles	Division Titles	League Series	World Season	Winning Pct.	Season Total
19	14	2344	1287	0.547	3	3	0	14	0.769	Points
14	9	6.5	6.5	4	7.5	9	0	8	20	85.5

Combination Player / Managerial

Playing Career Points	33.250
Post Season A	0.000
World Series Points	7.150
Writers Association Pts.	0.000
Military/Lifetime Achievement	0.000
Managerial Points	85.500
Grand Total HOF Points	125.900

The Baseball Hall of Fame

Piniella, Lou "Sweet Lou"

Personal Life

Louis Victor Piniella was born on August 28, 1943, to Louis Piniella Sr. and Margaret Magadan in Tampa, Florida.

Pinella married Anita Garcia in 1968 and the couple have three children, Lou Jr., Kristi, and Derek.

Baseball Career

In 1962. Pinella started his professional career playing in the Alabama-Florida League. After one year in the minors, Piniella's was taken by the Senators in the first-year player draft following the 1962 season. He hit .310 in Class A in 1963, establishing himself as one of the game's best hitting prospects. During the 1964 season, Piniella served in the National Guard at the beginning of the year and did not play for the Senators. He was traded to the Orioles on August 4 and assigned to the Aberdeen Pheasants of the Class-A Northern League. At the end of the 1968 season, Piniella had spent seven years in the minors and was 25 years old. In 1969 he was chosen by the Seattle Pilots in the expansion draft and felt this would be his last chance.

During spring training Piniella was dealt to another expansion team, the Kansas City Royals. Here is where Piniella found a home in Kansas City. On Opening Day, April 8, 1969, at Kansas City's Municipal Stadium, Piniella led off the bottom of the first with a double to left. This was the first hit of his major-league career and the first at-bat and base hit for the Royals. Piniella scored the franchise's first run and hit safely the next three times to start the season. Piniella became a key member of the expansion Royals batting .282 and named the American League Rookie of the Year. He was the first player to win the award playing with an expansion team in its inaugural season. In 1970 Piniella had a foot injury, but improved his average to .301, eighth in the American League, with a career-high 88 RBIs. Over 18 years, Piniella retired in the middle of the 1984 season finishing with 705 hits, 305 doubles, 102 home runs, 786 runs batted in, a .291 batting average, on base % of .333, SLG% of .409 and an OPS% of .741.

Manager Career

Piniella learned the game from every manager he played for. "Earl Weaver taught me some important lessons about winning when I played for him as a kid, and now Billy Martin taught me about team chemistry." Piniella transmitted his desire and will to win to his players as he turned three struggling franchises into contenders. He liked players who were like him, who had a fire in their bellies, cared deeply about the game and who could back it up. He took indifference and lack of emotion as not caring. He has been described by his players as tough but fair.

Piniella had a quick temper that he inherited from his parents. As a player, he broke helmets and bats, damaged water coolers, and broke lights in the runway. As a manager, he kicked dirt and threw bases. His tantrums are legendary; they were sometimes used to motivate his players but sometimes embarrassed his family. He led the league in ejections three times as a manager. All the kids would tell you he would throw his glove, swing his bat. There are guys who ae bullies and hotheads, but he was just tough on himself, he never took it out on others. His teammates loved him."

Piniella was named Yankees manager prior to the 1986 season. He won 90 and 89 games in two seasons in New York before being promoted to general manager in 1988, with another stint as Yankees manager that same year. "I guess the hardest thing for me is to learn how to relax," Piniella said. "After every game, I go over in my mind: 'Could I have done it differently?

New York Yankees

George Steinbrenner signed his management team to personal services contracts so he could fire and bring them back in various capacities, and Piniella was no exception. Steinbrenner made him the manager in 1986. He promised Piniella that he would not meddle in his decisions, but that did not last. After two seasons as manager, Piniella became GM, chief evaluator of talent, manager again, then spent a year in the broadcast booth. Steinbrenner offered Piniella the manager's job for a third time, but Piniella turned it down. Steinbrenner let Piniella out of his personal-services contract to manage the Cincinnati Reds.

Cincinnati Reds

In doing so, Piniella had taken over a Reds team that had lost 87 games the year before, but he believed they had good young talent and could win in 1990. Piniella surrounded himself with veteran NL coaches to help him make the league transition. This helped lead the Reds to a wire-to-wire National League West title for the first time in National League history. The Reds then won the

NLCS against the Pittsburgh Pirates and met the heavily favored 103-win Oakland A's in the World Series. The Reds upset the A's with Piniella being credited for getting the Reds over the top by the force of his personality, his unwillingness to let up on his players, and his passion for winning. Piniella added, "To win this thing is a great feeling. It's much more meaningful to me as a manager than as a player. You're more involved, more responsible. It's the total picture. You have got to make decisions. In 1991 the injury-plagued Reds regressed but won 90 games in 1992 but finished in second place. He had not been offered a contract for 1993 and owner Marge Schott was talking about cutting payroll. When Piniella's contract was up, he joined the Mariners, a team that had experienced only one winning season in its 16 years.

Seattle Mariners

The Seattle Mariners wanted Piniella, but he had concerns about the position. Piniella agreed to manage the Mariners and negotiated an unlimited travel budget for his wife. The Mariners were 64-98 in 1992, the worst record in the American League, but had a nucleus of good young talent. Piniella said, "Winning is an attitude just like losing is. We plan on bringing in a winning attitude and have it permeate the clubhouse. In 1993 the Mariners finished 82-80, their second winning season in franchise history. 1994 was strike shortened and the Mariners regressed to a 49-63 record. However, in 1995, Piniella led the Mariners into the Postseason, where they defeated the Yankees in a thrilling Division Series matchup. For his efforts, Piniella received his first Manager of the Year Award. In 1995 the Mariners overcame a 13-game deficit on August 2 to tie the California Angels and force a one-game tiebreaker. The Mariners won, 9-1, behind the pitching of Randy Johnson. In the best-of-five Division Series, the Yankees jumped out to a commanding 2-0 lead in games. Piniella remained positive and declared, "We are going to win this thing." The Mariners won the next two games, setting up the deciding game in the Kingdome. The Yankees took a 5-4 lead in the top of the 11th inning, but the Mariners won on a walk-off two-run double by Edgar Martinez in the bottom of the inning. Ken Griffey Jr. slid into home plate to score the winning run. The Mariners lost the ALCS to the Cleveland Indians, four games to two.

The Mariners remained competitive the next five years, winning the AL West in 1997 and the wild card in 2000. They lost core talent including Alex Rodriguez, Randy Johnson, and Ken Griffey Jr., but in 2001, they signed Ichiro Suzuki as a free agent from Japan and employed a small-ball offense. Piniella guided the Mariners to another American League West title in 1997 and a Wild

Card berth in 2000. Then in 2001, Piniella and the Mariners tied one of the game's oldest records by winning 116 games, matching the 1906 Cubs and setting a new AL standard. Piniella was named Manager of the Year. The Mariners won an AL record 116 games, topping the 1998 New York Yankees (114) and tying the major-league mark set by the 1906 Cubs. The Mariners defeated the Cleveland Indians in the Division Series but lost to the Yankees in the ALCS, four games to one. Although the Mariners won 93 games in 2002, they finished third in the AL West and Piniella needed a change. He was under contract but eventually the Mariners worked out a trade of Piniella to the Tampa Bay Devil Rays.

Tamp Bay

After 10 seasons in Seattle, Piniella took over for the Devil Rays in 2003 – the only one of his five stops where he did not post a winning record. Piniella went to Tampa in part to be close to his family but after three seasons, the team was below .500 in each of Piniella's three years there, which is the only team he managed that had an overall sub-.500 record. Piniella hated losing and what made matters worse was that it was in his hometown. Piniella was frustrated that ownership did not increase payroll, and he and the club agreed to buy out the last year on his contract.

Chicago Cubs

Piniella took 2006 off from managing before he became the manager of the Chicago Cubs in 2007, a team with the worst record in the National League. GM Jim Hendry was impatient like Piniella and the Cubs were willing to spend on free agents when they hired him. The team started out 22-29 and were described as an "overpriced, slapped together mess" in the media. However, the team turned it around and won the division and were swept by the Arizona Diamondbacks in the Division Series. In 2008 the Cubs finished with the best record in the National League, the first Cubs team to make back-to-back postseason appearances since 1908. In the Division Series they were swept by the Dodgers. The Cubs' high-priced stars underperformed their contracts and the Cubs struggled in both 2009 and 2010. The 66-year-old Piniella had planned to retire at the end of the season, but his mother was ailing. August 22, 2010, was Piniella's last game.

Achievements

- NL Pennants: 1 (Cincinnati 1990) & NL World Series: 1 (Cincinnati 1990).
- MLB Record 116 Wins: (Seattle 2001)

- 8-Times guided teams to 90, or more wins: (Yankees 1986, Cincinnati 1991 & 1992, Seattle 1997, 2000, 2001 & 2002, Chicago 2008)
- 7 Times guided teams to Playoff Appearances:(1-Cincinnati, 4-Seattle & 2-Chicago)

In 23 seasons as a manager, Piniella was named Manager of the Year three times, led seven teams to the postseason, winning one World Series, and won 1,835 games, 16th all-time. He received Manager of the Year votes in 14 of his 23 seasons and led his teams to six division titles. In virtually all of his managerial stops, Lou Piniella turned struggling teams into pennant contenders

Hall of Fame

Piniella has been a candidate for election to the Baseball Hall of Fame by the Veterans Committee three times, in 2016, and 2023 but has thus far failed to be elected.

Summary

Lou Piniella has a Hall of Fame Statistical Point Total of 135.300 for the "Proposed" new category of Player/Manager category. His total is higher than the proposed 120.000 Induction threshold and should be a benchmark for future Induction or election. Piniella was a true franchise changer for each team he managed and played for.

A Fan's Perspective

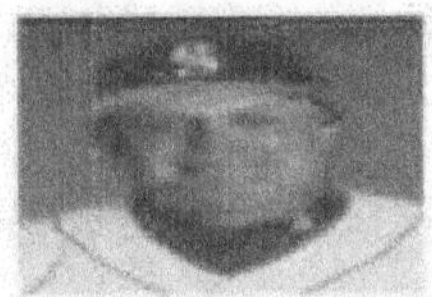

Player-Manager Hall of Fame Criteria Points

Piniella, Lou

Position	Outfielder			
Born :	August 28, 1943	Height	6' 0" USC 183 cm	
From:	Tampa, Fla.	Weight	182 lbs. 82 Kg.	
Bats:	Right	Debut	September 4, 1964	
Throws:	Right	Final Game	June 16, 1984	

Playing Career

Years Ages	G	PA	AB	R	H	2B	3B	HR	RBI	SB	CS	BB	SO	BA	OBP	SLG	OPS	TB	HBP	Pts
162 Games Av	162	590	544	60	158	28	4	9	71	3	4	34	50	0.291	0.333	0.409	0.741	222	3	
18 Years	1747	6362	5867	651	1705	305	41	102	766	32	41	368	541	0.291	0.333	0.409	0.741	2398	31	
	4.500	0.000	0.000	1.500	2.000	0.000	0.000	1.500	2.500	0.500	0.000	0.000	0.000	4.500	2.000	1.500	3.000	2.000	0.000	25.500

Post Season Points

Years Ages	G	PA	AB	R	H	2B	3B	HR	RBI	SB	CS	BB	SO	BA	OBP	SLG	OPS	TB	HBP	Post Season Pts.
None	18	71	69	8	20	5	0	3	9	0	0	2	6	0.225	0.319	0.325	0.564	65	1	
	0.400	0.000	0.000	0.250	0.400	0.000	0.000	0.400	0.400	0.000	0.000	0.250	0.000	0.000	0.400	0.000	0.000	0.800	0.000	3.300

World Series Points

Years Ages	G	PA	AB	R	H	2B	3B	HR	RBI	SB	CS	BB	SO	BA	OBP	SLG	OPS	TB	HBP	World Series Pts.
None	22	74	72	7	25	2	0	0	10	2	0	4	4	0.319	0.324	0.347	0.672	25	1	
	0.800	0.000	0.000	0.400	0.800	0.000	0.000	0.000	0.600	0.400	0.000	0.250	0.000	1.200	0.000	0.000	0.250	0.800	0.000	5.500

Managerial Career

					Regular Season						Post Season			World Series			
Rk	Year	Age	Team	League	Won	Lost	Ties	PCT %	Games	Finish	Won	Lost	PCT %	Won	Lost	PCT %	Comments
1	1986	42	N. Y. Yankees	AL	90	72	0	0.556	162	2	0	0	0.000	0	0	0.000	Did Not Qualify for Playoffs
2	1987	43	N. Y. Yankees	AL	89	73	0	0.549	162	4	0	0	0.000	0	0	0.000	Did Not Qualify for Playoffs
3	1988	44	N. Y. Yankees	AL	45	48	0	0.484	93	5	0	0	0.000	0	0	0.000	Did Not Qualify for Playoffs
					224	193	0	0.537	417		0	0	0.000	0	0	0.000	0 - Playoff Appearances
4	1990	46	Cinc. Reds	NL	91	71	0	0.562	162	1	4	2	0.667	4	0	1.000	Won World Series.
5	1991	47	Cinc. Reds	NL	74	88	0	0.457	162	5	0	0	0.000	0	0	0.000	Did Not Qualify for Playoffs
6	1992	48	Cinc. Reds	NL	90	72	0	0.556	162	2	0	0	0.000	0	0	0.000	Did Not Qualify for Playoffs
					255	231	0	0.525	486		4	2	0.667	4	0	1.000	1 - Playoff Appearances
7	1993	49	Sea. Mariners	AL	82	80	0	0.506	162	4	0	0	0.000	0	0	0.000	Did Not Qualify for Playoffs
8	1994	50	Sea. Mariners	AL	49	63	0	0.438	112	3	0	0	0.000	0	0	0.000	Did Not Qualify for Playoffs
9	1995	51	Sea. Mariners	AL	79	66	0	0.545	145	1	5	6	0.456	0	0	0.000	Lost A. L. Championship Series
10	1996	52	Sea. Mariners	AL	85	76	0	0.528	161	2	0	0	0.000	0	0	0.000	Did Not Qualify for Playoffs
11	1997	53	Sea. Mariners	AL	90	72	0	0.556	162	1	1	3	0.250	0	0	0.000	Lost A. L. Division Series
12	1998	54	Sea. Mariners	AL	76	85	0	0.472	161	3	0	0	0.000	0	0	0.000	Did Not Qualify for Playoffs
13	1999	55	Sea. Mariners	AL	79	83	0	0.488	162	3	0	0	0.000	0	0	0.000	Did Not Qualify for Playoffs
14	2000	56	Sea. Mariners	AL	91	71	0	0.562	162	2	5	4	0.556	0	0	0.000	Lost A. L. Championship Series
15	2001	57	Sea. Mariners	AL	116	46	0	0.716	162	1	4	6	0.400	0	0	0.000	Lost A. L. Championship Series
16	2002	58	Sea. Mariners	AL	93	69	0	0.574	162	3	0	0	0.000	0	0	0.000	Did Not Qualify for Playoffs
					840	711	0	0.512	1551		15	19	0.441	0	0	0.000	4 - Playoff Appearances
17	2003	59	T. Bay Rays	AL	63	99	0	0.389	162	5	0	0	0.000	0	0	0.000	Did Not Qualify for Playoffs
18	2004	60	T. Bay Rays	AL	70	91	0	0.435	161	4	0	0	0.000	0	0	0.000	Did Not Qualify for Playoffs
19	2005	61	T. Bay Rays	AL	67	95	0	0.414	162	5	0	0	0.000	0	0	0.000	Did Not Qualify for Playoffs
					1880	1707	0	0.511	3587		0	0	0.441	0	0	0.000	0 - Playoff Appearances
20	2007	63	Chicago Cubs	NL	85	77	0	0.525	162	1	0	3	0.000	0	0	0.000	Lost N. L. Division Series
21	2008	64	Chicago Cubs	NL	97	64	0	0.602	161	1	0	3	0.000	0	0	0.000	Lost N. L. Division Series
22	2009	65	Chicago Cubs	NL	83	78	0	0.516	161	2	0	0	0.000	0	0	0.000	Did Not Qualify for Playoffs
23	2010	66	Chicago Cubs	NL	51	74	0	0.408	125	5	0	0	0.000	0	0	0.000	Did Not Qualify for Playoffs
					316	293	0	0.519	609		0	6	0.000	0	0	0.000	2 - Playoff Appearances
			N. Y. Yankees	3 years	224	193	0	0.537	417	3.4	0	0	0.000	0	0	0.000	0 - Playoff Appearances
			Cincinnati Reds	3 years	255	231	0	0.525	486	2.7	4	2	0.667	4	0	1.000	1 - Playoff Appearances
			Sea. Mariners	10	840	711	0	0.542	1551	2.3	15	19	0.424	0	0	0.000	4 - Playoff Appearances
			T. Bay Rays	3 years	200	285	0	0.412	485	4.7	0	0	0.000	0	0	0.000	0 - Playoff Appearances
			Chicago Cubs	4 years	316	293	0	0.519	609	2.1	0	5	0.000	0	0	0.000	2 - Playoff Appearances
				23	1835	1713	0	0.517	3548	3.8	19	27	0.413	4	0	1.000	7 - Playoff Appearances

	Total Years	Total Full Sea.	Total Games	Won	Pct	Division Titles	League Titles	World Series	Winning Seasons	Pct	Total
	23	21	3548	1835	0.517	6	1	1	14	0.609	Points
	17.000	14.000	17.000	9.000	4.000	15.000	3.000	4.000	9.000	9.000	101.000

Combination Player / Managerial

Playing Career Points	25.500
Post Season Points	3.300
World Series Points	5.500
Writers Association Pts.	0.000
Military/Lifetime Achievement	0.000
Managerial Points	101.000
Grand Total HOF Points	135.300

Johnson, David "Davey"

Personal Life

David Allen Johnson born January 30, 1943 in Orlando, Florida to Frederick and Mary Lue Johnson. He graduated from Alamo Heights High School in San Antonio, Texas. .

Johnson married Mary Nan in the early days of his baseball career and the couple had three children, David Jr., Dawn, and Andrea with the marriage ending in divorce. Johnson married his second wife, Susan, in 1993. In 2011, his stepson Jake died from pneumonia at the age of 34. Johnson's daughter, Andrea, died in 2005 from septic shock and complications from schizophrenia.

Baseball Career

After making his major-league debut in 1965, Johnson became a starter for the Baltimore Orioles team that won the World Series in 1966. He also started for the club that won three straight American League pennants from 1969 to 1971 and a second World Series title in 1970. After the 1972 season, he was traded to the Atlanta Braves in a six-player deal. In 1973, playing for the Braves, he hit 43 home runs and set a new Major League Baseball record for homers by a second baseman.

After being let go by the Atlanta Braves in April of 1975, he played for the Tokyo Giants in Japan in 1975 & 1976. Johnson was a four-time All-Star and won three Gold Gloves during a 13-year career in the majors. His final numbers were 1435 games, 1252 hits, 136 home runs, 609 runs batted in, and a 261-batting average.

Managing

Johnson made his managerial debut in 1979 with the Miami Amigos, leading that team to the best record in the short-lived Inter-American League. In 1981 he was skipper of the Jackson Mets of the Texas League and in 1983 he led the Tidewater Tides. In 1984, Johnson became manager of the New York Mets and their record improved by 22 games in his first season with the team, as they went from last place to second. Two years later, in 1986, he led the team to their best record ever and a World Series title.

A Fan's Perspective

Johnson retired with a managerial winning percentage of .588. In 15 full seasons, he led his teams to 6 first place finishes and 7 second-place finishes. Johnson retired with a managerial winning percentage of .588. In 15 full seasons he led his teams to 6 first place finishes and 7 second-place finishes. The only three times his clubs did worse was when he was in his first year with a new team. Just fifteen managers have finished with a record of 300 or more wins above .500. Johnson finished with a record of 1,372–1,071–2 to finish 301 games above .500 as a manager. In all but one full season as a manager, he won at least 85 games. He is also tenth all-time in winning percentage for managers with 1,000 wins. All but Johnson have been inducted into the Hall of Fame.

Achievements

- 2-time Manager of the Year Award (1997/AL & 2012/NL)
- Division Titles: 6 (1986, 1988, 1994, 1995, 1997 & 2012)
- Other post-season appearances: 1 (1996 wild card)
- NL Pennant & World Series Champion with the New York Mets in 1986
- 100 Wins Seasons as Manager: 2 (1986 & 1988)

Hall of Fame

Dave Johnson in spite of his impressive record has been passed over for Hall of Fame election four previous times by the Veterans Committee in 2008, 2010, 2017 and 2018. He is next up for this committee in 2024.

Summary Analysis

Dave Johnson's Hall of Fame Statistical Point Total of 97.850 for the "Proposed" new category of Player / Manager category Baseball Hall of Fame. His total is lower than the proposed 120.000 Induction threshold but his ability to change losing teams into winners deserves to be enshrined in the Hall of Fame.

The Baseball Hall of Fame

Player-Manager Hall of Fame Criteria Points

Johnson, Davey

Position		**Born:**	January 30, 1943	**Height** 5'1" **USC** 185 cm
First Baseman		**Died:**	N/A	**Weight** 170 lbs. 77 Kg.
Second Baseman		**From:**	Orlando, Fla	**Debut** April 13, 1965
		Bats:	Right	**Final Game:** September 29, 1978
		Throws:	Right	

Playing Career

Year Ages	G	PA	AB	R	H	2B	3B	HR	RBI	SB	CS	BB	SO	BA	OBP	SLG	OPS	TB	HBP	
162 Game Ave.	162	617	542	54	141	27	2	15	69	4	3	63	76	0.261	0.340	0.4	0.744	219	5	
13 Years	1435	5465	4797	564	1252	242	18	136	609	33	25	559	675	0.261	0.340	0.4	0.744	1938	40	Career Pts.
	2.500	0.000	0.000	1.000	0.000	0.000	0.000	2.000	1.500	0.500	0.000	1.000	0.000	2.000	2.500	1.000	3.000	1.500	0.000	18.500

Post Season Points

Year	G	PA	AB	R	H	2B	3B	HR	RBI	SB	CS	BB	SO	BA	OBP	SLG	OPS	TB	HBP	
None	10	45	38	8	11	2	0	2	6	0	0	1	0	0.29	0.400	500	0.900	10	1	Post Season Pts.
	0.250	0.000	0.000	0.250	0.250	0.000	0.000	0.250	0.250	0.000	0.000	0.250	0.000	0.600	1.200	0.800	0.800	0.250	0.000	5.150

World Series Points

Year *	G	PA	AB	R	H	2B	3B	HR	RBI	SB	CS	BB	SO	BA	OBP	SLG	OPS	TB	HBP	
None	21	81	73	5	14	3	0	0	6	0	2	7	5	0.192	0.272	0.233	0.505	17	1	World Series Pts.
	0.800	0.000	0.000	0.400	0.600	0.000	0.000	0.000	0.400	0.000	0.000	0.400	0.000	0.000	0.000	0.000	0.000	0.600	0.000	3.200

Managerial Career

Rk	Year	Age	Team Managed	League	Won	Lost	PCT	Ties	Games	Finish	Post Season Wins	Post Season Losses	World Series Wins	World Series Losses	Comments
1	1984	41	New York	NL	90	72	0.556	0	162	2	0	0	0	0	Did Not Qualify for Playoffs.
2	1985	42	New York	NL	98	64	0.605	0	162	2	0	0	0	0	Did Not Qualify for Playoffs.
3	1986	43	New York	NL	108	54	0.667	0	162	1	4	2	4	3	Won East Division,N.L/ Pennant & World Series
4	1987	44	New York	NL	92	70	0.568	0	162	2	0	0	0	0	Did Not Qualify for Playoffs.
5	1988	45	New York	NL	100	60	0.625	0	160	1	3	4	0	0	Won N.L. East & Lost League Championship
6	1989	46	New York	NL	87	75	0.537	0	162	2	0	0	0	0	Did Not Qualify for Playoffs.
7	1990	47	New York	NL	20	22	0.476	0	42	2	0	0	0	0	Did Not Qualify for Playoffs.
					595	417	0.588	0	1012	12	7	6	4	3	2 Playoff Appearances
8			Cincinnati												
	1993	50	Reds	NL	53	65	0.449	0	118	5	0	0	0	0	Did Not Qualify for Playoffs.
9	1994	51	Reds	NL	66	48	0.579	1	115	1	0	0	0	0	1st N.L. Central. No Playoffs due to strike
10	1995	52	Reds	NL	85	59	0.590	0	144	1	3	4	0	0	1st N.L. Central. Won Division, & Lost Championship
					204	172	0.543	1	377	7	3	4	0	0	2 Playoff Appearances
11	1996	53	Balt. Orioles	AL	88	74	0.543	1	163	2	4	5	0	0	WC-Won Division Series and Lost Championship
12	1997	54	Balt. Orioles	AL	98	64	0.605	0	162	1	5	5	0	0	1st AL East - Won Division & Lost Championship
					186	138	0.574	1	325		9	10	0	0	2 Playoff Appearances
13	1999	56	L. A. Dodgers	NL	77	85	0.475	0	162	3	0	0	0	0	Did Not Qualify for Playoffs.
14	2000	57	L. A. Dodgers	NL	86	76	0.531	0	162	2	0	0	0	0	Did Not Qualify for Playoffs.
					163	161	0.503	0	324		0	0	0	0	0 Playoff Appearances
15	2011	68	Wash.	NL	40	43	0.482	0	83	3	0	0	0	0	Did Not Qualify for Playoffs.
16	2012	69	Wash.	NL	98	64	0.605	0	162	1	2	3	0	0	1st NL East & Lost Division Series
17	2013	70	Wash.	NL	86	76	0.531	0	162	2	0	0	0	0	Did Not Qualify for Playoffs.
					224	183	0.550	0	407		2	3	0	0	1 Playoff Appearance
			Mets	7 years	595	417	0.588	0	1012	1.7	11	8	4	3	2 Playoff Appearances
			Reds	3 years	204	172	0.543	1	377	2.3	3	4	0	0	2 Playoff Appearances
			Balt. Orioles	2 years	186	138	0.574	1	325	1.5	9	10	0	0	2 Playoff Appearances
			L. A. Dodgers	2 years	163	161	0.503	0	324	2.5	0	0	0	0	0 Playoff Appearances
			Nationals	3 years	224	183	0.550	0	407	1.8	2	3	0	0	1 Playoff Appearance
					1372	1071	0.563	2	2445	1.9	25	26	4	3	7 Playoff Appearance & 1 World Series Win

	Total Years	Total Full Sea.	Total Games	Won	Pct	Division Titles	League Titles	World Series	Winning Seasons	Total
	17	15	2445	1372	0.562	6	1	1	13	Points
	11.5	9	6.5	6.5	6.5	15	3	4	0	71

Combination Player / Managerial

Playing Career Points	18.500
Post Season Points	5.150
World Series Points	3.200
Writers Association Pts.	0.000
Military/Lifetime Achievement	0.000
Managerial Points	71.000
Grand Total HOF Points	97.850

A Fan's Perspective

The Baseball Hall of Fame

Martin, Alfred "Billy"

Personal Life

Alfred Manuel Pesano, Jr. was born in Berkeley, California, on May 16, 1928, to Alfred Manuel and Joan (Salvini) Pesano. Joan, who went by the nickname Jenny, was of Italian descent, and Alfred Sr. was born in the Azores. He abandoned the family when Billy was 8 months old, and Jenny later married a nightclub singer named Jack Downey. Alfred Jr.'s maternal Italian grandmother called him Belli or Bellitz when he was an infant and this name eventually evolved into Billy. Soon after, his mother changed the family name to Martin. Martin would have no further contact with his father until he was in his thirties, and the conflict between his parents likely left him with emotional wounds.

Martin was married four times with his first marriage was to Lois Berndt, who was the mother of Kelly Ann. She divorced him in 1955. Martin married Gretchen Winkler in 1961 with son Billy Joe Being born of that marriage. His third marriage was to Heather Ervolino who he divorced. His fourth marriage was to Jillian Guiver, in January,1988. On December 25, 1989, the 61-year-old Martin was killed in a pickup truck accident.

Baseball Career

After graduating from high school in 1946, Martin signed with the Idaho Falls Russets of the Class D Pioneer League. Martin was sent to the Pacific Coast League Oakland Oaks and he learned much from Casey Stengel, the man who would manage him both in Oakland and in New York. Martin played eleven years in the majors, and appeared in five World Series (all with the Yankees), slugging .566. He missed the 1954 season and most of 1955 while serving in the militaryMartin's spectacular catch of a wind-blown Jackie Robinson popup late in Game Seven of the 1952 World Series saved that series for the Yankees, and he was the hitting star of the 1953 World Series, earning the Most Valuable Player award in the Yankee victory. In Martins Five World Series (28 games), he collected 33 hits, two doubles, three triples, five home runs, and 19 RBIs while posting a .333 batting average. He missed most of two seasons, 1954 and 1955, after being drafted into the Army, and his abilities never fully returned. Martins career batting numbers were 1021 games, 877 hits, 64 home runs, 333 runs batted in and a .257 batting average.

Managing Career

Billy Martin built a reputation as a manager who would make bad teams good, before ultimately being fired amid dysfunctions. In each of his stints with the Yankees he managed them to winning records before being fired by team owner George Steinbrenner or resigning under fire. Martin had an exceptional record in turning teams, often bad teams, into winners. Also, part of the legacy of Billy Martin is he fought with management, players, umpires, and the media. Due to many factors, including his own titanic temper, chaos often ensued on the teams he managed. His managerial career consisted of 1253 wins, 1013 losses, 1 tie, .553 winning %, covering five different franchises (not counting the four times with the Yankees).

Achievements

- 5-Times Led Teams to a Division Title-(1968 Twins, 1972 Tigers, 1976, 1977 Yankees, & 1981 Oakland).
- 2-Times Led Teams to A.L. Pennant - (1976, 1977 Yankees).
- 1-Time Led Team to World Series Championship – (1977 Yankees)
- 6-Times Led Teams to 90 Wins – (Twins 1969, Tigers 1971, Yankees 1976, 1977, 1983 & 1985).
- 5-Times Led Teams to improving W/L record in First Year as Manager – (Twins 1969, Tigers 1971, Rangers 1974, Yankees 1976, & Oakland A's 980).

Hall of Fame

Billy Martin was considered by the Veterans Committee four times between 2003 and 2010, Martin has been considered for the Expansion Era Committee both times it's met so far, ahead of the 2011 and 2014 inductions and didn't receive enough votes.

Summary Analysis

Billy Martin's Hall of Fame Statistical Point Total of 111.850 for the "Proposed" new category of Player/Manager category. His total is lower than the proposed 120.000 Induction threshold but his career should be reviewed by the Veterans Committee and elected to the National Baseball Hall of Fame.

The Baseball Hall of Fame

Player-Manager Hall of Fame Criteria Points

Martin, Billy

Position	2nd Base	**Born:**	May 16, 1928
	Shortstop	**Died:**	December 25, 1989
		From:	Berkely, CA
		Bats:	Right
		Throws:	Right

Height:	5' 11"	USC	180	cm
Weight:	165	lbs.	74	Kg.
Debut	April 18, 1950		April 18, 1950	
Final Game	October 1, 1961		October 1, 1961	

Playing Career

Years / Ages	G	PA	AB	R	H	2B	3B	HR	RBI	SB	CS	BB	SO	BA	OBP	SLG	OPS	TB	HBP	
162 Game Ave.	162	560	542	87	139	32	4	10	53	5	6	30	56	0.257	0.300	0.369	0.669	200	5	
11 Years	1021	3719	3419	425	877	137	29	64	333	34	29	188	355	0.257	0.300	0.369	0.669	1252	32	Career Pts.
	1.000	0.000	0.000	0.500	0.000	0.000	0.000	1.000	0.000	0.500	0.000	0.000	0.000	1.500	0.500	0.000	1.500	0.000	0.000	5.000

Post Season Points

Years / Ages	G	PA	AB	R	H	2B	3B	HR	RBI	SB	CS	BB	SO	BA	OBP	SLG	OPS	TB	HBP	
None	0	0	0	0	0	0	0	0	0	0	0	0	0	0	0	0	0	0	0	Post Season Pts.
	0.000	0.000	0.000	0.000	0.000	0.000	0.000	0.000	0.000	0.000	0.000	0.000	0.000	0.000	0.000	0.000	0.000	0.000	0.000	0.000

World Series Points

Years / Ages	G	PA	AB	R	H	2B	3B	HR	RBI	SB	CS	BB	SO	BA	OBP	SLG	OPS	TB	HBP	
None	28	305	99	15	33	2	3	5	19	1	5	5	15	0.333	0.371	0.556	0.937	56	1	Post Season Pts.
	1.000	0.000	0.000	0.800	1.200	0.000	0.000	1.000	1.000	0.250	0.000	0.400	0.000	1.400	1.800	1.000	1.000	2.000	0.000	12.850

Managerial Career

Rk	Year	Age	Team	League	Won	Lost	Ties	PCT %	Games	Finish	Post Won	Post Lost	Post PCT %	WS Won	WS Lost	WS PCT %	Comments
1	1969	41	Minnesota	AL	97	65	0	0.599	162	1	0	3	0.000	0	0	0.000	Lost League Championship
					97	65	0	0.599	162		0	3	0.000	0	0	0.000	1 - Playoff Appearances
2	1971	43	Detroit	AL	91	71	0	0.562	162	2	0	0	0.000	0	0	0.000	Did Not Make Playoffs
3	1972	44	Detroit	AL	86	70	0	0.551	156	1	2	3	0.400	0	0	0.000	Lost League Championship
4	1973	45	Detroit	AL	71	63	0	0.530	134	3	0	0	0.000	0	0	0.000	Did Not Make Playoffs
					248	204	0	0.549	452		2	3	0.400	0	0	0.000	1 - Playoff Appearances
5	1973	45	Texas	AL	9	14	0	0.391	23	6	0	0	0.000	0	0	0.000	Did Not Make Playoffs
6	1974	46	Texas	AL	84	76	1	0.525	161	2	0	0	0.000	0	0	0.000	Did Not Make Playoffs
7	1975	47	Texas	AL	44	51	0	0.463	95	3	0	0	0.000	0	0	0.000	Did Not Make Playoffs
					137	141	1	0.493	279		0	0	0.000	0	0	0.000	0 - Playoff Appearances
8	1975	47	N. Y.	AL	30	26	0	0.536	56	3	0	0	0.000	0	0	0.000	Did Not Make Playoffs
9	1976	48	N. Y.	AL	97	62	0	0.610	159	1	1	2	0.600	0	4	0.000	Lost World Series
10	1977	49	N. Y.	AL	100	62	0	0.617	162	1	1	2	0.600	4	2	0.667	Did Not Make Playoffs
11	1978	50	N. Y.	AL	52	42	0	0.553	94	1	0	0	0.000	0	0	0.000	Lost Division Series
12	1979	51	N. Y.	AL	55	40	0	0.579	95	4	0	0	0.000	0	0	0.000	Did Not Make Playoffs
					134	232	0	0.500	566		6	4	0.500	4	6	0.400	2 - Playoff Appearances
13	1980	52	Oakland A's	AL	83	79	0	0.512	162	2	0	0	0.000	0	0	0.000	Did Not Make Playoffs
14	1981	53	Oakland A's	AL	37	23	0	0.617	60	1	3	0	0.500	0	0	0.000	Won Division Series
15	1981	53	Oakland A's	AL	27	22	0	0.551	49	2	0	3	0.500	0	0	0.000	Lost League Championship
16	1982	54	Oakland A's	AL	68	94	0	0.420	162	5	0	0	0.000	0	0	0.000	Did Not Make Playoffs
					215	218	0	0.497	433		3	3	0.500	0	0	0.000	1 - Playoff Appearances
17	1983	55	N. Y.	AL	91	71	0	0.562	162	3	0	0	0.0000	0	0	0.000	Did Not Make Playoffs
18	1985	57	N. Y.	AL	91	54	0	0.628	145	2	0	0	0.0000	0	0	0.000	Did Not Make Playoffs
19	1988	60	N. Y.	AL	40	28	0	0.588	68	5	0	0	0.0000	0	0	0.000	Did Not Make Playoffs
					222	153	0	0.592	375		0	0	0.0000	0	0	0.000	0 - Playoff Appearances

	Team		Won	Lost	Ties	PCT %	Games	Finish	Post Won	Post Lost	Post PCT %	WS Won	WS Lost	WS PCT %	Comments
1	Minn. Twins	A.L.	97	65	0	0.599	162	1	0	3	0.000	0	0	0.000	1 Playoff Appearances
3	Detroit	A.L.	248	204	0	0.549	452	1	2	3	0.400	0	0	0.000	1 Playoff Appearances
3	Texas	A.L.	137	141	1	0.493	279	1.7	0	0	0.000	0	0	0.000	0 Playoff Appearances
3	Oakland	A.L.	215	218	0	0.497	433	3	3	3	0.500	0	0	0.000	1 Playoff Appearances
6	N. Y	A.L.	556	385	0	0.591	941	2.2	10	10	0.500	4	6	0.400	2 Playoff Appearances
	16 years		1253	1013	1	0.553	2267	2.3	15	18	0.441	4	6	0.400	5 - Playoff Appearances

Total Years	Total Full Sea.	Total Games	Won	Pct	Division Titles	League Titles	World Series	Winning Season Seasons	Pct	Total
16	7	2267	1253	0.553	8	2	1	14	0.875	Points
11.500	4.000	14.000	6.500	6.500	15.000	6.000	4.000	13.000	30.000	88.000

Combination Player / Managerial

Playing Career Points	5.000
Post Season Points	0.000
World Series Points	12.850
Writers Association Pts.	0.000
Military/Lifetime Achievement	6.000
Managerial Points	88.000
Grand Total HOF Points	**111.850**

A Fan's Perspective

Murtaugh, Danny

Personal Life

Daniel Edward Murtaugh was born October 8, 1917 born to Daniel and Nellie McCarey in Chester, Pennsylvania. He was the middle of five children and the only boy which had Murtaugh working with his father at Sun Shipbuilding & Drydock Co. after he graduated from Chester High School.

Murtaugh married Kathleen "Kate" Clark on November 29,1941 with the couple having three children. Sons, Daniel Edward Murtaugh Jr., Timothy and a daughter Kathy.

Baseball Career

After signing with the St. Louis Cardinals, he joined the Redbirds' extensive farm system. In June1941, the Phillies purchased his contract, and he made his MLB debut on July 3. As a rookie, Murtaugh led the National League in stolen bases with 18, even though he played only 85 games. Murtaugh joined the United States Army in August 1943 for World War II service and served in combat with the 97th Infantry in Germany.

Returning to baseball in 1946, he played in only six games for Philadelphia before he was sold back to the Cardinals' organization. He did get his biggest break on November 18, when Boston traded him to the Pirates, where he spent the rest of his big-league career. Murtaugh was a .254 career lifetime batter with 661 hits, eight home runs and 219 RBI in 767 games. Murtaugh appeared in all or parts of nine big-league seasons, initially for the Philadelphia Phillies (1941–43, 1946) and Boston Braves (1947) before joining the Pirates (1948–51). He played 416 of his 767 MLB games with the Pirates.

Managing

After retiring as a player, in 1956 he returned to the Pirates as a coach. In his second year on the job, , he succeeded was named as skipper on August 4, 1957. Under Murtaugh, the Pirates won 26 of their final 51 games. In his first full season, 1958, Murtaugh led the Pirates to a second-place finish in the National League. And a fourth-place finish in 1959 with a 78-76 record. In 1960, Murtaugh guided the Bucs to the first World Series championship they won under his command. The Pirates stunned the heavy-hitting Yankees in the 1960 World Series.

A Fan's Perspective

After the conclusion of the 1964 campaign, Murtaugh stepped down as manager. Then, in 1967, Murtaugh returned as interim pilot for the remainder of the 1967 season. Well aware of the abundance of talent in the Pittsburgh system, Murtaugh asked to reclaim the managing job at end of the 1969 season. He began his third term as skipper of the Pirates on October 9, 1969. He went on to hold the Pittsburgh job for all or parts of fifteen seasons over four different terms (1957–64, 1967, 1970–71, 1973–76). Murtaugh's first two clubs won the 1970–71 National League East Division titles. On September 1, 1971, Murtaugh fielded a starting lineup consisting of nine black players. Murtaugh's 1971 Pirates would bounce back and defeated the San Francisco Giants in the NLCS and then captured the 1971 World Series against the Baltimore Orioles.

Murtaugh had a 29-year association with the Pittsburgh Pirates, with whom he won two World Series as manager and compiled a 1,115–950–3 record in 2,068 games (.540). In addition to his two National League pennants and world championships, he won four Eastern Division titles (1970–71, 1974–75),..

Achievements

- 2 - National League 2 -World Series: 2 (Pittsburgh 1960 & 1971).
- 2-Times named Manager of the Year (Pittsburgh 1960 & 1971)
- 5-Times led the Pirates to 90 Win Seasons: (1960, 1962, 1971, 1975 & 1976).
- 4-Times led the Pirates to Eastern Division Titles (1970, 1971, 1974 & 1975)

Hall of Fame

Danny Murtaugh was not elected by the Golden Days Era Committee in 2021..

Summary Analysis

Danny Murtaugh's Hall of Fame Statistical Point Total of 101.000 for the "Proposed" new category of Player /Manager category. His total is lower than the proposed 120.000 Induction threshold but Murtaugh's place in baseball history was cemented by his strong 15-year managerial tenure with Pittsburgh.

The Baseball Hall of Fame

Player-Manager Hall of Fame Criteria Points

Murtaugh, Danny

Position	Infield	Born :	October 7, 1917	Height:	5' 9" USC	175	cm
		Died:	December 2, 1976	Weight:	165 lbs.	74	Kg.
		From:	Cheter, PA	Debut	July 3, 1941		
		Bats:	Right	Final Game	September 6, 1951		
		Throws:	Right				

Playing Career

Years Ages	G	PA	AB	R	H	2B	3B	HR	RBI	SB	CS	BB	SO	BA	OBP	SLG	OPS	TB	HBP	
162 Game Ave.	162	621	549	56	140	20	4	2	46	10	10	61	45	0.25	0.331	0.317	0.648	174	2	
9 Years	767	2942	2599	263	661	97	21	8	219	49	46	287	215	0.25	0.331	0.317	0.648	824	9	Career Pts.
	0.000	0.000	0.000	0.000	0.000	0.000	0.000	0.000	0.000	0.500	0.000	0.000	0.000	1.500	2.000	0.000	1.000	0.000	0.000	5.000

Post Season Points

Years Ages	G	PA	AB	R	H	2B	3B	HR	RBI	SB	CS	BB	SO	BA	OBP	SLG	OPS	TB	HBP	
None	0	0	0	0	0	0	0	0	0	0	0	0	0	0	0	0	0	0	0	Post Season Pts.
	0.000	0.000	0.000	0.000	0.000	0.000	0.000	0.000	0.000	0.000	0.000	0.000	0.000	0.000	0.000	0.000	0.000	0.000	0.000	0.000

World Series Points

Years Ages	G	PA	AB	R	H	2B	3B	HR	RBI	SB	CS	BB	SO	BA	OBP	SLG	OPS	TB	HBP	
None	0	0	0	0	0	0	0	0	0	0	0	0	0	0	0	0	0	0	0	World Series Pts.
	0.000	0.000	0.000	0.000	0.000	0.000	0.000	0.000	0.000	0.000	0.000	0.000	0.000	0.000	0.000	0.000	0.000	0.000	0.000	0.000

Managerial Career

Rk	Year	Age	Team	League	Won	Lost	Ties	PCT %	Games	Finish	Won	Lost	PCT %	Won	Lost	PCT %	Comments
							Regular Season						**Post Season**			**World Series**	
1	1957	39	Pittsburgh	NL	26	25	0	0.51	51	7	0	0	0.000	0	0	0.000	Did not Win Pennant
2	1958	40	Pittsburgh	NL	84	70	0	0.545	154	2	0	0	0.000	0	0	0.000	Did not Win Pennant
3	1959	41	Pittsburgh	NL	78	76	1	0.506	155	4	0	0	0.000	0	0	0.000	Did not Win Pennant
4	1960	42	Pittsburgh	NL	95	59	1	0.617	155	1	0	0	0.000	4	3	0.000	Won World Series
5	1961	43	Pittsburgh	NL	75	79	0	0.487	154	6	0	0	0.000	0	0	0.000	Did not Win Pennant
6	1962	44	Pittsburgh	NL	93	68	0	0.578	161	4	0	0	0.000	0	0	0.000	Did not Win Pennant
7	1963	45	Pittsburgh	NL	74	88	0	0.457	162	8	0	0	0.000	0	0	0.000	Did not Win Pennant
8	1964	46	Pittsburgh	NL	80	82	0	0.494	162	6	0	0	0.000	0	0	0.000	Did not Win Pennant
9	1967	49	Pittsburgh	NL	39	39	1	0.500	79	6	0	0	0.000	0	0	0.000	Did not Win Pennant
10	1970	52	Pittsburgh	NL	89	73	0	0.549	162	1	0	3	0.000	0	0	0.000	Lost League Championship
11	1971	53	Pittsburgh	NL	97	65	0	0.599	162	1	3	1	0.750	4	3	0.571	Won World Series
12	1973	55	Pittsburgh	NL	13	13	0	0.500	26	3	0	0	0.000	0	0	0.000	Did Not Qualify for Playoffs
13	1974	56	Pittsburgh	NL	88	74	0	0.543	162	1	1	3	0.250	0	0	0.000	Lost League Championship
14	1975	57	Pittsburgh	NL	92	69	0	0.568	161	1	0	3	0.000	0	0	0.000	Lost League Championship
15	1976	58	Pittsburgh	NL	92	70	0	0.568	162	2	0	0	0.000	0	0	0.000	Did Not Qualify for Playoffs
	15 years				1115	950	3	0.540	2068	3.3	4	10	0.286	8	6	0.571	5 - Playoff Appearances

Total Years	Full Sea.	Total Games	Total Won	Game Pct	Division Titles	League Titles	World Series	Winning Seasons	Season Pct.	Total
15	12	2068	1115	0.540	5	2	2	11.5	0.747	Points
9.000	6.500	6.500	6.500	6.500	12.500	6.000	8.000	6.500	20.000	88.000

Combination Player / Managerial

Playing Career Points	5.000
Post Season Points	0.000
World Series Points	0.000
Writers Association Pts.	0.000
Military/Lifetime Achievement	8.000
Managerial Points	88.000
Grand Total HOF Points	101.000

A Fan's Perspective

Scioscia, Michael "Sosh" or "El Jefe"

Personal Life

Michael Lorri Scioscia was born November 27, 1958, in Upper Darby, Pennsylvania, to Fred Scioscia and Florence. Scioscia has an older brother friend, and a sister Gail. He played High School football, basketball, and baseball at Springfield, in Pennsylvania.

Scioscia married Anne Mellqueham, January 26, 1985, with the couple having two children Matthew and daughter Taylor.

Baseball Career

Scioscia was drafted by the Los Angeles Dodgers in the first round (19th overall pick) of the 1976 amateur. Scioscia was assigned to Bellingham (Washington) in the Class-A Northwest League. The following year, 1977, Scioscia played in 121 games, five at first base. He improved his defense behind the plate, and continued to be a patient hitter, walking 79 times and achieving a .385 OBP. He made his big league debut in 1980 and was the Dodgers' regular catcher for a decade. He was signed by the San Diego Padres after the 1992 season but suffered a torn rotator cuff the following year but retired before making it to the majors. His batting numbers were 1441 games, 1131 hits, 68 home runs, 446 runs batted in, and a batting average of .259.

Managing

After his playing career ended, Scioscia spent several seasons as a minor league manager and major league coach in the Dodgers organization before being hired as the Angels manager after the 1999 season. Under the leadership Scioscia, the Angels ended their 16-year playoff drought in 2002, winning the AL Wild Card and ultimately winning the franchise's first World Series against the San Francisco Giants. In winning the series, Scioscia became the 17th person to win a World Series as both a player and a manager. Scioscia was honored as 2002 American League Manager of Year by the Baseball Writers' Association of America.

The Angels under Scioscia would go on to enjoy a period of on-field success never before seen in franchise history, winning five American League West division titles in six years. Scioscia's Angels broke the franchise single-season win record with 99 wins in 2002, and again with 100 wins in 2008. However, they have yet to win another American League pennant or World Series. Scioscia is the

A Fan's Perspective

Angels' all-time leader in wins and games managed Scioscia was honored as 2009 American League Major League Manager of Year by the Baseball Writers' Association of America.

He is the Angels' all-time managerial leader in wins, games managed, and division titles. Scioscia was honored with the American League Manager of the Year Award in 2002 and 2009. He continued to lead the Angels the following decade, returning to the postseason regularly, but failing to advance deep into the postseason, with two losses in the ALCS, in 2005 and 2009 being the best results. After 19 seasons as manager, Scioscia announced his retirement as manager of the Angels on September 30, 2018. He finished with a record of 1650 wins and 1428 losses.

Achievements

- 2-time AL Manager of the Year Award (2002 & 2009)
- 6-Division Titles: (2004, 2005, 2007-2009 & 2014)
- 1-AL Pennant: 1 (2002) & 1-Managed one World Series Champion with the Anaheim Angels in 2002
- 100 Wins Seasons as Manager: 1 (2008)
- 7-Times guided teams to 90 plus wins: (2002, 2004, 2005, 2007-2009, & 2014).
- 7-Times guided teams to Playoff Appearances:

Hall of Fame

Mike Scioscia was ignored by The Hall of Fame Committee when they ignored Mike Scioscia with a list of managers who can be inducted into the Hall of Fame in 2024.

Summary Analysis

Mike Scioscia Hall of Fame Statistical Point Total of 105.000 for the "Proposed" new category of Player/Manager category. His total is lower than the proposed 120.000 Induction threshold but his career should be reviewed by the Veterans Committee for future election into the National Baseball Hall of Fame.

The Baseball Hall of Fame

Player-Manager Hall of Fame Criteria Points

Scioscia, Mike

Position: Catcher

Born :	November 27, 1958	
From:	Upper Darby, PA	
Bats:	Right	
Throws:	Right	

Height	6' 2"	USC	188	cm
Weight	200	lbs.	90	Kg.
Debut	April 20, 1980			
Final Game	October 2, 1992			

Playing Career

Years	Ages	G	PA	AB	R	H	2B	3B	HR	RBI	SB	CS	BB	SO	BA	OBP	SLG	OPS	TB	HBP	
162 Game Ave.		162	569	492	45	127	22	1	8	50	3	3	64	35	0.259	0.344	0.356	0.700	175	2	
11 Years		1441	5057	4373	398	1131	198	12	68	446	29	24	567	307	0.259	0.344	0.356	0.700	1557	22	Career Pts.
		2.500	0.000	0.000	0.000	0.000	0.000	0.000	1.000	0.500	0.500	0.000	1.000	0.000	1.500	2.500	0.000	2.000	0.500	0.000	9.500

Post Season Points

Years	Ages	G	PA	AB	R	H	2B	3B	HR	RBI	SB	CS	BB	SO	BA	OBP	SLG	OPS	TB	HBP	
None		22	75	66	6	16	1	0	2	5	0	0	8	5	0.246	0.324	0.410	0.734	23	0	Post Season Pts.
		0.600	0.000	0.000	0.250	0.400	0.000	0.000	0.250	0.250	0.000	0.000	0.400	0.000	0.250	0.400	0.400	0.400	0.400	0.000	4.000

World Series Points

Years	Ages	G	PA	AB	R	H	2B	3B	HR	RBI	SB	CS	BB	SO	BA	OBP	SLG	OPS	TB	HBP	
None		7	20	18	1	4	0	0	0	1	0	1	1	2	0.222	0.263	0.222	0.485	4	0	World Series Pts.
		0.250	0.000	0.000	0.250	0.250	0.000	0.000	0.000	0.250	0.000	0.000	0.250	0.000	0.000	0.000	0.000	0.000	0.250	0.000	1.500

Managerial Career

Rk	Year	Age	Team	League	Won	Lost	Ties	PCT %	Games	Finish	Won	Lost	PCT %	Won	Lost	PCT %	Comments
					Regular Season						Post Season			World Series			
1	2000	41	Anah. Angels	AL	82	80	0	0.506	162	3	0	0	0.000	0	0	0.000	Did not Qualify for Playoffs
2	2001	42	Anah. Angels	AL	75	87	0	0.463	162	3	0	0	0.000	0	0	0.000	Did not Qualify for Playoffs
3	2002	43	Anah. Angels	AL	99	63	0	0.611	162	2	7	2	0.778	4	3	0.571	Won World Series
4	2003	44	Anah. Angels	AL	77	85	0	0.475	162	3	0	0	0.000	0	0	0.000	Did not Qualify for Playoffs
5	2004	45	Anah. Angels	AL	92	70	0	0.568	162	1	0	3	0.000	0	0	0.000	Lost A. L. Division Series
6	2005	46	L. A. Angels	AL	95	67	0	0.586	162	1	4	6	0.400	0	0	0.000	Lost A.L. Championship
7	2006	47	L. A. Angels	AL	89	73	0	0.549	162	2	0	0	0.000	0	0	0.000	Did not Qualify for Playoffs
8	2007	48	L. A. Angels	AL	94	68	0	0.58	162	1	0	3	0.000	0	0	0.000	Lost A. L. Division Series
9	2008	49	L. A. Angels	AL	100	62	0	0.617	162	1	1	3	0.250	0	0	0.000	Lost A. L. Division Series
10	2009	50	L. A. Angels	AL	97	65	0	0.599	162	1	5	4	0.456	0	0	0.000	Lost A.L. Championship
11	2010	51	L. A. Angels	AL	80	82	0	0.494	162	3	0	0	0.000	0	0	0.000	Did not Qualify for Playoffs
12	2011	52	L. A. Angels	AL	86	76	0	0.531	162	2	0	0	0.000	0	0	0.000	Did not Qualify for Playoffs
13	2012	53	L. A. Angels	AL	89	73	0	0.549	162	3	0	0	0.000	0	0	0.000	Did not Qualify for Playoffs
14	2013	54	L. A. Angels	AL	78	84	0	0.481	162	3	0	0	0.000	0	0	0.000	Did not Qualify for Playoffs
15	2014	55	L. A. Angels	AL	98	64	0	0.605	162	1	0	3	0.000	0	0	0.000	Lost A. L. Division Series
16	2015	56	L. A. Angels	AL	85	77	0	0.525	162	3	0	0	0.000	0	0	0.000	Did not Qualify for Playoffs
17	2016	57	L. A. Angels	AL	74	88	0	0.457	162	4	0	0	0.000	0	0	0.000	Did not Qualify for Playoffs
18	2017	58	L. A. Angels	AL	80	82	0	0.494	162	2	0	0	0.000	0	0	0.000	Did not Qualify for Playoffs
19	2018	59	L. A. Angels	AL	80	82	0	0.494	162	4	0	0	0.000	0	0	0.000	Did not Qualify for Playoffs
	19 years				1650	1428	0	0.536	3078		21	27	0.471	4	3	0.571	8 - Playoff Appearances

	Total	Total	Total		Division	League	World	Winning	Season	
Years	Full Sea.	Games	Won	Pct	Titles	Titles	Series	Seasons	Pct	Total
19	19	3078	1650	0.536	6	1	1	12	0.632	Points
14.000	14.000	9.000	9.000	4.000	15.000	3.000	4.000	6.500	11.500	90.000

Combination Player / Managerial

Playing Career Points	9.500
Post Season Points	4.000
World Series Points	1.500
Writers Association Pts.	0.000
Military/Lifetime Achievement	0.000
Managerial Points	90.000
Grand Total HOF Points	105.000

A Fan's Perspective

Statistical Review of Potential Player/Coach for the Hall of Fame

Player	Years Played	Years Managed	Years Coached	Career Points	P.S. & W.S. Pts.	Coaching Points	Military Points	HOF Points	Comments
Players Needing to be Inducted									
Becker, Joe	2	0	16	4.000	0.000	0	0.000	122.000	Inducted
Duncan, Dave	12	0	32	3.000	3.250	0	0.000	156.250	Inducted
Harder, Mel	20	0	22	52.000	0.000	0	0.000	137.000	Inducted
Mazzone, Leo	0	0	18	0.000	0.000	0	0.000	131.500	Inducted
Perranowski, Ron	13	0	17	46.750	3.250	0	0.000	133.000	Inducted
Righetti, Dave	16	0	18	46.250	2.400	0	0.000	131.650	Inducted
Sain, Johnny	11	0	17	38.750	5.550	0	12.000	154.800	Inducted
Stottlemeyer, Mel	11	0	22	53.500	7.750	0	0.000	222.750	Inducted
Turner, Jim	9	0	23	32.000	1.500	0	0.000	182.000	Inducted
Players Needing to be Voted into the Hall of Fame by the BBWAA									
Black, Bud	5	16	6	32.000	3.050	30.000	0.000	98.500	Need Voting
Brecheen, Harry	12	0	11	51.000	8.650	45.000	0.000	104.650	Inducted
Players Not Meeting the Statistical Requirements									
Bamberger, Geo.	3	7	10	0.000	0.000	0	0.000	N/A	DMR
Beres, Ray	11	0	18.5	0.000	0.000	0	0.000	N/A	DMF
Gullet, Don	9	0	13	48.750	10.800	0	0.000	N/A	DMR
Miller, Ray	0	4	21	0.000	0.000	0	0.000	N/A	DMR
Root, Charlie	17	0	6	55.000	1.850	0	0.000	N/A	DMF

Hall of Fame Statistical Requirements:

All Players achieving the total of 120.000, or greater, Total Hall of Fame Points, shall be Inducted after five (5) years of retirement. This provision can be waived due to the death by a 75% vote of the 25 Panel BBWAA's. Individuals receiving less than the required 120.000 Hall of Fame Points are eligible for Election after five (5) years of retirement. A 25 person BBWAA will determine the Players that will be Inducted and vote on the Players needing to be elected. An example of those needing to be elected are as follows: Player "A" has a total of 95 Hall of Fame Points and will need 25 of the (25) BBWAA votes to be Elected in the following year.

Player/Coaches Needing to be Inducted.

1. Joe Becker
2. Dave Duncan
3. Mel Harder
4. Lee Mazzone
5. Ron Perranoski
6. Dave Righetti
7. Johnny Sain
8. Mel Stottlemyre
9. Jim Turner

110.000 Hall of Fame Statistical Induction Criteria

Becker, Joe

Personal Life

Joseph Edward Becker was born June 25, 1908 in St. Louis, Missouri and served in the United States Navy during World War II. No information is available on Beckers family life or marriage(s).

Baseball Career

Becker started his professional career in the St. Louis Cardinals minor league system, and played for various clubs between 1930 and 1933. After not playing in 1934, he spent 1935 with the San Francisco Seals as a catcher. Becker played two seasons for the Cleveland Indians in 1936 and 1937 got his big league break after hitting .372 for the San Francisco Seals in 1935. He was then picked up by the Cleveland Indians, and played for them for two seasons. In his major league career, he played in 40 games as a backup catcher and had a .241 batting average. After serving in the Navy during World War II, missing 1944-1945, he managed in the minors for a decade. He proved much more successful as a manager and coach.

Becker became the highly effective pitching coach of the Brooklyn and Los Angeles Dodgers (1955-1964), St. Louis Cardinals (1965-1966) and Chicago Cubs (1967-1970). The Dodgers won their first three World Championships (1955, 1959 and 1963) with Becker tutoring the pitching staff. Fine condition.

Achievements

- Coached 10 pitchers who won 20, or more games in a season: (Dodgers 4, Cardinals 1, & Cubs 5).
- Coached 4 Cy Young Winners with the Brooklyn/Los Angelas Dodgers: (1956, 1962, 1963 & 1964).
- Coached 5 Pitching Staffs that led the league in ERA: (1955, 1956, 1962, 1963 & 1964)
- Coached 3 Pitching Staffs that led the league in Saves: (1955, 1957, & 1962)
- Coached 5 Pitching Staffs that led the league in WHIP: (1955, 1956, 1962, 1963 & 1964.
- Coached 8 Pitching Staffs that led the league in Strikeouts: (1955, 1956, 1957, 1959, 1960, 1961, 1962, & 1963),
- Coached 4 Pitching Staffs whose team won the Pennant: (1955, 1956, 1959 & 1963).

- Coached 4 Pitching Staffs whose team won the World Series: (1955,1959 & 1963).

Summary

Becker was a member of the small fraternity of former catchers who became celebrated throughout baseball as pitching coaches (which included men such as Ray Berres, Dave Duncan, Rube Walker and Mike Roarke).

From 1955-1964, Becker oversaw a Dodgers pitching staff that was one of the best in baseball during his tenure. Working with pitchers such as Don Newcombe, Carl Erskine, Johnny Podres, Roger Craig, Sal "The Barber" Maglie, Don Drysdale and Sandy Koufax, Becker and manager Walter Alston worked magic together, collecting four NL championship Dodger clubs, including the 1955, 1959 and 1963 world series champions. He also doubled as the Dodgers' first-base coach during the early 1960s. Becker left the Dodgers in 1964. Becker would later coach for the St. Louis Cardinals1965 and 1966 and Chicago Cubs in 1967 o 1970, helping along the development of Ferguson Jenkins, Ken Holtzman and Joe Niekro.

Becker's coaching career ended in August 1970, when he was felled by a heart ailment while in uniform for the Cubs at Wrigley Field, forcing his retirement at age 62. He survived his 1970 illness, and died on January 11, 1998, at age 89 in Sunset Hills, Missouri.

Hall of Fame

Joe Beckers Hall of Fame Statistical Point Total was 112.000 based on an Induction Criteria on 120.000. Though his catching career wasn't Hall of Fame material, his knowledge and handling of Pitching Staffs was. He needs a place in the Hall of Fame.

Player/Coach Hall of Fame Criteria Points

Becker, Joe

Position	Born :	June 25, 1908	Height:	6' 1" USC	185 cm
Catcher	Died:	January 11, 1998	Weight:	180 lbs.	81 Kg.
	From:	St. Louis, Mo.	Debut	May 10, 1936	
	Bats:	Right	Final Game	September 14, 1937	
	Throws:	Right			

Playing Career

Years	Ages	G	AB	R	H	2B	3B	HR	RBI	SB	CS	BB	SO	BA	OBP	SLG	OPS	TB	HBP	
162 Game Avg.		162	373	336	32	81	20	8	4	53	0	0	32	32	0.241	0.32	0.386	0.701	130	
2 Yrs		40	83	8	20	5	2	1	13	0	0	8	8	0.241	0.315	0.39	0.701	32	1	Career Pts.
		0.000	0.000	0.000	0.000	0.000	0.000	0.000	0.000	0.000	0.000	0.000	####	0.500	1.000	0.500	2.000	0.000	0.000	4.000

Post Season Points

Years	Ages	G	AB	R	H	2B	3B	HR	RBI	SB	CS	BB	SO	BA	OBP	SLG	OPS	TB	HBP	
		0	0	0	0	0	0	0	0	0	0	0	0	0	0	0	0	0	0	Post Season Pt
		0.000	0.000	0.000	0.000	0.000	0.000	0.000	0.000	0.000	0.000	0.000	####	0.000	0.000	0.000	0.000	0.000	0.000	0.000

World Series Points

Years	Years	G	AB	R	H	2B	3B	HR	RBI	SB	CS	BB	SO	BA	OBP	SLG	OPS	TB	HBP	World Series P
		0	0	0	0	0	0	0	0	0	0	0	0	0	0	0	0	0	0	0.000
		0.000	0.000	0.000	0.000	0.000	0.000	0.000	0.000	0.000	0.000	0.000	####	0.000	0.000	0.000	0.000	0.000	0.000	0.000

Coaching Career

Year	Team	Coach of	Accomplishments	20 Game Winners	Cy Young	Rank ERA	Rank Saves	Rank WHIP	Rank S.O.'s	Teams League	Comments
1955	Brooklyn Dodgers	Pitching	1955 - N.L. Pennant Winner	1	0	1	1	1	1	8 Teams	
1956	Brooklyn Dodgers	Pitching	1955 - World Series Winner	1	1	1	2	1	1	8 Teams	
1957	Brooklyn Dodgers	Pitching	1956 - N.L. Pennant Winner	0	0	1	1	1	1	8 Teams	
1958	Los Angelos Dodger	Pitching	1959 -N. L. Pennant Winner	0	0	8	2	8	5	8 Teams	
1959	Los Angelos Dodger	Pitching	1959 - World Series Winner	0	0	3	3	3	1	8 Teams	
1960	Los Angelos Dodger	Pitching	1963-N. L. Pennant Winner	0	0	3	3	2	1	8 Teams	
1961	Los Angelos Dodger	Pitching	1963- World Series Winner	1	0	7	2	5	1	10 Teams	
1962	Los Angelos Dodger	Pitching		1	1	3	1	6	1	10 Teams	
1963	Los Angelos Dodger	Pitching		0	1	1	6	1	1	10 Teams	
1964	Los Angelos Dodger	Pitching		0	1	1	8	1	2	10 Teams	
				4	4	5	6	6	9		

Coaching Career

Year	Team	Coach of	Accomplishments	20 Game Winners	Cy Young	Rank ERA	Rank Saves	Rank WHIP	Rank S.O.'s	Teams in League	Comments
1965	Stl. Cardinals	Pitching		1	0	6	4	5	6	10 Teams	
1966	Stl. Cardinals	Pitching		1	0	2	5	3	8	10 Teams	
				1	0	1	0	1	0		

Coaching Career

Year	Team	Coach of	Accomplishments	20 Game Winners	Cy Young	Rank ERA	Rank Saves	Rank WHIP	Rank S.O.'s	Teams in League	Comments
1967	Chicago, Cubs	Pitching		1	0	7	5	6	8	10 Teams	
1968	Chicago, Cubs	Pitching		1	0	9	3	6	9	10 Teams	
1969	Chicago, Cubs	Pitching		2	0	5	7	6	2	12 Teams	
1970	Chicago, Cubs	Pitching		1	0	5	6	6	3	12 Teams	
				5	0	0	1	0	2		

Years Coached	CY Winner	20 Game Winners	Top 25% ERA	Top 25% Saves	Top 25% WHIP	Top 25% S.O.'s	Top 25% Titles	Division Titles	League Titles	WS Titles	
16	4	10	6	6	6	11	4	4	3		Coaching Pts.
9	11.500	30.000	6.500	6.500	6.500	14.000	10.000	12.000	12.000		118.000

Hall of Fame Points

Playing Career Points	4.000
Post Season Points	0.000
World Series Points	0.000
Writers Association Pts.	0.000
Military/Lifetime Achievement	0.000
Coaching Points	118.000
Grand Total HOF Points	**122.000**

The Baseball Hall of Fame

Duncan, Dave

Personal Life

David Edwin Duncan was born September 26,1945 to Clarence Edwin Duncan and Evelyn Louise Rabun. No information found for any siblings.

Duncan has two daughters from his first marriage (no information available), Tiffany Duncan and Devannie Duncan. Duncan married his second wife Jeanine Grove in 1974 with the couple having two sons, David Shelley, born in 1979, and Chris, born in 1981. Jeanine passed away on June 6, 2013. Duncan's son, Chris, died from brain cancer in Tucson on September 6, 2019

Baseball Career

In an eleven-year major league career, Duncan played in 929 games, accumulating 617 hits in 2,885 at-bats for a .214 career batting average along with 109 home runs, 341 runs batted in and an on-base percentage of .279. While he was a light-hitting player, he excelled as a defensive catcher, ending his career with a .984 fielding percentage. He was respected during his playing career for his defensive skills and for his knowledge of the game of baseball. During his time with the Athletics, he met future manager Tony La Russa, then a utility infielder with the club. The two of them teamed up with Dave McKay and began a long-term association from the midpoint of the 1986, when LaRussa and Duncan took over their respective positions with Oakland, through 2011 with the Cardinals. The three were on staff for six pennant-winning and three world championship teams-the 1989 Athletics, 2006 & 2011 Cardinals.

Achievements

- Coached 12 pitchers who won 20 + games:(White Sox 2, Athletics 5, & Cardinals 5).
- Coached 5 Cy Young Winners (White Sox 1, Athletics 4).
- Coached 4 Pitching Staffs that led the league in Saves: (1988, 1989, 1990, & 2005).
- Coached 4 Pitching Staffs that led the league in WHIP: (1983, 1989, 1990 &1904).
- Coached 2 Pitching Staff that led the league in Strikeouts: (1982 & 1985).
- Coached 5 Pitching Staffs that won the Pennant – (1988, 1989, 2004, 2006 & 2011).
- Coached 4 Pitching Staffs whose team won the World Series – (1989, 2006 & 2011).

A Fan's Perspective

Summary Analysis

Duncan began his coaching career in 1978 with the Cleveland Indians. After a stint as a pitching coach for the Seattle Mariners in 1982, he joined former teammate La Russa, then the manager of the Chicago White Sox. From that time they worked in tandem as manager and pitching coach, joining Oakland in 1986 and then the Cardinals in 1996. Beginning in 1986, first base coach Dave McKay also began a long tenure of working with Duncan and La Russa. The three men continued to work together until the Cardinals won the 2011 World Series. La Russa retired immediately after that World Series and Duncan retired from coaching less than three months later.

Pitchers on Duncan's staffs won four Cy Young Awards: LaMarr Hoyt in 1983; Bob Welch in 1990; Dennis Eckersley in 1992; and Chris Carpenter in 2005. Dave Stewart, who had not found consistent success before signing with Oakland as a free agent in 1986, won 20 or more games and pitched 250 or more innings four straight seasons from 1987 to 1990. From 1988 through 1990, Oakland pitchers had the lowest earned run average (ERA) in the American League, and the 2005 St. Louis staff had the lowest ERA in the majors. La Russa regularly credits Duncan as being a key factor in the success of the teams he managed for over 25 years.

Hall of Fame

Dave Duncan's Hall of Fame Statistical Point Total is 154.800 based on an Induction Criteria on 120.000. It is a shame that there is no room in Cooperstown for someone who gained fame and accomplished much as a pitching coach. That seems to be a hole in the system. Yes, the case can be made that Johnny Sain is the best pitching coach of all time, but there are others worthy of mention, too. The Hall should find a way to open its doors to great contributors to the sport that don't fit into narrower definitions.

The Baseball Hall of Fame

Duncan, Dave

Position	Catcher	**Born:** September 26, 1945	**Height:** 6' 2" USC 188 cm
		From: Dallas, TX	**Weight:** 190 lbs. 88 Kg.
		Bats: Right	**Debut:** May 6, 1964
		Throws: Right	**Final Game** October 1, 1976

Playing Career

Years / Ages	G	AB	R	H	2B	3B	HR	RBI	SB	CS	BB	SO	BA	OBP	SLG	OPS	TB	HBP	
162 Game Avg.	102	503	48	108	14	1	19	59	1	2	44	118	0.214	0.279	0.96	0.636	180	2	
13 Yrs	929	2885	274	617	79	4	77	341	5	13	252	677	0.214	0.279	0.96	0.636	1031	14	Career Pts.
	0.500	0.000	0.000	0.000	0.000	0.000	1.500	0.000	0.000	0.000	0.000	0.000	0.000	0.000	0.000	1.000	0.000	0.000	3.000

Post Season Points

Years / Ages	G	AB	R	H	2B	3B	HR	RBI	SB	CS	BB	SO	BA	OBP	SLG	OPS	TB	HBP	
2 Years 25 & 26	4	9	0	3	1	0	0	2	0	1	1	1	0.375	0.444	0.500	0.944	4	0	Post Season Pts.
	0.250	0.000	0.000	0.250	0.000	0.000	0.000	0.250	0.000	0.000	0.250	0.000	0.250	0.250	0.250	0.250	0.250	0.000	2.250

World Series Points

Years	G	AB	R	H	2B	3B	HR	RBI	SB	CS	BB	SO	BA	OBP	SLG	OPS	TB	HBP	
1 Year	3	3	0	1	0	0	0	0	0	0	1	1	0.200	0.333	0.200	0.533	1	0	World Series Pts.
	0.250	0.000	0.000	0.250	0.000	0.000	0.000	0.000	0.000	0.000	0.250	0.000	0.000	0.000	0.000	0.250	0.000		1.000

Coaching Career

Year	Team	Coach of	Accomplishments	20 Game Winners	Cy Young	Rank ERA	Rank Saves	Rank WHIP	Rank S.O.'s	Teams League	Comments
1981	Cleveland Indians	Pitching	Dropped Team ERA from 4.68 to 3.88	0	0	13	11	3	8	14 Teams	
				0	0	0	0	1	0		

Coaching Career

Year	Team	Coach of	Accomplishments	20 Game Winners	Cy Young	Rank ERA	Rank Saves	Rank WHIP	Rank S.O.'s	Teams League	Comments
1982	Seattle Mariners	Pitching	Dropped Team ERA from 4.23 to 3.88	0	0	4	4	0	1	14 Teams	
				0	0	0	0	0	1		

Coaching Career

Year	Team	Coach of	Accomplishments	20 Game Winners	Cy Young	Rank ERA	Rank Saves	Rank WHIP	Rank S.O.'s	Teams League	Comments
1983	Chicago White Sox	Pitching	Led A.L. in Whip	2	1	3	2	1	3	14 Teams	1983 - A. L. West Title
1984	Chicago White Sox	Pitching		0	0	11	11	3	7	14 Teams	
1985	Chicago White Sox	Pitching	Led A.L. in S.O.'s	0	0	7	7	7	1	14 Teams	
1986	Chicago White Sox	Pitching		0	0	0	0	0	0	14 Teams	1/2 Season
				2	1	1	1	2	2		

Coaching Career

Year	Team	Coach of	Accomplishments	20 Game Winners	Cy Young	Rank ERA	Rank Saves	Rank WHIP	Rank S.O.'s	Teams League	Comments
1986	Oakland Athletics	Pitching		0	0	0	0	0	0	14 Teams	
1987	Oakland Athletics	Pitching		1	1	5	4	4	3	14 Teams	
1988	Oakland Athletics	Pitching	Led A.L. in ERA and Saves	1	1	1	1	3	2	14 Teams	A.L. West & Pennant Winner. Lost W.S.
1989	Oakland Athletics	Pitching	Led A.L. in ERA, Saves, and WHIP	1	1	1	1	1	4	14 Teams	A.L. West, Pennant & World Series Winner
1990	Oakland Athletics	Pitching	Led A.L. in ERA and WHIP	2	1	1	2	1	11	14 Teams	A.L. West Winner
1991	Oakland Athletics	Pitching		0	0	13	11	6	9	14 Teams	
1992	Oakland Athletics	Pitching	Led A.L. in Saves	0	0	4	1	9	10	14 Teams	
1993	Oakland Athletics	Pitching		0	0	14	9	14	11	14 Teams	
1994	Oakland Athletics	Pitching		0	0	8	5	7	4	14 Teams	
				5	4	3	4	3	2		

Coaching Career

Year	Team	Coach of	Accomplishments	20 Game Winners	Cy Young	Rank ERA	Rank Saves	Rank WHIP	Rank S.O.'s	Teams in League	Comments
1995	Stl. Cardinals	Pitching		1	0	8	6	7	13	14 Teams	
1996	Stl. Cardinals	Pitching		0	0	8	6	5	7	14 Teams	N. L. Central Winner
1997	Stl. Cardinals	Pitching		0	0	5	8	5	8	14 Teams	
1998	Stl. Cardinals	Pitching		0	0	8	9	12	14	16 Teams	
1999	Stl. Cardinals	Pitching		0	0	11	10	15	13	16 Teams	
2000	Stl. Cardinals	Pitching		1	0	7	10	5	6	16 Teams	N. L. Central Winner
2001	Stl. Cardinals	Pitching		1	0	3	9	7	11	16 Teams	
2002	Stl. Cardinals	Pitching		0	0	4	8	5	12	16 Teams	N. L. Central Winner
2003	Stl. Cardinals	Pitching		0	0	11	9	10	12	16 Teams	
2004	Stl. Cardinals	Pitching	Led N.L. in Saves & WHIP	0	0	2	1	1	10	16 Teams	N. L. Central & Pennant Winner. - Lost W.S.
2005	Stl. Cardinals	Pitching	Led N.L. in ERA	1	0	1	3	2	13	16 Teams	N. L. Central Winner
2006	Stl. Cardinals	Pitching		0	0	9	9	6	14	16 Teams	N. L. Central, Pennant & World Series Winner
2007	Stl. Cardinals	Pitching		0	0	11	14	10	15	16 Teams	
2008	Stl. Cardinals	Pitching		0	0	7	8	8	16	16 Teams	
2009	Stl. Cardinals	Pitching		0	0	4	7	3	12	16 Teams	N. L. Central Winner
2010	Stl. Cardinals	Pitching		1	0	4	15	6	13	16 Teams	
2011	Stl. Cardinals	Pitching		0	0	8	7	10	13	16 Teams	N. L. Central, Pennant & World Series Winner
2012	Stl. Cardinals	Pitching		0	0	6	9	8	9	16 Teams	
				5	0	6	2	3	0		

Hall of Fame Points

Playing Career Points	3.000
Post Season Points	2.250
World Series Points	1.000
Writers Association Pts.	0.000
Military/Lifetime Achievement	0.000
Coaching Points	150.000
Grand Total HOF Points	156.250

Years Coached	CY Winners	20 Game Winners	Top 25% ERA	Top 25% Saves	Top 25% WHIP	Top 25% S.O.'s	Division Titles	League Titles	WS Titles	
32	4	7	10	7	9	5	12	8	3	Coaching Pts.
20	11.500	20.000	11.500	9.000	11.500	6.500	30.000	18.000	12.000	150.000

A Fan's Perspective

Harder, Mel "Chief"

Personal Life

Melvin Leroy Harder (October 15, 1909 – October 20, 2002) Harder was born in Beemer, Nebraska, to Klaus Harder and Clara Jeutel (Skala). He graduated from Tech High School in North Omaha, Nebraska and had sisters, Jennie and Beatta.

Harder married Sandy Schmidt in 1932 and had two daughters, Gay and Penny. His wife, Sandy, died in 1989.

Baseball Career

Pitcher Mel Harder spent his entire career of twenty years with the Cleveland Indians and made the All-Star team four times. He was in the top ten in the league in ERA six times in his career, all during the 1930s; he led the league in 1933 with a 2.95 ERA. He was also in the top ten in the league in wins six times in his career, also all during the 1930s. Harder is one of only four pitchers to pitch at least twenty seasons with one team. His peak years were in the early and mid-1930s. He set franchise records for wins (223), games started (433) and innings pitched (3426⅓) which were later broken by Bob Feller, and he holds the club record of 582 career games pitched. He was among the American League's career leaders in wins (9th), games (8th) and starts (10th) when he retired. He was also an excellent fielder, leading AL pitchers in putouts four times. Harder ended his career in 1947 with 1160 strikeouts and a 3.80 ERA. Harder's 223 victories and 186 losses remain club records.

Achievements

- Coached 16 pitchers that won 20, or more games: (Indians 1951 – 1956 & 1962).
- Coached 7 Pitching Staffs that led the league in ERA – (1948-1952, 1954 & 1956).
- Coached 3 Staffs that led the A.L. in Saves:(Indians 1948 & 1954, Reds 1968).
- Coached 8 Pitching Staffs that led the league in WHIP: (1948 – 1952, 1954 – 1956).
- Coached 4 Pitching Staffs that led the league in Strikeouts: (Indians 1955, 1956, & 1963 & Reds 1963).
- Coached 2 Staffs that won the Pennant: (1948 & 1954) & World Series: (1948).

A Fan's Perspective

Hall of Fame

Mel Harder's Hall of Fame Statistical Point Total was 138.500 based on an Induction Criteria on 120.000. Harder was a very good pitcher for 20 years but his knowledge and handling of Pitching Staffs was outstanding. He needs a place in the Hall of Fame. There was a push to have Mel Harder elected to the Hall of Fame in the 1990s, when he was still alive and the Veterans Committee still functioned as a small, largely unaccountable club; the effort did not reach fruition before the Committee was disbanded. However, his name still comes up in discussions of players to be considered for future induction in the Hall.

Summary Analysis

Harder was one of the game's most highly regarded pitching coaches from 1948 to 1969. As a coach, Harder molded Indians staffs that produced seven pitchers who won at least 20 games in a season, Even before he formally became a pitching coach, Harder successfully transformed Bob Lemon from an infielder in the mid-1940s into a top Hall of Fame pitcher. From 1948 into the 1950s, he guided the Indians' "Big Four" pitching rotation, featuring Feller, Bob Lemon, Early Wynn and Mike Garcia. He taught future 300 game-winner Wynn the breaking ball and changeup, who had a losing record (72-87) before being traded to the Indians. Herb Score was named Rookie of the Year in 1955 after Harder helped to develop his curveball. When Sal Maglie was struggling with the Indians, Harder watched some films of Maglie pitching with the Giants and figured out that he wasn't swiveling his foot like he normally did, which kept him from following through with his delivery.

Bob Feller, Early Wynn and Mike Garcia, all of whom achieved great success pitching in Cleveland, also praised the help Harder gave them when they played with the Indians. He was the pitching coach under manager Al Lopez when the Indians racked up a then-record 111 wins in 1954. Late in his tenure, prominent young pitchers as Sam McDowell, Tommy John and Luis Tiant would come under his guidance. Harder was dismissed by the Cleveland general manager after the 1963 season. He later coached with the New York Mets (1964), Chicago Cubs (1965), Cincinnati Reds (1966–68) and the Kansas City Royals (1969).

Player/Coach Player/Coach Hall of Fame Criteria Points

Harder, Mel

Position	Born : October 15, 1909	Died:	October 20, 2002
Pitcher	From: Beemer, NE	Height:	6' 1" USC 185 cm
	Bats: Right	Weight:	195 lbs. 88 Kg.
	Throws: Right	Debut	April 24, 1928
		Final Game	September 7, 1948

Playing Career

Years / Ages	W	L	PCT	ERA	G	GS	GF	CG	SHO	SV	IP	H	R	ER	BB	SO	BF	WHIP	Career Pts.
162 Game Avg.	15	12	0.545	3.8	39	29	6	12	2	2	230	248	115	97	75	78	996	1.408	
20 Yrs	223	186	0.545	3.80	582	433	94	181	25	24	3426.1	3706	1714	1447	1118	1161	14861	1.408	52.000
	9.250	0.000	4.500	3.000	5.500	5.750	1.000	4.500	2.500	0.500	9.250	0.000	0.000	0.000	0.000	3.750	0.000	2.500	52.000

Post Season Points

Year / Age	W	L	PCT	ERA	G	GS	GF	CG	SHO	SV	IP	H	R	ER	BB	SO	BF	WHIP	Post Season Pts
None	0	0	0	0	0	0	0	0	0	0	0	0	0	0	0	0	0	0	0.000
	0.000	0.000	0.000	0.000	0.000	0.000	0.000	0.000	0.000	0.000	0.000	0.000	0.000	0.000	0.000	0.000	0.000	0.000	0.000

World Series Points

Years / Ages	G	PA	AB	R	H	2B	3B	HR	RBI	SB	CS	BB	SO	BA	OBP	SLG	OPS	TB	World Series Pts.
	0	0	0	0	0	0	0	0	0	0	0	0	0	0	0	0	0	0	0.000
	0.000	0.000	0.000	0.000	0.000	0.000	0.000	0.000	0.000	0.000	0.000	0.000	0.000	0.000	0.000	0.000	0.000	0.000	0.000

Coaching Career

Year	Team	Coach of	Accomplishments	20 Game Winners	Cy Young	Rank ERA	Rank Saves	Rank WHIP	Rank S.O.'s	Teams League	Comments
1948	Cleveland Indians	Pitching	Led A.L. in ERA, Saves & WHIP	0	0	1	1	1	3	8 Teams	Won A. L. Pennant & World Series
1949	Cleveland Indians	Pitching	Led A.L. in ERA & WHIP	0	0	1	2	1	4	8 Teams	
1950	Cleveland Indians	Pitching	Led A.L. in ERA & WHIP	0	0	1	6	1	2	8 Teams	
1951	Cleveland Indians	Pitching	Led A.L. in ERA & WHIP	3	0	1	6	1	2	8 Teams	
1952	Cleveland Indians	Pitching	Led A.L. in ERA & WHIP	3	0	1	6	1	2	8 Teams	
1953	Cleveland Indians	Pitching		1	0	4	8	3	5	8 Teams	
1954	Cleveland Indians	Pitching	Led A.L. in ERA & WHIP & Record 111 Wins	2	0	1	2	1	3	8 Teams	Won A.L. Pennant - Lost World Series
1955	Cleveland Indians	Pitching	Led A.L. in Saves, WHIP & S.O.'s	3	0	3	1	1	1	8 Teams	
1956	Cleveland Indians	Pitching	Led A.L. in ERA, WHIP & S.O.'s	3	0	1	2	1	1	8 Teams	
1957	Cleveland Indians	Pitching		0	0	6	5	7	2	8 Teams	
1958	Cleveland Indians	Pitching		0	0	5	7	6	3	8 Teams	
1959	Cleveland Indians	Pitching		0	0	4	5	6	3	8 Teams	
1960	Cleveland Indians	Pitching		0	0	6	3	6	4	8 Teams	
1961	Cleveland Indians	Pitching		0	0	5	7	7	7	10 Teams	
1962	Cleveland Indians	Pitching		1	0	8	6	8	9	10 Teams	
1963	Cleveland Indians	Pitching		0	0	6	9	4	1	10 Teams	
				16	0	7	5	8	7		

Coaching Career

Year	Team	Coach of	Accomplishments	20 Game Winners	Cy Young	Rank ERA	Rank Saves	Rank WHIP	Rank S.O.'s	Teams League	Comments
1964	New York Mets	Pitching		0	0	10	10	10	10	10 Teams	
				0	0	0	0	0	0		

Coaching Career

Year	Team	Coach of	Accomplishments	20 Game Winners	Cy Young	Rank ERA	Rank Saves	Rank WHIP	Rank S.O.'s	Teams League	Comments
1965	Chicago Cubs	Pitching		0	0	7	5	8	9	10 Teams	
				0	0	0	0	0	0		

Coaching Career

Year	Team	Coach of	Accomplishments	20 Game Winners	Cy Young	Rank ERA	Rank Saves	Rank WHIP	Rank S.O.'s	Teams League	Comments
1966	Cincinatti Reds	Pitching		0	0	8	3	8	2	10 Teams	
1967	Cincinatti Reds	Pitching	Led the N. L. in S.O.'s	0	0	2	2	4	1	10 Teams	
1968	Cincinatti Reds	Pitching	Led the N. L. in Saves	0	0	10	1	10	5	10 Teams	
				0	0	1	2	0	2		

Coaching Career

Year	Team	Coach of	Accomplishments	20 Game Winners	Cy Young	Rank ERA	Rank Saves	Rank WHIP	Rank S.O.'s	Teams League	Comments
1969	Kansas City Royals	Pitching	Expansion Team	0	0	8	9	6	7	12 Teams	
				0	0	0	0	0	0		

Years Coached	CY Winners	20 Game Winners	Top 25% ERA	Top 25% Saves	Top 25% WHIP	Top 25% S.O.'s	Division Titles	League Titles	WS Titles	Coaching Pts.
22	0	16	8	7	8	9	2	2	1	
11.5	0.000	20.000	5.000	9.000	9.000	11.500	5.000	6.000	4.000	85.000

	Hall of Fame Points
Playing Career Points	52.000
Post Season Points	0.000
World Series Points	0.000
Writers Association Pts.	0.000
Military/Lifetime Achievement	0.000
Coaching Points	85.000
Grand Total HOF Points	137.000

A Fan's Perspective

Mazzone, Leo

Personal Life

Leo David Mazzone was born October 16, 1948, in West Virginia to Anthony "Tony" Mazzone and Maxine Malone. He has a younger sister, Mary Frances.

Mazzone married Rebecca (no information available) with the couple having three sons Tony, Chris, and Nick

Baseball Career

A left handed pitcher, Mazzone made his professional debut in 1967 with the Medford Giants, a class-A farm team of the San Francisco Giants. In all, he pitched seven seasons in the Giants organization, reaching as high as the Double-A Amarillo Giants, for whom he played four seasons from 1970 to 1973. He three seasons in the Oakland Athletics chain, reaching Triple-A with the Tucson Toros in 1975.

Summary Analysis

Shortly after joining the Braves, Mazzone discovered a mentor in Johnny Sain, who took the green pitching coach under his wing. Atlanta hired Mazzone in 1979 and he coached with the Durham Bulls (1983-1984), Sumter Braves (1986), Greenville Braves (1987), and Richmond Braves (1988-1990). He was named the pitching coach of the Braves in June 1990.

He arrived in Atlanta as the team was nurturing a generation of extremely talented young pitchers. Led by Tom Glavine, John Smoltz, Steve Avery, Derek Lilliquist, and Pete Smith. Under his tutelage, Glavine and Smoltz blossomed into Hall of Famers, and were soon joined by free agent Greg Maddux to form a remarkable "Big Three" that dominated the National League for years. The results were almost immediate. Twenty-one-year-old phenom Steve Avery went from three wins in 1990 to 18 in 1991. Smoltz's ERA dipped by nearly a full run between '91 and '92. The team's ERA went from a major league worst 4.58 in 1990 to third-best 3.49 in 1991, to a big-league best 3.14 in 1992. In 1991, Glavine, who had only won 10 games the previous year, went 20-11, the first of three straight 20-win seasons for the lefty. Even free agent Greg Maddux, who had won the NL Cy Young with Chicago in '92, bought into the program and went on to win his second Cy with the Braves in 1993. Mazzone's pitching staffs anchored 14 division title winners in Atlanta as he served as pitching coach of the Atlanta Braves from 1990-2005. During his tenure, the Braves won 14 consecutive division titles (1991-2005). Mazzone earned the reputation as being one of the best pitching coaches in the modern era. Mazzone's pitching philosophies state that pitchers should throw more between starts and be able to throw strikes on the low and outside corner of the strike zone.

Following the 2005 season, became the pitching coach of the Orioles in 2006. However following the 2007 season Mazzone was let go by the Orioles and he retired after that.

Achievements

- Coached 8 pitchers that won at least 20 games in a season: (Braves 1990 – 1993, 1996 – 1998, & 2003).
- Coached 10 Pitching Staffs that led the league in ERA: (Braves 1992, 1993, 1995, 1997-2002 & 2004).
- Coached 2 Pitching Staffs that led the league in Saves: (Braves 2000 & 2002).
- Coached 7 Cy Young winners: (1991-1996 & 1998.
- Coached 8 Pitching Staffs that led the league in WHIP: (Braves 1991, 1993, 1995-2000 & 2002).
- Coached 4 Pitching Staffs that led the league in Strikeouts: (Braves 1994-1996 & 1998).
- Coached 4 Pitching Staffs that won the Pennant: (Braves 1992, 1995,1996, 1999 & 1 Pitching Staff that won the World Series: (1995).

Hall of Fame

Leo Mazzone's Hall of Fame Statistical Point Total was 149.000 Though his pitching career did not lead to the major Leagues, his knowledge and handling of Pitching Staffs was. This is verified with Maddux, Glavine, and Smoltz all being inducted into the National Baseball Hall of Fame. Mazzone's impact on many pitchers' careers is quantifiable and had such an impact that he is deserving of Hall of Fame Induction.

The Baseball Hall of Fame

Player/Coach Hall of Fame Criteria Points

Mazzone, Leo

Position	Born :	October 16, 1948	Height: 5' 10: USC cm
None	From:	Keyser, WV	Weight: 165 lbs. Kg.
	Bats:	Left	Debut Did Not play MLB
	Throws:	Left	Final Game Did Not play MLB

Playing Career

Years Ages	G	PA	AB	R	H	2B	3B	HR	RBI	SB	CS	BB	SO	BA	OBP	SLG	OPS	TB	HBP	Career Pts.
162 Game Avg.	0	0	0	0	0	0	0	0	0	0	0	0	0	0	0	0	0	0	0	0.000
No MLB Exp.	0.000	0.000	0.000	0.000	0.000	0.000	0.000	0.000	0.000	0.000	0.000	0.000	0.000	0.000	0.000	0.000	0.000	0.000	0.000	

Post Season Points

Years Ages	G	PA	AB	R	H	2B	3B	HR	RBI	SB	CS	BB	SO	BA	OBP	SLG	OPS	TB	Post Season Pts.
No MLB Exp.	0	0	0	0	0	0	0	0	0	0	0	0	0	0	0	0	0	0	0.000
	0.000	0.000	0.000	0.000	0.000	0.000	0.000	0.000	0.000	0.000	0.000	0.000	0.000	0.000	0.000	0.000	0.000	0.000	

World Series Points

Years Ages	G	PA	AB	R	H	2B	3B	HR	RBI	SB	CS	BB	SO	BA	OBP	SLG	OPS	TB	World Series Pts.
No MLB Exp.	0	0	0	0	0	0	0	0	0	0	0	0	0	0	0	0	0	0	0.000
	0.000	0.000	0.000	0.000	0.000	0.000	0.000	0.000	0.000	0.000	0.000	0.000	0.000	0.000	0.000	0.000	0.000	0.000	

Coaching Career

Year	Team	Coach of	Accomplishments	20 Game Winners	Cy Young	Rank ERA	Rank Saves	Rank WHIP	Rank S.O.'s	Teams League	Comments
1990	Atlanta Braves	Pitching		1	0	13	11	12	5	12 Teams	Did not make playoffs
1991	Atlanta Braves	Pitching	Led N. L. in WHIP	1	1	3	3	1	6	12 Teams	Won N.L. West, Championship - Lost World Series
1992	Atlanta Braves	Pitching	Led N. L. in ERA	1	1	1	7	2	7	12 Teams	Won N.L. West & Pennant. Lost World Series
1993	Atlanta Braves	Pitching	Led N. L. in ERA & WHIP	1	1	1	7	1	4	14 Teams	Won N.L. West & Lost N. L. Championship
1994	Atlanta Braves	Pitching	Led N. L. in WHIP	0	0	7	12	2	1	14 Teams	Did not make playoffs.
1995	Atlanta Braves	Pitching	Led N. L. in ERA, WHIP & S.O.'s	0	0	1	10	1	1	14 Teams	Won N.L. East, Division Series, Championship Series & Won World Series
1996	Atlanta Braves	Pitching	Led N.L. in WHIP & S.O.'s	1	1	2	4	1	1	14 Teams	Won N.L. East, Division Series, Championship Series & Lost World Series
1997	Atlanta Braves	Pitching	Led N. L. in ERA & WHIP	1	1	1	10	1	2	14 Teams	Won N.L. East, Division Series,& Lost Championship Series
1998	Atlanta Braves	Pitching	Led N. L. in ERA, WHIP & S.O.'s	1	1	1	5	1	1	14 Teams	Won N.L. East, Division Series,& Lost Championship Series
1999	Atlanta Braves	Pitching	Led N. L. in ERA & WHIP	0	0	1	4	1	3	16 Teams	Won N.L. East, Division Series, Championship Series & Lost World Series
2000	Atlanta Braves	Pitching	Led N. L. in ERA, Saves & WHIP	0	0	1	1	1	7	16 Teams	Won N.L. East & Lost Division Series
2001	Atlanta Braves	Pitching	Led. N. L. in ERA	0	0	1	7	3	6	16 Teams	Won N.L. East & Division Series Lost Championship Series
2002	Atlanta Braves	Pitching	Led. N. L. in ERA	0	0	1	1	2	10	16 Teams	Won N.L. East & Lost Division Series
2003	Atlanta Braves	Pitching		1	1	9	2	9	11	16 Teams	Won N.L. East & Lost Division Series
2004	Atlanta Braves	Pitching	Led N. L. in ERA	0	0	1	5	9	12	16 Teams	Won N.L. East & Lost Division Series
2005	Atlanta Braves	Pitching		0	0	6	13	10	16	16 Teams	Won N.L. East & Lost Division Series
				8	7	13	6	12	7		

Coaching Career

Year	Team	Coach of	Accomplishments	20 Game Winners	Cy Young	Rank ERA	Rank Saves	Rank WHIP	Rank S.O.'s	Teams League	Comments
2006	Baltimore Orioles	Pitching		0	0	13	13	13	11	16 Teams	
2007	Baltimore Orioles	Pitching		0	0	13	13	12	5	16 Teams	
				0	0	0	0	0	0		

Years Coached	CY Winners	20 Game Winners	Top 25% ERA	Top 25% Saves	Top 25% WHIP	Top 25% S.O.'s	Division Titles	League Titles	WS Titles	Coaching Pts.
18	7	13	6	12	12	7	15	5	1	Coaching Pts.
9	20.000	20.000	6.500	14.000	14.000	9.000	20.000	15.000	4.000	131.500

<u>Hall of Fame Points</u>

Playing Career Points	0.000
Post Season Points	0.000
World Series Points	0.000
Writers Association Pts.	0.000
Military/Lifetime Achievement	0.000
Coaching Points	131.500
Grand Total HOF Points	131.500

Perranoski, Ron

Personal Life

Ronald Peter Perranoski was born April 1, 1936, to Peter Perranoski and Emily Yates in Paterson, New Jersey. Ron has a sister Pat and he attended Fair Lawn High School. He pitched for a team that won a high school state baseball championship. No record was found.

Perranoski attended Michigan State University after accepting a scholarship and turning down a bonus to sign with the White Sox following his 1954 graduation. At MSU, he won 16 of 19 decisions from 1957-58.

Perranoski married his first wife, Sue Ellen, with the couple having three sons (Ron, Brad and Michael). The couple divorced without no information found and later Perranoski and married Sarah (no information ground).

Baseball Career

Perranoski was signed by the Cubs in June 1958 and was pitching in their minor league system when he was traded to the Dodgers. Over 13 seasons (1961-1973) with the Dodgers, Twins, Tigers, and Angels, he pitched in five postseasons and three World Series — earning championship rings with Los Angeles in 1963 and 1965. He saved 178 games and earned Fireman of the Year recognition twice.

Summary Analysis

After his playing career, Perranoski spent 16 years as a respected pitching coach, winning two more World Series with the Dodgers in the 1980s. Perranoski was the Dodgers' minor league pitching coordinator (1973–80), then the MLB pitching coach under Tommy Lasorda for Los Angeles for 14 seasons (1981–94). He joined the San Francisco Giants as minor league pitching coordinator in 1995, was promoted to bench coach in 1997 and then to pitching coach in 1998-99. During Perranoski's tenure, Fernando Valenzuela and Orel Hershiser won NL Cy Young Awards, Alejandro Peña led the league in ERA, and Ramón Martínez developed into a 20-game winner.49 Although Dodger pitchers finished first or second in the circuit in team ERA in nine of his 14 years as coach,

Perranoski was unceremoniously terminated when the team expanded minor league pitching instructor Dave Wallace's duties to include working with his young proteges at the big-league level. "If there had been any communication, if I had known they were even thinking about it, I'd have been able to get my ducks in a row," Perranoski lamented. Perhaps having second thoughts about the way they fired such a loyal, long-term employee, Los Angeles owner Peter O'Malley, general manager Fred Claire and Lasorda helped Perranoski get hired about two months later as the Giants' coordinator of minor league pitching in 1997. He served as

Baker's pitching coach in 1998 and 1999 and counseled staff members Shawn Estes, Russ Ortiz and Robb Nen. Perranoski retired in 2014 to Vero Beach, Florida when Sabean became executive vice president of baseball operations.

Achievements

- Coached 3 pitchers that won at least 20 games in a season:(Dodgers 1986, 1988, & 1990).
- Coached 5 Pitching Staffs that led the league in ERA: (Dodgers 1985, 1983, 1985, 1989 & 1991).
- Coached 1 Pitching Staff that led the league in Saves: (Dodgers 1988).
- Coached 2 Cy Young winners: (Dodgers 1981 & 1988).
- Coached 5 Pitching Staffs that led the league in WHIP: Dodgers 1981-1983, 1985 & 1989).
- Coached 1 Pitching Staff that led the league in Strikeouts: (Dodgers 1984).
- Coached 2 Pitching Staffs whose team won the Pennant: (Dodgers 1981 & 1988).
- Coached 2 Pitching Staffs whose team won the World Series:(Dodgers 1981 & 1988).

Hall of Fame

Ron Perranoski Hall of Fame Statistical Point Total was 133.000. Though his pitching career did not lead to the Hall of Fame, his knowledge and handling of Pitching Staffs that had an impact on many pitchers' careers is quantifiable and deserving of Hall of Fame Induction.

The Baseball Hall of Fame

Player/Coach Hall of Fame Criteria Points

Perranoski, Ron

Position	Born : April 1, 1936
Pitcher	Died: October 2, 2020
	From: Paterson, N. J.
	Bats: Left
	Throw: Left

Height:	6' 0" USC 183 cm
Weight:	180 lbs. 81 Kg.
Debut	April 14, 1961
Final Game	June 17, 1973

Playing Career

Years Ages	W	L	W-L%	ERA	G	GS	GF	CG	SHO	SV	IP	H	R	ER	BB	SO	BF	WHIP	HBP	
162 Game Avg.	7	7	0.516	2.79	68	0	42	0	0	16	108	101	41	34	43	63	463	1.332	2	
13 Yrs	79	74	0.516	2.79	737	1	458	0	0	178	1174.2	1097	442	364	468	687	5023	1.332	24	Career Pts.
	2.000	0.000	3.750	12.500	9.250	0.000	6.750	0.000	0.000	4.500	1.500	0.000	0.000	0.000	0.000	2.000	0.000	4.500	0.000	46.750

Post Season Points

Years	W	L	W-L%	ERA	G	GS	GF	CG	SHO	SV	IP	H	R	ER	BB	SO	BF	WHIP	HBP	
2 Years	0	1	0.000	10.29	5	0	4	0	0	0	7	13	8	8	1	5	33	2.000	0	Post Season Pts.
	0.000	0.000	0.000	0.000	0.600	0.000	0.400	0.000	0.000	0.000	0.250	0.000	0.000	0.000	0.000	0.250	0.000	0.000	0.000	1.500

World Series Points

Years	W	L	W-L%	ERA	G	GS	GF	CG	SHO	SV	IP	H	R	ER	BB	SO	BF	WHIP	HBP	
3 Years	0	0	0.000	5.87	5	0	3	0	0	1	7.2	6	5	5	5	4	36	1.696	0	Post Season Pts.
	0.000	0.000	0.000	0.000	0.600	0.000	0.400	0.000	0.000	0.250	0.250	0.000	0.000	0.000	0.000	0.250	0.000	0.000	0.000	1.750

Coaching Career

Year	Team	Coach of	Accomplishments	20 Game Winners	Cy Young	Rank ERA	Rank Saves	Rank WHIP	Rank S.O.'s	Teams League	Comments
1981	L. A. Dodgers	Pitching	Led N.L. in WHIP	0	1	2	5	1	2	12 - Teams	Won N.L. Division Series & Championship Series & Won World Series
1982	L. A. Dodgers	Pitching	Led N.L. in ERA & WHIP	0	0	1	12	1	5	12 - Teams	Did not make Playoffs.
1983	L. A. Dodgers	Pitching	Led N.L. in ERA & WHIP	0	0	1	8	1	3	12 - Teams	Won N.L. West & Lost N.L. Championship
1984	L. A. Dodgers	Pitching	Led N.L. in S.O.;s	0	0	2	11	5	1	12 - Teams	Did not make Playoffs.
1985	L. A. Dodgers	Pitching	Led N.L. in ERA & WHIP	0	0	1	8	1	3	12 - Teams	Won N.L. West & Lost N.L. Championship
1986	L. A. Dodgers	Pitching		1	0	5	12	6	4	12 - Teams	Did not make Playoffs.
1987	L. A. Dodgers	Pitching		0	0	2	11	5	2	12 - Teams	Did not make Playoffs.
1988	L. A. Dodgers	Pitching	Led N.L. in Saves	1	1	2	1	3	3	12 - Teams	Won N.L. West, N.L. Championship, and Won World Series
1989	L. A. Dodgers	Pitching	Led N.L. in ERA & WHIP	0	0	1	9	1	3	12 - Teams	Did not make Playoffs.
1990	L. A. Dodgers	Pitching		1	0	7	12	4	3	12 - Teams	Did not make Playoffs.
1991	L. A. Dodgers	Pitching	Led N.L. in ERA	0	0	1	7	2	2	12 - Teams	Did not make Playoffs.
1992	L. A. Dodgers	Pitching		0	0	6	12	12	4	12 - Teams	Did not make Playoffs.
1993	L. A. Dodgers	Pitching		0	0	3	10	7	3	12 - Teams	Did not make Playoffs.
1994	L. A. Dodgers	Pitching		0	0	9	14	9	6	12 - Teams	Did not make Playoffs.
				3	2	10	1	7	6		

Coaching Career

Year	Team	Coach of	Accomplishments	20 Game Winners	Cy Young	Rank ERA	Rank Saves	Rank WHIP	Rank S.O.'s	Teams League	Comments
1997	S. F. Giants	Pitching		0	0	9	4	10	12	14 - Teams	
1998	S. F. Giants	Pitching		0	0	6	7	8	10	14 - Teams	
1999	S. F. Giants	Pitching		0	0	10	8	10	9	14 - Teams	
				0	0	0	0	0	0		

Years Coached	CY Winners	20 Game Winners	Top 25% ERA	Top 25% Saves	Top 25% WHIP	Top 25% S.O.'s	Division Titles	League Titles	WS Titles	
17	2	3	10	1	7	6	4	4	2	Coaching Pts.
9.000	6.500	9.000	11.500	1.500	9.000	6.500	10.000	12.000	8.000	83.000

Hall of Fame Points

Playing Career Points	46.750
Post Season Points	1.500
World Series Points	1.750
Writers Association Pts.	0.000
Military/Lifetime Achievement	0.000
Coaching Points	83.000
Grand Total HOF Points	**133.000**

A Fan's Perspective

Righetti, Dave "Rags"

Personal Life

David Allan Righetti was born November 28, 1958 in San Jose, Californiato to Leo Righetti and . He has an older brother, Steve, Dave and Steve starred for their Lincoln Glen Little League team and attended Pioneer High School. As a senior, he was named to the All-League team. Righetti enrolled in San Jose City College, where he continued his development as a pitcher and named the junior college player of the year.

Righetti married Kandace Owen on February 11,1989. They have non-identical triplets, daughters, Natalee and Nicolette, and son Wesley born in 1991 with Righetti's sister-in-law, Kayla, serving as a surrogate mother through an in vitro fertilization.

Baseball Career

Righetti was selected by the Rangers in the first round (10th overall pick) of the draft in 1977. Righetti was included in a 10-player deal that sent him to the New York Yankees on November 10, 1978. A left-handed pitcher, Righetti played in Major League Baseball from 1979 through 1995 for the New York Yankees, San Francisco Giants, Oakland Athletics, Toronto Blue Jays, and Chicago White Sox. Righetti began his career as a starting pitcher but was chosen to become the team's closer when Goose Gossage left via free agency. On the outside, he made the move without complaint, putting the team's needs first. Righetti really didn't want to become a reliever but did it for the team. He could possibly have been a 20-game winner for five or six years and made twice as much money. However, the transition was a smooth one for Righetti because of his tram-first attitude.

He won the American League Rookie of the Year Award in 1981 as a starter and threw a no-hitter on July 4, 1983. As a closer, he was twice named the AL Rolaids Relief Man of the Year and pitched in two MLB All-Star Games. He was the first player in history to both pitch a no-hitter and also lead the league in saves in his career. On November 9, 1995, Righetti retired and ended his 16-year career with 252 saves, a 3.46 ERA, and a record of 82–79 in 718 games.

Achievements

A Fan's Perspective

- Coached 2 Pitching Staffs that produced a Cy Young Winner - (Giants 1980 & 1981)
- Coached 1 Pitching Staffs that led the league in ERA – (Giants 2010).
- Coached 1 Pitching Staffs that led the league in Saves – (Giants 2010).
- Coached 4 Pitching Staff that won the Pennant: (Giants 2002, 2010, 2012, & 2014).
- Coached 3 Pitching Staff that won the World Series: (Giants 2010, 2012, & 2014).

Hall of Fame

Dave Righetti's Hall of Fame Statistical Point Total was 133. Though his pitching career did not accrue enough statistics to lead to the Hall of Fame, the combination of his pitching statistics and his knowledge in handling Pitching Staffs was more than worthy. Righetti's impact on many pitchers' careers is quantifiable and had such an impact that he is deserving of Hall of Fame Induction.

Summary Analysis

In 1999, he rejoined the Giants organization as a pitching instructor and was the club's pitching coach for the Giants from 2000 through 2017. Righetti's pitchers helped the Giants win the 2002 National League pennant, although the Giants would lose the World Series in seven games to the Anaheim Angels. from 2000 to 2017, a span of 18 seasons that included three World Series titles. He was the pitching coach for the pitching staff that included Matt Cain, Madison Bumgarner, Tim Lincecum, Jonathan Sánchez, and Brian Wilson that won the 2010, 2012, and 2014 World Series.

After 18 seasons of working under managers Dusty Baker, Felipe Alou, and Bruce Bochy, Righetti was removed from his role as pitching coach on October 21, 2017, and moved into a front-office role with the Giants. He was dismissed along with a number of other coaches following a dismal 2017 season that saw the team finish last, but was offered a job in the front office as a special assistant to General Manager Bobby Evans.

Player/Coach Hall of Fame Criteria Points

Righetti, Dave

Position	Born : November 28, 1958
Pitcher	From: San Jose, CA
	Bats: Left
	Throw: Left

Height:	6' 4"	USC	193	cm
Weight:	195	lbs.	88	Kg.
Debut	September 16, 1979			
Final Game	September 19, 1995			

Playing Career

Years	Ages	W	L	W-L%	ERA	G	GS	GF	CG	SHO	SV	IP	H	R	ER	BB	SO	BF	WHIP	HBP	
162 Game Avg.		7	7	0.509	3.46	61	7	40	1	0	21	118	108	51	46	50	94	505	1.338	2	
16 Yrs		82	79	0.509	3.46	718	89	474	13	2	252	1403.2	1287	602	540	591	1112	5988	1.338	21	Career Pts.
		2.500	0.000	3.000	5.750	9.250	1.000	6.750	0.500	0.500	8.000	2.000	0.000	0.000	0.000	0.000	2.500	0.000	4.500	0.000	46.250

Post Season Points

Years	W	L	W-L%	ERA	G	GS	GF	CG	SHO	SV	IP	H	R	ER	BB	SO	BF	WHIP	HBP	
1 Year	2	0	1.000	1.000	2	1	0	0	0	0	9	8	1	1	3	13	38	1.222	0	Post Season Pts.
	0.250	0.000	0.250	0.250	0.000	0.000	0.000	0.000	0.000	0.000	0.250	0.000	0.000	0.000	0.000	0.400	0.000	0.250	0.000	1.400

World Series Points

Years	Ages	W	L	W-L%	ERA	G	GS	GF	CG	SHO	SV	IP	H	R	ER	BB	SO	BF	WHIP	HBP	
1 Year		0	0	0	13.5	1	1	0	0	0	0	2	5	3	3	2	1	14	3.5	1	World Series Pts.
		0.000	0.000	0.000	0.000	0.250	0.250	0.000	0.000	0.000	0.000	0.250	0.000	0.000	0.000	0.000	0.250	0.000	0.000	0.000	1.000

Coaching Career

Year	Team	Coach of	Accomplishments	20 Game Winners	Cy Young	Rank ERA	Rank Saves	Rank WHIP	Rank S.O.'s	Teams League	Comments
2000	S. F. Giants	Pitching		0	0	4	4	7	8	16 Teams	Won N.L. West & Lost Division Series
2001	S. F. Giants	Pitching		0	0	7	4	9	12	16 Teams	Did not make Playoffs
2002	S. F. Giants	Pitching		0	0	2	6	4	13	16 Teams	Won N.L. West & N.L. Championship Series. Lost in World Series
2003	S. F. Giants	Pitching		0	0	2	6	3	9	16 Teams	Won N.L. West & Lost Division Series
2004	S. F. Giants	Pitching		0	0	11	8	10	13	16 Teams	Did not make the Playoffs
2005	S. F. Giants	Pitching		0	0	11	4	12	13	16 Teams	Did not make the Playoffs
2006	S. F. Giants	Pitching		0	0	12	11	8	13	16 Teams	Did not make the Playoffs
2007	S. F. Giants	Pitching		0	0	5	12	5	11	16 Teams	Did not make the Playoffs
2008	S. F. Giants	Pitching		0	1	9	7	13	2	16 Teams	Did not make the Playoffs
2009	S. F. Giants	Pitching	Led N.L. in S.O.'s	0	1	2	8	2	1	16 Teams	Did not make the Playoffs
2010	S. F. Giants	Pitching	Led N.L. in ERA, Saves & S.O.'s	0	0	1	1	3	1	16 Teams	Won N.L. West, Division Series, N.L. Championship. Won World Series
2011	S. F. Giants	Pitching		0	0	2	2	2	2	16 Teams	Did not make the Playoffs
2012	S. F. Giants	Pitching		0	0	5	2	7	7	16 Teams	Won N.L. West, Division Series, N.L. Championship. Won World Series
2013	S. F. Giants	Pitching		0	0	13	7	5	4	16 Teams	Did not make the Playoffs
2014	S. F. Giants	Pitching		0	0	6	5	2	12	16 Teams	Won N.L. West, Division Series, N.L. Championship. Won World Series
2015	S. F. Giants	Pitching		0	0	7	9	5	11	16 Teams	Did not make the Playoffs
2016	S. F. Giants	Pitching		0	0	4	7	4	7	16 Teams	Won Wild Card Game and Lost in Division Series.
2017	S. F. Giants	Pitching		0	0	7	16	10	14	16 Teams	Did not make the Playoffs
				0	2	7	6	7	5		

Years Coached	CY Winners	20 Game Winners	Top 25% ERA	Top 25% Saves	Top 25% WHIP	Top 25% S.O.'s	Division Titles	League Titles	WS Titles	
18	2	0	7	5	7	5	5	4	3	Coaching Pts.
	9.000	6.500	1.500	9.000	6.500	9.000	6.500	12.500	12.000	12.000 / 84.500

<u>Hall of Fame Points</u>

Playing Career Points	46.250
Post Season Points	1.400
World Series Points	1.000
Writers Association Pts.	0.000
Military/Lifetime Achievement	0.000
Coaching Points	84.500
Grand Total HOF Points	133.150

A Fan's Perspective

Sain, Johnny

Personal Life

John Franklin Sain was born in the tiny town of Havana, Arkansas on September 25, 1917, to Eva and John Sain. No information on siblings was available. Starting in late 1942, Sain served in the United States Navy during

Sain married his first wife Doris May McBride on October 1, 1945, and had four children: John Jr., Sharyl, Ronda, and Randy. The couple divorced in 1970. Sain married his second wife Mary Ann Zaremba, on August 24, 1972. They had no children together.

Baseball Career

Sain pitched for 11 years, winning 139 games and losing 116 in his career and compiled an earned run average of 3.49. Sain went 20-14 in 1946, 21-12 in 1947, and 24-15 in 1948 and was the first Braves' pitcher in franchise history to record three consecutive twenty-win seasons. Sain started 245 games and threw 140 complete games, 57.1% of the games he pitched. His best years were those immediately after World War II, when he won 100 games for the Boston Braves, before being traded to the New York Yankees during the 1951 season. .

Achievements

- Coached 16 pitchers who won at least 20 games in a season: (Yankees 1, Twins 2, Tigers 2. White Sox 7).
- Coached 3 Cy Young Winners (1 Yankees & 2 Yankees).
- Coached 2 Pitching Staffs that led the league in Saves: (1961 & 1974).
- Coached 2 Pitching Staffs that led the league in WHIP: (1962 & 1963).
- Coached 1 Pitching Staff that led the league in Strikeouts: (1969),
- Coached 5 Pitching Staffs that won the Pennant: (1961 - 1963, 1965 & 1968).
- Coached 3 Pitching Staffs that won the World Series: (1961, 1963 & 1968).

Hall of Fame

Johnny Sains Hall of Fame Statistical Point Total was 154. It is a shame there is no current room in Cooperstown for someone who accomplished so much as a player and pitching coach. There is a hole in the system. Yes, the case can be made that Johnny Sain is the best pitching coach of all time, but there are others worthy of mention, too. The Hall should find a way to open its doors to great contributors to the sport that don't fit into narrower definitions.

Summary Analysis

As good a pitcher as Sain was as a player, he was a better teacher. Sain spent many years as a well-regarded but outspoken pitching coach for the Athletics, Yankees, Minnesota Twins, Detroit Tigers, Chicago White Sox and Atlanta Braves. During the 1960s, Sain coached pitchers of five of the American League's pennant-winning teams.

While serving as the Yankees pitching coach, Sain picked up an apple one day and poked a broken car antenna through it. Spinning the apple, Sain came to the idea that he could do the same with a baseball by inserting a wooden rod into it, enabling him to spin the ball differently, imitating the spins used for different pitches. Sain eventually patented the idea and sold it from his home in Arkansas. An independent thinker among coaches, Sain tended to be admired by his pitchers, but he battled with at least two of his managers, Sam Mele of the Twins, and Mayo Smith of the Tigers when he disagreed with them. In each case, Sain was fired, but soon followed when his pitching staff suffered from Sain's absence. Sain was also well known for ignoring running drills that pitchers despised. He frequently told pitchers and managers "You don't run the damn ball across the plate. If running did it, they'd look for pitchers on track teams.

Jim Bouton, in his book *Ball Four*, expressed unreserved admiration for Sain, who had been his pitching tutor in New York during his first two Major League seasons, 1962 and 1963. Bouton openly wished to pitch for the 1969 Tigers in order to have a chance to again benefit from Sain's coaching. Sain and Bouton were briefly reunited in the Atlanta Braves system in 1978. Bouton has been said that Sain was the best pitching coach he ever encountered. "If he had an idea that he thought could be of value to you, he would tell you about it to try to help you. But by the time he finished visiting with you about it, you would think that you'd thought of it yourself". Many Pitchers won 20 or more games under Sain's coaching including Hall of Fame pitchers Jim Kaat and Whitey Ford.

The Baseball Hall of Fame

Player/Coach Hall of Fame Criteria Points

Sain, Johnny

Position: Pitcher

Born : September 25, 1917
Died: November 7, 2006
From: Havana, AR
Bats: Right
Throws: Right

Height: 6' 4"   USC 193 cm
Weight: 195 lbs.   88 Kg.
Debut: September 16, 1979
Final Game: September 19, 1995

Playing Career

Years	Ages	W	L	W-L%	ERA	G	GS	GF	CG	SHO	SV	IP	H	R	ER	BB	SO	BF	WHIP	HBP	
162 Game Avg.		14	17	0.545	3.49	43	25	13	14	2	5	220	222	98	85	64	94	3	931	1.300	Career Pts.
11 Yrs		139	116	0.545	3.49	412	245	125	140	18	53	2125.2	2145	947	824	619	910	30	8998	1.300	38.750
		3.750	0.000	4.500	5.750	3.000	1.000	1.500	3.000	2.000	1.000	3.750	0.000	0.000	0.000	0.000	2.000	0.000	0.000	5.500	

Post Season Points

Years	W	L	W-L%	ERA	G	GS	GF	CG	SHO	SV	IP	H	R	ER	BB	SO	BF	WHIP	HBP	Post Season Pts.
None	0	0	0	0	0	0	0	0	0	0	0	0	0	0	0	0	0	0	0	0.000
	0.000	0.000	0.000	0.000	0.000	0.000	0.000	0.000	0.000	0.000	0.000	0.000	0.000	0.000	0.000	0.000	0.000	0.000	0.000	

World Series Points

Years	Ages	W	L	W-L%	ERA	G	GS	GF	CG	SHO	SV	IP	H	R	ER	BB	SO	BF	WHIP	HBP	
2	2	0.500	2.64	8	2	2	2	1	0	30.2	27	9	9	6	15	1	127	1.076			World Series Pts.
0.400	0.000	0.000	1.200	0.400	0.250	0.250	0.400	0.250	0.000	0.600	0.000	0.000	0.000	0.000	0.400	0.000	0.000	1.400			5.550

Coaching Career

Year	Team	Coach of	Accomplishments	20 Game Winners	Cy Young	Rank ERA	Rank Saves	Rank WHIP	Rank S.O.'s	Teams League	Comments
1959	Kansas City	Pitching		0	0	8	7	7	7	8 Teams	Did not Make the Playoffs
				0	0	0	0	0	0		

Coaching Career

Year	Team	Coach of	Accomplishments	20 Game Winners	Cy Young	Rank ERA	Rank Saves	Rank WHIP	Rank S.O.'s	Teams League	Comments
1961	New York Yankees	Pitching	Led A.L. in Saves	1	1	2	1	2	4	10 Teams	Won A.L. Pennant & Won World Series
1962	New York Yankees	Pitching	Led A.L. in WHIP	2	0	3	2	1	6	10 Teams	Won A.L. Pennant & Lost World Series
1963	New York Yankees	Pitching	Led A.L. in WHIP	2	0	2	4	1	3	10 Teams	Won A.L. Pennant & Won World Series
				5	1	2	2	3	0		

Coaching Career

Year	Team	Coach of	Accomplishments	20 Game Winners	Cy Young	Rank ERA	Rank Saves	Rank WHIP	Rank S.O.'s	Teams League	Comments
1965	Minnesota Twins	Pitching		1	0	3	3	4	6	10 Teams	Won A.L. Pennant & Lost World Series
1966	Minnesota Twins	Pitching		1	0	2	9	2	4	10 Teams	Did not Make the Playoffs
				2	0	1	0	1	0		

Coaching Career

Year	Team	Coach of	Accomplishments	20 Game Winners	Cy Young	Rank ERA	Rank Saves	Rank WHIP	Rank S.O.'s	Teams League	Comments
1967	Detroit Tigers	Pitching		1	0	6	3	2	3	10 Teams	Did not Make the Playoffs
1968	Detroit Tigers	Pitching		1	1	7	3	2	3	10 Teams	Won A.L. Pennant & Won World Series
1969	Detroit Tigers	Pitching	Led A.L. in S.O.'s	0	1	4	8	4	1	12 Teams	Did not Make the Playoffs
				2	2	0	0	2	1		

Coaching Career

Year	Team	Coach of	Accomplishments	20 Game Winners	Cy Young	Rank ERA	Rank Saves	Rank WHIP	Rank S.O.'s	Teams League	Comments
1971	Chicago White Sox	Pitching		1	0	4	5	8	3	12 Teams	Did Not Make Playoffs
1972	Chicago White Sox	Pitching		2	0	8	2	5	3	12 Teams	Did Not Make Playoffs
1973	Chicago White Sox	Pitching		1	0	7	5	8	5	12 Teams	Did Not Make Playoffs
1974	Chicago White Sox	Pitching	Led A.L. in Saves	2	0	11	1	10	6	12 Teams	Did Not Make Playoffs
1975	Chicago White Sox	Pitching		1	0	8	2	11	7	12 Teams	Did Not Make Playoffs
				7	7	0	3	0	2		

Coaching Career

Year	Team	Coach of	Accomplishments	20 Game Winners	Cy Young	Rank ERA	Rank Saves	Rank WHIP	Rank S.O.'s	Teams League	Comments
1977	Atlanta Braves	Pitching		0	0	12	10	12	4	12 Teams	Did Not Make Playoffs
1985	Atlanta Braves	Pitching		0	0	12	11	12	11	12 Teams	Did Not Make Playoffs
1986	Atlanta Braves	Pitching		0	0	10	8	11	8	12 Teams	Did Not Make Playoff
				0	0	0	0	0	0		

Years Coached	CY Winners	20 Game Winners	Top 25% ERA	Top 25% Saves	Top 25% WHIP	Top 25% S.O.'s	Division Titles	League Titles	WS Titles	
16.5	1	16	3	5	6	3	5	5	1	Coaching Pts.
9.000	9.000	20.000	4.000	6.500	6.500	4.000	12.500	15.000	12.000	98.500

Hall of Fame Points

Playing Career Points	38.750
Post Season Points	0.000
World Series Points	5.550
Writers Association Pts.	0.000
Military/Lifetime Achievement	12.000
Coaching Points	98.500
Grand Total HOF Points	154.800

A Fan's Perspective

Stottlemyre, Mel

Personal Life

Melvin Leon Stottlemyre was born on November 13, 1941, in Hazleton, Missouri, to Vernon and Lorene Ellen Miles. He was the third of five children.

Stottlemyre married Jean, in 1964, and the couple had three sons, Todd, Mel Jr., and Jason, died of leukemia at the age of 11. Todd & Mel Jr. followed their father by becoming major-league pitchers.

Baseball Career

Stottlemyre was called up midseason in 1964, and went 9–3 to help the Yankees to their fifth consecutive pennant. In the 1964 World Series, Stottlemyre faced Bob Gibson of the St. Louis Cardinals three times in the seven-game Series. Stottlemyre was named to the American League's All-Star team and won 20 games in the 1965 season. In addition, he led the AL with 18 complete games, 291 innings pitched, and 1,188 batters faced. In 1966, Stottlemyre was an All-Star and won 20 games in the 1968 and 1969 seasons and threw 40 shutouts in his 11-season career which ties for 44th best all-time. After enduring years of regular cortisone shots in his shoulder to numb the pain, Stottlemyre was diagnosed with a torn rotator cuff after 15 starts in 1974, ending his career at the age of 32. The Yankees released Stottlemyre before the 1975 season and he retired with 164 career wins and a 2.97 ERA.

Achievements

- Coached 7 pitchers who won 20 plus games in a season – (Yankees 4, Mets 3).
- Coached 3 Cy Young Winners (1 Yankees & 1 Yankees).
- Coached 6 Pitching Staffs that led the league in Saves – (129697, 1998, 1996, 1999, 2001, 2004).
- Coached 2 Pitching Staffs that led the league in WHIP – (1989 & `).
- Coached 3 Pitching Staff that led the league in Strikeouts – (1988, 1989 & 1991),
- Coached 7 Pitching Staffs whose team won the Pennant – (1986, 1996, 1998,1999, 2000, 2001 & 2003).
- Coached 5 Pitching Staffs whose team won the World Series – (1986, 1996, 1998,1999, & 2000).

A Fan's Perspective

Hall of Fame

Mel Stottlemyre's Hall of Fame Statistical Point Total was 238.250. It is a shame that there currently is no room in Cooperstown for someone who has accomplished so much as a pitcher and pitching coach. There is a hole in the system where a great contributor like Mel Stottlemyre fell into. His great career was cut short due to injury which made his total numbers less than they could have been, but he re-invented his career as a pitching coach. Stottlemyer is a case for The Hall of Fame to create a way to open a door to great contributors that don't fit into narrower definitions. Mel Stottlemyre is a Hall of Famer and needs to be Inducted, or elected, so his family can enjoy his status as one of the best of all-time.

Summary Analysis

In 1977, Stottlemyre became a roving instructor for the Seattle Mariners. He spent five seasons in that position and was hired by the New York Mets as their pitching coach in November 1983. He oversaw Dwight Gooden's National League Rookie of the Year and Cy Young Award seasons in 1984 and 1985. Stottlemyre served in the role for ten years (including the 1986 World Series championship team) and then followed that by serving a two-year stint as the Houston Astros pitching coach.

In 1996, Stottlemyre joined the Yankees coaching staff along with the incoming manager Joe Torre. Stottlemyre helped lower the team ERA from 4.65 in 1996 to 3.84 in 1997. Under Stottlemyre, the Yankee team averaged an ERA of 4.23 from 1996 to 2005. The pitching staff was regarded as a major factor in the team's dynasty years when they won four World Series Championships in five years.

After 10 seasons, Stottlemyre resigned his coaching position on October 12, 2005, following the Yankees' defeat in the 2005 American League Division Series.
Stottlemyre was named pitching coach of the Seattle Mariners the 2008 season. Following the season, Stottlemyre retired from baseball.

Player/Coach Hall of Fame Criteria Points

Stottlemeyre, Mel

Position
Pitcher

Born : November 23, 1941	Height:	6' 1" USC 185 cm
Died: January 13, 2019	Weight:	178 lbs. 80 Kg.
From: Hazelton, Mo.	Debut	August 12, 1964
Bats: Right	Final Game	August 16, 1974
Throw Right		

Playing Career

N. Y. Mets	L	W-L%	ERA	G	GS	GF	CG	SHO	SV	IP	H	R	ER	BB	SO	BF	WHIP	HBP	
N. Y. Mets	13	0.541	2.97	34	34	0	14	4	0	253	231	95	83	77	119	4	1042	1.219	
164	139	0.541	2.97	360	356	3	152	40	1	2661.1	2435	1003	878	809	1257	44	10972	1.219	Career Pts.
5.500	0.000	4.500	11.500	2.500	4.500	0.000	3.750	4.500	0.000	4.500	0.000	0.000	0.000	0.000	3.000	0.000	0.000	9.250	53.500

Post Season Points

Years	W	L	W-L%	ERA	G	GS	GF	CG	SHO	SV	IP	H	R	ER	BB	SO	BF	WHIP	HBP	
	0	0	0	0	0	0	0	0	0	0	0	0	0	0	0	0	0	0	0	Post Season Pts.
	0.000	0.000	0.000	0.000	0.000	0.000	0.000	0.000	0.000	0.000	0.000	0.000	0.000	0.000	0.000	0.000	0.000	0.000	0.000	0.000

World Series Points

Years	Ages	G	PA	AB	R	H	2B	3B	HR	RBI	SB	CS	BB	SO	BA	OBP	SLG	OPS	TB	
		1	1	0.500	3.15	3	3	0	1	0	0	20	18	8	7	6	12	0	84	1.200
		0.250	0.000	0.000	1.000	0.250	4.000	0.000	0.250	0.000	0.000	0.400	0.000	0.000	0.000	0.000	0.400	0.000	0.000	1.200

World Series points total: **7.750**

Coaching Career

Year	Team	Coach of	Accomplishments	20 Game Winners	Cy Young	Rank ERA	Rank Saves	Rank WHIP	Rank S.O.'s	Teams League	Comments
1984	N. Y. Mets	Pitching		0	0	8	2	10	11	12 Teams	Did not make playoffs.
1985	N. Y. Mets	Pitching	Led N.L. in S.O.'s	1	1	3	7	2	1	12 Teams	Did not make playoffs.
1986	N. Y. Mets	Pitching	Led N.L. in ERA	0	0	1	3	2	2	12 Teams	Won N.L. East, N.L. Championship & World Series.
1987	N. Y. Mets	Pitching	Led N.L. in Saves	0	0	4	1	2	4	12 Teams	Did not make playoffs.
1988	N. Y. Mets	Pitching	Led N.L. in Saves	1	0	4	1	3	4	12 Teams	Won N.L. East & Lost in N.L. Championship
1989	N. Y. Mets	Pitching	Led N.L. in ERA, WHIP & S.O.'s	0	0	1	2	1	1	12 Teams	Did not make playoffs.
1990	N. Y. Mets	Pitching	Led N.L. in S.O.'s	1	0	4	6	2	1	12 Teams	Did not make playoffs.
1991	N. Y. Mets	Pitching		0	0	4	9	4	2	12 Teams	Did not make playoffs.
1992	N. Y. Mets	Pitching		0	0	10	9	4	2	12 Teams	Did not make playoffs.
1993	N. Y. Mets	Pitching		0	0	6	14	6	12	14 Teams	Did not make playoffs.
10 Years				3	1	3	5	6	6		

Coaching Career

Year	Team	Coach of	Accomplishments	20 Game Winners	Cy Young	Rank ERA	Rank Saves	Rank WHIP	Rank S.O.'s	Teams League	Comments
1994	Houston Astros	Pitching		0	0	5	6	5	5	14 Teams	Did not make playoffs.
1995	Houston Astros	Pitching		0	0	5	12	7	3	14 Teams	Did not make playoffs.
2 Years				0	0	0	0	0	1		

Coaching Career

Year	Team	Coach of	Accomplishments	20 Game Winners	Cy Young	Rank ERA	Rank Saves	Rank WHIP	Rank S.O.'s	Teams League	Comments
1996	New York Yankees	Led A.L. in Saves		1	0	5	1	4	2	14 Teams	Won A.L. East, Div. Champ., A.L. Championship & Won World Series
1997	New York Yankees	Led A.L. in ERA		1	0	1	5	3	2	14 Teams	Lost A.L. Division Series.
1998	New York Yankees	Led A.L. in ERA & WHIP		0	0	1	2	1	4	14 Teams	Won A.L. East, Div. Champ., A.L. Championship & Won World Series
1999	New York Yankees	Led A.L. in Saves		0	0	2	1	2	3	14 Teams	Won A.L. East, Div. Champ., A.L. Championship & Won World Series
2000	New York Yankees			0	0	6	7	2	4	14 Teams	Won A.L. East, Div. Champ., A.L. Championship & Won World Series
2001	New York Yankees	Led A.L. in Saves & S.O.'s		1	1	3	1	3	1	14 Teams	Won A.L. East, Div. Champ., A.L. Championship & Lost World Series
2002	New York Yankees			0	0	4	2	2	2	14 Teams	Won A.L. East & Lost Division Series
2003	New York Yankees			1	0	3	2	3	2	14 Teams	Won A.L. East, Div. Champ., A.L. Championship & Lost World Series
2004	New York Yankees	Led A.L. in Saves		0	0	6	1	5	5	14 Teams	Won A.L. East, Div. Champ., & Lost A.L. Championship
2005	New York Yankees			0	0	9	4	8	6	14 Teams	Won A.L. East Division & Lost Division Championship
10 Years				4	1	6	9	8	8		

Coaching Career

Year	Team	Coach of	Accomplishments	20 Game Winners	Cy Young	Rank ERA	Rank Saves	Rank WHIP	Rank S.O.'s	Teams League	Comments
2006	Seattle Mariners			0	0	11	4	11	9	14 Teams	

Years Coached	CY Winners	20 Game Winners	Top 25% ERA	Top 25% Saves	Top 25% WHIP	Top 25% S.O.'s	Division Titles	League Titles	WS Titles	
23	2	7	9	15	14	15	9	7	5	Coaching Pts.
14.000	6.000	21.000	11.500	20.000	17.000	20.000	22.500	21.000	20.000	173.000

Hall of Fame Points

Playing Career Points	53.500
Post Season Points	0.000
World Series Points	7.750
Writers Association Pts.	0.000
Military/Lifetime Achievement	0.000
Coaching Points	173.000
Grand Total HOF Points	**234.250**

A Fan's Perspective

Turner, Jim" Colonel or Milkman Jim"

Personal Life

James Riley Turner was born August 6, 1903, in Antioch, Davidson County, TN to Charles Turner and Hattie Thomas Bess. He was the fourth of six children.

He married Annie Pauline Sanford in 1926 with the couple having two daughters, Dorothy Jean, and Jacquelyn Ann.

Baseball Career

Jim Turner's Major League did not reach the big leagues until he was 33 years old, after 14 seasons of minor league ball. After making his big-league debut in 1937 at age 33, Turner enjoyed his most successful season that year, winning 20 games and leading the National League in complete games with 24, shutouts 5, and ERA with 2.38. In 231 career regular season games, Turner won 69 and lost 60 with a 3.22 lifetime, and 329 strikeouts. From 1937 through 1945, he played for the Boston Braves (1937–1939), Cincinnati Reds (1940–42) and New York Yankees (1942–45). He was a member of two World Series championship teams, the 1940 Reds and the 1943 Yankees, as well as the 1942 Yankees team that won the American League pennant. In two postseason appearances, Turner was 0–1 with a 6.43 ERA and 4 strikeouts in 7 innings pitched.

Achievements

- Coached 14 pitchers who won at least 20 games in a year:(Yankees (8) & Reds (4).
- Coached 5 Pitching Staffs that led the league in ERA:(Yankees 1952, 1953, 1955, 1957, 1958).
- Coached 7 Pitching Staffs that led the league in Saves: Yankees 1949, 1950, 1953, 1954, 1956 - 1958).
- Coached 1 Cy Young winners: (Yankees 1958).
- Coached 1 Pitching Staffs that led the league in WHIP:(Yankees 1953).
- Coached 6 Pitching Staffs that led the league in Strikeouts:(Yankees 1949 - 1951 & 1957, & 1959).
- Coached 8 Pitching Staffs that won the Pennant: (Yankees 1949 – 1953, 1955, 1957 & Reds 1961).
- Coached 6 Pitching Staffs that won the World Series:(Yankees 1949-1953 & 1956).

A Fan's Perspective

Hall of Fame

Jim Turners Hall of Fame Statistical Point Total was 182. His knowledge of Pitching Staffs had an impact on many pitchers' and deserving of Hall of Fame Induction.

Summary Analysis

When Casey Stengel took over the New York Yankees in 1949, Turner became their pitching coach until 1959. He helped Allie Reynolds, Vic Raschi, Eddie Lopat, Don Larsen, Johnny Sain, Ralph Terry, Whitey Ford, and many others develop their pitching skills. After the 1959 season, Club President, Dan Topping, fired Turner, even though he had been a major reason for the Yankees success for eleven years.

Turner wasn't out of Baseball long when he was hired to manage the Nashville Vols on October 27,1960. After the year Turner was hired by the Cincinnati Reds as their pitching coach. In his five years there, he helped six pitchers become 20-game winners and the 1961 team win the National League Pennant only to lose to the Yankees.

Turner returned to the Yankees in 1966 but it was a team that had been in decline since 1964. One of his students, Jim Bouton criticized Turner by claiming Turner (his pitching coach with the Yankees from 1966 to 1968) was a front-runner, who only wanted to be associated with successful pitchers. He was not his biggest fan and had the impression Turner only liked the big stars and didn't seem interested in lesser pitchers. Turner tried hard to get Bouton to throw a curveball the way Whitey Ford did – but he couldn't grasp the technique which was not easy to teach. Bouton admitted he was also a kid and maybe he should have tried a little harder to listen to Milkman Jim.

Jim Turner served for 24 seasons as pitching coach with the Yankees and Reds. He coached on seven Yankees world championship teams (1949 - 1953, 1956, 1958 & 1966–73)) and Reds (1961–65 as their pitching coach, working for ten pennant-winning clubs over a 24-year span. He retired in 1973 after 51 consecutive years in Baseball.

Player/Coach Hall of Fame Criteria Points

Turner, Jim
Position
Pitcher

Born:	August 6, 1903
Died:	August 6, 1903
From:	Antioch, TN
Bats:	Left
Throw	Right

Height	6' 0" USC	183	cm	
Weight:	185 lbs.	83	Kg.	
Debut	April 30, 1937			
Final Game	September 13, 1945			

Playing Career

Years	W	L	W-L%	ERA	G	GS	GF	CG	SHO	SV	IP	H	R	ER	BB	SO	BF	WHIP	
162 Game Avg.	13	12	0.535	3.22	45	23	17	13	2	4	220	218	94	79	55	64	913	1.242	
9 Yrs	69	60	0.535	3.22	231	119	86	69	8	20	1132	1123	482	405	283	329	4697	1.242	Career Pts.
	2.000	0.000	4.500	8.500	1.500	1.000	1.000	1.500	1.000	0.500	1.500	0.000	0.000	0.000	0.000	1.000	0.000	8.000	32.000

Post Season Points

Years	W	L	W-L%	ERA	G	GS	GF	CG	SHO	SV	IP	H	R	ER	BB	SO	BF	WHIP	HBP
None	0	0	0	0	0	0	0	0	0	0	0	0	0	0	0	0	0	0	Post Season Pts.
	0.000	0.000	0.000	0.000	0.000	0.000	0.000	0.000	0.000	0.000	0.000	0.000	0.000	0.000	0.000	0.000	0.000	0.000	0.000

World Series Points

Years	W	L	W-L%	ERA	G	GS	GF	CG	SHO	SV	IP	H	R	ER	BB	SO	BF	WHIP	
2 Years	0	1	0.000	6.43	2	1	1	0	0	0	8	8	5	5	1	4	0	28	World Series Pts.
	0.000	0.000	0.000	0.000	0.250	0.250	0.250	0.000	0.000	0.000	0.250	0.000	0.000	0.000	0.000	0.250	0.000	0.250	1.500

Coaching Career

Year	Team	Coach of	Accomplishments	20 Game Winners	Cy Young	Rank ERA	Rank Saves	Rank WHIP	Rank S.O.'s	Teams League	Comments
1949	New York Yankees	Pitching	Led A.L. in saves & S.O.'s	0	0	2	1	4	1	8 Teams	Won A.L. Pennant & World Series
1950	New York Yankees	Pitching	Led A.L. in saves & S.O.'s	0	0	3	1	3	1	8 Teams	Won A.L. Pennant & World Series
1951	New York Yankees	Pitching	Led A.L. S.O.'s	2	0	3	2	3	1	8 Teams	Won A.L. Pennant & World Series
1952	New York Yankees	Pitching	Led. A.L. in ERA	1	0	1	2	3	4	8 Teams	Won A.L. Pennant & World Series
1953	New York Yankees	Pitching	Led. A.L. in ERA, Saves & WHIP	0	0	1	1	1	6	8 Teams	Won A.L. Pennant & World Series
1954	New York Yankees	Pitching	Led A.L. in Saves	1	0	3	1	3	5	8 Teams	
1955	New York Yankees	Pitching		0	0	1	2	3	2	8 Teams	Won A.L. Pennant
1956	New York Yankees	Pitching	Led A.L. in Saves	0	0	2	1	3	3	8 Teams	Won A.L. Pennant & World Series
1957	New York Yankees	Pitching	Led. A.L. in ERA, Saves &S.O.'s	0	0	1	1	3	1	8 Teams	Won A.L. Pennant
1958	New York Yankees	Pitching	Led. A.L. in ERA, Saves &S.O.'s	1	1	1	1	2	1	8 Teams	
1959	New York Yankees	Pitching	Led A.L. S.O.'s	0	0	3	2	4	1	8 Teams	
1966	New York Yankees	Pitching		0	0	5	7	6	9	10 Teams	Did not make playoffs
1967	New York Yankees	Pitching		0	0	4	9	9	8	8 Teams	Did not make playoffs
1968	New York Yankees	Pitching		1	0	5	10	6	9	8 Teams	Did not make playoffs
1969	New York Yankees	Pitching		1	0	2	17	2	12	10 Teams	Did not make playoffs
1970	New York Yankees	Pitching		1	0	3	2	3	11	10 Teams	Did not make playoffs
1971	New York Yankees	Pitching		0	0	7	12	3	12	10 Teams	Did not make playoffs
1972	New York Yankees	Pitching		0	0	6	3	12	12	10 Teams	Did not make playoffs
1973	New York Yankees	Pitching		0	0	3	4	3	11	10 Teams	Did not make playoffs
19 Years				8	1	8	12	3	7		

Coaching Career

Year	Team	Coach of	Accomplishments	20 Game Winners	Cy Young	Rank ERA	Rank Saves	Rank WHIP	Rank S.O.'s	Teams League	Comments
1961	Cincinatti Reds	Pitching	Led N.L. in Saves	1	0	3	1	2	3	10 Teams	1961 - N. L. Pennant - Lost World Series
1962	Cincinatti Reds	Pitching		2	0	5	4	7	8	10 Teams	Did not make playoffs
1963	Cincinatti Reds	Pitching		1	0	5	4	7	3	10 Teams	Did not make playoffs
1964	Cincinatti Reds	Pitching	Led N.L. in S.O.'s	0	0	2	4	2	1	10 Teams	Did not make playoffs
1965	Cincinatti Reds	Pitching	Led N.L. in S.O.'s	2	0	9	6	9	1	10 Teams	Did not make playoffs
5 Years				6	0	1	1	2	2		

Hall of Fame Points

Playing Career Points	32.000
Post Season Points	0.000
World Series Points	1.500
Writers Association Pts.	0.000
Military/Lifetime Achievement	0.000
Coaching Points	148.500
Grand Total HOF Points	**182.000**

Years Coached	CY Winners	20 Game Winners	Top 25% ERA	Top 25% Saves	Top 25% WHIP	Top 25% S.O.'s	Division Titles	League Titles	WS Titles	
24	1	14	9	13	5	9	8	8	5	Coaching Pts.
14.000	4.000	20.000	11.500	17.000	6.500	11.500	20.000	24.000	20.000	148.500

A Fan's Perspective

The Baseball Hall of Fame

Black, Harry "Bud"

Personal Life

Harry Ralston "Bud" Black was born June 30, 1957 to Harry Black Sr. in Northern California. No information was found on his mother. Black is a graduate of Mark Morris High School in Longview, Washington. Black attended San Diego State University, pitching for the Aztecs in his junior and senior seasons and graduating in 1979

Black married Nanette Steffen on February 9, 1985. The couple have two daughters, Jamie, and Jessie.

Baseball Career

Black was selected by the Seattle Mariners in the 17th round of 1979 Major League Baseball draft, the 417th overall pick. The Mariners assigned him to the San Jose Missions of the California League, where he pitched in 17 games, mostly in relief, and posted a 3.00 ERA. Black played in MLB from 1981 through 1995, most notably for the Kansas City Royals and Cleveland Indians,

Achievements

- Postseason Appearances: 2 (2017 & 2018 - Wild card)
- Coached 2 Pitching Staffs that led the league in Saves – (1990 & 1992).
- Coached 2 Pitching Staffs whose team won their Division – (2004 & 2005).
- Coached 1 Pitching Staff whose team won the World Series – (2004).
- Managed 2 Teams that played in the NL Wild Card Game – (2017 & 2018)
- National League Manager of the Year in 2010 for the Colorado Rockies.
- Coach 1 Cy Young Winner (Bartolo Colon in 2005).

Hall of Fame

Bud Blacks Hall of Fame Statistical Point Total was 98.550 based. He is still managing so his numbers may continue to grow. Black may become a case where his overall career could lead him to the Hall of Fame when he is finished. He has substantial statistics as a player, coach and manager that cannot be discounted when the final tabulation is in.

Summary Analysis

On November 23, 1999, Anaheim Angels manager Mike Scioscia hired Black to be the team's pitching coach. Black took over an Angels starting rotation that was considered subpar by the media in the previous season. He worked with young pitchers like Jarrod Washburn, Ramón Ortiz, and Scott Schoeneweis. He became the pitching coach for the Anaheim Angels and under Black's direction in 2002, Angel's pitchers combined for a 3.69 ERA and a .247 both good for 4th best in the league. He was often mentioned as a candidate when managerial jobs opened up after the Angels won the 2002 World Series. On October 24, 2003, the Angels gave Black a one-year contract extension to remain with the team through the 2004 season. Black remained with the Angels and coached Bartolo Colón in 2005 during his AL Cy Young-winning season. and after the 2006 season, he was named skipper of the San Diego Padres

Black was hired on November 8, 2006, to manage the Padres. Despite a last-place finish for the Padres in 2008, Black returned to finish his contract in 2009. During the 2009 season, Black was given a contract extension for the 2010 season with a club option for 2011. During the 2010 season, the Padres gave Black another three-year extension through 2013, with club options in 2014 and 2015. In 2010, Black presided over the worst collapse in Padres history when they went on a ten-game losing streak with a little over a month left in the season, and squandered a 6+½-game lead over the Giants for the NL West title. Black was the winner of the 2010 National League Manager of the Year Award, On June 15, 2015, Black was fired after eight-plus seasons with the Padres after the team started 2015 at 32–33 and was six games behind in the National League West. He finished with a record of 649 wins and 713 losses.

On November 7, 2016, the Colorado Rockies hired Black as its new manager and is still the manager of the team going into the 2024 season.

The Baseball Hall of Fame

Player/Coach Player/Coach Hall of Fame Criteria Points

Black, Bud

Position	Pitcher	Born: June 20, 1957	Height: 6' 2" USC 188 cm
		From: San Mateo, CA	Weight: 180 lbs. 81 Kg.
		Bats: Left	Debut September 15, 1981
		Throw Left	Final Game July 9, 1991

Playing Career

Years	Ages	W	L	W-L%	ERA	G	GS	GF	CG	SHO	SV	IP	H	R	ER	BB	SO	HBP	BF	WHIP	
162 Game Avg	12	11	0.511	3.84	39	29	4	3	1	1	201	194	96	86	21	61	5	845	1.267		
15 7Yrs	121	116	0.511	3.84	398	296	42	32	12	11	2033	1978	982	876	217	623	49	8627	1.267	Career Pts.
	3.750	0.000	3.000	3.000	3.000	3.750	0.500	1.000	1.500	0.500	3.750	0.000	0.000	0.000	0.000	1.500	0.000	0.000	6.750	32.000

Post Season Points

Years	Ages	W	L	W-L%	ERA	G	GS	GF	CG	SHO	SV	IP	H	R	ER	BB	SO	HBP	BF	WHIP	
None		0	1	0.000	3.45	4	2	0	0	0	0	15.2	18	7	6	2	5	0	70	1.468	Post Season Pts.
	0.000	0.000	0.000	0.250	0.400	0.250	0.000	0.000	0.000	0.000	0.400	0.000	0.000	0.000	0.000	0.250	0.000	0.000	0.250	1.800

World Series Points

Years	Years	G	AB	R	H	2B	3B	HR	RBI	SB	CS	BB	SO	BA	OBP	SLG	OPS	TB	HBP	World	
Years	Ages	W	L	W-L%	ERA	G	GS	GF	CG	SHO	SV	IP	H	R	ER	BB	SO	HBP	BF	WHIP	
None		0	1	0.000	5.06	2	1	1	0	0	0	5	4	3	3	5	4	0	23	1.68	World Series Pts.
	0.000	0.000	0.000	0.000	0.250	0.250	0.250	0.000	0.000	0.000	0.250	0.000	0.000	0.000	0.000	0.250	0.000	0.000	0.000	1.250

Coaching Career

Year	Team	Coach of	Accomplishments	20 Game Winners	Cy Young	Rank ERA	Rank Saves	Rank WHIP	Rank S.O.'s	Teams League	Comments
2000	Anaheim Angels	Pitching	Led A.L. in Saves	0	0	9	1	11	14	14 Teams	Did Not Make Playoffs
2001	Anaheim Angels	Pitching		0	0	5	7	7	10	14 Teams	Did Not Make Playoffs
2002	Anaheim Angels	Pitching	Led A.L. in Saves	0	0	2	1	3	8	14 Teams	Did Not Make Playoffs
2003	Anaheim Angels	Pitching		0	0	5	6	6	10	14 Teams	Did Not Make Playoffs
2004	Anaheim Angels	Pitching	Led A.L. in S.O.'s.	0	0	4	3	3	1	14 Teams	Won A.L. West & Lost Divisional Series
2005	Anaheim Angels	Pitching	Led A.L. in S.O.'s	1	1	3	4	5	1	14 Teams	Won A.L. West Divisional Series & Lost Championship
				1	1	3	4	2	2		

Years Coached	CY Young Winner	0 Game Winner	Top 25% ERA	Top 25% Saves	Top 25% WHIP	Top 25% S.O.'s	Division Titles	League Titles	WS Titles	
6	1	1	3	4	2	2	2	1	1	Coaching Pts.
1.5	4.000	1.500	4.000	4.000	1.500	1.500	5.000	3.000	4.000	30.000

Managerial Career

Regular Season

Year		Lg	Won	Lost	Ties	W-L%	G	Finish	Post Season Won	Post Season Lost	World Series Won	World Series Lost	Comments
2007	San Diego Padres	NL	89	74	0	0.546	163	3	0	0	0	0	Did Not Make Playoffs
2008	San Diego Padres	NL	63	99	0	0.389	162	5	0	0	0	0	Did Not Make Playoffs
2009	San Diego Padres	NL	75	87	0	0.463	162	4	0	0	0	0	Did Not Make Playoffs
2010	San Diego Padres	NL	90	72	0	0.556	162	2	0	0	0	0	Did Not Make Playoffs
2011	San Diego Padres	NL	71	91	0	0.438	162	5	0	0	0	0	Did Not Make Playoffs
2012	San Diego Padres	NL	76	86	0	0.469	162	4	0	0	0	0	Did Not Make Playoffs
2013	San Diego Padres	NL	76	86	0	0.469	162	3	0	0	0	0	Did Not Make Playoffs
2014	San Diego Padres	NL	77	85	0	0.475	162	3	0	0	0	0	Did Not Make Playoffs
2015	San Diego Padres	NL	32	33	0	0.492	65	3	0	0	0	0	Did Not Make Playoffs
			649	713	0		1362		0	0	0	0	0 Playoff Appearances

Regular Season

Year		Lg	Won	Lost	Ties	W-L%	G	Finish	Post Season Won	Post Season Lost	World Series Won	World Series Lost	Comments
2017	Colorado Rockies	NL	87	75	0	0.537	162	3	0	1	0	0	Lost N.L. Wild Card Game
2018	Colorado Rockies	NL	91	72	0	0.558	163	2	1	1	0	0	Won N.L. Wild Card Game & Lost Division Series
2019	Colorado Rockies	NL	71	91	0	0.438	162	4	0	0	0	0	Did Not Make Playoffs
2020	Colorado Rockies	NL	26	34	0	0.433	60	4	0	0	0	0	Did Not Make Playoffs
2021	Colorado Rockies	NL	74	87	0	0.460	161	4	0	0	0	0	Did Not Make Playoffs
2022	Colorado Rockies	NL	68	94	0	0.420	162	5	0	0	0	0	Did Not Make Playoffs
2023	Colorado Rockies	NL	40	62	0	0.392	102	5	0	0	0	0	Did Not Make Playoffs
			457	515	0		972		1	4	0	0	2 Playoff Appearances

	Won	Lost	Ties	W-L%	G		Post Won	Post Lost	WS Won	WS Lost	
9 years	649	713	0	0.477	1362		0	0	0	0	0 Playoff Appearances
7 years	457	515	0	0.47	972		1	4	0	0	2 Playoff Appearances
16 years	1106	1228	0	0.474	2334		1	4	0	0	2 Playoff Appearances

Years	Full Season	Total Games	Total Won	Winning Pct	Division Titles	League Titles	W.S. Titles	Win Season	Win Pct	Total
16	14	2334	1106	0.474	0	0	0	4	0.250	Points
11.500	9.000	6.500	6.500	0.000	0.000	0.000	0.000	0.000	0.000	33.500

Hall of Fame Points

Playing Career Points	32.000
Post Season Points	1.800
World Series Points	1.250
Managing Points	33.500
Writers Association Pts.	0.000
Military/Lifetime Achievement	0.000
Coaching Points	30.000

A Fan's Perspective

Brecheen, Harry "The Cat"

Personal Life

Harry David Brecheen was born October 14, 1914, in Broken Bow, Oklahoma to Texans Tom Brecheen and Lucy Tyree who had settled in the small town near the Texas border when Oklahoma was still a territory. He was the first of three children and by the time Harry was 10, his family had relocated to Ada. More interested in sports than school, little Harry seemingly always had a bat, glove, fishing rod, or gun in his hand while growing up on the family farm.

He married his high-school *Vera Caperton* Sept. 16, 1933. The couple did not have any children.

Baseball Career

Brecheen was acquired by the Cardinals in 1938 from the Chicago Cubs after two minor league seasons, but made only three relief appearances during 1940 and did not pitch again at the major league level until 1943. Cardinals beat writer Roy Stockton began referring to rookie Brecheen as "The Cat" because of his quick, feline-like reflexes on the mound and excellent fielding. "Harry the Cat" became such a recognizable nickname that papers did not need to mention Brecheen's surname. Brecheen led or co-led the NL with a 1.000 fielding percentage three times (1944, 1948, and 1950), and had four additional errorless seasons (1940, 1943, 1952, and 1953) in which he did not have enough innings to qualify for the crown. He committed only eight errors in more than 1,900 major-league innings in his 12-year big-league career, Brecheen established his reputation as a big-game pitcher. "He was a real pressure guy," said Joe Cronin of the Red Sox. "When he walked out onto the field, you knew a 'take-charge' guy was in the game."

Brecheen compiled a 133-92 record and impressive 2.92 ERA in 1,907⅔ innings in the regular season. He won 114 games and logged 1,715 innings in eight minor-league seasons. Bracheen's career World Series earned run average of 0.83 was a major league record from 1946 to 1976.

Coaching

After his playing career with the Browns ended in 1953, Brecheen stayed with the club in its move to Baltimore, becoming the pitching coach for the Orioles for the next 14 seasons. In 1954 they relocated to Baltimore, where they were renamed the Orioles in honor of the city's team in the

A Fan's Perspective

International League. The Orioles developed into a model franchise grounded on fundamentals and smart pitching. During Brecheen's 14-year tenure as pitching coach, the Orioles' staff ranked in the top four in ERA for ten years in a row from 1957-1966 and led the league four times. Brecheen helped veterans as he converted 36-year-old Hoyt Wilhelm into a starter in 1959 and the knuckleballer promptly led the league in ERA. Under the Cat's guidance, Robin Roberts, considered washed up in 1961, enjoyed a rebirth. In an era defined by hard-throwing strikeout pitchers, Brecheen preferred fundamentally sound pitchers with good control.

During his career as coach, Brecheen mentored many young pitchers who eventually became All-Stars with the group winning a World Series title in 1966 over the Los Angeles Dodgers. In Baltimore's four-game sweep of the Los Angeles Dodgers in the 1966 World Series, the Orioles yielded just two earned runs in 36 innings. Brecheen retired following the 1967 season.

Achievements

- Coached 1 Pitchers who won 20, or more games in a season:(Orioles 1964).
- Coached 4 Pitching Staffs that led the league in ERA:(Orioles 1960 - 1962 & 1965).
- Coached 2 Pitching Staffs that led the league in Saves:(Orioles 1963 & 1966).
- Coached 3 Pitching Staffs that led the league in WHIP:(Orioles 1958, 1959 & 1961).
- Coached 1 Pitching Staff whose team won the Pennant:(Orioles 1966).
- Coached 1 Pitching Staff whose team won the World Series:(Orioles 1966).

Hall of Fame

Harry Brecheen's Hall of Fame Statistical Point Total was 104.650. Though his pitching career did not accrue enough statistics to lead to the Hall of Fame, his knowledge and handling of Pitching Staffs along with his pitching career was worthy. Brecheen's impact is quantifiable and had such an impact that he is deserving of Hall of Fame Induction.

The Baseball Hall of Fame

Player/Coach Hall of Fame Criteria Points

Brecheen, Harry

Position	Born :	October 14, 1914
Pitcher	Died:	Jauary 17, 2004
	From:	Bethany, OK
	Bats:	Left
	Throws:	Left

Height:	5' 10"	USC 178 cm
Weight:	160 lbs.	72 Kg.
Debut	April 22, 1940	
Final Game	September 13, 1953	

Playing Career

Years	Ages	W	L	W-L%	ERA	G	GS	GF	CG	SHO	SV	IP	H	R	ER	BB	SO	BF	WHIP	
162 Game Avg.		16	11	0.591	2.92	39	29	6	15	3	2	232	211	85	75	14	65	7	110	
12 Yrs		133	92	0.591	2.92	318	240	53	125	25	18	1907	1731	701	618	536	901	7821	1.188	Career Pts.
		3.75	0.000	9.250	11.500	2.000	2.500	1.000	2.500	2.500	0.500	3.000	0.000	0.000	0.000	0.000	2.000	0.000	10.500	51.000

Post Season Points

Years	W	L	W-L%	ERA	G	GS	GF	CG	SHO	SV	IP	H	R	ER	BB	SO	BF	WHIP	
None	0	0	0	0	0	0	0	0	0	0	0	0	0	0	0	0	0	0	Post Season Pts.
	0.000	0.000	0.000	0.000	0.000	0.000	0.000	0.000	0.000	0.000	0.000	0.000	0.000	0.000	0.000	0.000	0.000	0.000	0.000

World Series Points

Years	Years	G	AB	R	H	2B	3B	HR	RBI	SB	CS	BB	SO	BA	OBP	SLG	OPS	TB	HBP	World Series Pts.
	Years	W	L	W-L%	ERA	G	GS	GF	CG	SHO	SV	IP	H	R	ER	BB	SO	BF	WHIP	
	2 Years	4	1	0.8	0.83	7	3	4	3	1	0	32.2	28	3	3.000	12	18	129	1.224	World Series Pts.
		0.800	0.000	1.400	2.000	0.400	0.400	0.400	0.500	0.250	0.000	0.600	0.000	0.000	0.000	0.000	0.600	0.000	1.200	8.650

Coaching Career

Year	Team	Coach of	Accomplishments	20 Game Winners	Cy Young	Rank ERA	Rank Saves	Rank WHIP	Rank S.O.'s	Teams League	Comments
1957	Balltimore Orioles	Pitching		0	0	3	2	2	3	8 Teams	
1958	Balltimore Orioles	Pitching	Lead A.L. in WHIP	0	0	2	2	1	6	8 Teams	
1959	Balltimore Orioles	Pitching	Lead A.L. in WHIP	0	0	2	2	1	5	8 Teams	
1960	Balltimore Orioles	Pitching	Lead A.L. in ERA	0	0	1	6	2	2	8 Teams	
1961	Balltimore Orioles	Pitching	Lead A.L. in ERA and WHIP	0	0	1	3	1	2	10 Teams	
1962	Balltimore Orioles	Pitching	Lead A.L. in ERA	0	0	1	5	3	3	10 Teams	
1963	Balltimore Orioles	Pitching	Lead A.L. in Saves	0	0	4	1	6	7	10 Teams	
1964	Balltimore Orioles	Pitching		1	0	4	3	2	9	10 Teams	
1965	Balltimore Orioles	Pitching	Lead A.L. in ERA	0	0	1	3	2	6	10 Teams	
1966	Balltimore Orioles	Pitching	Lead A.L. in Saves	0	0	4	1	4	2	10 Teams	1966 Pennant & World Series Champions
1967	Balltimore Orioles	Pitching		0	0	6	6	5	4	10 Teams	
				1	0	6	5	7	3		

Years Coached	CY Winners	20 Game Winners	Top 25% ERA	Top 25% Saves	Top 25% WHIP	Top 25% S.O.'s	Division Titles	League Titles	WS Titles	
11	0	1	6	5	7	3	1	1	1	Coaching Pts.
4	1.500	4.000	6.500	6.500	9.000	4.000	2.500	3.000	4.000	45.000

Hall of Fame Points

Playing Career Points	51.000
Post Season Points	0.000
World Series Points	8.650
Writers Association Pts.	0.000
Military/Lifetime Achievement	0.000
Coaching Points	45.000
Grand Total HOF Points	**104.650**

Statistical Review of Accused Steroid Users Before & After Suspected Usage

Player	Years Played	Career Pts.	Post Season Pts.	World Series Pts.	Add-On Pts.	Mil/LT Pts.	Total HOF Pts.	Needed HOF Votes	Comments
Bonds, Barry	22	176.250	3.185	6.875	196.000	0.000	387.310	0	Total Career
Bonds, Barry	14	93.750	4.100	0.000	105.000	0.000	202.850	0	Pre-Steroids
Canseco, Jose	17	64.000	5.300	4.100	56.00	0.000	129.400	0	Total Career
Canseco, Jose	15	54.250	5.300	4.100	34.000	0.000	97.650	0	Pre-Steroids
Clemens, Roger	24	120.500	10.800	8.200	130.000	0.000	269.500	0	Total Career
Clemens, Roger	16	86.050	4.850	5.050	119.000	0.000	114.950	0	Pre-Steroids
Giambi, Jason	20	80.500	10.050	4.000	35.000	0.000	129.550	0	Total Career
Giambi, Jason	5	43.750	0.000	0.000	0.000	0.000	43.750	0	Pre-Steroids
McGwire, Mark	16	86.750	5.650	2.600	65.000	0.000	160.000	0	Total Career
McGwire, Mark	14	68.000	4.850	3.000	63.000	0.000	138.850	0	Pre-Steroids
Palmiero, Raphael	20	113.250	4.500	0.000	12.000	0.000	129.750	0	Total Career
Palmiero, Raphael	14	60.250	4.500	0.000	12.000	0.000	76.750	0	Pre-Steroids
Ramirez, Manny	19	118.500	17.400	7.450	51.000	0.000	194.350	0	Total Career
Ramirez, Manny	7	36.250	7.200	7.450	13.000	0.000	63.900	0	Pre-Steroids
Rodriguez, Alex	22	155.500	13.250	6.050	106.000	0.000	280.8000	0	Total Career
Rodriguez, Alex	6	34.500	3.300	0.000	0.000	0.000	37.800	0	Pre-Steroids
Sosa, Sammy	19	91.000	5.600	0.000	54.000	0.000	150.600	0	Total Career
Sosa, Sammy	13	42.750	5.600	0.000	29.000	0.000	77.350	0	Pre-Steroids
Tejada, Miguel	16	55.750	2.750	0.000	15.000	0.000	73.500	0	Total Career
Tejada, Miguel				0.000		0.000		0	Pre-Steroids

Baseball: The Changing Game

The Different Eras of Baseball History

If you know about baseball history, you realize that several significant events and rule changes throughout the 20th century have divided baseball statistics into different eras which each have their own distinctions.

Dead-Ball Era

Hitters in the 1900s decade were in the dead ball era. The league lacked the modern machinery to tightly stitch baseballs and stadium lights were nonexistent. The results were poor hitting conditions and a ball that did not go as far

WWII Era

The development of a new baseball broke the game out of the dead ball era and things remained moderately stable statistics-wise through the 20s and 30s until World War II caused a major shakeup. In addition to personnel changes, the composition of the ball changed during the World War II era due to materials being used in the war effort.

Age of the Pitcher

Following World War II, the game remained relatively the same from the mid-40s into the late 60s. Throughout the 60s there was a trend evolving in the MLB as pitchers became more dominant and hitting statistics deteriorated. Some baseball traditionalists liked this defensive style of baseball, but most fans called the lack of offense a problem. This "problem" reached its peak in 1968, which is dubbed "*The Year of the Pitcher*". Bob Gibson was the league's best pitcher that year, leading the St. Louis Cardinals to the World Series. In '68 Gibson had a record of 22-9 with a sparkling ERA of 1.12 and a WHIP of 0.85. Gibson was not the only pitcher dominating that year as the league ERA in '68 was 2.98 and was the lowest since 1918. Batting averages were much lower as an average of 301 was the lowest batting average to ever lead a league.

Lowering the Mound

Major League Baseball League officials the league lowered their mounds from 15 inches to 10 inches, the height that is still in use today. This forced pitcher to throw off a shorter mound with the results being the offense began to increase.

The Designated Hitter Enters the American League

League officials made another rule change to introduce even more offense into the game and created the designated hitter. Prior to the 1976 season, pitchers batted for themselves in every single game in both leagues. In 1976, the American League gave teams the designated hitter option by allowing them to put a hitter in the lineup in place of any defender. Getting to replace your weakest hitting player with an athlete whose sole responsibility is hitting the baseball was another major source of inflation for offensive stats. In 2023, the National League incorporated the designated hitter.

The Steroid Era

The game remained relatively the same until the 90s when steroid use became widespread. Many sluggers rose to fame during this era. They were beloved at the time until it was later found out that they were taking performance enhancing drugs. This led to the most controversial era in baseball, power stats exploded in the late 90s and early 2000s before the media uncovered the performance-enhancing drug use behind the explosion. It was obvious when the steroid usage stopped in the MLB as offensive stats returned to pre-steroid levels.

The Launch Angle Era

The game remained the same through the 2000s and the early 2010s until offensive numbers began exploding late in the 2010s and in 2019 saw more home runs than any other season in MLB history. With 4 of the top-5 home run seasons in history happening within the past 5 years, long balls are undeniably trending right now. Many players and fans believed that the MLB changed baseballs to showcase more home runs. This may have been true but the approach to hitting also changed and lower batting averages came into play. The league batting average remained pretty steady through the late 70s, 80s, and even through a lot of the steroid ERA of the 90s and early 2000s. In the 11-season stretch from 1994-2004, Barry Bonds posted a batting average of .315. Sammy Sosa hit

.287 during those same seasons while Mark McGwire also hit .287 from 1994 until his retirement in 2000. Suddenly batting averages began to tumble at the end of the 2000's decade.

Launch Angle Hitting?

The launch angle theory of hitting became popular around the time batting averages began declining. The theory is that a perfectly squared up baseball results in a line drive. Line drives have the highest chance of resulting in a hit of the three hit types (ground ball, line drive, flyball) but rarely result in home runs. For the longest time baseball players were trying to hit line drives. Line drives rarely result in home runs and fly balls are the most common hit resulting in a home run. There is a school of thought in baseball that a home run was a mistake by the hitter. If a hitter is trying to hit a line drive, but gets under the ball, and lifts a fly ball that goes over the fence, it's a good result but actually a mis-hit ball.

Hitters began to hit fly balls as their primary goal instead of line drives. This shift in hitting philosophy created a new term, launch angle. Launch angle refers to the angle of elevation of the ball leaving the bat. This shift in philosophy coincided with the new Statcast sensor system that began being installed in MLB stadiums and used by all 30 teams by 2015. The Statcast sensors calculate the launch angle of every hit. Hitting coaches soon data which showed the optimal launch angle for hitting home runs. The result was a new surge of hitters whose goal was to not hit a line drive but instead to strike the ball from below and create an optimal launch angle that would give them the best chance of hitting a home run.

This approach to hitting results in more home runs but also results in lower rates of getting on base. If a hitter is trying to square the ball up and hit a line drive and he succeeds, the result will be a line drive. If he misses it and gets under the ball, he might still hit a fly ball. If he misses and hits on top of the ball a little bit, he might still find a hole with a hard grounder. By intentionally trying to hit under the ball you reduce your margin for error. Now, hitting too low on the ball results in weak pop-ups or even swings and misses. In certain stadiums, well-hit fly balls will not always result in home runs.

Strikeouts Are Viewed as Just Another Out

With hitters enjoying increased home runs on their stat line and coaches giving them the green light to hit for a lower average, teams look to stock their lineups with guys strong enough to hit home runs, not necessarily well-rounded hitters. The stigma around striking out has disappeared.

A Fan's Perspective

Coaches from Little League to the Major Leagues had always implored their players to shorten up and just look to make contact when you get behind in the count, citing that anything can happen once you put the ball in play and that nothing good can happen if you strike out.

Getting three singles to score a run is difficult and managers began to change their thinking about striking out versus going for the home run. Managers began giving hitters approval to continue swinging hard throughout their at-bats, sacrificing a few singles for the increased chance of hitting a home run and driving in multiple runs with one swing. Looking at strikeout rates over the past 25, seasons shows a dramatic uptick in batters returning to the dugout empty handed. Strikeouts went from being the worst embarrassment for a hitter to a side effect expected in the pursuit of home runs.

In the past, teams could put up with having one all-or-nothing slugger, who could hit 40+ home runs with an average barely above .200. In today's game, managers are routinely penciling in 3 or 4 all-or-nothing hitters into their lineup in the hopes of getting a 3-run homer from one of them. With batting averages declining across the league, the .300-club has become more exclusive than it was in the 90s or 2000s. The MLB produced 40 plus .300 hitters every season up until the launch angle era began at the end of the 2000s decade. Hitters went from having 42 .300 hitters in 2009 to just 23 in 2010.

Most of the other hitters atop the batting average leaderboards are the league's continuing contact hitters. In past decades, each MLB team would have a few .300 hitters with many more in the .290s or high .280s. Those days may be depleted, so maybe fans should appreciate a hitter who can keep their average well into the .300.

This next graphic is the number of players per season that have hit 35 home runs. As home runs have risen in the 2010s, the number of 35-home run seasons should have risen but that has not. More players hit 35 home runs in the 90s or 2000s than in the 2010s. Even in 2016, 2017, and 2018, which were the top-5 home run seasons of all time, there were fewer 35 home run seasons than in previous years. Today a weak hitting shortstop might knock 12 home runs in a season where the same type of player in the 90s would hit 2 or 3. A backup catcher might hit 8 home runs now whereas he might hit 1 or 2 in 1995.

There were many 35-home run seasons in 2019 but the 2020 season only lasted 60 games. There were over 25 players on pace to reach 35 home runs. The top hitters are not any more powerful today than they were in the 80s or 90s. What qualified as an excellent season in 1980 is more or less still the criteria today? Even though we are setting league records in home runs there has not been a single-player home run or RBI record broken in a very long time.

As baseball became populated with stars, and it grew in popularity, the need to distinguish between players became more important and baseball rules changes came with it. Most significantly, in 1917, earned run statistics were defined and began being recorded. This was the first of many changes in baseball that focused on the pitching strategy. In successive years, rules were changed to ban spitball (1920), changed again to ban any moistened pitch (1968); and then in rapid succession the strike zone was shrunk, the pitcher's mound was lowered, and the save rule was changed two times.

The most major way that baseball has changed over the years is, the erasing of the color line that split baseball into the Major League and the Negro League. When Jackie Robinson came onto the Major League's in 1947, it marked the introduction of equality for sport but for the country as well. One of the major paths baseball has changed over the years is that as money escalated in other industries it arrived in baseball with advent of televised games. Night games became increasingly more prevalent to catch viewers at their home after work. Free agency was fought for and introduced in the 1970s, which drove up player contracts and ended an era when teams had a player's right to their career unless they decided otherwise. The money throughout the system has continued to increase and the construction of new stadiums has replaced the majority of the original ballparks with the number of teams going up from 16 to 30.

Baseball statistics should be kept on the backs of baseball cards with a bubble gum scent. In addition, there is no team loyalty anymore. During baseball's professional history, any time an opportunity arose to leave a team for another to make more money, the players took it. When the American League went major, they raided the National League rosters and players were quite willing to jump to the new league for more money, violating their contract with the old. The same happened with the Federal League, the Players League, etc. Players in the past stayed "loyal" to their teams because the owners' interpretation of the reserve clause (which an arbitrator ruled was incorrect) gave them no choice. Ted Williams and Joe DiMaggio had no choice but to be "loyal" to the Red Sox and Yankees. But the "loyalty" of the owners didn't stop them from discussing a trade for the two. Why was it so admirable for Ted Williams to spend his entire career with the Sox when he had no choice? And why is there no similar expectation for owners?

Today's players are better conditioned, the equipment is better, the grounds keeping is better. Baseball was great when Honus Wagner played on a pebbly infield. It's great with Derek Jeter playing on the manicured fields of today. But the players of today are no better or worse, morally, than the players of a hundred years ago. But to think that this is a comment on the weaknesses of the modern player and the valor of the players of the past is a case of willful foolishness. The Media use to hide player's flaws and weaknesses but with today's vast media presence, look to dig up and exploit them. With the creation of the Baseball Hall of Fame in 1936, the media's Baseball Writers Association of America (BBWA) has acted as Judge and Jury for the Election of Players. Since there is over 150 years of data available, the time is now for the Hall of Fame to create Automatic Induction Criteria for all disciplines of the sport and take the bias out of the election process.

Baseball has gradually become less central to American culture over the last 50 years as football's popularity has skyrocketed and other sources of entertainment have come about. Even dedicated fans have grumbled in recent years about games being longer and less exciting. To an extent, M.L.B. executives say they agree, and they believe that last year's rule changes helped reduce the time of a game. The changes, including the pitch clock, did increase action and have led to much faster games with more hits, more stolen bases, and less down time. Whether the changes will increase interest in baseball is another question.

The evolution of the game in equipment, physical strength of players, rules and emergence of other sports will continue to be challenges Baseball will face in order to grow, or even maintain relevant in society. In an effort to speed up the game, and make it exciting, the new pitch clocks installed in stadiums that now countdown between every pitch, forcing pitchers and batters into action. It's a radical change for a sport defined by its leisurely pace, but league executives believed was necessary to grow baseball's popularity. This is an area of contention that separates older fans from the fans over the last 30 years. Older fans believe the game is a lot of the past, with many of the important reasons below. The Hall of Fame could be used as a means to promote the games generational connection with our forefathers by maintaining consistency that can be shared going forward. Listed below are areas needing attention."

The Baseball Hall of Fame

1. **Pitching**:
    a. Too many relief specialists. Relief Pitchers were mostly players that were not good enough to start. Now they are being groomed since little league.
    b. Too many changes in-game. New three-batter, or end of inning rule change is addressing this issue.
    c. Too many unqualified major leaguers Pitchers have been brought up and used before they were at least close to being major league ready.
    d. Too much time between pitches. Both the batter and the pitcher have fault in this. Note: The introduction of the "pitch clock", this is being addressed.
    e. They are taught a "throw as hard as you can, for as long as you can." This mentality has increased the number of arm injuries, shorter starting pitcher innings, and the need for a larger relief staff.
    f. Pitchers need to learn to pace their velocity and "bear down" when needed, thus lessening the stress on the pitchers' arm.

2. **Strike-Outs & Bases on Balls**:
    a. Longer pitch counts forcing starting pitchers to rarely pitch a complete game.
    b. Pitchers Velocity valued for strikeout ability more than pitch-to-contact.
    c. Control pitchers often overlooked for lower than desired velocity.

3. **Batters:**
    a. Needless "swinging from the heels" and better bat control.
    b. Bunting is becoming a lost art. Re-introduce this exciting and tactical aspect of the game.
    c. Learning to play "small ball" has almost become non-existent.
    d. The batter specific shift of the fielders designed to place the most fielders where the batter historically hit a batted ball.

4. **Basic "Old-Time" Fundamentals:**
    a. Fundamentals are not being taught extensively.
    b. Need better bat control.

   c. With two strokes, choke up on the bat for better control and put the ball in play instead of swinging for the home run.

   d. Strike-outs should be viewed as being awful and not as just another out.

   e. Placement hitting by shifting of the feet based on fielder's position.

   f. Situational hitting by take a team-first attitude into the batter's box. Knowing when to bunt, hit and run, position of the fielders, etc. The mental part of hitting.

   g. Pitchers need to play long-toss more, build-up their throwing muscles, run more to build up their legs and throw more in between starts. Strive to pitch 9 innings.

When it comes to game duration, the amount of time between the first pitch and the last pitch, M.L.B.'s new rules have been a success. For decades, outings at the ballpark had been getting longer and longer. When Babe Ruth played in the 1920s, nine innings of play lasted less than two hours. Over time, as it became more common for at-bats to last longer, the average game time ticked up. It ultimately peaked at 3 hours 11 minutes in 2021. That trend has sharply reversed in 2023 with reducing the time in between pitches as the average game fell to 2 hours and 42 minutes, a reduction of 29 minutes from 2022. MLB is looking to shorten the clock even more for 2024.

Average game duration

It means that all of the runs, hits, strikeouts, and errors occur during a shorter period of time, making the game feel more action-packed. The time reduction can be mostly credited to the implementation of the pitch clock. The timer means that at-bats now move faster, though fans who are scrolling through social media, or are in line for a hot dog are now more likely to miss something.

The second, and more important, goal that baseball is trying to accomplish with its new rules is to make the games more entertaining. The M.L.B. commissioner, Rob Manfred feel that baseball's problems were at least partly a result of the sport's recent obsession with analytics. Teams over the past two decades have raced for a statistical edge: They use more pitchers, and those pitchers throw faster, while batters have tuned their swings to hit the long ball, leading to more strikeouts and more home runs, but fewer balls hit in play. Many Fans want the game to look like the way it used to look like. The sport's new rules, including requirements about where certain defensive players can stand, are designed to increase the game's action, and entertainment value, with more hits, more steals and more impressive defensive plays. Last years increased major league batting

The Baseball Hall of Fame

average, up to .248 in 2023 from .243 in 2023 is statistically insignificant and still means that hits are still less common than they were in the mid-2000s. Teams over the past two decades have raced for a statistical edge: They use more pitchers, and those pitchers throw faster, while batters have tuned their swings to hit the long ball, leading to more strikeouts and home runs, but fewer balls hit in play.

Though the changes have had an impact, they are not enough to solve baseball's troubles. Hitting a baseball has always been incredibly hard. In the modern era, when pitchers are stronger and more informed by data, it is only getting harder. "Pitchers are only getting better, and I don't know how they're really going to limit strikeouts." MLB is increasing base sizes in order to promote player safety and make bang-bang plays less dangerous for defenders and runners. There is slightly less distance between bases now, so there may be more stolen bases, but that would not necessarily be a "feature" of the new sizes.

In 2021, it was reported on the contents of an MLB memo stating it would be deadening its official Rawlings baseballs, in part by loosening the tension on the first of three wool windings within the ball. Lab reports stated the new balls would fly one to two feet shorter on balls hit over 375 feet. Future changes of the will be driven over the next several years. Some changes will occur but mostly in the pitching categories. Listed below is a cursory view of categories used for Induction into The Baseball Hall of Fame:

Pitching Categories – Projected Future
- Games – Starting Pitchers are trending to the lower side.
- Games Started - Starting Pitchers are trending to the lower side.
- Complete Games – Starting Pitchers rarely go more than 7 innings.
- Shut-Outs – Starting Pitchers rarely complete a game even when giving up no runs.
- Wins – Career Totals will be much lower as importance as been diminished.
- Wins PCT – May trend higher due to less overall decisions.
- Saves – May have leveled off but career saves may be raised much higher.
- Innings - Starting Pitchers are trending to the lower side.
- WHIP – May need to be separated into two categories for starters and relievers.
- Strike-Outs – May have reached historic highs due to less innings being pitched.

- Earned Run Average – Trending much higher career wise.
- Games Finished – Career Totals will go higher for relievers.
- Pitcher's HOLD - Potential New Category – when a relief pitcher enters a game and maintains his teams led for the next relief pitcher, while recording at least one out.
- Quality Start – Potential New Category – 6 innings & 3 earned runs, or less.

Hitting Categories - Projected Future

- Games – Players are playing less per season.
- Batting Average – Career Batting Averages will continue to be lower.
- Runs – No Change
- Hits – No Change,
- Total Bases – No Change.
- Home Runs - No Change.
- Runs-Batted-In - No Change.
- Bases-On-Balls - No Change.
- On-Base-Percentage – No Change.
- Slugging Percentage – No Change.
- Stolen Bases – No Change

The Game of baseball needs to revisit what made the game great and different from other sports. This writer believes it to be a connection with the past, not trying to compete with other sports in the present. Baseball is worldwide with more players coming from ALL continents than ever before. Instead of tampering with the rules, regulations, and equipment, maybe the key for future growth and success is going back to the basics and re-introducing the BASICS of the game to the world and future generations. Baseball needs to expand to include more teams and allow the cream of the talent to rise to the heights achieved in the early years and through the 1940's when they had the last .400 hitters. Fans enjoy superstars, dominance, underdogs, gaudy statistics, and unpredictability. Baseball needs to remember the past in order to fuel the present and drive the future. Doing this would continue making Baseball generational and merge the past, present and the future. The Baseball Hall of Fame should be the key to maintaining that core goal.

Proposed Revised Hall of Fame Election Requirements

Authorization - By authorization of the Board of Directors of the National Baseball Hall of Fame and Museum, Inc., the Baseball Writers' Association of America (BBWAA) is authorized to hold an election and/or automatic Induction every year for the purpose of inducting members to the National Baseball Hall of Fame from the ranks of retired baseball players.

Electors - Only active and honorary members of the Baseball Writers' Association of America, who have been active baseball writers for at least ten (10) years, shall be eligible to vote. They must have been active as baseball writers and members of the Association for a period beginning at least ten (10) years prior to the date of election in which they are voting.

Eligible Candidates - Candidates for eligibility must meet the following requirements:

1. A baseball player must have been active as a player in the Major Leagues at some time during a period beginning for a minimum of ten years before and ending five (5) years prior to election.
2. Players must have played in each of ten (10) Major League championship seasons, some part of which must have been within the period described in 2 above. Note: Should a player fall short of the ten (10) Major League championship seasons due to death, or permanent disablement, an amendment may be proposed and voted on for the player to become eligible by a 75% vote of the Electors.
3. Player shall have ceased to be an active player in the Major Leagues at least five (5) calendar years preceding the Induction, or election, but may be otherwise connected with baseball.
4. In case of the death of an active player, or a player who has been retired for less than five (5) full years, a candidate who is otherwise eligible shall be eligible in the next regular election held at least six (6) months after the date of death or after the end of the five (5) year period, whichever occurs first.
5. Any player on Baseball's ineligible list shall not be an eligible candidate for induction. Their career statistics will be displayed in a special area for the public to view.
6. Equal Categories have been given to Pitchers and Position Players to ensure the Election Criteria are fair and non-biased.
7. Player is to meet the minimum statistical analysis of 110.000 Hall of Fame Points based on the criteria set for in the following categories: **Note:** The proposed new categories of <u>Player/Coach & Player/Manager</u> to meet the minimum statistical analysis of 120.000 Hall of Fame Points.

8. **Hall of Fame Points:**

Career Points for Position Players - are awarded points based on their accumulated points for each of 12 categories for their careers. There is a total of 240 total points available for career statistics.

- Games Played - Given 0 - 20 points based on career totals on the statistical chart.
- Batting Average - Given 0 - 20 points based on career totals on the statistical chart.
- Hits - Given 0 - 20 points based on career totals on the statistical chart.
- Runs - Given 0 - 20 points based on career totals on the statistical chart.
- Total Bases - Given 0 - 20 points based on career totals on the statistical chart.
- Home Runs - Given 0 - 20 points based on career totals on the statistical chart.
- Runs-Batted-In – Given 0 - 20 points based on career totals on the statistical chart.
- Bases-On-Balls – Given 0 - 20 points based on career totals on the statistical chart.
- On Base % – Given 0 - 20 points based on career totals on the statistical chart.
- Slugging % - Given 0 - 20 points based on career totals on the statistical chart.
- Stolen Bases – Given 0 - 20 points based on career totals on the statistical chart.
- On-Base-% + Slugging % - Given 0 - 20 points based on career totals on the statistical chart.

Career Points for Pitchers - are awarded points based on their accumulated points for each of 12 categories for their careers. There is a total of 240 total available points for career statistics.

- Games Played - Given 0 - 20 points based on career totals on the statistical chart.
- Games Started - Given 0 - 20 points based on career totals on the statistical chart.
- Complete Games - Given 0 - 20 points based on career totals on the statistical chart.
- Shut-Outs - Given 0 - 20 points based on career totals on the statistical chart.
- Wins - Given 0 - 20 points based on career totals on the statistical chart.
- Winning % - Given 0 - 20 points based on career totals on the statistical chart.
- Saves - Given 0 - 20 points based on career totals on the statistical chart.
- Innings Pitched – Given 0 - 20 points based on career totals on the statistical chart.
- WHIP – Given 0 - 20 points based on career totals on the statistical chart.
- Strike-Outs - Given 0 - 20 points based on career totals on the statistical chart.
- Earned Run Average – Given 0 - 20 points based on career totals on the statistical chart.
- Games Finished - Given 0 - 20 points based on career totals on the statistical chart.

9. **Seasonal Add-on Points** – Both pitchers and position players are awarded points based on leading their respective leagues for each of the following categories per season of play:

The Baseball Hall of Fame

<u>Pitchers (17 Categories)</u>

- Most Valuable Player Award – Awarded 7 points.
- Rookie of the Year – Awarded 5 points.
- Cy Young Award – Awarded 5 points.
- Gold Glove Award – Awarded 3 points.
- All-Star Selection - Awarded 2 points.
- Leading respective league in the following categories
- Earned Run Average (E.R.A) – Awarded 3 points.
- Wins - Awarded 3 points.
- Saves - Awarded 3 points.
- Strike-Outs– Awarded 2 points.
- Games – Awarded 2 points.
- Games Started - Awarded 2 points.
- Complete Games - Awarded 2 points.
- Shut-Outs – Awarded 2 points.
- Winning Pct. - Awarded 2 points.
- Innings Pitched - Awarded 2 points.
- WHIP – Walks and Hits per Inning Pitched – Awarded 2 points.
- Games Finished - Awarded 2 points.

<u>Position Player (17 Categories)</u>

- Most Valuable Player Award – Awarded 7 points.
- Rookie of the Year – Awarded 5 points.
- Triple Crown Award – Awarded 5 points.
- Gold Glove Award – Awarded 3 points.
- All-Star Selection - Awarded 2 points.
- Leading respective league in the following categories
- Batting Average – Awarded 3 points.
- Home Runs - Awarded 3 points.
- Runs Batted in– Awarded 3 points.
- Hits - Awarded 2 points.
- Runs - Awarded 2 points.
- Games – Awarded 2 points.

- Total Bases - Awarded 2 points.
- Base-On-Balls – Awarded 2 points.
- On-Base % – Awarded 2 points.
- Slugging % - Awarded 2 points.
- Stolen Bases – Awarded 2 points.
- OPS% - Awarded 2 points.

10. **<u>Post Season Points</u>** - Both pitchers and position players are awarded points based on their career accumulated Post Season points for each of 12 categories for their careers. There is a total of 24 total points for career statistics. The categories are listed below:

i. <u>Pitchers </u>(12 Categories)
- Games – Awarded from 0 to 20 points.
- Games Started – Awarded from 0 to 20 points.
- Complete Games – Awarded from 0 to 20 points.
- Shut-Outs – Awarded from 0 to 20 points.
- Wins – Awarded from 0 to 20 points.
- Winning % – Awarded from 0 to 20 points.
- Games Saved - Awarded from 0 to 20 points.
- Innings Pitched – Awarded from 0 to 20 points.
- Earned-Run-Average (ERA) – Awarded from 0 to 20 points.
- Strike-Outs – Awarded from 0 to 20 points.
- WHIP – Walks + Hits / Innings Pitched – Awarded from 0 to 20 points.
- Games Finished – Awarded from 0 to 20 points.

ii. <u>Position Players </u>(12 Categories)
- Games – Awarded from 0 to 20 points.
- Batting Average – Awarded from 0 to 20 points.
- Runs Scored - Awarded from 0 to 20 points.
- Hits – Awarded from 0 to 20 points.
- Total Bases – (1 for single, 2 for double, 3 for triple, 4 for home run added up ten divided by At-Bats)) Awarded from 0 to 20 points.
- Home Runs – Awarded from 0 to 20 points.
- Runs Batted in – Awarded from 0 to 20 points.

The Baseball Hall of Fame

- Base-On-Balls - Awarded from 0 to 20 points.
- On-Base % – Awarded from 0 to 20 points.
- Slugging % – (Total Bases / At-Bats) - Awarded from 0 to 20 points.
- Stolen Bases – Awarded from 0 to 20 points.
- OB+SL% – On-Base % + Slu % - Awarded from 0 to 20. points.

11. **<u>World Series Points</u>** - Both pitchers and position players are awarded points based on their career accumulated World Series points for each of 12 categories for their careers. There is a total of 20 total points for career statistics. The categories are listed below:

<u>Pitchers</u> (12 Categories)

- Games – Awarded from 0 to 2 points.
- Games Started – Awarded from 0 to 2 points.
- Complete Games – Awarded from 0 to 2 points.
- Shut-Outs – Awarded from 0 to 2 points.
- Wins – Awarded from 0 to 2 points.
- Winning % – Awarded from 0 to 2 points.
- Games Saved - Awarded from 0 to 2 points.
- Innings Pitched – Awarded from 0 to 2 points.
- Earned-Run-Average (ERA) – Awarded from 0 to 2 points.
- Strike-Outs – Awarded from 0 to 2 points.
- WHIP – Walks + Hits / Innings Pitched – Awarded from 0 to 2 points.
- Games Finished – Awarded from 0 to 2 points.

<u>Position Players</u> (12 Categories)

- Games – Awarded from 0 to 2 points.
- Batting Average – Awarded from 0 to 2 points.
- Runs Scored - Awarded from 0 to 2 points.
- Hits – Awarded from 0 to 2. points.
- Total Bases – (1 for single, 2 for double, 3 for triple, 4 for home run added up ten divided by At-Bats)) Awarded from 0 to 2 points.
- Home Runs – Awarded from 0 to 2 points.
- Runs Batted in – Awarded from 0 to 2 points.
- Base-On-Balls - Awarded from 0 to 2 points.

- On-Base % – Awarded from 0 to 2 points.
- Slugging % – (Total Bases / At-Bats) - Awarded from 0 to 2 points.
- Stolen Bases – Awarded from 0 to 2 points.
- OB+Sl% – Awarded from 0 to 2 points.

12. **Revolution of the Game Points** – Designed to reward individuals that had a dramatic revolutionary impact on the game. This can be achieved through contributions pertaining to health, safety, sportsmanship, social responsibility, and yet-to-be recognized events of the game a 75% majority must be achieved through the voting of 25 Senior Sports Writers.

13. **Method of Induction/Election** – An individual shall automatically be scheduled for inducted into the Baseball Hall-Of-Fame by reaching the total accumulation of 110.000 Career Points upon their retirement based on the following:
- Career Statistical Points
- Post Season Points
- Word Series Points
- Yearly Add-On-Points
- Writers Association Points
- Military / Lifetime Achievement Points

14. **Military Service** – EVERY player that loses MLB Service time due to USA Military commitments receives four (4) points for every full year. All partial years missed will be prorated by quarters.

15. **Lifetime Achievement** – Points awarded for contributions to the game outside of coaching, playing, or managing. Example: Jackie Robinson integrating the Major League's = 20 Points. **Note:** There will be a five (5) year waiting period prior to the induction ceremony. Individuals that are within 20 points of the necessary Hall of Fame Point Total will be forwarded to the BBWAA section below.

16. **BBWAA Screening Committee** - A Screening Committee consisting of baseball writers will be appointed by the BBWAA. This Screening Committee shall consist of six members, with two members to be elected at each Annual Meeting for a three-year term. They will perform the following duties:

- Screening Committee shall be:
  1. Prepare a ballot listing in alphabetical order the eligible candidates:
  2. Review the accuracy of the Total Hall of Fame Points for each individual.

3. Review each individual for Character Clause Violations, which would downgrade an individual to not being allowed a plaque in the Hall of Fame.

- The Results of the Screening Committee:
    a. **Induction**: Upon retirement, individuals that have achieved the Induction status of 110.00, or more, in the accumulation of the Hall of Fame Point System, the individual will be inducted into the Hall of Fame the following year.
    b. **Election:** Upon retirement, individuals that have not achieved the Induction status of 110.00 in the accumulation of the Hall of Fame Point System will be eligible to acquire the additional Points votes ballots cast in the preceding election or (2) are eligible for the first time and are nominated by any two of the six members of the BBWAA Screening Committee.   Designed for players that are within 25 points of the automatic induction threshold of 110.000 Hall of Fame Points.   A panel of 25 Senior Sports Writers will review the career contributions of the individual and vote with a yes or no ballot.
    c. **Hall of Very Good:** All individuals that have Hall of Fame Career Point Totals less than 90.000 shall be removed from the Baseball Writers Association (BBWAA) and placed in this Category. A player can be placed back into active voting by a 75% Vote of the 25 panel BBWAA.

17. Baseball Writers Association (BBWAA)

If an individual is still short of the necessary point threshold the first year, they will continue to be on the ballot for up to two additional years. After the end of the three-year Writers Association Vote and they are still short of the Hall-of-Fame Points Threshold, they will be removed from this panel and become eligible in five (5) years for a vote consisting of the Living Hall-of-Famers with a 75% majority needed for Induction.

18. Election Criteria for the BBWAA

- **An elector** will vote for no more than ten (10) eligible candidates deemed worthy of election. Write-in votes are not permitted.

- **Any candidate** receiving enough BBWAA votes added to their Total Hall-Of-Fame and brings the points over the 110.000-point threshold shall be Inducted to membership in the National Baseball Hall of Fame the following year if there are no Character Clause violations.

3) **Voting** shall be based upon the player's record, playing ability, integrity,

sportsmanship, character, and contributions to the team(s) on which the player
played accumulated during their career in Baseball. Non-Career related
activities activities such as political views, gender identity after retirement, and
Unites States Constitutional Rights shall not be infringed upon.
Note: Conviction of Illegal Activities and Domestic Abuse shall constitute a
character clause violation and will result in the elimination, or removal, of the
Individual plaque being exhibited in the Baseball Hall of Fame. The individuals'
records will be exhibited in a special section of the Baseball Hall of Fame for
Public Review along with others who have Character Clause violations.

4) **<u>Automatic Elections</u>** for specific Achievements - No automatic elections based on
performances such as a batting average of .400 or more for one (1) year, pitching a
perfect game or similar outstanding achievements shall be permitted.

5) **<u>Time of Election</u>** The duly authorized representatives of the BBWAA shall prepare date
and mail ballots to each elector no later than the 15th day of January in each year in
which an election is held. The elector shall sign and return the completed ballot within
twenty (20) days. The vote shall then be tabulated by the duly authorized
representatives of the BBWAA.

- **Certification of Election Results** - The results of the election shall be certified by a representative of
the Baseball Writers' Association of America and an officer of the National Baseball Hall of Fame and
Museum, Inc. The results shall be transmitted to the Commissioner of Baseball. The BBWAA and
National Baseball Hall of Fame and Museum, Inc. shall jointly release the results for publication.

- **Amendments** - The Board of Directors of the National Baseball Hall of Fame & Museum, Inc.
reserves the right to revoke, alter or amend these rules any time.

19. Proposed New Categories of Induction/Election

Due to history and evolution of the game, additional categories to the Baseball Hall of Fame
should be added to include individuals that have spent their careers in the game and have
held multiple positions such as player, coach, and manager over a minimum fifteen (15)
years. Their contributions should be captured, honored, and enshrined to show everyone
their impact on the game. There are two categories that can be quantified at this time,
Player/Manager and Player/Coach. These individuals may not have the overall statistics as
a player but transitioned into a great coach, or manager, and should be included. Below
are the new categories with the quantifying statistics that can be used for Induction and, or

The Baseball Hall of Fame

election of these great individuals.

1. Player/Manager - Statistical Evaluation for the following ten (10) Categories

a) **Yrs.** = Years managed a season with a ball club & part of a calendar year with one or   more teams. Example: 12 full seasons with Chicago, one ½ year dismissed & ½ hired by another team) equals 14 years that were managed in. **Note:** Point totals achieved from 0 to 20.00 over eight (8) point levels.

b) **FS** = Full Seasons Managed a team for a complete Calendar Year. Example: 2 full seasons managed plus 2 partial seasons equals will show only the12 full years that were managed in. **Note:** Point totals achieved from 0 to 20.00 over eight (8) point levels.

c) **G** = Accumulated games managed (Wins + Losses + Ties) over the entire Career. **Note:**   Point totals achieved from 0 to 20.00 over eight (8) point levels.

d) **W** = Accumulated games won for a career includes all full and partial Seasons. **Note:** Point totals achieved from 0 to 20.00 over eight (8) point levels.

e) **PCT** = Percentage of accumulated Games Won vs. games lost with ties given .5 points each. Example: 1274 games won, 1198 games lost, and 4 ties and equals 2476 total games. 1276/2000 would have a .5153 PCT. **Note:** Point totals achieved from 0 to 20.00 over eight (8) point levels.

f) **WS/LS** =Total Years with a winning record for the time managed including all partial seasons. **Note:** If a manager is involved with multiple teams during a year, the accumulated wins/losses will be used. Example: Manger X had a 33-37 record with team #1 and a 40-25 record with team 2. The accumulated total for the year would be 73 wins & 62 losses in 135 total games which would be considered a winning year. **Note:** Point totals achieved from 0 to 20.00 over eight (8) point levels.

g) **WS%** = Total Seasons where the games won exceeds the games lost divided by the total number of seasons managed. Example: 15 seasons managed – 7 seasons with a winning record – 7 seasons with a Losing record – one season with the same number of wins & losses would be a .500 PCT by dividing 7.5/15.Partial seasons are included. Note: Point totals achieved from 0 to 20.00 over eight (8) point levels

h) **DT** = Divisional Titles managed for a career. Must be the Manager at the end of the the regular season to count on the record. The number of titles times 2.5 equals the number of points the manager is awarded. Note: No Maximum points. Example: 4 Division Wins times 2.5 would equal 10 points for this category.

i) **LT** = League Titles Total managed for a career. Must be the Manager at the end of the the regular season to count on the record. The number of titles times 3.0 equals the number of points the manager is awarded. Note: No Maximum points. Example: 5 League Titles times 3.0 equals 15 points for this category.

j) **WS** = World Series Titles Total managed for a career. Must be the Manager at the end of the regular season to count on the record. The number of titles times 4.0 equals the number of points the manager is awarded. Note: No Maximum   points. Example: 5 League Titles times 4.0 equals 20 points for this category.

Example Hall of Fame Player/Manager Point Totals

Total Years	Cy Young Winners	Total Games	Total Won	Winning PCT.	Division Titles	League Titles	World Series Titles	Winning Seasons	Winning Seasons PCT.	Total Manager Points
18	16	2610	1405	.538	8	4	3	15	.667	
11.500	11.500	9.000	9.000	4.000	20.000	12.000	12.000	9.000	14.000	112.000

Manager Points	112.000
Coaching Points	0.000
Total Player Pints	6.500
Post Season Points	1.250
World Series Points	0.250
Seasonal Add-On Points	0.000
Military/Lifetime Achievement	0.000
Total Hall of Fame Points	120.000

Statistical Assumptions to account for the number of teams and Playoff Series Introductions

- Prior to 1969, ALL Pennant Winners were given Pennant Winning Points of 5.5 (Division Title Points of 2.5 plus League Championship Pints of 5.5.

- With the introduction of Divisional Play in 1969, this system set up a two-team Playoff System. ALL Division Winners were given Division Title Points of 2.5 and the Pennant Winner was given an additional 3.0 Points.

- With the realignment of the Divisional Playoff set-up in 1994 came the introduction of the Wild Card team. This system maintained a two-tiered Playoff System. Only Division Winners were given Division Title Points of 2.5 and the Pennant Winner was given an additional 3.0 Points.

The Baseball Hall of Fame

- With the realignment of the Divisional Playoff set-up in 1997 came the introduction of the Wild Card team. This system created a two-tiered Playoff System. Only Division Winners were given Division Title Points of 2.5 and the Pennant Winner was given an additional 3.0 Points.

- In 2012, a second Wild Card team was added and had play one-game to get into the Playoffs. No points were awarded to either team. Only Division Winners were given Division Title Points of 2.5 and the Pennant Winner was given an additional 3.0 Points.

- Winning the World Series awarded 4.0 points to the winning team Manager. No Points were awarded to the losing team.

Player/Coach. - Statistical Evaluation for the following ten (10) Categories:

- **Yrs**.= Years coached a full season with the same ball club & part of a calendar year with one or more teams. Example: 12 full seasons with one ½ year dismissed & ½ hired next year by another team) equals 14 years that were coached in.
  Note: Point totals achieved from 0 to 20.00 over eight (8) point levels.

- **CY** = Must be the Coach for the entire regular season to count on the record. The number of times one of their coached players wins the Cy Young times 3.0. points will be awarded. **Note:** No Maximum points.

- **20 G** = Must be the Coach for the entire regular season to count on the record. The number of times one of their coached players wins 20 games in a season times. points will be awarded. **Note:** No Maximum points.

- **ERA** = Team finishing in the Top 25% of the League in ERA for the complete year.
  Note: Point totals achieved from 0 to 20.00 over eight (8) point levels. Levels adjusted due to expansion starting the years expansion takes Place.

- **SV** = Team finishing in the Top 25% of the League in Saves for the complete year.
  Note: Point totals achieved from 0 to 20.00 over eight (8) point levels. Levels adjusted due to expansion starting the years expansion takes Place.

- **WHIP** = Team finishing in the Top 25% of the League in WHIP for the complete year.
  Note: Point totals achieved from 0 to 20.00 over eight (8) point levels. Levels adjusted due to expansion starting the years expansion takes Place.

- **S.O** = Team finishing in the Top 25% of the League in Strike Outs for the complete year. Levels adjusted due to expansion starting the years expansion takes place.
Note: Point totals achieved from 0 to 20.00 over eight (8) point levels.

- **DT** = Divisional Titles coached for a career. Must be the Coach for the entire regular season to count on the record. The number of titles times 2.5 equals the number of points the coach is awarded.
Note: No Maximum points. Example: 5 Division Wins times 2.5 would equal 10 points for this category.

- **LT** = League Titles Total coached for a career. Must be the Coach for the entire regular season to count on the record. The number of titles times 3.0 equals the number of points the coach is awarded.
Note: No Maximum points. Example: 5 League Titles times 3.0 equals 15 points for category.

- **WS** = World Series Titles Total coached for a career. Must be the Coach at the end of the regular season to count on the record. The number of titles times 4.0 equals the number of points the manager is awarded. **Note:** No Maximum points. Example: 5 League Titles times 4.0 equals 20 points for this category

Example Hall of Fame Player/Coach Point Totals

Total Years	Cy Young Winners	20 Game Winners	E. R. A. Top 25%	Saves Top 25%	WHIP Top 25%	Strike Outs Top 25%	Division Title	League Titles	*World Series Titles*	Total Coach /Player Points
20	2	3	6	5	5	6	5	4	3	
11.500	6.000	9.000	6.500	6.500	9.000	6.500	12.500	12.000	12.000	91.500
Coaching Points										91.500
Total Player Points										28.500
Post Season Points										4.250
World Series Points										0.250
Seasonal Add-On Points										2.000
Military/Lifetime Achievement										0.000
Total Hall of Fame Points										126.500

Statistical Assumptions to account for the number of teams and Playoff Series Introductions

- Prior to 1969, ALL Pennant Winners were given Pennant Winning Points of 5.5 (Division Title Points of 2.5 plus League Championship Pints of 5.5.

- With the introduction of Divisional Play in 1969, this system set up a two-team Playoff System. ALL Division Winners were given Division Title Points of 2.5 and the Pennant Winner was given an additional 3.0 Points.

- With the realignment of the Divisional Playoff set-up in 1994 came the introduction of the Wild Card team. This system maintained a two-tiered Playoff System. Only Division Winners were given Division Title Points of 2.5 and the Pennant Winner was given an additional 3.0 Points.

- With the realignment of the Divisional Playoff set-up in 1997 came the introduction of the Wild Card team. This system created a two-tiered Playoff System. Only Division Winners were given Division Title Points of 2.5 and the Pennant Winner was given an additional 3.0 Points.

- In 2012, a second Wild Card team was added and had play one-game to get into the Playoffs. No points were awarded to either team. Only Division Winners were given Division Title Points of 2.5 and the Pennant Winner was given an additional 3.0 Points.

- Winning the World Series awarded 4.0 points to the winning team Pitching Coach. No Points were awarded to the losing team.

Proposed Charts for Hall of Fame Criteria

Position Players

Pitchers

Player/Manager

Player/Coach

Hall of Fame Statistical Charts

Career Statistics - Position Players

Total Games			Career Average			Total Runs			Total Hits			Total Bases			Total Runs		
From	To	Points	From	To	Points	From	To	Points	From	To	Points	From	To	Points	From	To	Points
800	934	0.500	0.240	0.246	0.500	400	489	0.500	1300	1429	0.500	1300	1579	0.500	25	59	0.500
935	1069	1.000	0.247	0.253	0.550	490	579	1.000	1430	1559	1.000	1580	1859	1.000	60	94	1.000
1070	1204	1.500	0.253	0.259	1.050	580	669	1.500	1560	1689	1.500	1860	2139	1.500	95	129	1.500
1205	1339	2.000	0.260	0.266	1.550	670	759	2.000	1690	1819	2.000	2140	2419	2.000	130	164	2.000
1340	1474	2.500	0.266	0.272	2.050	760	849	2.500	1820	1949	2.500	2420	2699	2.500	165	199	2.500
1475	1609	3.000	0.273	0.279	2.550	850	939	3.000	1950	2079	3.000	2700	2979	3.000	200	234	3.000
1610	1744	3.750	0.279	0.285	3.300	940	1029	3.750	2080	2209	3.750	2980	3259	3.750	235	269	3.750
1745	1879	4.500	0.286	0.292	4.050	1030	1119	4.500	2210	2339	4.500	3260	3539	4.500	270	304	4.500
1880	2014	5.500	0.292	0.298	5.500	1120	1209	5.500	2340	2469	5.500	3540	3819	5.500	305	339	5.500
2015	2149	6.750	0.299	0.305	6.750	1210	1299	6.750	2470	2599	6.750	3820	4099	6.750	340	374	6.750
2150	2284	8.000	0.305	0.311	8.000	1300	1389	8.000	2600	2729	8.000	4100	4379	8.000	375	409	8.000
2285	2419	9.250	0.312	0.318	9.250	1390	1479	9.250	2730	2859	9.250	4380	4659	9.250	410	444	9.250
2420	2554	10.500	0.318	0.324	10.500	1480	1569	10.500	2860	2989	10.500	4660	4939	10.500	445	479	10.500
2555	2689	11.750	0.325	0.331	11.750	1570	1659	11.750	2990	3119	11.750	4940	5219	11.750	480	514	11.750
2690	2824	13.000	0.331	0.337	13.000	1660	1749	13.000	3120	3249	13.000	5220	5499	13.000	515	549	13.000
2825	2959	14.250	0.338	0.344	14.250	1750	1839	14.250	3250	3379	14.250	5500	5779	14.250	550	584	14.250
2960	3094	15.500	0.344	0.350	15.500	1840	1929	15.500	3380	3509	15.500	5780	6059	15.500	585	619	15.500
3095	3229	16.750	0.351	0.357	16.750	1930	2019	16.750	3510	3639	16.750	6060	6339	16.750	620	654	16.750
3230	3364	18.250	0.357	0.363	18.250	2020	2109	18.250	3640	3769	18.250	6340	6619	18.250	655	689	18.250
3365	>	20.000	0.364	>	20.000	2110	>	20.000	3770	>	20.000	6620	>	20.000	690	>	20.000

Runs-Batted-In			Bases-On-Balls			On-Base Percentage			Slugging Percentage			Stolen Bases			O.B.% + SLG%		
From	To	Points	From	To	Points	From	To	Points	From	To	Points	From	To	Points	From	To	Points
400	489	0.500	400	489	0.500	0.300	0.309	0.500	0.375	0.389	0.500	10	64	0.500	0.595	0.621	0.500
490	579	1.000	490	579	1.000	0.310	0.319	1.000	0.390	0.404	1.000	65	119	1.000	0.622	0.648	1.000
580	669	1.500	580	669	1.500	0.320	0.329	1.500	0.405	0.419	1.500	120	174	1.500	0.649	0.675	1.500
670	759	2.000	670	759	2.000	0.330	0.339	2.000	0.420	0.434	2.000	175	229	2.000	0.676	0.702	2.000
760	849	2.500	760	849	2.500	0.340	0.349	2.500	0.435	0.449	2.500	230	284	2.500	0.703	0.729	2.500
850	939	3.000	850	939	3.000	0.350	0.359	3.000	0.450	0.464	3.000	285	339	3.000	0.730	0.756	3.000
940	1029	3.750	940	1029	3.750	0.360	0.369	3.750	0.465	0.479	3.750	340	394	3.750	0.757	0.783	3.750
1030	1119	4.500	1030	1119	4.500	0.370	0.379	4.500	0.480	0.494	4.500	395	449	4.500	0.784	0.810	4.500
1120	1209	5.500	1120	1209	5.500	0.380	0.389	5.500	0.495	0.509	5.500	450	504	5.500	0.811	0.837	5.500
1210	1299	6.750	1210	1299	6.750	0.390	0.399	6.750	0.510	0.524	6.750	505	559	6.750	0.838	0.864	6.750
1300	1389	8.000	1300	1389	8.000	0.400	0.409	8.000	0.525	0.539	8.000	560	614	8.000	0.865	0.891	8.000
1390	1479	9.250	1390	1479	9.250	0.410	0.419	9.250	0.540	0.554	9.250	615	669	9.250	0.892	0.918	9.250
1480	1569	10.500	1480	1569	10.500	0.420	0.429	10.500	0.555	0.569	10.500	670	724	10.500	0.919	0.945	10.500
1570	1659	11.750	1570	1659	11.750	0.430	0.439	11.750	0.570	0.584	11.750	725	779	11.750	0.946	0.972	11.750
1660	1749	13.000	1660	1749	13.000	0.440	0.449	13.000	0.585	0.599	13.000	780	834	13.000	0.973	0.999	13.000
1750	1839	14.250	1750	1839	14.250	0.450	0.459	14.250	0.600	0.614	14.250	835	889	14.250	1.000	1.026	14.250
1840	1929	15.500	1840	1929	15.500	0.460	0.469	15.500	0.615	0.629	15.500	890	944	15.500	1.027	1.053	15.500
1930	2019	16.750	1930	2019	16.750	0.470	0.479	16.750	0.630	0.644	16.750	945	999	16.750	1.054	1.080	16.750
2020	2109	18.250	2020	2109	18.250	0.480	0.489	18.250	0.645	0.659	18.250	1000	1054	18.250	1.081	1.107	18.250
2110	>	20.000	2110	>	20.000	0.490	>	20.000	0.660	>	20.000	1055	>	20.000	1.108	1.134	20.000

Hall of Fame Statistical Charts

League Series Add-Ons - Position Players

Total Games			Batting Average			Total Runs			Total Hits			Total Bases			Home Runs		
From	To	Points	From	To	Points	From	To	Points	From	To	Points	From	To	Points	From	To	Points
1	10	0.250	0.240	0.259	0.250	1	8	0.250	1	12	0.250	1	21	0.250	1	2	0.250
11	20	0.400	0.260	0.279	0.400	9	16	0.400	13	24	0.400	22	42	0.400	36	37	0.400
21	30	0.600	0.280	0.299	0.600	17	24	0.600	26	38	0.600	43	63	0.600	71	72	0.600
31	40	0.800	0.300	0.319	0.800	25	32	0.800	39	51	0.800	64	84	0.800	106	107	0.800
41	50	1.000	0.320	0.339	1.000	33	40	1.000	52	65	1.000	85	105	1.000	141	142	1.000
51	60	1.200	0.340	0.359	1.200	41	48	1.200	66	79	1.200	106	126	1.200	176	177	1.200
61	70	1.400	0.360	0.379	1.400	49	56	1.400	80	93	1.400	127	147	1.400	211	212	1.400
71	80	1.600	0.380	0.399	1.600	57	64	1.600	104	107	1.600	148	168	1.600	246	247	1.600
81	90	1.800	0.400	0.419	1.800	65	72	1.800	108	122	1.800	169	189	1.800	281	282	1.800
91	>	2.000	0.420	>	2.000	73	80	2.000	123	>	2.000	190	>	2.000	316	317	2.000

Runs-Batted-In			Bases-On-Balls			On-Base Percentage			Slugging Percentage			Stolen Bases			O.B.% + SLG%		
From	To	Points	From	To	Points	From	To	Points	From	To	Points	From	To	Points	From	To	Points
1	5	0.250	1	5	0.250	0.300	0.316	0.250	0.375	0.407	0.250	1	2	0.250	0.625	0.699	0.250
6	10	0.400	6	10	0.400	0.317	0.333	0.400	0.408	0.440	0.400	3	4	0.400	0.700	0.774	0.400
11	15	0.600	11	15	0.600	0.334	0.350	0.600	0.441	0.473	0.600	5	6	0.600	0.775	0.849	0.600
16	20	0.800	16	20	0.800	0.351	0.367	0.800	0.474	0.506	0.800	7	8	0.800	0.850	0.924	0.800
21	25	1.000	21	25	1.000	0.368	0.384	1.000	0.507	0.539	1.000	9	10	1.000	0.925	0.999	1.000
26	30	1.200	26	30	1.200	0.385	0.401	1.200	0.540	0.572	1.200	11	12	1.200	1.000	1.074	1.200
31	35	1.400	31	35	1.400	0.402	0.418	1.400	0.573	0.605	1.400	13	14	1.400	1.075	1.149	1.400
36	40	1.600	36	40	1.600	0.419	0.435	1.600	0.606	0.638	1.600	15	16	1.600	1.150	1.224	1.600
41	45	1.800	41	45	1.800	0.436	0.452	1.800	0.639	0.671	1.800	17	18	1.800	1.225	1.299	1.800
46	>	2.000	46	>	2.000	0.453	>	2.000	0.672	>	2.000	19	>	2.000	1.300	>	2.000

World Series Add-Ons - Position Players

Total Games			Batting Average			Total Runs			Total Hits			Total Bases			Home Runs		
From	To	Points	From	To	Points	From	To	Points	From	To	Points	From	To	Points	From	To	Points
1	10	0.250	0.240	0.259	0.250	1	8	0.250	1	12	0.250	1	21	0.250	1	2	0.250
11	20	0.400	0.260	0.279	0.400	9	16	0.400	13	24	0.400	22	42	0.400	36	37	0.400
21	30	0.600	0.280	0.299	0.600	17	24	0.600	26	38	0.600	43	63	0.600	71	72	0.600
31	40	0.800	0.300	0.319	0.800	25	32	0.800	39	51	0.800	64	84	0.800	106	107	0.800
41	50	1.000	0.320	0.339	1.000	33	40	1.000	52	65	1.000	85	105	1.000	141	142	1.000
51	60	1.200	0.340	0.359	1.200	41	48	1.200	66	79	1.200	106	126	1.200	176	177	1.200
61	70	1.400	0.360	0.379	1.400	49	56	1.400	80	93	1.400	127	147	1.400	211	212	1.400
71	80	1.600	0.380	0.399	1.600	57	64	1.600	104	107	1.600	148	168	1.600	246	247	1.600
81	90	1.800	0.400	0.419	1.800	65	72	1.800	108	122	1.800	169	189	1.800	281	282	1.800
91	>	2.000	0.420	>	2.000	73	80	2.000	123	>	2.000	190	>	2.000	316	317	2.000

Runs-Batted-In			Bases-On-Balls			On-Base Percentage			Slugging Percentage			Stolen Bases			O.B.% + SLG%		
From	To	Points	From	To	Points	From	To	Points	From	To	Points	From	To	Points	From	To	Points
1	5	0.250	1	5	0.250	0.300	0.316	0.250	0.375	0.407	0.250	1	2	0.250	0.625	0.699	0.250
6	10	0.400	6	10	0.400	0.317	0.333	0.400	0.408	0.440	0.400	3	4	0.400	0.700	0.774	0.400
11	15	0.600	11	15	0.600	0.334	0.350	0.600	0.441	0.473	0.600	5	6	0.600	0.775	0.849	0.600
16	20	0.800	16	20	0.800	0.351	0.367	0.800	0.474	0.506	0.800	7	8	0.800	0.850	0.924	0.800
21	25	1.000	21	25	1.000	0.368	0.384	1.000	0.507	0.539	1.000	9	10	1.000	0.925	0.999	1.000
26	30	1.200	26	30	1.200	0.385	0.401	1.200	0.540	0.572	1.200	11	12	1.200	1.000	1.074	1.200
31	35	1.400	31	35	1.400	0.402	0.418	1.400	0.573	0.605	1.400	13	14	1.400	1.075	1.149	1.400
36	40	1.600	36	40	1.600	0.419	0.435	1.600	0.606	0.638	1.600	15	16	1.600	1.150	1.224	1.600
41	45	1.800	41	45	1.800	0.436	0.452	1.800	0.639	0.671	1.800	17	18	1.800	1.225	1.299	1.800
46	>	2.000	46	>	2.000	0.453	>	2.000	0.672	>	2.000	19	>	2.000	1.300	>	2.000

Hall of Fame Statistical Charts

Yearly Add-On Points

Position Players

Awards	Times	Add-On		Awards	Times	Add-On	Points	Hall of Fame Point Total	
MVP		7	0	Hits		2	0	Category	Points
R.O.Y		5	0	Games		2	0	Career Points	
Triple Crown		5	0	Total Bases		2	0	Post Season Points	
Gold Glove		3	0	Bases-On-Balls		2	0	World Series Points	
Batting Average		3	0	Stolen Bases		2	0	Career Add-On Points	0
Home Runs		3	0	OBP %		2	0	Writers-Association Points	
R.B.I.'s		3	0	SLG %		2	0	Military/Lifetime Achievement	
Runs		2	0	OBPS+		2	0		
All-Star		2	0						
			0				0	Total Hall of Fame Points	

Yearly Add-On Points

Pitchers

Awards	Times	Add-On	Points	Awards	Times	Add-On	Points	Hall of Fame Point Total	
MVP		7	0	Games		2	0	Category	Points
R.O.Y		5	0	Games Started		2	0	Career Points	
Cy Young		5	0	Complete Games		2	0	Post Season Points	
Wins		3	0	Shut-Outs		2	0	World Series Points	
Saves		3	0	Winning PCT.		2	0	Career Add-On Points	0
ERA		3	0	Innings Pitched		2	0	Writers-Association Points	
Gold Glove		3	0	WHIP		2	0	Military/Lifetime Achievement	
All-Star		2	0	Games Finished		2	0		
Strike-Outs		2	0						
			0				0	Total Hall of Fame Points	

Hall of Fame Statistical Charts

Career Statistics - Pitchers

Total Games			Games Started			Complete Games			Shutouts			Games Won			Winning Percentage		
From	To	Points	From	To	Points	From	To	Points	From	To	Points	From	To	Points	From	To	Points
100	154	0.500	41	80	0.500	5	25	0.500	1	4	0.500	1	20	0.500	0.426	0.44	0.500
155	209	1.000	81	120	0.550	26	50	1.000	5	10	1.000	21	40	1.000	0.441	0.455	1.000
210	264	1.500	121	160	1.050	51	75	1.500	11	15	1.500	41	60	1.500	0.456	0.47	1.500
265	319	2.000	161	200	1.550	76	100	2.000	16	20	2.000	61	80	2.000	0.471	0.485	2.000
320	374	2.500	201	240	2.050	101	125	2.500	21	25	2.500	81	100	2.500	0.486	0.5	2.500
375	429	3.000	241	280	2.550	126	150	3.000	26	30	3.000	101	120	3.000	0.501	0.515	3.000
430	484	3.750	281	320	3.300	151	175	3.750	31	35	3.750	121	140	3.750	0.516	0.53	3.750
485	539	4.500	321	360	4.050	176	200	4.500	36	40	4.500	141	160	4.500	0.531	0.545	4.500
540	594	5.500	361	400	5.500	201	225	5.500	41	45	5.500	161	180	5.500	0.546	0.56	5.500
595	649	6.750	401	440	6.750	226	250	6.750	46	50	6.750	181	200	6.750	0.561	0.575	6.750
650	704	8.000	441	480	8.000	251	275	8.000	51	55	8.000	201	220	8.000	0.576	0.59	8.000
705	759	9.250	481	520	9.250	276	300	9.250	56	60	9.250	221	240	9.250	0.591	0.605	9.250
760	814	10.500	521	560	10.500	301	325	10.500	61	65	10.500	241	260	10.500	0.606	0.62	10.500
815	869	11.750	561	600	11.750	326	350	11.750	66	70	11.750	261	280	11.750	0.621	0.635	11.750
870	924	13.000	601	640	13.000	351	375	13.000	71	75	13.000	281	300	13.000	0.636	0.65	13.000
925	979	14.250	641	680	14.250	376	400	14.250	76	80	14.250	301	320	14.250	0.651	0.665	14.250
980	1034	15.500	681	720	15.500	401	425	15.500	81	85	15.500	321	340	15.500	0.666	0.68	15.500
1035	1089	16.750	721	760	16.750	426	450	16.750	86	90	16.750	341	360	16.750	0.681	0.695	16.750
1090	1144	18.250	761	800	18.250	451	475	18.250	91	95	18.250	361	380	18.250	0.696	0.71	18.250
1145	>	20.000	801	>	20.000	476	>	20.000	96	>	20.000	381	>	20.000	0.711	>	20.000

Total Games Saved			Total Innings Pitched			WHIP			Strike-Outs			Earned Run Average			Games Finished		
From	To	Points	From	To	Points	From	To	Points	From	To	Points	From	To	Points	From	To	Points
5	24	0.500	750	799	0.500	1.555	1.526	0.500	100	244	0.500	4.38	4.29	0.500	10	50	0.500
25	49	1.000	800	999	1.000	1.525	1.496	1.000	245	489	1.000	4.28	4.19	1.000	51	99	1.000
50	74	1.500	1000	1249	1.500	1.535	1.466	1.500	490	734	1.500	4.18	4.09	1.500	100	149	1.500
75	99	2.000	1250	1499	2.000	1.545	1.436	2.000	735	979	2.000	4.08	3.99	2.000	150	199	2.000
100	124	2.500	1500	1749	2.500	1.555	1.406	2.500	980	1224	2.500	3.98	3.89	2.500	200	249	2.500
125	149	3.000	1750	1999	3.000	1.565	1.376	3.000	1225	1469	3.000	3.88	3.79	3.000	250	299	3.000
150	174	3.750	2000	2249	3.750	1.575	1.346	3.750	1470	1714	3.750	3.78	3.69	3.750	300	349	3.750
175	199	4.500	2250	2499	4.500	1.585	1.316	4.500	1715	1959	4.500	3.68	3.59	4.500	350	399	4.500
200	224	5.500	2500	2749	5.500	1.595	1.286	5.500	1960	2204	5.500	3.58	3.49	5.500	400	449	5.500
225	249	6.750	2750	2999	6.750	1.605	1.256	6.750	2205	2449	6.750	3.48	3.39	6.750	450	499	6.750
250	274	8.000	3000	3249	8.000	1.615	1.226	8.000	2450	2694	8.000	3.38	3.29	8.000	500	549	8.000
275	299	9.250	3250	3499	9.250	1.625	1.196	9.250	2695	2939	9.250	3.28	3.19	9.250	550	599	9.250
300	324	10.500	3500	3749	10.500	1.635	1.166	10.500	2940	3184	10.500	3.18	3.09	10.500	600	649	10.500
325	349	11.750	3750	3999	11.750	1.645	1.136	11.750	3185	3429	11.750	3.08	2.99	11.750	650	699	11.750
350	374	13.000	4000	4249	13.000	1.655	1.106	13.000	3430	3674	13.000	2.98	2.89	13.000	700	749	13.000
375	399	14.250	4250	4499	14.250	1.665	1.076	14.250	3675	3919	14.250	2.88	2.79	14.250	750	799	14.250
400	424	15.500	4500	4749	15.500	1.675	1.046	15.500	3920	4164	15.500	2.78	2.69	15.500	800	849	15.500
425	449	16.750	4750	4999	16.750	1.685	1.016	16.750	4165	4409	16.750	2.68	2.59	16.750	850	899	16.750
450	474	18.250	5000	5249	18.250	1.695	0.986	18.250	4410	4654	18.250	2.58	2.49	18.250	900	949	18.250
475	>	20.000	5250	>	20.000	1.705	>	20.000	4655	>	20.000	2.48	<	20.000	950	>	20.000

Hall of Fame Statistical Charts

Player/CoachStatistical Evaluation

Total Years			Top 25% - ERA			Top 25% Saves			Top 25% WHIP			Top 25% Strike-Outs		
From	To	Points	From	To	Points	From	To	Points	From	To	Points	From	To	Points
4	7	1.500	1	2	1.500	625	1250	1.500	400	724	1.500	0.475	0.514	1.500
8	11	4.000	3	4	4.000	1250	1875	4.000	725	1049	4.000	0.515	0.539	4.000
12	15	6.500	5	6	6.500	1875	2500	6.500	1050	1374	6.500	0.540	0.579	6.500
16	19	9.000	7	8	9.000	2500	3125	9.000	1375	1699	9.000	0.580	0.619	9.000
20	23	11.500	9	10	11.500	3125	3750	11.500	1700	2024	11.500	0.620	0.659	11.500
24	27	14.000	11	12	14.000	3750	4375	14.000	2025	2349	14.000	0.660	0.699	14.000
28	31	17.000	13	14	17.000	4375	5000	17.000	2350	2674	17.000	0.700	0.739	17.000
32	>	20.000	15	>	20.000	5000	>	20.000	2675	>	20.000	0.740	>	20.000

Manager Statistical Evaluation

20 Game Winners			Cy Young Winners			Division Titles			League Titles			World Series Titles		
From	To	Points	From	To	Points	From	To	Points	From	To	Points	From	To	Points
0	0	1.500	0	0	1.500	1	1	1.500	1	1	3.000	1	1	4.000
1	1	4.000	1	1	4.000	2	2	4.000	2	2	6.000	2	2	8.000
2	2	6.500	2	2	6.500	3	3	6.500	3	3	9.000	3	3	12.000
3	3	9.000	3	3	9.000	4	4	9.000	4	4	12.000	4	4	16.000
4	4	11.500	4	4	11.500	5	5	11.500	5	5	15.000	5	5	20.000
5	5	14.000	5	5	14.000	6	6	14.000	6	6	18.000	6	6	24.000
6	6	17.000	6	6	17.000	7	7	17.000	7	7	21.000	7	7	28.000
7	>	20.000	7	>	20.000	8	8	20.000	8	8	24.000	8	8	32.000

NOTE: Before Divisional Play Started in 1969, ALL Pennant Winers were given Divison Title Points as well.

Title	Full Meaning	Explanation
Years	Total Years Manageing a Team - Full & Part of a Calendar Year	
Full Seasons	Total Full Seasons Managed a team for a complete Calendar Year.	
Games	Total Accumulated Games Managed (Wins plus Losses) over entire career	
Won	Total Games Won Accumulated games won for career	
PCT	Percentage of Games Won vs. Percentage of Games Won vs. lost	
Division Titles	Total Division Titles Won Total Dividional Titles Years managed for career.	
League Titles	Total League Titles Won Total League Championships managed for career.	
WS Title	Title World Series Titles Won Total World Championsips managed for career.	
Winning Seasons	Total Winning Seasons Managed when the tam won more than they lost for career	
WS/LS Pct.	PCT of Winning Seasons Managed Percentage more than they lost while manager for career	

<u>Reasoning for the above Omissions</u>

1. Before Divisional Play started in 1969, All Pennant Winners were given Division Title Points as well.
2. Losses - Captured with the Ewinning Percentage.
3. Wild Card Teams - Omitted as only Division Titles are recognized. However, if the team advances they are given the subsequent Titles they win (Division, League Pennant, and World Series Titles)

Hall of Fame Statistical Charts

Manager Statistical Evaluation

Total Years			Full Seasons			Total Games			Total Wins			Wining Percentage		
From	To	Points	From	To	Points	From	To	Points	From	To	Points	From	To	Points
4	6	1.500	4	6	1.500	625	1250	1.500	400	724	1.500	0.475	0.514	1.500
7	9	4.000	7	9	4.000	1250	1875	4.000	725	1049	4.000	0.515	0.539	4.000
10	12	6.500	10	12	6.500	1875	2500	6.500	1050	1374	6.500	0.540	0.579	6.500
13	15	9.000	13	15	9.000	2500	3125	9.000	1375	1699	9.000	0.580	0.619	9.000
16	18	11.500	16	18	11.500	3125	3750	11.500	1700	2024	11.500	0.620	0.659	11.500
19	21	14.000	19	21	14.000	3750	4375	14.000	2025	2349	14.000	0.660	0.699	14.000
22	24	17.000	22	24	17.000	4375	5000	17.000	2350	2674	17.000	0.700	0.739	17.000
25	>	20.000	25	>	20.000	5000	>	20.000	2675	>	20.000	0.740	>	20.000

Manager Statistical Evaluation

Winning Seasons			WS/LS PCT			Division Titles			League Titles			World Series Titles		
From	To	Points	From	To	Points	From	To	Points	From	To	Points	From	To	Points
4	6	1.500	0.475	0.514	1.500	1	1	1.500	1	1	3.000	1	1	4.000
7	9	4.000	0.515	0.539	4.000	2	2	4.000	2	2	6.000	2	2	8.000
10	12	6.500	0.540	0.579	6.500	3	3	6.500	3	3	9.000	3	3	12.000
13	15	9.000	0.580	0.619	9.000	4	4	9.000	4	4	12.000	4	4	16.000
16	18	11.500	0.620	0.659	11.500	5	5	11.500	5	5	15.000	5	5	20.000
19	21	14.000	0.660	0.699	14.000	6	6	14.000	6	6	18.000	6	6	24.000
22	24	17.000	0.700	0.739	17.000	7	7	17.000	7	7	21.000	7	7	28.000
25	>	20.000	0.740	>	20.000	8	8	20.000	8	8	24.000	8	8	32.000

NOTE: Before Divisional Play Started in 1969, ALL Pennant Winers were given Divison Title Points as well.

Title	Full Meaning	Explanation
Years	Total Years Manageing a Team - Full & Part of a Calendar Year	
Full Seasons	Total Full Seasons Managed a team for a complete Calendar Year.	
Games	Total Accumulated Games Managed (Wins plus Losses) over entire career	
Won	Total Games Won Accumulated games won for career	
PCT	Percentage of Games Won vs. Percentage of Games Won vs. lost	
Division Titles	Total Division Titles Won Total Dividional Titles Years managed for career.	
League Titles	Total League Titles Won Total League Championships managed for career.	
WS Title	Title World Series Titles Won Total World Championsips managed for career.	
Winning Seasons	Total Winning Seasons Managed when the tam won more than they lost for career	
WS/LS Pct.	PCT of Winning Seasons Managed Percentage more than they lost while manager for career	

Reasoning for the above Omissions

1. Before Divisional Play started in 1969, All Pennant Winners were given Division Title Points as well.

2. Losses - Captured with the Ewinning Percentage.

3. Wild Card Teams - Omitted as only Division Titles are recognized. However, if the team advances they are given the subsequent Titles they win (Division, League Pennant, and World Series Titles.

Hall of Fame Statistical Charts

League Series Add-Ons for Pitchers

Total Games			Games Started			Complete Games			Shutouts			Games Won			Winning Percentage		
From	To	Points	From	To	Points	From	To	Points	From	To	Points	From	To	Points	From	To	Points
1	5	0.250	1	2	0.250	1	8	0.250	0	0	0.250	1	2	0.250	2-1		0.250
6	10	0.400	3	4	0.400	2	16	0.400	1	1	0.400	3	4	0.400	2-0		0.400
11	15	0.600	5	6	0.600	3	24	0.600	2	38	0.600	5	6	0.600	3-1		0.600
16	20	0.800	7	8	0.800	4	32	0.800	3	51	0.800	7	8	0.800	3-0		0.800
21	25	1.000	9	10	1.000	5	40	1.000	4	65	1.000	9	10	1.000	4-1		1.000
26	30	1.200	11	12	1.200	6	48	1.200	5	79	1.200	11	12	1.200	5-2		1.200
31	35	1.400	13	14	1.400	7	56	1.400	6	93	1.400	13	14	1.400	5-1		1.400
36	40	1.600	15	16	1.600	8	64	1.600	7	107	1.600	15	16	1.600	6-2		1.600
41	45	1.800	17	18	1.800	9	72	1.800	8	122	1.800	17	18	1.800	5-0		1.800
46	>	2.000	19	>	2.000	10	>	2.000	9	>	2.000	19	>	2.000	6-0 >		2.000

League Series Add-Ons for Pitchers

Total Games Saved			Total Innings Pitched			WHIP			Strike-Outs			Earned Run Average			Games Finished		
From	To	Points	From	To	Points	From	To	Points	From	To	Points	From	To	Points	From	To	Points
1	5	0.250	1	10	0.250	1.525	1.465	0.250	1	10	0.250	4.71	4.37	0.250	0.625	0.699	0.250
2	10	0.400	11	23	0.400	1.465	1.405	0.400	11	20	0.400	4.36	3.92	0.400	0.700	0.774	0.400
3	15	0.600	16	28	0.600	1.405	1.345	0.600	21	30	0.600	3.91	3.57	0.600	0.775	0.849	0.600
4	20	0.800	29	41	0.800	1.345	1.285	0.800	31	40	0.800	3.56	3.23	0.800	0.850	0.924	0.800
5	25	1.000	34	46	1.000	1.285	1.225	1.000	41	50	1.000	3.21	2.87	1.000	0.925	0.999	1.000
6	30	1.200	39	51	1.200	1.225	1.165	1.200	51	60	1.200	2.86	2.50	1.200	1.000	1.074	1.200
7	35	1.400	44	56	1.400	1.165	1.105	1.400	61	70	1.400	2.49	2.13	1.400	1.075	1.149	1.400
8	40	1.600	49	61	1.600	1.105	1.045	1.600	71	80	1.600	2.12	1.75	1.600	1.150	1.224	1.600
9	45	1.800	54	66	1.800	1.045	0.985	1.800	81	90	1.800	1.74	1.01	1.800	1.225	1.299	1.800
10	>	2.000	59	>	2.000	0.985	>	2.000	91	>	2.000	1.00	>	2.000	1.300	>	2.000

World Series Add-Ons for Pitchers

Total Games			Games Started			Complete Games			Shutouts			Games Won			Winning Percentage		
From	To	Points	From	To	Points	From	To	Points	From	To	Points	From	To	Points	From	To	Points
1	2	0.250	1	2	0.250	1	1	0.250	0	0	0.250	1	2	0.250	2-1		0.250
3	4	0.400	3	4	0.400	2	2	0.400	1	2	0.400	2	2	0.400	2-0		0.400
5	6	0.600	5	6	0.600	3	3	0.600	2	3	0.600	3	3	0.600	3-1		0.600
7	8	0.800	7	8	0.800	4	4	0.800	3	4	0.800	4	4	0.800	3-0		0.800
9	10	1.000	9	10	1.000	5	5	1.000	4	5	1.000	5	5	1.000	4-1		1.000
11	12	1.200	11	12	1.200	6	6	1.200	5	6	1.200	6	6	1.200	5-2		1.200
13	14	1.400	13	14	1.400	7	7	1.400	6	7	1.400	7	7	1.400	5-1		1.400
15	16	1.600	15	16	1.600	8	8	1.600	7	8	1.600	8	8	1.600	6-2		1.600
17	18	1.800	17	18	1.800	9	9	1.800	8	9	1.800	9	9	1.800	5-0		1.800
19	>	2.000	19	>	2.000	10	>	2.000	9	>	2.000	10	>	2.000	6-0 >		2.000

Total Games Saved			Total Innings Pitched			WHIP			Strike-Outs			Earned Run Average			Games Finished		
From	To	Points	From	To	Points	From	To	Points	From	To	Points	From	To	Points	From	To	Points
1	2	0.250	1	15	0.250	1.525	1.465	0.250	1	8	0.250	4.71	4.37	0.250	1	2	0.250
3	4	0.400	16	30	0.400	1.465	1.405	0.400	9	16	0.400	4.36	3.92	0.400	3	4	0.400
5	6	0.600	31	45	0.600	1.405	1.345	0.600	17	24	0.600	3.91	3.57	0.600	5	6	0.600
7	8	0.800	46	60	0.800	1.345	1.285	0.800	25	32	0.800	3.56	3.22	0.800	7	8	0.800
9	10	1.000	61	75	1.000	1.285	1.225	1.000	33	40	1.000	3.21	2.87	1.000	9	10	1.000
11	12	1.200	76	90	1.200	1.225	1.165	1.200	41	48	1.200	2.66	2.50	1.200	11	12	1.200
13	14	1.400	91	105	1.400	1.165	1.105	1.400	49	56	1.400	2.49	2.13	1.400	13	14	1.400
15	16	1.600	106	120	1.600	1.105	1.045	1.600	57	64	1.600	2.12	1.75	1.600	15	16	1.600
17	18	1.800	121	135	1.800	1.045	0.985	1.800	65	72	1.800	1.74	1.01	1.800	17	18	1.800
19	>	2.000	136	>	2.000	0.985	>	2.000	73	>	2.000	1.00	>	2.000	19	>	2.000

Summary

Baseball Fans have a great time interacting with people whose love of baseball is equal to or surpasses their own. They learn a lot about the game that for over 150 years has been considered "The National Pastime". This has allowed this great sport to come up with new ideas, new possibilities, and new friendships. Cooperstown should be a fan first adventure for individuals able to enjoy the game. Baseball needs this museum for people who are passionate about history, the game, and everything that to do with it.

This is the only game in the United States that is generational where today's youth could interact, understand the game with the fathers, grandfathers, and even some with their great-grandfathers. Each generation could sit and tell stories from their life to the rest of the family. Baseball and the American Culture should be a blue-ribbon program for the people who love the game. They give us ideas, create, and present areas of history that are just a lot of fun. The Baseball Hall of Fame can create an honors class by expanding the membership by remaking the Criteria for entrance based more on the history of statistics of the game with the creation of statistical guidelines that allow the best to be Inducted within five years after they played their last game without going through the election process. The" Hall of Fame Point System" will assist in separating the superstars, great players, and the "Hall of Very Good Players" for the BBWAA.

Everyone that has played, managed, or coached in the game at the highest level should be given the same statistical overview as the players the media prefer. By leveling the playing field, the small market players and those that excel in their overall career, post season success, and/or World Series success can achieve their rightful status. In addition, these statistical guidelines consider the times a player leads their league in the different specific categories in a year and will often make a difference in shortened careers like Sandy Koufax and Kirby Pucket for being inducted, and or elected. The current system of voting by the BBWAA hasn't helped put two deserving individuals like Thurman Munson and Don Mattingly into the Hall of Fame many years after their last game was played. One died and the other had a congenital back defect BUT both were awesome for large parts of their careers.

Fans will never tire of coming back come back to the most famous small town in the world with the greatest Hall of Fame in the world. Growing up in a small town myself, I would find an attraction here

The Baseball Hall of Fame

to meet with other lovers of baseball, scholars, and all fans to share an opportunity to talk about our common love.

Professional baseball writers have played the main role in deciding if former Major League Baseball players will be enshrined in the Hall of Fame. This time-honored tradition has become more complex and should be updated with statistical history separating the "No Doubt" players that should be Inducted after their five-year wait, and those that are close but should be elected by the BBWAA. In addition, several players from the "Steroids Era" have become eligible for consideration and have divided writers and fans across the country. The Hall of Fame should offer unbiased guidance for the writers to follow, so a player meeting the criteria, but in violation of the "Character Clause", during their time in Major League Baseball, be penalized but not left out of the Hall of Fame. If in violation, their statistics should be enshrined in a different section of the Hall of Fame for the fans to look at and review, but a Plaque denied.

The BBWAA would not be replaced but enhanced using the statistical history of baseball that would legitimize their voting decisions for individuals. It also encourages that new rules and regulations could not be applied to players prior to their implementation.   The BBWAA present their voting decisions in a variety of ways that primarily adhere to principles of legitimacy and ethical opinion. However, there are areas identified that need improvement and demand that baseball writers explain their ballot decisions. Those areas include a more consistent use of fact-based arguments, more thorough presentation of context about players, steroid use, and a greater effort to create a balance of understanding between them and the public. The Baseball Hall of Fame should never be used to communicate an agenda, political ideology, bias, suppress information, but display only the facts and truths about this great game. Baseball is a bridge that should be used to connect the origins of the past, the game in the present, and what the future may present for both the game and the United States of America. instead of a short 1–2-day visit, it can be a Disney-like stay of multiple days, or a week for generations to come.

Works Cited

The following websites and books were used in obtaining the material in the research and writing of this book. All the biographies were condensed using multiple sources from Baseball-Reference.com, Stathead Baseball, The Baseball Hall of Fame and Wikipedia. Family information not available in the above references was obtained through the My Heritage and Legacy websites.

All the statistical data was acquired through the use of downloads from the Stathead Baseball and the Baseball-Reference.com websites with certain statistics eliminated and condensed, for the purpose of easier understanding for the readers. Due to the extensive research, fact checking and condensing done for this book, some information may have been imitated for the readers to follow the flow and understanding of the purpose of the book. Footnotes were not used for referencing.

1. **Baseball-Reference.com**

   Owner – Sports Reference

   Created by – Sean Forman

   Website – www.baseball-reference.com - Country of Origin – United States

2. Stathead Baseball Website – Baseball Monthly Subscription Started April 16, 2023

   Owner – Sports Reference LLC.

   Created by – Sean Lahman's Baseball Database

   Website – Stathead.com//baseball - Country of Origin – United States

3. Wikipoedia

   Owner – Wikipedia Foundation

   Created by – Jimmy Wales, Larry Sanger

   Website – www,Wikipedia.org.   - Country of Origin – United States

4. My Heritage

   Owner – MyHeritage Ltd

   Created by – Gilad Japhet

   Website – myheritage.com -_   Country of Origin – Israel

5. Legacy

   Owner – Privately Held

   Created by – 1,500 Newspaper Affiliates   - Website – legacy.com

6. The Baseball Hall of Fame – Various Committees

   Owner – Privately Held

   Created by – Stephen Carlton Clark

   Website – https://baseballhall.org - Country of Origin – United States

7. Interviews with Tommy John

   Done over multiple phone calls.

   June 15, 2003, through March 5, 2024.

8. Discussions with Jeff Santo

   Done over multiple phone calls.

   June 15, 2003, through March 5, 2024. - Podcast: peanutspopcornandcrackerjacks.com

9. Who are the best managers in MLB History?

   Author - Sanjesh Singh

   Published October 24, 2023

   Digital Editor and Analyst, NBC Sports

10. The 50 Best MLB Pitching Coaches of All-Time

   Author – Doug Mead

   February 1, 2012

   Google Article

11. The Baseball Encyclopedia: The Complete and official Record of Major League Baseball

   Author – David PreBenna

   MacMillan Publishing

   Sold by EKG Books

12. The New Bill James Historical Baseball Abstract

   Author – Bill James

   Free Press – Publishing - June 13, 2003